Employment Rights in Britain and Europe

Selected Papers in Labour Law

Lord Wedderburn

LAWRENCE AND WISHART
in association with the Institute of Employment Rights
LONDON

Lawrence and Wishart Limited
144a Old South Lambeth Road
London SW8 1XX

First published 1991

Photoset in North Wales by
Derek Doyle and Associates, Mold, Clwyd
Printed and bound in Great Britain by
Dotesios, Trowbridge

Contents

CONTENTS

Acknowledgements

It would be impossible to name all those persons to whom I owe thanks in connection with the papers which appear in this volume. They include so many scholars and students in universities and colleges in Britain and elsewhere (especially France, Germany, Spain, North America and, above all, Italy), trade unionists, managers, legal practitioners and, indeed, lawyers who are now on the bench.

I have profited greatly from colleagues with whom I have worked in Cambridge and at the London School of Economics, and from other scholars with whom I have published joint works. In this last category I must record my debt especially to the members of the Comparative Labour Law Group (Ben Aaron, Xavier Blanc-Jouvan, Gino Giugni, Thilo Ramm and Folke Schmidt, and the group's co-founder Otto Kahn-Freund) and to Silvana Sciarra for her long-standing aid in comparative legal understanding, as well as the other members of the 'Pontignano seminars'. I also owe particular thanks, that reach back to the labour movement of the 1960s, to Jack Jones and David Lea, and in the world of legal scholarship in Britain to Paul Davies.

I am particularly happy that the Institute of Employment Rights is associated with the volume and that it will receive part of the benefits resulting from it. My warm thanks go to colleagues in the Institute who first proposed its publication.

But above all, these papers like the years they span, owe most, beyond all thanks, to the love, wisdom and patience of my wife Frances ... 'like the dazzle on the sea ...'.

Bill Wedderburn
March 1991

1

Introduction: From Rookes *v.* Barnard *to Social Charter*

In 1960 British labour law appeared to be in a state of calm equipoise. Yet in the thirty years that followed it has suffered a series of volcanic disruptions. Its political masters have changed its course like a mountain zig-zag. All the different governments, alternate Labour and (two different species of) Conservative governments, have tried to change the basic structure. Yet none of this has produced a stable system. A glance across the Channel discloses a different picture. In many countries, Germany for example, labour law has undergone no structural change in this period. Nor is it legal change itself which destroys stability. For example, despite profound changes a stability which has evaded us survived the Workers' Statute of 1970 in Italy and the reforms of 1982 (the *lois Auroux*) in France. Looking ahead to the next century, in order to produce a fair and stable system in Britain it may be necessary to renovate our system by reforms that go to its very roots.

The chapters that follow were written as contributions to the legal debate during this period. They contain a few guidelines: for example, it has become increasingly clear that, in order to understand a country's laws about employment and industrial relations, it is necessary to set that system of labour law in the frame of its social origins and above all of its labour movement. That at any rate is the lesson of a comparative study of the systems in Western Europe, a method of study which is useful to put the British system into perspective. There is a particular need today to examine our system in this comparative manner and, even more important, not to misunderstand foreign systems by applying our tests to their different logic, or vice versa. The comparative approach can teach us how others deal with familiar problems in unfamiliar ways – dismissal of an employee, for example, or collective bargaining. We need to assess British labour law in two changing dimensions: changes in British law and society, and developments in neighbouring systems across the Channel, including the needs of a labour market and capital structures which are increasingly international.

The changes in British law and policy over these years have certainly been profound. The proposals of the Labour government in 1969 (*In Place of Strife*), the Industrial Relations Act of 1971 of the Heath government, the Labour government's Trade Union and Labour Relations Act 1974, and the Thatcher legislation of the 1980s: each of these tried to swivel the direction and shift the balance of our system to its own design. There is, therefore, a special need to understand the system with which we now start the 1990s: to understand its past in order to plan its future and to appreciate, at least in elementary outline, some of the neighbouring European systems of labour law, if only because these are fellow member states of the European Community. Indeed after 2000, like it or not, we may find more labour laws enacted at Community level.

These papers, then, form part of the accelerating debate on labour law over this period and for the future. But their substance is not for lawyers alone. If a few technical terms are unravelled, labour law is a subject accessible to non-lawyers. Indeed, the social issues are often more important than the legal technicalities. Not infrequently, a worker more readily understands the problem of a dismissal or redundancy than the lawyer or the judge. True, there are a few special terms to be mastered. For example, there is the civil wrong called a 'tort'; that means a wrong (other than a breach of contract or breach of trust) for which civil remedies are available in the courts – damages or an 'injunction' (an order prohibiting it). It is useful for the non-lawyer to keep in mind the distinction between a crime, a breach of contract and a 'tort'. An act may be both a crime for which a prosecution can be brought and a tort for which a civil action can be launched; that is the case, for example, with an assault.

The period since 1960 has been a remarkable historical period for our system in terms of both the rules laid down by parliament and those designed by the courts (that is the 'common law' which is pronounced by the judges and is of crucial importance in labour law). Today there are many volumes of Acts of Parliament and two specialist series of law reports on the judges' decisions in labour law; yet only three decades ago it was agreed that British industrial relations stood out 'compared with those of the other democracies', because they were 'so little regulated by law'.[1] That feature, the comparative absence of legal regulation which had become part of our system by the 1920s, was thought thirty years ago to be a source of stability and strength.

There was indeed a lot to be said for that analysis. We had relatively little regulatory legislation outside the area of safety, health and welfare at work (where there was a lot). The relationship between the employee and employer was governed largely by the common law of 'master and servant', but in practice that had become increasingly modified by collective bargaining. The law had little to say about patterns of bargaining (there were no obligatory works councils, no national minimum wage, no duty to bargain in good faith) and even less about the collective agreement that resulted. Workers' liberties to organise and to strike were protected, but not by 'rights' to organise or to strike as in many other countries. Instead the struggles of the labour movement in the nineteenth and early twentieth century had given us legal 'immunities' in the Trade Disputes Act 1906 – protection from liability in tort for trade unions' funds, and protection for their officials and many other organisers of strikes in trade disputes from the central liabilities in tort – or so it was thought in 1960.

The trade union movement had survived its defeats, as in the General Strike of 1926, to reach the era after the Second World War as a powerful, respected institution. Few important innovations by judges had been experienced in the common law since the 1920s, at any rate none in the manner of the notorious judgments delivered in the first decade of the century when they had manipulated various doctrines of the common law to repress the unions, as in the *Taff Vale* judgment 1901 or the cases that created liability for the tort of 'conspiracy'. The mood of the Law Lords in the 1960s was thought (wrongly, as it turned out) to be opposed to a repetition of such excesses. In the one big case on strikes in the 1950s the Court of Appeal refused an injunction to a publisher to prohibit a union boycott against him because he banned trade unionism among his employees, the judges almost ostentatiously refusing to indulge in novel interpretations of the common law in his favour.[2]

In 1946 the post-war parliament had repealed the nasty little Act limiting trade union rights that had followed the General Strike – how modest it looks today! The ill-judged decision in 1951 of Lord Shawcross (then Labour Attorney-General) to activate surviving wartime regulations that made strikes into crimes, led to their repeal; but the accompanying machinery which enabled unions unilaterally to take claims about terms and conditions to arbitration was retained. Later adopted by a Conservative administration in 1958, this could be presented, along with the Fair Wages Resolution in the public sector and the Wages Councils in certain industries which depressed pay and conditions, as part of a statutory 'floor' which, though it had no general minimum wage, propped up the voluntary system of collective bargaining. With the command of a master, Kahn-Freund, the leading comparative labour lawyer of his day, rationalised all this as a system where the law 'abstained', or a system one might dub, 'if you like, *collective laissez-faire*'.[3] Those who inquired after the British system of labour law in the 1950s – it was then a recognised subject of study in only three universities (by 1966 it had reached thirteen) – found in his 'abstention of the law' a revealing insight into what had been going on. Yet this period turned out to be merely a prolonged truce, a pause in the pendulum of trade union law swinging between the courts' tort-creation and parliament's immunities. Indeed, before the Social Contract model of the 1970s could be tested, combining as it did old immunities with new interventions actively to promote trade unions and collective bargaining, political control of parliament changed again in 1979 and its role was turned inside out.

But it was in *Rookes* v. *Barnard* in 1964 that the old peace was shattered. That was clear at the time, though those who said so tended to be thought extremists. Other interventionist judgments followed in the 1960s, constricting what had been thought to be union liberties. This is what set off the Donovan Royal Commission, 1965-68, and the battle around *In Place of Strife* one year later; then with the Heath government came the Industrial Relations Act 1971, opposed alike by gaoled dockers' shop stewards and (eventually) TUC leaders. Its repeal and replacement by the Trade Union and Labour Relations Act (TULRA) in 1974 was followed, after the Labour government achieved a majority in parliament, by a completed version in 1976. In this period too came legislative efforts to extend employment rights, new inroads by the courts into trade union rights, the breakdown of the 'Social Contract' and the abortive Bullock inquiry into industrial democracy in 1977.[4] In 1979 the Thatcher victory brought a new perspective on the role of judges and parliament. Now judicial and legislative policies pointed in the same direction on trade union rights; the pendulum was one-way. The Acts (major legislation in 1980, 1982, 1984, 1986, 1988, 1989 and 1990) led to creeping 'deregulation' of workers' rights (such as protection against unfair dismissal), repeal of the 'floor' of bargaining rights and a 'step-by-step' attrition of trade union liberties. Paradoxically the Thatcher parliaments found it easier to make use of the old machinery of 'immunities' to achieve their ends than to construct, in the manner of the 1971 Act, new and overarching institutions (see Chapter 8, below).

By 1989 the British system, which had begun in the 1950s with relatively few positive rights but in practice extensive liberties for unions, was made the subject of an unprecedented condemnation by the Committee of Experts of the ILO for contravening minimum international standards of 'freedom of association' (not least in legitimising the dismissal of workers for the act of going on strike, in banning union membership at GCHQ, in fettering the liberty to strike and other union freedoms, and in banning collective bargaining by teachers). The Thatcher government responded in 1990 by giving employers more powers to dismiss unofficial strikers and extended the powers of the CROTUM (a commissioner whose sole job is to spend public funds to help workers sue their own unions).

It is important to appreciate that the trigger of change was pulled in the courts, not by Parliament. This underlines the importance of the common law and its 'ordinary courts'. *Rookes* v. *Barnard* was decided by Sachs J in 1961 and on final appeal by the (judicial) House of Lords in 1964. It showed that the old judicial habit of creating new liabilities for unions in the common law (thought to be dead, not least by Kahn-Freund) was still alive and kicking when the climate of middle-class opinion required it.[5]

Perhaps seduced by a belief in the permanence of the abstention which he had discovered, he came to believe that the judges had changed: 'Until 1964 I had always imagined that the 1906 Act contained an exhaustive list of such "economic" torts.'[6] This conclusion had been stimulated in part by his occasional habit of reducing the class content of English experience, as when he rationalised the history of the factory legislation as a process of 'trial and error'.[7] But it must be added that in 1960 there was little evidence to disprove the thesis that the High Court and appellate tribunals would never again play the *Taff Vale* game. In 1961 there was evidence, and by the end of 1964 it was convincing, that judicial abstention was crumbling.

The decision of Sachs J sitting with a jury on 19 May 1961 was that the three defendants – two employees of BOAC, Alfred Barnard and Trevor Fistal, members of the union (a forerunner of MSF) and their local full-time union official, Reg Silverthorne – were liable in £7,500 damages to Douglas Rookes (who had once been a militant member but was now a non-unionist after a bitter series of disputes at the workplace) for threatening that a strike would take place unless he was removed (said to be actionable 'intimidation'). Rookes had been suspended and later dismissed with notice. It was very difficult to interest a wider public, or even some trade unionists, in what seemed to be a rather technical decision in 1961. Yet the case was from the outset manifestly of central importance. Interest grew when in April 1982 the Court of Appeal unanimously allowed the defendants' appeal; Kahn-Freund believed this judgment would hold, but on 21 January 1964 the Law Lords unanimously reversed it.[8]

During those three years the significance of the issues had reached a wider audience. Articles had appeared in the legal journals. Within a fortnight of the Lords' decision it was being widely claimed that the law was now in some 'confusion', rather unnecessarily because the issues were clear. Whenever the courts create a new area of liability for unions, the voice of the establishment takes refuge in the existence of 'confusion', doubt as to what the common law 'is' – one need only look at the literature in the period after 1901. This takes attention away from the manner in which the judges have created a new principle and sees to it that the common law 'is' what (to appeal to Bentham) Judge and Co. say it is. And of course, the law *is* what the judges say it is (that is why today there is a debate about who the judges should be, even about 'labour courts'). This makes it doubly difficult to demand a return to the *status quo ante* because it is now assumed that the common law always 'was' whatever it is the judges say it 'is'. A plea for protection against the new liability created by the High Court or its appellate courts (Court of Appeal and the Law Lords in the House of Lords) is now made to look like a claim for 'privilege' above 'the ordinary law of the land'. In the *Rookes* case the TUC eventually recognised the new liabilities created by the judges as a threat to the 'right to strike'. Others, including the British Employers' Federation (predecessor to the CBI) said that new legislation was needed to clear up the confusions but restrict the 'immunities' of unions still further, with compulsory registration and perhaps obligatory strike ballots.[9] The debate about labour law was on.

In March 1964 the Conservative government committed itself to set up an inquiry into trade union law after the coming election. It lost the election, but within a year the ensuing Labour administration appointed a Royal Commission under Lord Donovan, simultaneously introducing a Bill to reverse the narrow liabilities created by the House of Lords decision in *Rookes* v. *Barnard* (these were based on the tort – 'intimidation' – created out of a threat to strike in a trade dispute). That, it was said, achieved 'the restoration of the law as we had thought it had existed for over 50 years ... to create the right atmosphere for the Royal Commission to look at the whole scene'.[10]

True, the points of law at issue in *Rookes* were shrouded in a certain semantic complexity. The last clear case of 'intimidation' as a tort had been in 1793. Yet the two main issues were from the outset simple and they have been central to the law ever since 1964. First, did the threat to strike give rise to a liability, i.e. common law civil liability in tort (by definition, a liability other than one for breach of a contract), and, if it did, were all three of the defendants liable in tort? Secondly, was there a defence under the Act of 1906? Before 1906 a union official who organised his members in a stoppage was liable for the tort of '*inducing* a breach of contract' (i.e. inducing breach of the contract of employment by the employees who left their work). If he threatened to induce them, he could be made liable to an injunction to stop him, a so-called *quia timet* injunction to stop him threatening to commit a wrong. To allow for some lawful organisation of strikes, parliament, in section 3 of the 1906 statute, enacted that an act done in furtherance of a trade dispute was not actionable on the ground only that it (i) *induced* a breach of a contract of employment, or (ii) *interfered* with the trade, business or employment of another person. These things a defendant could lawfully do, or threaten to do, so long as he acted in furtherance of a trade dispute.

But the two limbs of statutory 'immunity' were needed only if the three defendants were liable at common law. The three defendants argued they were not liable to Rookes. They had committed no tort against him – or no tort which was not protected by the Act. Barnard and Fistal had merely threatened to break their own contracts with BOAC, their employers. They might be liable for that to BOAC; but the law did not allow Rookes, a third party, to take an advantage from a contract made not with him, but with someone else (this is the well known English doctrine of 'privity' of contract). If C cannot sue B for an actual breach of a contract made between A and B (and that is the law) it would be 'inherently absurd', said the Court of Appeal, to allow C to sue B for the threat to break the same contract. The Law Lords disagreed. There is a tort of 'intimidation', they held, which includes a threat by B to do *any* kind of illegal act to the intended damage of C. True, the previous cases were few and usually involved violence (the leading case of 1793 concerned attempts by a sea captain to keep customers away from a rival ship by firing cannons at them). But in the modern law the principle applied to breach of contract just as it did to violence. Anyone threatening a breach of contract to the deliberate damage of another person committed the tort. What is more, the Act did not provide an immunity for this tort; Parliament had not mentioned it.

But it was argued for Silverthorne that he had not threatened, and could not have threatened, to break these employment contracts. He had no such contract with BOAC. As a union official, he had acted in concert with his members and at most *induced* them to threaten to break their employment contracts with BOAC. For that inducement he was given immunity by the Act (the Law Lords agreed with that in terms; it was agreed this was a trade dispute). Yet on this issue too the Law Lords reversed the Court of Appeal, holding that Silverthorne had acted jointly with his members, as a 'conspirator' with them, in committing their tort of 'intimidation'. In retrospect, it is interesting to note that Sachs J had asked the jury whether there was a 'conspiracy to threaten strike action' and whether Silverthorne was a party; to which the jury replied: 'There was', and 'He was'. Trade union opinion was particularly struck by the fact that, not only did the findings in the House of Lords enlarge the liabilities of workers, they also made perilous the day-to-day work of union officials.

But there was a final point. If none of the defendants was protected by the first limb of section 3 of the Act (inducing breach of contract), did not the second limb protecting 'interference with employment' offer a defence? The difficulty with this limb of the section was to know what tort liability it was passed to protect. In 1906 it had been feared that the Law Lords' judgments at the turn of the century might have introduced very wide and uncertain liabilities for intentional interference with the employment or trade of another person. Later it seemed likely that there was no such liability, though the point is still uncertain as the litigation about the dock strike in 1989 made clear.[11] At the time of the *Rookes* case, therefore, two options were open to the judges. They could either interpret 'interference' in the Act to mean interference by unlawful economic pressure, such as intimidation by threatened breach of contract, or apply the words to 'an interference which is lawful anyway'. The Court of Appeal chose the first meaning. As Donovan LJ observed, if the second meaning were adopted, 'why bother to enact it?' The Law Lords chose the second meaning, acknowledging that this made that part of the section pointless, 'nugatory' and unnecessary. It also made the defendants in the case liable.

Two schools of thought at once emerged. To one (to which the writer contributed) this decision was as Kahn-Freund put it in an analysis that did not beat about the bush, a 'frontal attack upon the right to strike'; it reopened the old issues in such a way that 'only new legislation can effectively restore the right to strike'.[12] To the other school, the Law Lords had been right to interpret the 1906 Act as they did and to ensure that the tort of intimidation was 'extended to cover threats to break a contract' (though on whether it should cover cases where only the employer suffered damage – i.e. thereby undoubtedly making every threat to strike illegal – they tended to be divided).[13] Any suggestion that the Law Lords' decision incorporated an anti-union element was met with indignant denial.

Hindsight suggests that the second school had much the weaker arguments, certainly on the Act and probably on the common law. Even if the 'technical' argument about privity of contract admitted of two views, the Law Lords in *Rookes* were so obviously determined to adopt the old policy of extending tort law to the disadvantage of the unions which many observers had believed they had abandoned. It was no accident that towards the close of the 1950s murmurings of individualist discontent had been heard, with demands that unions should be 'subject to the law of contract like everybody else', or that the 'privileges' in the statutory immunities (without which, unions would in the British system be unlawful) should be restricted to 'official' or registered unions – those themes carry on through the Industrial Relations Act 1971 into the literature of the 1980s and eventually into the litigation on the dock strike of 1989.[14] *Rookes* can now be seen as a crucial point in this history, reviving the campaign to curb the unions which had been unnecessary in the 1930s, undesirable during the war but adumbrated again late in the 1950s.[15]

The relationship of technicalities to policies was made unusually clear in this episode. Lord Devlin and the supporters of the Law Lords' decision admitted that their objective was to develop new tort liability in the common law. One objective was to outflank the solitary maverick judicial bulwark which had put a limit to some union liabilities at the turn of the century (*Allen* v. *Flood* in 1898). Attitudes to *Allen* v. *Flood* are a litmus test of a lawyer's place on the spectrum of labour law politics. In that case, a majority of the Law Lords had refused to make a union official liable in tort for calling out members in a demarcation dispute without any breach of their employment contracts.[16] One lawyer in this school, a future judge, wrote when justifying the *Rookes* decision:

> In a sense therefore, *Allen* v. *Flood* was a political decision in which the need for justice to individuals, outside the sphere of labour disputes, was sacrificed to the particular needs of the trade unions. In 1897 ... this may have been a proper attitude for the House of Lords to take

when the unions were 'politically weak'. But in 1964 he said, 'the situation was very different. The trade unions are a powerful pressure group who can have little difficulty in securing the passage of any legislation reasonably necessary to protect their interests.'[17] The analysis passed for moderate in the Temple. It is not known whether the learned judge has made known his later views on trade union law in the 1980s.

There is a second problem, more closely connected with legal principles. The *Rookes* judgment laid it down that a breach of contract is an 'unlawful act' for the purposes of the law of tort. That was the kernel of the decision. As Lord Devlin put it: 'I find nothing to differentiate a threat of a breach of contract from a threat of physical violence *or any other illegal threat.*' If that be so, then the infliction of damage by the act must be a tort, just as much as by the threat. Lord Reid indeed commented: '... it would be absurd to make him liable for threatening to do it but not for doing it'. That must mean that all strikes as breaches of contract give a right of action for the unlawful act to anyone intentionally injured. No trade dispute immunity had ever been granted to the actual act of breaking employment contracts by the workers themselves when taking industrial action (that is still a key issue, as we shall see, in the 1990s).[18] This line of reasoning, which would make all strikes unlawful despite the statutory immunities, and other difficulties inherent in the new doctrine were foreseen by Lord Devlin who, hedging his bets, declared that breach of contract might not be 'unlawful means' for the purposes of the tort of 'conspiracy' even though it was for the tort of 'intimidation' (though he did not explain why or how he could come to that extraordinary conclusion).

But the problem applies more generally in tort, not just to intimidation or conspiracy. Once breach of contract is 'unlawful means' for the law of tort, parallel to violence, then a vast new area of arguable liabilities is opened up. It is important to note that this is put as an 'arguable' point of liability because today all that an employer needs to prove to obtain an injunction to stop industrial action is such an 'arguable' case. *Rookes* was an unusual case in this one respect only: it was an action for damages whereas most cases about strikes involve the remedy of injunction (a remedy, as is argued later in this book, which it is particularly difficult for the legislature to control). Here parliament was eventually alerted to the dangers of the range of breach of contract as 'unlawful means'. In 1974, therefore, it inserted subsection (3) into section 13 of TULRA when the Labour government re-enacted the immunities in a modernised form. This provided:

> For the avoidance of doubt it is hereby declared that ... (b) a breach of contract in contemplation or furtherance of a trade dispute shall not be regarded as the doing of an unlawful act or as the use of unlawful means for the purpose of establishing any liability in tort.

Since this subsection was regarded (with reason) as a legitimate offspring of the present writer, his unconfined joy can be understood when it was not opposed by the then Opposition despite their amendments to other parts of the Bill against the then minority government; but his remorse was greater when it was repealed by section 17(8) of the Employment Act 1980. It had been limited enough. A worker remained liable and could still be sued by his employer (for breach of contract). All that the subsection did was stop the waves of illegality lapping over into the law of tort. But it had been expressed in the 1974 Act (despite the writer's strongest endeavours) as 'for the avoidance of doubt'. The wishes of parliamentary draftsmen are dominant on such matters. Yet that phrase was not technically correct. 'Avoidance of doubt' is an expression which means that the law is not being changed; but paragraph (b) of section 13(3) was meant to change it. It reversed the deepest principle enunciated by the Law Lords in *Rookes* v. *Barnard*. That is why the repeal of the subsection in 1980 caused such difficulties.

In 1983 Lord Denning MR felt sure the repeal of s.13(3) was intended 'to throw us back into the era of doubt which had existed before 1974'. In consequence he held – in perhaps one of the most amazing labour law judgments of our time – that all threats of strikes were unlawful once again and afforded rights of action to third persons. But Lord Diplock led the Lords to reverse that decision, which could not have been intended by parliament, he said, because it meant that the last two lines of section 17 in the 1980 Act introduced liabilities wider than all those in the rest of that long section on secondary action.[19]

But if Lord Denning was wrong, the problem of breach of contract as an 'illegal act' remained – and it does still remain. Thus, when in 1987 Henry J came to the problem again in a leading case involving strikes by a civil service union, he noted that: 'Philosophers may delight in the implications of the repeal of a provision passed "for the avoidance of doubt", but there is no pleasure for those who must grapple with doubt reborn.'[20] He felt constrained to hold that there was indeed now an 'arguable case that a striker's breach of his contract of employment may be an unlawful means' generally in the law of tort, though he avoided making the defendants liable there for other reasons. This ability of the common law to engender new threats to the legality of trade union activities which lie like landmines until a plaintiff activates them and in the interim create uncertainty, has been a contributory factor in the growing interest in specialist 'labour courts' in Britain.

Another theme central to *Rookes*, which reappears in the essays that follow, is the legal categorisation of collective union action in relation to the individual contract of employment. Ideologically, that is the key point at which the 'individual' meets the collective interest. Legally, it is where the contract of the employer and employee meets the right or liberty of workers collectively to organise and to strike. Here we must remember that the private 'employer' is normally a collectivity of capital endowed by the law with a fictional 'individual' personality as a company, while in the public sector he appears in various 'individual' forms from the parish council to the Crown. This issue – the meaning of the 'employer' – and the need to concentrate upon centres of power that affect the worker whether or not they are technically the 'employer' (such as a parent company in a group) in the eye of the common law, are aspects which are greatly illuminated by comparative legal research. The reader will find, it is hoped, passages in what follows that indicate such areas. It is, of course, in the insistence upon comparative method that Kahn-Freund's greatest legacy to us is found.

Comparatively, though, this is the point where practice and law in Britain tend to diverge significantly from most of the Continental European systems. In the history of British labour law it has been an area which has received much more attention after *Rookes* v. *Barnard*. Indeed, before 1964 and even after, one can find confident assertions that industrial principle is identical with legal principle, so that it could be said: 'Where proper notice is given, the right to strike in civilian industry is unquestionable.'[21] And even Kahn-Freund often toyed with the idea that such notice (which was not a notice to terminate the contracts) might render a strike free from any breach of the contract. There was no authority to support this widely shared misconception; but many had hoped they could bring the judges round to it. But the *Rookes* decision was the end of any hope that the judges might one day feel free to create some principle (except for the idiosyncratic judgments of Lord Denning) equivalent to the dominant principle in Western Europe: '*la grève ne rompt pas le contrat de travail sauf faute lourde imputable au salarié.*'[22] This principle could never become law without legislation. It is often forgotten that in 1966 the Ministry of Labour Evidence to Donovan proposed that, in the light of *Rookes*, a strike on due notice should be permitted by legislation to suspend the contract – whilst reserving to the employer however a right to terminate contracts in suspense without notice.[23]

It was at just this same intersection that the legislation of the 1980s picked up one of the threads dropped from the spool of conservative thinking in the 1970s. The debate about the Donovan Report had concentrated on legal ways to control unofficial strikes. It rejected a variety of legal mechanisms (including compulsory strike ballots) and concluded that the first priority was

> a change in the nature of British collective bargaining and a more orderly method for workers and their representatives to exercise their influence in the factory; and for this to be accomplished, if possible, without destroying the British tradition of keeping industrial relations out of the courts.

although a bare majority also favoured confinement of the modernised immunities in trade disputes to industrial action by official (and registered) trade unions.[24] The Report favoured a new jurisdiction over individual employment disputes for industrial tribunals (which had been created in 1964 by civil servants who had in mind the creation of labour courts); but it rejected the demand of the Conservative Lawyers' Society for new 'Industrial Courts' (with a High Court judge and lay members from a panel nominated by the TUC and CBI) which would be given a wide competence including cases on collective agreements, industrial disputes, trade union affairs and 'restrictive practices in the use of labour'.[25]

Significantly the Society also saw the interlocutory injunction – especially 'immediate interlocutory relief' – as the 'principal weapon' in collective labour law, including injunctions on application by the Minister for a 60 day cooling off period in labour disputes creating grave national loss.[26] This last proposal was of course modelled on the 'Taft-Hartley' law in the United States; and it is perhaps a testimonial to civil service pertinacity that parallel ideas, after being rejected by Donovan, turned up again in Labour's plan, *In Place of Strife*, in 1969. Moreover, a similar mechanism was enacted in the Conservative Industrial Relations

Act in 1971 (though it was used only once in 1972 when a work to rule on the railways was made more protracted and turned into a union victory by the obligatory ballot). Indeed, similar proposals were at the centre of the enormous public row between the Labour government and the TUC in 1969, from which the government backed away after fruitlessly considering a short Bill composed mainly of the objectionable 'penal clauses' (especially those enabling the Secretary of State to order those striking in breach of agreed procedure or after inadequate discussion to desist for 28 days, or to require a union to hold a strike ballot – without even going to any court), ending in the 'solemn and binding' undertaking by the TUC to take modest steps about industrial action.[27]

Similarly, from the proposed 'Industrial Courts', via the Conservative proposals of 1968, may be traced the lineage of the National Industrial Relations Court – 'the NIRC for short'[28] (and so it became). Indeed, future historians may be puzzled by the fact that they find the Labour Party, having succeeded in its fight to repeal the Act and the NIRC three years after 1971, and not having shown any interest in creating such a court in the 1980s, suddenly in 1990 proposing 'a new Industrial Court', chaired by a High Court judge with 'expert industrial members' and (with three exceptions) using normal High Court procedures – something which would 'bring us closer to the rest of Europe'.[29] Some of the chapters that follow will inquire further into these important questions.

One reason why such proposals did not surface in the Thatcher government's programme for the 1980s was the different nature of that Conservative government. The administration of 1970–74 was in great measure corporatist in instinct, attempting in its Act of 1971 to draw the unions in to a regulated and regulatory system of industrial relations law. Indeed, that Act was said to have 'two different phantom draftsmen', one concerned with individual rights (such as the right not to join a union, which Donovan had demonstrated to be something other than the obverse side of the coin bearing the right to join), the other concerned with order and discipline. The 'unifying theme' was the weakening of trade union power.[30] Neither theme was perhaps fully tested in the short period of the Act's life. Union opposition (refusal to register, for example) was matched by management's reluctance to take the steps the authors of the law expected from it (failure to demand legal effect for collective agreements, for instance).[31]

These twin obstacles to the Act's implementation led many observers to adopt the maxim – indeed, who can honestly say he wholly escaped? – that British employers would not make significant use of legal weapons against their own workers and unions, that here the law itself was shown to be a 'secondary' phenomenon. The 1980s proved the maxim to be unreliable. Now government pursued with relentless vigour an anti-union policy of a different kind. Corporatist elements were ejected and the principles of Hayek for the defence of market forces were stamped on the evolving legislation.[32] It was seen early on that, 'having learned the skills of manipulating "non-interventionist" institutions in the service of restricting trade union activity, the new policy may have no need for the legislature to introduce new concepts'[33] (though it took some time to convince a wider audience of its policy due in part to the intense reasonableness of Mr (now Lord) Prior, Secretary of State in 1980, who never seemed fully to appreciate the manner in which his Act was the base on which the Hayek programme was enacted by the later Bills). The introduction of a specialist court, in place of the courts of the 'ordinary law of the land', would for the Thatcher government have been an act of corporatist eccentricity.

The aspect of *Rookes* v. *Barnard* which most sharply put the unions on the defensive was perhaps the dismissal of non-unionists in a closed shop. It is also the aspect where the law has changed the most over the last three decades. Also when Rookes was suspended and then dismissed there was no question of his complaining about the dismissal; once given his notice he had no further claim. The history is intertwined therefore with the introduction of the new remedies for 'unfair dismissal', the one bi-partisan aspect of the 1971 Act; having been part of Labour's final Bill one year before. Comparison with other systems, made in many of the chapters that follow, demonstrates how difficult it is to make the remedy of reinstatement work for those who are unlawfully dismissed, and how weak the British system is even comparatively in this respect. 'Employment protection' laws are futile in the absence of adequate remedies, available at low cost and with speed for the workers concerned. Interestingly enough, one system which meets that challenge, the Italian, has specialist judges but no 'labour courts'. Concern with such questions will lead us to ask again just who 'judges' are.

It is to be observed that *Rookes* was decided before even the first legislation on redundancy payments went on the statute book in 1965. It left its mark there too, though. Earlier legislation of 1963 had attempted to distinguish strikes in breach of contract from those that were not in breach, for the purposes of continuity of employment and rights to minimum notice. After *Rookes* it was clearer, as it should perhaps have been before, that even after due notice most strikes would be in breach. This realisation meant that the proposals to deprive strikers of redundancy payments or other seniority rights had to be argued on their merits to Donovan, which 'had little difficulty in showing that such a sanction against unconstitutional action would operate in an arbitrary and capricious way'.[34] When the Thatcher government sought to deprive strikers' families of benefits, it preferred to do so in the relative shadow of social security adjustments.

Although union security practices themselves received some support from Donovan, the posture of *Rookes* as David, the non-unionist, fighting the union Goliath not only matched language used by many judges in this era, especially Lord Denning MR whose favourite image that was; it also fed the lurid campaigns of the media on which is now based the folk legend of 'union power' known to children before they have ever heard of unemployment or a shop steward.[35] Nor was the cause of reasonable union security assisted by practices in a few industries in the 1970s, such as the insistence by railway management and unions that religious conscientious objectors alone could be exempt from union membership and then only if they could point to a passage in their sacred text to justify their refusal to join.[36] Trade union roots are ancient but not as ancient as that.

Gradually the legislation narrowed down the ambit of 'fair' dismissals of non-unionists in closed shops and it made their validity subject to ballots with remarkable requirements (80 per cent support of the electorate or 85 per cent of those voting). In 1988 came another twist; the ballots were abolished, no such dismissals at all were henceforth to be lawful and industrial action to secure 'discrimination' in favour of union members was deprived of immunity. In 1990 a refusal to hire on grounds of union membership or non-membership was made illegal, though blacklists based on union activity remain lawful. Although a closed shop agreement is not in itself unlawful, the legislation has by now made any such attempts to enforce it illegal.

Trade union membership had by 1990 fallen sharply away from its high point ten years before. Mergers of unions had come to be dictated as much by survival as anything else. The draughtsmen's union of which Barnard and Fistal were members has long been part of the large conglomerate MSF. Perhaps it was inevitable too that, although its programme would still 'fully support and advocate 100 per cent trade union membership at the workplace', the Labour Party should now come to accept for the first time that the legality of the closed shop in all its forms had to be jettisoned. This change of policy was ascribed to the Community Social Charter's 'freedom not to join a trade union' without personal or occupational damage.[37] In return for the absolute right not to join, it was stressed, 'the Social Charter guarantees freedom of association and collective bargaining.' The TUC General Council agreed to accept the Charter, adding somewhat optimistically that it would need to discuss with the Labour government 'how unions can most effectively pursue 100 per cent membership in ways consistent with the Charter'.[38] There having been no reservation on the point, in legal terms this would now not be free from difficulty. Indeed, one could predict that any attempt by a government to legislate support for a form of union security would even be met by legal action in the Council of Europe Court of Human Rights (at Strasbourg) where any unconditional commitment to the Community's Social Charter on the rights of non-unionists would obviously be prayed in aid.

For many, the Social Charter was an oasis in the Thatcherite desert of the decade. It held out many attractive principles. But it is a rather more limited declaration than some of the publicity for it suggested. For example, the proposed Directives for part-time workers the protection of whose position was thought to be central to the 'social dimension' under the Charter turned out to make no proposal to protect their rates of pay. More, many believed that the minimum standards of the Charter, such as a 'right' to collective bargaining, would be automatic fruits of the 'social dimension' of the Community's internal market of 1992. But it was clear that such 'rights' were in the eyes of the European Commission, in its 'Action Programme' published at the time of the Charter, subject to the principle of 'subsidiarity'. That is, they would *not* be the subject of legislation at Community level. There is not, for example, to be any action at Community level on rights to freedom of association nor, probably, on a minimal wage.

Similarly, the critical parts of collective labour law – whether an employer should be obliged to bargain, the nature of the right to strike, the regulation of internal union affairs – all these were to be left to each member state. This is the subject of concern in some of the later chapters.[39] But on the closed shop, the complex arguments about union security practices and the 'functional justifications' found for them in scholarly analysis, or about the place of 'free riders' (which had caused even the 1971 Act to permit 'agency shops' to avoid non-unionists making an unfair profit from collective bargaining)[40] these arguments were all abruptly ended early in 1990 by a simplistic statement about the rights of non-unionists.

The price for this abnegation was a series of standards each of which was in the Charter but the implementation of which still needed the same struggle at national level. Perhaps some moral support had been gained from the Charter; but on these matters (union rights to bargain, for instance) the same battle had to be fought. No new Community obligation had arisen. Moreover, some parts of the Charter were not fully understood (for example, its confinement of the right to strike to 'conflicts of interests', put into the Charter even though the Community's own comparative study had shown this limitation to be central to the law and practice in only three member states).[41] But whether fully argued or not, the dumping of the closed shop was the first major effect the Social Charter had in Britain on political policies. The battle about the legal status of the non-unionist, which many non-lawyers had understandably seen as the core of *Rookes* v. *Barnard*, appeared, as a matter of political reality, suddenly to have ended. Precisely how this happened will be known only when all the dossiers of the time are opened to public gaze.

Many of these threads in the pell-mell changes overtaking British labour law lead back to *Rookes* v. *Barnard*. The innovations by the Law Lords in tort liability still echo beneath the battlements like old Hamlet throughout the plot. They are not of course the social reason for the later developments. They did not 'cause' the Thatcherite legislation. But the decision fits in as the legal base of a resumption of hostilities in the 1960s against strong trade unionism. Indeed, it is for consideration whether it was rooted in that peculiarly English refusal to accept the trade union as part of a consensual sharing of power in society.

And the decision reaffirmed the power of the common law in this policy. It was to the common law that the policies of the 1980s increasingly consigned the governance of employment relations, stripping bare the immunities and deregulating other protections long established, such as controls on night work for young workers. A Thatcher government in Italy or Germany, if such can be imagined, would not have the same common law residue to which to refer. Furthermore, certain areas of trade union activity were perceived by the Thatcher government to be in need of special regulation in order to protect 'market forces'. For its philosophy saw it as the task of the state to intervene when needed; as Hayek makes abundantly clear there was no contradiction between abstaining from the operation of the market and intervening to safeguard market forces against 'obstacles'.

The state intervened, therefore, massively in internal union affairs, industrial action and closed shop arrangements. Again, comparison with Western European systems of our law on strikes focuses on the central feature in *Rookes:* the common law principle of breach of the employment contract which industrial action invariably involves in Britain.[42] The comparison naturally raises again the questions reopened at the time of *Rookes* and of Donovan: whether we need a right to strike, and whether that means 'the establishment of a Labour Court'.[43] In the past such issues had been debated in an insular setting. In the 1990s a comparative glance at other systems is happily more common.

Such questions are, of course, part of wider issues. Whether we are dealing with individual employment rights – unfair dismissal, wage deductions or discrimination – or with collective issues – the right to bargain or to consult, or the incorporation of the terms of a collective agreement into a worker's contract – the question inevitably arises how far the tribunal which eventually determines the meaning of these employment rights is meant to have, and can achieve, some 'autonomy' from the common law. Concretely, that can be expressed in terms of a jurisdiction (for example, whether a 'labour court' is subject to the ordinary Court of Appeal); but in a more general and perhaps more important sense discussed in later chapters, the question can be expressed by asking how far labour law, in its concepts and imagination and in the hands of an 'ordinary' judge, is free from the constraints of a common law philosophy alien to its policies which emphasises the employee's subordination and the supremacy of managerial prerogative despite the camouflage of contractual equality. This is a question which arises in all systems, but it receives peculiarly little attention in England because of the prejudice which has long held that the common law by virtue of being 'the ordinary law of the land' must be correct in its appreciations of all types of social issue.

The papers which follow were contributions to debates on such issues at various times since 1960, during which time the writer has taught, researched and practised labour law. He has remained convinced that the subject is a place where law, politics and social assumptions meet in a person; those who believe they are so 'objective' or 'impartial' as to be above policies or prejudices deceive themselves.[44] Considerations of space have led to the omission of detailed commentary on *Rookes* in the 1960s and papers written in the period of the Industrial Relations Act 1971 and TULRA 1974. After a brief account of the Donovan Report we proceed, therefore, to the period which ended with the defeat of the Labour government in 1979. The remaining chapters were written in the 1980s and in 1990-91 (and, although no question of copyright arises, the writer is glad to have the support of the various journals to their publication here). Some papers assess the Thatcher legislation, others the basic operation of our legal machinery, not least injunctions and their place in the class entangled machinery of labour law. Some reach out to other systems of labour law in Europe and to international standards, especially on 'freedom of association' and 'the right to strike' (the latter is the subject of an unpublished and revised paper). Many are relevant to a possible reform of labour law and with that in mind discuss themes relevant to a new approach, from 'positive rights' to 'labour courts'. Even in the trough of the 1980s it was not believable that the then current policies of employment law could last for ever.

It is of course the rich variety of labour movements and industrial relations systems which makes this area of law so fruitful for the comparative method, seeking from the foreign systems not answers to our problems but different questions for our agenda. One purpose of comparative law is the stimulation of our imagination; to some extent it is the insularity of English legal culture and of the common law which most ties down advocates, judiciary, employers, trade unionists and government in their unimaginative resistance to new analyses in labour law. Of these, a special role is played in Britain by the judiciary. Innovative judges are found everywhere (we shall see especially strong examples in France). But in no other European system does the process have the regressive influence on the legal structure as a whole that the common law courts have had in Britain.

Long ago, one member of the Donovan Commission wrote:

> A thing that worried me all through the deliberations of the Commission ... was this: supposing we made all the right recommendations, and supposing the government gave effect to them all in legislation, how long would it be before the judges turned everything upside down? They have done it periodically over the past century, most notably in 1867, 1872, 1901, 1910 and 1964.[45]

One further puzzle, indeed lies in a related but unanswerable question: what difference would it have made in the ensuing decades if the Law Lords had gone the other way and agreed with the Court of Appeal in *Rookes* v. *Barnard* itself?

Finally, two points about the chapters which follow. First, the published papers are reproduced as they were at the date of publication. The chapter on the right to strike in an international and European setting is hitherto unpublished and has been amended to January 1991 as far as the materials were available in an exceptionally important year (not least in Italy, France and Ireland). No attempt has been made to conceal changes of view or of emphasis over time. These publications must speak and argue for themselves. There are of course changes. It would be a poor legal scholar who learned nothing new from new learning over the years.

But certain values, it is hoped, can be found constant in all of them. One such is the belief that the task of the law in employment – however 'flexible' it has to be in a modern and changing labour market – is primarily the protection of the worker whose living is obtained, in high technology or in low, by the sale of labour power in the 'work-wage bargain'. From that relationship itself springs the need and the right of workers to organise and to take action in free and effective trade unions. The predominance of that need and that right remains, in Western and in Eastern Europe. An understanding of collective freedoms which are crucial for workers' self-protection, men and women, young and old, must be rekindled in the 1990s after a decade in which the values of fraternity and community have been swept aside in favour of an ideology of commercialised individualism. With that goes the need, finally, for free research. The causes of employment protection and trade union freedom are advanced not by heads buried in the sand but by liberal inquiry and free expression to which both employers and trade unions contribute.

To these ends – and especially the last – it is hoped that these chapters can make some small contribution.

Notes

1. H. Phelps Brown, *The Growth of British Industrial Relations* (1959), p. 355.
2. *D. & C. Thomson* v. *Deakin* [1952] Ch. 646, CA. It is significant that in 1952 there was not the flood of commentary on the case which would be expected today.
3. O. Kahn-Freund, 'Labour Law' in M. Ginsberg (ed.), *Law and Opinion in England in the Twentieth Century* (1959), p. 224.
4. See Chapter 2 below.
5. See K. Wedderburn, 'Labour Law and Labour Relations in Britain', (1972) X BJIR 270, 277; see too, Chapters 3, 8 and 11 below. On the growth and range of judicial interventionism in the 1960s, see Chapters 1 and 8, *The Worker and the Law* (1986 3rd ed.). On the ILO, see K. Ewing, *Britain and the ILO* (1989, Institute of Employment Rights); and for the 1991 ILO case, p. 353 below.
6. O. Kahn-Freund, *Labour Law: Old Traditions and New Developments* (1968), p. 69.
7. 'At one time I called it "trial and error" but Bill Wedderburn quite rightly persuaded me that I was wrong in talking as if there was deliberate experimentation.' *Sir Otto Kahn-Freund QC FBA, 1900-1979* (1979) 8 ILJ 193, 201.
8. *Rookes* v. *Barnard* [1964] AC 1129, HL, reversing [1963] 1 QB 623, CA, and restoring [1962] 2 All E.R. 579, and *Times*, 5 and 20 May 1961, Sachs J.
9. A programme for legislation which resembled the later Industrial Relations Act 1971 appeared in the *Economist*, 8 February 1964.
10. R. Gunter MP, Minister of Labour, on the *Trades Disputes Bill*, Parl. Deb. HC 16 February 1965 col.1032. The announcement of the Royal Commission was made by the Prime Minister on 2 February 1965.
11. For the authorities, see the writer's Chapter 15 in *Clerk and Lindsell on Torts* (1989 16th edn, R. Dias ed.); also Wedderburn, *The Worker and the Law* (1986 3rd ed.) Chapter 8. On the dock strike case: *Associated British Ports* v. *TGWU* [1989] 1 WLR 939, CA, and (reversed on other grounds) HL, and [1989] IRLR 288, Millett H, below Chapters 10 and 11. Ironically, nearly 20 years after the *Rookes* decision, the HL ruled that a plaintiff cannot make use of a contravention of a penal statute as 'unlawful means' in tort unless the breach of the statutory duty was one for which he could bring a civil action: *Lonrho* v. *Shell Petroleum Co.* (No. 2) [1982] AC 173, HL (in contract no such action can be brought by the third party).
12. Respectively, O. Kahn-Freund (1964) 14 Federation News 30, and K. Wedderburn (1964) 27 MLR 257, 281. See too, K. Wedderburn (1961) 24 MLR 572, (1962) 25 MLR 513; and 'From Rookes v Barnard to a Royal Commission?' (1964) 14 *Federation News* 83; I. Christie (1964) 42 Can. BR 464 and (1967) 13 McGill LJ 101.
13. L. Hoffman (later Hoffman J) (1965) 81 LQR 116, 139-40; C.J. Hamson [1961] CLJ 189 and [1964] CLJ 159; D. Thompson (1963) 41 Can. BR 167; A. Weir [1964] CLJ 225; and see D. Smith (1966) 40 Aus. LJ 81.
14. See discussion of the common law attitude in Chapters 3, 8 and 11 below, especially the Court of Appeal decision in *Associated British Ports* v. *TGWU* [1989] 1 WLR 939 (reversed on other grounds, ibid. HL); see *Clerk and Lindsell on Torts* (1989, 16th ed.) para. 15-20 note 45; B. Simpson (1989) 18 ILJ 234.

15. See Inns of Court Conservative Society, *A Giant's Strength* (1958) p. 54; amidst a mass of articles at the time, notably A. Crawley, *Sunday Times*, 1 March 1964; one of the early 1980s pieces, R. Tur in Wedderburn and W. Murphy, *Labour Law in the Community* (1982), pp. 155, 160-3.

16. *Allen* v. *Flood* [1896] AC 1, HL; see Lord Devlin, *Samples of Lawmaking* (1962), pp. 11-12, and see pp. 370-1 below.

17. Hoffman, ibid., note 13, p. 139.

18. See the discussion of 'European standards' on strikes, Chapter 10.

19. See Lord Denning MR *Hadmor Productions* v. *Hamilton* [1983]1 AC 191, CA 204; and Lord Diplock, ibid. HL, 232. For another (ingenious) view, see S. Auerbach, *Legislating for Conflict* (1990).

20. *Barretts and Baird (Wholesale) Ltd.* v. *IPCS* [1987] IRLR 3, pp. 9-10, approving Wedderburn, *The Worker and the Law* (1986 3rd ed.) 637-8.

21. J. Anderson, 'Fair Shares at Law', *Guardian*, 23 February 1964.

22. 'A strike does not break the contract of employment unless there is serious misconduct on the part of the employee': Law of 11 February 1950, art. 4 (now art. L.521-1 *Code du Travail*); see O. Kahn-Freund, *Labour Law: Old Traditions and New Developments* (1968) pp. 64-7, and in G. Wilmer (ed.) *Jus et Societas* (1979): 'Those who participate in a strike break their contracts, unquestionably if they do not give the prescribed notices, and very probably if they do.' The attempt to build the outline of a doctrine of suspension by Lord Denning MR came too late and could not have been successful without legislation: *Morgan* v. *Fry* [1968] 2 QB 710, 724-8; but compare R. Rideout, 'Strikes' (1970) Current Legal Problems 137. See too, Chapters 3, 4, 5 and 10 below.

23. Ministry of Labour *Royal Commission on Trade Unions and Employers' Associations Written Evidence* (1965) p. 77-8.

24. *Donovan Report* (Cmnd 3623, 1968) paras 190, 430-56, 576.

25. Inns of Court Conservative and Unionist Society, *Minutes of Evidence, Royal Commission on Trade Unions and Employers' Associations*, Day 35, 26 April 1966, paras. 26-34.

26. On the crucial importance of the interlocutory injunction, see Chapter 7 below. *Rookes* v. *Barnard* [1964] AC 1129, HL, was unusual in being a leading case where the claim was by an employee, not an employer or customer, and for damages not for an injunction.

27. *In Place of Strife* (Cmnd 3888, 1969); compare the Conservative Political Centre proposals, *Fair Deal at Work* (1968).

28. *Professor Wedderburn on the Industrial Relations Bill* (TUC 1971, a speech at the Albert Hall Rally, 12 January 1971): 'I see opposition to this Bill not as something negative, but as based upon a positive affirmation that only a strong, free trade union movement can secure for working people, blue collar or white, deliverance from the status of second-class citizenship at work.' (p. 6).

29. Labour Party, *Looking to the Future* (1990), p. 34. The exceptions would be a conciliation role for the Court, limitations on sequestration of unions' property and amendments of injunction procedure (an end to *ex parte* injunctions, and a right for either party to require a speedy 'hearing on the full merits' where a court grants an interlocutory order). On the need to be clear about a 'labour court' and its procedures, and on the position in Western Europe, see Chapter 11.

30. K. Wedderburn, op. cit. above n. 5, (1972) X BJIR pp. 281-2.

31. See B. Weekes, M. Mellish, L. Dickens, J. Lloyd, *Industrial Relations and the Limits of Law* (1975).

32. See Chapter 8 on the legislation from 1979 to 1988. The Employment Acts of 1989 and 1990 amply confirmed the analysis.

33. J. Clark and Wedderburn in Wedderburn, R. Lewis and J. Clark (eds.), *Labour Law and Industrial Relations* (1982) p. 215. On the judiciary in different systems, see Chapters 10, 11 below.

34. P. Davies and M. Freedland, *Labour Law: Text and Materials* (1984 2nd ed.)

30   *Employment Rights in Britain and Europe*

p. 933, on the Contracts of Employment Act 1963, Sched. 1, and s. 37 Redundancy Payments Act 1965; Donovan *Report* op. cit. paras 495-9.
35. See generally Wedderburn, *The Worker and the Law* (1986 3rd ed.) Chap. 4.
36. See S. Dunn and J. Gennard, *The Closed Shop in British Industry* (1984) Chapter 7; *Saggers* v. *BR* [1987] ICR 809.
37. *Looking to the Future*, pp. 34-5; the Charter offered 'historic opportunities' in this respect: speech of T. Blair MP, Labour Party Employment Spokesman, 17 December 1989.
38. TUC *Employment Law: A New Approach* (June 1990).
39. See Wedderburn, *The Social Charter, European Company and Employment Rights* (1990 Institute of Employment Rights), and Chapter 11 below. On the 'right to strike' see Chapters 5, 10 and 11.
40. See the classic study by W.E.J. McCarthy, *The Closed Shop in Britain* (1964).
41. See especially Chapter 10 below.
42. See Chapters 3, 10 and 11. The case raised a further related issue, namely whether a no-strike clause in a collective agreement can become part of the individual employment contracts of workers employed on the terms of that agreement (as s. 18(4) TULRA 1974 suggests it can, though only under certain conditions). Kahn-Freund never wholly shed the belief that the incorporation of the no-strike obligation in *Rookes* v. *Barnard* [1964] A C 1129, was 'artificial and strained': *Labour and the Law* (1988 3rd ed. P. Davies and M. Freedland eds.) p. 176; compare Wedderburn, *The Worker and the Law* (1986 3rd ed.) pp. 329-43.
43. See for example, Stephen Fay, 'Will the TUC Accept a Labour Court?', *Sunday Times*, 3 September 1967. Compare Chapters 5 and 11 below.
44. For the best known demonstration of the profound complexities surrounding the 'negative' right to dissociate, and the 'shallow legalism' of simple answers, see O. Kahn-Freund, *Labour and the Law* (eds. P. Davies and M. Freedland, 1983 3rd ed.) Chapter 7; and on the 'right to be a non-unionist', Wedderburn, Chapter 6 in Folke Schmidt (ed.) *Discrimination in Employment* (1978).
45. Eric Whigham, 'But Would the Judges Turn It Upside Down?' *Times*, 18 June 1968.

2

The Report of the Donovan Royal Commission: The End of an Era

It is not possible in a short note to do justice to the baker's dozen of curate's eggs enshrined in the Donovan Report[1] and its twelve research papers.[2] Inevitably the Report of the first Royal Commission on labour law and industrial relations since 1906 attracts attention; but the research papers, produced by the unit under Dr McCarthy, specially created by the wisdom of the commission, could in the long run turn out to be of even greater significance. The commission unfortunately became known as a commission on 'trade unions'; but its terms of reference were incomparably wider, including all 'relations between managements and employees'. This brief note concentrates upon features of the report of special interest to lawyers, and must perforce ignore many individual dissents by particular commissioners all of whom signed the report.

The report is most important for its analysis of the character of British industrial relations. In legal terms, the process which began with the *exclusion* of common law and allied doctrines from industrial affairs between 1871 and 1906 (because the ordinary doctrines would have made a modern system of collective bargaining impossible without constant risk of illegality for workers' organisations) was rationalised between 1920 and 1950 into the principle of 'voluntarism' or 'abstention of the law' from collective labour relations. It is important to understand that this notion is not equivalent to an *absence* of labour law. It means that labour law assumes a special form. The statutes protecting rights to take industrial action are 'negative' not 'positive', i.e., do not set out rights to strike, etc., but exclude doctrines which would make some acts unlawful in trade disputes. Laws about collective bargaining do not regulate its forms; they act as props to the

First published in (1968) 31 Modern Law Review 674.

system of voluntary negotiation, as in the case of the Terms and Conditions of Employment Act 1959. (The Prices and Incomes Acts 1966-1968 are the first major exception here since the repeal of the unused and repealed Act of 1927.) As for individual employment law, we have had a lot of it; Factories Acts from 1833 to 1961 (currently about to be recodified), and more recently the Acts on contracts of employment and redundancy of 1963 and 1965. But none of these has inhibited collective bargaining *above* the floor of rights thereby established for each worker, unionist or not. A failure to appreciate this character of British labour law legislation vitiates, in the writer's opinion, much of the dissenting report (for that is what it is) by Mr A. Shonfield where he counterposes to that of the majority a rather different analysis and very different proposals.

The basic problem, the commission found, was the existence of two systems of industrial relations in Britain, the one formal and largely industry-wide, the other informal, dominated often by unwritten 'custom and practice', operating largely at plant level.

> What is needed first of all is a change in the nature of British collective bargaining, and a more orderly method for workers and their representatives to exercise their influence in the factory; and for this to be accomplished, if possible, without destroying the British tradition of keeping industrial relations out of the courts. (para. 190).

The basic choice for the commission was this: should that reform be attempted by use primarily of legal sanction, or by other methods, using law where appropriate to create new machinery? The critical feature of the report is its crushing weight of argument in favour of the second means to achieve its stated objective.

Thus it proposes that an Industrial Relations Commission be established (though without legal 'teeth'); and that companies of a certain size must register their collective agreements with the Department of Employment. The purpose of the latter idea is obscure, as is its practicability in view of the oral nature of many plant agreements. (Nor is it clear why the 'civil service' should escape the obligation to register (para. 197).) Under the prodding influence of the IRC companies would reform their bargains, recognising the reality of the dominance of the 'factory' or plant agreement, adopting wherever possible the principles outlined in the vital paragraph 203 of the report; management recognising its responsibility to take the lead; the trade unions closing the gap between officials and shop stewards (who come out of the report with flying colours) in order to 'integrate' the latter into the 'orderly' system. As important as the reform of bargaining institutions is the *extension* of the range of collective bargaining. But, again, except for recommending that the 'yellow dog' employment contract be illegal, the report proposes few legal sanctions for the job. Employers ought to recognise unions; but the IRC would be able only to guide and encourage, not compel, recalcitrant employers (para. 256). Unions should have a right to unilateral arbitration restored to them (similar to Order 1376 of 1951); but it would relate to substantive claims not to recognition itself, and should be exercisable only when the Secretary of State certifies on the advice of the IRC (the arbitral body being the Industrial Court). One is left doubtful that these proposals would alter the practice of the small and foreign firms described in the TUC Report of 1967.[3] One specific proposal is that no Friendly Society should be allowed to forbid members to join a trade union – a proposal aimed at the Foreman and Mutual Staff Benefit Society; but already ASTMS has anticipated the commission by a cunning use of private Act procedure in its private Bill introduced in 1967. Otherwise, the report scarcely discusses 'company unions', which is odd.

Given this base, it is not surprising that in the lengthy chapters devoted to current problems which affect the relations between British management and employees, the commission rarely proposes any major use of legal sanctions as the way out. A careful review of the problems of manpower utilisation, for example, includes a reasoned rejection of a 'Restrictive Labour Practices Tribunal' (paras 312-7); and the questions of training and re-training (perhaps the most critical facing British industry) and of women workers (the most exploited group of all) lead to many positive proposals with few legal dimensions. Indeed, there is not even a proposal for new law on equal pay for women, nor even on compulsory committees and workers' safety delegates in connection with industrial accidents – a subject glaringly omitted from the report. Further, the majority strikingly reject compulsory introduction of 'workers' directors' in industry as the way forward, and insist that the extension of collective bargaining is the route to greater 'industrial democracy', in the writer's opinion a correct assessment of the perspective for the private sector of the economy (Chap. XV).

The more 'legal' proposals of the commission may be summarised under four headings. First, as regards 'individual' employment law two major suggestions are made. Employees should have the right to challenge 'unfair' dismissals before independent tribunals, in accordance with ILO Recommendation 119. Certain reasons should be declared invalid grounds for dismissal, such as race; colour; religious or political opinion (though no equivalent proposal is made to stop unions barring members from office on that ground); sex or marital status; and trade union membership or activity. In these cases the employer should be 'obliged to explain' the dismissal; in others the worker should prove the grounds of unfairness. Most trade unionists seem to take the view that employers can always find a 'valid' reason if they want to – a view partly supported by the experience of the Redundancy Payments Act 1965; but such a statute would probably do something to improve the protection of millions of unorganised workers. The report differs from the report of the committee of the NJAC which preferred voluntary methods to statutory tribunals.[4] But the difference is more apparent than real because the Commission recommends that the Secretary of State on the advice of the IRC could 'exempt' workers covered by a 'satisfactory' voluntary procedure from their right to go to the tribunal (para. 560). One can foresee grievances being felt by such workers if they feel that their case has not been properly handled by their union. Even workers who had such a right would have to complain within five days of dismissal (an extraordinarily narrow margin) and would have no right to be merely suspended during the hearing of the case (paras 546-7). The right to strike about dismissals should be unimpaired; but the major remedy would be not reinstatement but compensation – the reverse of the normal position under voluntary procedures, which would have to include compensation provisions before they could be 'exempted' – and the compensation should not include any 'punitive' element, being limited to a maximum of two years' wages (scarcely a princely sum for a worker deprived of his livelihood for reasons which the law declares invalid).

All such disputes and all other individual employment disputes should, the commission proposes, be heard by Labour Tribunals – subject to certain rights to go to the ordinary courts. These would be, in fact, the present Industrial Tribunals; but they should in all appropriate cases adopt a conciliation procedure before adjudicating the case, to try to get an agreed settlement. In this welcome recommendation the commission reflects the influence of the French system of Conseils de Prud'hommes.[5] It is, therefore, strange that the commission appears not to have asked itself why such tribunals need a 'legally qualified' chairman between the lay wingmen; for the Conseils have operated for a century and a half largely – and best – without the intervention of lawyers as judges. Further, since the Labour Tribunals are to be based on the present Industrial Tribunals, and since the commission rightly insists on speed and informality in their proceedings, it is notable that the one gap in the research papers is a full account of the workings of the tribunals now in existence. Early experience of redundancy cases suggested in 1967 that such cases were taking about ten weeks from receipt of Form 1, and about three to four months from the dismissal to adjudication.[6] The time might be even longer if an unsuccessful conciliation session intervened – a long time for an 'unfairly' dismissed worker to wait for his compensation. Lastly, all experience of labour courts shows that appeals to the ordinary courts bring out the worst in the judiciary – both France and Germany are examples. Yet the report conventionally proposes that appeals on points of law should lie to the High Court. At least, however, it adds that British lawyers are ill-equipped for the task of understanding labour law and firmly calls on the professions and universities to give lawyers 'at least an elementary knowledge of industrial relations'.

Secondly, the commission suggests new machinery to help solve the problems of industrial life, including unofficial and unconstitutional strikes. The IRC, for example, in addition to the functions previously described, should investigate such problems and supplement the present methods of investigation and inquiry under the Acts of 1919 and 1896. Nearer the ground, the local Industrial Relations Officers should have new powers to demand information and inquire into difficult stoppages (para. 448). (There are currently only 55 such officers, and they have a multitude of conflicting functions already; this new task of acting as local 'mini-Scamps' might be the last straw. The work of Scamp himself, by the way, seems to be rather briefly dismissed by the report.) Further, it is proposed that all arbitrators should give reasons for their awards,[7] and in all cases be *legally* bound to observe current government demands on 'incomes policy' (para. 285). This type of thinking stems from a 'monolithic' model, where incomes policy and industrial law are combined into a single unity. But even under the present Acts, the British model has been a 'two-tier' system – the collective bargaining operating first, and the government's fluctuating policies coming in later. The report itself makes this distinction in an earlier passage where it describes the 'short-run' nature of changing incomes policies (para. 208). The proposal in paragraph 285 could spell the death of a valuable tradition of voluntary arbitration.

These proposals for new machinery stem, however, partly from the masterly analysis in Chapters VII and VIII, to which justice cannot be done here, in which it is demonstrated that most of the fashionable remedies for strikes by way of new legal sanction (compulsory strike ballots, cooling-off periods, etc.) would be of little profit to anyone. In particular, Chapter VIII overwhelmingly shows that no good could come from making collective agreements legally enforceable as such (though a majority favours the repeal of section 4 of the 1871 Act). No benefit can come from legally enforcing defective 'procedure' agreements when the priority is to improve them. Employers do not use their right to sue workers now (e.g., for breach of employment contract). Sanctions against unions would not cure unofficial action; and as the Devlin Report put it, unions cannot be made into industry's 'policemen'. Automatic sanctions against strikers by way of loss of social security rights are useless after the first occasion for afterwards the men have nothing to lose. Other sanctions against individual strikers are shown not to be relevant to the *causes* rather than the symptoms of stoppages, although, as we shall see, a bare majority of commissioners later made a proposal inconsistent with this view. Indeed the argument in Chapter VIII is so strong that it is surprising to find the report going on to say that in a few years' time it may be necessary to reconsider the point. By then, either procedures for settling grievances will be improved as the commission hopes; or they will not, in which case all the objections of Chapter VIII to legal sanction will continue to apply. One final point may be made here. It is sometimes said that, with the removal of section 4 of the 1871 Act, the 'ordinary law of contract' will apply and therefore no new element would be introduced if employers enforced collective agreements against unions in the courts.[8] This can be misleading. At present the collective industrial parties are taken *not* to 'intend to make a legally binding contract' (para. 470). Therefore, the employer must buy legal enforceability if he can. If the presumption were by law reversed, the union would always have to buy off legal sanction, and its position at the bargaining table would be materially altered.

Thirdly, what of trade union law as such? Most welcome is the proposal to codify the law and have it kept under review by a committee attached to the IRC. New legal definitions should be enacted for employers' associations (on which the report has very little to say) and for trade unions. In a flight of realist jurisprudence, which pays scant regard to Professor Herbert Hart, the report commits itself to Dicey's view that a trade union 'by the very nature of things differs from the individuals of whom it is constituted' as being 'true'. A trade union should be obliged to register and thereupon receive corporate status. An odd attempt is made to justify this on the ground that the clarification of the current procedural muddle about unregistered unions would involve some measure of registration; whereas, of course, partnerships have in England managed very well without such a law but with appropriate Rules of the Supreme Court. The demand for compulsory registration is likely to be viewed with suspicion by the unions, especially as it is usually discussed, as it was in 1894, in connection with enforcement of collective agreements. The change in the definition proposed is not great (mainly omitting 'temporary' combinations). What then of Mr Woodcock's famous seven men who decide to become a union? They would have to register before the law recognised them as such – with one exception. The report proposes that sections 2 and 3 of the 1871 Act should continue to apply to all trade unions as *now* defined. So there would be two definitions after all.

In Chapter XI important proposals are made to govern the rules and the practices of trade unions. Rule books should be modernised and made less ambiguous; and the Registrar should have a stronger right to demand rules matching up to certain standards on admission; discipline and expulsion; disputes between member and union; and the place of shop stewards. New requirements for audit of union funds should be enacted; but the present system of contracting out of the political fund should be retained as in the Act of 1913 (a special Appendix 7 refutes in detail proposals for changes in this law). Few unions would object to all this. But the report goes on to recommend new regulation. No person accepted as a member for two years should be allowed to be shown to be ineligible for membership in a closed shop situation unless guilty of fraud on admission. On the whole, the closed shop is shown to be a reasonable objective reasonably administered by most unions. But closed shop or not, the report recommends that a new 'Review Body' be established (two trade unionists; and the inevitable lawyer as chairman – why?). To this any member should have the right to complain of breach of union rules or of principles of natural justice; of election malpractices or irregularities under statutes such as the 1913 Act; and of unfair penalties involving 'substantial injustice'. An appeal would lie too against 'arbitrary rejection' of an application for admission. The list escalates into the most controversial proposals. No definition of 'arbitrary', for example, is attempted, although the section on training makes it clear that the proposal is aimed at craft unions who refuse membership to a man suitably qualified to conduct his trade. But the report also speaks of a man's 'right to use the skills which he has acquired' (para. 618). The right to control admission to the union is often part of the union's share in job-control. If this is to be subject to the jurisdiction of a review body, it plainly should follow that an applicant for a job for which he is suitably skilled should have the right to appeal against an *employer's* refusal to employ him. The report makes no such balancing recommendation. On problems such as multi-unionism and the place of shop stewards (including the important phenomenon of inter-plant stewards' committees) the report is less interventionist and makes proposals for progress which the unions themselves could make effective, with the aid if necessary of the IRC.

Lastly, a rather confused chapter makes proposals on the law governing trade disputes. Socially, the most important could be that which suggests narrowing the scope of disqualification from unemployment benefit of workers unemployed due to a stoppage at their place of work. In a long section (paras 953-96) the most important suggestions are that members in the same grade or class as the strikers should no longer be disqualified; and that a worker should not be regarded as 'financing' a strike merely because he is in the same union as the strikers. As for trade dispute law proper, various minor amendments are proposed: section 2 of the 1906 Act should be strengthened to allow peaceful persuasion of customers by pickets; any risk of liability for conspiracy to break contracts (resting on *Rookes* v. *Barnard*) should be removed; sections 4 and 5 of the 1875 Act should be retained, apparently for no better reason than that their repeal might be 'construed as an express licence to do' what is now forbidden. The unions' immunity in tort under section 4 (1) of the 1906 Act would apply only to registered unions; it should protect against damages and (contrary to some modern judicial views) also injunctions; but it should be restricted to acts done in contemplation or furtherance of trade disputes. One expects, therefore, an extended consideration of the modern cases in which judges have been restricting the scope of the golden formula of 'trade dispute' defined in section 5 (3), especially in cases of inter-union rivalry. The report disappoints such expectations. The term 'workmen' should be revised to include all 'employees'. (In passing, it is bizarre that nowhere do the Commissioners turn their minds to the burning question of who exactly *is* an 'employee' in these days of growing 'self-employment'.)[9] Otherwise the report regards the definition in section 5 (3) as adequate (except for three commissioners who would restrict its application in inter-union cases, a dissent which seems to overlook the fact that the courts are well on the way to producing that result already). The reasonable proposal for restriction of section 4 (1) to trade disputes is likely to be opposed by unions who feel that the definition in section 5 (3) is not being interpreted today in the same way as it was between 1920 and 1964.

The most remarkable recommendation, however, is that of a majority of seven commissioners concerning inducing breach of contracts of employment and section 3. First, it must be remarked that the commission agrees unanimously that section 3 must be extended to cover inducing breach of commercial contracts to protect the right to strike after recent decisions such as *Stratford* v. *Lindley*. But ironically, much of the report's discussion has here been overtaken by judicial creativity effected before the ink on its pages was dry. For example, much of its advice as to what can and cannot be done without tortious liability (e.g., para. 891) is open to grave doubt in the light of recent judicial opinion extending the notion of 'inducement'; putting indirect and direct inducement on the same footing; and finding liability even where there was no breach of contract induced.[10] Similarly, the report seems to accept that at least some strike notices are no more than notices of *breach* of employment contracts rather than of termination. It therefore considers whether the introduction of a doctrine of 'suspension' of such contracts in trade disputes (in the European manner) is the answer, and concludes that it is not, giving eight strong objections to the concept (para. 943). Yet Lord Denning MR has recently conjured such a doctrine out of the interstices of the common law, without consideration of any of the eight points.[11] In this confusion, the majority of seven drop their bombshell. Section 3 (as reformed), they say, should apply only to registered trade unions and employers' associations and persons 'acting in an authorised capacity' on their behalf.[12] The problems are immediately apparent. When is a shop steward an 'authorised agent'? Does ratification by the union relate back? As the minority of five energetically point out (para. 804) the proposal would leave ordinary workers, even if union members, without the protection of either section 3 or section 1 of the 1906 Act; and it is clearly 'incompatible with the proposals made in this report for the reform of the collective bargaining system'. Indeed it is. But worse than that, it involves a theoretical shift in trade dispute law of fundamental importance. Since 1906, 'any person' has received the protection of the Trade Disputes Acts. The majority would allow it only to those who registered on state imposed terms. Perhaps it is old-fashioned liberalism to dislike the corporate flavour of such recommendations. Certainly few suggestions could do more to inflame the industrial temperature.

Despite these criticisms, the Donovan Report is fundamentally a document based on a common sense analysis. There is, however, a problem latent even in its unanimous recommendations. The objective is to make the system more 'orderly' and to 'integrate' plant bargainers into the system. This can mean two very different things. It may aim at the improvement of procedures for grievances and a strengthening of bargaining on the shop floor. Many passages show that some commissioners had this in mind (e.g., those which insist that management must give stewards proper facilities). But it may mean that the bargainers are to be wrapped up in a package of state regulation, the stewards 'integrated', the arbitrators bound by incomes policy, all neat and tidy. Much will depend upon the interpretation put upon the objective by the Industrial Relations Commission when it comes to be established as, no doubt, it will be very soon.

Notes

1. Report of Royal Commission on Trade Unions and Employers' Associations 1965-1968, Chairman Rt. Hon. Lord Donovan (Cmnd 3623).
2. Research Papers 1 to 11 (listed in Appendix 4), and 'Workplace Industrial Relations' (Government Social Survey. SS. 402).
3. TUC Report 1967, pp. 130-5 (General Council's Report) and pp. 444-6 (debates). A motion on foreign firms was also passed at the 1968 Conference.
4. *Dismissal Procedures* (1967) noted by Judith Reid (1968) 31 MLR 64.
5. See W.H. McPherson and F. Meyers, *The French Labour Courts: Judgment by Peers* (Illinois, 1960); G. Camerlynck and G. Lyon-Caen, *Droit du Travail* (Dalloz, 1966), Chap. VI.
6. Reported in K.W. Wedderburn and P. Davies, *Employment Grievances and*

Disputes Procedures in Britain (UCLA), Part 4.

7. The Commission was in error in saying that voluntary arbitrators do not give reasons (para. 286). Some bodies and single arbitrators invariably do give reasoned decisions. The Industrial Court normally does not do so, on the good grounds explained by the President in his Evidence to the Commission, Day 45, paras 4-8, which are not discussed in the Report. On incomes policy, see the same Evidence, paras 9-20; and for an explanation of the 'political' character of such policies, see A. Shonfield, *Modern Capitalism* (1965), pp. 218-9.

8. See, for example, the arguments in *Fair Deal at Work* (Conservative Political Centre 1969), pp. 32-5.

9. The problem in regard to the building industry is discussed in the Phelps Brown Committee of Inquiry (Cmnd 3714, 1968), especially in Appendix III by Dr R.W. Rideout.

10. Respectively in *Square Grip Reinforcement Ltd.* v. *MacDonald*, 1968 SLT 65 (noted *ante* (1968) 31 MLR 550); *Daily Mirror Newspapers* v. *Gardner* [1968] 2 WLR 1239 (CA), *per* Lord Denning MR at p. 1250 (noted *ante* (1968) 31 MLR 440); and *Torquay Hotel Co. Ltd.* v. *Cousins* [1968] 3 All E.R. 43 (noted *ante* (1968) 31 MLR 555, A.S. Grabiner).

11. *Morgan* v. *Fry* [1968] 3 WLR 506 (CA). I am indebted to Mr B. Thompson for drawing to my attention the decision, as yet unreported, of the Inner House of the Court of Session in *Cummings* v. *Charles Connell & Co. Ltd.*, on 23 May 1968, in which the court held that a lock-out by certain employers did not have the effect of 'suspending' the contracts of employment but was in the circumstances of that case a breach of contract. The judges did there advert to some of the eight problems raised in the Royal Commission Report.

12. This is the phrase used by Lord Tangley in his separate Note, at p. 287. With respect to the other members of the majority, this is the only place in which the proposal is put in a manner which is legally intelligible and clear; and Lord Tangley understood this to be the intended meaning of his colleagues in the majority of seven.

3

Industrial Relations and the Courts: The Judges' Response

The relationship between courts and industrial relations in Britain, compared with developments in other Western European countries, serves, because of its special character, to illustrate a general thesis. In the comparable capitalist societies of Europe the differences in labour law which determine the approach by courts to issues involving industrial relations (especially collective labour relations) appear to a great extent to derive from different solutions to a common problem, one which all the countries discussed below – France, Italy, Germany, Sweden and Great Britain – faced (as did others) at different dates but at comparable periods of their industrial revolutions. That problem was the illegality of trade unions and the illegalities attendant upon industrial struggle conducted by workers through trade unions. Those legalities did not derive essentially from judges' dislike of trade unions (though most judges in the relevant periods had no affection for such associations). They were the natural consequence of systems of law based upon rights of property derived from legal concepts of the seventeenth and eighteenth centuries, allied in some countries to relics of paternalism or feudal status for certain workers (especially in the public sector, for example the German *Beamte*).[1]

The solution offered to that common problem is a central feature of each system of collective labour law. The first stage of the solution was everywhere of the same character. The most repressive, penal restrictions upon organisations of workers were removed as each country proceeded into an era of industrialisation to face the emergence of a proletarian class, troublesome to those in control of social and economic power but necessary for their

First published in (1980) 31 *Rivista Giuridica del Lavoro e della Previdenza Sociale* 3 and in English in (1980) 9 Industrial Law Journal 65.

new economy. In Britain – the first to experience the industrial revolution – the repressive Combinations Acts of 1799 and 1800 were repealed in 1824.[2] In France the law of 21 March 1884 swept aside the prohibitions placed on associations of workers by the Loi le Chapelier 1791. In Germany the old penal sanctions were ended by the Trade Order of 1869; and the same effect was achieved in Sweden by the Degree of 1864. In Italy the old laws forbidding agreements between workers to increase wages and combinations to strike were repealed by the Codice Zanardelli of 1889.

These laws, however, created only narrow areas of *liberty* of association for workers. Other types of illegality remained and were sometimes extended (as in 1825 in Britain), especially in respect of strikes and industrial struggle. The second stage of development ultimately gave rise to various positive *rights* for workers in all of these countries – except Great Britain. Such rights – a right to associate, to organise or to strike – came to be expressed in constitutional or other laws as the basis from which courts in those other countries became obliged to approach problems of modern industrial relations.[3]

Some Continental Systems

In France, for example, the Preamble to the Constitution[4] declares that everyone has the *right* to strike,[5] the right to defend his interests by trade union action and the right 'to belong to the trade union of his choice'. This element of a right of 'choice' between trade unions illustrates the law reflecting at the very highest level the social substructure – the reality of French trade unionism, namely a system of ideological pluralism.[6] Despite attempts to create a unified trade union movement, French trade unions have for most of their history been divided into groups which have been closely related in structure and in policy to the divided political parties of the left.[7] After the First World War French trade unionism was overcome by a series of schisms, the more important being those of 1919 and 1921; other splits followed in 1947 and 1964. On each occasion the events reflected to some extent ideological struggles of political parties of the left (despite a continuing assertion in the trade unions since the Congress of Amiens in 1906 of the 'apolitical' nature of the industrial movement in terms of control by those parties). The important point is that from its inception the modern labour movement was accustomed, in both its industrial and its political wing, to speak the language of political ideology and rights. The two wings grew up together.

In Italy, too, the trade union movement has been based upon ideological pluralism both before its oppression by Fascist laws of 1926 and 1931 and in the last thirty years (after a short period of structural unity between 1944 and 1948) – although today unity in action is commonly achieved between the three main confederations, CGIL, CISL and UIL.[8] More important for our purpose, however, the various trade union groups have been allied to, and their policies intertwined with the different political parties of the working class, especially after the establishment of the Italian Socialist Party in 1892, the emergence of rival Catholic movements in 1906, and the split of the working-class political parties in 1922.[9] Because these industrial and political elements of the labour movement had grown together and an ideological base had existed in the movement from the beginning, it was natural for the post-war constitution of democratic Italy to establish positively the freedom to organise in trade unions (Art. 39) and the right to strike (Art. 40).[10] Trade unions have been concerned to defend these constitutional rights in the courts; and it is from the base of these rights that the courts consider legal aspects of industrial relations, after the development of autonomous collective bargaining in Italy in the 1960s, together with the legal problems derived from the great Workers' Statute of 1970.[11]

In Germany the trade union movement was heavily involved with the various political parties of the left from its early origins,[12] beginning with the formation of the Social Democratic Party in 1875 and the split in that party in 1917, which led to 'fratricidal conflict within the working class itself'.[13] Under the influence of a labour movement active on both the industrial and political front, the Weimar constitution of 1919 established various *rights* for workers, such as the right to organise in trade unions (Art. 159), and the right of parity representation on various 'economic-political' bodies (Art. 165) to which was added the Works Councils Law of 1920.[14] This tradition of positive rights is now expressed in the Constitutional Basic Law 1949, of today's Federal Republic of Germany, Article 9 (3), as 'the right to form associations to safeguard and improve working and economic conditions'. In Germany today, of course, the trade union movement is very different from that of the Weimar period, being divided not ideologically but between the largest confederation (DGB) and the smaller, mainly white-collar grouping (DAG). Highly integrated into German society, it has shed many of the characteristics of class struggle in favour of legal rights for workers in Works Councils and in the enterprises subject to the régimes of co-determination[15] and submitting to severe control by the Labour Courts of the right to strike.[16]

Sweden presents an even more interesting study.[17] After the defeats suffered by the early trade union movement – especially in the 1909 General Strike – and the 'December Compromise' of 1906 – the first central collective agreement – the growth of trade union membership proceeded steadily until, in the 1920s, 'the unions began their collaboration with other popular movements,' especially the co-operative movement and the Social Democratic Party.[18] The Confederation of Trade Unions (LO) was founded in 1898, and now comprises the major trade unions, other than the predominantly white-collar unions in the TCO, and a few in smaller groupings. In 1928 the labour movement was forced unwillingly to accept the establishment of a Labour Court to administer binding collective agreements. But, largely because of the close relationship between the LO and the Social Democratic Party and the translation in 1932 of the latter into the party of government, by 1936 Swedish trade unions had not only accepted the Labour Court but also supported a law of that year on the right of association which broadly established legal rights to organise and bargain. The labour movement consolidated its industrial strength in legal rights by way of the acquisition of political power by the Social Democratic Party. The first central 'Basic Agreement' between the trade unions and the employers' confederation followed in 1938. The characteristic, delicate admixture of statutory rights and autonomous collective bargaining used by the Swedish labour movement is now amply illustrated by the Joint Regulation of Working Life Act 1976, which protects the right to organise and extends the area in which trade unions have the right to demand negotiation of collective agreements.[19]

The British System

When we turn to Great Britain, however, we find that even today no *positive* rights exist parallel to those found in those countries. The ordinary courts in Britain, therefore, stand at once in a very different relationship to collective industrial relations. In strict juridical terms, there does not exist in Britain any 'right' to organise or any 'right' to strike. The law still provides no more than a 'liberty' to associate in trade unions and certain 'liberties' of action by which trade unions can carry on industrial struggle. Statutory provisions protect trade unions[20] or workers' strikes and other industrial action[21] from illegalities which would otherwise be imposed upon them by the law, largely by the common law created by judicial decisions. When he goes into court in 1980 to defend himself, the trade union official believes he is defending his 'rights'; but he finds that judges see his statutory protections as some form of 'privilege'. Such an attitude on the part of the judiciary at once becomes the source of tension, even hostility, between British trade unions and the ordinary courts. Judges – taking the statute for what it seems to be – note that

when Parliament granted immunities to the leaders of trade unions, it did not give them any *rights*. It did not give them a *right* to break the law or to do wrong by inducing people to break contracts. It only gave them immunity if they did ... [such statutes] are to be construed with due limitations as so to keep the immunity within reasonable bounds.[22]

That has been the natural approach of the judiciary since the 'immunities' were first enacted in 1871. By 1979 the House of Lords recognised that these judicial 'limitations' had gone too far, and, in a new 'trilogy' of judgments, restored the plain and ordinary meaning of the golden formula – 'acts done in contemplation or furtherance of a trade dispute'.[23] Even so, some Law Lords made it clear that they too still regarded these statutory provisions (whereby industrial action ceases to be unlawful to the extent that they exclude common law liabilities) as 'privileges'[24] – and even 'repugnant' in their scope to boot.[25] To this we must return below.

It is, of course, quite false to see the 'negative statutory protections' which exclude common law liabilities for acts done in furtherance of a trade dispute as essentially some kind of privilege. There are no more than the curious British method of affording to workers in a modern democratic society what in many other countries are positive rights. 'In substance, behind the form, the statute provides liberties or rights which the common law would deny to unions. The "immunity" is mere form.'[26]

But why did this strange British legal pattern ever emerge? What was so *different* about Britain that no positive rights were created for trade unions? After all, British trade unions were at least as strong at the comparable point in their industrial revolution as unions in the other countries. Why did they not demand and obtain a right to organise and a right to strike?

The central reason is surely to be found in the nature of the labour movement in the *formative* period of our labour law. That period in Britain lies between 1867 (the year of the first great Royal Commission) and 1906 (when the Trade Disputes Act was passed). In that period the organic relationship between law and industrial relations was established. In just that period the nature of the British working-class movement was uniquely different from its European counterparts during *their* 'formative' periods:

The essential feature of that period was a labour movement which was relatively strong; but which was *wholly* an industrial movement. Unlike its European counterparts it had, as yet, no ideological political wing. The Labour Party was not born until 1906. It was, therefore, a movement which made pragmatic not ideological demands. And those demands registered upon bourgeois parties in Parliament as they encountered a gradual extension of the political franchise in 1867 and 1884 – although of course universal franchise did not come until after the end of this formative period.[27]

The British Formative Period

Innumerable factors contribute to the evolution of an industrial relations system[28] and its relationship to law. For example, the character of employers' associations;[29] events in war-time; the presence or absence of a written constitution;[30] and many other threads go into the fabric of that relationship. But whereas capital flows easily across most frontiers and company laws of developed[31] (even developing) countries have tended to converge, labour relations and its laws are more deeply rooted in national or regional social and economic structures.

The formative period saw a unique conjunction of three elements in Britain: i) a relatively strong but wholly industrial labour movement; ii) the absence of a working class political party, with the political ideology of which the unions might have been associated; and iii) the first, but gradual extensions to men of political franchise. It was this conjunction which gave rise to the strange base of British labour law, the 'negative statutory protection' or 'imunity'.[32] It is true that leaders of British trade unions played a role in the formation of international, more ideological organisations, such as the International Working Men's Association in 1864; but, as Marx well recognised, [33] their personal association did not ally their movement to its revolutionary purposes; to them it 'meant no more than a gesture of sympathy with continental movements of the oppressed'.[34]

The statement that the British movement did not make 'ideological' demands is not meant to deny that its 'pragmatic' approach can be said to be itself an 'ideology'. Indeed, the British movement in part shared the prevailing 'ideology' of *laissez-faire* in the years after 1850. The word is merely convenient to distinguish the British and the continental movements. It is, on the other hand, sometimes said that the 'immunities' express a *legal* aspect of *laissez-faire*, the common law approach: 'You may do anything unless it is expressly unlawful.' But this appeal to legal style is no explanation in itself of the special trade union 'immunities'. The common law is not *so* different from some other systems of law; the United States, Canada, Australia and New Zealand received common law but have developed legally regulated collective labour relations (though not always, it is true, with many positive 'rights'); and the word 'unlawful', in any event, renders the whole argument suspect when new common law illegalities are born of new judges from age to age.

As for British trade unions, it is true that in 1880 to 1900 they had some leaders (of the general workers' 'New Unions',) who were of a more socialist inclination. But they, too, eventually 'prided themselves that their approach to industrial problems was of a practical and not of a theoretical character'.[35] The movement as such did not develop before 1906 a political platform from which a demand for collective industrial rights could be launched. Nor did the socialist leaders 'as a rule like the degree to which continental unionists were tied up with Marxist politics'.[36] For most of them the class-conscious militancy with which they set out turned, by the end of the century, into a stance of 'moderation and conciliation' which 'assisted the process of their assimilation into the wider trade union movement'.[37] That 'practical' approach was the bequest of the earlier 'New Model' Unions of the 1850s. The 'period of the trade union legislation of 1867-75' was also that of 'the transformation of militant Chartist workers into respectable aristocrats of labour'.[38] The 'political commitment' (which, in this context, 'need not necessarily mean Socialism: the French Christian unions provide evidence of an alternative')[39] strong among 'Continental trade unions during their formative stages ... (for) changing the very structure of society' was absent in Britain except in a form of no more than 'temporary and superficial significance'.[40]

The absence of universal franchise during the whole of the formative period in Britain is worth even greater emphasis if one contrasts the solution in the United States.[41] The 'New Deal' legislation of 1932 and 1935[42] depended on the fact that the labour unions (so different from any European trade union movement, but lacking, like the British unions before 1906, a distinct, working-class political wing) reached the point where they could 'fully appreciate the importance of co-ordinated political pressure to achieve their ends' in a positive manner.[43]

It is to be noted that there *was* in Britain in the formative period some tradition of regulatory or protective legislation on individual employment matters.[44] Nor can it be denied, as the Webbs wrote in 1897, that 'an Act of Parliament has, at all times, formed *one* of the means by which British trade unionists have sought to attain their ends.'[45] The labour movement *might* have demanded additions to that corpus of law in order to acquire collective rights of organisation and industrial action. It is often suggested that this did not happen because of the 'fundamental change' that overcame the labour movement in the 1830s with 'the failure of ... Owen's Grand National Consolidated Union'.[46] But this ignores the Chartists. The political demands of the Chartists for universal franchise could perhaps have led to such industrial demands if the Chartist movement had continued to be effective in the 1850s,[47] though such a speculation must be tempered by the knowledge that the Chartists failed to find a base in the earlier, less well organised trade unions.[48] The years in which revolutionary industrial demands were adumbrated in Britain were much later – 1911 to 1913, when there developed 'for the first time a class war in which all its [the labour movement's] component parts were involved'[49] and which 'led to scenes of industrial strife on a scale undreamed of since the days of Chartism'.[50] But by then the formative years were over.[51]

After 1850 the demise of the Chartist movement and the rise of the 'New Model' trade unions had left the British labour movement with a wholly industrial character. The unions' leadership, the so-called 'Junta', 'interested itself in politics but not in the sense in which politics had been understood by the Chartists. Its members ... fell often enough into the most glaring opportunism because of their lack of any clearly formulated political philosophy'.[52] Opportunist or not, this pragmatic characteristic persisted to the end of the century.[53] By the end of it, when 'reformism had driven its roots so deeply into the British working class', the comparison with Europe was clear: 'On the continent mass movements could develop on the basis of a political attitude which in Britain merely isolated a militant minority, which in turn reacted to its isolation by exalting it.'[54]

Modern British Labour Law

The British solution, therefore, of the common problem of illegality was unique primarily because of the special historical development of its working class movement at a particular phase of the industrial revolution. So when, in 1871, parliament turned its mind, under pressure from the growing trade union movement, to the problem posed by judges who had – quite naturally – decided that the civil status of trade unions was unlawful because they were 'in restraint of trade',[55] it did not solve the problem by enacting a right to organise. Nor did the trade unions demand such a 'right' as part of any ideological programme.[56] Instead, Parliament enacted a law which purported to exempt trade unions from the application of the doctrine of 'restraint of trade' – and the modern law still takes that form.[57] This was the first of the modern 'immunities'. So, too, in 1875 and 1906 no right to strike was promulgated; but acts done 'in contemplation or furtherance of a trade dispute' were – and are today – exempted from certain criminal and tortious common law liabilities, such as 'simple' conspiracy.[58]

Organising a strike, before 1906, invariably involved its authors in civil liability in tort, especially liability for inducing breaches of contracts of employment of the workers involved. In 1906, therefore, parliament provided that the organisation of a strike 'in contemplation or furtherance of a trade dispute'[59] was to be immune both from that civil liability – *and* from any tortious liability for 'interference with trade business or employment' or with 'the right of some other person to dispose of his capital or his labour as he wills'.[60] The social function of such a law is provision of freedom to organise strikes. The legal form, however, is an 'immunity'; and the legal form naturally moulds the approach of the judge to it. A strike for wholly 'political' purposes cannot qualify in such a system of law as a 'trade dispute' because the statutory definition refers only to industrial matters.[61] Contrast the position in Italy. Because of the constitutional *right* to strike, a 'political' strike is not in Italy automatically unlawful. Indeed, provisions of the penal code were declared unconstitutional in 1974 in so far as they penalised 'a political strike not aimed at subverting constitutional order nor at hindering or obstructing the free exercise of the legal powers in which popular sovereignty is expressed'.[62] And the right to strike excludes without difficulty liability for the non-performance of contracts.[63] The difference of approach for the Italian and the British courts relates to the basic structure of the law, and that has its roots deep in the history of the working-class movements in the evolution of capitalism in the two countries.

In Britain, once the organic relationship was fashioned, it became the legal framework within which the modern British system of 'voluntary' collective bargaining developed.[64] Eventually the legal structure was rationalised by jurists – and even by the parties to collective bargaining – as a system of 'abstention' of the law;[65] or of 'collective *laissez-faire*' or 'non-intervention' by the law.[66] Such rationalisations can be helpful. They help, for example, to explain the otherwise mysterious development of the legal status of collective agreements in Britain.[67] They also help to understand why so much British labour legislation implicitly accepts the 'primacy' of voluntary collective bargaining;[68] why it is still true that 'the first objective of any Wages Council should be to commit suicide';[69] how it is still true of a great part of British labour legislation that it is, 'in a sense, a gloss or a footnote to collective bargaining'.[70] But the same rationalisations can be dangerous, because they easily give comfort to the fallacious belief that the so-called 'immunities' put British trade unionists 'above' or 'outside' the law – a belief scarcely to be sustained in the last two decades in face of a stream of labour injunctions issuing from the High Court.

This special relationship of 'negative statutory protection' for trade union rights inevitably creates even greater tension if judges develop the common law in new ways – as they do from time to time – and impose liabilities not foreseen by parliament at the time of the statutory enactment. This has happened frequently. The major Acts of 1875, 1906, 1913, 1965, 1974 and 1976 all included important provisions the purpose of which was to protect trade unions from some new judge-made liability. British labour law is characterised by this 'pendulum' that has swung between judge-made law and parliament's enactments.[71] And it is of significance that the eras of judicial 'creativity', of new doctrines hostile to trade union interests, have been largely, though not entirely, coterminous with the periods of British social history in which trade unions have been perceived by middle-class opinion as a threat to the established social order. That was certainly true of the judge-made law of the periods 1961 to 1969, and 1976 to 1979. The lack of such 'creativity' by the courts in the 1930s can similarly be related to the extreme weakness of trade unions in that decade.[72]

In the 1960s the statutory 'immunity' for strike action in contemplation or furtherance of a trade dispute extended under the 1906 Act only to inducing breach of contracts of employment. In that decade, however, a series of judicial decisions extended tort liability as it had been previously understood. Threats to break contracts were held to be unlawful; and interference with *commercial* contracts of employers was extended to the disadvantage of trade unionists.[73] It was never very clear why the Trade Disputes Act 1906, s. 3, protected inducing breach only of *employment* contracts in trade disputes, a provision introduced in an amendment by Sir Charles Dilke. The 'Donovan' Royal Commission in 1968 was puzzled by this restriction and could only offer the explanation that: 'The contracts of which trade union officers were most likely to induce breach were contracts of employment; and the cases decided in the courts against trade unions seem to have been cases of that kind,' so that in 1906 it seemed 'there was no present need to go further.'[74] That explanation is reinforced by the parliamentary debates on Dilke's amendment. Speakers both for and against it clearly assumed that protection against interfering with employment contracts would not leave trade unionists liable for interference with other contracts.[75] That was why some regarded it as 'the most important clause of the Bill'. [76] Moreover, the Lord Chancellor of the day, Lord Loreburn, expressed his own view that 'to induce a man to break a contract ought not in itself to be an actionable wrong' in any circumstances,[77] and he must have thought (as did others) that, with Dilke's amendment, the section was sufficient to exclude *all* liability for economic torts in trade disputes, certainly liabilities for 'indirect' procurement or threat of breach of contract which the judiciary introduced in the 1960s – let alone interference *short* of causing breach.[78]

Given the judicial extensions of liability, however, for interference with commercial contracts in the judicial decisions of the 1960s, the Donovan Royal Commission, in 1968, recommended that the statutory immunity should be similarly extended[79] otherwise most industrial action might well be unlawful. This recommended rewording of the 'immunity' was finally effected in 1976.[80]

From Donovan to TULRA

There have, of course, been many proposals for changes in the basic structure of British labour law. In 1968 the Report of the Donovan Royal Commission of Inquiry considered the conflicting arguments of two main schools of thought about the law. In essence, the first argued that the peculiar traditional framework of British labour law should be retained but reformed; the other school demanded that British industrial relations should be reformed by regulation of a new legal system with a far greater element of compulsion than the traditional 'voluntary' system.[81] The Donovan Commission (for the most part) favoured the first school of thought.[82] Despite the commission's conclusion the Conservative government proceeded to follow the second policy, and enacted the Industrial Relations Act 1971. That statute had the objective, as the government openly put it, of using the law as 'the main instrument' for reforming industrial relations structures.[83]

The resistance to the Act on the part of trade unions had one consequence of special importance for their attitudes to the courts of that period. In order to enforce the new 'unfair industrial practices', the Act created a special court, the 'National Industrial Relations Court' (NIRC). The judges of the NIRC became a focal point in the conflict between trade unions and the government. The NIRC was naturally perceived by the unions as an instrument of class justice; there was little prospect of its ever being accepted by them as Swedish trade unions had accepted the Swedish Labour Court between 1928 and 1938. The NIRC was forced in 1972 to imprison shop stewards who refused to obey its orders, a step which precipitated the threat of a national strike;[84] and in 1973 the NIRC fined and seized the assets of the engineering workers' union (the second largest in the country) which refused to recognise the jurisdiction of the court in disputes connected with a prohibited strike and its refusal to admit a worker to membership of the union.[85] Indeed, the whole style of the NIRC was such as to suggest that its president, at least, believed that industrial class conflicts were justiciable issues appropriate for courts of law to resolve.[86] The Act and its Court caused concern to senior lawyers who felt that this overt use of the legal process to settle fundamental social conflicts could only lead to loss of respect for the law.[87] The Act itself failed not *only* because of trade union opposition and the undue enthusiasm of the NIRC. The Act attempted to wrench the law at a stroke into a new pattern, to change its organic historical relationship with industrial relations. That was what the industrial body politic rejected – to a great extent management as well as workers, as the surveys of the period show – like an unsuccessful heart transplant operation.[88]

TULRA 1974 and Collective Labour Law

The minority Labour government of 1974 repealed the 1971 Act (except, in effect, for the provisions on unfair dismissal) and restored the non-interventionist structure of collective labour law based upon the 'immunities'. By 1976, when it acquired a majority, the government was able to repeal provisions enacted against its wishes in 1974, such as the restriction of the trade dispute 'immunity' to inducing breach of *employment* contracts, and the judicial control of 'arbitrary or unreasonable discrimination' in expulsions from or refusals to admit persons to a trade union.[89] But meanwhile, in its Employment Protection Act 1975, it had acceded to demands for more 'positive rights' even in the sphere of *collective* labour relations, some of which had first been put forward by two bold trade unionists in 1968.[90] Of these, the obligation of an employer to disclose certain information for collective bargaining[91] and an obligation to consult about proposed redundancies (required by an EEC Directive)[92] could fit into the non-interventionist structure as 'props' to collective bargaining. So too – just – could the establishment of a right of unilateral arbitration against an employer undercutting not merely 'recognised terms and conditions' but also the 'general level' of conditions in his industry.[93]

But another part of the EPA 1975 cut across the path of 'non-intervention' by granting to ACAS the power to make legally binding recommendations obliging an employer to 'recognise' (i.e. to bargain with) a trade union.[94] The sad story of the emasculation of this procedure by recalcitrant employers and totally unsympathetic judges (plus, perhaps, too ready a use of it by some unions, when it was meant only to be fall-back procedure) is now well documented.[95] Sometimes the very understandable expectations placed upon this procedure were perhaps too great;[96] and, although a modern democracy ought to establish a legal duty on an employer to recognise his workers' trade union, the 'British paradox' seems to be that 'even this small degree of intervention may be too strong a burden for the traditionally "voluntary" system of collective labour law to bear.'[97]

But it may be asked, why not replace the 'immunities' of the traditional system with other rights – say, a right to strike? The Donovan Commission considered this suggestion, but concluded: 'we do not think it [the present situation] can be improved by granting the right [to strike] in express terms.'[98] The technical legal problems involved for the British system would be formidable, not least for the introduction of a doctrine of 'suspension' of the individual contract of employment in strikes and in other (all?) types of industrial action.[99] The experiments in this direction of the 1971 Act were clearly unsuccessful.[100] The attempt by Lord

Denning to invent such a doctrine at common law did not even confront the problems[101] and has not been adopted.[102] Nor have proposals for a positive right to strike (still less to take other industrial action) ever faced the difficulties posed by a comparative glance at the Continent: for example, would 'peace obligations' (absolute or relative 'no-strike' clauses) in collective agreements risk illegality because they 'fetter' the inalienable right to strike, as in France?[103] Even more important, in the debates before the Donovan Commission

> it became clear that ... proposals for positive 'rights' were much more commonly found on the lips of those who wanted a quite new, legally regulated system of collective bargaining, in which trade unions would be constricted by many legal 'duties' as the price of the 'rights' and which would be alien to an essentially voluntary system.[104]

There is in Britain today no *consensus* about the price trade unions should pay for a 'right' to strike. In 1980 the CBI floated the idea that, in order to achieve a 'better balance' in industry, the 'unsatisfactory nature of the trade union immunities' might be replaced – 'even perhaps by a positive right to strike, *subject to reasonable limitations*'.[105] Perhaps – but what *are* those 'limitations'?

The Floor of Rights in Individual Employment Law

The legislation of 1974 and 1976 also expanded the 'floor of rights' in individual labour law, the employment protection legislation which has always been a part of the British system and which, as the Webbs said, British trade unions have always accepted as a method of advance – though they have not, contrary to popular belief, always been in the vanguard of demanding such legislation even in modern times.[106] Indeed, it is interesting to note that whereas in other countries a similar expansion of employment protection rights often consolidates a set of norms already achieved by collective bargaining,[107] in Britain it has largely been introduced to reach the parts of the system which voluntary bargaining could not effectively reach. The contrast should cause us no surprise. Whereas in other countries the negotiated norms were seen to be consolidated at the higher, legislative plane, the method of substantive, legislative enactment was, in Britain, normally called upon where the primary method of autonomous bargaining could not achieve the objective. What the primary method of collective bargaining had achieved needed no legitimisation by law.

Since 1963 such legislation, partly consolidated in the 1978 Act,[108] has rapidly increased in Britain. The relationship between

the Industrial Tribunals (and Employment Appeal Tribunal)
enforcing these laws and trade unionists is not initially one of
tension or hostility, if only because one of the three 'judges' is a
trade unionist – though whether that will continue to be so in 1980
if the government forces through its employment legislation
remains to be seen. But it must not be forgotten that ultimately
appeals in individual labour law lie to the Court of Appeal and
House of Lords, where no trade unionists sit. It is too early to say
whether the tribunals 'have won the confidence of working
people'.[109]

Of course, it would be surprising if the new laws – on unfair
dismissal; redundancy; maternity rights; health and safety; equal
pay;[110] racial and sexual discrimination – have had no effect upon
the objects and mechanism of autonomous collective bargaining.
But precisely what their impact has been upon collective practices
research has yet to tell us. Without doubt, more lawyers and more
legalism appear today in British labour relations than two decades
ago, largely because of the 'floor of rights' legislation. But it seems
premature to conclude that there is a 'fundamental trend' in the
'ever-increasing extent of the legal regulation of the British *system*
of industrial relations'.[111] Even the new individual employment
legislation acknowledges, in its *structure*, the primacy of voluntary
collective bargaining. That is why collective agreements, approved
by ministerial order, can elevate groups of workers from statutory
rights (e.g. on guaranteed lay-off payments) to the superior plane
of collectively bargained norms.[112] That is why the jurisdiction of
Industrial Tribunals about unfair dismissals is excluded where (in
the absence of victimisation of any employee) an employer
dismisses all the workers on strike,[113] in order that the courts
should not be given the task of deciding what is a 'just' or
'reasonable' strike and so invade the area of collective labour
relations.[114] And, as we have seen, collective labour law appears
unable to carry the weight even of an elementary obligation to
bargain. Nor is there any overall compulsory arbitration or
conciliation.[115]

Among the 'individual' rights, however, some in every system
fall into an intermediate category. The British statute of 1975
provided that a worker is not to be dismissed, or penalised in a
manner short of dismissal by his employer by reason of his
membership of, or his taking part in the activities at an
'appropriate time' of an independent trade union,[116] and provided
rights for workers to take time off from work in respect of their
trade union activities – in the case of trade union officials
(including shop stewards) rights to time-off with pay.[117] This use of
individual employment legislation to protect collective organisational rights may be described as 'building a collective "right to
associate" out of the bricks of certain "individual" employment

rights'.[118] Articles 15 and 16 of the Italian Workers' Statute of 1970 fulfil essentially the same functions as the British law,[119] prohibiting actions of the employer which discriminate against a worker by reason of his being a member of an independent trade union or taking part in its activities.[120] Article 15, however, goes further than the British law in explicitly rendering unlawful dismissal of a worker, or other discriminatory acts against him, 'by reason of his membership of a trade union or of his trade union activity *or of his participation in a strike*'.[121] This last protection is clearly related to the constitutional *right* to strike, a point of reference which can have no counterpart in the British system. Nor does it seem likely that the sponsors of a 'right to strike' in Britain would grant to workers such a blanket protection against dismissal or discrimination on the part of their employer.

Prospects for the 1980s

So far, the present government has not proposed any constitutional right to strike – though it will be interesting to see whether its promised 'Green Paper' in 1980 leans in that direction and whether it answers the questions prompted by comparative studies. Instead it has set about fundamental restriction of traditional trade unionists' rights in five main ways.

First, it aims to restrict the right of peaceful picketing to a worker's 'own place of work' (or the employer's premises where that is 'impracticable' or the worker has no one place of work).[122] A right to picket peacefully at or near *any* place in furtherance of a dispute, which it took decades to establish before 1906, and which has never protected against liability for violence, intimidation, 'wilful obstruction' of the highway or obstruction of the police and the like, will be emasculated at the very time when trade unionists' desire to take sympathetic action with brother workers has become 'commonplace and may be thought to be a necessary weapon in the armoury of workers'.[123] Secondly, it plans to exclude the 'immunity' from tortious liability of workers taking industrial action in order to compel another's employees, at a different place of work (e.g. a subcontractor's workers), to be members of a union.[124]

Thirdly, in a response to the new trilogy of House of Lords judgments, it will restrict the immunity against torts based on actual or threatened interference with commercial contracts for 'secondary actions', i.e. action 'in relation to a trade dispute' (an odd formula) when a person interferes with an employment contract or threatens to do so or induces another person to do so, *if* the employer concerned is not a party to the dispute. Secondary action which interferes with a commercial contract will be lawful if: a) its principal purpose was the prevention or disruption of

supplies of goods or services under a 'subsisting contract' between
the employer in dispute and the 'secondary' employer, or supplies
under such a contract by an 'associated' employer to (not from) a
recipient in 'substitution' for supplies which would have been
supplied by the employer in dispute;[125] *and* b) the secondary action
is 'likely to achieve that purpose', along with other secondary
action taken against the same secondary employer. The latter
qualification takes away from *this* area of secondary action the
subjective test of 'furtherance' of a trade dispute which has existed
since 1906 and restores the novel meaning given to the golden
formula by Lord Denning MR.[126] Another type of secondary
action which is lawful is action taken in the course of picketing
declared lawful by the Act; but in this case 'furtherance' of a trade
dispute is not given the new, restrictive meaning. The Bill does
not, however, restrict the range of possible plaintiffs. Once the
'secondary action' fails at any of these hurdles, any person injured
may sue under the ordinary principles of the relevant economic
torts, and that will often include the very employer in dispute.
Fourthly, the new clause strikes at *all* types of industrial action by
proposing to repeal totally section 13 (3) of TULRA. This
subsection was enacted in order to prevent reliance of any
interference with contract or on a breach of contract *itself* as
'unlawful means' in the law of tort in trade disputes. Without such
a protection it is more than arguable – despite the government's
protestations to the contrary – that all industrial action ('primary'
or 'secondary') could be held to be unlawful for making use of this
'unlawful means' to damage a plaintiff.[127] Fifthly, the intention of
the government is that industrial acts done to counter-attack the
new liabilities imposed by some clauses of the Bill, should also
amount to 'unlawful means' for the purposes of the law of tort.[128]
This adds a new dimension to the Bill, a veritable minefield of
illegalities through which trade union officials will daily tread at
their peril.

These proposals were put forward mainly on the basis that the
House of Lords decisions in the new trilogy rendered 'virtually
unlimited' the extent of the trade dispute immunity as
re-established in 1976 to include commercial contracts which: 'The
Conservative Party as HM Opposition in Parliament fought
vigorously ... and ... was dangerously wide.'[129] Neither in
opposition nor in government were the authors of these proposals
apparently convinced by the reasoning of the Donovan
Commission which concluded in 1968 that the tort immunities had
to be extended to commercial contracts,[130] because of the judicial
extensions of liability in the common law. The 'immunity' was not
in substance 'extended' in 1976 any more than it was 'extended' in
1965 when Parliament provided a defence in trade disputes against
the extension of the tort of 'intimidation' in *Rookes* v. *Barnard*.[131]

It has been authoritatively stated of the 1974 Act, as amended in 1976: 'Briefly put, the law now is back to what Parliament had intended when it enacted the Act of 1906 – but stronger and clearer than it was then.'[132] To push statutory 'immunities' back into their 1906 shape, after 'the restraints of judicial review which the courts have been fashioning one way or another since the enactment of the Trade Disputes Act 1906',[133] is to throw trade unions back into a legal position equivalent to that of 1905, as the Earl of Halsbury wished in 1906, when he attacked the 1906 Bill itself for creating an 'immunity' for a 'privileged class' ... 'a Bill for the purpose of legalising tyranny ... likely to produce commercial distress'.[134]

The Working Paper refrained from arguing that the law should be what it was in 1905. Instead, it merely stated that anyone whose commercial contracts are hindered by workers employed by persons outside the magic circle of first suppliers and customers must no longer be 'deprived of their common law rights',[135] including even the employer in dispute. The 1980 Bill, especially clause 16, although drafted in different terms from the Working Paper, will put into the hands of judges potent new weapons to control, and powers to assess the merits of industrial action – and in labour injunction cases at that, where the evidence in interlocutory proceedings is hastily assembled on affidavit and the court has an elastic 'discretion' to grant the remedy.[136]

The proposed legislation does not repeat the more obvious mistakes of the 1971 Act. In particular, it will establish no special court like the NIRC. Despite their distrust of ordinary High Court and appellate judges, British trade unions have over the last century obeyed – perhaps to a surprising extent – the judgments and orders of the ordinary courts, even when they considered that those judgments infringed basic trade union liberties. That tradition of obedience was strained to the limit in *Duport Steels Ltd.* v. *Sirs*,[137] where the inability of the Court of Appeal to apply the meaning of the golden formula, 'acts done in furtherance of a trade dispute' (reasserted only weeks before by the House of Lords in *Express Newspapers Ltd.* v. *McShane*)[138] caused one of the most moderate trade union leaders in Britain to declare that he would go to prison rather than obey the injunctions requiring him to withdraw the call for strike action, if his union executive committee decided to defy the injunctions.[139]

In reaching their decision to reverse the Court of Appeal in *Duport Steels* v. *Sirs* [140] the House of Lords took great account of the factor which had worried Lord Devlin about the NIRC in 1972,[141] namely, respect for the law itself. If injunctions are granted by judges when it is 'highly probable that the acts that they are enjoining are perfectly lawful, it is unlikely that voluntary respect for the law as laid down and applied by courts of justice will continue to have any influence in controlling industrial action.'[142]

It is little less than astonishing that, after a century of labour injunctions,[143] English courts of law should need to be reminded of such a proposition. But the scrupulous care with which the Law Lords in 1979 and 1980 restated the interpretation of the immunities – especially the 'subjective' meaning of 'furtherance'[144] – was not matched by restraint in their comments on the social propriety of the law. For trade unionists to have these rights to cause 'disastrous loss' to a 'stranger' to the dispute, said Lord Diplock, would 'not surprisingly, have tended to stick in judicial gorges'; [145] and he came to his decision 'with considerable reluctance' in the steel case because the law as it stood was 'intrinsically repugnant to anyone who has spent his life in the practice of the law or the administration of justice' – instincts which he 'shared'.[146] Lord Salmon criticised pickets outside a hospital (about whom he presumably drew his knowledge from the media) and said, if they were within the law: 'surely the time has come for it to be altered.'[147] Lord Edmund-Davies described the present law as 'unpalatable to many'; and Lord Keith saw trade unionists as 'privileged persons' able to 'bring about disastrous consequences with legal impunity'.[148] The premises of these value judgments clearly rest upon the same belief as Lord Devlin's in 1964, that the imbalance previously found in the 'scales' between labour and capital has been 'redressed'.[149] In abundant dicta, they expressed a social judgment, no less apparent for being unargued, similar to the traditional British middle class belief that 'labour' was oppressed once, in the dim past of history, but 'today' – whenever today is – has become a 'tyrant'.[150] Indiscriminate law-making by the Master of the Rolls led the Law Lords to their insistence in 1980 that the law would fall into disrepute unless interpreted by the usual rules of the game. But for some of them, social instinct led them also to call, explicitly or impliedly, for fundamental change in that law, because of the 'disastrous' damage which trade unions can do to an 'innocent' third party or 'stranger'.

In an increasingly interdependent society, however, it is a matter of delicate political judgment how far such 'innocent' parties must be shielded by the law against all economic harm in a strike. The simplistic notion of enterprises 'unconcerned'[151] with a dispute begs many questions. How far does the need of some countervailing power for workers bargaining with increasingly powerful concentrations of capital imply a need for wide legal rights? How far are the interests of various groups of workers interdependent? And what of the interdependence of employers? The CBI Steering Group in 1980 significantly suggested that few of them are really strangers to disputes, even though British employers do show undue 'independence' – a 'strategically unsound' attitude causing them to 'avoid involvement in issues with which they are not immediately concerned'. They should turn, like their European colleagues, to 'collective action' in disputes, and not 'take commercial advantage of the plight of others' hit by industrial action, since 'the long-term interests of individual employers are closely bound up with the general interests' of employers and the economy.[152]

The *dominant* judicial philosophy of the judgments in the new trilogy was again one exhibiting 'the habits' in which those judges were trained, and a 'generally unsympathetic attitude' to trade union rights which, as in earlier years and not surprisingly, 'reflected that of the middle class' of the time.[153] To assert, however, that 'innocent third parties' cannot settle a trade dispute poses, but does not answer the questions. Workers who strike in sympathy with other workers may not gain and may be able to lend no more than moral support to the strikers; but why does that prove they shall have no liberty to strike and thereby interfere with contracts? Those trained in the habits of a constitutional positive *right* to strike might want better reasons than these for drawing a narrow limit today around its permitted exercise.

Two Law Lords – Lord Fraser and Lord Scarman – refrained from appeals, open or tacit, for changes in the law. The latter (indicating that he knew well that he was dealing, in substance, not with 'immunities' but with a clash of social 'rights') was 'relieved' that the courts were not called upon to be 'some sort of a backseat driver in trade disputes'.[154] Later, realising that the government was obviously about to change the law in that direction. Lord Scarman called for clarity and an end to 'open-ended' expressions in the new law[155] – a call so far largely unheeded by the government.

At the time of the new trilogy, parliament conveniently had before it the Employment Bill of a government whose spokesmen shared with the majority of the judges the belief that the 'immunities' are all 'privileges'. The Bill aimed, it claimed, at 'restoring to employers and others who are harmfully affected by the consequences of people acting as pickets inducing breaches of contract *their common law rights that statute has taken away*'.[156] But every economic common law right 'restored' is an industrial trade union right destroyed. Historians will surely find fascinating the dates of the delicate game of law-making and the roles of the various players.[157] In that context, the question inevitably arises whether the relationship between British trade unionists and the *ordinary* courts – the traditional obedience to their orders even when workers felt judicial decisions infringed their basic rights – will be secure in the 1980s. Will this obedience continue if a struggle against the new legislation, applied by judges made (in some cases willingly) into front-seat drivers adjudicating the industrial merits of disputes, becomes part of an over-all battle about social and economic policies?[158] Will even the industrial tribunals and the Employment Appeal Tribunal escape distrust when their role is politicised by the Employment Bill.[159] In a deepening crisis of recession, unemployment and inflation, how will British trade unions and their members relate to judges who have often figured, in working class culture and legend,[160] among their oldest enemies?

The homogeneity of British society and, with it, the relationship between the ordinary courts and trade unionists, will be put to novel tests when the courts have to apply the new legislation. In the same period it will be of equal interest to see how far *positive* industrial rights survive in the relationship between other European labour movements and their courts of law.[161] Whatever the system of labour law, it is unlikely that those relationships will anywhere remain unaffected by the economic and social crisis into which Western Europe and, indeed, the world has plunged.

Notes

1. On the problems encountered in allowing civil servants and public employees to have industrial rights to organise or to strike, see B. Aaron and K.W. Wedderburn (eds.), (1972), Chap. 6, pp. 364-77 (hereafter *Industrial Conflict*, 1972). On the law in Britain before 1824, see R. Hedges and A. Winterbottom, *The Legal History of Trade Unionism* (1930), Chaps. I-III.
2. O. Kahn-Freund significantly described the legislation of 1824 and 1825 as passing 'from the stage of suppression to that of abstention': (1943) 7 MLR 192, 193, 'The Illegality of a Trade Union'. This appears to be the first use by him of the term 'abstention' of the law, which he later applied to modern British labour Law: see below, notes 65 and 66. (For brevity the main works of Kahn-Freund will be referred to below as follows: Chap. II, 'Legal Framework', in *The System of Industrial Relations in Britain* (A. Flanders and H. Clegg, eds. 1954): 'System 1954'; 'Labour Law' in *Law and Opinion in England in the Twentieth Century* (M. Ginsberg, ed., 1959) (reprinted as Chap. 1 of *Selected Writing* 1978): 'Ginsberg 1959'; *Labour Law: Old Traditions and New Developments* (1968); 'Traditions 1968'; *Labour and the Law* (1st ed., 1972; 2nd ed. 1977): 'Labour 1972' or '1977'; *Labour Relations, Heritage and Adjustment* (1979): 'Heritage 1979'.)
3. For a brief account of the various trade union movements and the legal developments see Wedderburn, Chap. 6 in Folke Schmidt, (ed.) *Discrimination in Employment* (1978), pp. 370-90 (hereafter *Discrimination*, 1978). To the legal sources in the text which follows must, of course, be added for most European countries, other than Britain, the International Labour Organisation Conventions 89 and 98 (of 1948 and 1949 respectively) establishing rights to organise and bargain collectively.
4. Of 27 October 1947, reaffirmed in that of 4 October 1958. See too *Code du Travail* (1974 ed.), Art. L. 411-2 and 412-2.
5. Within the ambit of laws regulating that right: see H. Sinay, *La Grève* (1966), Chap. II. On the Constitutional rights generally, see G. Camerlynck and G. Lyon-Caen, *Droit du Travail* (1976), para. 40. But see below, note 62.
6. See J.D. Reynard, *Les Syndicats en France* (1975), Vol. 1, pp. 122 *et seq.* The major trade union groups are now the CGT (Communist and 'left' Marxist), CGT-FO (Social-democrat) and CFDT (of which the roots were in Catholic trade unionism and the syndicalism of the French movement, but which is now a secular, often radical, federation). The broadly equivalent groups in Italy are the

CGIL, UIL and CISL. In both countries other groups exist, e.g. CISNAL (neo-fascist) in Italy; and in France, CFTC (Catholic) and CFT (alleged to be employer-dominated). Such ideological 'pluralism' creates a system markedly different from British 'multi-unionism': see W. Kendall, *The Labour Movement in Europe* (1975), Chaps. 4, 5 and 7.

7. See G. Camerlynck and G. Lyon-Caen, *Droit du Travail* (1976), paras 509-32; J.C. Javillier, *Droit du Travail* (1978), pp. 126-42; J.D. Reynaud, *Les Syndicats en France*, Vol. 1, Chap. III (the schism of 1919, for example, was bound up with that which split the Left in France: p. 72). On the importance of political action to French unions, see H. Clegg, *Trade Unions Under Collective Bargaining* (1976), Chap. 8.

8. See G. Giugni, 'Recent Developments in Collective Bargaining in Italy', *International Labour Review* (1965), pp. 273-91, for the beginning of this tendency. On developments in Italy strikingly parallel to British experience, see S. Sciarra, 'The Rise of the Italian Shop Steward' (1977) 5 ILJ 35, who points out how the new *consigli di fabbrica* (shop stewards' committees) have led to greater co-operation between the three conferederations: pp. 42-3.

9. See W. Kendall, op. cit. pp. 143-58. Cf. on the period 1914-24 A. Davidson, *Antonio Gramsci* (1977), Chap. III, and P. Spriano, *Storia del Partito Comunista Italiano* (1976), Vol. I, especially Chaps. XV-XVIII. on the 'autonomy' of trade unions today in the context of 'class unity', see B. Trentin, *Da Sfruttati a Produttori* (1977), pp. 271-330.

10. A right, as in France, guaranteed 'within the ambit of laws that regulate it': see G. Giugni, *Diritto Sindacale* (1979), pp. 181-2; and T. Treu et al., *Commentario della Costituzione* (ed. G. Branca, 1979) pp. 257-325, on Arts. 39 and 40. On the effect of such a 'right', see, infra, notes 62, 63, and p. 103.

11. Law No. 300, 20 May 1970. For a survey of problems arising under this law, see below G. Giugni, (ed.), *Lo Statuto dei Lavoratori: Commentario* (1979).

12. See for a general account of the German labour movement, W. Kendall, op. cit., pp. 89-105. Catholic trade unionism played a role here too, as in France and Italy.

13. Ibid., p. 101. But before 1918, it seems that neither German trade unions nor the Social Democratic Party subscribed to demands for positive rights in respect of collective bargaining and collective agreements (with the exception of Professor H. Sinzheimer). I am much indebted on this point to R. Lewis and J. Clark (eds.), *Labour Law and Politics in the Weimar Republic: Selected German Writings of O. Kahn-Freund* (1981). This point makes even more interesting, of course, the emergence of a programme for wide-ranging positive rights in the Weimar period. See below note 41.

14. See H. Spiro, *The Politics of German Codetermination* (1958), pp. 44-60.

15. See generally S. Simitis, 'Workers' Participation in the Enterprise – Transcending Company Law' (1975) 38 MLR 1; P. Davies, 'Employee Representation on Company Boards' (1975) 39 MLR 254. Since then the proportion of workers' representatives on supervisory boards of large companies has been increased by the Co-determination Act 1976; only in the 'Montan' industries of coal and steel, however, is there parity representation on supervisory boards.

16. See generally B. Aaron, G. Giugni and T. Ramm, Chaps. 2, 3 and 5 of *Industrial Conflict* (1972).

17. On what follows, see especially Folke Schmidt, *The Law of Labour Relations in Sweden* (1962), pp. 14-34.

18. L. Forsebäck, *Industrial Relations and Employment in Sweden* (1976), p. 16: by 1919, the 48-hour week was established through legislation. See, too, Folke Schmidt, 'From Socialism to Labourism' (1977) *Scandinavian Studies in Law* 243, and *Industrial Conflict* (1972), p. 28, on the earlier periods; for a few years after 1898 affiliation to the LO was conditional upon affiliation to the party.

19. See the lucid account in Folke Schmidt, *Law and Industrial Relations in Sweden*

(1977), especially Chaps. 4 to 15. In certain cases, trade unions are given statutory rights even to veto acts proposed by the employer: see Arts. 38-40 of the 1976 Act. This Act, extending the right to bargain, must be set in the context of two other prongs of the labour movement's programme, first the right to (minority) representation on company boards of directors, and, secondly, the 'Meidner' proposal that unions should by law be allotted an increasing proportion of shares in private companies: see Alan Neal, 'A New Era of Collective Labour Law in Sweden' (1978) 26 Am.J.Comp.L. 101; H.G. Myrdal, 'The Swedish Model – Will It Survive?' (1980) XVIII BJIR 57 (an employer's rection).

20. Now, the Trade Union and Labour Relations Act 1974 ('TULRA'), s. 14 (1), in effect re-enacting s. 4 (1) of the Trade Disputes Act 1906, which protects unions from liability in tort. In the light of current debates, it is worth recalling that Kahn-Freund called the immunity of a trade union in tort, 'the British solution of the problem of the "labour injunction" ': *System* 1954, pp. 110-11.

21. Acts done 'in contemplation or furtherance of a trade dispute' protected from certain criminal or civil liabilities: see Conspiracy and Protection of Property Act 1875, s. 3 (now overtaken by Criminal Law Act 1977, ss. 1, 3, 5) on criminal conspiracy; and in the civil law, Trade Disputes Act 1906, ss. 1, 2 and 3 (now replaced by TULRA 1974, ss. 13, 15 and 17, as amended in 1976).

22. Lord Denning MR, *Express Newspapers* v. *McShane* [1979] ICR 210, 218 (emphasis in original). On the Court of Appeal decisions between 1976 and 1979, restricting the 'immunities' to their narrowest ambit, see K. Ewing (1979) 8 ILJ 133. Until 1979 it could be said that almost every major decision of the House of Lords, too, had not favoured or had failed to understand collective trade union interests since *Allen* v. *Flood* [1898] AC 1 (a decision itself thought to be unfortunate by Lord Devlin: *Samples of Lawmaking* (1962), pp. 11-12). The one major exception, in war time, was *Crofter Hand Woven Harris Tweed* v. *Veitch* [1942] AC 435 (where the interests of the big union, coincided with those of the big employers). It is noteworthy that 'immunities' of other bodies have been approached much more cautiously by judges; see, e.g. *Harold Stephen Ltd.* v. *Post Office* [1978] 1 All E.R. 939 (CA).

23. *NWL* v. *Woods* [1979] ICR 867 (see Simpson (1980) 43 MLR 327); *Express Newspapers Ltd* v. *McShane* [1980] ICR 42 (in [1980] 1 All E.R. 65, *MacShane*) (see *Benedictus* (1980) 9 ILJ 45; Wedderburn (1980) 43 MLR 319; *Duport Steels Ltd* v. *Sirs* [1980] 1 All E.R. 529. On the 'trilogy' of 1892-1901, see Viscount Cave, *Sorrell* v. *Smith* [1925] AC 700, 711.

24. See e.g. Lord Keith in the *Sirs* case, p. 550.

25. Lord Diplock in the *Sirs* case, ibid. p. 541.

26. K.W. Wedderburn, *The Worker and the Law* (2nd ed. 1971), p. 314 (hereafter WATL). See too P. Davies and M. Freedland, *Labour Law: Text and Materials* (1979), pp. 590-624 (hereafter Davies and Freedland).

27. Wedderburn, 'The New Structure of Labour Law in Britain' (1978) 13 *Israel Law Review* 435, 437. The Liberal Party, the 'Lib-Labs' and the Labour Representation Committee did not provide a political base in the manner of working-class parties on the Continent.

28. On recent European developments, see J.D. Reynaud (1980) XVIII BJIR 1; and on the importance of the *structure* of collective bargaining in Britain, H. Clegg, *The Changing System of Industrial Relations in Britain* (1979).

29. See H. Clegg, *Trade Unions under Collective Bargaining* (1976).

30. See O. Kahn-Freund, 'The Impact of Constitutions on Labour Law' [1976] CLJ 240. Events in both World Wars (e.g. the Whitley Committee 1917, and Order 1305 cf. 1940) contributed much to the evolution of the British system – as did the fact (and now the disappearance) of the Empire.

31. Not only *via* transnational corporate structures. Even differences in national company laws decrease in comparable countries: see A. Levy, *Private Corporations and their Control* (1950); cf. Gower, *Modern Company Law* (4th ed., 1979),

Chap. 4 (EEC developments). On transnational industrial action, Wedderburn (1972) 1 ILJ 12.

32. See further O. Kahn-Freund, *Ginsberg* (1959), pp. 215 *et seq.*; R. Lewis, 'The Historical Development of Labour Law' (1976) XIV BJIR 1; K.W. Wedderburn, 'Labour Law and Labour Relations in Britain' (1972) X BJIR 270. On ways in which the British trade union movement came to be in this situation in the nineteenth century, see S. and B. Webb, *The History of Trade Unionism* (1920) (hereafter 'Webbs, *History*'); E.P. Thompson, *The Making of the English Working Class* (1963); E.J. Hobsbawm, *Labouring Men* (1964); A. Briggs, *The Age of Improvement* 1783-1867 (1979 ed.), Chap. 6.

33. See a letter to Engels, 4 November 1864, explaining why his famous *Inaugural Address* to the IWMA had to 'appear in a form acceptable from the present standpoint of the workers movement. In a few weeks, the same people will be holding meetings for the franchise with Bright and Cobden,' *Karl Marx: Selected Works* (1945), Vol. 2, p. 606. See too ibid. p. 618, where in 1871 he fears that the working class may remain a 'plaything' in the 'game Messrs. Gladstone and Co. are bringing off in England'. He could hardly foresee that Disraeli would do even better in 1875: Wedderburn, WATL, p. 312. On British unions and *laisser faire*, see Folke Schmidt [1974] CLJ 246, 252.

34. G.D.H. Cole, *A Short History of the British Working Class* (1948), p. 193. On the rapid decline of English Branches of the International, see H. Collins, *Essays in Labour History*, Chap. 7 (A. Briggs and J. Saville, eds, 1960).

35. H. Pelling, *A History of British Trade Unionism* (1963), p. 117, quoting Tillett's remark about the 'hare-brained chatterers and magpies of Continental revolutionists'. See too Webbs, *History*, pp. 383-415; E. Hobsbawm, *Labouring Men* (1964), pp. 181-91.

36. H. Pelling, op. cit., p. 116.

37. H. Clegg, A. Fox and A. Thompson, *A History of British Trade Unions Since 1889* (1964), Vol. 1, p. 96; see pp. 87-96 generally on this development. In 1892, Engels saw the working class in France and Germany as 'well ahead' of England, where it 'moves, like all things in England, with a slow and measured step'. *Socialism Utopian and Scientific* (1950 ed.), Intro., p. xxxviii.

38. E. Hobsbawm, op. cit., p. 319; the seminal legislation: Trade Union Act 1871 and Conspiracy and Protection of Property Act 1875.

39. Folke Schmidt, *Industrial Conflict* (1972), p. 65

40. O. Kahn-Freund, *Heritage* (1979), p. 44.

41. On the important fact that 'the industrial revolution preceded the extension of the Parliamentary franchise to the working class' in Britain, see O. Kahn-Freund, *Labour* (1977), p. 39; and *Traditions* (1968), pp. 2-9. After the Reform Act of 1884, and Redistribution Act 1885, more working men gradually satisfied the conditions for voting; but only in 1918 did statute enact universal male franchise at 21 (30 for women). Universal male suffrage was established in France in 1870, Sweden in 1907, and Italy in 1912; in Germany men of 25 were enfranchised in 1871, but they elected a Lower Chamber with very restricted powers: see C.L. Mowat (ed.), *The New Cambridge Modern History* (1968) Vol. XII, pp. 22-3, 473-88. In all these countries the industrial revolution, of course, came later than in Britain.

42. The Norris La Guardia Act 1932 and the National Labor Relations 'Wagner' Act 1935; before that, of course, the unions had experience of the Railway Labor Act 1926. Ironically, the one major, ideological (eventually syndicalist) American union (the IWW) founded in 1905, finally died in 1932 with 'exactly $29 cash' as assets: P. Renshaw, *The Wobblies* (1967), p. 214. On the transformation of the 'old voluntarist ideology' of most American unions by reason of *'favourable experience of legal support'*, see A. Flanders, 'The Tradition of Voluntarism' (1974) XII BJIR 352 366-70.

43. C. Gregory, *Labor and the Law* (2nd ed., 1961), p. 184. The labour unions thus came to see their relationships with the courts as based upon legislation, legiti-

mated by universal suffrage, which had liberated them from judicial labour injunctions and given them new collective bargaining *rights* (though these were later restricted). Cf. D. Bok (1971) 84 Harv. L.R. 1394, who points out that exclusive bargaining units of the Wagner Act 1935 were made to fit the shape of the bargaining patterns of the old AFL unions (pp. 1426 *et seq.*).

44. e.g. the Truck Act 1831 and the various Factories Acts from 1833 onwards: see Hutchins and Harrison, *A History of Factory Legislation* (1903).

45. S. and B. Webb, *Industrial Democracy* (1914 ed.), p. 247, on 'The Method of Legal Enactment' (emphasis supplied). See O. Kahn-Freund, *Labour*, 1977, pp. 39-41; and *infra* p. 83. Later, towards the turn of the century, 'parliamentary methods' for industrial purposes became the 'main weapon' only of *public* servants; with the possible exception at times of the railwaymen, it remained for other unions a weapon supplementary to industrial action: H. Clegg, A. Fox and A. Thompson, op. cit., Chap. 6.

46. O. Kahn-Freund, *Heritage*, 1979, p. 45.

47. On the Chartist movement, which played the 'most important part in working-class annals from 1837 to 1842' (Webbs, *History*, p. 174) see R. Gammage, *The History of The Chartist Movement* (1894); A. Briggs (ed.), *Chartist Studies* (1959); and N. Gash, *Aristocracy and People* (1979), Chap. 7. The claims of the Owenite and Chartist movements before 1850 'implied also further claims: a new way of reaching out by the working people for *social control* over their conditions of life and labour': E.P. Thompson, *The Making of the English Working Class*, p. 828. The Chartist movement came to a peak in 1842; declined into relative unimportance after 1848; and disappeared as a movement in 1857.

48. Even in their prime – despite their part in the campaign over the Tolpuddle martyrs – 'the Chartists could never point to any solid backing from the trade unions – this was one of the major weaknesses especially when they entertained plans of calling a general strike': G.D.H. Cole and A.W. Filson, *British Working Class Movements: Selected Documents* (1965), p. 392. Cf. *Robert Lowery: Radical and Chartist* (B. Harrison and P. Hollis, eds, 1979), pp. 82-90. But it was a near thing in one sector – the cotton unions, which spanned the earlier and later periods: see H.A. Turner, *Trade Union Growth, Structure and Policy* (1962), pp. 99-107.

49. S. Beer, *History of British Socialism* (1929), Vol. 2, p. 362 (who contrasts the organising capacity of the movement then with 'the years 1839-42'). Syndicalist influences helped to give the 'workers' rebellion' of those years a higher ideological content: see R. Rayner, *The Story of Trade Unionism* (1929), Chap. VI; Lord Askwith, *Industrial Problems and Disputes* (1920), Chaps. XIV-XXXIII, much drawn upon by G. Dangerfield, *The Strange Death of Liberal England* (1935), Part II, Chap. 4.

50. P. Mathias, *The First Industrial Nation* (1969), p. 172.

51. The one important Act of that period, the Trade Union Act 1913 (legitimising trade union political expenditure after the *Osborne* case [1910] AC 87, HL) did not, interestingly enough, assume the form of a statutory 'immunity'.

52. A.L. Morton, *A People's History of England* (1968), p. 444. The Webbs described this 'opportunism' of the Junta less critically in *History*, Chap. V, although they approve Harrison's criticism of the Junta's adoption of 'the capitalist cry of "non-interference" ' (pp. 296-8). In the Junta's cry of 'non-interference' may be seen the *fons et origo* of the modern doctrine of legal 'non-intervention', see below notes 65 and 66.

53. Webbs, *History*, p. 362: between 1875 and 1885, the union leaders 'carried on the traditions of the Junta ... the same shrewd caution and practical opportunism'. As for the more socialist leaders of some of the General Unions in 1880-1900, see above, notes 35 to 37.

54. Hobsbawm, op. cit., pp. 236-7, pointing out that the achievements of Hyndman's Social Democratic Federation should nevertheless not be overlooked. See further E.P. Thompson, 'Homage to Tom Maguire,' Chap. 8, *Essays in Labour History* (A. Briggs and J. Saville, eds, 1960), p. 288.

55. *Hornby* v. *Close* (1867) LR 2 QB 153.
56. For the ingenious demand which *was* put forward (legal status under the Friendly Societies Acts, with immunity from legal suit) devised by Harrison, see Webbs, *History*, pp. 261-74.
57. Trade Union Act 1871, ss. 2 and 3 (now TULRA 1974, s. 2 (5), strengthened by the repeal of s. 5 in 1976), after the 'Minority' Report of the Royal Commission 1869, pp. 51-60, and the interim Trades Union Funds Protection Act 1869.
58. Conspiracy and Protection of Property Act 1875, s. 3 (now overtaken by Criminal Law Act 1977, ss. 1-5); Trade Disputes Act 1906, ss. 1, 2 and 3 (now TULRA 1974 and 1976, ss. 13 and 15). On s. 4, see note 20 above. On the history leading to the Act of 1906, see F. Bealey and H. Pelling, *Labour and Politics, 1900-1906* (1958); H. Clegg, A. Fox and A. Thompson, *A History of British Trade Unions Since 1889* (1964), Vol. I, pp. 305-96; B.C. Roberts, *The Trades Union Congress* (1958), Chaps. 4-6.
59. On this golden formula of British trade union law, see Davies and Freedland, pp. 611-38; Wedderburn, WATL, pp. 327-37; Simpson (1977) 40 MLR 16; and the new 'trilogy' in the House of Lords, above, note 23.
60. This 'second limb' of s. 3 of the 1906 Act (of which the wording derived from Sir William Erle's famous *Memorandum on Trade Union Law*, Report of the Royal Commission 1869, pp. 65-89) was intended to protect residual forms of liability for 'economic torts'. But the House of Lords, in *Rookes* v. *Barnard* [1964] AC 1129, held that it did not protect threats to break contracts or indeed, any other liability under the modern law, and was, therefore, 'otiose' (p. 1216), 'unnecessary' (p. 1177), 'nugatory' (p. 1192) or 'pointless' (p. 1236); see (1961) 24 MLR 589; (1964) 27 MLR 270-280. Cf. below, notes 79 and 28.
61. Now s. 29, TULRA 1974 and 1976; see *BBC* v. *Hearn* [1977] ICR 685, CA, approved in *Express Newspapers* v. *McShane* [1980] ICR 42, HL; *NWL* v. *Woods* [1979] ICR 867, HL. The *Hearn* case, however, might have been presented as a 'trade dispute', as Pain J. held it was: (1978) 41 MLR 80. See now *Express Newspapers Ltd* v. *Keys, Times*, 9 May 1980.
62. *Corte Costituzionale*, 27 December 1974, n. 290; reported in (1978) 1 *International Labour Law Reports* 51, 54. Contrast the position in France, Camerlynck and Lyon-Caen, op. cit., pp. 651 *et seq.*
63. Giugni, *Diritto Sindacale* (1979), p. 185; L. Mengoni, 'Lo Sciopero nel diritto civile', in *Il diritto di sciopero* (1964).
64. See, for example, E.H. Phelps Brown, *The Growth of British Industrial Relations* (1959); on the 1960s, the '*Donovan*' *Royal Commission Report on Trade Unions and Employers' Associations* (Cmnd 3623, 1968); today, H.A. Clegg, *The Changing System of Industrial Relations in Britain* (1979); E. Batstone, I. Boraston, S. Frenkel, *Shop Stewards in Action* (1977).
65. O. Kahn-Freund, *System* 1954, p. 123. See note 2 above.
66. O. Kahn-Freund, *Ginsberg* 1959, pp. 225-44. The present writer came to prefer 'non-intervention' (WATL, p. 17); but perhaps that term, too, is rather abstract to describe what was no conscious decision, but the exclusion of common law liabilities in a special manner by reason of the social forces discussed above. See on 'abstention', etc., the very interesting discussion 'Kahn-Freund and Labour Law: An Outline Critique', by R. Lewis (1979) 8 ILJ 202.
67. Not normally contractual because of lack of intention: *Ford Motor Co* v. *AUEFW* [1969] 2 QB 303 (see G. de N. Clark (1970) 33 MLR 117); now s. 18 (1) TULRA 1974. Cf. R. Lewis, 'Collective Agreements: The Kahn-Freund Legacy' (1979) 42 MLR 613; Davies and Freedland, pp. 127-46; and Kahn-Freund's recollection just before his death of his thinking on the point: (1979) 8 ILJ 200.
68. See A. Flanders, *Management and Unions* (1970), p. 97 (reprinting his paper of 1965, 'Industrial Relations – What is Wrong with the System?'). See, too, p. 99, on the British 'lack of concern for the distinction between conflicts of interest and conflicts of right, which is fundamental in European labour law'. That distinction has now begun to appear more prominently in procedures bargained under the

influence of protective, 'individual' employment legislation (e.g. on disciplinary matters or dismissals); note 12 above.

69. Wedderburn, WATL, p. 210.

70. Kahn-Freund, *System* 1954, p. 66, who applied the dictum then to 'all' British labour legislation.

71. Wedderburn, WATL, p. 371. See Davies and Freedland, pp. 607-9, on the vulnerability of statutory immunities to judicial erosion. It is notable that judicial 'creativity' did far more to extend workers' liabilities in practice than the Trade Disputes and Trade Unions Act 1927 (repealed 1946).

72. See Wedderburn (1972) 10 BJIR 270, 276-8. The judges were 'creative' in other areas of the common law in this period: J.A.G. Griffith, *The Politics of the Judiciary*, p. 62, and *passim*. Contrast the curious period of 1920 to 1924; see Wedderburn, WATL, p. 28. On the period 1976 to 1979, above, note 22.

73. *Rookes* v. *Barnard* [1964] AC 1129 HL (threat of breach); *Stratford* v. *Lindley* [1965] AC 269, HL (extension of direct and indirect procurement of breach); *Torquay Hotel Ltd.* v. *Cousins* [1969] 2 Ch. 106, CA (interference short of causing breach; *per* Lord Denning MR pp. 137-8). The Trade Disputes Act 1965 was Parliament's answer to the *Rookes* case. The Employment Bill 1980 largely rescinds that answer: p. 55 above.

74. *Report*, Cmnd 3623, 1968, para. 887; on s. 3, see also note 60 above.

75. See in particular: Parl. Deb., Vol. 162, 4 ser., cols. 1678 (Lord R. Cecil); 1684, 1691 (Sir John Walton, Att.-Gen.); 1687-8 (Mr Atherley Jones); 1702 (Sir E. Carson); Vol. 164 ibid. cols. 145-7 (Sir Frederick Banbury); 150 (Sir John Walton); 151 (Lord R. Cecil); 152 (Mr Clement Edwards); 156 (Viscount Castlereagh); Vol. 166, ibid. cols. 711-2 (Lord Coleridge); 716-8 (Lord James).

76. Sir Gilbert Parker, Vol. 164, ibid. col. 899.

77. See Vol. 167 ibid. col. 295: 'I always thought it [*Lumley* v. *Gye* (1853) 2 E&B 216] was bad law and so did a great many of my confrères and many occupants of the Bench.' It is not conceivable that a lawyer of his quality would, thereafter have supported the clause as amended if he believed that organising strikes involved liability for other forms of interference with contracts (see note 60 above) especially commercial contracts. His speeches in Vol. 167, ibid. cols. 295-296, and *Conway* v. *Wade* [1909] AC 506, are consistent with that conclusion. Some legal systems know of no liability for inducing breach of contract, e.g. Sweden (Folke Schmidt, *Law and Industrial Relations in Sweden* (1977), pp. 184-6); in others, e.g. Italy, the right to strike excludes such liability, see above, note 63.

78. See above, n. 73.

79. Op. cit. Cmnd 3623 (1968), paras. 803; 804; 893; 894 (where the majority – seven to five – recommended a limitation on the exemption for interfering with contracts which would have left 'unofficial' industrial action at risk of illegality; but the Royal Commission was unanimous that some such extension had to be enacted).

80. TULRA 1974, s. 13 (1), (3), as amended by TULR Amendment Act 1976, s. 3 (2). It was included in the Labour government's Bill of 1970, after acceptance of the recommendation in 'In Place of Strife' (Cmnd 3888, 1979) para. 100.

81. See the arguments reviewed in C. Crouch, *Class Conflict and the Industrial Relations Crisis* (1977), Chap. 6; and W.E.J. McCarthy and N. Ellis, *Management by Agreement* (1973), Chaps. 3, 4 and 5 (in relation to the Industrial Relations Act 1971).

82. Op. cit. Cmnd 3623 (1968), especially Chaps. VI to XIV.

83. Para. 8, *Industrial Relations Bill: Consultative Document* (5 October 1970, Department of Employment). On the operation of the Industrial Relations Act 1971, see B. Weekes, M. Mellish, L. Dickens and J. Lloyd, *Industrial Relations and the Limits of Law* (1975); A. Thomson and S. Engleman, *The Industrial Relations Act: A Review and Analysis* (1975). The present writer's doubts about the wisdom, justice and practicability of the 1971 Bill were dismissed by the *Times* as 'rather

implausible misgivings' 13 January 1971. The Employment Bill 1980 (as amended) now bears striking similarities to it.

84. For the legal and other problems of the dockworkers' dispute, see P. Davies (1973) 36 MLR 78. See too B. Hepple (1972) 1 ILJ 197, on *Heaton's Transport Ltd* v. *TGWU* [1973] AC 15, HL.

85. On the strike case, *Con-Mech. Ltd* v. *AUEW* (No. 3), ICR 464, see N. Lewis 'Con-Mech: Showdown for the NIRC' (1974) 3 ILJ 201; and the exclusion from the union, *Goad* v. *AUEW* (No. 3) [1973] ICR 108. On the role of the NIRC, see J.A.G. Griffith, *The Politics of the Judiciary* (1977), pp. 70-6, and pp. 199-201.

86. This belief was fortified by a lecture by the President, Sir John Donaldson, after the court was abolished, 'Lessons From The Industrial Court' (1975) 91 LQR 181, pp. 191-2; '... courts could be given their traditional role of investigating the merits of disputes and helping the party who is right.... Ought [the public] not to know who is right? ... they *would* know, for the court which investigated the dispute would tell them.' This astonishingly naïve view of the nature of industrial conflict illuminates in retrospect the judgments of 1971 to 1974 when he presided over the NIRC.

87. See, for example, Lord Devlin, *Sunday Times*, 6 August 1972, quoted in Griffith, *The Politics of the Judiciary*, pp. 190-1. For 1980, see above, notes 43 and 59.

88. On the 'transplantation' analogy, see the remarkable lecture by O. Kahn-Freund, 'On The Uses and Misuses of Comparative Law' (1974) 37 MLR 1; for the surveys see Weekes *et al.*, op. cit. note 83.

89. TULR Amendment Act 1976, ss. 3 (2) and 1 (a). On the second point, in 1976 the TUC set up its own Independent Review Committee (of which the writer is Chairman) to monitor exclusions from affiliated unions in closed shop situations. On the work of the Committee, see (1979) 208 *Industrial Relations Review and Report* 2; Davies and Freedland, pp. 548-57. The Employment Bill 1980 proposes to restore the legal obligation in closed shops not to exclude 'unreasonably': Cll. 3, 4. On the other main change in 1976, protection in respect of commercial contracts, see above notes 72 to 80.

90. C. Jenkins and J. Mortimer, *The Kind of Laws the Unions Ought to Want* (1968).

91. Employment Protection Act ('EPA') 1975, ss. 17-21. (H. Gospel (1976) 5 ILJ 223).

92. Directive 75/129; EPA, ss. 99-107 (M.R. Freedland (1976) 5 ILJ 24).

93. EPA, Sched. 11 (Penny Wood (1978) 7 ILJ 65). This replaced the Terms and Conditions of Employment Act 1959, s. 8 (see K.W. Wedderburn and P.L. Davies, *Employment Grievances and Disputes Procedures in Britain* (1969)), which replaced Order 1376 of 1951, which replaced Order 1305 of 1940 (on both see O. Kahn-Freund, *System* 1954, pp. 91-101).

94. EPA ss. 11-16. See O. Kahn-Freund, *Labour*, 1977, pp. 77-88; Davies and Freedland, pp. 61-110, especially pp. 102-4; and M. Hart (1978) 7 ILJ 201 on the duty to bargain and analogies in the United States.

95. See especially Simpson, 'Judicial Control of ACAS' (1979) 9 ILJ 69 (from *Grunwick* v. *ACAS* [1978] AC 655, HL to *UKAPE* v. *ACAS* [1979] ICR 303, CA). Ironically, now that ss. 11-16 are to be repealed (Employment Bill 1980, cl. 18), the House of Lords has liberated ACAS to use its discretion more widely in order to improve industrial relations: *UKAPE* v. *ACAS* [1980] 1 All E.R. 612; *EMA* v. *ACAS* [1980] 1 All E.R. 896.

96. For example, that it would 'vitally affect the very structure of collective bargaining'. R. Lewis (1976) XIV BJIR 14. It was in part because ACAS could not fulfil that role, that the chairman wrote to the Secretary of State on 29 June 1979, more or less inviting the Government to repeal ss. 11-16: see Working Paper of 24 September 1979.

97. Wedderburn, op. cit. (1978) 13 *Israel Law Review* 456.

68   *Employment Rights in Britain and Europe*

98. Op. cit. Cmnd 3623, p. 243, para. 935: 'No doubt if the law is codified, as we recommend, the matter will receive further consideration.'
99. Ibid. p. 244, para. 943, setting out just eight of the many difficulties.
100. In s. 147 of the Industrial Relations Act 1971. See the brilliant analysis of s. 147, in a comparative context, by X. Blanc Jouvan, *Industrial Conflict* (1972), pp. 196-210.
101. *Morgan* v. *Fry* [1968] 2 QB 710, 726; *Tramp Shipping* v. *Greenwich Marine* [1975] ICR 261. On strike notices cf. P. O'Higgins [1968] CLJ 223; Wedderburn WATL, pp. 109-11.
102. All the case law since *Simmons* v. *Hoover Ltd* [1977] ICR 61, shows that the doctrine has 'failed to win general acceptance': B. Napier (1977) 6 ILJ 1, 12.
103. See Camerlynck and Lyon-Caen, op. cit., p. 671; Javiller, op. cit., pp. 584-5, (even an imprecise or unreasonably long obligation to give strike notice is unconstitutional because it fetters that right). On the parallel debate in Italy, see G. Giugni, *Industrial Conflict* (1972), pp. 151-3; and *Diritto Sindacale* (1979), pp. 158-63.
104. Wedderburn, WATL, p. 401.
105. *Trade Unions In A Changing World: The Challenge for Management* (a discussion document), Confederation of British Industry 'Steering Group' (February 1980), p. 22, (emphasis supplied). On Art. 11 of the European Convention on Human Rights, see *infra*, note 17.
106. They often – and understandably – preferred collective bargaining to legislation until a very late stage. See the attitude of the TUC to what became the Redundancy Payments Act 1965, in Congress *Report* 1961, pp. 131-2; 1963, pp. 138-40; 1964, p. 143; 1965, pp. 144-5; and on what became the unfair dismissal provisions of the 1971 Act, *Report* 1963, p. 219; 1964, p. 144; and the participation of the TUC representatives in Report of Committee of NJAC, Ministry of Labour, 1967: 'strong arguments against the introduction at an early date of legislation', para. 195.
107. See for example the Swedish Employment Protection Act 1974 (Folke Schmidt, *Law and Labour Relations in Sweden* (1977), p. 27); and the Italian Law No. 604 on Job Security July 14, 1966 (G.F. Mancini, Chap. 1, *Causa e Giustificati Motivi Nei Licenziamenti Individuale*, G. Mazzoni, ed., 1967).
108. Employment Protection (Consolidation) Act 1978 ('EPCA'). (The Italian paper included a more detailed discussion of 'individual' labour legislation; but, for brevity, the British reader is referred to the excellent accounts in B. Hepple and P. O'Higgins, *Employment Law* (4th ed., 1979), Pts. II and III, and Davies and Freedland, pp. 199-477, for details of laws with which he will be familiar.)
109. Wedderburn, WATL, p. 481. Research is beginning to bear fruit on the problems here raised: see e.g. L. Dickens, 'Unfair Dismissal Applications and the Industrial Tribunal System' (1978) 9 *Industrial Relations Journal* 4; M. Mellish and N. Collis-Squires 'Legal and Social Norms in Discipline and Dismissal' (1975) 5 ILJ 164; B. Weekes, 'ACAS – An Alternative to Law?' (1979) 8 ILJ 147. On the practice of the tribunals, see Davies and Freedland, pp. 726-44; and a fascinating contrast with *conseils de prud'hommes*. B. Napier, 'The French Labour Courts – An Institution in Transition' (1979) 42 MLR 270.
110. Is such a law operable without strong trade union and, indeed, other social support? On the Equal Pay Act 1970, Art. 119 of the EEC Treaty and their context of sex discrimination generally, see O. Kahn-Freund, *Labour* 1977, pp. 154-7.
111. R. Lewis (1976) XIV BJIR at p. 15 (emphasis supplied) and see (1979) 8 ILJ 218-21: compare Kahn-Freund, *Labour* 1977, p. 46. The Employment Bill 1980 will, of course, add strength to this argument.
112. See EPCA 1978, ss. 18, 65 (dismissal), 96 (redundancy), 140 (2) (a), (c), (f); and EPA 1975, s. 107 (consultation about redundancies).
113. EPCA 1978, s. 62. Compare ibid. s. 63 (industrial pressure to be ignored in unfair dismissal claims). See the remarkable decision of the EAT in *McCormick* v. *Horsepower Ltd*, 176 IDS Brief, March 1980, p. 6.

114. But cll. 9 and 14 (as amended) of the Employment Bill 1980 transgress into just that area and will cause tribunals (and appellate courts) to decide how reasonable industrial pressure is, in determining the 'just and equitable' contribution payable by a union or its officials to an employer guilty of unfair dismissal or discrimination induced by union pressure.

115. Indeed the government's stance in 1980 of 'non-intervention' in industrial matters has withdrawn from the 1980 scene the meta-legal pressures of a 'social contract'. For the best modern review of British procedures, see P. Davies, 'Arbitration and the Role of Courts' (UK National Report), Ninth International Congress, *International Society for Labour Law and Social Security* (1978), pp. 281-346. In France obligatory procedures of conciliation, mediation and arbitration exist in law but, in practice, are 'dead', G. Camerlynck and G. Lyon-Caen, op. cit., p. 711.

116. As to union membership agreements, trade union rights and dismissals, see s. 58 of the EPCA 1978. The present writer has essayed a comparative treatment of the closed shop and 'union security' in *Discrimination*, 1978, Chap. 6. The closed shop 'cannot be attacked or defended in terms of general ethical sentiments but only in terms of social expediency': O. Kahn-Freund, *Labour* 1972, p. 201. The European Commission and Court on Human Rights may prefer the German approach of implying a right to 'dissociate' into the right of association established by Art. 11 of the Human Rights Convention when it decides *Young, James and Webster* v. *UK* (cf. *Discrimination*, p. 368); that would limit the legality of the closed shop far more even than clause 6 of the Employment Bill 1980.

117. See generally EPCA, 1978, ss. 27-32.

118. Wedderburn (1975) 39 MLR 169. *Quaere* whether judicial interpretations adequately recognise the collective aspect of these 'individual rights'; see, e.g. *Chant* v. *Aquaboats Ltd* [1978] ICR 643.

119. On the future relationship in Italy of such legislation and collective bargaining, see G. Arrigo *et al.*, *Per Una Politica del Lavoro* (1979).

120. The Italian statute also protects the worker from discrimination penalising his *not* joining a trade union, as one would expect in a system of trade union 'pluralism' where the right to choose between unions, or against all of them, is deeply embedded in the labour movement itself. So, too, in France, union 'pluralism' leads to a prohibition of discrimination by the employer against a worker for joining or not joining a trade union: *Code du Travail*, Art. 412-2 (as amended in 1956). But such systems of law have fulfilled many of the objects of 'union security' arrangements by giving certain rights only to 'representative' trade unions. 'Union security' becomes important for trade union movements that have traditionally relied on *membership* for strength (Britain, United States) and have not then acquiesced in integration (Germany) or solved the problem by very high 'density' of organisation (Sweden). See Wedderburn in *Discrimination* 1978, pp. 385-90, 401-66.

121. On Arts. 15 and 16, see E. Trigiani in *Lo Statuto dei Lavoratori: Commentario* (G. Giugni, ed., 1979), pp. 209-36 (especially at pp. 210-2 on the relationship between Art. 15 of the Statute, Art. 39 of the Constitution, and the ILO Convention 98); and T. Treu, *Condotta Antisindacale e Atti Discriminatori* (1974). It is worth noting also that Art. 28 of the 1970 statute gives to Italian workers the remedy of injunction whereby they obtain reinstatement, an Article much used by workers in industrial disputes. For similar but rather less extensive protection of workers in France: see J.C. Javaillier, *Droit du Travail* (1978), pp. 518-24.

122. Employment Bill 1980, cl. 15. It will be much discussed whether this clause (with a Government 'Code of Practice') will affect in practice the criminal as well as civil liability of pickets especially in view of cl. 2 (8). Union 'officials' may accompany a member picketing lawfully *only* if they 'represent' the member, a limitation full of legal hazards in view of the new s. 15 (4) of TULRA in cl. 15 (1).

123. Templeman J., *Camellia Tanker Ltd SA* v. *ITWF* [1976] ICR 274, 289

(affirmed on other grounds by CA 291). See the CBI strategy for employers, below note 152.

124. Employment Bill 1980, cl. 17. This would reimpose only liability for interference with contracts (s. 13 (1), TULRA); whereas cl. 15 on picketing would remove the protection of the whole of s. 13, including s. 13 (4) on 'simple' civil conspiracy to injure. For a critical analysis of Conservative Government proposals in 1979, relevant to the Bill, see R. Lewis, P. Davies and Wedderburn, 'Industrial Relations Law and the Conservative Government' (1979, Fabian Society).

125. Cl. 16 added on Report in the House of Commons. The definitions ('directly', 'supply', and the 'representation' of employers by an employers' association) leave a lot of questions unanswered, especially in the light of the law on 'indirect' interference with commercial contracts: Clerk and Lindsell on *Torts* (14th ed., 1975), pp. 404-10. So too, the doctrine of 'principal purpose' seems to reverse in this area the decision in *NWL* v. *Woods* [1979] ICR 867 HL, in so far as it decided that furtherance of a trade dispute did not require a 'predominant' purpose to further the dispute 'connected with' the matters set out in s. 29 (1) TULRA 1974; see Simpson (1980) 43 MLR 327.

126. See *Express Newspapers Ltd* v. *McShane* [1980] ICR 42, HL (see Wedderburn (1980) 43 MLR 319); *Duport Steels Ltd* v. *Sirs* [1980] 1 All E.R. 529 HL.

127. Cl. 16 (8). On the need for s. 13 (3) of TULRA 1974, see Clerk and Lindsell, op. cit., p. 443; Wedderburn (1974) 37 MLR pp. 541-3; (1968) 31 MLR p. 560; Grabiner (1969) 32 MLR p. 437; and see Templeman J. in *Camellia Tanker* v. *ITWF* [1976] ICR 274, 285-8; affirmed on other grounds by CA. The range of tortious 'interference by use of unlawful means' has been growing and includes breach of statutory provisions: *Carlin Music* v. *Collins* (1979) FSR 548 CA (*quaere* all such breaches?). Breach of contract was not regarded as unlawful means in tort until *Rookes* v. *Barnard* [1964] AC 1129, HL. Now other new species of wrongdoing are being elaborated by the courts which may not even be *torts* at all, thereby allowing for evasion not just of s. 13 but even of s. 14 (1) of TULRA: see e.g. *Universe Tankships* v. *ITF*, *Times*, 10 April 1980 (the extension of 'duress', and claims for 'restitution').

128. For example, industrial action which includes a demand that an employer reimburse a shop steward whom he 'joined' in proceedings before an industrial tribunal under cl. 9 or the amended cl. 14, and from whom he thereby recovered hundreds, perhaps thousands, of pounds. That this *is* the intention of the Government was confirmed by the Under-Secretary of State for Employment (Mr P. Mayhew) in Committee, Parl. Deb., *Standing Committee A*, 11 March 1980, cols. 1093-1100.

129. Working Paper, 19 February 1980, paras. 7 and 10. The government also argues (ibid. para. 5) that TULRA 1974, s. 13 (3) gave a 'wider immunity' than under the 1906 Act by legitimating inducement of breach of employment contracts as an indirect way of lawfully interfering with commercial contracts. But s. 13 (3) is a critical requirement if 'primary' strikes are not to be at risk of illegality. See above note 125.

130. Above, note 79 for the proviso of the majority to the statement: '... we recommend that the protection of section 3 be extended so as to cover all contracts.'

131. [1964] AC 1129, HL; Clerk and Lindsell, op. cit., pp. 419-21; 445-6. See, too, the doubts of the Canadian Supreme Court as to the correctness of that decision at common law: *Central Canada Potash* v. *Govt. of Saskatchewan* (1979) 68 DLR 3d. 609, 636. The *Rookes* decision amounted to a 'frontal attack upon the right to strike': O. Kahn-Freund, *Federation News* (1964), Vol. 14, pp. 30, 41.

132. Lord Scarman, *NWL* v. *Woods* [1979] ICR at p. 886. Contrast Lord Diplock's belief that the 1974 and 1976 Acts had led to real extensions of the 'immunities' compared with the 1906 Act, in the *Express* case [1980] ICR 56 (see (1980) 43 MLR 324) and *Duport Steels Ltd.* v. *Sirs* [1980] 1 All ER 541.

133. Ibid. This is the first major judicial recognition of the true effect of the judicial decisions.

134. Parl. Deb., Vol. 166, cols. 705 and 709: 'Was there ever such a thing heard of in a civilised country?' Dicey asked a meeting to oppose a Bill that would allow the 'caprice' of a trade union to govern the employment conditions of 'women – domestic servants for instance': *Times*, 3 October 1906.

135. Working Paper, para. 7; at a time when collaboration between associated groups of employers, nationally and transnationally, has never been greater, and the CBI is pressing ahead with plans for its strike-insurance scheme; see below n. 152.

136. The Bill, especially cl. 16 (3) (4), will impose upon judges 'the strange and embarrassing task' of being 'called upon to review the tactics of a party to a trade dispute', which Lord Scarman was 'relieved to find' he did not have in the *Express* case: [1980] ICR 65. As to uncertainty, see the difference in applying the 'objective' test in *Express Newspapers Ltd.* v. *McShane*, between Lord Wilberforce's minority opinion [1980] ICR at pp. 54, 56, and Lawton and Brandon LJJ [1979] ICR 210, 220-3. On the great importance of procedural considerations in this area of law, see O. Kahn-Freund, *Labour* 1977, p. 274; Wedderburn (1980) 43 MLR 319; Simpson (1980) 43 MLR 327. The new trilogy of decisions leaves great doubt about the range of the discretion – which permits an injunction even if the defendant seems 'likely' to prove a trade dispute defence.

137. [1980] 1 All E.R. 529. This extraordinary case will go down in legal history. The judge in chambers refused injunctions on Friday afternoon 25 January because the case was clearly covered by the *Express* decision. The Court of Appeal, sitting on Saturday 26, granted the injunctions *and* refused leave to appeal to the House of Lords, 'somewhat surprisingly' as Lord Diplock later said (p. 544). The Law Lords granted leave to appeal (without requiring any argument from defendants' counsel) on 31 January. After only three hours of argument, in the course of which counsel for the employers stated he felt unable to rely on *any* of the reasons given by the Court of Appeal in their three judgments, the House of Lords gave judgment for the defendants at 2.00 p.m., Friday 1 February. But the injunction, wrongly granted by the Court of Appeal, had caused great confusion among steel workers in the week following 26 January. The Law Lords gave the reasons for their decision in speeches delivered on Thursday 7 February, completing what must surely be a record for celerity in their court.

138. [1980[ICR 42 (HL 13 December 1979).

139. Mr W. Sirs of ISTC: see *Times* and *Financial Times*, 29 January 1980. After the CA decision on 26 January, the executive committee delayed its decision to withdraw its instructions (by first class post) until Tuesday 29 January. By the evening of Friday 1 February, the day of the HL decision, it had renewed them. See too below note 158.

140. See above note 137.

141. See note 87 above.

142. *Per* Lord Diplock [1980] 1 All E.R. 529, 547; and p. 542: 'It endangers continued public confidence in the political impartiality of the judiciary which is essential to the continuance of the rule of law, if judges, under the guise of interpretation, provide their own preferred amendments to statutes ...' So too, Lord Keith on risks to 'the standing and the degree of respect commanded by the judicial system' (p. 550); Lord Scarman: 'Justice ... is not left to the unguided, even if experienced, sage sitting under the spreading oak tree' (p. 551). The Court of Appeal, in *Beaverbook* v. *Keys* [1978] ICR 582; *Star Sea Transport* v. *Slater, The Camilla M.* [1978] IRLR 507; *ANG* v. *Wade* [1979] ICR 664; *Express Newspapers* v. *McShane* [1979] ICR 210; *PBDS* v. *Filkins* [1979] IRLR 356; and the *Sirs* case, had indeed brought respect for the law into danger by its interpretations of the trade dispute 'immunities'. Contrast Goulding J. in *Health Computing Ltd.* v. *Meek, Times*, 5 March 1980.

143. See on British developments, P. Davies and S. Anderman, 'Injunction Procedure and Labour Disputes' (1973) 2 ILJ 213, (1974) 3 ILJ 30; O. Kahn-Freund, *Labour* 1977, pp. 271-4. The classic work is Frankfurter and Greene, *The Labor Injunction* (1932).

144. Professor A. Goodhart, in his persuasive argument for the legality of the 1926 General Strike, clearly agreed with that meaning: see (1927) 36 Yale L.J. 464, 471 (*Essays in Jurisprudence and the Common Law* (1937), p. 235). One of the problems posed by the Employment Bill is when, if ever, a general strike will in future be lawful.

145. *Express* [1980] ICR 57. The first indication of this line of thought by Lord Diplock in the trilogy was in the *NWL* case [1979] ICR 867, 878, where he speaks about wage claims that aimed to bring down the 'present economic system' (see Simpson (1980) 43 MLR 330). His attitude to 'what is popularly known as industrial action' and 'industrial muscle' was more clearly evinced in *Express* [1980] ICR 56-7, and in *Sirs* (1980) 1 All E.R. 541-2 and 547.

146. The *Duport Steels* case [1980] 1 All E.R. 541.

147. *Express* [1980] ICR 60-1. The picketing of the hospital was indeed abhorrent to many people; but the dispute was a very complex one and it was less than fair to condemn the pickets unheard as guilty of 'inhuman conduct' (p. 60).

148. *Duport Steels* [1980] 1 All E.R. 548, and 550. Lord Wilberforce in the *Express* case [1980] ICR 53, adopted the objective test partly to protect an 'innocent and powerless third party' from 'action by enthusiasts, extremists and fanatics'.

149. *Rookes* v. *Barnard* [1964] AC 1219. On the judicial policies in *Stratford* v. *Lindley* [1965] AC 269, see (1965) 28 MLR 205.

150. See *supra*, note 35 on the Earl of Halsbury and Dicey in 1906. See too, *A Giant's Strength*, Inns of Court Conservative and Unionist Society (1958). Compare H. Clegg, *The Changing System of Industrial Relations* (1979), Chaps. 5 to 11, on trade union power today.

151. Lord Diplock, *Duport Steels* [1980] 1 All E.R. 541.

152. Op. cit. above, note 105, pp. 22-3: They should copy the 'mutual financial support schemes' successful in Europe, and the similar practices of the Engineering Employers' Federation. 'The work of that company [hit by a dispute] should not be done by others nor should gaps created in a market be filled by competitors.' This remarkable statement seems to mean that normal market forces do not include competitive opportunities caused by withdrawals of labour. Does this need for employers' solidarity stop at the Channel? Or are all employers' 'long-term' interests today transnational?

153. As Kahn-Freund said of the judges in 1900-10 (*Ginsberg* 1959, p. 241). On such 'habits' imparting a 'certain class of ideas', see the famous remarks of Scrutton LJ [1923] CLJ 8. To advert to such matters is not, of course, to deny 'the obvious point, which some modern Marxists have overlooked, that there is a difference between arbitrary power and the rule of law.' E.P. Thompson, *Whigs and Hunters* (1975), p. 266; cf. J.A.G. Griffith, *The Politics of the Judiciary* (1977), Chaps. 8, 9.

154. *Express*, above, n. 145, at p. 65. (But see the criticisms of Simpson (1980) 43 MLR 327) Lord Scarman's speech in *UKAPE* v. *ACAS* [1980] 1 All E.R. 612, 615-22, is an illustration of a Law Lord applying the law (without stretching it) with a deep understanding of the conflict of values and related problems in industrial relations.

155. *Duport Steels*, above, at p. 554 (a phrase he adopted from Lord Wilberforce in *Express* [1980] ICR 54). Such expressions 'bring the judges inevitably into the industrial arena exercising a discretion which may well be misunderstood by many and which can damage confidence in the administration of justice'.

157. P. Mayhew, Under-Secretary of State for Employment, H.C. Deb., Vol. 976, No. 89, col. 162, 17 December 1979 (emphasis supplied). Compare Lord Diplock's description of trade union rights as a power 'to inflict *by means which are contrary to the general law* untold harm' ... (emphasis supplied) [1980] 1 All E.R. 541.

157. The dicta of some Law Lords in effect calling for changes in the law increased as the story unfolded: Reasons in the *NWL* case, 25 October 1979; Bill printed, 6 December; *Express* speeches, 13 December; Second Reading of the Bill, 17 December; first sitting of Standing Committee on the Bill, 24 January 1980; *Duport Steels* decision 1 February, and speeches 7 February; further proposals in the government's Working Paper, 19 February. The government has hinted that it may even repeal s. 14 (1) of TULRA; clauses 9 and 14 of the Bill seem to be preparing the ground for this further fundamental attack upon trade unions which will reopen the wounds of the *Taff Vale* decision [1901] AC 426, and expose unions to the inappropriate vagaries of vicarious liability. See above, note 20.

158. A straw blew in the wind when a printing union General Secretary defied an injunction granted under the *existing* law: *Times*, 9 May 1980. See too the remarkable speech of the Attorney-General to the House of Commons Committee on the Bill: Parl. Deb., 18 March 1980, Standing Committee A, cols. 1346 *et seq*.

159. By extending their task to include assessment of the merits of parties to *collective* industrial disputes, e.g. under cll. 9 and 14; see above, notes 113 and 114. The Bill overlooks the crucial principle that such tribunals cannot hope to function properly in *individual* employment disputes if they also deal with disputes between unions and members (see cl. 3), or between employers and trade unions: Donovan Report, Cmnd 3623, para. 576.

160. On this aspect of 'working class culture', and the demands in 1906 that immunities should be so clear that judges (especially Law Lords) could find 'no possible loophole' whereby 'they may wriggle out of the plain intention of the Act of Parliament' (Keir Hardie, *Times*, 7 September 1906), see Wedderburn, WATL Chaps. 7, 8; H. Laski, *Trade Unions in the New Society* (1950), pp. 103-36.

161. Such a comparison is fraught with difficulties, not least the different character of the *judiciary*: see F. Mancini (1980) 43 MLR 1 (especially his discussion of the *Magistratura Democratica*). In France it is of note that a court recently ordered a union to pay damages to 150 workers excluded from work by pickets; the union said it would appeal in the face of this 'serious obstacle imposed on the right to strike'; *Le Monde*, 9, 10 March 1980. Cf. G. Lyon-Caen, *Rec. D.*, 1979, XXXIX *Chronique* 255-8; H. Sinay and O. Drague, *Droit Social*, March 1980; and the attempt to limit the right to strike in Italy by concepts of 'bona fides' and 'proportionality' in pending proceedings brought by the engineering employers against three unions, described in A. Lettieri, F. Caffé and G. Ghezzi, *Libertà di Sciopero o Libertà d' Impresa* (1979, De Donato).

4

The New Politics of Labour Law: Immunities or Positive Rights?

I have never found any reason to retract the view that labour law must and should expose political attitudes.

> It is a place where law, politics and social assumptions meet in a man; and whoever believes that he is so 'objective' or 'impartial' as to be above policies and prejudices is either arrogantly naïve or dishonest with himself and others.[1]

But it is sadly strange that one needs almost to apologise today for the use of the word 'politics' in scholarly circles. It is as though John Stuart Mill had never written on the *Principles of Political Economy*;[2] nor Ruskin on *The Political Economy of Art*;[3] that Aristotle had not declared that man 'is a political animal by nature';[4] or Marx not offered his *Capital* as a contribution to the critique of 'Political Economy'.[5] And if one dwells in the London School of Economics and Political Science one is ready to accept from Gramsci that: 'Everything that is of real importance in sociology is nothing other than political science' – unless, perhaps, one is a Professor of Sociology.[6]

In this broad sense of 'political', the time is ripe for a reassessment of the politics of that part of the legal system which controls or interacts with industrial relations. The limited aim of this lecture is to offer a contribution for that agenda, first in connection with the nature of some changes which we have recently witnessed and, secondly, about the structure of our labour law and the debate on ways in which it might be changed – whether we should concentrate, for example, on 'positive rights' rather than 'immunities'. Clarification of that agenda should be useful

---

The revised text of a lecture given at the Faculty of Law, University of Durham on 1 March 1983. Later published in W.E.J. McCarthy, *Trade Unions* (1985 2nd ed. Penguin).

both in itself and for the subsequent consideration of the relationship of labour law to wider debates on planning and industrial democracy where different, if parallel, problems arise.

The Public Policy of Labour Law

There can be little doubt that a continuity of public policy which persisted for nearly three-quarters of a century has now been ruptured. There was such a policy. Some governments paid lip service to it; others embraced it; but none jettisoned it as this administration has done since 1979. The change may be measured by attempting to guess that date of a Ministerial pronouncement on labour law policy:

A great argument upon which we rely ... is decent provision for industrial workers. 'General low wages' said Mill, 'never caused any country to undersell its rivals'; nor did high wages ever hinder it.

In the 'great staple trades ... powerful organisation on both sides' promotes 'healthy bargaining', and increases 'competitive power':

But where you have what we call sweated trades, you have no organisation, no parity of bargaining, the good employer is undercut by the bad, and the bad employer is undercut by the worst ... and ignorance generally renders the workers an easy prey to the tyranny of the masters and middle men.

That was not an Opposition speech against the Employment Bill 1982, but – as perhaps the words 'sweated trades' reveal – Winston Churchill, President of the Board of Trade, introducing the Trade Boards Bill in 1909, from which sprang today's Wages Councils.[7] Measures to support and to promote collective bargaining (but *not* to regulate or control it) were already becoming an accepted feature of the system, as far back as the Fair Wages Resolution 1891 and the Conciliation Act 1896 – the *fons et origo* of ACAS.[8] After the Reports of the Whitley Committee 1917, consultation between employers and workers organised collectively became acceptable to, and even favoured by, government as a method of resolving industrial disputes. It was, of course, no accident that the same year saw the last reports of the Commissioners on Industrial Unrest.

This was the system of industrial relations which Kahn-Freund ultimately rationalised as one based on 'abstention' of the law or as 'collective *laissez faire*', a structure to which, in his brilliant descriptions in the 1950's, he ascribed the virtues of 'a state of maturity' through non-reliance on the State or legal sanction.[9] This was (at any rate in peace-time) the supreme 'voluntary' system. His analysis and his influence – for example on the law affecting collective agreements – is well recognised by every labour law scholar to have been 'brilliant and compelling'.[10] True, we begin now to see more confidently what may prove to be the transitional character of this system, with its insistence upon the primacy of collective bargaining; to acknowledge that the stability and 'equilibrium' so vital to Kahn-Freund rested often upon 'a middle class acquiescence in the current balance of industrial power'.[11] Even so, it was a long transition, from the Trade Disputes Act 1906 to the new policies of 1979. Even the vindictive little statute passed in 1927 to punish the unions defeated in the General Strike the year before, looked little more than a side-wind; Baldwin after all refused to abolish trade union 'legal immunities' as the employers demanded.[12]

Kahn-Freund saw the Industrial Relations Act 1971 as an event in which:

> The law has now – to some extent – abandoned the previous policy [of 'abstention'] ... we shall see whether legal compulsion or its threat is capable of remoulding industrial relations.[13]

The failure of the Act to achieve its objectives before its repeal in 1974 is well documented.[14] More to my present purpose, it is important to stress that the abandonment was intended only '*to some extent*'. For the authors and protagonists of the 1971 Act believed that it would produce:

> the improvement of industrial relations in Britain [which could] only be secured by collective effort on the part of Government, managements, unions and workers within a new framework of law which (i) sets national standards for good industrial relations; (ii) safeguards those who conform to them; (iii) protects industrial rights ... and (iv) provides new methods of resolving disputes.[15]

The government desired 'collective bargaining between employers and strong representative trade unions supported by orderly procedures';[16] unions had only to register and accept the new National Industrial Relations Court in order to participate. Moreover, the Act was, they claimed, in line of descent not only from the Conservative Party's *Fair Deal at Work* (1968) but, in great measure, from the Labour government's *In Place of Strife*, and from the great Donovan Report itself.[17] The Act was, of course, meant to clip the wings of the trade unions, and in that it carried the seeds of the strife to come. Even so, it was an ambiguous statute; it appeared to have two 'phantom draftsmen': one concerned with reform to produce greater 'order'; the other obsessed with 'individual rights'.[18] But it could be, and was, presented – not altogether without legitimacy – as pursuing the politics of 'reform', even if that meant greater elements of 'corporatism'.[19] Indeed, some radical commentators saw the 1971 Act as a 'Tory approach to reform' and thought more generally that 'reformism', by the mid 1970s, stood 'at something of an impasse'.[20] I could not myself agree that the 'reformism' of the 1971 Act had much in common with the Social Contract legislation of 1974-76; but it is obvious that both appealed, though in very different ways, to sentiments of the traditional politics in a manner not shared by the legislation of 1979 to 1982.

The New Policy of Restriction

Jon Clark and I have recently suggested that the old traditional public policy which was partly replaced in 1971 has now been 'ruptured' and largely replaced by a new policy of 'restriction'. The *essence* here is to 'restrict the social power of trade unions' and:

> as part of a wider strategy to increase the power of employers and strengthen managerial control in industrial relations as a means of promoting greater efficiency and productivity in the economy

in a policy which considers that:

> trade unions are a distortion of the market relation between employer and employee, and trade union aspirations to regulate jobs and labour markets, even by way of *joint* regulation, are incompatible with individual liberty.[21]

By 1980 the new policy had been seen by others as one of 'coercion' of trade unions;[22] and recently Davies and Freedland, in a tentative but fascinating analysis of labour law through the window of 'anti-wage inflation strategies', see the 'policy of restriction' as complemented by that of 'Control by the Market', i.e. 'direct attack upon the economic conditions which create union strength, rather than by use of positive law'.[23]

It is clear that the new policy relies upon economic forces in what Professor Kaldor has called its aim 'to break real wage resistance'.[24] The doctrines of Professor Hayek are central to it: there can be 'no salvation for Britain until the special privileges granted to the trade unions three-quarters of a century ago are revoked'. Such nostrums have been adopted as part of a policy for a substitute 'incomes policy', where the policies of reform offered little to satisfy conventional wisdom which is convinced of the root evil of 'wage-push'.[25] But the 'free market' element operates mainly in the private sector; and the policy of 'restriction' must, in my view, lead inevitably to legal restrictions bordering on the authoritarian against the industrial rights of workers and effective, autonomous trade unionism in the *public* sector. To this we return later.

What, after all, have we seen in these four extraordinary years since 1979?[26] Let us look at the five headings.

First, the protective legislation for individual employees was severely restricted, by adjusting the qualifying period and other rules about unfair dismissal and by narrowing maternity rights for women, restrictions often put forward on grounds which research had shown to be unfounded (such as the idea that, especially in small firms, employers refused to hire workers because of such legislation).[27] Secondly, the traditional policy of favouring union organisation has been discarded. The non-unionist, secure in the knowledge that if dismissed as such he can claim the new minimum £12,000 from either his employer or, in the case of industrial pressure, from the union or its officials has been promoted to a legal status equal, if not superior, to that of the trade union member. The 1982 Act completed, the Secretary of State declared: 'the most comprehensive and the most effective statutory protection for non-union employees that we have ever had in this country,' and he followed through by asserting not only that requirements for work to be done by 'union labour only' are 'deliberately stifling completition' leading to 'loss of jobs' (another statement short on proof) but that 'the lump' is, if 'properly managed, ... a very effective institution'.[28]

Thirdly, the 1982 Act creates a new statutory tort in respect of employers' commercial pressure or trade union industrial pressure – pressure which is otherwise in every respect lawful – if one of the grounds for such pressure upon another employer party to a contract for goods or services is that the latter does not or is not likely to recognise, negotiate or consult with a trade union. Pressure on another employer *not* to bargain is lawful. Pressure upon him to bargain, or even to consult with unions, is unlawful. And the ban remains even if he is under a legal duty to consult recognised union representatives – as in the case of safety committees or impending redundancies. Moreover, anyone 'adversely affected' can sue for an injunction and for damages the miscreant business or trade union which has thereby tried to extend the range of collective bargaining. Naturally, the trade unions and their officials are stripped of their normal 'immunities' in trade disputes in such cases. These sections are the clearest illustration of the reversal of the public policy favouring collective bargaining normally followed since 1917.[29] The statute declared a policy not even of neutrality. It is *against* the extension of collective consultation.

Fourthly, a great range of 'auxiliary' laws which have traditionally been 'props' or 'encouragements' for collective bargaining has now been swept away. These include the right of a union to unilateral arbitration for low paid workers which (in some form) has existed since 1940 and the right of ACAS to require recognition of a union by an employer. Convention 94 of the ILO has been denounced and the Fair Wages Resolution rescinded – the first time since 1891 that contractors with government are not required to observe minimum conditions of employment. The 'fair wages' protection in the Road Haulage Wages Act 1938 is repealed. The government has declared that, when it can review its ILO obligations in 1985, we can expect the role of Wages Councils to be 'slimmed down'.[30] It has reduced the implementation of the EEC 'Transfer of Undertakings' Directive on employment protection to farcical Regulations[31] and is known to be bitterly opposed to the 'Vredeling' draft Directive which aims to improve union rights to information and consultation in large, and especially transnational, enterprises in the Community.

As for industrial action – the fifth area – a new legislative technique has now been employed. Traditionally it has been the judges who have 'eroded' the immunities or (to use Davies and Freedland's happy phrasing) diminished 'the exclusion of common-law regulation'[32] which parliament has attempted to impose via the 'immunities'. Indeed, in many respects, the 'immunities' from civil liability in trade disputes (on which alone rests the legality of workers' withdrawal of their labour in whole or in part) are in many ways narrower now than under the Trade Disputes Act 1906. That is incontrovertibly the case with picketing. The uncertain protection in regard to 'interference with trade or business' has been repealed. The right of the strong to aid the weak has been emasculated, first by restoration of common law liabilities for so-called 'secondary action' in 1980, and then in 1982 by the redefinition of 'trade dispute' and especially of the term 'worker'. Even the traditional aid rendered altruistically by British workers to the enslaved crews of 'flag of convenience' ships is now regularly dubbed unlawful in our courts.[33] The new definition will also cause some disputes to be seen by the courts not as 'trade' but as 'political' disputes, for example disputes about government 'privatisation' of nationalised enterprises. In 1982, furthermore, common law liability in tort was re-imposed upon the trade union itself, a very real threat to the depleted funds of contemporary unions (despite the ceiling on damages in a particular 'proceeding') and one reinforced by the imposition of a special statutory code in place of the common law principles of vicarious liability when an 'industrial' or 'economic' tort is alleged. The union and its officials are also threatened by new liabilities for industrial pressure by way of 'joinder' in the tribunals when non-unionists sue for unfair dismissal.

Similar though it may be to the policy of 1971 in its desire to reduce the influence of trade unions and of workers' collective action and to increase the rights of a somewhat reified 'individual', the new policy is nevertheless startlingly different from that of

1971. There is on the table no corporatist 'offer' of a 'deal' to trade unions. No new structure is envisaged into which they might be 'integrated'. Instead the effect of the statutes of 1980 and 1982 has been to whittle away the right to withdraw labour to a level below that which is acceptable in most pluralist democracies today.

Indeed, it has become 'difficult to define the natural boundaries of the new strategy'.[34] Events have moved too fast for the ink to dry. In 1982, no sooner did one think that the Fair Wages Resolution might be rescinded than it was abruptly swept away with little apology. As one wondered whether the 1913 compromise on political funds of trade unions would 'still be sacred', up popped a Green Paper to show that the government was out to scrap that too.[35] No sooner had the logic of the market sunk in that it was made clear that it would indeed apply to the 'sweated trades' and Wages Councils. In 1982 we asked: 'Will the restriction strategy lead inevitably to legislation on the maintenance of "public" or "essential services"?' Now that the legislature had 'learned from the judges the central technique of "modifying" the immunities' and of manipulating 'non-interventionist' instititions in the service of restricting trade union activity, it seemed logical that it should use the new weapon of removing 'immunities' (coupled perhaps with compulsory arbitration, or even an 'up-to-date' version of criminal liabilities) against workers in the public sector or in 'essential services'. To government eyes they would no doubt appear to be using their 'monopoly powers' to obstruct the economic and social market, and especially to hinder the proper 'pricing' of jobs.[36] Such developments go hand in hand with 'the true deliberate policy, since 1979, of taking government off its pedestal as a model for progressive labour relations policies'.[37] Even in industrial training the record of government in the last three years has been one of dismantling tripartite machinery set up by law.

Today one finds that both the Prime Minister and the Secretary of State do indeed have in mind new legal measures against workers in the public sector, the natural drift of the policy of 'restriction' – legislation in relation to such 'abuse of monopoly power' as was envinced in the 1983 national strike by water workers possibly to enforce arbitration agreements or (since these can be broken or not concluded) to impose 'a statutory duty to continue the supply of essential services'.[38] At this point, there are present the seeds of a dangerously illiberal, even authoritarian, thread in the skein of the market-orientated restriction policy. The services that are 'essential' to a modern community are hard to define; they clearly range from power-stations, electrical and nuclear, through fire stations, gasworks and ambulance stations on to doctors, nurses, police and sewerage workers.[39] But why end there? The government observed in 1981:

[The] interdependent nature of industry means that a case can now be made for regarding a strike by most groups of workers as threatening essential services or supplies.[40]

A statutory duty to ensure services entails, of course, the risk of introducing forced labour.

Other writers have adverted to the dangers of authoritarianism that lurk both in the government's ill-defined powers to use troops and in the demands of new (especially nuclear) technology.[41] Ironically, it was the Heath government that repealed the special and 'selective' criminal sanctions under the 1875 Act applicable to gas, water and electricity workers because it believed that 'the necessary safeguard against action leading to serious harm is provided by section 5' – the section of that Act which makes it criminal to strike in breach of contract causing risk to life or property.[42] No doubt it is instructive that no prosecution has apparently ever been launched under that section. But recent experience suggests we should not rely on that. Certainly it is increasingly difficult to designate just what is an 'essential' service or industry, or even which disputes may create an 'emergency', in our type of society.[43] It seems inevitable that, if continued, the policy of restriction will feel compelled to use special legal weapons, which it has so far kept largely in reserve, to abate 'real wage resistance' to its policies by public sector workers. Yet it is more than fifty years since Harold Laski rejected Leon Duguit's claim that the state may and must make strikes illegal where stoppages would dislocate enterprises 'at the very heart of social organisation'. Not only would such a law be futile; Laski added, in words which Kahn-Freund echoed even in his last pessimistic years: 'I do not think the right to strike can be denied to any vocation.'[44]

Even more worrying, in terms of liberty and democracy, is the character of the debate promoted in the 1983 Green Paper. This carries various traits of authoritarianism; it accuses the trade union movement of fraud and malpractice in general terms, which history will show to be false; and it is prepared to consider legal measures that go to any lengths to compel trade unions to submit, such as providing, for unions which fail to comply with new statutory provisions on rule books, 'for the taking over by an outside authority of the running of the business of the trade union in the interest of its members'.[45] If that sanction applied in respect of failure to meet standards set for the rules, it would *a fortiori* be logical to apply it in respect of breaches of other parts of the restrictive legislation. The plan seems to be for the state, having shackled political activities and industrial action by trade unions, to be ready with a team of Trade Union Receivers to take over any that refuse to submit. One wonders what the response would be to parallel proposals for the seizure of companies formed by capital. No doubt, the army of consultants who have recently arrived from the United States to advise employers how to *resist* unionisation would prosper in this framework – especially in the absence even of statutory reporting provisions.[46] More important, one is reminded of one of the last sentences written by Kahn-Freund – for a German audience:

> The German reader of this book, who is acquainted to some extent with the history of Germany over the last half century, will not need to be reminded of the immense general political significance of the maintenance of internally active trade unions.[47]

Alternative Policies

There are alternative policies. If one envisages a general change or deflection of direction, what is the lawyer likely to contribute? It is no part of my purpose to place this question here in the context of particular party-political programmes. But most alternatives to the market economics and labour law policy of restriction now on offer by government have certain features in common: they would operate a more 'managed', less market-orientated economic policy, above all in order to fight unemployment; and to that end, and in seeking to rediscover wider areas of social *consensus*, they would attempt to involve the trade unions in a common effort. 'Tripartitism' would find renewed favour, more, at any rate, than it now receives in Whitehall. Of course, the political programmes which would require extensive legislation in favour of rights of consultation and participation for workpeople and their trade unions necessarily rely, in the current crisis, on tripartite structures. Such policies diverge too (though not always explicitly) from the 'individualist' ethic of current policies. In particular both 'corporatist' forms of 'tripartitism' and policies which aim to reduce 'corporatism' by maintaining decentralised, direct democratic structures acknowledge that individual workers gain freedom largely by collective organisation. More radical attitudes perceive the *individual* employment relationship, as Kahn-Freund thought, to be a relation of *subordination* and *submission* concealed by the 'figment' of a contract.[48] It would be inevitable (to put it at its lowest) that in the presence of such policies the price of trade union co-operation would be the revision, if not the total repeal, of the statutory measures of 1980 and 1982 and a return to something more like traditional labour law policy. No doubt the return cannot resurrect the old 'abstentionist' system. But there must be a return to the acceptance of collective organisation and strong trade unionism. But a return in what legal form? To the 'immunities'? It is my belief that we are witnessing the beginnings of an unhappily formalistic debate on that question. My objective here is to suggest that a formalistic debate on that issue will be counter-productive and may even obscure the real problems.

Some aspects of the issues can be dealt with quickly. For example, it is sometimes suggested that the laws of 1974-76, simply by being enacted, in some way 'caused' the retrogressive legislation of 1980 and 1982. This mistakes the place of law, its 'secondary force in human affairs, and especially in labour relations'.[49] I have, for example, heard it said that section 23 (1) (c) of the Employment Protection Act 1975 somehow 'facilitated' the law enacted by the Employment Act 1980 section 15 (1), which by repealing four words of the 1975 section totally changes its meaning and function. It seems hardly likely that the draftsmen of 1980 would have been incapable of composing the laws they wished to have even if there had never been a 1975 Act. Of course, precisely what the *social* effect of the individual 'employment protection' legislation had and is having is not clear, not least in the ways it has affected industrial bargaining and behaviour. The evidence so far does not suggest that it has 'juridified' the system to the disadvantge of trade unions; and it has certainly not had any effect remotely comparable with the forces of the labour market.[50]

But let us return to the 'immunities'. It is now widely accepted that they too were the product not of legal, but of social causes. The difference between Britain's legal 'immunities' and the legal 'rights' available to French, German or Austrian trade unions, said Kahn-Freund, 'reflects the histories of the various working-class movements'.[51] Our 'unique legal solution to the common problem of trade union illegality' rested upon the unique conjunction of three *social* events in Britain's industrial revolution: comparatively strong unions at an early date; the absence in the formative period of a working-class political party; and the absence of universal male franchise – all emerging in a *laissez-faire* society.[52] The legal protections – it is now generally agreed, even by the 1981 Green Paper *Trade Union Immunities*[53] – were the British method of providing the elementary social 'rights' which in other legal systems are sometimes – not always and not all – provided by legal rights (and obligations): especially in three rights always claimed by trade unionists – the rights to combine, to be recognised by employers for bargaining and to withdraw labour.[54] Of course, the form of our general law did play a role in this history, not least the absence of a written constitution; it contributed, but it was a relatively minor cause. The critical factors that gave to shareholders *rights* to associ-ate in limited liability companies after 1855 but provided the right to associate collectively to trade unionists after 1871 primarily by way of *immunities*, were not legal but social. The nature of these statutory 'immunities' must never be misunderstood, and the prob-lems inherent in their form are well-known:

In substance, behind the form, the statute provides liberties or rights which the common law would deny to unions. The 'immunity' is mere form ... One of the problems inherent in this way of doing things is that the judges remain in a strategically very powerful position.[55]

The question remains of course how far a change of form might affect their powers.

Judging the Immunities

Recently, writers on labour law have once again suggested that the 'immunities' should be scrapped in favour of a system of statutory 'positive' rights. The Donovan Committee considered the point – not a new one even in 1968 – but it believed that nothing would be 'improved by granting the right to strike in express terms'.[56] Indeed, the fact is that proposals for positive rights to strike, etc., have normally been put forward in recent times by those who have wished to see a more legally regulated system of collective bargaining; and, of course, the right should be subject to 'reasonable limitations' as a CBI report put it.[57] Such limitations are now, we should note at once, less likely to find agreement in our society in the 1980s than twenty years ago.[58]

But this is not a sufficient answer to those who, having worked hard to master the techniques of a complex system of law and watched the judiciary time and again subvert its very purposes, conclude that: 'Over 70 years' experience has shown that no amount of legislative tinkering with the "golden formula" will remedy the imbalance of industrial power' – and who call for the 'total exclusion of industrial relations' (or at least of interlocutory processes) from injunctive relief.[59] So, too, a policy of:

legislative pirouettes attempting to circumvent the legal perspective by stipulating immunity in defined circumstances is inadequate ... A statute which in principle prohibited the employer from carrying on his operation in the circumstances of a trade dispute would resolve the problems of picketing to a very large extent.[60]

One can readily understand and share the emotions raised by the century or more of legal struggle for effective trade union rights. Moreover, much of this writing approaches the issue pragmatically, asking after the effect of the law on particular industrial power relationships. This is surely right. The debate about 'immunities' or 'positive rights' must be neither wholly technical nor theological. Secondly, however, such propositions, if put into legislative form, would still require a definition of 'industrial relations' or 'trade dispute'. To this we return. Such definitions of basic concepts of labour law constitute 'limiting factors'

determining the scope of rights available to employers, workers
and trade unions.

Thirdly, one can sympathise with the impatience that shines
through much modern commentary at the role of our judges for
over a century in labour law. The invention of special doctrines on
criminal conspiracy in 1872; on civil liability and conspiracy in
1901; *ultra vires* and political activity in 1910; the apparent
conversion of the judges to an understanding of 'non-intervention'
when 'Labour says: "Where are your impartial judges?" ', and
when the balance of power lay with employers, or later synthesised
in a war-effort; the re-emergence of judicial erosion of the
'immunities' in the 1950s and 1960s above all by way of the
economic torts; the invention of new torts such as 'intimidation' in
1964 (a 'frontal attack' Kahn-Freund held 'on the right to strike');
the granting of labour injunctions not only in interlocutory
proceedings but even *ex parte* – this is a small part of a tale
well-known and often told.[61] So too, the statutory protection of
peaceful picketing was approached by judges determined to decide
rights of workers in the law of nuisance and obstruction as though
they were on a par with persons 'carrying banners advertising some
patent medicine or advocating some political reform' in 1967; or
with hitch-hikers in 1974; implicitly confirming the pronouncement
of Lindley LJ in 1896: 'You cannot make a strike effective without
doing more than is lawful.'[62] Those who doubt whether 'many
judges have yet learned the simple historical truth' that immunities
are not *ipso facto* 'privileges'[63] must then ask how many of today's
judicial hearts do not still beat in rhythm with the robust and
masterly declaration of Lord Bramwell in 1891 in the legislature: 'I
have said and do say there is nothing unlawful in picketing,
provided that it is lawfully practised, but that is what it never is.'[64]
In three quick strokes, game set and match to the common law.

Even when they were rectifying a line of cases in the Court of
Appeal that were little less than outrageous distortions of the
'golden formula',[65] most of the Law Lords in the famous modern
trilogy of decisions of 1979-80 took the occasion to state that,
properly interpreted, the immunities (which, as Lord Scarman
demonstrated, effectively reproduced the 1906 protections) were
'intrinsically repugnant'; tending 'to stick in judicial gorges' –
'unpalatable'; and above all 'privileges'; and when Lord Salmon
said: 'surely the time has come for it [the law on trade disputes] to
be altered', he knew that government proposals to do just that
were on their way to the statute book.[66] Indeed, the 'emotively
charged illustrations' of what might be within the golden formula
(driving an employer out of business, or demands fierce enough 'to
bring down the fabric of the present economic system') led some
commentators understandably to see these ostensibly liberal
decisions as 'thinly disguised justifications for changing the law if

not an invitation to the government to propose changes to Parliament'.[67]

Moreover, even when one examines those English decisions on civil conspiracy which are thought to prove that 'judicial hostility' has not always been a constant feature,[68] one finds that even these decisions favoured 'the big battalions of labour and capital' standing against the small militant union or small producers: corporatist, not radical, decisions.[69] Indeed, it is scarcely possible to discover in the long history of the 'golden formula' an important reported judgment which advanced the collective interests as such of workers effectively and unequivocally on a critical point of law. Even the two decisions in which Lord Scarman's thoughtfully informed opinion on industrial relations led the Law Lords to that attitude in judgment were made in the context of the repeal of the relevant legislation,[70] a posthumous endorsement of a more liberal stance. Even the refusal of the Law Lords in 1982 to adopt the most Draconian view of remaining trade union freedoms left commentators doubtful,[71] especially when a majority of the Law Lords subsequently refused to include a world-wide trade union industrial practice as giving rise to a 'trade dispute', preferring in the classical style to equate a trade union demand for payments to a workers' welfare fund to a demand for payment to guerrillas in El Salvador (a view that Lord Scarman found little less than 'cynicism').[72] That decision, it is to be remembered, was rendered under the old definition before the 1982 Act's changes in the definition of 'trade dispute'. And to rub the point home, it is always open for the judges to say with Lord Denning MR with Hohfeldian accuracy:

> [When] Parliament granted immunities to the leaders of trade unions, it did not give them any *rights*. It did not give them a *right* to break the law or to do wrong by inducing people to break contracts. It only gave them immunity if they did.[73]

The language of 'immunities' gives judges easy, semantic points of entry. But that is the beginning, not the end, of our enquiry. Some judges never lack points of entry to ground they mean to occupy.

Unavoidable Problems

So it is perhaps an understandable feeling of impotence in the face of this century of obstructive interpretation (now joined by the parliamentary policy of restriction) that has caused some commentators recently to declare that 'the present immunities represent a very insecure foundation for the freedom to strike'. Such writers advance the argument that the best method of guaranteeing 'the freedom to strike' today may be by way of 'a positive right to strike', a method 'which has a number of virtues though they should not be exaggerated'. The method is, however, thought to be virtuous enough to reverse the burden of proof: 'So whatever may be the arguments against a right to strike they have yet to be convincingly made.'[74]

One objective in choosing 'positive rights' is of course to secure the clear formulation of minimum standards for the rights to associate, to bargain and to strike – as well as the semantic advantages of 'rights' over 'immunities'. The facts of economic recession do not necessarily preclude such progressive measures. The great labour law reforms in France illustrated that last year.[75] But rights cannot be discussed in the abstract. The arguments *for* 'positive rights' must themselves meet certain standards if they are on the agenda. It is not clear that this has yet been achieved.

For example, what is to be the definition of a 'strike'? That very definition is a limiting factor in any labour law system. The Donovan Report in 1968 asked whether it would apply to 'unofficial' or 'unconstitutional' strikes?[76] The 'golden formula' has always applied to *any person* acting in furtherance of a trade dispute, a very liberal tradition that has avoided the granting of industrial rights to 'official' action, or to unions approved by the state. In this respect, it is not the case that an explicit decision is made 'in any legal system' on the status of 'unofficial' action,[77] or at least not in the traditional British system. One of the rocks on which the 1971 Act foundered was its insistence that only official action by state-licensed trade unions could be lawful. We want no more positive rights of that sort.

So, too, the traditional formula applies to lesser forms of industrial action, to a 'go-slow' to a 'work to rule', to 'working without enthusiasm'. Would the new positive right? Existing British legislation refrains from defining generally the phrase 'strike or other industrial action'; but the courts have held (to the detriment of workers' rights) that it includes an overtime ban which is *not* a breach of workers' employment contracts, because that is a 'combined application of pressure' on the employer.[78] There is no obvious or common international meaning even for these basic concepts. As for concepts, the French constitutional 'right to strike' sees a 'go slow' or 'work to rule' as not a 'strike' at all; it is only 'defective execution of work' and not a 'concerted cessation'. German law accepts a 'work to rule' as a 'strike'. Swedish law accepts a stoppage by even one worker as a 'strike' if he acts on union instruction. As for legality, the Italian constitutional 'right to strike' extends to strikes for political objectives but the French does not, except for 'demonstration' strikes. An Italian 'strike' requires a concerted stoppage for common ends but permits as lawful 'rolling', intermittent or 'hiccup' strikes by groups of workers (*sciopero articolato* or *a singhiozzo*); these are within the pale in France only so long as they *are* real stoppages (*grèves tournantes*) or even *débrayage répété* (repeated short-term disengagements) except in respect of public sector workers for whom rolling strikes are forbidden.[79]

These matters are not technicalities. The concepts of 'strike' and the legality provided by each system reflect the social and historical roots of its own labour law and its own society. It is therefore, quite pointless to propose a discussion of a 'positive right to strike' *in principle*. Discussion can be meaningful only if the proponents make clear what kind of *right*, what kinds of *strikes*, what extent of *legality*, they have in mind.

I note in parenthesis that it is highly arguable that the central core of these legal concepts on industrial conflict tends to be established at a time or over a period of strong consensus when a labour movement is strong, as in Italy in the years following the constitution of 1948, or when the labour movement is too weak to oppose a system which it later comes to accept, as happened with the Labour Court and binding collective agreements in Sweden in 1928 and did not happen here in 1971-74. Perhaps our unwillingness or our inability in Britain to achieve a shared definition of 'strike or other industrial action' in 1974-78 says something about the continuing social division which followed the defeated attempt to impose alien labour law concepts on trade unions in 1971. It may also be a reason why, with our society fragmented as never before in the post-war period, today – or even tomorrow – may not be the right moment to make another attempt.

But protagonists of 'positive rights' have no choice. One must define the rights which one proposes. This is particularly true if one argues (as perhaps one should)

> The essence of a *right* to strike as opposed to a liberty to strike is that those exercising the right are protected against any prejudice or detriment in consequence of having struck, particularly at the hands of their employer.[80]

This raises *inter alia* the issue of the effect of industrial action upon individual employment contracts. Whether or not notice is given, English law regards a strike and most other forms of industrial action as a breach of the relevant employment contracts.[81] The failure of Lord Denning's attempt to introduce a doctrine of 'suspension' resulted not only from the clear precedents against it, but also from his failure to answer most of the major questions posed on this matter in 1968 by the Donovan Report: was a strike notice required? If so, of what length to bring about suspension? Could the employer dismiss or discipline the workers during suspension? Could the suspended strikers take other jobs? How could we know when the strike had terminated? Suppose it went on for years? Or for ever? Could the parties 'contract out' of the doctrine, either individually or through collective agreements?[82] It is well known that in French law (as in many other systems) a strike does not *per se* break the employee's contract but that the employer can dismiss for *faute lourde* (grave misconduct); less is known about the complex case law concerning *faute lourde individuelle, faute lourde collective* (let alone *faute grave* and *faute légère*).[83] What would English judges make of all that?

The problem of dismissal by the employer goes to the root of the issue. Our employment protection legislation has long provided that the tribunals shall have no jurisdiction if the employer dismisses without discrimination *all* the workers taking part in the industrial action.[84] Though this provision has now been greatly amended so as to favour the managerial interests of the employer[85] the primary reason for this odd legal structure remains unchanged. If dismissal by reason of a strike without victimisation were made justiciable, the principles by which a strike is to be accounted 'reasonable' would be placed squarely into the hands of the tribunals, and before long therefore into the hands of the judges of the Court of Appeal and House of Lords. How do proponents of 'positive rights' deal with that issue? How should – or could – the legislation effectively guide the courts on that issue? How far would judicial principles on 'reasonable strike' invade the rest of labour law? And what is to happen to the employment contract – and the power to dismiss – in a lock-out? Would the current equivalence of strikes and lock-outs be continued? Many would argue that withdrawal of labour should be treated with more liberality than a withdrawal of the opportunity to work. If so, would a 'positive rights' system distinguish the two rights in its approach?

I am not suggesting that these questions might not be satisfactorily answered. But proposals that fail to confront them do not contribute to the debate. Instead, the introduction of 'rights' without thinking through such questions in detail could result in handing to judges who so often call for greater 'clarity' in labour law[86] an easier opportunity to control the legality of industrial action by way of *a priori* concepts of 'fault'. The concepts are ready to hand; and part of the judiciary is eager to apply them, so as to say who is 'right' in a dispute.

> The public suffers from every industrial dispute. Ought they not to know who is right? Adopting this new approach they *would* know, for the court which investigated the dispute would tell them.[87]

We have a good comparative example to hand of a modern labour law system in which a 'right' to strike has been limited by judicial concepts of 'social adequacy' or 'disproportionality' (i.e. the judges' view of who is socially 'right'). German labour law illustrates the manner in which the right can be reduced to the narrow range of judicially moulded 'ultima ratio', exercisable by official trade unions alone in a narrow compass. 'Thus the court fills the gap which exists through the lack of compulsory settlement or even of statutory settlement procedures in German law.'[88] Nothing is worse than the assumption that 'positive rights' *necessarily* afford a wider area of industrial legality than a statutory 'immunity'. Both the historical and the comparative study of labour law systems prove any such assumption to be false.

Moreover the problem of 'suspension' of employment contracts cannot be relegated to a footnote as something which may or may not be 'desirable'.[89] No one familiar with the brilliant analysis of the effect of industrial action upon individual employment rights by Professor Blanc-Jouvan in 1972[90] can fail to recognise the subtly diverse answers which can be given in comparable legal systems to this problem. Such scholarship imposes an obligation to come forward with a specific, concrete answer on the point for British proposals. The same study shows that these issues concern not only the employee's interface with his employer; social security law (at the very least unemployment benefit law) must be confronted. Again, is a 'right to strike' to be subrogated to the right of trade unions and employers to extinguish or modify it in collective agreements and their 'peace clauses'? If one relies upon the European Social Charter, Art. 6 as an international source of the 'right to strike', it must be noted that that Article specifically makes the right to strike subject to 'obligations that might arise out of collective agreements', and applies it only to 'conflicts of interest' – in both respects a less liberal doctrine than the traditional British formula. Foreign systems vary enormously, of course, on this point. Swedish law is based upon the binding force of the negotiated peace obligation; in both France and Italy some clauses of this kind risk being unconstitutional; while German law relies on them at collective level but traditionally does not incorporate them into individual contracts of employment.[91] When should English courts incorporate from the collective agreement a 'procedure' or 'no-strike' clause into the individual employment contract of (say) a non-union worker whose terms and conditions otherwise stem from that agreement, as they so often do? Would the requirements of s. 18 (4), TULRA, 1974 be varied?

These are just a few of the items on the agenda. The Green Paper of 1981, for all the poverty of its intellectual quality, raised others. No doubt it would be true that 'a positive rights system' might succeed in changing the 'language and concepts' of industrial conflict law so that the law would be easier, superficially at least, to understand.[92] But would that in itself stop the misrepresentation of trade unionists' rights to 'privileges' – a process which has reached a new peak in the 1983 Green Paper.[93] The 1981 Green Paper gave good reason for the belief that in practice: 'a positive rights system could be at least as restrictive as the immunities and possibly more so'.[94]

It opened up, for example, the prospect of a prohibition on unions' disciplining members who refuse to strike on the basis of the fallacy that a positive 'right to strike' implies the negative 'right not to strike'. This consideration poses the question of the relationship with a 'Bill of Rights'. Here the 'positive rights' argument intersects with the 'shallow legalism' that equates the right to associate in unions with the right to dissociate as a non-unionist[95] and with the unsatisfactory character of the European Convention on Human Rights (which establishes no right to strike at all).[96] These and other international sources have sometimes led even those judges who are sensitive to industrial relations to declare that the 'negative' right is part of English law.[97] Other judges have exulted in its application in Britain to protect individual rights: 'even though it could result in industrial chaos'.[98] If some 'Bill of Rights' is to be part of a 'positive rights' system, there seems on present experience little reason to believe that it will 'help remove the unions' traditional suspicion of the courts' or that 'the courts might seem more neutral in interpreting the rights of management, unions and workers', as the Green Paper stated. In any event, if trade union rights are not to be restored or enlarged, why *should* such suspicion be removed other than as part of a confidence trick.

Quis Custodiet Opificibus Leges?

The truth is that a formal switch from 'immunities' to 'positive rights' cannot by itself produce judicial 'neutrality'. The root problem is not the form of the law. It is its administration. 'A change in its semantic presentation does not alter the fundamental problem.'[99]

This is an issue, however, which has been joined by advocates of positive rights. Sometimes they give the impression of believing that they can, as the Green Paper put it, 'insulate [the] legal right to strike from the common law'. The claim seems to be that, whereas the 'immunities', even in 'more sophisticated and complex terms', cannot halt the 'relentless march and new liabilities' of the common law, now:

> The advantage of a rights based system is that the right could exist regardless of common law developments. So even if the judges developed new causes of action, this would be largely irrelevant in the labour field because they would always be secondary to the primary statutory rights ... it may be that the development of the common law would come to a virtual standstill.[100]

This is a bold pronouncement. If it were correct, it could hold the key to the format of an alternative strategy. The ability to regulate developments of the common law has been long sought in various areas of our law. But some questions arise. What is the definition to be, in precise terms, of this *'labour field'* into which common law will not now venture? Will it be that of 'trade disputes'? How is it to be made more judge-proof than a revised golden formula?

Secondly, does the historical evidence suggest that the semantics of 'positive' rights secure workers' rights from judicial novelty or incursion like St George from the dragon? From 1906 to 1971 and 1974 to 1983 we have had one basic right expressed in positive form, even though its content since the 1980 Act has been restricted to a minimum ambit. The right to picket peacefully, which stemmed from the proviso to the crime of watching and besetting in the Conspiracy and Protection of Property Act 1875, section 7 – a proviso at once interpreted in a customarily hostile manner by the courts – was subsequently enunciated in the 1906 Act in different, *positive* form. '*It shall be lawful ...*' said the statute (and later statutes said the same), to attend in furtherance of a trade dispute at or near a place (now, of course, the place) of work merely for the purpose of informing, or of persuading not to work. Yet the judges regularly turned the flanks of this positive provision just as easily as they had restricted the proviso; pickets who committed nuisance or obstruction on the highway were placed, as we have seen, outside the bounds of attendance declared to be 'lawful', equated to hitch-hikers or to persons carrying banners advertising patent medicines.[101] Even Kahn-Freund saw some of these judicial limitations as 'obvious', for example in 'mass'-picketing on which, in the words of one chief constable, one sometimes gets 'a very jaundiced picture from the news media'.[102] The judicial attitude to the positive right to picket in fact incorporated the old tradition that *effective* demonstrations by workers are presumptively wrong. The attitude was not materially affected by the change from immunity in 1896 (*Lyons* v. *Wilkins*) to right in 1967 (*Tynan* v. *Balmer*). What is more, the House of Lords made it quite clear in dealing with the 'mixed' form of the statutory picketing section in the Industrial Relations Act 1971 (section 134, which can be seen as part 'immunity', part 'right') that the form was immaterial.[103] Indeed, faced with parliament's desire to create an effective 'right' of peaceful picketing it remained true in face of all forms of statutory expression that:

> the courts have adopted the curious approach of hunting for some minimal activity that the section protects and then reasoning that parliament can have intended to create no greater protection.[104]

This approach is indeed the normal judicial approach to the social rights of trade unionists whenever they infringe the contractual or property rights of others or invade the realm perceived by judges to be that of 'public order', both areas on which workers' collective action must trespass to be effective. (Indeed, on occasions when they have been unable to discover any such minimal activity to be protected, judges have even been prepared to declare the entire statutory provision to be 'unnecessary', 'pointless' or 'nugatory'.)[105] Given a century of interpretation, though, of the positive right to picket peacefully, what ground is there to believe that a right to strike would fare materially better?

Again the apparent 'right' to recognition hardly modified the application of the power of judicial review in respect of ss. 11-27 of the Employment Protection Act. 1975.[106] Equally, consider more generally the treatment of the limiting factor of 'recognition' itself in our modern labour law. A number of positive rights for trade unions, their officials and members require that the union be 'recognised', the rights to information, for example, or to time off or to undertake trade union activity. The statutory definition of 'recognition' has remained broadly the same since 1975;[107] but few would claim that they foresaw the restrictions placed upon it by the courts, by such devices as inflating the distinction between 'representations' and negotiations or, most of all, by placing ponderous weight upon the subjective intention of managers (representing the 'employer').[108]

The approach of our judges to limiting factors that are required in any system of industrial jurisprudence is unlikely to change. Their minds will turn naturally to the needs of management, of property, of capital, and of the hypothetical 'individual' long before they consider those of trade unionists. Indeed, one is compelled to inquire further and ask what magical quality of draftsmanship will by the enactment of positive rather than negative phrases immediately halt relentless developments in 'economic duress'. True, in that case a majority of the Law Lords indicated that they would not (probably) allow the new common law doctrine to invade the territory of labour relations that is guarded from tort liability – by the immunities.[109] Could a 'positive right' have hoped to fare better? It might have fared worse. In the same case, would a 'positive right' have stood a better or worse chance of resisting the decision that this was not a 'trade dispute' (or the *'labour field'*), or of pacifying the desire of some of the judges to encumber labour law with the mysteries of resulting trusts?[110] Why would a new doctrine of 'economic duress' necessarily be 'irrelevant' to a right to strike and payments made in connection with its exercise?

It is, of course, difficult to assess precisely how a 'positive rights' system would fare. But the agenda demands some elaboration. Would a new format prevent a judge from ever again perceiving the law giving workers the right to bargain collectively as one which, like some compulsory purchase order, snatched away their rights to bargain individually?[111] Indeed, the mere mention of experiments of this sort in the 1975 legislation reminds us that no proposal has yet advanced a solution to the fearsome problems inherent in a 'right to collective bargaining' – with the morass of difficulties illustrated by the huge corpus of American litigation on the 'duty to bargain in good faith' – a formulation rightly said to raise 'as many problems as it solves'.[112] Does the proposal of a positive right to strike not require an attendant, positive 'right to bargain' – with at least a tentative description of its character? The difficulties encountered by the 'duty to bargain' have very little to do with the literary form of the legislation, and much, perhaps everything, to do with industrial reality and, in Britain at least, with the judiciary.

A simple return to the classical tradition of the 'voluntary' industrial relations system is hardly possible in the 1980s. But if a new policy is to replace the current policy of restriction, its greatest challenge will be the construction of an adequate and positive role for effective and autonomous trade unions. Such a policy should use whatever drafting format is appropriate to particular problems. That would not exclude 'positive rights', any more than the use, where beneficial, of negative rights, freedoms, liberties, or, where appropriate, immunities. New ventures in democracy generally in industrial relations may make use (may have to make use) of legislation with rights blended as far as possible into the system. There we stand on the frontier of the wider debate which must be for another occasion.

But whatever 'formula' is chosen, the common law – that means the judges – will have to be excluded from certain areas of industrial life. They, as John Griffith has put it, are 'concerned to preserve and to protect the existing order'. If they move with the times, 'their function in our society is to do so belatedly'.[113] Demands that trade unions must be placed under 'the rule of law' (meaning the common law) 'are not legal demands. They are ideological demands.'[114] The ideology of the common law is stronger than that of most statutes; and it is more dangerous because of the mystifying pretence that it does not exist. There can be no *a priori* assumption that judges will abstain or be less 'jealous' of their jurisdiction because a statute tells them that their common law is 'secondary' to a primary statutory right. Proponents must demonstrate just what the statutory form of words would be to establish that the primary right prevails against all doctrines (existing and yet to be discovered) of the common law and judicial review? For many years our colleagues in public and administrative law have been telling us that such control of the judiciary is difficult, if not impossible[115] – unless perhaps we can dress up the union as David facing Goliath (and avoid its being perceived as a 'troublemaker').[116]

Judges (whatever they may say) are not 'jealous' of their jurisdiction primarily because of the forms of immunities. Misunderstanding as to their nature as 'privileges' at most compounds the 'jealousy' carried in the very blood of the common law towards collective organisations by workpeople who had to fight their way to legality against its civil and criminal liabilities. The 'insecure foundation' for the freedom to strike in our society today is *not* primarily the form of the present immunities. It is the attitude of the courts and of the common law – now ably reinforced by the mass media and the myths of 'trade union power' in a powerfully projected market analysis.

In truth, a philosophical confrontation between doctrines of 'immunities' and 'positive rights' is no more useful today as a contribution to the politics of labour law than a dispute about the number of shop stewards able to dance on the head of a pin. The approach to drafting should be pragmatic. No doubt, wherever it is advantageous, a form of words will be chosen which cannot easily allow a fundamental human freedom to be misrepresented as a 'privilege', whether in Grimsby or in Gdansk. Perhaps at times in the past, draftsmen did not always keep that point adequately in mind. But, by itself, consideration of the statutory *form* of the law is secondary – a matter not of strategy but of tactics.

More important are the substantive liabilities of the common law. Should the approach to these be bolder? It was suggested in 1965 in connection with the new tort of intimidation:

> Instead of creating what looks like another privilege for trade disputes ... it might be preferable ... for the statute to repeal the novel doctrine ... for the law of tort.[117]

That is to say, some areas of common law liability might simply be abolished. Similarly, Davies and Freedland think there would 'seem a lot to be said for restructuring s. 13 [TULRA] on the model of s. 14'[118] though the difficulties in respect of torts that cover violence, assault, and other similar acts are obvious.[119] We should certainly think about the repeal of certain common law doctrines altogether, leaving it to parliament to revive such parts of the liability as are needed for commercial, family or property transactions. That is roughly what we did with the common law crime of conspiracy in 1977. It is arguable that the same technique should be used as an antidote to some parts of the poison which the common law brings to its treatment of trade unions and industrial action? But we should not be surprised if we find a need to utilise the limiting factor of 'trade disputes', as the 1977 legislation did on certain minor issues.

The right to strike is always expressed, in practice in the legal systems of societies comparable to ours, by reference to some limiting factors. These may be *intérêts professionelles* as in France or, as has been the case in Germany, 'social adequacy' or 'proportionality'. Even in Italy, where the right is perhaps at its widest, it is confined to actions which are: 'not aimed at subverting constitutional order nor at hindering or obstructing the free exercise of the legal powers in which popular sovereignty is expressed.'[120]

Unless one goes that far – and British labour law seems unlikely to do so – one is left with the hard task of drawing a new line between 'state' and 'society', in the full knowledge that in any such edifice of law (as Kahn-Freund concluded in 1954) 'the foundations are shaky'. But whether or not they are wholly defensible philosophically, they are drawn because they represent 'the social and political convictions on which all law-making rests'.[121] A 'trade dispute' may not exist, like God; but, perhaps, like Him, it needs to be invented.

Social Substance and Forms of Law

The task of building a new labour law will be difficult. The difficulties do have a little, but relatively only a little, to do with the form of 'rights' and 'immunities'. They have more to do with practical enforcement of areas of legality for effective and autonomous trade unionism as part of a transition to social advance, the re-establishment of opportunities for employment, and industrial participation and democracy. At the level of the courts, particular attention must be paid to ending – whether by positive rights, immunities or (perhaps more important than either) procedural adjustments – the preposterous practice of interlocutory labour injunctions (an area where our judges still claim indefensible rights of jurisdiction).[122] Most of all it has to do with finding a new boundary, sufficiently based upon social *consensus* but sufficiently broad in its class terms, which will prevent the ideology of the common law torpedoing the trade union contribution. What is more, that structure must face a world of internationalised trade, where localised trade unions face transnational capital. We must ask: what role can national law play in promoting the development of effective trade unionism on an international plane?

Perhaps, too, it is time to inquire anew into the nature and functions of our specialised system of labour courts, not least the role of the lay members of the tribunals, and ask whether the 'wing persons' should be invested, in French fashion, more directly with a representative character.[123] We certainly cannot wait for the problems of the judiciary (and the profession from which it comes) to fade away in face of a 'new generation of lawyers', trained to a new sensitivity of 'industrial relations', which was the hope of both Donovan and Kahn-Freund.[124] We must do our best with the judges we have and utilise whatever shape of statute seems most suitable to the time. Perhaps we have spent so long trying to explain to them the true nature of the 'immunities' that we failed to realise that all along it was not the form but the substance that mattered to them.

There may well be a case for more positive rights in areas of our labour law. But arguments for them will be convincing only if based upon something more concrete than their idealised virtues. The critical issue for 'rights' and for 'immunities' is: how will they fare in court and on the shop floor? Judges in courts determine the meaning of the law in action. And the law will have some effect – though one much more difficult to determine – upon bargaining and industrial behaviour. Moreover, comparative study which goes beyond the form of foreign laws will demonstrate why we must not be led astray by the functioning of positive rights in *other* systems to assume that those rights must produce the same results here. Comparison with Italy is particularly useful. No British court could produce the judgment of the Italian Constitutional Court on 'political' strikes unless specifically directed by parliament to do so – and who knows even then? On the other hand, the 'right' not to be unfairly dismissed in Italy does, in very many cases, lead to re-engagement. In Britain that remedy is notoriously rare. Why has the British 'right' fared so much worse?[125] Equally important, the interplay of the industrial and social forces does not always produce qualitatively similar results out of parallel pressures. It has, for instance, been said of Italian trade unions that their 'general weakness' has tended recently to nurture hopes of 'long-term goals' and:

> leads the unions to link themselves to and depend upon political parties. From this, as from the ideological propensity to be orientated towards long-terms ends, the predominance of political action or of political aspirations over narrowly union ones is born.[126]

Most observers would make the very opposite judgment of tendencies in British trade unions over the last decade. This has direct relevance for legal developments; for there can be no doubt that judicial cognisance and understanding of the political dimension of the labour movement has at times been a critical factor in the interpretation of the constitution by Italian courts. No such cultural influence would be felt in Britain. British judges do not always recognise that a democratic trade union movement cannot, in a free society, be excluded from the 'politics' from which capital does not abstain. Comparative legal inquiry must take account of such factors, therefore, in considering the forms of foreign law, and recognise the need to judge the meaning of law primarily by reference, not to its formal drafting but to the entire social and cultural context that determines its meaning and effect in application.

Finally, to those who are not lawyers I add this: these are not merely technical issues, delights savoured only by the sharp tastes of academics or in the briefs of their brethren in professional practice. The role of law remains limited; as Otto Kahn-Freund put it in 1954: 'The first duty of a lawyer about to discuss the legal framework of industrial relations is to warn his readers not to overestimate its importance.'[127] But the procedure, the substance and the very concepts of the law frequently reflect the dissonance or harmony of the social substructure. Where there is industrial dissonance, you must not expect the lawyer to solve problems beyond the law's competence. In his turn, the lawyer must not present the technicalities of his craft, the mysteries of 'rights' and 'immunities', as if they are primary rather than subsidiary items on the agenda of social and legal reform, as if the form determined the substance. For the politics of his laws are the politics of the wider society and his laws cannot as such solve political confrontations. Nor could anything be more absurd today than that lawyers should impede the urgent, concrete debate about such priorities of the crisis as unemployment with some alien, abstract argument on juridical formalities.[128] The law is, in the last resort, never a substitute for politics.[129]

Notes

1. K.W. Wedderburn, *The Worker and the Law* (1965), p. 339, (2nd ed. 1971), p. 479.
2. Especially, 1852 edn, with the additional and relevant chapter on 'The Future of Labouring Classes'.
3. In 1857, later incorporated into *A Joy for Ever*.
4. *Politics I*. 1253 a.10.
5. (1938; ed. Dona Tor), Marx's Preface, p. xv.
6. Antonio Gramsci, *Selections from Prison Notebooks* (1971, ed. Q. Hoare and G. Nowell Smith), p. 243.
7. Parl. Deb. HC 28 April 1909 cols 387-8; see now Wages Councils Act 1979.
8. See on the clause, O. Kahn-Freund, 'Legislation through Adjudication' (1948) 11 MLR 269 and 429; on conciliation K.W. Wedderburn and P.L. Davies, *Employment Grievances and Disputes Procedures in Britain* (1969); and 'Arbitration and the Role of Courts' P.L. Davies (UK National Report to 9th International Congress of International Society for Labour Law, Heidelberg 1978).
9. See respectively *Law and Opinion in England in the 20th Century* (1959, ed. Ginsberg) p. 224; *The System of Industrial Relations in Great Britain* (1954, ed. A. Flanders and H. Clegg), p. 43.

10. See 'Otto Kahn-Freund and British Labour Law' by Wedderburn, Chap. 3, in Wedderburn, R. Lewis and J. Clark (eds), *Labour Law and Industrial Relations; Building on Kahn-Freund* (1983) (hereafter cited as *Labour Law and IR*).

11. K.W. Wedderburn, 'Labour Law and Labour Relations in Britain' (1972) 10 BJIR 270.

12. See the Special Study by G. McDonald in M. Morris, *The General Strike* (1976), pp. 289 *et seq*.

13. *Labour and the Law* (1st ed. 1972), p. 270; contrast (2nd ed. 1977), p. 276 after repeal of the Act in 1974.

14. B. Weekes, M. Mellish, L. Dickens and J. Lloyd, *Industrial Relations and the Limits of Law* (1975); A. Thomson and S. Engleman, *The Industrial Relations Act: A Review and Analysis* (1975).

15. *Consultative Document Industrial Relations Bill*, Department of Employment, 5 October 1970.

16. R. Carr, Secretary of State for Employment, Preface to Draft *Code of Industrial Relations Practice*, June 1971. The CBI believed the legislation would 'have a major influence on the future development of our industrial relations system' and stressed 'the importance of employers and their organisations taking the initiative' for reform: *Guidance to Employers on the Industrial Relations Bill* (1971), pp. 1, 3.

17. Respectively Cmnd 3888, 1969, and Cmnd 3623, 1968.

18. Wedderburn, op. cit. (1972) 10 BJIR, p. 282.

19. See C. Crouch, *Class Conflict and the Industrial Relations Crisis* (1977), Parts III and IV.

20. J. Goldthorpe in *Trade Unions Under Capitalism* (eds. J. Clarke and L. Clements, 1978), p. 215.

21. Clark and Wedderburn, Chap. 6, 'Modern Labour Law: Problems, Functions and Policies' in *Labour Law and IR* (1983), pp. 130-1 and 135 (emphasis supplied). See that chapter for elaboration of these and other points in what follows below.

22. R. Lewis and B. Simpson, *Striking A Balance? Employment Law After the 1980 Act* (1981).

23. 'Labour Law and the Public Interest – Collective Bargaining and Economic Policy', Chap. II in *Labour Law and the Community* (1983, eds. Wedderburn and W.T. Murphy, IALS), pp. 17-8.

24. Nicholas (Lord) Kaldor, *The Economic Consequences of Mrs Thatcher* (Fabian Tract 486, 1983) p. 9 (reprint of his speech in the House of Lords on 16 April 1980).

25. F. Hayek, *1980s Unemployment and the Unions* (1980), p. 58; and see the discussion by Wedderburn, Chap. I, 'Introduction: A 1912 Overture' in *Labour Law and the Community*, pp. 4-7.

26. What follows summarises the main effects of the Unfair Dismissal (Variation of Qualifying Period) Order S.I. 1979 No. 959; Employment Act 1980 ss. 4-19; Employment Act 1982 ss. 2-19. On the 1980 Act see Lewis and Simpson, op. cit.; on the 1982 Act R. Lewis and B. Simpson, 'Disorganising Industrial Relations' (1982) 11 ILJ 227; K. Ewing, 'Industrial Action: Another Step in the "Right" Direction' (1982) 11 ILJ 209; Wedderburn, Chap. 15, Part 5, Clerk and Lindsell on *Torts* (15th ed. 1982 and First supp. 1983); and Clark and Wedderburn, Chap. 6, *Labour Law and IR*, n. 10 above.

27. See W. Daniel and E. Stilgoe, *The Impact of Employment Protection Laws* (1978); and W. Daniel, 'A Clash of Symbols: the Case of Maternity Legislation' (1981) 2 Policy Studies 74. The Department of Employment was widely believed to be in part responsible for non-publication of an authoritative survey of the closed shop by a research team led by Professor J. Gennard during the passage of the Employment Bill 1982.

28. Parl. Deb. HC 8 February 1982 cols 742-4.

29. For further discussion see Clark and Wedderburn, Chap. 6, 'Modern Labour

Law; Problems, Policies and Functions' in *Labour Law and IR*, especially pp. 162-3, 210 and note 379; Lewis and Simpson, op. cit. (1982) 11 ILJ 228-33; Wedderburn in Clerk and Lindsell on *Torts* (1982) 15th ed; supplement (1983) Chap. 15 para. 15-29 (2).

30. See Parl. Deb. HL 22 March 1982, col. 892. Within a fortnight of this lecture being given the Secretary of State showed that he was determined to prevent the traditional operation of Wages Councils when, in an unprecedented intervention, he objected to an 8 per cent increase proposed by the Non-Food Wages Council for shop workers (raising the minimum wage to £67.50 per week) and was instrumental in securing the Council's agreement to only a 6 per cent rise: *Financial Times*, 12 March 1983. [See now Wages Act 1986, below Chapter 10, pp. 211-2.]

31. See P. Davies and M. Freedland, *Transfer of Employment* (1982); B. Hepple, 'The Transfer of Undertakings (Protection of Employment) Regulations', (1982) 11 ILJ 29.

32. Davies and Freedland, *Labour Law, Text and Materials* (1979), p. 596. On what follows see especially ss. 16, 17 of the 1980 Act and ss. 7, 11 and 15-19 of the 1982 Act.

33. As to the illusory nature of the much-vaunted 'exceptions' in s. 17 (3) (4), Employment Act 1980, see *Marina Shipping Ltd.* v. *Laughton* (1982) QB 1127, CA; *Merkur Island Shipping* v. *Laughton* [1983] 2 WLR 45 CA; see Wedderburn 'Secondary Action and Primary Values' [1982] 45 MLR 317, and (1981) 10 ILJ 113; Benedictus and Newell (1982) 11 ILJ 111.

34. Clark and Wedderburn, *Labour Law and IR*, p. 210. On the importance of s. 15 of the 1982 Act and the lack of a 'command structure' in the trade unions upon which vicarious liability can be structured: see ibid., pp. 199-206, and on 'joinder' crossing a 'legal and ideological Rubicon', p. 207.

35. Clark and Wedderburn, ibid., p. 211; *Democracy in Trade Unions*, Cmnd 8778, Chapter 4.

36. Clark and Wedderburn, ibid., pp. 211-4 (where the role of the media is also mentioned); and see G. Morris, Chap. III, 'Essential Sources, the Law and the Community' in *Labour Law and the Community* (eds. Wedderburn and W.T. Murphy, 1983), especially pp. 25-6 on s. 5, Conspiracy and Protection of Property Act 1975 and the proposals of the Centre for Policy Studies.

37. B. Hepple, Chap. VII, 'Labour Law and Public Employees' in *Labour Law and the Community*, p. 78.

38. Margaret Thatcher, Prime Minister, Parl. Deb. HC 24 February 1983; N. Tebbit, Secretary of State for Employment, Evidence to HC Employment Committee, *Times*, 17 February 1983 (referring to the proposals in the Green Paper, *Trade Union Immunities*, Cmnd 8128, 1981).

39. All these are named by the Centre for Policy Studies which has recommended a ban on strikes in essential services with rights of action for those suffering (including next of kin) and for the Attorney General: see *Times* and *Guardian*, 19 February 1983. See now the Centre's *The Right to Strike in a Free Society*, March 1983.

40. *Trade Union Immunities*, Cmnd 8128, 1981, para. 334. Most legal systems do differentiate in respect of 'essential service' workers: G. Morris, *Labour Law and the Community*, op. cit., Chap. III citing Pankert, 'Settlement of Labour Disputes in Essential Services' (1980) Int. Lab. Rev., November, p. 723. The SDP proposes legislation on 'life and limb' risks, to impose a pause for arbitration: SDP, *Reforming the Unions*, p. 27.

42. See e.g. C. Whelan, Chapter IV, *Labour Law and the Community* and (1979) 8 ILJ 222 on troops; on the police G. Morris (1980) 9 ILJ 1; and on nuclear power workers R. Lewis (1978) 7 ILJ 1. See too, P. Elias, B. Napier and P. Wallington, *Labour Law Cases and Materials* (1980), pp. 290-3.

42. *Industrial Relations Bill Consultative Document*, Dept. of Employment, 5 October 1970.

43. For a comparison of different systems see *Industrial Conflict – A Comparative Survey* (eds. B. Aaron and K.W. Wedderburn, 1972) Chap. 6, Wedderburn, pp. 342 *et seq.*; and on North America, S. Anderman in *Labour Law and the Community*, op. cit., Chap. VIII. On the British experience 1971-74, Weeks *et al.*, op. cit., pp. 213-8; *Sec. of State* v. *ASLEF* (No. 2) [1972] ICR 19, CA.
44. *A Grammar of Politics* (1925), pp. 254-5, 515. See Kahn-Freund, *Labour Relations, Heritage and Adjustment* (1979), pp. 75-88.
45. *Democracy in Trade Unions*, Cmnd 8778, 1983.
46. See C. Craver, 'The Application of the LMRDA "Labour Consultant" Reporting Requirements to Management Attorneys', 73 NWUL Rev 605 (1978).
47. O. Kahn-Freund, Chap. 1 in *Labour Law and IR*, p. 7 (translated after his death from the German). See too, his *Labour Relations – Heritage and Adjustment* (1979), p. 20 for a similar statement.
48. *Labour and the Law* (1977), p. 6. On plans for future tripartitism and rights of unions on a decentralised basis, see the joint TUC/Labour Party *Economic Planning and Industrial Democracy* (1982).
49. O. Kahn-Freund, *Labour and the Law* (1977), p. 2.
50. See Clark and Wedderburn, *Labour Law and IR*, pp. 184-98, for the arguments on the effects of the 'Social Contract' legislation. Simpson has suggested that such a framework could 'easily be amended in pursuit of policies contrary to those for which it was envisaged' (1979) 8 ILJ 69, 83.
51. O. Kahn-Freund, Renner's *Institutions of Private Law and their Function* (1949) p. 172, note 154. Later he slightly changed the emphasis, see *Labour and the Law* (1977), p. 39.
52. See Wedderburn, *Labour Law and IR*, Chap. 3, pp. 36-9; and 'Industrial Relations and the Courts' (1980) 9 ILJ 65.
53. Op. cit., Cmnd 8128, 1981, Chap. 5.
54. The three rights claimed by the TUC in 1982 with which Mr Tebbit, Secretary of State, said he had 'no quarrel' as his 1982 Bill did not interfere with them: Parl. Deb. H.C. 8 February 1982, col. 744.
55. K.W. Wedderburn, *The Worker and the Law* (1971), p. 314.
56. *Report* Cmnd 3623, 1968, para. 935. For early proposals of 'positive rights' by trade unionists, see C. Jenkins and J. Mortimer, *The Kind of Laws the Unions Ought to Want* (1968).
57. *Trade Unions in a Changing World; The Challenge for Management* (discussion document; CBI, 'Steering Group' 1980), p. 22.
58. Wedderburn, op. cit. (1980) 9 ILJ pp. 82-3; *The Worker and the Law* (1971) p. 401.
59. B. Doyle (1979) 42 MLR 458, 462; to the same effect, K. Ewing (1982) 11 ILJ 209, 218.
60. B. Bercusson, 'One Hundred Years of Conspiracy and Protection of Property' (1977) 40 MLR 268, 292. See too his interesting, 'Labour Law and the Public Interest: A Policy Appraisal', Chap. XVIII, *Labour Law and the Community*, op. cit.; and cf. (1980) 9 ILJ 215, 232.
61. See respectively *Quinn* v. *Leathem* [1901] AC 495, HL; *Taff Vale Rly Co.* v. *Amal. Soc. of Rly Servants* [1901] AC 426, HL; *Amal. Soc of Rly Servants* v. *Osborne* [1910] AC 87, HL; Scrutton LJ [1923] Camb. LJ p. 8; *Crofter Hand Woven Harris Tweed Co.* v. *Veitch* [1942] AC 435, HL; *Cunard SS* v. *Stacey* [1955] 2 Lloyd's Rep. 245 CA; *Torquay Hotel Ltd* v. *Cousins* [1969] 2 Ch. 106, CA; *Square Corp. Reinforcement Ltd* v. *MacDonald*, 1968 SLT 65; O. Kahn-Freund (1964) 14 *Federation News*, 30, 41; K.W. Wedderburn, *The Worker and the Law* (1971), Chap. 8.
62. Respectively *Tynan* v. *Balmer* [1967] 1 QB 91; *Broome* v. *DPP* [1974] AC 587, 597; *Lyons* v. *Wilkins* [1896] 1 Ch. 811, 825.
63. Clark and Wedderburn, *Labour Law and IR*, p. 168. See too Davies and Freedland, op. cit., Chaps. 8, 9; J.A.G. Griffith, *The Politics of the Judiciary* (2nd

102   *Employment Rights in Britain and Europe*

ed. 1981) Chap. 3; Wedderburn, *The Worker and the Law* (1971) Chaps 1, 7, 8; Lewis and Simpson, op. cit., Chaps 9, 10; Wedderburn (1980) 9 ILJ 65.

64. Debate on the 'Scotch Railway Strike', Parl. Deb. HL, 6 March 1891, col. 371. Nobody could object if 'the picketers ... had merely met their fellow workmen in a friendly way and asked them to join, with nothing but a kind persuasiveness in their manner' (ibid.). The parallel in tone with the 1981 *Code* on Picketing is remarkable.

65. See on the Court of Appeal cases, K. Ewing, 'The Golden Formula, Some Recent Developments', (1979) 8 ILJ 133, concluding that, if unions' rights were established, 'the present formula will need major revisions or ... a fresh statutory initiative will have to be offered' (p. 146). The Court of Appeal went to the brink of unconstitutional behaviour in its insistence upon making union officials liable: *Duport Steels Ltd* v. *Sirs* [1980] 1 All ER 541.

66. See *Express Newspapers Ltd* v. *McShane* [1980] AC 672, 687 (Lord Diplock), 690 (Lord Salmon); *Duport Steels Ltd* v. *Sirs* [1980] ICR 161, 177, 184 (Lord Diplock), 186 (Lord Edmund-Davies), 188 (Lord Keith). Contrast Lord Scarman's analyses in [1980] ICR 189-93; and in *NWL* v. *Woods* [1979] ICR 867, 885-9; and see Wedderburn (1980) 45 MLR 319.

67. R. Simpson (1980) 45 MLR 327, 335-6, especially on Lord Diplock's opinion *NWL* v. *Woods* [1979] ICR at p. 878.

68. See R. Tur, Chap. XVI 'The Legitimacy of Industrial Action' in *Labour Law and the Community*, op. cit., p. 156, offering *Reynolds* v. *Shipping Fedn* [1924] 1. Ch. 28; and the *Crofter* case, above, note 61.

69. See Wedderburn, *The Worker and the Law*, p. 30.

70. *UKAPE* v. *ACAS* [1981] AC 424, HL; *EMA* v. *ACAS* [1980] ICR 215, HL, on ss. 11-16 of the 1975 Act, repealed by s. 19 (b) Employment Act 1980. Compare too the posthumous relation of *GAS* v. *TGWU* [1976] IRLR 224, HL with *Heatons Transport* v. *TGWU* [1973] AC 15, HL.

71. *Hadmor Production Ltd* v. *Hamilton* [1982] 2 WLR 322 HL; Simpson (1982) 45 MLR 447 who doubts whether 'the integrity of [the legal non-interventionist] framework could ever be restored' (p. 454).

72. *Universe Tankships of Monrovia Inc.* v. *ITWF* [1982] 2 WLR 803, HL; see Wedderburn (1982) 45 MLR, 556; Lord Diplock felt it necessary to apologise (pp. 818-9) to the lower courts for his formulation of the law on the golden formula in the *NWL* case, above, thereby again envincing the unpredictability of judicial temperament in this area. See below note 109.

73. *Express Newspapers Ltd.* v. *McShane* [1979] ICR 210, 218 CA. Oddly in jurisprudential terms this view was inconsistent with Lord Denning's view that acts rendered 'not actionable' by the immunities were 'lawful' (see e.g. *Stratford* v. *Lindley* [1965] AC 269, 285) contrary to Lord Pearce's view (ibid., p.336) which was later held to be 'wrong' in the *Hadmor* case, above.

74. P. Elias and K. Ewing, 'Economic Torts and Labour Law' (1982) Camb. L.J. 32, 356-8 (who summarise the case which other writers have supported). Their account of the torts was overtaken by some later developments: see Wedderburn 'Rocking the Torts' (1983) 46 MLR 224.

75. See J.M. Verdier, 'Les Réformes et le Droit Syndical' (1982) Droit Social 291; J.C. Javillier, Y. Delamotte and C. Morel, 'Les Projets de Loi Auroux' *Regards Sur L'Actualité*, 1982, Juillet-Août 3, 11 and 19; J.C. Javillier, *Les Réformes du Droit du Travail Depuis le 10 Mai 1981* (Paris 1982). The French reforms introduce a new right to bargain.

76. *Report*, Cmnd. 3623, para. 943 (in the context of 'suspension' of employment contracts). References below are to this paragraph of the Report.

77. Elias and Ewing, op. cit., p. 357. It is of course true that the extent of a positive right to strike 'would depend to a very large extent on the government in power'; ibid.

78. *Power Packing Casemakers Ltd* v. *Faust* [1983] 2 WLR 439, CA (no jurisdic-

tion therefore in respect of unfair dismissal). The definitions in Employment Protection (Consolidation) Act 1978, Sched. 13, para. 24 (1) of 'lock-out' and 'strike' are for the purposes only of determining 'continuous employment' (s. 151). It has been used, however, as guidance generally: *Coates* v. *Modern Methods and Materials Ltd* [1980] IRLR 318, 321; *McCormick* v. *Horsepower Ltd* [1980] ICR 278, 281. But contrast *Rasool* v. *Hepworth Pipe* [1980] ICR 494, 509 (definition no help on 'other industrial action').

79. See H. Sinay, *La Grève* (1966, mise à jour 1979, Dalloz) paras 60-65, 74-5, 85-91; G. Carmerlynck and G. Lyon-Caen, *Droit du Travail* (10th ed. 1980) paras 691-712, 735-40; J. C. Javillier, *Droit du Travail* (1981), mise à jour (1982) paras 635-69; G. Giugni, *Diritto Sindacale* (1979) pp. 179-213; G. Ghezzi and U. Romagnoli, *Il Diritto Sindicali* (1982) paras 321-41; G. Halback, A. Martins, R. Schwedes, O. Wlotzke, *Ubersicht Recht der Arbeit* (1981), p. 236; W. Daübler, *Das Arbeitsrecht* (1976), Chap. 5; Folke Schmidt, *Law and Industrial Relations in Sweden* (1977), Chap. 11. especially pp. 164-6. See, too, ibid., the different understandings in these systems of the term 'lock-out'; cf. on Britain, B. Hepple, 'Lockouts in Great Britain' (1980) *Recht der Arbeit*, s. 25 [Chapter 10 below].

80. P. O'Higgins, 'The Right to Strike – Some International Reflections', Chap. 3 *Studies in Labour Law* (ed. J. Carby-Hall, 1976) relying especially upon the European Social Charter, Art. 6 of which both the Industrial Relations Act 1971 and TULRA 1974, he alleged, were in breach: p. 117.

81. *Simmons* v. *Hoover Ltd.* [1977] 1 QB 284; see Davies and Freedland, op. cit., pp. 246, 651-9.

82. *Report*, op. cit. para. 943; see Lord Denning MR *Morgan* v. *Fry* [1968] 2 QB 710, 728-30; Hepple and O'Higgins, op. cit., p. 227. In rare cases the notice may be the basis of a variation of the terms of employment: see Davies LJ *Morgan* v. *Fry* above, at p. 731; but contrast Lord Donovan in *Stratford* v. *Lindley* [1965] AC at p. 342. Lord Denning MR, op. cit., did suggest an answer on the length of the notice required, i.e. the same as that needed to terminate the employment contract. It is not obvious that the two periods should necessarily be the same.

83. See J.C. Javillier, op. cit. paras. 346-8, 634; Camerlynck and Lyon-Caen op. cit. paras 727-8.

84. Now s. 62 Employment Protection (Consolidation) Act 1978.

85. See s. 9 Employment Act 1982; P. Wallington, 'Section 9 of the Employment Act 1982 – A Recipe for Victimisation?' (1983) 46 MLR (May).

86. See Sir John Donaldson MR, *Merkur Island Shipping Corpn* v. *Laughton* (1983) 2 WLR 45, 66. The objectives of Lord Scarman were different in that he did not wish to be made a 'back seat driver' in trade disputes, *Duport Steels Ltd* v. *Sirs* [1980] ICR at p. 193; *Express Newspapers Ltd* v. *McShane* [1980] AC at p. 694.

87. Sir John Donaldson, 'Lessons from the Industrial Court' (1975) 91 LQR 181, 192.

88. T. Ramm, 'Federal Republic of Germany', *International Encyclopaedia for Labour Law and Industrial Relations* (ed. R. Blanpain, 1979), para. 617.

89. See Elias and Ewing, op. cit., p. 358 note 58.

90. X. Blanc-Jouvan, 'The Effect of Industrial Action on the Status of the Individual Employee', Chap. 4 in *Industrial Conflict. A Comparative Legal Survey* (eds B. Aaron and K.W. Wedderburn, 1972) written when the 'suspensory' s. 147 Industrial Relations Act 1971 was in force, on which see especially pp. 198-210.

91. See G. Aubert's useful study of seven systems, *L'Obligation de Paix du Travail* (Geneva 1981), and especially on Germany pp. 98-100. See too G. Giugni in *Industrial Conflict. A Comparative Legal Survey* (1972), Chap. 3 'The Peace Obligation'.

92. *Trade Union Immunities*, Cmnd 8128, 1981, para. 379. The quotations that follow are also from paras 351, 345, 376. The parallel problems of labour courts (paras 365-71) are not discussed here.

93. *Democracy in Trade Unions*, Cmnd 8778, 1983, especially para. 52 (d). See generally Wedderburn (1980) 9 ILJ 65.

94. Lewis and Simpson, *Striking a Balance?* op. cit., p. 226, who point out the relevance of the Code of Practice on Closed Shops, para. 54.
95. O. Kahn-Freund *Labour and the Law* (1977), p. 196; and see Wedderburn Chap. 6 in *Discrimination in Employment* (ed. Folke Schmidt, 1978).
96. For the unsatisfactory application of Article 11 (1) (after the withdrawal by the UK of defence under Art. 11 (2) see *Young, James and Webster* v. *UK* [1981] IRLR 408 (ECHR).
97. See Lord Scarman, *Report of A Court of Inquiry ... Into a Dispute (at) Grunwick Processing Laboratorieds Ltd*, Cmnd. 6922, 1977, paras. 56-8 (where he recognises 'all rights and freedoms for which each side contends').
98. Lord Denning MR, *Cheall* v. *APEX* [1982] ICR 543, 557 (the CA decision was reversed by the HL [1983] 2 AC 180). Compare reliance by Lord Denning and Lord Scarman on the Convention in *UKAPE* v. *ACAS* [1979] ICR at pp. 316-7; [1980] ICR at p. 214.
99. Clark and Wedderburn, *Labour Law and IR*, p. 157.
100. Elias and Ewing, op. cit., p. 358.
101. Trade Disputes Act 1906 s. 2; TULRA s. 15 (also in form as substituted in 1980); Employment Act 1980, s. 16. See the cases in note 62 above; and recently on 'nuisance'. *Mersey Dock and Harbour Co.* v. *Verrinder* [1982] IRLR 152; *Norbrook Labs Ltd* v. *King* [1982] IRLR 456 (NI).
102. Chief Constable of South Wales, J. Woodcock, Evidence to H.C. Employment Committee, 27 February 1980. See Kahn-Freund, *Labour and the Law* (1977) pp. 261-2; (1974) 3 ILJ at p. 200.
103. *Broome* v. *DPP* [1974] AC 587; see above, n. 62.
104. Davies and Freedland, *Labour Law: Text and Materials*, p. 677; cf Clark and Wedderburn, *Labour Law and IR* (1983), pp. 58-9, 168-9; B. Bercusson, 'One Hundred Years of Conspiracy and Protection of Property' (1977) 40 MLR 268.
105. See *Rookes* v. *Barnard* [1964] AC 1129, 1177, 1192, 1236, in respect of s. 3 (second limb) of the 1906 Act, the same provision as s. 13 (2) TULRA 1974, now repealed by s. 19, Employment Act 1982.
106. As in the *Grunwick* case, [1978] AC 655, HL; see the invaluable case study in Chapter 1 of Elias, Napier and Wallington, *Labour Law, Cases and Materials* (1980).
107. See now Employment Act 1980, sched. 1, para. 6; Employment Protection Act 1975 s. 126; s. 29 TULRA 1974, (as amended now, however, by s. 18 Employment Act 1982, especially subsection (6)).
108. *USDAW* v. *Sketchley* [1981] ICR 644, EAT; NUGSAT v. *Albury Bros.* [1979] ICR 84, CA; *R* v. *CAC ex parte Tioxide* [1981] ICR 843, EAT; and cf. *NALGO* v. *National Travel* [1978] ICR 598.
109. *Universe Tankships of Monrovia Inc.* v. *ITWF* [1982] 2 WLR 803; see the doubts especially of Lord Brandon at p. 833; and the extraordinary majority decision that the facts disclosed no trade dispute; Wedderburn (1982) 45 MLR 556. For the view that unions should not be protected against liability for 'economic duress' when statutory protection applies only to tort, see G. Jones (1983) Camb L.J. 47-8.
110. See B. Green (1982) 45 MLR 564 and (1983) 46 MLR (March).
111. Browne-Wilkinson J *Powley* v. *ACAS* [1978] ICR 123, 135.
112. Davies and Freedland, op. cit., p. 103.
113. J.A.G. Griffith, *The Politics of the Judiciary*, p. 241.
114. Wedderburn in *Labour Law and the Community* p. 6. Oddly, the greatest exception to judicial interference was a case which involved no statutory rights or immunities at all: *Ford Motor Co.* v. *AUEFW* [1969] 2 QB 303.
115. See the contrasts in Chapter 10, Griffith, op. cit.
116. Lord Denning MR saw the parties as 'David and Goliath' in *UKAPE* v. *ACAS* [1979] ICR 303, 310 and *PO* v. *Crouch* [1973] ICR 366, 375; but he turned against the small group confronting the TGWU in *Morgan* v. *Fry* [1968] 2 QB 710, 729, because they were 'troublemakers who fomented discord in the docks'.

117. K.W. Wedderburn in *Labour Relations and the Law – A Comparative Study* (ed. O. Kahn-Freund, 1965) p. 153, note, proposing an answer to *Rookes* v. *Barnard* (1964) AC 1129.
118. *Labour Law: Text and Materials*, p. 607, cited by Elias and Ewing, op. cit., p. 356.
119. Elias and Ewing, op. cit., p. 356.
120. *Public Prosecutor* v. *Antenaci*, Constitutional Court, 1974, Vol. 1 Int. Lab. Law Rep. at p. 54.
121. O. Kahn-Freund, *System of Industrial Relations*, op. cit. (1954), p. 127; see Clark and Wedderburn, *Labour Law and IR*, pp. 155-65, 198-206.
122. See *Express Newspapers* v. *McShane*, above; *NWL* v. *Woods*, above; Wedderburn (1982) 45 MLR 319 325-7; Simpson (1982) 45 MLR 327, 330-2.
123. On the industrial tribunals, see Clark and Wedderburn, op. cit., *Labour Law and IR*, pp. 173-84.
124. *Report* Cmnd 3623, 1968, para. 583; O. Kahn-Freund, 'Industrial Relations and the Law – Retrospect and Prospect' (1969) 7 BJIR 301, 316. See on this problem, Clark and Wedderburn in *Labour Law and IR*, op. cit., pp. 166-73.
125. See Clark and Wedderburn, *Labour Law and IR*, p. 208 and authorities cited notes 364-9.
126. A. Pizzorno, 'Azione di classe e sistemi corporativi' in *I Spoggetti del Pluralismo* (1980) p. 198; quoted and discussed P. Lange, G. Ross and M. Vannicelli, *Unions, Change and Crisis, French and Italian Union Strategy 1945-1980* (1982), pp. 268-86.
127. *The System of Industrial Relations in GB*, op. cit., (1954), p. 43.
128. In Italy, the leading labour lawyer Professor Gino Giugni said recently, in the context of his role as chairman of an expert committee which helped to negotiate the new social compact amending the 1975 agreeements on the *scala mobile* (indexation of wages), that each epoch has its own 'model' for labour law: 'In the 60s, with an economic boom, it was right to concentrate on a system of collective bargaining to increase wages. Today, with unemployment and crisis, objective number one in industrial relations must be the defence of employment' (*Panorama*, 31 January 1983, p. 95). Compare the conclusion of Clark and Wedderburn in *Labour Law and IR*, op. cit., that labour law must, 'so long as the democratic principle of maintaining effective, independent trade unions remains paramount' (p. 219), now be based upon policies addressed to 'low incomes and, especially, to mass unemployment. The policy for labour law must find its appropriate place in that immediate enterprise.' (p. 220)
129. This message is, of course, best spelled out in J.A.G. Griffith's *The Politics of the Judiciary*, op. cit., and in 'The Political Constitution' (1979) 42 MLR 1 (the Seventh Chorley Lecture).

5

Labour Law – From Here to Autonomy?
A Franco–British Comparison

The father of modern French labour law, Paul Durand, wrote in 1945 of labour law's 'distinctive quality': *le particularisme du droit du travail*. First, the legal rules on dependent labour became a distinct discipline and the subject of industrial legislation. Then separation became more complete. 'Labour law detaches itself from the civil law and is established as an independent juridical system.'[1] A similar development to that giving rise to *le droit maritime* or *le droit fiscal*; or he might have added, as contemporaries did, *le droit professionel* or *droit commercial*.[2] In this sense one could, therefore, speak of the emergency 'autonomy' of labour law (*l'autonomie du droit du travail*).

Autonomy and Labour Law

The existence of, or need for, 'autonomy' in labour law has since been a staple diet of French scholarship, one which 'generates a good deal of controversy' between those who lean towards the application of techniques of the civil law, *le droit commun*, and those who would adopt 'modes of reasoning specific to labour law', usually protective of workers, a debate which 'remains open' and is likely to continue so.[3] The need to categorise precise divisions of the law may, no doubt, be greater in such civil law systems than it is in England. There the law student must know at once whether he is working within the walls of *le droit publique* or *le droit privé*, the kind of distinction which has not traditionally been so profound here, at any rate until the concoctions of Lord Diplock which led our judges 'to pass off unpalatable common law left-overs as delicacies from the classic French cuisine'.[4]

This article is based upon a paper presented to the Industrial Law Society Summer School, 26 September 1986, at St Catherine's College, Oxford. First published in (1987) 16 Industrial Law Journal 1.

Not that the word 'autonomy' should be used lightly. Strictly, Durand accepted, *particularisme* was preferable. No branch of law can be 'completely autonomous, within the body of the juridical order as a whole'.[5] Fortress labour law, like Fortress Wapping, cannot survive in total isolation. One leading modern scholar, Gérard Lyon-Caen, makes the same point: labour law cannot wholly escape (at any rate at the present stage) from the institutions of *droit civil*, for they constitute a major part of the legal environment and 'infrastructure'. Complete independence would place labour law in 'a juridical void'.[6] The way to *l'autonomie* resembled the way that the jurists of old had taken to fashion 'French customary law' out of Roman law, out of its concepts but distinct from it. Durand later wished to refashion that law as a modern law of the enterprise on a rather unitary basis, Lyon-Caen to break from it profoundly on a much more conflictual model.[7] But both, and many others, joined in the view that 'autonomy' was the more forceful, more revealing word: better to risk imprecision for the sake of the idea, 'the sooner to liberate labour law'.[8]

If the terms of this ambition begin to sound almost familiar to us, the reason may be that we have stumbled into that same debate in England without appreciating fully either the character or, more important, the difficulty of the venture. Certainly, parallels with the French debate can now be found here. French writers, both those who urge that labour law must cut adrift from the rules and methods of civil law which prejudice workers, for example on payment of wages, and those who argue against 'autonomy' on the ground that the common law is sufficiently capable of the development necessary to meet new social needs,[9] are more familiar to us now than to our forbears. But it may be that our literature lacks an attempt to prescribe the overall dimensions of any 'autonomy' which our labour law might have in freedom from the common law and its concepts, such as that attempted by Lyon-Caen in 1974 in France. In any attempt to do so, the care exhibited in the French literature deserves attention. If labour law remains part of the legal order, as it will, it cannot be wholly 'free'. That is part of the problem. Not only will it have some contact with the 'ordinary' law and 'ordinary' courts; it will of necessity have close relationships with the positive rules elsewhere – how could it escape co-habitation, for example, with the law on social security?[10]

Such factors are common ground. What may make the undertaking more difficult, perhaps more necessary, in England than in France is the legal and social place of the 'ordinary' courts and their 'ordinary' common law. Indeed, the strength of common law may be such that straightforward reforms (changes in the concept of 'dismissal', for example, or extension of employment protection to all workers beyond the range of the 'employee' *stricto sensu* – straightforward only in the sense of being in themselves less than root-and-branch changes) may be destined to disappoint, even founder, unless they are forged in the crucible of more profound adjustments which give some 'autonomy' to the principles and, more important, to the procedures and enforcement mechanisms of labour law.

A glance (only a summary is possible) at the range of Lyon-Caen's remarkable agenda in 1974 shows how searching such a project might be.[11] Labour law must break free from the assumptions of underlying institutions of the civil law, the property rights of the employer, through which he controls work and the enterprise, the prerogative of the proprietor to organise and distribute work, and the status of subordination attached to the worker. The contract of employment could be retained as representing a free choice to enter an employment relationship; but it must be modified, on the base rather of agreement (*un ordre concerté*) than of hierarchic subordination. Above all labour law was distinguished from civil law by its collective character, its umbilical cord to the social facts. It must deal in categories of collective negotiation rather than contract; the base, and source, of the law itself is derived from *l'autonomie collective*. Recognising the social facts of conflict, it must avoid the trap of legally imposed solutions. Providing the required minimum protections, it must recognise the dominant source of industrial negotiation. In the enforcement of the laws, the aim must always be the search for acceptable, collective compromises: *moins l'ordre de l'Etat qu'un ordre autonome, mal connu du juge* (not so much the state order as an autonomous order, one not well understood by judges).

The agenda is in comparative terms interesting in a number of ways. First, the English labour lawyer finds familiar this insistence upon the priority of 'autonomy for the industrial parties', even if he may now sometimes fear for the survival of such notions. When he reads about labour law as '*un Droit collectif nouveau, fondé sur la conciliation, la discussion plus que sur la "juridiction"* ' (a new collective law, based on conciliation, talks rather than judgements) or finds: '*C'est là une des originalités du Droit du travail, le role de l'Ètat, loin de s'accroitre, en cette matière tend plutot à s'effacer,*' (in this we find one of the original features of Labour Law; the role of the state, so far from increasing, tends to fade away)[12] he can hardly fail to be reminded a little of Kahn-Freund: 'British industrial relations have, in the main, developed by way of industrial autonomy.' The 'free play of collective forces ... if you like collective *laissez faire*'. The primacy or 'priority of autonomous over statutory methods'. Even, rather optimistically: 'What the State has not given the State cannot take away.'[13]

Not that the two attitudes wholly coincide. French writing of this *genre* tends often to aim more unequivocally at the protection of workers, at the 'extension of rules protective of employed labour'.[14] Kahn-Freund, too, saw the 'main object of labour law' to be a force counteracting the 'inequality of bargaining power ... inherent in the employment relationship'; but only a few pages away he describes its 'principal purpose' as regulating, supporting and restraining 'the power of management *and* the power of organised labour'.[15] This comparative point is broader; for there are many British labour lawyers who would have less truck with the position of Kahn-Freund in analysing today's problems who nevertheless wish to distance labour law more sharply from the common law.[16] For them, too, the need for 'autonomy' is critical. The autonomy of labour law has a wider sweep than the autonomy of the industrial parties.

Common Law Control

In neither country do the protagonists of the need to divorce labour law from control by common law partake of one, homogeneous, ideological colour, though (like most issues within labour law) this debate can never itself be independent of ideological content. The divide is not between 'voluntarists' and 'regulators', not even between 'left' and 'right', but between those who do, and those who do not, find the dominance of common law inappropriate for their purpose. The old rules of contract, for example, based upon 'will' and 'agreement', however 'modernised', meet objections from many who agree at least in perceiving them to constitute 'that indispensible figment of the legal mind, known as the contract of employment' shrouding a relationship of subordination: 'the mask of a contract ... the fiction through which [the law] exorcises the incubus of "compulsory labour".'[17] In general, the story is part of a wider realisation that the common law is by itself unable significantly to support new forms of modern social relationship.[18] In particular, though, the labour lawyer's attitude is frequently a reaction to the restriction, nullification or evasion of purposive legislation by the application of inappropriate concepts or doctrines, so often based upon the 'contract of service'.

By 1966 Rideout found that this 'cornerstone' of employment law (as Kahn-Freund had rightly called the employment contract in positive terms) comprised a 'core of rubble'.[19] More recently, in different ways, Leighton[20] and Hepple[21] have raised the issue of its utility. The latter persuasively renews the pressure for a root and branch solution, a new code of labour law based upon alternative concepts. In so doing, the lawyer calls in aid the sociologist; few would now recoil from the view that 'The nature of the exchange relationship in work cannot be gauged by reference to the so-called contract of employment.'[22] But once the concept of the contract of employment is rejected, the need to rebuild labour law more generally inescapably emerges.

Replacing the concept of 'employee', with a contract of 'service' as opposed to 'services', is necessary but not sufficient. As a concept it has long been in crisis, one created by changes in relations of production that are not recent. The 'control' test was already fragile in the late nineteenth century not long after it was adopted from concepts that had their roots in that medieval servant in whom the master had his property or *servitium*.[23] But the crisis has been reinforced in recent decades by a rapid fragmentation of the labour market, especially by the growth of myriad, so-called 'a-typical' or 'marginal' relationships between workers and those for whom they produce value – the worker part-time, casual, temporary, lump labour, homeworker, outworker, or the subcontractor, let alone the trainee or the police cadet who are, unless special laws are passed, left unprotected because they are, in the eye of the judges as reflected in the common law glass, *sui generis*, 'in a class by themselves', as Lord Denning said. Their own legal tests for 'employee' and 'self-employed' have splintered in the hands of the judges.[24] Bad is compounded by worse when this concept is used to define the bearers of most of the statutory employment protection rights. Worse still, common law concepts restrict labour law in even less predictable ways – as when young trainees, for example, for whom society can provide no proper employment and who manifestly should have been given status and protections equivalent to those anciently accorded to apprentices, are left with uncertain protection even by legislation on race and sex discrimination (despite the fact that they work for others) because they do not satisfy the test of a contract *either* for service *or* for services 'personally to execute work or labour'.[25] It is little less than bizarre that only a long legal battle enabled young work-experience trainees, engulfed by flames at work, to establish the duty of their employer to inform and instruct them in their hazardous work even though they were not 'employees'.[26] No wonder it is said:

> We need a new concept which can match the underlying purposes of labour legislation. The contract of service should be replaced by a broad definition of an 'employment relationship' between the worker and the undertaking by which he is employed.[27]

This is a call for autonomy, for freedom from civil law categories. It now receives a wide and favourable response.

All this – the masking of subordination by the terms of contract, the fragmentation of the concept of 'employee' along with the social forms of dependent labour and the curbing of legislation by the bridle of common law interpretation – remains true for the newest as for the oldest relationships. There is no absence of subordination in 'telework' or 'distance employment'. Indeed, the new information, like the new nuclear technologies, introduce their own peculiar risks of exploitation for many workers. Nor have other legal systems found it impossible to base their labour law upon wider concepts of the worker's subordinate relationship.[28] Where they have done so, their legal system has been more, not less, capable of meeting new trends in the labour market.

Within the stockade of employment protection in Britain, the erosion of workers' rights by common law orientations in meaning and interpretation (sometimes by the very adoption in the statute itself of common law terms) is now notorious. In determining whether there was a 'dismissal', said Lawton LJ optimistically in 1978: 'The statutory provisions which have been under consideration have brought social justice into labour relations; but this new and desirable factor must be based on justice not on whimsy or sentimentality.'[29] That justice meant, he immediately found, that the statutory concept of 'dismissal' had to be fashioned in accordance with the common law of contract (and it must be admitted the legislature had not clearly said otherwise). Thence were introduced the rules on repudiation and discharge by breach, to be grandly re-named 'constructive dismissal', along with the complexities of acceptance of repudiatory breach and election. Acceptance of breach in the law of dismissal has indeed now become a 'knotty problem' under the statutes.[30] It is no good asking the common law how to render void the unjust dismissals of ordinary workers. The answer to that problem must be the one given to the man who asked the way to York: 'You do not start from here.'

Courts and Precedents

Nor is it true that such developments can be put down exclusively to reactionary control by the Court of Appeal over an enlightened EAT, as even a few recent examples indicate. Although the Court of Appeal agreed with that tribunal in depriving a university lecturer of his redundancy claim because the university's termination was not a 'dismissal' in the light of his application under the Premature Retirement Compensation Scheme (therefore a termination by mutual agreement), it was the EAT which tried to extend that notion of termination by 'consent' to the case of Mrs Igbo, who was late back at work after her holiday, having signed a paper acknowledging that failure to return meant automatic termination.[31] This was a termination by consent, said the EAT. It took the Court of Appeal to reject such an unjust result, and to exclude it from a range of other cases, it seems, by the conclusion that such an automatic termination clause concerning future events limits the operation of sections 54 and 55 of the 1978 Act and is therefore void under the terms of section 140. Nor has the EAT always exhibited better industrial judgment than the Court of Appeal. It is the EAT which has obstructed the continuity qualification of part-time workers under short separate contracts, allowed automatic termination of employment by reason of the impecuniosity of an employer[32] and limited 'equal value' claims to situations where men and women do not do like work.[33] More, it is hard to imagine that any three Lords Justices of Appeal could be assembled who would agree to do such injury to industrial autonomy, employment protection and juridical logic as that produced by Popplewell J when he mixed together the enforceability of collective agreements, incorporation of terms in employment contracts and the 'intention' of the various parties (at different levels) to conjure up the result that collectively agreed redundancy arrangements, although firmly 'incorporated into the applicant's terms of employment', were still not legally enforceable there by reason of a TINALEA (this is not a legally enforceable agreement) clause in the collective agreement.[34] It was 'regrettable' and 'bad for industrial relations'. Fortunately the Court of Appeal saw it was wrong on any footing. The character and record of the EAT, not least its attitude to common law concepts, must be assessed carefully in considering any proposals to make it either a final court of appeal or a court of wider jurisdiction in labour law.[35] In terms of labour law autonomy the case for that is not yet proven.

The charge of reinforcing the retrogressive character of common law control over statutory employment protection cannot, however, be answered by proof of occasional Court of Appeal moderation over EAT excesses. Under some Presidencies (or perhaps the influence of new wingpersons – we cannot tell) the EAT has leaned modestly the other way. It is in the House of Lords and, largely, in the Court of Appeal as the controlling judicial body, that the dominant skein of statutory law on employment protection has usually been woven, by way of such concepts as 'constructive dismissal' and common law implied terms. A new code demanding, for example, co-operation from the worker has been constructed, reaching often far beyond the terms of the contract he or she thought – or even an officious bystander might think – had been concluded. This is an area that reminds us that the common law is, indeed, as the Master of the Rolls has it, a 'living thing'.[36] As Lord Reid said, we do not believe any more in the fairy tale 'that in some Aladdin's cave there is hidden the Common Law in all its splendour and that on a judge's appointment there descends on him knowledge of the magic words Open Sesame'.[37] There is such a thing as judicial creativity, even a capability in judges to move with the times – though 'their function in our society is to do so belatedly'.[38] The 'living thing' of the common law is the judiciary; the principles are changed in application; but the underlying philolsophy is not.

This area reminds us too that it is the very function of the common law to preserve subordination inherently within employment, and if necessary to do so creatively. True, we do not find judges deciding today that a servant has impliedly agreed not to sue the employer for injury negligently caused by a fellow servant who is in 'common employment'[39] (though it is sometimes forgotten just how far judges took that doctrine).[40] The invention of that class doctrine smacks of its time, but like other common law developments it cannot be ascribed to some personality defect in the British judges involved. Indeed they found understandable comfort in the fact that courts in other common law jurisdictions at the time had adopted these same 'principles of universal application'.[41]

What we do find, though, is that in 1956 the Law Lords, by a majority, departed from testing the 'intention of the parties' and applied tests based on the 'necessary condition of master and man' to enforce an implied term whereby a negligent employee must indemnify the employer's insurance company. The language was of its time, updating Lord Abinger. Not to do this would 'tend to create a feeling of irresponsibility in a class of persons from whom, perhaps more than any other, constant vigilance is owed to the community'.[42] So too, in the last decade or so the Court of Appeal has enlarged the duty of co-operation, extending even to a worker's obligation to 'serve the employer faithfully with a view to promoting those commercial interests for which he is employed',[43] a model of unitary labour relations.[44] In the same period has come the implicit duty of the worker to accept the employer's changes in search of 'improved business methods' so long as there is a 'sound business reason', an implication which both in redundancy and in unfair dismissal (not least by manipulation of the magical SOSR 'some other substantial reason') has transformed the statutes.[45] In SOSR, Parliament gave the courts a mighty weapon; but it was the courts' choice how they used it. Such decisions shaped the statutes to undermine expectations of workers based upon contracts and collective agreements which those laws were meant to improve.[46] In the dinner ladies' cases, 1985, they made it clear that breach of a national collective agreement did not shut out the employer from proving SOSR, that 'belt and braces which sustains [managerial prerogative] in business reorganisations'.[47] In addition, compelled by EEC sources, Parliament placed in the hands of the judges ETOR (justification of dismissal through an 'economic, technical or organisational reason') in transfers of undertakings, rightly said to be a 'most searing attack on principles of job security'.[48] But there have been few protests that such a formula is unpalatable to judicial gorges.

This expansion of the worker's duty to cooperate, an illustration of continuing common law insistence upon his subordination and upon the employer's right to legislate at the workplace, has been untiringly pursued by High Court judges. His obligation to re-train in 'new methods and techniques' when required has been matched by the imposition on teachers (scarcely over-paid for their work) of all those implied obligations which would be expected by 'the public' of professional persons, combined with a skilful manipulation of the old law of abatement and set-off.[49] Nor has the Court of Appeal failed to give a similar lead elsewhere. The obvious dangers of allowing the employer to argue that the absence of the employee has automatically terminated his contract by frustration – rather than by 'dismissal' which can be tested against 'fairness' – are well documented in labour law.[50] The EAT has in part understood them. But such considerations are absent from the Court of Appeal's decisions even today. Dillon LJ can see 'no reason in principle' why an indeterminate employment contract determinable on short notice should not be held to have terminated automatically 'according to the accepted and long established doctrine of frustration'.[51] How else could it strike the common law, even if that precludes the court from examining the reasonableness of the employer's conduct where it is he who purported to give 'notice' to the absent worker?

A French Lesson?

The dominant, though by no means exclusive, role of the Court of Appeal as the infiltrator of an expanding common law back into labour law, both statutory and non-statutory, suggests that any replacement for the 'contract of employment', however desirable, might encounter problems at that level, if nowhere else. If we take the view that the key to reform lies in the enactment of a code based upon an alternative concept of the employment relationship[52] we must ask what the new law would look like in action, above all in court.

It may be useful here to note that in all this we are not entirely alone. French labour lawyers, in the struggle to exclude doctrines of *le droit civil*, have faced problems not wholly dissimilar. Take *la resolution judiciaire* (individual rescission). The *Code Civil* enshrines the doctrine that a party against whom a synallagmatic contract is broken has the choice either to demand performance or to claim rescission, but that claim must be made in a legal action. This principle has been applied to individual dismissals under a contract of employment, not always to the liking of French labour lawyers since it may outflank special laws about dismissal.[53] The gravest of such conflicts, though, arose over the complex legal protections given to workers' representatives, such as those elected to the *comité d'enterprise* (works council) and the *délégués syndicaux* (union delegates). For them, the law lays down formidable additional protection, with procedures involving consultation with the *comité d'enterprise* and authorisation by the labour inspectorate, to which collective agreements may add but not detract, in both 'individual' and collective (or 'economic') dismissals. These buffers against dismissal are naturally retained by the representatives on transfer of the enterprise.[54] Such technicalities are not allowed to displace them. Dismissal in breach of the procedure is a nullity, sanctioned by heavy damages and reinstatement.

But in 1952 the 'Social Chamber' of the *Cour de Cassation* (High (civil) Court of Appeal) held that the employer could avoid these procedures by way of *resolution judiciaire* to terminate the representative's employment contract under that Article of the *Code Civil*. True, in his capacity as representative he had the statutory protections; but as a worker his contract was subject to the 'common law of contract'.[55] So contract law still applied permitting the employer to seek rescission for breach. Although the 'Criminal Chamber' took a different view, it was not until the judgment of the specially convened 'mixed' Chamber of the court in 1974 that the judges generally changed their view. The employer was then forbidden to utilise *resolution judiciaire* against a workers' representative protected by the special legislative provisions.[56] The *Cour de Cassation* held the statutory protections could not be displaced; they were for the benefit of all the workers represented, exclusive of the civil law remedy, *incompatible avec le caractère autonome de la protection spéciale* (which was incompatible with the autonomous character of the special protection). That was 'the intention of the legislature' from 1945, the court found. What is more, the very commencement by an employer of proceedings for *resolution judiciaire* became a penal misdemeanour (*délit d'entrave*) – 'one of the rare cases where the fact of starting a legal action constitutes a criminal offence'.[57] Some lower courts still resisted, citing principles of 'equality' in the *Code du Travail*, the constitution and the Declaration of the Rights of Man, refusing, as it was put in language worthy of Lord Denning, to accept *'une caste de citoyens priviligiés'* (a caste of privileged citizens). But the *Cour de cassation* in full plenary assembly confirmed its position in 1983.[58] Common law and labour law had done battle for 22 years. At the end writers saw a victory for 'the autonomy of labour law in respect of the civil law of contracts and obligations'.[59] Such instances of *particularisme* are not confined to civil law; the criminal courts have also pursued a logic of independent labour law.[60]

Judges, Autonomy and Flexibility

It would of course be quite inadmissible from the point of view of comparative method to read into that story from France direct lessons for Britain. But some reflections may be permissible. First, if we are not alone in encountering such issues, are our problems perhaps even more difficult? In the two countries, for example, judges are not necessarily comparable. The French judge chooses to be a judge in his twenties; his relationship with the bar is not the father and son bond of the Temple but with practising lawyers who are equal but separate. It could be that there is more chance for new generations to bring in a breath of fresh air in such a system, not least when *la doctrine* occupies a rather higher place among acknowledged sources. Further, although it would be wrong to say that concepts of 'precedent' are unknown in France, they do not play the role there which they have in our courts. One may legitimately ask whether it would take more than 22 years for our appellate judges to accept equivalent changes, to expel fundamental common law institutions from employment law. The learning curve is not very favourable, not merely among appellate judges but among High Court puisne judges and, even more important for tomorrow's bench, among many members of the bar. What matters here is the judiciary as a body, as an institution. No matter that a small proportion of judges now come from state schools, Scrutton LJ is still right: 'they are all educated and nursed in the same ideas as the employers'.[61] Not (or not only) because of their formal education, but because these are the same ideas of contract, property and employer's prerogative that are central to the common law.

The question is not the personality of the man on the bench, certainly not the problem of personal good faith or 'bias' (though some still set up those Aunt Sallies). The question concerns deeply rooted common law institutions which mould both training and judgment. The mere creation of courts with a labour jurisdiction does not necessarily change that. By itself such a step does not provide a magistracy with different reference points and traditions, let alone, as in Italy since 1973, make provision for annual study and training that may be needed for judges in industrial and trade union affairs.[62] A move towards 'autonomy' for labour law in Britain perhaps depends in part upon the appointment to its administration of those who have not grown comfortable in wig and gown and who are willing to take regular socio-legal refreshers in the subject as an autonomous discipline.[63] (Conventional wisdom might give such an idea the headline: 'Labour law grab for immunity from law of the land' – but that is the habitual English description for the rescue of labour law from common law.) Such an idea does not imply, though, that a new system for administration of labour law would not contain 'lawyers'. Experience abroad – France, Sweden and Italy, for example – suggests that lawyers of different types are able to adapt to ways of thought relatively independent of ancient, native traditions. There is no reason to assume that we lack young (perhaps even some not so young) lawyers who might do the same here. But we cannot expect the bulk of the existing profession to rescue labour law from their own training.

Current developments in Britain have run contrary to any such rescue. It is well documented that the so-called 'deregulation' of labour law between 1979 and 1986 has introduced to a great degree a legal framework resting 'upon a withdrawal of legislative resistance to the common law. This reintroduces a corpus of rules for social relationships that is by no means "ordinary", certainly not neutral between contending social classes.'[64] And, as Lewis puts it: 'Why should reforms designed to make the task of the unfair dismissal claimant more difficult ... be counted as examples of deregulation?'[65] Indeed, common law is capable of adding layers of 'juridification', a feature often overlooked in the debate on that issue.[66] The same pressure towards 'deregulation' and 'flexibility' has blossomed in France since the government in 1984 deflected the engines of reform which, through the *lois Auroux* two years earlier, aimed to usher in an era of '*citoyenneté dans l'enterprise*' (citizenship at work) for workers.[67] Journals once full of debate about the autonomy of labour law now sprout symposia entitled: *Faut-il brûler le code du travail?* (should we burn the Labour Law Code?). The talk is of flexibility via decentralised bargaining, of loosening rules about dismissal, of rescinding protections in the Code, of a new enterprise law: some say, 'quite simply, *le droit civil*' (civil common law).[68] At the same time, it is interesting to find French courts renewing and enlarging restrictions on lawful strikes, despite the Constitutional guarantees, in a way not unfamiliar to the British student.[69] Creativity is not confined to Britain when social pressures mount.

Characteristically, Gérard Lyon-Caen has attacked this 'rigged' debate, arguing that there was plenty of flexibility in existing labour law.[70] What is being demanded in France as in Britain, is the surrender of statutory protections placed around the contract of employment to lead, with a fragmentation of bargaining into enterprise units, to a greater individuation of employment relations. This is the context in which labour law now faces common law – on the latter's ground. Because we have no *Code du Travail* (Labour Law Code), the task of introducing a code to govern the rights and duties of all types of workers – attractive though that suggestion is – would be even greater in Britain, whether or not it adopted the practice of applying collective agreements as an automatic base from which only improvements

could be contracted, together with optional norms from which
contracting away would be more free.[71] The issue upon which we
have stumbled here goes not only, or not so much, to the substance
of a reformed labour law, but to its application and procedures.
Unless the tribunals to whom it is entrusted understand and
sympathise with its purposes, the autonomy of the new law (from
its definitions of 'workers' or rules on formation and termination of
work relationships to the express and implied obligations of the
parties or its specific principles governing the work-wage bargain)
would drown beneath its own complexity. The fate of a code that
cannot trust its courts is intolerable prolixity and, ultimately,
defeat.

Rights, Immunities and Autonomy

Two areas illustrate the daunting nature of the task in Britain.
First, the well-known problem of rights to organise, to bargain and
to strike.[72] Many now believe – and in principle there is a good
case for it – that some or all of these social rights must be dealt with
through a framework of express rights. Why not express social
rights as legal rights? The view that we might profitably set out
such rights positively and clearly is not wholly confined to those
who wish to extend them, as a glance at the CBI committee of 1980
illustrates.[73] The desire to move to industrial rights according to
their 'substance' was expressed even by Viscount Radcliffe in
1965.[74] Fortunately, the related, but different, antithesis between
the forms of statutory 'positive rights' and 'negative immunities'
has now been largely jettisoned. Any British draftsman clearly
needs both legal forms in constructing effective social rights. The
main problems do not arise from an inherent weakness in the
syntactical character of legislation, nor even from the absence of a
constitution in which such rights might be entrenched, though both
factors can exacerbate the difficulties. They stem from the refusal
or inability (or both) of judges to bow the knee of the common law
to a balance of power that offends its philosophy. That was the
issue with trade dispute 'immunities' which, as Lord Diplock said,
stuck in 'judicial gorges' whenever organised workers appeared too
strong, long before the legislation of the 1980s came along
(legislation that has had no such fishbone effect).[75] Rights in the
form of 'rights' have fared little better; take the right to picket.[76]

The obstacles in the path of such statutory rights are legion.
Take the right to strike. If all or some industrial action is to rest
upon a 'right', it must exclude a host of common law doctrines,
above all allow for suspension, rather than breach, of workers'
employment contracts. The well-known questions in the Donovan
Report at once arise: Can the employer ever dismiss? Can the
workers take second jobs? What if the strike goes on for ever? –

and so on.[77] After that, what guarantee is there that existing or new liabilities will not prove destructive of the new rights? It is a bold aspiration to say that 'the right would override any tortious or other liability at common law';[78] that the new rights would operate 'regardless of common law developments'; or that judges would accept them as 'primary' so that the common law 'would come to a virtual standstill'.[79] It would need a good draftsman to accomplish that; it might need also the abolition of some torts altogether, perhaps something parallel to the truncation by statute of conspiracy as a common law crime in 1977. Experience demonstrates that even the most discriminating common law mind does not see constitutional rights or freedoms of this kind as deserving of broad interpretation; a 'freedom of association' is interpreted as not guaranteeing liberty for workers to *act* in combination.[80] Nor is there any suggestion to alter that approach in the case made by lawyers and judges who advocate the adoption of a Bill of Rights.[81] The new, quasi-constitutional labour law rights would still be in these hands when the day came for judgment.

History bids us remember the evidence about common law power. This century we have seen judicial invention of tortious conspiracy, of trade union quasi-corporate liability, of illegality for unions taking political activity; the transmutation of a statutory 'right' to picket into a weak immunity; the many constrictions of the 'trade dispute' golden formula; the expansion of tort liability for inducing breach of contract (itself invented in 1853) and for 'interference'; the creation of tortious intimidation out of a threat to strike – to mention but the headlines. If we seek to bring that process to a standstill, we must say how we will close down the rule-making factory buzzing away creatively at the heart of that legal tradition. Normally, moreover, common law interpretation of collective rights for workers puts them at their lowest. It seems to be common ground that there will be limitations to the new rights. True, a positive right to strike 'can be as wide or as narrow as the political climate dictates'; and 'technically' it could have no limits. But 'political expediency may' (surely will) 'dictate that there shall be some'.[82] Obviously, these could vary widely. They might relate to trade disputes, ballots, strike notices, secondary action, forms of picketing – quite apart from trespass, 'violence', 'force' and the like. Whatever they are, those boundaries will be the first areas to attract judicial intervention. Where is the guarantee that common law courts will cease to apply their creative energies in the normal way?

More, the common law tradition, faced with a workers' trade union, is quite genuinely capable of adopting contradictory methods of reasoning along the path of judgment. Take section 3 (second limb) of the Trade Disputes Act 1906, later re-enacted ('for the avoidance of doubt') in section 13 (2) of TULRA 1974. It purported to protect acts done in furtherance of trade disputes which 'interfered with trade, business or employment' – part of the tort that Sir William Erle wanted to create in 1869. In order to prevent the section protecting interference by workers' threats to break employment contracts in a strike the Law Lords in 1964 decided that it 'protected' nothing – merely applied to interference that was lawful anyway. Lord Reid held 'that what Parliament did in enacting the second part of section 3 was to put in a provision which would be necessary to achieve their object if the law should go one way, but unnecessary if it went the other way'.[83] Twenty years later, in cases where the 1964 decision was extensively discussed, precisely the opposite construction was adopted. Lord Diplock averred: 'the interference there referred to must involve interference by unlawful means', something that would be 'actionable' if not done in furtherance of a trade dispute – a construction 'too plain and unambiguous to justify resort to legislative history'.[84] The latter interpretation not only provided reasons why section 13 (2) should be repealed, it flew in the face of the 1964 decision and, more important, fuelled the flames of the expanding liabilities for 'unlawful interference' with trade or business.

A parallel aspect of the problem is illustrated by other expansions of liability. Labour law always stands at risk of new common law liabilities created in areas which had little or nothing to do with the employment relationship. The foundations of its fortress are, as things stand, defenceless against their penetration. There are many such in the common law pipeline. So, in commercial law judgments of the late 1970s judges expanded the doctrine of 'economic duress' to include novel cases where a party's 'will is overborne' (though quite how this works in the multinational corporation remains to be explored). This newly expanded wrong was translated into labour law in 1982; and so strong is the seamless web of common law that counsel was compelled to concede its entry. Now it applies when an employer has 'no alternative' but to submit in face of industrial action – that is, he would suffer economic loss which in the eye of the court is unacceptable. True, the Law Lords hinted that they might temper this doctrine where some remaining trade dispute protection would still be available had the action been based on an equivalent tort. But this uncertain concession, granted by common law grace and favour, does little to detract from the enormity of its transplantation from commercial relations into employment relations with such a radically different social significance.[85] Nor was it a surprise to find in 1986 that the will of a worker about to lose his job was not seen as overborne; in the common law framework, he had 'a very clear alternative, namely to complain to an Industrial Tribunal and to draw social security meanwhile'. Such a view was inevitable if the common law was not to be led into denial of the legitimacy of workers' economic subordination.

In truth, the twenty years after 1964 suggest that such 'abstention' as there was by judges between 1918 and 1960 (and there was some) may in the longer perspective come to be seen as exceptional. Faced with what it perceives as a threat to the established social order, the common law creates its response, whether it is the mutilation of the Factory Act by Parke B in 1850 or Lord Denning's explicit 'extension' of tort liability in 1969.[86] Labour law cannot resist because it has no autonomy. Nor are its statutes immune from creative erosion. In the long run the common law may sometimes give way; but even then it possesses formidable interlocutory sanctions against social change.

Secondly, though, there are more fundamental problems. The essence of intervention by the High Court in collective labour relations often lies less in substantive than in procedural law. For what does it profit a defendant to have great bundles of 'positive rights', if he loses at a hearing where the judge defers examination of them until a notional full trial, meanwhile granting the plaintiff on proof merely of an arguable case the interlocutory labour injunction which he seeks against the strike or the overtime ban? The deficiencies of our procedures which make them unjust to workers and trade unions in industrial conflict are well known.[87] Amelioration by way of statutory fetters upon judicial discretion or even on procedure can be useful, but has been shown to be of limited value.[88] Further progress might be made by penalising plantiffs who make extravagant use of interlocutory procedures in costs. But any such measures will apply within judicial interpretation of the limiting factors (such as 'trade dispute'). Judges do not know about 'labour injunctions', only about injunctions; and they are likely to continue in the habit of squeezing such limiting factors until the pips squeak.

More fundamentally, the judge exercises his discretion in a particular case. This the statute finds it hard to reach. Left to strike a 'balance' in a case of industrial conflict, the common law judge is bound, by reason of training and tradition out of his (rarely her) very being, to lean instinctively in favour of exercising an 'interim' discretion to prevent damage to property. It is unrealistic to expect anything else, especially at times when the social 'climate' is hot. The use of injunctions to help employers or others stop strikes, though, must be put at the door of the common law itself as a system, not in the persons of its judges. If parliament cannot have confidence in the courts in this respect, it has little option but to remove that discretion and put certain decisions (about the existence of a 'trade dispute', for example) elsewhere. The same is true of the repeated judicial insistence upon a 'residual discretion' to issue injunctions in the public interest, of the invention of new sanctions against trade unions, like 'interim declarations' and novel receiverships, or of extensions of third party liability for aiding and abetting contempt.[89] This suggests that the disease of the labour injunction, a running sore in our society for a century, can be cured only by bringing in some other tribunal.

Behind these commonly discussed issues are others less commonly recognised as labour law problems. Why, for instance, do we continue to talk of 'the employer'? The term is normally a mystification of reality. The worker usually has legal links in the private sector with a personified aggregation of capital, a company given legal personality 'to enable business to be undertaken with limited financial liability'.[90] Such a company may, often will, be one of a group, maybe a transnational group; but it retains its own legal personality. This unreality is the pivot of the traditional lawyer's world. The workers may not even know which company in the group is his 'employer'.[91] The problem recurs throughout labour law from strikes and secondary action to unfair dismissal and transfers of undertakings, where, as Hepple says, our law already knows of the alternative concept of 'undertaking'; and it is accentuated by the inadequate definition of 'associated employers' and the even sadder interpretation of that formula.[92]

Measures to pierce the veils of grouped or associated companies, however, are only a first step. Proposals now made to apply 'transfer of undertaking' protections to company takeovers by shares hint at a broader agenda, one concerned to identify the various points of power by which the worker is in reality confronted. Similarly, the 'Vredeling' draft directive is (or was originally) concerned not merely with lifting multinational corporate veils, but with attaching responsibility to the ultimate focus of decision making, including the parent corporation.[93] This too was on Lyon-Caen's agenda in 1974. In place of the 'employer', as party to the employment relation, he proposed that we should substitute notions of centres of decision and of power.[94] Labour law obligations should rest upon the real decision takers. A decade later he reminded us also that the 'relative autonomy' of labour law may rest upon hollow formulae if it does not affect other areas of law. If labour law obligations to consult workers are broken, for example, why should company law still permit a takeover to proceed.[95] As with social security, so with company law: labour law cannot remain in a watertight compartment. The parallel English agenda here is not hard to set.

In Britain the base of the mystified 'employer' rests, it is too often forgotten, largely upon judicial decision. No statute conclusively bound the House of Lords in 1897 to deny, as the Court of Appeal had unanimously affirmed, that his company was an agent or trustee for Mr Salomon. Corporate personality is largely a creation of the judges over which parliament has often been reluctant to take sovereignty. The plea of the Cork Committee in 1982 for fundamental changes in the liability of parents for subsidiary companies' debts has gone unheeded even by the legislature.[96] When reform comes in company law, as it must, the need to make its interests felt will be a necessary, if paradoxical condition of labour law's 'autonomy'.

Autonomy in Action

These considerations suggest that, alongside a new substantive code, a new framework for British labour law may need institutions not merely administrative like ACAS but judicial, too, which take their stand initially on some ground other than the common law. Otherwise that very reform of substantive law may encounter severe limitations by reason of the concepts, procedures and assumptions brought to it by a judiciary moulded, if not trapped, in its tradition. In the contest between labour law and common law, the latter's judges hold the high ground. But it may be said: 'Labour law surely cannot in this sense ever escape from the common law. That will always reappear, if in nothing else than in the form of judicial review by the High Court. Look at what happened to ACAS, the CAC, even the EOC and CRE.[97] The small bonuses offered to superior "public" employees, by the novel enforcement of status or expectations, will be the price of overall control of labour agencies and tribunals, either by review or through appeals to the normal appellate courts.[98]

Curiously, there have existed jurisdictions in our labour law which were more autonomous. From 1913 the Registrar of Friendly Societies had power to decide complaints by aggrieved union members about the operation of political fund rules by a final order 'without appeal', orders 'not removable into any court of law or restrainable by injunction'.[99] So too, his decisions about procedures in union mergers were originally conclusive unless he saw fit to agree to seek the opinion of the High Court.[100] Only in 1975 were these decisions tidily shunted into the judicial machinery via appeal on points of law to the EAT and onwards (and looking back, there seems to have been little better apparent reason than tidiness, for the Registrar had scarcely ever been challenged).[101] Even today the High Court is excluded from making decisions on union 'independence' until the Certification Officer has reached a decision about the matter.[102] What else are these instances but an assertion of autonomy for labour law, an insistence that juridical decisions on industrial issues be made in suitable special procedures and by those best qualified to make them? Those precedents were not condemned as constitutional outrages. Procedures could no doubt be reformed in a complementary direction in all courts. It is sometimes proposed, for example, that all types of employment litigation should permit intervention by the trade union, even in actions by individual workers, whenever collective interests are at stake. One finds such juridical 'space' for trade unions in other countries.[103]

But the introduction of such procedural devices (sensible though they are) would by itself do little to change the character of the court or tribunal. The British industrial tribunals, for example, are in essence highly ambiguous institutions. They are cheaper, quicker and more informal than the ordinary courts.[104] But they were set up in 1964 (after scarcely any debate) to be a 'nucleus of a system of labour courts'.[105] They have lay members. But those judges, authority insists, are not allowed to be in any way 'representatives'. They are cut off from the roots of their constituencies, contrasting markedly with the elected judges of the French *Conseils de prud'hommes*.[106] Unlike the *Conseils*, where the lay representatives sit in equal numbers, the tribunals have a legal chairman (in the EAT even a High Court judge) to whom, except in rare instances, the lay judges defer. The *Conseils* had, Marcel David once put it, the aim of operating outside the dominant social system by inserting democratic concepts into the domain of industrial relations – hardly the core of our tribunals' ambition.[107] So great has concern become about our tribunals that some now propose their replacement by informal arbitration.[108] Why is this? Not merely because they are today more legalistic, formal and tardy than was hoped for or because they frustrate other expectations, such as the provision of effective remedies like reinstatement. More profound disquiet has arisen because they have, in these and other ways, become part of the traditional judicial system, absorbed into the procedures and ways of common law institutions. They have been more easily absorbed because of the refusal of any representative status to their lay judges.[109] Part of the disappointment about the tribunals and EAT concerns their lack of autonomy – an autonomy which by their nature in present form they can never have.

There is more than one way for courts, tribunals or arbitration bodies with labour jurisdiction to achieve a degree of autonomy. A labour court may grow up with the modern social and industrial system peaceably, as in Sweden,[110] or in dynamic tension, as in France. It may emerge technically as part of the ordinary hierarchy of courts yet operate nevertheless as part of an increasingly autonomous labour law, in substance and procedure, as with the Italian *Pretore*.[111] Independence may be gained by institutions that express established collective autonomy on which, by reason of the balance of social forces, the State does not trample, as with our 'Industrial Court' and Central Arbitration Committee in their heyday.[112] There may be other examples in Britain.[113] But what is virtually impossible is to expect a new tribunal dumped into the system as an inferior court, divorced from representative contact with the collective social forces involved in its cases (no matter how 'individual' the litigation is said to be), controlled by the ordinary judiciary, spatchcocked into a complex industrial relations system with a motley menu of 32 assorted jurisdictions, to develop that kind of autonomy.

Autonomy and Agony

Where then is the guiding star for those who seek a new map for labour law in Britain, to make it relatively independent in action of common law direction? How to make a reality of any 'intelligible framework which promotes collective bargaining and is freed from the contract of service'?[114] Such a code, freed from the 'dead weight of tradition in the common law' with its 'simple contractual account of the employment relation', might be based upon an analogy with 'governmental power' in order to control both the rules at work and 'bureaucratic power' in their exercise, according to standards of 'reasonableness', with a 'public law' content.[115] But who will guarantee the concrete exercise of that jurisdiction in some tradition other than that which now reigns, not least in the interpretation of 'reasonableness'? If labour law is to escape from the clutches of common law thinking and procedures, the compass seems to point in a direction in which few instinctively wish to travel. That is (dare one say it?) towards labour courts.[116]

The term 'labour courts' means different things to different people. In our context it cannot mean Diplock-courts to which trade union rights are 'unpalatable', nor Donaldson-courts which aim to tell the public which side is 'right' in an industrial dispute. Nor could reform rest upon a sole 'Labour Court' rather than a system of separate specialised bodies with diverse tasks, from informal arbitration or dispute resolution machinery to more formal tribunals, all speaking an autonomous language of labour law, *fondé sur la conciliation, la discussion plus que sur la juridiction.* There is neither need for, nor advantage in advocating a 'son-of-NIRC' to make the *merits* of labour disputes justiciable, though some already make that equation.[117] Somewhere, however, in such a structure there will be need for a body sufficiently tall in its independence to repel appeals to, or review by, the High Court and the common appellate courts. At the frontier, there would be need of a tribunal (however composed) with Supreme Court status, one that can repel common law jurisdictions whose logic it is the purpose to exclude, if you like, a 'Labour Court'.

Such a court could pursue the objective of autonomy only if staffed from the outset in a new way. Its judiciary could not from its very nature comprise common law Trojan horses without robes. It would be necessarily very different from the EAT. It could not operate under the presidency of peripatetic justices on leave from the High Court. This problem of staffing cannot be discussed fully here;[118] but these judges, whether laymen or lawyers, would be no less 'judicial' than common law judges, merely tuned to a different logic, experience and policy. Unless this problem is faced, separate 'labour courts' can add little or nothing to the autonomy of labour law. Indeed, we may well see the legal and industrial establishment move in behind proposals for such a court precisely in order to sanitise them by retaining the traditional High Court judiciary. One could also expect initial trade union distrust of the idea, bred from the fear that such courts would necessarily involve their further integration and legal control. Few could deny that experiment with any form of labour court would be a high risk strategy. On the other hand, the concept of a new judiciary chosen from different professions and social groups, with a different sex and ethnic balance, is likely to seem less objectionable a decade from now when solicitors, barristers, accountants and others will have moved towards multi-profession partnerships. Without some such step, how can labour law ever be administered on any basis other than the common law?

The issue of the new judiciary for such a court is distinct from the pressing need to reform the existing, common law judiciary itself.[119] Nor does it rest upon the existence of 'bias' in existing judges.[120] It is different from the first and more difficult than the second. New roles, therefore, for existing institutions (the EAT or CAC, for example) can be measured only *after* clarification of the proposed nature of the new tribunals to administer labour law. Debate about a 'labour court' is an empty formality unless we know the proposed composition of its membership, just as opposition to the idea that rests on traditional theory alone may seem to our grandchildren little more than sclerotic fear.

Of course, whatever regulatory competence the new bodies, or some of them, acquired, it might well be presented in public debate as a renewal of threats to the autonomy of collective bargaining, even if the opposite were intended. Unions and employers, remembering the NIRC, might take fright, saying: 'Better the judges we know ...'. Critics might identify further 'juridification' (even if they remembered the juridifying potential of the common law) or an undue promotion of legal sanction in industrial relations (even if they remembered the prominence of such sanction today). Others would predict that 'the lawyers' of traditional ilk would always end up in control; and if they did not think that, they would be told so by entrenched interests. Implacable opposition could be expected from those to whom labour law is still little more than the 'ordinary law of the land', the common law which they have cossetted out of 'a kind of nostalgia for the law as it stood before ... the Trades Disputes Act of 1906'.[121] Irrespective of such opposition new procedures and new fora could arguably be introduced only step by step; but nothing at all could be achieved without clarity and determination of purpose at every stage.

The argument presented here is not an immediate proposal for labour courts. It is a proposed agenda for re-examination of the structures of labour law process to which scholars and practitioners can now devote the ingenuity and variety of approach they have deployed upon a critique of labour law substance. Whether or not it is of immediate programmatic moment, the topic must lose its taboo. It can then at least test the mettle of more conventional proposals, especially those that advocate other 'new tribunals' or new roles for existing courts. We may well not end up with autonomous 'labour courts'. But if so, we ought to know why.

There, then, is the agony at the point of a new departure. A code based upon a logic diverse from that of common law could not, experience suggests, be administered according to its purposes by the existing common law courts. But the effective exclusion of their jurisdiction appears to be practicable only by bringing out that skeleton in the industrial relations cupboard, a superior labour court. From that unpalatable dilemma comes the need to match proposals on a new law with ideas for new procedures so that expectations raised by the former should not be disappointed. It may well be that a new and constructive relationship between law and industrial relations in Britain depends in tomorrow's labour market and social conditions even more upon reform of labour tribunals than upon substantive law reform.

The call for a modern labour law is indeed a call for its autonomy. The renewed quest for reform may be seen as a natural consequence of four decades of socio-legal scholarship and research without previous parallel in British employment relations. In 1945 our labour law existed but was largely unrecognised as a discipline. Now it is recognised but it is not, in Durand's sense, liberated. Current proposals for radical change mark the commencement of a new phase, beyond the immediate, sometimes mundane, debates into which we have been plunged since Donovan by rapid alternations of the legislative roundabout. With sights now raised at new horizons, at Labour Law 2000, we may recall the spirit of Durand's concluding words:

> It would doubtless be easier to continue along the traditional road, and to go on building labour law on common law principles. But does not the creation of a new law have its own intellectual attraction? It should tempt all those who resolutely stand at the prow of the ship carrying society to new shores, who watch for the thousand traces that will reveal to them the face of land as yet

unknown, and whose hearts miss a beat when in the glittering night
they see a new star rise in the heavens or an old familiar constellation
imperceptibly disappear as, little by little, the new firmament takes
shape beneath which they will henceforth live their lives.[122]

Notes

1. P. Durand, *Le Particularisme du Droit du Travail* 1945 Dr.Soc. 298: *un
système juridique indépendant*.
2. See M. Duverger, '*Essai sur l'autonomie du droit professionel*' 1944 Dr.Soc.
276 and 1945 Dr.Soc. 20; G. Lyon-Caen, '*A la Recherche d'une Définition du
Droit Commercial*' (1949) Rev.Trim. de Droit Commercial 577. The frontiers
between *droit professionel* and *droit commun* were even the subject of decisions
by the Conseil d'Ètat: 19 January 1945, Dr.Soc. 1945, 154.
3. X. Blanc-Jouvan in S. Edlund (ed.), *Labour Law Research in Twelve
Countries* (1986) pp. 145-6.
4. Carol Harlow, 'Public and Private Law: Definition Without Distinction' (1980)
43 MLR 241, 265.
5. Durand, op. cit., n. 1, p. 298. It cannot have escaped such a scholar, that
particularisme referred also to that sect of Calvinists who held that only the elect
would go to Heaven.
6. Gérard Lyon-Caen, 'Du Rôle des Principes Généraux du Droit Civil en Droit
du Travail (Première Approche)' (1974) Rev.Trim. de Droit Civil 229, 231: 'Le
processus conduisant à l'autonomie est en tous points comparable à celui que les
juristes de l'ancienne France ont connu, dans l'élaboration d'un Droit coutumier,
distinct du Droit romain dans ses concepts et ses termes.' (The process
leading to autonomy is in every way comparable to that known to the jurists of
oldern France in their elaboration of a customary law distinct from Roman Law in
its concepts and its terms.)
7. See N. Catala, *L'Enterprise* (1980) pp. iv-ix.
8. Durand, op. cit., n. 1: 'C'est en ce sens que l'on pourrait parler d'une
autonomie du droit du travail. Dans une terminologie rigoureuse l'expression
n'est cependant pas exacte. Aucune branche du droit ne peut se construire
isolément: aucune n'est complètement autonome au sein de l'ordre juridique. Le
terme de particularisme et plus juste. Mais, si celui d'autonomie devait avoir une
force de suggestion plus grande, et prendre par un aspect plus tranchant, une
valeur de manifeste, mieux vaudrait payer de l'imprecision du terme la conquete
de l'idée, et libérer plus tot le droit du travail.' (It is in this sense that one can
speak of an autonomy of labour law. That expression, though, is not exact if one
maintains a rigorous use of terminology. No branch of the law can be developed
in isolation; none is completely autonomous within the bosom of the legal order.
The most exact term would be particularity. But, since autonomy has a stronger
power of suggestion and puts it into a sharper perspective as a demonstration of
values, it is perhaps better to sacrifice precision of the term so that the idea may
triumph, the sooner thereby to liberate labour law.)
9. See, e.g. G.H. Camerlynck, 'L'autonomie du droit du travail (La prescription
abrégée de la créance de salaires)' 1956 D.Chron. 23; G. Couturier, 'Les
techniques civilistes et le droit du travail' 1975 D.Chron. 151 and 221 (civil law
reasoning could continue to bring 'une certaine cohérence technique' (a certain
technical coherence): p. 228).
10. On the difficulty of drawing the line between the two in France: G.
Camerlynck, G. Lyon-Caen, J. Pélissier, *Droit du Travail* (1986, 13th ed.) pp.
45-6; compare J.C. Javillier, *Droit du Travail* (2nd ed. 1982) pp. 16-17. So too,
changes in British social security complement changes in labour law, e.g. the

'deemed' union strike pay deducted from supplementary benefit: Social Security (No. 2) Act 1980, s. 6.

11. Op. cit., n. 6 above.

12. Lyon-Caen, op. cit., n. 6, p. 243 and p. 248.

13. O. Kahn-Freund in A. Flanders and H. Clegg (eds.), *The System of Industrial Relations in Great Britain* (1954), p. 44; and in M. Ginsberg (ed.), *Law and Opinion in England in the Twentieth Century* (1959) p. 244; 'Intergroup Conflicts and their Settlement' (1954) V B.Jo. of Sociology 193, 217. See generally now Wedderburn, *The Worker and the Law* (3rd ed. 1986) Chaps. 1, 4, 10; and Chapters 3, 4, 5 in Wedderburn, R. Lewis and J. Clark (eds.), *Labour Law and Industrial Relations: Building on Kahn-Freund* (1983). Kahn-Freund was not unaware of the need for labour law to transcend common law analysis (see, e.g., *Labour and The Law* (1972) pp. 21-9); but he never quite applied to judge-made common law the razor which (as a judge) he took to the German Labour Court judges: see 'The Social Ideal of the Reich Labour Court' and 'The Changing Function of Labour Law', Chaps. 3 and 4 in R. Lewis and J. Clark (eds.), *Labour Law and Politics in the Weimar Republic* (1981).

14. X. Blanc-Jouvan, op. cit., n. 3, p. 146. Labour law as an 'autonomous doctrinal sphere' need not be pro-union: see H. Hurvitz 'American Labor Law and the Doctrine of Entrepreneurial Property Rights' (1986) 8 Ind.Rels. Law Jo. 307, 308.

15. *Labour and the Law* (1972) pp. 5, 8; now ibid., P. Davies and M. Freedland (eds. 1983, 3rd ed.), pp. 15, 18. For critical evaluations of Kahn-Freund see R. Lewis (1979) 8 ILJ 202, and A. Wilson (1984) 13 ILJ 1.

16. See for example: S. Deakin, 'Labour Law and the Developing Employment Relationship' [1986] Camb.Jo.Econ. 1; H. Collins, 'Market Power, Bureaucratic Power and the Contract of Employment' (1986) 15 ILJ 1; B. Bercusson, 'A New Framework for Labour Law' (1982) 9 Jo. Law Soc 277; F. von Prondzynski, 'Changing Functions of Labour Law' Chap. 7, P. Fosh and C. Littler (eds.), *Industrial Relations and the Law in the 1980s* (1985).

17. O. Kahn-Freund, *Labour and The Law* (1972), p. 8, p. 15; (3rd ed. 1983) p. 24; earlier 'a command under the guise of an agreement' in Intro. to Renner, *The Institutions of Private Law and Their Social Functions* (1949), p. 28.

18. See, e.g. W. Friedmann, *Law and Social Change in Contemporary Britain* (1951), pp. 34-55, and *Law in a Changing Society* (1959), pp. 89-100; compare B. Napier in R. Lewis (ed.), *Labour Law in Britain* (1986), pp. 327-30.

19. R. Rideout, 'The Contract of Employment' (1966) *Current Legal Problems* 111, 127. On the 'cornerstone of the edifice', Kahn-Freund in A. Flanders and H. Clegg (eds.), *The System of Industrial Relations in Great Britain* (1954), p. 45.

20. See e.g. P. Leighton, 'Observing Employment Contracts' (1984) 13 ILJ 86.

21. B. Hepple, 'Restructing Employment Rights' (1986) 15 ILJ 69, based upon his lecture in 1985, 'Do We Need the Contract of Employment?' The developments of 'public' law principles in the last decade, much applauded by some commentators, do aim not to replace the employment contract, but to protect those who have a sufficiently high status, appearing 'to refine the class distinctions of private law': Wedderburn, *The Worker and The Law* (1986), p. 163.

22. A. Fox, *Beyond Contract: Work, Power and Trust Relations* (1974), p. 191; see too, P. Davies and M. Freedland, *Labour Law: Text and Materials* (1984, 2nd ed.), pp. 318-47.

23. Clark and Wedderburn in *Labour Law and Industrial Relations*, n. 13 above, pp. 144-55: 'A Crisis in Fundamental Concepts: The Contract of Employment'.

24. *Wiltshire Police Authority* v. *Wynn* [1980] ICR 649, 656 (police cadets). On the cases, see Wedderburn, *The Worker and the Law* (1986), Chap. 2; B. Napier, Chap. 12 and P. Leighton, Chap. 18 in R. Lewis (ed.), *Labour Law in Britain* (1986).

25. *Daley* v. *Allied Suppliers Ltd.* [1983] IRLR 14; orders of 21 July 1983 have remedied this situation; see Wedderburn *The Worker and the Law*, pp. 507-8; M. Freedland, 'Labour Law and Leaflet Law: The YTS of 1983' (1983) 12 ILJ 220.

26. *Carmichael* v. *Rosehall Engineering Works Ltd* [1983] IRLR 480 (Scot: leading to a fine of £800, ibid., p. 482).

27. Hepple (1986) 15 ILJ p.74.

28. As in Italy, where 'subordinated labour' is the basis under art. 2094 cod.civ ('a subordinated worker is one who agrees to provide his work for a wage, rendering dependent work, intellectual or manual, under the direction of the employer'). Problems, of course, arise even then such as the position of 'parasubordinated' workers to whom certain rights are extended: G. Ghezzi and U. Romagnoli, *Il diritto sindacale* (1982), pp. 59-61; G. Giugni, *Diritto Sindacale* (1984 7th ed.), pp. 222-3; generally G. Santoro Passarelli, *Il lavoro parasubordinato* (1979). On 'telework', see U. Huws (1984) *Employment Gazette* 13; M. Braun, '*Le Télé-travail*', 1981 Dr.Soc. 569.

29. *Western Excavating (ECC) Ltd* v. *Sharp* [1978] ICR 221, 230 (CA). On election. *Shook* v. *Ealing LB* [1986] IRLR 46; see, too, *Harrison* v. *Norwest Host Group* [1985] IRLR 240 (CA); P. Kerr (1984) 47 MLR 30; on 'dismissal' see s. 55 EPCA 1978.

30. H. Carty (1986) 49 MLR 240, 243 on *Bliss* v. *SE Thames* v. *RHA* [1985] IRLR 308. On the 'public law' approach, perhaps overrated in its effect, see Wedderburn, *The Worker and the Law*, pp. 153-71.

31. *Birch* v. *University of Liverpool* [1985] IRLR 165 (CA); *Igbo* v. *Johnson Matthey Chemicals Ltd.* [1986] IRLR 215, 218. Compare now s.10 Social Security Act 1986.

32. See *Lewis* v. *Surrey CC* [1986] IRLR 11, rv'sd. [1986] IRLR 455 (CA); and *Brown* v. *Knowsley BC* [1986] IRLR 102.

33. *Pickstone* v. *Freemans plc* [1986] IRLR 335.

34. *Marley* v. *Forward Trust Group* [1986] IRLR 43, 45; reversed [1986] IRLR 369 (CA). Compare *Robertson* v. *British Gas Corpn.* [1983] ICR 351; and on the problems posed by *Cadoux* v. *Central Regional Council* [1986] IRLR 131 (Ct. Sess.), Wedderburn, *The Worker and the Law*, pp. 333-6.

35. See, e.g. B. Hepple (1986) 15 ILJ p. 83; compare K. Ewing (1986) 15 ILJ 143, 158-9, considering adaptation of the EAT in some cases with 'two trade union nominees'.

36. Sir John Donaldson MR *Hennessy* v. *Craigmyle* [1986] IRLR 300, 304 (CA): 'Its principles may not change but its application conforms to changing circumstances.'

37. 'The Judge as Lawmaker' (1972) 12 Jo. SPTL 22.

38. J.A.G. Griffith, *The Politics of The Judiciary* (3rd ed. 1985), p. 234.

39. 'In fact, to allow this sort of action to prevail would be an encouragement to the servant to omit that diligence and caution which he is in duty bound to exercise on behalf of his master, to protect him against the misconduct or negligence of others who serve him': Lord Abinger CB *Priestley* v. *Fowler* (1837) 3 M. & W. 1. The doctrine was abolished by the Law Reform (Personal Injuries) Act 1948, though before that many judges saw it as 'a doctrine which lawyers who are gentlemen have long disliked'; *per* MacKinnon LJ, *Speed* v. *Thomas Swift* [1943] KB 557, 569. In these 100 years judges did of course develop the employer's 'personal' duty to provide safe working conditions.

40. See *Wilson* v. *Merry and Cunninghame* (1868) LR 1 Sc. & Dir. 326, where managing directors of railway and factory companies were seen as fellow servants of the injured workers; see the accounts by R. Howells (1963) 26 MLR 367 and P. Bartrip and S. Burman, *The Wounded Soldiers of Industry* (1983), pp. 103-25.

41. See *Bartonshill Coal Co.* v. *Reid* (1858) 4 Jur.N.s. 767 (HL), 772, where Lord Cranworth relied upon American decisions adopting common employment.

42 *Lister* v. *Romford Ice etc. Company* [1957] AC 555, p. 579, Viscount Simmonds.

43. *Sec. of State for Employment* v. *ASLEF* (No. 2) [1972] ICR 19; *per* Buckley LJ p. 62.

44. See B. Napier, 'Working to Rule' (1982) 1 ILJ 125.

45. *Hollister* v. *National Farmers' Union* [1979] IRLR 238 (CA); *Woods* v. *WM Car Services* [1982] ICR 693 (CA); s. 57 (1) (b) EPCA 1978.
46. See S. Anderman in R. Lewis (ed.), *Labour Law in Britain* (1986), p. 428.
47. See Wedderburn, *The Worker and the Law*, p. 242.
48. H. Collins (1985) 14 ILJ 61, 62, on Reg. 8, Transfer of Undertakings (Protection of Employment) Regulations 1981. Contrast the distaste for immunities, below note 75.
49. *Cresswell* v. *Board of Inland Revenue* [1984] ICR 508; *Sim* v. *Rotherham MBC*, [1986] IRLR 391 (where Scott J met the argument that to allow employers to set off deductions against alleged default by workers, even though a grievance procedure was available to test it, by saying this had 'sociological rather than legal weight': p.405). But defiance of the *Cresswell* judgment led to a useful technology agreement: Wedderburn, *The Worker and the Law*, p. 185. The employer can of course still break the contract by other ill-advised actions: *Rigby* v. *Ferodo Ltd*, *Times*, 15 October 1986. [The HL reviewed this area on appeal from *Miles* v. *Wakefield MDC* [1985] ICR 363 (CA): [1987] AC 539.]
50. See P. Davies and M. Freedland, *Labour Law: Text and Materials* (2nd ed., 1984) pp. 454-6.
51. *Notcutt* v. *Universal Equipment Co. Ltd* [1986] IRLR 218, 221. See too, *Shepherd & Co. Ltd* v. *Jerrom* [1986] IRLR 358, where an impeccable survey of three centuries of precedents led to application of the doctrine, such that it might have *more*, not less, severe effects on employment than on commercial contracts: *per* Mustill LJ, p. 366.
52. See, e.g. Hepple op. cit. (1986) 15 ILJ 69, 74, 83.
53. Article 1184: also *résiliation judiciaire*, see J.-C. Javillier, *Manuel de Droit du Travail* (1986), p. 121; G. Camerlynck, G. Lyon-Caen and J. Pélissier, *Droit du Travail* (13th ed. 1986) pp. 298-9, 708-9; J.M. Verdier, *Droit du Travail* (7th ed. 1983), pp. 117-8. The courts had also used Art. 1142, Code civil to obstruct reinstatement: see Camerlynck, Lyon-Caen and Pélissier, op. cit., pp. 717-9.
54. *Code du Travail* (1985) L. 412-8; L. 425-1; L. 436-1 *et seq*; R. 436-1 *et seq*; see Javillier, op. cit., pp. 242-3 for a summary, and on the 'intense doctrinal battle'; p. 240. This special protection dates from the laws of 1945-6 and 1968; now 28 October 1982 (decree 83-470, 8 June 1983).
55. Camerlynck, Lyon-Caen and Pélissier, *Droit du Travail*, p. 708; on the jurisprudence before 1974, see Camerlynck and Lyon-Caen, *Droit du Travail* (10th ed. 1980), pp. 536-8; Javillier, *Droit du Travail* (2nd ed. 1982), pp. 499-500. For a more *civiliste* and detailed view, see N. Catala, *L'Enterprise* (1980) pp. 649-77 (though noting the 'brilliant' defence of the 1974 judgments by G. Lyon-Caen, op. cit. n. 6 above, this critique of the 1974 judgements and their 'immunity' for representatives bears a remarkable resemblance to English common-law reasoning).
56. The *arrêts 'Perrier'* Dr.Soc. 1974, 454, 593; JCP 74, II 17801; H. Sinay D. 1974, 237; two judgments of 21 June 1974.
57. Camerlynck, Lyon-Caen and Pélissier, *Droit du Travail*, p. 709.
58. e.g. Cour d'appel, Besançon, 10 March 1976, JCP 1977 II. 18520, note R. Jambu Merlin; Cass.As. plénière, 28 January 1983; D. 1983, p. 269.
59. Camerlynck and Lyon-Caen, *Droit du Travail* (10th ed. 1980), p. 538.
60. For example, in safety at work, rights of workers' representatives, and sex equality: see Antoine Lyon-Caen, 'Sur les fonctions du droit pénal dans les relations de travail' 1984 Dr.Soc. 438 (in using remedies to prevent future discrimination or accidents '*le juge pénal est en France ... un juge du travail moderne*' (in France the Criminal Law judge is a modern Labour Law judge): p. 445).
61. [1923] CLJ 1, 8. On judges' background, Griffith, *The Politics of the Judiciary*, pp. 25-31. It is an institutional, not a personal or motivational, problem; this makes it unfortunate to label the problem as one of 'judicial bias': L. Dickens and D. Cockburn in Lewis (ed.), *Labour Law in Britain*, pp. 553-4. On this issue, see

Griffith, op. cit., n. 59, pp. 184-92, 233-5; Wedderburn, *The Worker and The Law*, pp. 18-26, 32-3; below, note 21.

62. Law 533, 11 August 1973; but for criticisms of its non-application, see G. Ghezzi and U. Romagnoli, *Il diritto sindacale* (1982), pp. 303-5; see too 'Intervista su la giustizia del lavoro a dieci anni dalla riforma' (1984) 21 Gior.Dir. del Lav. e di Rel.Ind. 115.

63. See the tentative suggestions in Wedderburn, *The Worker and the Law*, p. 854.

64. Ibid., p. 94; so too, W. Brown and B. Hepple in P. Fosh and C. Littler (eds.), *Industrial Relations and the Law in the 1980s* (1985) p. xi, and Wedderburn, pp. 51-2.

65. R. Lewis, *Labour Law in Britain*, p. 15.

66. See on juridification J. Clark (1985) 14 ILJ 69; R. Lewis, op. cit., n. 64, pp. 34-6; Wedderburn, *The Worker and the Law*, pp. 856-61, with sources cited; and S. Simitis, 'The Juridification of Labor Relations', in (1986) 7 Comp.Lab. Law 93.

67. Notably the laws of 4 August (workers' rights in the enterprise), 28 October (workers' representatives), 13 November (collective bargaining and conflict), 23 December (safety) 1982; and 13 July 1983 (sex equality); J.-C. Javillier, *Les Réformes du Droit du Travail depuis le 10 Mai 1981* (1984); and *Droit Social, Numéro Spécial*, January 1983, *Les Réformes: Un nouveau droit du travail?* (intro. J. Auroux).

68. B. Boubli, 'A propos de la flexibilité de l'emploi; vers la fin du droit du travail?' 1985 Dr.Soc. 239, 240: 'Après tout il ne s'agirait que d'instituer le droit des gens dans l'enterprise, le droit civil tout simplement'. (After all, what is needed is only the institution of the General Law in the workplace, quite simply the Common (civil) Law.) B. Teyssié and others, 'Faut-il brûler le Code du Travail?' 1986 Dr.Soc. 559. For a fiercely contrary view, A. Roudil, 'Flexibilité de l'emploi et droit du travail: la beauté du diable' 1985 Dr. Soc. 84.

69. See J. Déprez, 'L'existence de revendications professionelles préalables, condition de licéité de la grève', 1986 Dr.Soc. 610, on Cour Cass. 16 October 1985, Moreau c. Ets. Villiers; 6 November 1985, Zekronfa c. Soc. Colas; 27 February 1986, Martin c. Soc. Lorgnet et Martin (right to strike conditional upon refusal by employer of industrial demand; until then workers must wait; a doctrine thought in the 1970s to be no longer applicable). The *Cour de Cassation* has now held that demands must be 'reasonable' to legitimise a strike (Cour Cass. 4 July 1986); a reference for which I am grateful to Prof. A. Lyon-Caen. [But now see below, pp. 286 and 315.]

70. G. Lyon-Caen, 'La Bataille Truquée de la Flexibilité' 1985 Dr.Soc. 801. For a cautious survey, see M. Vranken, 'Deregulating the Employment Relationship: Current Trends in Europe' (1986) 7 Comp. Lab. Law 143; and the perceptive analysis by Dominique Eustache, 'Individualisation des salaires et flexibilité' 1986, No. 29, *Travail et Emploi*, 17-42.

71. As suggested by B. Hepple, op. cit., (1986) 15 ILJ pp. 77-8. On this practice in France: *Code du Travail* art. L. 135-2; the terms have automatic effect, *not* by incorporation in employment contracts: Javallier, *Manuel de Droit du Travail*, p. 291. Note the different position in the United States, where the individual contract may not normally improve on the collective terms: W. Gould, *A Primer on American Labor Law* (1982), p. 68. Compare Napier, op. cit., n. 24, p. 344.

72. The right to bargain may be the most important, but it cannot be dealt with here: see Wedderburn, *The Worker and the Law*, pp. 278-89; Davies and Freedland, *Labour Law: Text and Materials*, pp. 127-43, 197-205; and L. Dickens and G. Bain, Chap. 3 in Lewis (ed.), *Labour Law in Britain*.

73. See CBI *Trade Unions in a Changing World: The Challenge for Management* (1980), p. 22.

74. *Stratford and Sons Ltd* v. *Lindley* [1965] AC 269, 330; but 'substance' is not a neutral category; the conflict is often about what the true 'substance' is. Judges sometimes think they should have power to say who is 'right' in a dispute, like Sir

John Donaldson LJ (1975) 91 LQR 181, 192, a particularly dangerous approach: *The Worker and the Law*, pp. 16-47.

75. Lord Diplock, *Express Newspapers Ltd* v. *McShane* [1980] AC 672, 687; see Lord Salmon p. 690; Simpson (1980) 43 MLR 327; Wedderburn (1980) 9 ILJ 65.

76. See generally Wedderburn, 'The New Politics of Labour Law', 1983, now in W. McCarthy (ed.), *Trade Unions* (1985), pp. 497-532; and *The Worker and the Law*, pp. 846-56: 'no system of labour law is either all "immunities" or all "rights" ' (p. 848) [see above Chapter 4].

77. *Report of Royal Commissions (etc.)* (1968, Cmnd 3623) para. 943; proposals for a positive right to strike were rejected: paras. 935-40. See too for proposals of this kind: C. Jenkins and J. Mortimer, *The Kind of Laws the Unions Ought to Want* (1968); P. O'Higgins, Chap. 3 in J. Carby-Hall (ed.), *Studies in Labour Law* (1976).

78. K. Ewing, 'The Right to Strike' (1986) 15 ILJ 143, 160, the best of the proposals so far advanced, who adds: 'the procedural and institutional reforms would help to ensure that this was not out-flanked by the judicial power of interpretation.' The right to strike is seen as operating at individual and collective level, as a 'right' not 'immunity', with some reform of injunction procedures. But this leads logically to his consideration of new judicial institutions: see below n. 116.

79. P. Elias and K. Ewing, 'Economic Torts and Labour Law' [1982] CLJ 321, 357-8, where there was rather greater concentration on changing the form of the statutory rights. On conspiracy, see Criminal Law Act 1977 ss. 1-5; and on other problems arising, Wedderburn, op. cit. n. 76 above.

80. See e.g. *Collymore* v. *Att.-Gen.* [1970] AC 538 (PC; Lord Donovan). So far this has been the normal fate of 'freedom of association' in the new Canadian Charter of Rights and Freedoms: see *Re Retail Wholesalers (etc.) Union* (1985) 12 DLR (4th 10, 18-24; *Dolphin Delivery* v. *Retail Wholesale (etc.) Union* (1984) 10 DLR (4th) 198; *Re Public Service (etc.) Act* (1985) 16 DLR (4th) 359 – though a much wider interpretation was evinced in *Re Retail Wholesale (etc.) Union and Government of Saskatchewan* (1985) 19 DLR (4th) 609 (where a majority of the Saskatchewan CA preferred non-legal sources, such as Thomas Aquinas, to cases like *Collymore*: see pp. 614-27, 639-41). For more liberal treatment of picketing tenants, see *Halifax Antiques Ltd* v. *Hildebrand* (1985) 22 DLR (4th) 120. The contrast of approach in Italy to *libertà sindacale*, or in France to *liberté syndicale*, is marked. The Supreme Court of Canada is expected to pronounce on the ambit of 'freedom of association' in appeals from some of the cases cited above.

81. The 'freedom of association' accorded by the European Convention on Human Rights, Art. 11, has received an interpretation predominantly protective of the 'negative right' to dissociate rather than of workers' rights to take action: see *Young, James and Webster* v. *UK* [1981] IRLR 408; Wedderburn, *The Worker and the Law*, pp. 376-8. No other interpretations are proposed by those who wish to make it law in Britain: see the Human Rights and Fundamental Freedom Bill discussed in *Parl.Deb*. HL 10 December 1985, Vol. 469, col. 156; 20 March 1986, Vol. 472, col. 1087; 9 April 1986, Vol. 473, col. 267.

82. Ewing, op. cit. (1986) 15 ILJ pp. 149, 155.

83. *Rookes* v. *Barnard* [1964] AC 1129, 1177; so too Lord Pearce p. 1236 (the section was 'pointless'); Lord Evershed p. 1192 ('nugatory'); Lord Devlin pp. 1215-6 (who did not decide about a tort of 'interference'; but the enactment would anyway be 'otiose but harmless').

84. *Hadmor Productions Ltd* v. *Hamilton* [1983] 1 AC 194, 229; and in *Merkur Island Shipping* v. *Laughton* [1983] 2 AC 570, 609-10. On his misunderstanding of that history, see Clerk and Lindsell *Torts* (15th ed., 4th Supp. (1986) para. 15-28. See too, *Plessey Co plc* v. *Wilson* [1982] IRLR 198 (Ct. Sess.); Wedderburn, *The Worker and the Law*, pp. 611-3.

85. See *Universe Tankships Inc. of Monrovia* v. *ITWF* [1983] 1 AC 366 (HL); on the development see Wedderburn (1982) 45 MLR 556: 'The very language of

"coercion" echoes the class judgments of earlier times' (p. 564). Canadian courts refused to import the doctrine into labour relations: *Mandalaysay* v. *The Oriental Victory* [1978] 1 FC 440, 446-7; Clerk and Lindsell, *Torts* (1982 15th ed.) Chap. 15; and generally Wedderburn *The Worker and the Law*, pp. 650-4. On the 'alternative' for a worker, see Donaldson MR, *Hennessy* v. *Craigmyle* [1986] IRLR 300, 304 (CA).

86. A law 'to restrain the exercise of capital and property ... must be construed stringently': *Ryder* v. *Mills* (1850) Parl. Pap. 67 Sess. 3, x/ii p. 479; *Torquay Hotels Ltd* v. *Cousins* [1969] Ch. 106, 138 (CA). Compare the treatment of a union's right to bargain, needing restrictive interpretation because it was 'compulsory acquisition of an individual's right to regulate his working life'; *Powley* v. *ACAS* [1978] ICR 123, 135 *per* Browne-Wilkinson J.

87. See P. Davies and S. Anderman, 'Injunction Procedure in Labour Disputes' (1973) 2 ILJ 213; Wedderburn, *The Worker and the Law*, Chaps. 8 and 9, and pp. 852-5; see too L. Dickens and D. Cockburn, Chap. 19 in Lewis (ed.), *Labour Law in Britain*.

88. See on the fate of s. 17 (2) of TULRA 1974; B. Simpsom (1984) 47 MLR 577, 578-9; Wedderburn, op. cit., pp. 692-6. It was, Lord Diplock found, only 'a reminder addressed by Parliament to English judges' to continue doing what they had done: *NWL* v. *Woods* [1979] ICR 867, 879-880. As Ewing says: 'the capacity of the judges to produce perverse or unanticipated results should never be underestimated' (1986) 15 ILJ p. 156; so too, he rightly alluded to the very limited impact of s. 17 (1) of TULRA, ibid., p. 154. In *Barretts & Baird Ltd* v. *IPCS*, *Financial Times*, 27 October 1986, the interlocutory injunction was issued *ex parte* without notice to the defendants and before a writ was issued, on a Sunday afternoon at the judge's home. It was discharged three weeks later after argument *inter partes* as there was no arguable case: [1987] IRLR 3.

89. See Wedderburn, op. cit., pp. 730-48. See too now, the sting in the tail, concerning third parties in *UK Nirex Ltd* v. *Barton*, *Times*, 14 October 1986.

90. Lord Diplock, *Dimbleby & Sons Ltd* v. *NUJ* [1984] 1 WLR 427, 435 (HL). See on this problem, B. Bercusson, Chap. 5, Lewis (ed.), *Labour Law in Britain*; Wedderburn, op. cit., pp. 96-105.

91. *Simpson* v. *Norwest Holst (Southern) Ltd* [1980] 2 All E.R. 471 (CA).

92. See s. 153 (4) of EPCA 1978; s. 30 (1) of TULRA 1974; now *South West Launderettes Ltd* v. *Laidler* [1986] IRLR 305 (CA: husband and wife each owning 50 per cent of shares; no 'control' of company to render it associated with husband's company); Hepple (1980) 15 ILJ p. 75.

93. See now C. Docksey, 'Information and Consultation of Employees; the UK and the Vredeling Directive' [1986] 49 MLR 281.

94. Op. cit., n. 6 above, p. 240: 'A la notion d'employeur droit être substituée celle de centre de décision ou de pouvoir.' (We must substitute for the notion of the 'employer' that of the centre of decision-making or of power.) On establishment of a 'group council', parallel to the *comité d'enterprise*, in corporate groups in the 1982 reforms: (1982) 107 EIRR 22.

95. G. Lyon-Caen, 'La Concentration du Capital et le Droit du Travail', 1983 Dr.Soc. 287, 301.

96. *Salomon* v. *Salomon & Co* [1897] AC 22 (HL); *Cork Report on Insolvency Law and Practice* (Cmnd 8558, 1982) para. 1952. The moves in 'public' law to reveal the true nature of the 'employer' (above n. 21) must be accounted a modest step forward which reinforces the need for equivalent reform in the rest of the law.

97. See the classic studies by B. Simpson, 'Judicial Control of ACAS' (1979) 8 ILJ 69; P. Davies, 'The Central Arbitration Committee and Equal Pay' (1980) *Current Legal Problems* 165; and see R. Townshend-Smith (1981) 1 Legal Studies 205, 208. On the CRE, J. Griffith, *The Politics of the Judiciary* (3rd ed. 1985) pp. 96-104, 213-5.

98. On 'public' law status: *R.* v. *East Berks. HA, ex parte Walsh* [1984] IRLR 278

(CA); *Council of Civil Service Unions* v. *Minister of Civil Service* [1985] ICR 14 (HL); Wedderburn, *The Worker and the Law*, pp. 153-71, 276-8.

99. Trade Union Act 1913, s. 3 (2). The High Court exercised a residual control if the Act was contravened: *Birsh* v. *NUR* [1950] Ch. 602. Ewing notes a contemporary parallel in the Interception of Communications Act 1985, s. 7 (8), where the Tribunal's decisions, including those on jurisdiction, are not subject to appeal or to question in any court: (1986) 15 ILJ p. 157.

100. Trade Union (Amalgamations, etc.) Act 1964, s. 4 (8), when the High Court decision was 'final'. These jurisdictions now vest, or course, in the Certification Officer.

101. EPA 1975, Sched. 16, IV, paras. 2 (3), 10 (3); and EPCA 1978, s. 136.

102. EPA 1975, s. 8 (12) (proceedings must be stayed until the CO makes a decision). See too Social Security Pensions Act 1975, s. 55 (4) (Occupational Pensions Board has exclusive jurisdiction).

103. In France, see *Code du Travail* Art. 411.11; union may enforce obligations in agreement owed to members and interpose in any litigation *pour la défense de l'interêt collectif* (for the defence of the collective interest): Camerlynck, Lyon-Caen and Pélissier, *Droit du Travail* (13th ed. 1986), pp. 624-5. In Sweden the union can sue on behalf of a member since the act on Labour Dispute Litigation, 1974. In Italy the union has a general ability to place information and argument before the court at the request of a party or the judge in individual cases (law of 11 August 1973, no. 533, arts. 421, 425: Ghezzi and Romagnoli, *Il diritto sindacale*, pp. 302-3); but it also appears in cases on the broad range of 'anti-union' activity as the protector of individual and collective interests: art. 28 Workers' Statute, 20 May 1970, no. 300; see M. Grandi and G. Pera, *Commentario breve allo Statuto dei lavoratori* (1985), pp. 157-73.

104. L. Dickens, M. Jones, B. Weekes and M. Hart, *Dismissed* (1985), p. 220.

105. Ministry of Labour, *Evidence to Donovan Commission* (1965), p. 92. The tribunals were established as a civil service policy in 1964 and adopted by the Donovan Report: Clark and Wedderburn in *Labour Law and Industrial Relations*, above n. 13, pp. 173-84.

106. On the *Conseils* see Camerlynck, Lyon-Caen and Pélissier, *Droit du Travail*, pp. 581-95; B. Napier (1979) 42 MLR 270.

107. M. David, 'L'évolution historique des Conseils de prud'hommes en France' 1974 Dr.Soc. No. 2 (numéro special) 3, 17: 'pour atteindre le plénitude de leur essence seulement lors de l'instauration de celui ci en système dominant et à la faveur de la pénétration des conceptions démocratiques dans la domaine des relations socio-professionnelles' (attaining their full character only by their establishment outside the dominant system and by support for the penetration of democratic conceptions into the domain of industrial relations).

108. See Dickens *et. al.*, op. cit. n. 104, Chap. 9. Compare Hepple (1986) 15 ILJ pp. 82-3; and the careful proposals by R. Rideout, 'Unfair Dismissal – Tribunal or Arbitration' (1986) 15 ILJ 84 (see especially pp. 92-4 on legal chairmen) and 'Arbitration and Public Interest: Regulated Arbitration' Chap. in Wedderburn and Murphy (eds.), *Labour Law and The Community* (1982). Some problems may benefit from use of administrative agency enforcement in place of individual complaint (see L. Dickens, 'Equal Opportunity – A More Encouraging Approach' (1986) *Employee Relations* 277) so long as it escapes hostile review in the courts.

109. See further Wedderburn, *The Worker and the Law*, pp. 261-8. But in cases on sex equality (or race discrimination) attempts are made to ensure a woman member (or a member experienced in race relations – *not* a black member) who is presumably more 'representative' in role. But Waite J, an ex-President of EAT, would restrict race and sex discrimination cases to a 'selected core' of legal chairmen and lay judges 'with particular training and experience' because those cases are 'sensitive and ... complicated', (1986) 15 ILJ 32, 41. *Quaere* whether the 'experience' would require their *being* a woman or black?

136   *Employment Rights in Britain and Europe*

110. Or, eventually peaceably: see Folke Schmidt, *The Law of Labour Relations in Sweden* (1962), pp. 14-54; *Law and Industrial Relations in Sweden* (1977), pp. 37-44: the court was accepted in the 1930s, after initial protests, by the unions.

111. The *Pretore* as 'labour judge' has jurisdiction in all cases concerning 'private subordinate relationships' (Law of 1973, no. 533, art. 409) which the Constitutional Court interprets as 'the socio-economic subordination of one of the parties': Cort. Cost. 19 February 1976, no. 29; Foro. It. 1976 I c. 508. A. Proto Pisani 'Lavoro, controversie individuali (in mat. di)'; *Appendice del Novissimo Dig. It.* (1983), p. 48; and n. 28 above.

112. K. Wedderburn and P. Davies, *Employing Grievances and Disputes Procedures in Britain* (1969), Chaps. 8, 9; Sir John Wood, 'The CAC; A Consideration of its Role and Approach' (1979) Employment Gazette 9; GAC *Annual Reports* 1981 (Chap. 1) and 1984.

113. On the 1917 munitions tribunals see, G. Rubin (1977) 6 ILJ 149, and (1985) 14 ILJ 33; a certain independence from the ordinary courts was found in these war-time bodies.

114. Hepple, op. cit. (1986) 15 ILJ p. 83.

115. See H. Collins, op. cit. (1986) 15 ILJ 1, 8-14.

116. See now similar proposals by K. Ewing, 'The Right to Strike' (1986) 15 ILJ p. 157, and the different proposals at p. 158; Hepple's proposal of a 'self-contained system of expert tribunals' to deal with unfair dismissal, with appeals to the EAT but not to the Court of Appeal (1986) 15 ILJ p. 83; Lord McCarthy, 'Freedom, Democracy and The Role of Trade Unions', (Jim Conway Lecture) 12 November 1986 ('a balanced framework of law must seek, as far as possible, to escape from the age-old logic of the common law. ... If we go down that road we have to face the fact that at the apex of such a structure there would have to be some kind of labour court ... to ensure that the will of Parliament prevails.'). The judges have joined in: see Waite J (1986) 15 ILJ pp. 33, 41, and Sir John Donaldson, *Martin* v. *MBS Fastenings* [1983] IRLR 198, 199; favouring (a minority of) lay members in the Court of Appeal, the former vigorously rejecting replacement of the tribunals by arbitration (ibid., p. 39); neither propose any change in the lay judges' role. One finds in most such proposals, a glitter of autonomy that is not gold.

117. Unhappily including Sir Pat Lowry, Chairman of ACAS, tying the court in to compulsory ballots, apparently with High Court judges: *Financial Times*, 25 October 1986. The 'son of NIRC' concept is as objectionable now as it was in 1975; see note 74 above, and B. Simpson (1986) 49 MLR 796, 813-5. Such proposals encourage the view that it is 'almost certainly, wishful thinking' to believe that a 'specialist labour court' would do other than 'legitimise and facilitate greater legal controls and restrictions over collective bargaining', A. Wilson, Chap. 2 in K. Coates (ed.), *Freedom and Fairness* (1986) pp. 41-2 (though he acknowledges that 'the ordinary courts' have developed common law and interpreted statutory law 'in a manner hostile to unions').

118. If such a step were ever considered by a government, and accepted by its Lord Chancellor, there is no reason to assume that individual lawyers (or even individual members of the present judiciary) would have no contribution to make, especially those with experience of non-common law jurisdictions. So too, the issue would arise whether part of an industrial judiciary should be elected.

119. See the persuasive case made by Carol Harlow in 'Refurbishing the Judicial Service', Chapter 5 in C. Harlow (ed.), *Public Law and Politics* (1986). See too, J.A.G. Griffith, op. cit., note 61 above; and 'Judges on Trial', *Labour Research*, January 1987 (of all the 465 judges, seventeen are women and one is black).

120. See notes 60, 61 above.

121. H. Laski, *Trade Unions in the New Society* (1950), p. 126.

122. P. Durand 1945 Dr.Soc. p. 303: 'Il serait sans doute plus facile de persévérer dans la voie de la tradition, et de continuer à construire le droit du travail sur les principes du droit commun. Mais cette création d'un droit ne prèsente-t-elle pas

intellectuellement un tout autre attrait? Elle mérite de tenter tous ceux qui, se plaçant délibérément à l'avant du navire, sur lequel une société est portée sur de nouveaux rivages, épient les mille signes qui leur révèleront le visage de cette terre encore inconnue et dont le coeur frémit quand, par les nuits étincelantes, ils voient monter au ciel une étoile nouvelle ou disparaitre insensiblement une constellation jusqu'alors familière, et se former, peu à peu, le firmament nouveau sous lequel ils vivront désormais. '

6

Freedom of Association or Right to Organise? The Common Law and International Sources

British law has never enshrined a positive 'freedom of association' giving workers a right to organise in trade unions. Yet collective bargaining in a democracy

> requires that workers have the liberty to organise in autonomous and effective trade unions and that employers should be willing and able to bargain with them.[1]

The recent, understandable tendency in Britain to suggest that the 'immunities' of labour law should be replaced by 'positive rights' has led some observers to welcome also the prospect of our adopting, as binding, domestic law, the European Convention of Human Rights, 1950. That convention provides that everyone 'has the right to freedom of assembly and freedom of association with others, including the right to form and to join trade unions for the protection of his interests' (Art. 11 (1)). Such a step may be incautious, and even dangerous, without further examination of the meaning put upon this provision. There is, in particular, need of an industrial relations input into the debate.

The European Convention on Human Rights and Fundamental Freedoms

The Context
The United Kingdom has ratified the European Convention on Human Rights and Fundamental Freedoms (ECHR), drawn up by the Council of Europe, and has agreed to the procedure whereby individuals can take complaints to the Commission and (if found

---

First published in (1987) 18 Industrial Relations Journal 244.

admissible by it) to the Court of Human Rights at Strasbourg. British governments and courts have accepted that our law should be construed, as far as possible, in conformity with the convention, as interpreted by that court.[2] But, in the absence of legislation at Westminster, it is not immediately binding law here (as distinct from European Community law, which derives from the EEC treaties and the binding judgments of the different European Court of Justice at Luxembourg, along with the European Commission in Brussels).

From 1968 onwards a campaign cutting across party lines has been mounted to have the ECHR adopted by parliament as domestic law, as a Bill of Rights immediately binding in the UK. In the most recent attempt such a Bill passed all its stages in the House of Lords (a famous Select Committee Report had by six to five reported favourably in 1978, just after the Northern Ireland Advisory Commission on Human Rights had done the same); and in 1987 it came within a handful of votes of passing a critical stage in the House of Commons.[3] Such an Act would make the principles of the ECHR overriding unless parliament expressly ousted them (politically no easy task). That step would amount to 'a new constitutional settlement', one which in the 1970s was often linked to other constitutional proposals, such as the new federal structure that could emerge from Scottish devolution.[4] The new rights or freedoms would have 'priority in social policy, legislative and administrative but [would be] still subject to some necessary restrictions'.[5] One of them would be the right to 'freedom of association' in Art. 11.

The general debate about the ECHR has largely turned upon the desirability of giving to judges new powers and control of policy inherent in the interpretation of the vague articles contained in it. Left and right – and even some judges – have combined to oppose this.[6] Other protagonists, like Lord Hailsham after his conversion, have accepted the 'political' role of judges and regarded the new package as a desirable way of stopping radical legislation.[7] It is important in what follows to remember that British judges have, on the whole, 'supported the conventional, established and settled interests' on most recent social, economic and political issues, in accordance with common law tradition.[8]

It is to be expected that in the present parliament new attempts will be made, from various sides of politics, to have the ECHR adopted as a British Bill of Rights. An initiative by the EEC European Commission in 1979 to have the ECHR adopted as European Community law (and so binding on Britain automatically) has petered out. And the EEC European Court of Justice (Luxembourg) has done no more than refer to such human rights provisions, in interpreting Community law under the treaties.[9]

In future debates, as in the past, protagonists will make much of those articles of the ECHR – the great majority – which protect the individual. They are indeed valuable and formidable, and have often caught out the UK government.[10] For example, there is the freedom from 'inhuman or degrading treatment or punishment' (art. 3) and from servitude and forced labour (Art. 4); the right to liberty and personal security, subject to conviction according to law and to certain standards (Art. 5, said to be 'worth a hundred Habeas Corpus Acts');[11] and to fair and public hearing by independent courts in proceedings (Art. 6). The 1952 protocol establishes the right of every person, including companies, to 'peaceful enjoyment of his possessions' (Art. 1; this allowed *Lithgows Ltd* to establish a right to compensation after nationalisation in 1977, though the court judged the amount in that case to be not unreasonable); and a 'right to education' without state discrimination against parents by reason of 'religious or philosophical convictions' (which some lawyers hold would invalidate legislation to end private education).[12]

The Restrictions

This flavour of liberal principle combined with uncertainty of meaning is compounded in Articles 8 to 11, ECHR. They establish the rights to respect for 'private and family life'; to 'freedom of thought, conscience and religion'; to 'freedom of expression' (the basis of the *Sunday Times* decision which rejected a Law Lords' judgment banning newspaper comment on pending litigation as 'contempt of court'); and to freedom of association (including forming and joining trade unions). But each article here is subject to a restriction couched in similar words. For example, Art. 11 (2) forbids restrictions on the rights in that article other than those 'prescribed by law' and 'necessary in a democratic society' in the interests of national security or for prevention of disorder or crime, protection of health or morals or 'for the protection of the rights or freedoms of others'.

The range of judicial control is at once apparent. The court (or the Commission in preliminary hearings) decides what is 'necessary in a democratic society', not parliament. On the *GCHQ* complaint, for example, the Strasbourg Commission, like the House of Lords in Britain, accepted that the prohibition of trade unions was defensible on grounds of 'national security', even if it was a breach (as it was) of the ILO Convention No. 87, 1948, on freedom of association. (The Commission was able to make use also of a further provision in Art. 11 (2), allowing the state to curtail the freedom of 'members of the administration of the state'.[13]) But in the famous 'Railwaymen's case', the court embarked upon an evaluation of the closed shop provisions in British Rail and the law permitting them in 1976. These, it held, infringed *both* Art. 11 (1), because they forced existing employees to join unions, *and* Art. 11 (2), because they failed to 'achieve a proper balance' between the union members and non-unionists involved, leading to detriment not 'proportionate to the aims being pursued'.[14] The policy character of this decision is manifest. Moreoever, the Labour government had pleaded that the law was 'necessary' in the interests of the majority of workers; but the Conservative administration withdrew that defence in 1980, half way through the case. So the court reached its conclusion without hearing argument upon it.

Freedom of Association and the International Conventions

The ECHR is part of a pattern of international conventions. For example, the words of Art. 11 (1) and (2) are parallel to those in Art. 22 (1) and (2) of the United Nations International Covenant on Civil and Political Rights, 1966. Both derive in part from the UN Universal Declaration of Human Rights, 1948, in which Art. 20 (1) established everyone's right to 'freedom of association' (but added also, (2): 'No one may be compelled to belong to an association'); and Art. 23 (4) declared everyone's 'right to form and join trade unions for the protection of his interests' (and also: (1) 'the right to work, to free choice of employment, to just and favourable conditions of work and to protection against unemployment'). Later conventions followed suit, such as the American Convention on Human Rights 1969 (Art. 16, right to associate freely) and the African Charter on Human Rights and People's Rights, 1981 (Art. 10). Meanwhile, the ILO, a specialist UN agency, had put more detailed flesh on the bones of *Freedom of Association and the Right to Organise* in Convention 87, 1948, and the *Right to Organise and Right to Bargain Collectively* in Convention 98, 1949. These set out standards of freedom and autonomy for workers' and employers' organisations and the impermissibility of state interference.

The ILO conventions, however, were significantly different from most of the rest. Whereas the provisions in such conventions as the ECHR were couched largely in terms of *individual* rights, the ILO conventions are concerned also with the elaboration of *collective* rights. Thus 'freedom of association' is seen in ILO industrial terms as a right to organise, leading to the right to bargain collectively, and (within limits) a right to withdraw labour. The Ministry of Labour in its evidence of 1966 put to the Donovan Royal Commission as documents binding Britain, both the ECHR, and the ILO Conventions 87 and 98, together with the 'European Social Charter'.

The Charter was adopted by the Council of Europe in 1961 and accepted by the UK. Article 5 commits a state to ensuring that there is freedom for workers and employers to form and join 'organisations for the protection of their economic and social interests'. Article 6 commits it to ensure effective collective bargaining, promotion of joint consultation and 'voluntary negotiations' for collective agreements. Article 6 (4) also guarantees a 'right to strike'; but only in regard to conflicts of interest (not of rights); not in breach of obligations in collective agreements; and subject to any restrictions imposed by the state (which are allowed by Art. 31 if 'prescribed by law and necessary in a democratic society for protection of the rights and freedoms of others or for the protection of public interest, national security, public health or morals'.[15] The parallel with Art. 11 (1) and (2), ECHR, is plain.

So, freedom of association in unions is protected both by ECHR, Art. 11, and the European Charter, Arts. 5 and 6. There is an overlap. This is found in parallel conventions also. Thus, the provision in Art. 22 of the UN International Covenant on Civil and Political Rights on freedom of association is matched by the International Covenant on Economic, Social and Cultural Rights, 1966, which provides in Art. 8 (a) for the right of everyone to form trade unions and join the union of their choice, subject only to the rules of the organisation concerned, for the promotion and protection of his economic and social interests (subject to restrictions prescribed by law and necessary in a democratic society for national security, public order and protection of the rights of others). Art. 8 (c) adds the right for trade unions to 'function freely' (subject to the same formula); and (d) the right to strike, subject to any laws of a particular country.

In other words, the function of conventions like the ECHR is largely to protect rights as they inhere in the individual. There, as Fawcett puts it, 'the individual is sovereign'.[16] But the collective end of the problem is filled out by the charter, which establishes a right to organise for certain purposes (collective bargaining etc.), and so protects those purposes for the protection of the individual interests. Viewed from this perspective, it is natural to regard, as the ILO does, the right to bargain freely with employers as 'an essential element in freedom of association'.[17] As Kahn-Freund put it:

> Freedom of organisation has two social and therefore two legal functions. It is a civil liberty, a human right, an aspect of freedom of association ... its existence and adequate guarantees for its exercise are, however, also indispensable conditions for the operation of collective labour relations.

It has a 'dual aspect'. The Charter is 'a supplement' to the ECHR.[18] Just as the collective freedom cannot function without the individual freedom, so the latter, where trade unions and protection of interests are concerned, is meaningless without the former.

The European Court of Human Rights

The duality would not matter so much if the mechanisms for enforcement of the ECHR and of the charter were the same, or even parallel. They are not. Whereas the former allows for complaint to the Commission and to the Court of Human Rights (which can, and does, award damages to individuals), the latter knows only of a complaint to the Committee of Experts, independent nominees whose reports are sent to the Committee of Ministers with recommendations for the attention of the states and parties concerned.[19] This means that when the court grapples with Art. 11 of the ECHR, its perspective is skewed towards an individualistic interpretation. Deprived of the collective standards expressed in the charter, the 21 judges (one each from countries as different as Malta and Norway, Turkey and Spain) are unable to develop a jurisprudence that reflects the needs of workers collectively organised, unless they import the charter by implication.

The judgments given since 1950 on Art. 11 (1), show that the court has recognised the problem but has failed to solve it. In the *Belgian Police Union* and *Swedish Engine Drivers' Union* cases,[20] the court concluded that states must make possible the protection of 'the occupational interests of trade union members by trade-union action'. But this did not 'secure any particular treatment of trade unions'. The judges did not accept the Commission's view that collective bargaining might be an essential part of the rights safeguarded. A public sector union, they held, had no right to make collective agreements with, or be consulted by, the state where it was the employer (as those cases), adding:

> Not only is this latter right not mentioned in Article 11 (1) but neither can it be said that all Contracting States incorporate it in their national law or practice, or that it is indispensable for the effective enjoyment of trade union freedom.

Each state was left a 'free choice', which might not include collective bargaining. Moreover, in *Schmidt and Dahlström* v. *Sweden* the Court held that the right to strike 'is not expressly enshrined in Article 11' and may be limited at large by national laws.[21] The convention requires no more than that unions should, under national law, 'be enabled, in conditions not at variance with ECHR 11, to strive for the protection of their members' interests'.[22] Even authoritarian legislation like the Pay and Conditions of Teachers Act, 1987, might not infringe that test (and might anyway be regarded as 'necessary' within Art. 11 (2)).

Otherwise, the court's approach inserts into 'freedom of association in trade unions' very little collective content at all. It is largely an individual right.

The Right to Dissociate

The individual and formalistic approach of most Strasbourg judges raised the question whether the 'positive' right to freedom of association incorporates a 'negative' right to dissociate, an absolute right to be a non-member. This approach is natural to industrial legal systems which enjoy ideologically pluralist unions (France, Italy, Holland, Spain). Such systems could not see Catholics forced to join a Communist union, or Communists pushed into a religious union. The right to choose must there include the right not to join. By contrast, systems based on unitary unions often permit union security practices (in Britain, Canada and United States, forms of union membership arrangements; in Sweden, union member-only recruitment; in Australia, union member preference)[23] – though not always (as in Germany and Ireland where constitutional provisions protect the right to dissociate).[24]

Differences in background in Strasbourg were apparent in the 'Railwaymen's case'. The British legislation of 1974-76 allowed British Rail fairly to dismiss three existing employees who refused to join any of the three rail unions when a closed shop agreement came into effect. The majority of the court held this to be an infringement of their right to freedom of association under Art. 11 (1). It did not finally decide whether the 'negative' right was implied in the 'positive' right to associate, though it did regard 'choice' of union to be essential.[25] But six judges within the majority – all from pluralist systems – wished to go further and imply into Art. 11 (1) a 'negative' right to dissociate. At the other end, three dissenting judges – all from unitary systems (Denmark, Sweden, Iceland) – held that there was 'no logical link' between the rights to associate and to dissociate. The latter might need protection on other grounds (as here, in regard to security of employment); but that was concerned with protection of the individual as such, not 'the individual as an active participant in social activities'. Moreover, like all other conventions after the Universal Declaration, 1948, the ECHR had deliberately omitted a right not to be a union member. This very division of opinion illlustrates the way that the 'meaning' of this freedom can acquire a different logic in different social systems.

The decision caused the UK government to pay compensation to other similar claimants to the court; and it was influential (often in garbled form) in the debates leading to the Employment Act 1982, with its retroactive compensation schedule. The majority judges of the court, which had not been willing to indulge in making positive rights to organise and to bargain part of the right to collective freedom of association, were willing to make social and political choices, some in favour of an implied 'negative' right for individual non-unionists, and all, as we have seen, under Art. 11 (2) that the closed shop arrangements were not 'necessary' because of their disproportionate effect on those individuals.

It must be added that the Strasbourg court is not here alone among international tribunals. Members of the Alberta Union of Provincial Employees met a similar fate when, after legislation deprived public employees of the right to strike, they appealed to the United Nations Human Rights Committee, alleging a breach of Article 22 of the International Covenant on Civil and Political Rights, 1966, which enshrines rights equivalent to ECHR, Art. 11 (1). The majority of the committee adopted a formal, legalistic approach, even though the complainants here were individuals. Art. 22 did not expressly include any right to strike. Nor were the three decisions of the ILO Freedom of Association Committee relevant which had called for amendments to this legislation. (That committee had held that a total ban, as opposed to limits, on the right to strike violated the freedom of association in ILO terms under Convention 87.) The majority insisted that 'each international treaty ... has a life of its own', and must be interpreted by itself. The Covenant was based, the drafting history showed, upon the Universal Declaration and that too included no express right to strike. Such a right could not be part of the right to freedom of association, even including the right to join unions. The case could not therefore be considered.[26]

The minority members (including the British member) dissented. The exercise, they thought, of the right of freedom of association 'required some measure of concerted activities'. The purpose of joining a union was expressed in Art. 22 to be protection of one's interests; and the ILO decisions were some guide on that. Some means of doing so must be included. The complaint, they thought, should at least be admitted for argument on the merits, e.g. on whether the right to strike was in this case a 'necessary element' in the protection of the interests of these workers. But they lost by thirteen votes to five.

Freedom of Association in National Courts

If the majority of international and European tribunals have tended to approach freedom of association on a formal and individualistic level with the minimum of collective content, what of national courts? The common law judges have certainly not displayed great enthusiasm for any different approach. In *Collymore* v. *Attorney-General* the Privy Council's Judicial Committee (effectively the Law Lords) confronted an appeal against Trinidad legislation which prohibited strikes and lock-outs and imposed compulsory arbitration of disputes before an industrial court.[27] The Trinidad constitution declared: 'the following human rights and fundamental freedoms ... (j) freedom of association and assembly'. Giving judgment, Lord Donovan denied that 'abridgement of the rights of free collective bargaining and of the freedom to strike are abridgements of the right of freedom of association'. Perhaps the main purpose of trade unions was bargaining to improve conditions. But 'these are not the only purposes which trade unionists as such pursue'. They often have other objects – 'social, benevolent, charitable, political' – as the ILO itself recognised. Moreover, bargaining was dealt with by ILO Convention 98, not Convention 87. The right to form trade unions was 'left untouched' by the Trinidad legislation.

This might be thought to reduce trade union freedom of association to a mere freedom of assembly, from which it is invariably distinguished. Yet the grim reduction of freedom of association to the right to associate together for some purpose or other, however restricted, still dominates the common law contribution to the subject. It is hardly the basis for any legal right to organise in effective trade unions. The Supreme Court of India, however, followed the same path, interpreting the constitutional right to 'form associations or unions' as not incorporating any rights to engage in collective bargaining, still less to strike.[28]

Canada
But in Canada the glimmer of a different approach briefly appeared after the adoption of the new constitution or 'Charter' in 1982. This established certain fundamental freedoms which can be displaced only by express legislative provision (which can last for only a limited period without re-enactment).[29] The scheme is not dissimilar to what would be involved in adopting the ECHR into UK law; and the list of rights and freedoms is also similar to that Convention. Section 2 states: 'Everyone has the following fundamental freedoms ... (d) freedom of association'. But like other freedoms, this 'guaranteed' freedom may be subjected to 'such reasonable limits prescribed by law as can be demonstrably justified in a free and democratic society' (s. 1). Again there is a broad parallel with ECHR, Art. 11 (1) and (2).

A mass of litigation has followed the Charter's adoption, including challenges by unions to legislation limiting union activities. Most have followed the formal common law logic. Incomes policy legislation limiting strikes was held to be not inconsistent with s. 2 (d) because all the latter did was guarantee unions the right to 'enter into consensual arrangements' with no protection of their objects. The right to picket was not protected, since the freedom was general, to associate for any purpose, 'from

political parties to hobby clubs', with no constitutional guarantee
for particular purposes. Alberta laws depriving public employees
of collective bargaining and strike rights were similarly held not to
be a breach of this guaranteed freedom.[30]

But the majority judges of the Saskatchewan Court of Appeal
suddenly refused in 1985 to accept this line of thinking. They
rejected provincial legislation banning bargaining, strikes and
lock-outs in the dairy industry, as being inconsistent with the
constitutional freedom in s. 2 (d). The Chief Justice rejected the
legal precedents in favour of many philosophical writings. '*To be* in
association', he declared 'means *to act* in association, for it is
metaphysically impossible for a human being to exist in a state of
inanimateness ... as it were, a state of mere beingness'. This he
based upon Thomas Aquinas (a novel legal source). The purposes
of an association must therefore be constitutionally protected,
subject to two limitations. First, where a person acting alone would
be forbidden to engage in the acts, no protection existed; and
second, if a single person were incapable of doing them, they were
not protected if the object was to 'inflict harm'. Neither limit
applied to bargaining or to strikes in this case.

The concurring judge reached the same conclusion by a less
esoteric route:

> the freedom to bargain collectively, of which the right to withdraw
> services is integral, lies at the very centre of the existence of an
> association of workers. To remove their freedom to withhold their
> labour is to sterilise their association.[31]

Into the individual freedom he built a protection also for collective
purposes.

The Chief Justice had also challenged the reasoning in cases like
Collymore with a homely parallel. Suppose there was legislation
'prohibiting the act of procreation'. Would that not infringe the
'freedom of association of marriage partners'? Would Lord
Donovan say that 'permitting the partners to have breakfast
together, to talk to each other regularly, to go to the theatre'
meant that such a law had not 'infringed their freedom of
association'? Both judges went on to to hold that, on the available
evidence, the legislation went beyond what was reasonable and
was therefore of no effect. They had found in the right to associate
a right to organise for the industrial purposes normal in a
democracy. For all the difficulties inherent in the approach and in
defining its limitations, it makes a reality out of a freedom which is
otherwise hollow.

This judicial shaft of light has, however, now been extinguished
by the Supreme Court in 1987, in judgments on three related
appeals concerning the Alberta laws prohibiting collective
bargaining and strikes, federal legislation banning bargaining by

public sector employees, and the same Saskatchewan dairy legislation.[32] In all three cases, by a majority of four to two, the court held that s. 2 (d) had not been infringed. In the Saskatchewan case one dissentient judge, Dickson CJ, accepted that the legislation, although an infringement, was reasonable and demonstrably justified under s. 1.

The most extensive Supreme Court judgment in the *Alberta* case points to the general character of the guaranteed 'freedom of association'. The freedom does not exist only for trade unions. It is a 'freedom belonging *to the individual* and not to the group formed through its exercise'. The group cannot acquire greater constitutional rights by its association. Otherwise legislation to ban guns would be inapplicable to gun clubs. Freedom of association is not concerned with 'the particular activities or goals themselves'; but it includes the right to 'establish and maintain organisation' to engage in constitutionally protected or other permitted activities. The right to strike could not acquire protection merely from a right to associate, even though in Canada a strike is not (as it is in England) 'either a breach of contract or termination of employment'; that result is the product of specific legislation on strikes. Restrictions on strikes did not aim at the 'associational character of trade unions'. The judgment harnesses an abstentionist philosophy to its reasoning. Labour law is 'an extremely sensitive subject'; and 'the courts, as a general rule, are not the best arbiters of disputes', in which 'political, social and economic questions frequently dominate'. The judges should not be asked to decide whether government intervention in collective bargaining is reasonable or not. Le Dain J, agreeing, commented: 'the modern rights to bargain collectively and to strike ... are not fundamental rights or freedoms'.[33]

The Canadian Supreme Court judgments will be quarried by legal commentators for many years, not least the dissenting judgment of Dickson CJ in the *Alberta* case (which analyses the international material and finds the prohibition of strikes *together with* no provision of a right to refer disputes to arbitration to be a contravention of s. 2 (d)) and his analysis there and in the *Saskatchewan* case of the permissible, justifiable limits allowed by s. 1.

It must be noted that the Canadian Constitution guarantees 'freedom of association' without expressly mentioning, as the ECHR does, any right to *join or form trade unions for the protection of one's interests*. But the reasoning of the Supreme Court majority is sufficiently close to the formal argument of Lord Donovan to suggest that few English judges would adopt a more collective or purposive interpretation of Art. 11 (1) ECHR merely by reason of the addition of those words. Forming and joining a union might be said to summarise the content given by the

Supreme Court to industrial freedom of association, though it says less about protection of interests. Moreover, the few heterodox comments by English judges up to now claiming that the common law 'recognises a right of association' in trade unions,[34] have shown, too, that no direct legal remedies are available in England to enforce any such right in the absence of specific legislation (such as that which now sanctions discriminatory penalties by the employer).[35] There is nothing to indicate that the judiciary in Britain would depart from the reasoning dominant in international and common law national tribunals.

Europe

On the other hand, not far away, the major systems of labour law on the Continent tend to take a different view and to recognise considerable collective content in the fundamental right to freedom of association. In West Germany the Constitutional Court has interpreted the constitutional right to 'form associations for the safeguarding and improvement of working and economic conditions' (Art. 9 III, Basic Law) as making sense only if the associations themselves are given the opportunity to engage in activities typically undertaken by such associations, such as collective bargaining.[36] In France the constitutional right to join a union of one's choice, in the context of other union rights and the overall *liberté syndicale*, 'implies a right to take normal union *activity* for the member or the activist'.[37] In Sweden the right of association, protected by the constitution and by s. 7 of the Joint Regulation of Working Life Act 1976, includes the right to 'make use of membership' of an organisation; the collective content is reinforced by allowing the union to sue for infringements. The right of association is inseparable from, indeed exists for, bargaining purposes.[38]

Italy is perhaps the strongest case. There the constitution of 1948, adopted in the period after liberation from fascism, incorporating numerous human rights, establishes the right 'to form associations without authorisation' (Art. 18) and also guarantees *libertà sindacale* (Art. 39: freedom of organisation in trade unions) and the right to strike (Art. 40),[39] To this has been added the list of workers' and union rights in the *Statuto dei Lavoratori* (Workers' Statute) 1970, including rights to carry on union activities (Art. 14) and not to be penalised for joining or not joining a union, for union activities, or for participating in a strike (Art. 15). Union activities is a phrase given a wide meaning, and a speedy remedy by injunction under Art. 28 provides effective sanctions. The 'representative' union has its own rights to be present at the workplace under the Statute.[40] British labour law, said by some to have indulged in such excesses in the 1970s, has never been within sight of the rights for workers and unions in the Italian *Statuto*.

In this structure *la libertà sindacale* is seen as both an individual and a collective freedom albeit that its exercise will often be individual (i.e. against discrimination). Trade union activity within the guarantee 'consists in a wide range of actions in three main categories: recruitment and organisation, self-protection and bargaining'.[41] Other authors see trade union freedom as broadly covering: 'organising, bargaining and striking'.[42] It is true, of course, that the constitution secures the right to 'form associations' in a different article from the right to organise in trade unions, and that this very fact leads to the concept that Art. 39 takes the 'right to organise' in unions beyond the normal compass of 'associations' within Art. 18, guaranteeing 'union purposes' and internal autonomy (i.e. union rules) as freedoms beyond the range of ordinary legislation.[43] That makes Italy a special case. But it is a case that shows that the right to associate in trade unions can be meaningful only as a right to organise for at least some normal trade union purposes.

Conclusion

The British parliament of 1987 is likely to be presented with yet more legislation to control trade unions' internal affairs and external activities.[44] In the same period another attempt is likely to be made to have the ECHR imported into our domestic law. The provisions in it relating to 'freedom of association' (Art. 11) are unlikely as they stand to receive any Italian-style interpretation from British judges. More probable would be a continuation of interpretations adopted by other common-law jurisdictions, including now the Canadian Supreme Court, which regard the right to such a freedom as essentially an individual right to meet together, with little or no protection of any collective purposes. This probability is heightened by the inability or unwillingness of the Strasbourg court when it has been confronted with Art. 11 ECHR, divided like a butchered Siamese twin from its brothers the European Social Charter (Arts. 5 and 6), to inject any serious measure of protection for collective action into its understanding of the right in Art. 11 (1).

With that attenuated interpretation, the 'freedom of association' proclaimed by the Convention is a false prospectus. Moreover two other dangers arise. First, the uncertainties surrounding the restrictions permitted by Art. 11 (2) would be dangerous in the hands of a British judiciary willing to give as great a latitude to the state as the Strasbourg court, if not more. Secondly, if the ECHR were adopted on this basis, it would open yet another avenue for individuals to litigate against trade unions – in the hope, for example, of convincing the English judges to read Art. 11 (1) (as the six hard-core Strasbourg judges wished in the 'Railwaymen's case')[45] to enshrine an absolute, 'negative' right to dissociate.

If, therefore, there is to be another debate about the adoption of the ECHR, Art. 11, into domestic law, practitioners in industrial relations and labour law would serve it best by injecting into it the realities of employment, a relationship in which most workers will continue to achieve greater 'freedom' in the labour market only in combination. Further, the bare right to freedom of association including the right to form trade unions' must be challenged in its sterilised form. Deprived of all collective purposes it is a sham formula. We need to judge that right in a concrete fashion, in the light of the facts.

Examples occur every month. Employers like IBM and Citibank refuse a union presence. New financial services are set up by banks in such a way as to displace the recognition of established unions.[46] Because of a strike, a macho and newly privatised employer deprives all employees of their expected benefits in profit sharing, strikers and non-strikers alike, though the effect on profits was 'negligible'.[47] Young workers in service industries do not join unions principally because of their 'restricted opportunity' even to encounter one.[48] These are the facts relevant to an assessment of workers' freedom to associate in trade unions for 'the protection of their interests', of their right to organise for that protection.

If the ECHR, Art. 11, is adopted as domestic law without some recognition of these realities, voices will be heard here in Britain, as they were recently in Canada, saying: 'I find it incomprehensible that a majority of justices would hold that freedom of association does not include the right to free collective bargaining.'[49]

Meanwhile the new individualism recoils from freedom of association the more it incorporates an effective right to organise. Hayek writes that the very term 'freedom of organisation' – a 'hallowed battle cry' of labour and political organisations – carries 'overtones ... in conflict with the reign of law on which a free society rests'. Their organisational powers 'will probably require limitations by general rules of law far more narrow than those it has been found necessary to impose by law on the actions of private individuals'.[50] Sponsors of the ECHR must be asked what defences they understand it to contain against yet further restrictions in Britain upon organisational liberties, and what opportunities it guarantees in real life for the organised protection of workers' interests.

Notes

1. See Wedderburn, *The Worker and the Law* (3rd ed. 1986), p. 276; and on 'positive rights' pp. 846-56 (and sources cited).
2. See the authorities in A. Lester, 'Fundamental rights: the UK Isolated?' [1984]

152   *Employment Rights in Britain and Europe*

Public Law 46, 66-71; M. Zander, *A Bill of Rights?* (3rd ed. 1985), pp. 31-6. For the first *GCHQ* judgment: R v. *Sec. of State for Foreign Affairs* [1984] IRLR 309, 323-4 (aff'd. *CSSU* v. *Min. Civil Service* [1985] AC 374, HL).

3. See Parl. Deb. HL, Vol. 469, 10 December 1985, col. 156; Vol. 472, 20 March 1986, col. 472; Vol. 473, 9 April 1986, col. 267; and HC Vol. 109, 6 February 1987, col. 1223. For the Reports see HL Paper 176, June 1978; N. Ireland Commission *Report*, Cmnd. 7009 (1977).

4. See Lord Scarman, *English Law: The New Dimension* (1974), pp. 76-85.

5. See James Fawcett, *Lights on Human Rights* (1987, Strasbourg), p. 6.

6. See the Solicitor General (Sir Patrick Mayhew MP) Parl. Deb. 109 HC, 6 February 1987, col. 1270 ('thrusting the judges far into the arena of political controversy'); Lord McCluskey, *Law, Justice and Democracy* (1987).

7. Lord Hailsham, *The Dilemma of Democracy* (1978), p. 172; and *Times*, 16 and 19 May 1975 (advocating a new written constitution).

8. J.A.G. Griffith, *The Politics of the Judiciary* (3rd ed. 1985), p. 233; on labour law, see Wedderburn (1987) 16 ILJ 1.

9. EC Bull. Supp. 2/79 (Commission). The EEC 'parliament' has more recently favoured adoption: OJ 1982 C 304/253. The ECJ: *Rutuli* v. *Interior Minister* [1976] 1 CMLR 140, 155; *National Panasonic* v. E. Comm. [1980] 3 CMLR 169. See M. Dauses, [1985] 10 Eur. L.R. 398.

10. On the detailed law under these provisions: J.E.S. Fawcett, *The Application of the European Convention on Human Rights* (2nd ed. 1987), pp. 33-420; P. Sieghart, *The International Law of Human Rights* (1983) Part III. On the ECHR and other international labour law treaties, see P. O'Higgins, Chap. 20 in R. Lewis (ed.), *Labour Law in Britain* (1986).

11. A. Lester, op. cit., note 2, p. 69.

12. See *Lithgow Ltd.*, 8 July 1986 (1984, Series A, 102); (1987) 12 Eur. L.R. 65. On education, Fawcett, op. cit., note 2, pp. 413-6 (but the UK, acceptance of Art. 2, Protocol I, is qualified).

13. Commission Minutes (11603/85) Session 184 (Strasbourg 19 March 1987) p. 2; see Law Society Gazette, 17 June 1987, p. 1807. *CCSU* v. *Minister for Civil Service*, above n. 2; ILO, Freedom of Association Committee, Report 234, case 1261, 226th Session, 1984, p. 87 (a decision rejected by the UK government).

14. *Young, James and Webster* v. *UK* [1982] 3 EHRR 38, 57-8. On the withdrawal of the defence in 1980, Sir I. Percival *Parl. Deb.* (HC) 6 February 1987, col. 1235. The TUC appeared but was permitted by the court to refer *only* to issues of 'fact and English law', not to the Convention.

15. See P. O'Higgins, Chap. 3 in J. Carby-Hall (ed.), *Studies in Labour Law* (1976), for the argument that the UK is in breach of the Charter for not having any positive right to strike.

16. Fawcett, op. cit., note 5, p. 11.

17. ILO Committee on Freedom of Association, 1970, case 559, 118th Report, para. 120. So too: Committee of Experts General Survey, 'Freedom of Association and Collective Bargaining' (1983) ILO 69th Session, III Part 4 (B) paras. 191-206, 286-97.

18. 'Labour Relations and International Standards: Some Reflections on the European Social Charter' in *Miscellanea: WJ Ganshof van der Meersch* (1972, Brussels), pp. 134, 138. (Sir Otto Kahn-Freund was a member of the Committee of Experts.)

19. Sieghart, op. cit., note 10, pp. 354-7, 430-2 (some recommendations have led to modifications in domestic laws).

20. *National Union of Belgian Police* v. *Belgium* (1975) 1 EHRR 578; *Svenska Lokmannaforbundet* v. *Sweden* (1976) 1 EHRR 617.

21. (1976) 1 EHRR 637 (penalisation of strikers on settlement of strike); see F. Schmidt, *Law and Industrial Relations in Sweden* (1977), pp. 63, 104-6. Also, see *X* v. *Germany* (10365/83) (1985) 7 EHRR 461 (teacher; no right to strike for public

servants; no contravention of Art. 11 (1); Commission); M. Forde (1983) 31 Am.,
Jo. Comp. Law 301.
22. Sieghart, op. cit., note 10, p. 351.
23. Wedderburn, Chap. 6 in F. Schmidt (ed.), *Discrimination in Employment*
(1978) (Britain, Germany, France, Italy, United States); W. Creighton, W. Ford,
R. Mitchell, *Labour Law, Materials and Commentary* (1983, Aus.) Chap. 28; O.
Kahn-Freund, *Labour and the Law* (3rd ed., 1983, eds. Davies and Freedland)
Chap. 7; R. Bean, *Comparative Industrial Relations* (1985), pp. 25-9.
24. See T. Treu, *Condotta Antisindacale e Atti Discriminatori* (1974), pp. 142-59;
F. von Prondzynski, *Freedom of Association and Industrial Relations* (1987) Chap.
10 (Germany and United States); A. Kerr and G. Whyte, *Irish Trade Union Law*
(1985), Chap. 1.
25. *Young, James & Webster* v. *UK* (1982) 4 EHRR 38; see Wedderburn, *The
Worker and the Law*, pp. 364-81; R. Lewis and B. Simpson, Chap. 2 in R. Lewis
(ed.), *Labour Law in Britain* (1986). The proposals in *Trade Unions and Their
Members* (1987, Cm. 95) would build on the Employment Act 1982, to create a
total right to dissociate in the U.K. The present law does not establish 'a clear right
not to join': P. Davies and M. Freedland, *Labour Law: Text and Materials* (1984
2nd ed.), p. 666. Since 'freedom of association can only be mutual', the right of the
union to reject a member is accepted both by English law (*Cheall* v. *Apex* [1983] 2
AC 180, though Lord Diplock leaves open a doubt in closed shops, p. 190), and by
the ECHR Commission: *Cheall* v. *UK* [1986] 8 EHRR 74. In the *Cheall* case, the
House of Lords rejected the claim by Lord Denning MR that the ECHR, Art. 11,
meant that restraints on the free choice of union such as the TUC 'Bridlington
Principles', were illegal even if that the ECHR, Art. 11, meant that restraints on the
free choice of union such as the TUC 'Bridlington Principles', were illegal even if
that 'should result in industrial chaos' [1982] ICR, p. 567. Donaldson LJ pointed
out that in the *Young James & Webster* decision, 'what degree of freedom of choice
was necessary was not spelt out other than in the context of the facts of that case'
(ibid., p. 564). But the hard core position has now received further support in
Canada where the express right to freedom of association in the constitution (below
n. 29) has been held to include an implied 'negative' right to dissociate: *Re Lavigne
and Ontario Public Service Employees* (1986) 29 DLR (4th) 321, 360-70 (Ont.).
26. *JB and others* v. *Canada*, Decisions of 18 July 1986, Reprint 7. Human Rights
Cttee., GAOR 41st Session, Suppl. No. 40, p. 151. On the Human Rights
Committee, see Sieghart, op. cit., note 10, pp. 381-90. For the three ILO decisions,
see *Canadian Labour Congress* v. *Canada (Alberta)* Case No. 893, 194th Report of
Committee on Freedom of Association, (1980) 43 Off. Bull. Series B, p. 28. For
comparison of decisions under Art. 11 ECHR, ILO Conventions 87 and 98, and the
European Social Charter, see Sieghart, op. cit., note 10, pp. 345-58; A. Pankert,
Chap. 10 in R. Blanpain (ed.), *Comparative Labour Law and Industrial Relations*
(1985, 2nd ed.). The ILO Committee has reaffirmed in over 100 decisions that a
right to strike is essential to freedom of association: *Freedom of Association, Digest
of Decisions and Principles* (1985, 3rd ed.) paras. 360-420.
27. [1970] AC 538 (PC).
28. *All India Bank Employees Assoc.* v. *National Industrial Tribunal* (1962) 49
AIR 171.
29. See P. Hahn, 'Canada's Charter of Rights and Freedoms' [1984] Public Law
530; J. Weiler and R. Elliott (eds.), *Litigating the Values of a Nation; The Canadian
Charter of Rights and Freedoms* (1986).
30. Respectively *Public Service Alliance* v. *Queen* (1984) 11 DLR (4th) 337, 392;
Dolphin Delivery v.*Retail, Wholesale (etc.) Union* (1984) 10 DLR (4th) 198, 209;
Re Public Service Employee Relations Act (1984) 16 DLR (4th) 359; see now note
32 below.
31. *Re Retail Wholesale (etc.) Union and Govt. of Saskatchewan* (1985) 19 DLR
(4th) 609, Bayda CJS, pp. 614-29, Cameron JA, pp. 639-52. See the similar

approach in *Re Service Employees (etc.) Union* (1983) 44 OR (2d) 392 ('freedom to associate ... includes the freedom to organise, to bargain collectively and, as a necessary corollary, to strike', per Smith J, p. 463).

32. *Alberta Union of Provincial employees* v. *Attorney-General of Alberta,* Transcript, 9 April 1987 (references are to this main judgment); *Public Service Alliance* v. *Queen,* Transcript, 9 April 1987; *Govt of Saskatchewan* v. *Retail, Wholesale (etc.) Union,* Transcript, 9 April 1987. [See now the main judgment reported as *Re Public Service Employees* (1987) 38 DLR (4th) 161.]

33. The *Alberta* case, McIntyre J, Transcript, pp. 7, 15-8, 20-30; Le Dain J, at p. 3. Compare the narrow interpretation of freedom of expression, under s. 2 (b) of the Charter, holding *inter alia* that injunctions against secondary picketing are not an infringement of that freedom: *Re Retail, Wholesale (etc.) Union* v. *Dolphon Delivery* (1986) 2 SCR 573 (Sup. Ct.); T. Christian and K. Ewing (1987) Camb. L.J. 195; J. Fudge (1987) 16 ILJ 188.

34. Lord Scarman, *UKAPE* v. *ACAS* [1980] ICR 201, 214; Lord Denning MR, ibid. [1979] ICR 303, 316.

35. Lord Scarman, *Report of Court of Inquiry on Grunwick Ltd* (1977 Cmnd 6922), p. 20. The Employment Protection (Consolidation) Act 1978, ss. 23, 58, protects the unionist and non-unionist against the employer's dismissal or action short of dismissal.

36. B. Verf, GE 19, 303, 30 Nov. 1965; von Prondzynski, op. cit., note 24, pp. 81, 91; T. Ramm 'Federal Republic of Germany' in R. Blanpain (ed.), *International Encyclopaedia for Labour Law.* Vol. 5, (1979), pp. 150-5.

37. J-M. Verdier *Syndicats et Droit Syndical* (2nd ed., 1987) Vol. 1, p. 398.

38. Folke Schmidt, op. cit., note 21, Chaps. 5, 8.

39. Art. 39 envisaged laws for registration of unions which have never been passed: see G. Giugni in G. Branca (ed.), *Commentario della Costituzione: Rapporti Economici* (1979), Vol. 1, pp. 257-88.

40. Wedderburn, op. cit., note 23, pp. 386-90.

41. Giugni, op. cit., note 39, pp. 273-4.

42. F. Carinci, R. de Luca Tamajo, P. Tosi, T. Treu, *Il Diritto Sindacale* (1983), p. 75. Many Italian writers see the 'negative' right to dissociate not as implied within the right to associate or organise, but as a separate individual right to dissent; and most analyse *libertà sindacale* in terms of a 'concrete power to act': e.g. G. Ghezzi and U. Romagnoli, *Il Diritto Sindacale* (2nd ed. 1987), pp. 40-1.

43. U. Carabelli, *Libertà e Immunità del Sindacato* (1984), pp. 146-54. The use of 'organise' in Art. 39 means that all activity to defend relevant collective interests is protected, very different from associations falling under Art. 18: G. Giugni, *Diritto Sindacale* (7th ed. 1984), pp. 57-9. Others put a rather more narrow view: e.g. S. Fois in G. Palma (ed.), *Profili Giuridici della Libertá Sindacale* (1986), pp. 129-40 ('unions are not, from a constitutional point of view, qualitatively different from associations within Art. 18': p. 130).

44. See the Green Paper, *Trade Unions and Their Members* (1987, Cm. 95).

45. See note 25 above.

46. *BIFU* v. *Barclays Bank,* [1987] ICR 495 (EAT).

47. *Times,* 19 June 1987, p. 25 (British Telecom).

48. M. Spilsbury, M. Hoskins, D. Ashton, M. Maguire, Trade Union Membership Pattern of Young Adults' (1987) 25 BJIR 267, 273.

49. Daryl Bean, President, Public Service Alliance of Canada, *Globe and Mail* (Toronto) 10 April 1987, p. 1.

50. F. Hayek, *Law, Legislation and Liberty* (1979), Vol. III, pp. 89-90 [and see below Chapter 8].

7

The Injunction and the Sovereignty of Parliament: Control of Judicial Discretion?

Lord Upjohn was a great master of Equity. It is not, therefore, inappropriate to fulfil the privilege of an address in his honour with a problem which is posed most acutely in the sphere of equitable remedies. Nor to link that problem with the question whether we as law teachers teach our students about the reality behind the form of those remedies.

We teach that parliament is sovereign, as in a democracy it should be. But we know that judges too make law. As Lord Reid observed, we must accept that fact for better or worse, for we no longer pretend that the common law is hidden in some Aladdin's cave waiting only for the judge to discover it by crying 'Open Sesame'.[1] But students are taught that, in the end, parliament is the master. Parliament believes it. The judges affirm it. Time and again they say: 'however wrong or anomalous the decision may be, it must stand until it is altered by parliament ... Parliament alone is the proper authority to change the law'; and they say, in interpreting parliament's statutes, no aids must 'restrict what is otherwise the plain meaning of the words of the statute'.[2] Judges must not distort its 'plain and unambiguous meaning' or try, as Lord Diplock said of Lord Denning in 1980, 'to invent some fancied ambiguities as an excuse for failing to give effect to its plain meaning because ... the consequences of doing so would be inexpedient, or even unjust or immoral'.[3] Yet that is not the whole story. Judges on occasion do interpret both the common law and the intention of parliament in pursuit of policies known only to – sometimes it would seem not even to – themselves. Some of the recent increase in judicial discretion may be explained by such

---

Based upon the Upjohn Lecture 1988, delivered to the Association of Law Teachers on 9 April 1988. First published in (1989) Vol. 23 The Law Teacher 4.

factors as the disappearance of the jury in civil cases.[4] But we must not overlook Bishop Hoadly's remark about the very power of the judicial function itself: 'whoever hath absolute authority to interpret any written or spoken laws, it is he who is truly the law-giver to all intents and purposes.'[5]

The question that arises is how far this theoretical supremacy of parliament has real content when it is applied to areas of the law – and, just as important, of procedure – which the judges feel instinctively and by training to be their own.[6] Grand, but rather suspect, statements are made by writers about this. For example, Dworkin says that in democratic countries, the people 'can elect legislators who have the power to impose their will on judges through one means or another'.[7] Yet one may wonder whether the judiciary is in every area so easily accountable.

That is why this paper concentrates upon the interlocutory injunction and the judicial powers over contempt of court which in this jurisdiction accompany it. It is not concerned with the conventions that are sometimes said to impose procedural limitations on the legitimation of parliament's 'sovereignty',[8] nor with the very real limitations now imposed by accession to the European Community which causes British courts, in areas from sex discrimination to fisheries protection, to enforce a law derived from Brussels and the court in Luxembourg, rather than Westminster.[9] This latter part of our new constitutional law is still only marginally relevant – though it may not long remain so – to the theme that follows. The object here is to ask how far it is realistic, whatever the theory, to affirm the 'sovereignty' of an omnicompetent parliament in the territory of interlocutory injunctions, and in particular interlocutory injunctions in industrial disputes, or as such a remedy is often called, 'the labour injunction'.[10]

The granting of such injunctions in the High Court is based on statutory authority and consquent rules of court, largely Order 29, rule 1, made in pursuance of what is now s. 37, Supreme Court Act, 1981. That basis for the jurisdiction to grant an injunction whenever the court finds it 'just and convenient' to do so has been broadly the same since s. 16 of the Judicature Act 1873, though it is significant that that section has usually been understood to have confirmed, rather than regulated, the inherent jurisdiction and equitable discretion of the courts themselves.[11] It is worth noting, too, the character of the legislative process itself on these matters. Effective debate on the 1981 Act and the Contempt of Court Act of the same year was provided largely by the Law Officers, their Opposition counterparts, the Lord Chancellor, Lord Advocate, ex-Lord Chancellors, Law Lords, and ex-Law Lords.[12] Furthermore, important reform is sometimes effected by the judiciary itself through the Rules Committee of the Supreme Court, as with

judicial review in 1977, enshrined in the form of a statutory
instrument and only later, as in that case, to be confirmed in
statute.[13] All these procedures tend to confirm the cultural
sentiment that this is judges' territory.

Injunctions and Discretion

More important, the life of the injunction and its associated
discretionary sanctions rests exclusively with the judiciary in court.
This is hardly surprising given their discretionary character. The
remarkable extension of the *Anton Piller* order after 1976 and the
parallel growth of the *Mareva* injunction after 1975[14] both testify to
the creativity of the judiciary in this field. It is the very discretion
attached to such remedies that allows them to be moulded into
flexible weapons – for example, to take five instances from 1987
alone: to assert the old principle that no interlocutory injunction
should restrain publication where a plea of justification or fair
comment is entered in answer to the cry of defamation, but to
cast it aside where the court thinks the publication (by flying an
aircraft with messages over the Cheltenham Gold Cup) is arguably
part of a 'conspiracy to injure' the plaintiff; or to refuse an
injunction to the Church of Scientology to stop disclosure of
confidential information because of its not inordinate delay in
bringing suit, but to grant one to the Crown on the same grounds
despite its having awaited worldwide publication; or to relax the
rule that a plaintiff must show detriment, in order to grant the
National Health Service an order banning disclosure of the names
of persons suffering from AIDS.[15]

Such discretionary decisions involve a high element of policy.
Each of us will approve the policies inherent in some of the
decisions and not in others. Let it be clear at the outset, though,
that the issue at stake is emphatically *not* one that turns on a
judge's personal 'bias'. It is concerned with judicially created
principle. It is the character of the basic guidelines for the
protection of property interests, created by the judiciary over a
long tradition, which causes much of the difficulty in labour
injunction cases. For in this sphere the judge is entitled, often
expected, to reach beyond strict application of principle. He has
the right, even the duty, to treat any particular case as special, as
unique or exceptional, especially if it seems to be urgent, involving
some extra element which allows him to displace the principle that
would normally apply.

It may be said that parliament could control all these principles
and their application 'through one means or another' if it really
wanted to do so. But that is too simple an answer. In one sense it is
obviously necessary for judges to have at hand some discretionary
power in interim and interlocutory cases so as to maintain the

status quo until a dispute between two parties can be properly heard and determined. Order 29, rule 1, springs from just that basic purpose, to preserve the '*status quo* until the rights of the parties have been determined in the action'.[16] Normally, an application should be made on motion with notice of two clear days and be heard *inter partes*; but judicial discretion here naturally applies to procedure as well as to substance. Where 'the case is one of urgency' application may be made *ex parte*, even before a writ is issued. Mandatory injunctions should not normally be sought in interlocutory proceedings; but exceptionally, of course, so long as the terms are clear they may be granted, for example where the defendant has attempted to 'steal a march' on the plaintiff.[17] Even in commercial cases there have been signs of a greater readiness to grant the remedy where the risk of commercial injustice is thought to demand the preservation not of the static, but of 'the dynamic status quo'.[18]

At root the model in the judge's mind is, and in our system must in the High Court be, linked to property, given the history of the 'equitable principles' which he is called upon to apply. In disputes over property the model is understandable. It would be a poor system of justice that provided no speedy remedy to stop a man who threatened at a moments' notice to bulldoze your house. At least the court should, you might think, preserve the *status quo* until the rights of the parties can be settled. 'It is on the ground of injury to property', observed Turner LJ in 1853, 'that the jurisdiction of this court must rest.' The landowner whose title is not disputed is normally entitled, for the same reason, to an injunction to restrain a trespass, even if it would cause him no damage.[19] But it is for the propertied rather than for the property-less that these principles do their work best. In *Kerr on Injunctions*, 1927, the author wrote (to take the main headings) about 'waste', property in timber, trespass, nuisance, patents, copyright, covenants, confidences, libel, trustees, partners, mortgages, and companies. Of the 678 pages only nine are devoted to 'clubs, societies and trade unions'. The proportion might need to be rather different today; but the principles applicable to the people in the associations would still be largely those transferred from the other headings.

It must be added that our assessment of the interlocutory discretion does not enter the lists in the struggle between the various writers on jurisprudence who dispute the extent to which recognition of 'principles' or 'rules' leaves the judge with a residue of 'discretion'.[20] That debate, like so many others, tends to be conducted on the basis of law as found at trial. Writers on jurisprudence show little interest in interlocutory process. Yet that earlier stage is in many disputes frequently a decisive phase. At that stage principles guide the exercise of discretion which are described by a long tradition, most of them coloured by the historical origins of equity itself, such as the refusal of the injunction where damages would be an adequate remedy. But – unlike trial – the judge is allowed, and expected, to exercise an over-riding discretion on evidence that is often much more flimsy. It is this area of judicial power which is inadequately represented to the law student in his training, both in regard to procedures and to the important social effects.

The law student may object that this unpredictable stream of judicial discretion could be blocked or channelled by a determined parliament. For parliament is sovereign. Was it not Lord Cairns' Act that gave the Chancery judges power to award damages despite the protests of some of them at the time that this made their courts into tribunals for 'legalising wrongful acts' by those able and willing to pay?[21] So too, from parliament comes section 52 of the Sale of Goods Act 1979 to govern the court's discretion or order specific performance of a contract to deliver specific or ascertained goods. But these are statutes that expand jurisdiction and discretion. What about legislation to cut the latter down, to rob it of its over-riding character? Is parliament equally sovereign there in practice as well as in theory? Or is its real power over that ocean of discretion better compared with the power of King Canute?

The Labour Injunction

The problem arises in its most acute form on the interlocutory labour injunction. The phrase 'labour injunction' is convenient to describe an injunction arising out of a trade dispute, sought against a defendant worker, trade union or union officials, in civil proceedings brought by an employer or third party or, sometimes, by a dissident member of the union itself. It is hardly necessary to explain why the problem is so acute. On the assumption that our society recognises a liberty of some kind for employed persons collectively to withdraw their labour, wholly or in part, and for an employer to lock his workers out, the question arises how far the courts will intervene *before or during* such a dispute to prohibit the organisation or continuance of the industrial action. That problem is not unique to Britain; it is a critical issue in many other systems of labour law. In such cases, it is obvious that a plaintiff employer or third party will generally be interested primarily in the interlocutory remedy, an order banning or delaying the action, rather that in the final trial. Moreover, it is apparent that he will be better placed to allege a threat of 'irreparable loss' to his business, his trade or his property than the workers or the union who, if enjoined, will lose the less tangible tactical opportunity to withdraw labour while the iron is hot.

Fifty years ago Judge Frankfurter and Professor Greene surveyed the extensive use of such injunctions against unions by American courts and concluded that in strikes there were present special difficulties of justice:

> The injunction cannot preserve the *status quo*; the situation does not remain in equilibrium awaiting judgment upon full knowledge. The suspension of activities affects only the strikers; the employer resumes his efforts to defeat the strike, and resumes them free from the interdicted interferences. Moreover, the suspension of strike activities, even temporarily, may defeat the strike for practical purposes ... The law's conundrum is which side should bear the risk of unavoidable, irreparable damage. Improvident denial of the injunction may be irreparable to the complainant; improvident issue of the injunction may be irreparable to the defendant.[22]

The judges' practices led to the banning in 1932 of labour injunctions in Federal courts. It is significant that they have reappeared since in new forms,[23] and that the judges in the Supreme Court are said to have 'emasculated the Act'.[24] The British parliament has never tried to go that far. Instead, in 1974 it aimed to limit the range of such injunctions. First it tried to curb *ex parte* injunctions in industrial conflict, where the employer obtains from the judge an order for a stated period or 'until further order', without the presence of, possibly without even notice to, the union. Secondly, it tried to moderate the use of labour injunctions in proceedings *inter partes*.

Ex Parte *Orders and Section 17(1)*

Although some judges had earlier thought any case involving a prospect of serious legal argument on the issues should not be the subject of an *ex parte* labour injunction, in the increasing labour litigation of the 1960s such injunctions were regularly granted. In that year Geoffrey Lane J granted *ex parte* famous injunctions which continued for eight days against unions at Fords for breach of a collective agreement which he later held, having considered it on argument, could not after all create any binding obligations.[25] By 1971 we find the High Court even granting mandatory orders in such *ex parte* proceeding. Although the Court of Appeal found them 'most unusual', they were effective in stopping the workers' industrial action.[26] In an *ex parte* proceedings, the defendant has no right to be heard, even if he hears about the application and arrives breathless at the door of the court in time. Moreover, a plaintiff may commence an *ex parte* motion against the defendant when they are in the middle of *inter partes* proceedings. This was the way in which the court granted an application for a receivership over union funds (another discretionary remedy) in the 1985 legal battles in the miners' strike, an 'unusual' proceeding, said Stephenson LJ, but one the court in its discretion approved. The first judge had stood over the motion for a week; but the very next day another judge had granted an *ex parte* application (these days known as an 'opposed *ex parte* application') making an order for seven days.[27] In all such cases the proof of exceptional 'urgency' is readily accepted.

In s. 17(1) of the Trade Union and Labour Relations Act 1974, parliament confronted the *ex parte* labour injunction for the first time. Such orders 'need to be very carefully examined', Scott J has said: 'Defendants are entitled, prima facie, not to have assumptions made against them and orders made against them without a hearing at which they can be represented and can put forward their case.'[28] Yet *ex parte* orders are regularly made in industrial disputes, though they are frequently not reported (that is another difficulty confronting the law teacher). Parliament therefore enacted in 1974 that in *ex parte* applications where the defendant claims, or the court thinks he would be 'likely to claim', that he *acted* in contemplation or furtherance of a 'trade dispute', no interlocutory injunction should be granted by the court unless it is satisfied that 'all steps which in the circumstances were reasonable' have been taken to give him notice and an opportunity of being heard. The section does not demand that the 'trade dispute' would afford him a defence, only that he would claim he acted in contemplation or furtherance of it. Since the defendant will not usually be present, the court is left to determine whether he would be 'likely' to make that assertion. True, counsel for the applicant is professionally obliged to bring all relevant facts and authorities to the notice of the court. Even so, it was only four years after the Act was passed that 'snap' injunctions were granted by Stocker J against the UPW without notice and on hearsay evidence;[29] and on appeal Lord Wilberforce was constrained to agree that the union's complaints about the procedure used were justified.

The law reports themselves show that little, if anything, has changed today (and we must remember that many such orders, and the compromises reached after threats to seek them, are not reported at all). A dispute about grading and salaries between members of a civil service union and the Meat and Livestock Commission, their employer, began in 1984. Two years later after two strike-ballots, and a one-day lightning strike, abattoir owners obtained an *ex parte* injunction banning further industrial action. The union moved to discharge the order, but pressure of business in the courts held up argument *inter partes* for a week. Two weeks later, a different judge decided after argument that there was no arguable case at all that the union had been guilty of any tortious conduct.[30]

For three weeks, therefore, the union had been subject to an injunction that rested on no wrongdoing whatever. It was, however, tactically forced to agree during the proceedings to organise industrial action for not more than one day at a time; and after the final judgment both the employers and the union claimed victory. The injunction, which had been obeyed, had been of great tactical advantage to the employer, even though the union ultimately won the point of principle. What is more, the original *ex parte* order had been granted by a judge to the employers before the issuing of a writ, at 3.30 p.m. on a Sunday afternoon, from his home – over the telephone. No doubt the judge was convinced of the special 'urgency' (under RSC. 0.29 r. 1(2)). But how it was acceptable to refrain from giving notice to the union (their solicitors' answering machine was notified *after* the order was made) remains a mystery. There is of course no law report of what was said on the telephone.

The case illustrates the reaction of High Court judges faced with a claim for urgent, discretionary relief against alleged prospective damage to property in the employer's business. The very clear words of parliament's s.17(1) by now have a distinctly Canute-like look. It is not a question of judicial bias at the weekend or at any other time. The judicial reaction is founded upon an ideology of property deep within the jurisdiction and the tradition. Parke B said in 1850 any law 'to restrain the exercise of capital and property ... must be construed stringently'.[31] This factor is still at work. Discretionary relief is readily available for allegations of damage to property, and the 'steps reasonable in the circumstances' in the section are interpreted as being subject to the requirements of 'urgency' as so understood. Moreover, the case of the Sunday injunction was not a one-off case. The general experience following parliament's attempt in 1974 to accomplish the relatively straightforward task of putting an end to regular *ex parte* injunctions in trade disputes increases the need to analyse the factors involved in any parallel attempt to control *inter partes* proceedings. Parliament's attempt to assert its sovereignty here has had very limited effects.

Inter Partes *Orders*

Although large numbers of labour injunctions begin as *ex parte* applications, they do not usually take quite as long to reach some kind of *inter partes* argument. It might be said that for the union to suffer a few days under a questionable injunction is not too high a price for the protection of an employer's trade against irreparable loss; but even a day or two can destroy the union's ability to seize the moment and 'to strike while the iron is still hot; once postponed it is unlikely that it can be revived'.[32] And when the union applies for discharge of the *ex parte* order, the first round of argument now falls upon it, not the employer. It is already one goal down, without having taken the pitch.

As the case goes on, the entire concept of the 'status quo' militates against the trade union side. Objections by workers keeping to old work schedules that the employer has been stepping up the rhythm in new production methods are met by the comment that this is the 'normal commercial way' for him to operate.[33] If unofficial action causes management to sack workers, then (in Lord Denning's words): 'So it must be.' That's life. Very rarely is the idea found that an injunction must not be granted to an employer because his hands are not clean by reason that the dismissals of workers were unfair.[34] The lack of industrial rights – of the union to recognition, or of workers to improved conditions or security of employment – gives the employer's property rights an even stronger look in court.[35] Most judges see the union's loss of the chosen moment to strike as just the loss of a 'bargaining counter'.[36] The interim pause required to 'suspend' the industrial action is spoken of as a temporary matter – for a stated period or, usually, until full trial – whereas in effect it may decide the dispute in the employer's favour.[37]

Industrial action which is 'reactive' to management's initiatives always has the air in court of aggression and its cessation of restoring normality; indeed, the judicial concept of the *status quo* has rightly been seen as conditioned in large part by 'a response to market forces and the maintenance of managerial prerogatives'.[38] Moreover, the procedure in a trade dispute case is almost as unsatisfactory *inter partes* as it is *ex parte*. Even when notice is given, it need be no more than two clear days; but even less is permitted with the leave of the court. The motion may be moved before issue of the writ, let alone service of any statement of claim. As recent cases illustrate,[39] the defendant union is fortunate to receive more than the main affidavit, frequently in draft; further affidavits often pour in during the proceedings, including new evidence in the Court of Appeal, often with bundles of prejudicial material. The nature of a trade union compounds these difficulties in knowing what the case is that it has to answer. Its solicitors need to take statements from officials who are often in various parts of the country. If counsel meanwhile objects to the court's dispensing with the writ, he will at best gain no more than an hour or two while one is drafted.

A 1986 case is a good example of the way things really work.[40] A grumbling dispute between production workers and their employers led to industrial action after a ballot. The employers dismissed five workers, and imposed sanctions including suspension of sick pay, time-off and retirement schemes. Negotiations took place but no agreement was reached. On 24 June official action (by 'working without enthusiasm') recommended. One week later on Tuesday 1 July the employers applied to Gatehouse J for an *ex parte* injunction without notice to the union and were granted it. That Friday the union appeared, but after argument *inter partes* the judge refused to lift the injunction, despite a proper ballot. On 8 July the Court of Appeal discharged the injunction, saying there was no case to argue for any remedy. For eight days injunctions had restrained lawful action. More important, if in that interim period the union had continued its lawful action (as it did), it was acting in contempt of court. The 1988 seamen's strike was the subject of similar *ex parte* injunctions. The NUS agreed to withdraw its instruction to members in a dispute held arguably to involve secondary action under the 1980 Act, and unsupported by a ballot which the 1984 Act required, and therefore without the immunity from liability in tort. The judge pointed out the case would be mentioned again a few days later and warned, if the union did not comply precisely and 'in the most efficient way', then: 'Watch out on Tuesday'.[41] Subsequently the union was found to be in breach of other injunctions and in contempt of court, with consequences to which we come later.

It is well known that for three reasons, the development of substantive labour law has played its own part, complementary to procedure, in the life of the labour injunction. First, the liberty of industrial action in Britain has historically taken the peculiar form of 'immunities' in trade disputes, rather than positive rights. It has been built upon exceptions to the primary rights of management and of property. Secondly, the tendency of judges in recent periods has been to create new liabilities out of old, torts like 'intimidation' by threats to strike, or the wider forms of tort liability for 'interference' with contracts, or of 'economic duress' where the will of one party is 'overborne' by the other (something which to many shop-stewards and even managers is of the essence of collective bargaining itself). Thirdly, in the Employment Acts 1980, 1982 and now 1988, and the Trade Union Act 1984, a 'trade dispute' has been more narrowly defined and the 'immunities' increasingly restricted to a narrow core.[42] Many of the leading decisions have sprung from applications for injunctions; and the appellate courts have often been only too ready to decide uncertain points of law 'creatively' in such cases.[43]

There is not, in other words, any consistency of meaning in the notion that where difficult issues of law and of fact are strongly contested and must be tried, the '*status quo*' should be maintained.[44] Sometimes, especially on claims for mandatory injunctions, that is found to be a reason for refusing an order.[45] More often it has been a reason for *granting* an injunction, the judge observing:

> a direct conflict of evidence ... is not the sort of conflict one can resolve on motion on affidavit evidence without cross-examination,

and before discovery, and I decline to do so ... (these) are things
that can only be ascertained by the court after hearing full oral
evidence ... [the defendant] fails in his contention that there is no
serious issue to be tried.[46]

The Judicial Legislation in Ethicon

It is usual to distinguish two stages in the reasoning in these cases,
though when discretion is so fluid there can be no rigid boundaries.
First, what must the plaintiff prove as to his rights? Second, what is
the way of striking the 'balance of convenience'?

Until a decade or so ago, although the test was not uniformly so
stated, judges appeared to be agreed that on the first point the
plaintiff had to prove a *'prima facie* case', or 'a probability' as to his
legal rights, though the proof that those rights had been infringed
was sometimes put at a slightly lower level. A *prima facie* case was
generally agreed to be 'an essential prelude to the granting of
interlocutory relief'.[47] Lord Upjohn himself, no slender authority
upon such matters, thought it 'clear' that a claimant 'seeking an
interlocutory injunction must establish a prima facie case of some
breach of duty by the (defendant) to him'.[48] This is hardly an
unreasonable limit to set upon the granting of an order which
restrains the defendant from doing what he claims is lawful. But in
the *Ethicon* case, 1975, the Law Lords changed all that. In an
action concerning a patent, Lord Diplock declared there was 'no
such rule' as the *prima facie* or any other similar test. It led to
'confusion'; the court must not try to resolve conflicts of evidence
at the interlocutory stage, involving itself in 'difficult questions of
law'; that was for the trial. But 'the court ... must ... be satisfied
that the claim is not frivolous or vexatious; in other words, that
there is a serious question to be tried'.[49]

This test – *'Is there a serious question to be tried?'* – was thus
brought into English law by 'judicial legislation of quite
exceptional importance.'[50] It has been dominant ever since, and
has put the plaintiff into an even safer driving seat. All he needs to
do is prove a serious argument. Led by Lord Denning MR the
Court of Appeal in one Division put up spirited resistance to the
new test, only to retreat in another, ultimately to surrender to
Lord Diplock's initiative.[51] Apart from a few areas where special
rules may still apply (such as injunctions to restrain a winding-up
petition) the *Ethicon* test has swept the board – except, in formal
terms, in Scotland. The decision, said Lord Fraser in 1979,

does not apply to Scotland ... [where] the court is in use to have
regard to the relative strength of the cases put forward in averment
and argument by each party at the interlocutory stage as one of the
many factors that go to make up the balance of convenience.

Whether the pursuer or the defender was 'likely to succeed' was part, in Scotland, of the balance of convenience.[52] But in England, the 'strength of the parties' cases' is now either excluded or reduced to a residual place in the assessment of balance of convenience. As Lord Scarman put it, the employer under such rules would in most cases have little difficulty in showing that the *status quo* should be preserved until full trial, and the 'trade union's bargaining counter would disappear'. Despite that the old 'prima facie test' rapidly gave way to the issue whether there is 'a serious question to be argued'.[53]

Parliament's Response to Ethicon *and Section 17(2)*

At the very time *Ethicon* was decided, an Employment Bill happened to be before parliament. This was almost a test-tube experiment on what parliament could really do. It was apparent that the judicial legislation in *Ethicon* made labour injunctions even more difficult for unions to defend. The TUC therefore approached the Labour government to insert a clause in the Bill to curb the practice. But while the Employment Secretary, as the present writer can testify, was willing to help, the Law Officers put up what can only be described as a very straight bat. The Attorney General doubted whether 'adverse consequences' could flow from the *Ethicon* decision for trade unions; we needed more 'experience' of its application; and the TUC's draft clause, which attempted to restore the *prima facie case* rule, could not be accepted. Eventually the Attorney-General agreed to speak to the Lord Chancellor. After that, with little further consultation, the parliamentary draftsman slipped a very different clause into the Bill. It became s. 17(2) of TULRA, 1974.[54]

The Temple – Labour government or no Labour government – believed it had hit the TUC for six, and it was right. There was a feeling in the legal establishment that such interference with discretionary remedies was partial, dangerous, even presumptuous. The occasion illustrated how difficult is the task of a Secretary of State for Employment who appreciates that there is a need to change a general rule of common law or procedure for the purposes of labour law. As often as not he will find ranged against him not only his political opponents in the House but (much more important) also the Lord Chancellor and the Attorney General in his own Cabinet and (more important still) the officials in their departments. The new section 17(2) was manifestly inadequate; but its effect was not improved by the predominant judicial reception. The section began: 'It is thereby *declared* for the avoidance of doubt ...' That mistaken drafting by itself was enough for judges like Lord Diplock to decide that it was no more than 'a reminder addressed by parliament to English judges' to consider the realities in exercising discretion, as they did anyway. A declaratory section is thought not to intend to change the law. The intention of the TUC and of the Secretary of State had been to change the law in *Ethicon*. Further, the section 'declared' that where in interlocutory applications the defendant claimed to have a defence because he had acted in contemplation or furtherance of a trade dispute, then in exercising its discretion the court must '... have regard to the likelihood of that party's succeeding at the trial of the action in establishing the matter or matters which would afford a defence to the action'. This meant it was only one factor, not a determining factor, to which the court should 'have regard'. And finally, s. 17(3) declared: 'Subsection (2) above shall not extend to Scotland'.

The judgments of 1979-80[55] and what followed on the new subsection can be understood only in the context of a struggle by the majority of judges to protect their discretion unimpaired. One or two of them, like Lord Scarman, were willing to see it as restoring 'the old law' by adding a third requirement: the judge should ask: 1. has the plaintiff shown a serious case to argue; 2. where is the balance of convenience?; 3. if the defendant relies on a trade dispute immunity, what is his likelihood of success? But Lord Diplock, and the majority of judges, treated the question of 'likelihood of a defence' as something to be 'put into the balance of convenience', just one more 'practical reality' that the judge must 'in weighing the respective risks' of injustice, consider in exercising his discretion. It was 'prudent' of the draftsman to remind the court to consider that likelihood; but it was not a 'paramount' factor. What is more, s. 17(2) did not apply to Scotland: 'Parliament cannot be taken to have intended that radically different criteria should be applied to English and Scots Courts.'[56]

Whether or not Lord Diplock's own formulation is the same as Scots law – it appears, in truth, not to be quite the same because it fails to give the strength of the defendant's case an adequately prominent position – what is clear is his reassertion that judicial discretion is trammelled only by a 'reminder' to have regard to 'reality', a step hardly worth parliamentary time. Moreover, whatever their differences over s. 17(2), Lords Diplock and Scarman joined hands with Lord Fraser in asserting that, even where the defendant showed that he *was* likely to succeed in his defence, the court still had a discretion to grant an interlocutory injunction in 'the public interest'. So, even if a union appears likely on an interim view to be acting lawfully, an injunction can be granted to a plaintiff who finds a point to argue that is not frivolous in a case

where the consequences to the employer or to third parties or the public or perhaps the nation itself may be so disastrous that the injunction ought to be [granted] unless there is a high degree of probability that the defence will succeed.[57]

The judges determine the public interest. This is, once again, judges' territory. Parliament is something of a trespasser.

Yet the persistent law student might still object that the trouble in this case was surely caused by the draftsman: by his unclear language, by his error in making s. 17(2) declaratory 'for the avoidance of doubt', by his muddying the border between England and Scotland. A clearly worded section could sort it all out, if parliament were really determined. Again the answer is not so simple. It is the end, as well as the means, which creates difficulty. What is it exactly that parliament wants to do? It cannot abolish judicial discretion altogether in such cases, at least not without declaring that in a trade dispute case one side or the other should always win in interlocutory proceedings. And even then, the designation of which 'side' is which in a particular case (say between two unions, or a union and breakaway members, or workers and two different employing interests) must be made by the court. Parliament's difficulty is manifest. And anyone who has ever attempted to raise these matters in one or other House at Westminster knows that before two minutes have passed he will be the target of conventional wrath for daring to 'criticise the judges'. They must be 'trusted'; for they *are* discretion personified in our highly personalised system of justice.

The Balance of Judicial Convenience

So far we have not fully identified the size of the real problem. The 'balance of convenience' or weighing of the 'risks of injustice' to one party and to the other before deciding whether to grant an injunction are phrases cloaking discretion in Protean forms. Grasp one layer and a dozen more slip away beneath you. Take, for instance, Hoffman J who laid it on the line when he granted a mandatory injunction in 1986. He followed the *Ethicon* decision; but he understood that Lord Diplock was not intending (as indeed he had said) to 'fetter the court's discretion by laying down any rules which would have the effect of limiting the flexibility of the remedy'. He allowed himself to weigh the 'qualitative' as well as the quantitative considerations in the risks of injustice to each side.[58] So too, the Court of Appeal in 1987 put all its eggs into the 'balance of convenience' basket, granting interlocutory orders where it appeared that the acts threatened might not be unlawful, leading litigants a year later even to argue (though unsuccessfully) that proof of damage is enough even if no wrongdoing can be seriously argued.[59] We can best appreciate what all this means in labour injunction cases by looking at eight moments in the interlocutory process.

i Notice

We have already seen that normal rules about notice or issue of the writ are regularly put aside in cases of 'urgency' (on the word of the plaintiff). The practice of making *ex parte* applications in what is manifestly a trade dispute, notwithstanding s. 17(1) of the 1974 Act, continues to militate against trade union defendants. This is a feature of practice which scarcely appears in the law reports at all but which dominates the procedures from which trade unions and their officials suffer regularly.

ii Mandatory Orders

Secondly, the presumption that only in 'rare cases' should mandatory injunctions be granted 'in the delicate mechanism of industrial disputes – and industrial negotiations',[60] often cited where the defendant is not a trade union, is rarely, if ever, applied to the full when the motion is against a union, not because the precept is broken but because the prospect of damage to the employer causes the court to find in its discretion that the case is sufficiently rare. Indeed, mandatory elements are common in the orders made in those proceedings, such as the injunction ordering the AEU to convene meetings and approve an election in 1976 (though there was 'no precedent' for such an order) and ordering the Yorkshire NUM in 1984 to hold elections (though it was later discovered the court had hastily fixed upon posts that were not vacant).[61]

iii Evidence

Next, the evidence in interlocutory proceedings is all on affidavit. It can therefore contain statements based on belief, not on the witnesses' knowledge. The grounds of the belief should be stated; but the *Supreme Court Practice* confirms these 'are frequently not stated'.[62] Cross-examination is therefore imperative. In other types of injunction proceedings the Court of Appeal has been willing to subject parties to cross-examination on their affidavits, though some judges are cautious where the plaintiff obtains an *ex parte* order.[63] And the court may, it seems, give leave for cross-examination on interlocutory applications, certainly in *inter partes* proceedings. Yet no case for a labour injunction is reported or known where a deponent was ever cross-examined. The reason is in practice well known. Experienced counsel do not make applications in such cases for fear of losing credit with the judge about to exercise his discretion. Anyone who has seen the procedure understands why they take that view. The plaintiff has usually had weeks to prepare those affidavits to make maximum impact on the court, whereas the union will have had a few days or hours to prepare its case, often searching for busy officials all over the country. Cross-examination should in these circumstances be normal procedure. It is not.

iv Appeals
Fourthly, the function of the appellate court is initially that of review. The modern rule is that it may not replace the discretion of the trial judge (though only fifty years ago it was stated in different terms). Yet appellate courts regularly do interpose their own discretion in labour injunction cases, either because it says the judge misunderstood the law or the evidence or an inference from the facts, or because of new evidence let in on the appeal, or because of a 'change of circumstances', or because the judge's decision was 'so aberrant that it must be set aside on the ground that no judge regardful of his duty to act judicially could have reached it'.[64] The last is, at any rate, a candid acceptance of fallibility of the judiciary in exercising discretion. The practice of denying a power to upset discretion below whilst exercising it in so many exceptional circumstances is especially objectionable in trade dispute cases where appellate judges rewrite the industrial facts in the light of new evidence introduced by the employer, as in the *Mercury Communications* case 1984. The union complained that the new material which had been let in was being seen out of context; yet the fact that it was not produced in the court below led the Court of Appeal to cast suspicion on the union for not referring to it earlier.

v Damages
An established guideline of equity on the balance of convenience is the principle that where damages would be an adequate remedy for the plaintiff and, as it was put in 1984, 'the defendant would be in a financial position to pay the damages,' no interlocutory injunction should be granted.[65] In that case, shareholders in a company injured by the wrong-doing of the Milk Marketing Board were told damages was all they could have. The prospect of greater loss increases the chance of an injunction; loss easily compensated goes the other way. Where the allegation is of irreparable loss to the employer, the court may even grant an order banning an experienced employee from working for a rival.[66]

It is difficult to find any decision where this principle has been applied in favour of trade union defendants. That is not because all plaintiffs are large corporations alleging irreparable loss, though many are. Both Megarry VC and Mervyn Davies J swept the principle aside in judgments given in favour of individual miners against the miners' unions during the 1984 strike. The former abruptly dismissed the test; the latter asserted that the plaintiffs needed 'an injunction to protect them, not damages for loss'.[67] If that broad equitable principle were to be used generally, the refusal of English judges to reinstate a worker unfairly dismissed by way of an injunction (a remedy they will employ, even in the modern decisions, only in those cases where the 'confidence' of the employer still subsists in the worker) would be inexplicable.[68] What the worker wants is not damages for loss but the protection of his job. The practice is otherwise. No injunction will issue. Courts do grant injunctions to union members against their trade unions where damages might, on normal principles, be thought adequate. But the dismissed employee can expect no such general remedy. The 'adequacy' of damages for the ordinary worker suffering 'wrongful' dismissal is part of the legal sustenance of the employer's proprietary power. The roots of that structure still lie in the law of 'master and servant', even in part in the law before 1875 when the breach of the contract of service was also a crime for which the servant could, but the master could not, be imprisoned.

A special problem arose in the substantive law on unions. The 1982 legislation made the union available as a defendant in tort actions reversing the protection first given in 1906 – the most significant change in labour law of the last decade. But the same Act recognised the problem set by the House of Lords in the *Taff Vale* decision in 1901 when it made the unincorporated union sufficiently corporate to be sued (to which parliament had responded in 1906) by restricting the amount of damages recoverable against a union in tort. This limit, however, was used by judges in the Court of Appeal in 1984 to *expand* liability to injunctions.[69] Where the plaintiff employer alleged irreparable loss as the likely result of the strike, the judges could not see how the damages could be adequate when the loss he alleged he was going to suffer might exceed the limit. A protection in damages inserted by parliament became, in the hands of the court, a widened vulnerability to the discretionary injunction. It is little wonder that union officials sometimes approach the law courts feeling wigs-they-win, robes-we-lose.

Some judges have gone even further. One union general secretary who had called out his printer members on a political 'day of action' was liable in tort for inducing the breach of their employment contracts; that was clear as no immunity has ever existed for 'political' strikes. But he argued that the employer newspapers would lose only one day's issue. That could and would, he offered, be compensated in damages. Griffith J rejected the plea. Whether or not the damages would be adequate, the court would not provide a 'licence to commit an unlawful act against the plaintiffs because the defendants can afford to pay damages.'[70] This was a curious echo of the ancient Chancery objections to Lord Cairns' Act and shows how directly a penal element, rarely found elsewhere, can creep into trade union injunction cases. One may compare Lord Diplock's maxim that if the national interest requires new laws to restrain 'industrial muscle', that 'effectively as well as constitutionally, can only be done by parliament, not by the judges'. Whence did Griffith J derive his power to set aside the principle about damages? The traditional answer is that it was not new law at all; it was part of his inherent discretion, whereby he was entitled to have regard to *his* concept of the 'public interest'.

Before leaving issues of damages, we may note the requirement of the plaintiff's 'undertaking'. Except where proceedings are brought by the Attorney-General on behalf of the Crown to restrain illegal acts, an interlocutory injunction will invariably be granted only on condition that the plaintiff undertakes that he will compensate the defendant in damages for loss suffered in consequence of it, if it turns out that the judge should not have granted it.[71] In some types of case this device can be effective. In industrial disputes it is normally useless to a defendant union. Even if a full trial takes place, that may be months even years later; and a decision that the initial injunction should not have been granted will not mean that the union or the workers involved can prove 'damage' known to the law. A claim for the better wages or safer conditions lost by reason of the abstention from collective pressure on the employer enforced by the temporary injunction would be laughed out of court.

vi Procedure and Reality

A similar question emerges from the use made by the judges of the principle of 'reality', that is to say, the fact that the labour injunction expressed to be temporary normally has more than interim effects. In 1979 Lord Diplock remarked that trade dispute cases were unusual, even 'unique'. The court should pay regard to the realities: to the fact that an injunction usually had the practical effect of disposing of the action, that industrial action was part of wider negotiations and that the union needed to strike while the iron was hot.[72]

This at least recognised that in most industrial cases, the employer or third party, whilst suing in form for an interim remedy until trial, is in reality seeking the one remedy he wants – the interlocutory injunction to stop the strike. Frequently, no trial ever takes place, and all the parties know it will not take place. Even if there is a trial, it will be months or years later, in a changed industrial relations situation.[73] Yet judges maintain the pretence – it is little more – of speaking in conditional terms, granting an injunction saying: 'The union may succeed at the trial but if it does it will have been a close run thing.'[74] The recognition of 'the realities', however, has led to no change. On the contrary, by 1984 Lord Diplock explained his statement away by saying it no longer applied, because the trade union itself (not just union officials) could after the Act of 1982 be sued for damages at trial and that, therefore, allowed an injunction to be granted not less, but more easily.[75]

In this setting, the Employment Act 1988 is of some significance.

In case there were any doubt about the High Court's jurisdiction to grant interlocutory injunctions against unions to dissident members or to employers, section 23 reaffirms the court's jurisdiction to grant such orders, for example in respect of contraventions of the duty to hold a ballot on industrial action (even where there is no tort committed), a failure to provide accounting records back over six years, or a failure to hold postal ballots in elections. The scope of the labour injunction is being gradually extended from a remedy for torts which no longer enjoy trade dispute immunity to the central remedy for enforcing a tight legislative code enfolding also the internal affairs of trade unions.

vii Finality

An interlocutory injunction should not be granted if its effect would be to determine finally the rights of the parties. Thus, an injunction was refused to one of two competing factions of shareholders in a take-over, because it would have given them control of the company board, settled the issues at the shareholders' meeting, and so stopped the defendants having their rights determined at a full trial. But when South Wales miners raised the same argument against an injunction to stop picketing, Scott J held that it did not apply. True, the case was 'unlikely' ever to go to trial but injunctions were still 'necessary to protect the plaintiffs' rights'.[76] The union could still come to the trial (one day) to contest the limit put on the right to picket *ad interim*. As we have seen, the interlocutory order is in industrial reality the final order in most labour disputes; but since it does not in formal terms decide final rights, here it is granted.

Other discretionary remedies parallel to the injunction have been expanded in trade union cases, not merely the use of receivership in the miners strike (a remedy also in the discretion of the court, though some novel features there too have emerged)[77] but also the remedy of declaration. This remedy is a declaration of the final rights of the parties. The normal rule has long been that a court cannot grant it in interlocutory cases; for if it did, and the defendant later won at trial, the court would presumably then have to 'undeclare' the rights retroactively. As Lord Upjohn observed in 1962, 'I simply cannot understand how there can be such an animal ... as an interim declaratory order, which does not finally declare the rights of the parties ... (one) only meant to preserve the status quo.'[78] But in the very first major case against the Nottinghamshire NUM in 1984 Megarry VC, in interlocutory proceedings and in the absence of the five defendants, was prepared 'after some hesitation' to make a *final* declaration of rights in favour of dissident miners, declaring invalid and 'void' acts done, and resolutions passed, by the union contrary to an earlier order. To grant yet another injunction would put the plaintiff to the task of returning to enforce it by contempt proceedings.[79] No doubt such decisions must be assessed in the 'climate of opinion' at the time. That does not make them any more defensible in principle.

viii The Plaintiff's Standing

It was once a principle that a member of an association, before coming to the court, should exhaust his 'domestic remedies' under the society's rules, at least where they imposed an obligation on him so to do.[80] By 1970 the courts had decided that they had a discretion to decide cases of discipline or expulsion of a member, whether or not he had exhausted his internal remedies and whatever the rules said.[81] Later they claimed the right to decide upon the propriety of such discipline in advance of the relevant union bodies' even meeting.[82] It is true that very recently some judges have drawn back, refusing an injunction for example to restrain the NUJ from disciplining a journalist who went to work at Wapping even though he appeared to raise a serious question to be tried, and have begun once more to insist that the 'appeals and internal machinery for resolving disputes in unions' must be followed before litigation is begun.[83] It is impossible to know whether these last decisions are a new summer of judicial 'abstention' or merely a few stray swallows.

There has been great variation, too, in the application of the maxim that a plaintiff will be denied equitable remedies if he comes, in the words of the old equitable maxim, without 'clean hands'. Although lack of manual cleanliness here normally requires a 'wrong-doing' in the legal sense, the authorities disclose instances of 'unconscionable' conduct being sufficient.[84] But no case is reported of an employer being refused an injunction by reason of his unclean hands. In the Wapping pickets' case the judge rejected the proposition that what some people would regard as the 'morally reprehensible' conduct of News International (in pretending to plan a new paper at Wapping) was an answer to an injunction for tortious conduct by dismissed workers and their union.[85] Such cases show the distance between equitable concepts and even modest concepts of industrial justice.

Contempt of Court

It has to be remembered that these illustrations of the ambit of judicial discretion are backed by the great, and again discretionary, power of the English High Court judge over a defendant found to be in breach of any order, and therefore to be in 'contempt of court'. Any wilful act which constitutes a failure to obey the order of the court in civil proceedings constitutes contempt. The judge can impose penalties upon the defendant – the same judge who made the order – either a fine or imprisonment (up to two years)[86] or, in the case of a company or trade union, sequestration of part or all of its property.[87] In industrial cases, punishment for contempt of court can backfire, making the union officials heroes suffering for the cause. In 1981 in order to avoid this 'martyrdom' problem and the risk that imprisonment of union officials may harden the attitude of members – as it has done in disputes all over the world – it was enacted that fines for contempt should be enforced as civil debts by the Queens' Remembrancer, thus putting prison for individuals as far away as possible. That policy was congruent, as we shall see, with judicial thinking in the era. An understanding of the interlocutory labour injunction is impossible without some inquiry into these remedies for contempt of court. For it is the court's wide power to punish for 'contempt' which makes the interlocutory injunction so effective.

a Contempt – A Necessary Fetish?

Common lawyers tend to take for granted these contempt powers of the High Court. It is therefore instructive to note that only a few miles from England civil justice is administered without a parallel concept. Take the equivalent of interlocutory labour injunctions in France. On 30 July 1987 the court at Creteil in interlocutory proceedings (the *juge des referés*, acting in his interlocutory jurisdiction under Article 809 of the *Code de Procedure Civile*) declared a threat to strike by the union of Air Inter pilots to be unreasonable and illegal – a rather new doctrine of uncertain ambit sitting uneasily with the constitutional right to strike. The trade unions protested, but the decision, based on a 'creative' precedent by the *Cour de Cassation* in 1986,[88] did not – even before its subsequent reversal on appeal – cause quite the stir it might have done here. The union was in a quite different situation than that which faced the British National Union of Seamen a few months later when it was held to be in contempt of court in seeking to ballot all its members after an injunction banning a strike call to some of them. One of the reasons was that, even if the pilots' union had not respected the judgment and pursued the strike notice (which it did not do), the court itself would have had no powers to punish it in the English manner. For the classic French doctrine is that, save for rare exceptions, the plaintiff, not the court, has the role of enforcing a civil judgment.[89] Where the defendant fails to respect a civil order, it is – especially in interlocutory proceedings – up to the plaintiff to demand payment of an *astreinte*, a sum payable to the plaintiff (not to the court). The *astreinte* may be either a fixed sum or (more usual in interim proceedings) an indefinite or 'provisional' amount. Although it is true that a civil court may pronounce an *astreinte* of its own motion, application by the plaintiff is essential before the penalty is actually 'liquidated' and enforced.

The plaintiff can, therefore, waive enforcement if the dispute is settled without impropriety or risk of further punishment to the defendant. The *astreinte* is calculated at so much per day of non-compliance and is enforced as a *peine privée*: 'a monetary sanction designed to enforce indirectly the court's decisions'.[90] The law of 1972 recognised that the courts make such orders to 'ensure compliance with their decisions'.[91] It is also possible for an appellate court to impose an *astreinte*, or to reduce one already imposed; but if the appeal court reduces an *astreinte*, the plaintiff must pay the difference back to the defendant. The tradition that it is not the job of the state through its courts to enforce or to profit from the enforcement of civil obligations, is so strong that a proposal in the Bill of 1972 for the Treasury to retain one-half of the money paid was roundly defeated in the Senate and did not become law.[92]

How different is this from the common law concept? What is particularly remarkable to English eyes is a modern system of justice in which judges, no matter how high the court, faced with a defendant who has disobeyed an order in a civil action, do not have power to punish, fine, imprison or sequestrate at their discretion. English lawyers frequently refuse to believe it can be so. Yet in France the orders of the courts are respected. The system of civil justice has not collapsed.

The English High Court judiciary, on the other hand, jealously guards its contempt powers as crucial to its potency. It is 'a great power – a power to imprison a person without trial', said Lord Denning in 1960, 'but it is a necessary power. So necessary, indeed, that until recently the judges exercised it without appeal.'[93] In a mood of eulogy, Dr Mann has called it 'one of the great contributions the common law has made to the civilised behaviour of a large part of the world beyond the Continent of Europe, where the institution is unknown'.[94] Yet, rather like cricket, the French, German, and Italian systems of justice seem to have no need of it.

b Civil and Criminal Contempt

The comparison suggests that the high claims made for the severe powers enjoyed in England by the judiciary should at least be scrutinised. For it is integral to the power of the interlocutory injunction that it is enforced on pain of contempt of court and its concomitant sanctions, whatever happens subsequently in the proceedings. If the defendant breaks the interlocutory order, he is punished even if the final hearing shows him to have been in the right all along, or if the plaintiff abandons the action because he sees he will lose at trial.

The classical law, though, has always distinguished between *criminal* contempt and *civil* contempt.[95] This is a distinction of great importance. A criminal contempt takes place in the face of the court or through some other act which interferes, or tends to interfere, with the administration of justice. A civil contempt is constituted by wilful disobedience to an order of the court in a civil action. It is at once apparent that, by suitable semantic juggling, every civil contempt could be turned into a 'criminal' contempt by extending the meaning of 'interference with the administration of justice' to include breach of a civil order. This the old – and some modern – authorities pointedly refuse to do. In truth, the ancient distinction is fundamental to the maintenance of civil liberties.

Many of the old procedural differences between the two forms of contempt have been abolished by parliament,[96] which also, after the judgment of the European Court of Human Rights, restructured the rules of criminal contempt about 'strict liability' on publications in the Contempt of Court Act 1981. But generally the judges control, and feel entitled to control, the law on contempt. So strong is this instinct that, seven years after the Act of 1981 laid down a maximum sentence of two years imprisonment, a stream of reported cases disclosed that the Court of Appeal is still called upon to invalidate custodial sentences on contemnors for longer, sometimes for indefinite, periods, and occasionally even decisions punishing them twice for the same offence.[97]

In the trade union cases after 1982 fines and sequestration of union assets have largely replaced the imprisonment of officials, mainly to avoid the 'risk that individuals may be moved to seek martyrdom by deliberately ignoring an injunction'.[98] That was the lesson of the dockers' shop stewards in 1972, when they had to be released to their cheering supporters on grounds of public policy without having 'purged' their contempt. Contempt takes many forms. Clearly the union must not give members a 'nod and a wink' when withdrawing instructions to strike in order to comply with an injunction. But other principles have been broadened. The test of vicarious liability, based on the common law notion that the union must not do an act contrary to the order either itself or 'by its servants or agents', has been made more flexible, especially in the extent to which it can be made to discipline its shop stewards to secure compliance.[99] Again the normal rules require precision in the terms of the order disobeyed and strict proof of service on the contemnor personally before an order, especially a mandatory order, can be enforced; yet such rules have been noticeably relaxed in recent decisions against union officials.[100]

More important, judges have in recent years come to deny the very distinction between civil and criminal contempt, especially in labour injunction cases. The first step was to assert that a civil contempt which was wilful and contained 'a measure of contumacy' bore a two-fold character – between the parties the liability was to submit to the judgment but there was also, Cross J said in 1964, 'as between the party in default and the state, a penal or disciplinary jurisdiction ... in the public interest'. In making such changes, they felt the need of no parliamentary approval. When they have wished to do so, they have simply asserted: 'the old distinctions [between civil and criminal contempt] ... do not apply'.[101] But in other cases, mainly not the labour injunction cases, they have upheld the old distinction, speaking of the 'very special field of civil contempt', holding that a breach of a civil order remains civil contempt 'albeit closely connected with criminal proceedings'; for example, questions of hearsay evidence under the Civil Evidence Act 1968, in proceedings between a bank and debtors were determined by rigorous application of the traditional distinction between criminal and civil contempts, which '*Halsbury's Laws of England* faithfully maintains'.[102] Yet it is that very distinction which has been jettisoned increasingly in the labour cases when judges have felt the urge to do so.

If judges were to change the 'old' law relating to defamation or to theft, saying that 'old distinctions' no longer applied, there would be criticism. Reform of such principles has been felt to lie with parliament. Yet little criticism is heard of judicial revision of the rules of punishable contempt. It is territory they have claimed as their own, a claim acknowledged deep in the psyche of the legal system and of the lawyers trained in its ways. Four examples must suffice of the ways in which this is particularly important to the problem of the labour injunction:

i Punishment and Coercion. The case for civil contempt must be proved to a criminal standard of proof, partly because it is said to involve a common law misdemeanour, partly because it can lead to penalties on the defendant, whether by fines, imprisonment, sequestration or receivership of assets.[103] The sanctions now normally bear a 'two-fold character',[104] first the penal element, punishing the contemnor and, secondly – traditionally the primary purpose – the coercion of the contemnor to obey the court.[105] Sequestration is primarily coercive; but it may also have the purpose of seizing property from which a penal fine is paid. A fine is primarily penal, not least because – by a tradition which is perhaps not wholly logical – a third party is permitted to pay it for the contemnor. In criminal contempts, on the other hand, the sanctions are all essentially penal.

In civil contempt it was long thought that fines were inappropriate, just because the central point was the coercion.[106] Gradually, however, judges have developed the notion that they are appropriate for civil contempt cases and some have built on to that base the doctrine that any civil contempt which involves a 'contumacious' disobedience of the court's orders constitutes a contempt of a criminal or quasi-criminal nature.[107] Much more prominence has gradually been given to the 'punishment' of the contemnor, to show people that those who disobeyed the court did so 'at their peril'.[108] The same common law development is found elsewhere. In 1986 the Australian High Court asserted its right to fine for penal purposes for any contempt where the contempt is wilful, as against 'casual, accidental and unintentional' (which contempt can in its nature rarely be) despite persuasive earlier authority to the contrary. Whether in England 'contumacious' civil contempt is now criminal, or in an intermediate category, is uncertain; but things are tending in that direction especially in the cases on trade unions and state secrets, and such contempts are now met with heavy punishment, whatever their exact nomenclature.[109]

ii Criminalisation and Waiver. This gradual criminalisation of civil contempt has far-reaching consequences for civil liberties. Take 'waiver'. It is of course no answer for the union which has already committed contempt by disobedience to an injunction to plead that the industrial dispute has now been settled.[110] So, too, the discontinuance of the original action does not by itself prevent the plaintiff or other parties (such as sequestrators who have taken possession of the defendant's property) from seeking further sanctions against the defendant for a contempt. Precisely that happened in the miners' cases.[111] The rule is so strict that in these cases the defendant does not have even the opportunity to prove that the original order for the injunction was wrong or misguided. But what if the employer and the union have settled *both* the industrial *and* the legal issues, and the former has *waived* any wrongdoing by the latter? The classical rule was that 'a civil contempt can be waived' by the plaintiff.[112] As Lord Diplock said in 1974:

> The order is made at the request and for the benefit of the other party to the civil action ... no sufficient public interest is served by punishing the offender if the only person for whose benefit the order was made chooses not to insist on its performance.[113]

In this, the classical English procedure shares, for all their differences, a conceptual heritage with the civil law in France. Civil actions are for the parties' interests, not the state. The principle is of special importance in industrial relations, for here the parties, union and employer, may well need to live together long after the judgment, unlike the protagonists in a criminal trial or even in a commercial dispute. For similar reasons, in family disputes the courts have allowed the complainant to settle the action and thereby to waive a contempt by the defendant – at any rate unless the Attorney-General appears to assert some over-riding public interest.[114] The notion of waiver has important procedural connotations. In particular in the principle that sanctions for contempt must normally be sought by the plaintiff, as the motive force to set the punitive court wheels in motion.

Gradually, though, some judges have set about unilaterally changing this structure, especially in the industrial cases. In the National Industrial Relations Court the law of contempt was reshaped between 1972 and 1974 by Donaldson P. He held point blank and more than once that 'It is not open to the parties to settle the matter of the contempt.'[115] Other judges in the last two decades have gradually cut down the 'waiver' principle, making it subject to the approval of the court (which 'as a rule would pay attention' to the plaintiff's wishes, but might not).[116] Lord Donaldson MR has also asserted recently that a plaintiff is under a *duty* to report a civil contempt to the court; and, then, that the court can move to punish the contemnor *of its own motion*.[117] That general approach to turn the court into its own policeman and prosecutor was favoured by other judges in cases arising out of the miners' strike (though there was never a lack of plaintiffs on that occasion to move the court). Megarry J, for example, believed the court had power to punish 'clear contempts' in cases where it was 'urgent and imperative', even if the plaintiff did not apply to it. The Attorney General could apply. But he complained that this power too was inadequate. The Attorney-General might be put off if there were 'political overtones'. If an order was 'openly flouted and the administration of justice is being brought into disrespect', the 'present restraint' of the judges should be relaxed so that they could enforce their own orders of their own motion.[118] In such judgments judges have made clear their willingness to use knowledge acquired from the media and to safeguard the law of contempt as their own, changing doctrine. The extension is nothing less than a massive inroad into the rule of law. But no word has been said by parliament.

The equation of civil contempt with criminal contempt was also made three decades ago by Canadian judges. They too started with the concept of 'contumacious' contempt. This led rapidly to a serious deterioration in the relationship between the courts and industrial relations.[119] So far have the courts there become entangled, that they have been sometimes even a primary target for picketing in disputes.[120] Studies of the judicial trends in those judgments demonstrate how easy it is for courts which feel their pride is at stake to mould out of the contempt power a weapon that threatens respect for the law itself.

iii Liability of Third Parties. The criminalisation of civil contempt has significant effects also on the position of third parties. An injunction is normally effective only against those named in it. That is why a new procedure had to be invented to secure repossession of property occupied by unknown squatters or against anonymous persons in a sit-in.[121] It is also the reason why plaintiffs often move for injunctions against 'representative defendants' since all the members of the class represented will then be bound. Traditionally, leave for representative proceedings has not been easily obtained; but in some – though not all – of the recent picketing cases, courts have relaxed the strict rule that persons cannot be represented if they may have different interests or separate defences,[122] as with the injunctions against leaders of Animal Aid and protestors against the dumping of nuclear waste.[123] The variations in applying this rule on representative defendants are significant. The ability to sue the union where it is responsible – either vicariously or through its 'control' over the pickets, as in the Wapping case – has decreased the need to use this method of imposing wider liability in some industrial cases.

But suppose a third party is not named in an injunction against pickets, and is not referred to, even as an 'agent or servant' of a named defendant. He may lawfully picket despite the order. He does not become liable for doing the same act as that envisaged in the order. True, he is liable for contempt if he 'aids or abets' the person enjoined to disobey the order, that is 'if, knowing the terms of the injunction, he wilfully assists the person to whom it was directed to disobey it'.[124] Wilful assistance by a third party of such disobedience has long been held to be an independent contempt of court and been regarded as an interference with the administration of justice. Such instances have therefore been a source for the somewhat confused idea that the third party is guilty of a *criminal* contempt in so doing (even though what he aids or abets is a breach of an order that is civil contempt), though there is also authority for the more logical view that his is a civil contempt, at least if 'contumacy' is not present.[125]

The tendency to criminalise and to extend the scope of both injunction and contempt together now constitutes a marked and dangerous feature in English law. There was a clear tendency of this kind in respect of third parties in the miners' strike litigation. It is true that assistance given to a fund to alleviate hardship among families of striking miners was scrupulously excluded by Scott J from the ambit of contempt as a form of assisting the union to continue to defy court orders.[126] But, rather more important, the TUC was deterred from giving money to a trust fund for the striking miners themselves by threats made by the sequestrators and receiver (who were agents of the court) to treat that as contempt.[127] It preferred to surrender this by no means certain point rather than fight it out in litigation. A more important precedent was established by not taking this issue to the courts.

What is more, in lifting the sequestration order over NUM assets, Nicholls J pointed out that he was aware that other unions had provided general financial assistance during the strike to the NUM (as they had) at a time when it was in contempt. He would not punish them this time. But others should not conclude that 'in the context of another sequestration, they will be treated with similar leniency'. He went on to make even more significant pronouncements: 'Secondly, those who give professional or other advice to a person against whom an injunction has been granted ... must be vigilant to see they are not assisting in a breach of the injunction.' Furthermore, he added: '... those who assist others to take steps intended to thwart orders which it is anticipated that a court may thereafter make should not regard themselves as necessarily unassailable.'[128]

Third parties, in other words, must now *anticipate* what may – one day – be a contempt of an order not yet made. This novel suggestion that advisers or others could be caught by such a wide contempt liability has been rightly challenged. There is not – or there has not previously been – any wrong of 'preparing' for a contempt known to English law.[129] But there are few practitioners who would confidently predict that a court would not act – in its discretion – on this concept now that it has been judicially stated. Its introduction was not unrelated to a certain irritation in some judges in the face of those who were attempting to advise the miners' unions. This interlocks with the expansion of parallel duties for third parties in the face (as there) of a sequestration order or receivership over the contemnor's property. The modern industrial cases have, in truth, greatly widened the third party's duty to co-operate with the sequestrators and the receiver, to disclose, for example, all requested information, however confidential.[130] The tendency in all these judgments has been to increase the obligations of the third party not to take any action favourable to the contemnor. They are more than consistent with the gradual judicial criminalisation of civil contempt and the most important steps have been taken against trade unions.

That is what makes one of the developments in the *Spycatcher* litigation so important. In addition to proceedings against certain newspapers (the *Guardian* and others) for interlocutory injunctions to prevent them publishing confidential information in alleged breach of duty by a former British security service officer – an action which rested upon the civil obligation of confidentiality imposed upon 'anyone else who receives confidential information knowing that it is confidential'[131] – the Attorney-General also brought proceedings against another group of newspapers (the *Independent* and others) which were not parties to the former proceedings. He alleged that their publication of some of that material, knowing of the initial injunction, constituted a (criminal) contempt of court. The Court of Appeal held there was indeed a contempt,[132] not because they had aided and abetted a breach of the first order – the *Independent* had done nothing to assist the *Guardian* to disobey it – but on other grounds. An act, it held, can prejudice the administration of justice if, after interlocutory orders have been made against another party, the defendant, knowing of those orders, destroys or damages the subject matter of the action. Here that was the 'confidentiality of the Wright material pending trial' (which the court intended to see preserved). So too if he 'disables the court from conducting the case in the intended manner'.[133] The court was not deterred by the fact that no English case could be found on which to base that new principle. Indeed, Lord Donaldson MR called for the complete jettisoning of the classification used 'in earlier times' of civil and criminal contempt – which 'now tends to mislead rather than to assist'.[134]

This is the way judges feel able to expand jurisdiction. The court could make orders to preserve the 'subject matter' of the action against all-comers pending trial, something Balcombe LJ noted the Canadian courts had done where in industrial cases injunctions were made against unions or pickets so expressed as to bind the defendants and *all* other persons having notice of the order – a departure from the principles of jurisdiction which Canadian commentators have long criticised severely.[135] This was also the basis of the labour injunctions issued by courts in the United States to be binding against the world – or against 'all persons whomsoever' – the abuse which led to the Norris La Guardia Act of 1932 banning the labour injunction. Frankfurter and Greene said of that kind of injunction:

> The imminent threat of irreparable harm to property, the basis of the Chancellor's restraint upon the persons who actually so threatened, does service against all persons, indefinable and undefined, who might subsequently injure or threaten to injure ... A particular controversy between particular parties – which is the limited sphere of judicial power – is made the occasion for a code of conduct governing the whole community.[136]

In a parallel way English judges began in 1987 to take power to make interlocutory injunctions binding against all the world.

The Court of Appeal was well aware of the likely impact of its doctrine upon labour relations. Lord Donaldson MR gave an example. An order restraining B from picketing A's premises does not make picketing by C unlawful as a contempt of court. But 'if picketing by C would lead to the irreparable collapse of A's business rendering a resolution of his dispute with B impossible or irrelevant, ... there would begin to be an analogy with the present situation'.[137] The likely impact of this doctrine upon the reality of interlocutory procedures for the labour injunction is obvious. First the plaintiff obtains his interlocutory injunction against the union to preserve the *status quo*. Then he gives the order maximum publicity. Picketing or industrial action by any other workers or unions, even if lawful in itself, will be presented as seriously impairing the subject matter of the interlocutory order so as to threaten contempt proceedings. To creeping criminalisation there is now added an oozing expansion of punishable offences. On no part of this development has parliament pronounced. Is it able to do so?

iv Sequestrators and Receivers. Before addressing that question, a word should be added about some other extensions of contempt, this time in the sequestration and receiver cases. The law says, for example, that where a party is in contempt the court will not hear him in those same proceedings except to appeal, contest jurisdiction or purge his contempt.[138] Yet in the miners' cases judges insisted that they had a discretion to refuse to hear the NUM in *different* proceedings from those giving rise to the contempt.[139] Further, the appointment of sequestrators or a receiver, and his subsequent management of them, has always required special care by the judge. For these persons are agents of the court, and in particular of the judge who appointed them. They therefore have direct and private access to the judge to seek his directions and his views. The same judge – by convention, it appears – will hear subsequent stages of the case in court, for example applications to discharge the sequestration or receivership, and in these proceedings the sequestrators or receiver may well appear as a party. In the miners' cases, judges let slip knowledge which they had clearly gained in those private conversations.[140] There is little justification for allowing the judge who speaks privately to the receiver or sequestrator to be the same judge who hears such later proceedings. That is hardly a procedure in which justice will be seen to be done.

Parliament, Injunctions and Contempt

Let us recall that this wide and growing jurisdiction exercised by the English judge in his own court is, in interlocutory cases, an inverted pyramid of penal power. It is built on the tip of the defendant's liability which is in itself a liability proved not fully, not even *prima facie*, but as an arguable point, a 'serious case' to be tried, when he may be told he might still win at the trial (if ever one takes place). As soon as the interlocutory order is made on that standard of proof, precise obedience is required sanctioned by massive deterrents which the defendant ignores at his peril. If he wins at a trial, or even if the plaintiff discontinues the action, he will not recover the fines or costs suffered as punishment, nor will he easily recover from a long period of sequestration of his assets after their return less the deduction of penalties and sequestrators' fees at top City accountants' rates.

We have seen from the history of section 17 of the 1974 Act that the High Court will construe strictly statutory limitations upon the discretionary remedy of the injunction and its associated contempt powers.[141] Not that parliament has ever pushed hard at this cuneated door. If by constitution and training the English judge feels at home with discretionary interlocutory injunctions, his power over contempt of court is his very castle. Those in the common law world to whom we have exported this alleged contribution to civilised law have not always seen it as uniformly beneficial. One authoritative survey in the United States pointed out how the labour injunction is contrary to principle because 'the judicial power has been used prematurely and unfairly to aid one party in a private dispute'.[142] Another writer has pointed out in 1987 how, at the contempt stage, the labour injunction means

> the parties and the court are emotionally focused upon remedial detail while ignoring the merits or demerits, as well as the solution, of the underlying disputes ... if the courts do not become more thoughtful and abstemious in using injunctions, they will once again be brought in widespread disrepute, reminiscent of the 1920s and 1930s.[143]

In Canada, as we saw, the bequest is questioned. So too in Australia:

> So long as the courts persist in applying legal concepts developed in the context of protecting proprietary interests ... to the activities of organized labour, they leave themselves open to charge of at best unconscious, at worst, crude union-bashing.[144]

In face of this tapestry of judicial law-making, one might imagine oneself as a minister (in a government of any political complexion whatever) compiling instructions to the parliamentary draftsman for a Bill with the modest aim of putting some new limits to the 'labour injunction'. Perhaps one could target the *ex parte* application in ways better than s. 171(1) did in 1974. But then could one totally exclude the judges' discretion in case of 'urgency'? It might be possible to amend the procedure (on notice, affidavits, cross-examination, etc.) – though one would be told that this is better done through general Rules of Court. A sterner effort might be made to reverse *Ethicon*, perhaps to require the plaintiff to prove a *prima facie* case. But this, one would be told, was tampering with a general rule that should be the same in all types of proceedings – for all injunctions, not just 'labour injunctions'. And would the judges whose remedies were being restricted not construe even more restrictively whatever substantive limiting factor was chosen for lawful action – 'trade dispute', or whatever it was?[145]

There would be other questions. Would the Bill apply to

Scotland? Would parliament try to pre-empt new developments by inserting, in Lord Reid's famous phrase, 'a provision which would be necessary to achieve their object if the law should go one way but unnecessary if it went the other way'.[146] If so, what clauses would one draft *ex abundanti cautela* (so as to be quite sure)? How could one guess what the judges would do next? Then again, one should consider third parties. Would the Bill have anything to say about liability for knowingly damaging the 'subject matter' of an injunction granted against a different defendant in an industrial dispute? If so, is one led into provisions creating special rules for contempt of court procedure, perhaps requiring that the judge who grants the injunction should not be the judge who hears applications for contempt? Or that a different judge should hear subsequent applications after sequestration? Would one declare – 'for the avoidance of doubt'? – that the court does not have competence to move *proprio motu* (of its own motion) against defendants for contempt? The draftsman will at this point go pale; for he, after all, is a barrister.

Sir Humphrey, your Permanent Secretary, will now point out gently that, while it is clear to *him* that your proposals have merit, with the admirable purpose of avoiding conflict between the courts and the system of industrial relations in the highest interests of the law itself (remembering as he does Lord Devlin's wise words about the law made by the judiciary: 'It is imperative that (their) high powers should not be used except in support of consensus law')[147] even so, will your proposals not be characterised in some quarters (most unfairly, of course) as an attack upon the 'rule of law' or even as a subversive trade union takeover of the constitution? The Prime Minister, who has other things on his mind, may not like that. Nor may the Lord Chancellor and Attorney General. Judges may speak out. After all, when Members of Parliament dared to criticise Lord Donaldson for his handling of a contempt by the AEU in 1973, the Lord Chancellor, Lord Hailsham, called on the public to note their names and alleged there had been 'a gross contempt of the House of Commons'.[148] It might go down badly in your own constituency if you were labelled as a friend of law-breakers or subversives in the tabloids.

Your legal advisers will warn of the great difficulty of legislating on discretionary remedies: each case is different. Parliament may try to fix boundaries to discretion, just as it can fix limits for damages; but the very character of discretionary remedies means, they will say, that one cannot draft clauses that control their application to a particular case when the plaintiff will work on the conscience of the court to show that his circumstances are 'exceptional' or 'urgent'. You might be advised to look at the leading work on *Equitable Remedies*. In all its 628 pages, you will find no discussion of the Trade Union and Labour Relations Act 1974 s. 17, (1) or (2), or indeed any other employment legislation. Nor does the index list 'Strikes', 'Trade Disputes' or 'Labour Injunctions' (though it *does* refer you to 'Senility of Party to Contract' and 'Proprietary Interest as Basis for Granting Injunctions'). More important, while the index of cases extends to 32 pages, there is no index of statutes at all. The author was doing his job; for this is perceived as a subject primarily for judges' law not parliament's law; it is about the 'proper application of equitable principles'.[149] The principles of discretion and, in marked degree, of contempt still rest upon the court's 'inherent jurisdiction', not upon statute; they are in Lord Goff's words 'unfettered by statute'.[150] You will be advised to consider, too, that your Bill, even if it can be drafted and survive a passage through Cabinet and both Houses, will be interpreted by those very judges whose wrath you may have incurred and who may (like Lord Diplock in 1979) strive to see it as little more than a 'reminder' to do what they said they were doing anyway. You will be asked whether it is all worth the candle, especially when the Department may have no more parliamentary time for a few years.

That is the kind of process which is involved in the reality, rather than the theory, of parliamentary control. Such difficulties have contributed to the recent conviction of some that a better solution to problems of the 'labour injunction' might be to remove certain issues, such as those relating to trade disputes from the High Court altogether and have them decided by a different body – not because of any personal judicial 'bias', but because the High Court judiciary is trapped, even if it wished to escape, in a land of procedure and remedies of which only the periphery is normally accessible to parliamentary supervision. Any such solution would lead, of course, to the creation of a separate, autonomous tribunal, perhaps even to some kind of 'labour court'.[151] That may well be an equally hard road to tread with equal, possibly greater, difficulties; but its appearance on the agenda of labour law reform testifies to the peculiar difficulty parliament would confront if it ever seriously attempted to set significant new frontiers to the labour injunction and other discretionary remedies in the High Court. Moreover, behind those remedies stand the massive powers of punishment and coercive sanctions for contempt of court, not known in many European systems of civil jurisprudence but regarded by the English judiciary as crucial and private to its majesty, wielded by the judge in the very same case he has heard before, sometimes after private conversation with those he has appointed to control the contemnor's property, with fierce sentences and seizures imposed in the name of law and order on a party against whom an arguable case was once proved and who may yet – in theory – show at the trial that he is in the right.

Here in the private law of discretionary remedies, where judicial creativity wears the distinguished cloak marked 'old equitable principles', parliament meets material which in real life by its very nature limits what it can do. Of all discretionary remedies, the injunction is the most discretionary. In turn the interlocutory injunction is the strongest remedy anyone can obtain on a weak case. A judge faced with the plaintiff's cry for 'urgent' protection against 'irreparable loss' is in this procedure prone to tell the defendant he may well win at the trial, but until then the *status quo* had better be maintained.

Given all this, must parliament not inevitably leave the interim decision to the discretion, the good sense of the courts? One reason why it should not do so is that the injunction as we know it assumes that all types of social conflict can be governed by the same type of discretion, the same code of equitable principles bequeathed from principles built on property, equally applied to disputes between husband and wife, buyer and seller, worker and employer, employer and union. In a modern society that approach is inadequate. Certainly in industrial disputes where the collective interests of workers are involved, this means that the employer invariably wins, and by winning in court he is helped to win in the plant. When a procedure produces that result there is something wrong, some might say something of a class skew, in its character. There is still more than an echo of Mr Dooley who in the United States at the height of the old 'whomsoever, whatsoever' injunctions spoke for employers when he said: 'I care not who makes the laws in a nation if I can get out an injunction.'[152]

No doubt discretionary equitable remedies are often employed by our judges to prevent great wrongs being done to individuals or groups. What is less noticed – though Mr Dooley spotted it – is that private judicial remedies in industrial disputes constrain not only the strength of workers and their unions but also the public power of parliament itself. We should be candid to our students and to ourselves about this apparent limitation on its real 'sovereignty' and on the subjection of certain types of defendant to a special deformity in the rule of law. It is legitimate and necessary to ask whether these ways of the judiciary should remain unquestioned in our democracy.

This paper has been concerned to evaluate the real difficulties that lie in the path of parliament. Unless they are understood, any attempt at reform will be as unsuccessful as the laws passed in 1974 and 1975. The problem is difficult but it is not insoluble, though the lines of the solution must await another occasion. The failure of parliament in the past to control the discretionary labour injunction only re-emphasises the urgency of devising, when the opportunity arises, some new procedure or jurisdiction to remedy the present injustices of the labour injunction. For, unfashionable though it may be to say so in 1988, those injustices are very real and quite indefensible.

Notes

1. 'The Judge as Lawmaker' (1972) JSPTL 22. See too J.A.G. Griffith, *The Politics of the Judiciary* (1985, 3rd ed.), Chap. 8.
2. Respectively, Lord Reid, *Knuller (Publishing) Ltd.* v. *DPP* [1972] AC 435, 455, and Lord Lane CJ *R.* v. *Galvin* [1987] 2 All E.R. 851, 855.
3. Lord Diplock, *Duport Steels Ltd.* v. *Sirs* [1980] ICR 161, 177.
4. See Sir Roger Ormerod, 'Judicial Discretion' (1987) Current Legal Problems 123, 129.
5. Quoted by D. Meiers in W. Twining, *Legal Theory and Common Law* (1986), p. 129.
6. On the different question of reform of the judiciary generally, see C. Harlow, Chap. 10 in C. Harlow (ed.), *Public Law and Politics* (1986).
7. R. Dworkin, *Law's Empires* (1986), p. 140.
8. See N. Lewis in I. Harden and N. Lewis, *The Noble Lie; The Rule of Law and the British Constitution* (1986), Chap. 2.
9. *EC Commission* v. *UK* [1982] ICR 578 (ECJ); *EC Commission* v. *UK* [1984] ICR 192 (ECJ); *R.* v. *Kirk* [1985] 1 All E.R. 453 (ECJ). An injunction may be obtained to enforce a right directly enforceable in Community law; *Garden Cottage Foods Ltd* v. *Milk Marketing Board* [1984] AC 130 (but damages were there an adequate remedy). Compare the availability of judicial review; *Bourgoin SA* v. *Ministry of Agriculture* [1985] 3 All E.R. 585.
10. See Wedderburn, *The Worker and the Law* (3rd ed. 1986), pp. 681-748; L. Dickens and D. Cockburn in R. Lewis (ed.), *Labour Law in Britain* (1986), pp. 545-55; P. Davies and M. Freedland, *Labour Law: Text and Materials* (2nd ed. 1984), pp. 765-76; J. Bowers and M. Duggan, *The Modern Law of Strikes* (1987), pp. 135-72. For an interesting account of parallel problems in Ireland, see A. Kerr and G. Whyte, *Irish Trade Union Law* (1985), Chap. 11.
11. On the development before and since 1873, see I. Spry, *Equitable Remedies* (3rd ed. 1984), pp. 312-23. 'The Judicature Acts have not altered the principles on which the Court acts in granting injunctions where principles have been established as just and convenient': *Kerr on Injunctions* (6th ed. J. Paterson 1927), p. 6.
12. Especially in the House of Lords, On Second Reading and in Committee speeches were made there on the Supreme Court Bill by the Lord Chancellor, an ex-Lord Chancellor, four Law Lords, two solicitors and a senior barrister; and on the Contempt of Court Bill by the Lord Chancellor, Lord Advocate, two ex-Lord Chancellors, two Law Lords, two ex-Law Lords, four senior barristers, one solicitor, a bishop and three journalists.
13. See s. 31, Supreme Court Act 1981, on judicial review. The Rules Committee itself derives its authority from ss. 84, 85 Supreme Court Act 1981. The 1977 Order (SI No, 1955) was largely based on the Law Commission's Report No. 73 (Cmnd 6407, 1976). On discretion, see Lord Goff in *South Carolina Insurance* v. *Assurantie Maatschappij* [1987] AC 24: *Re Oriental Credit* [1988] 2 WLR 172.
14. R. Ough, *The Mareva Injunction and Anton Piller Orders* (1987): M. Hoyle, *The Mareva Injunction and Related Orders* (1985); *Hanbury and Maudsley's Modern Equity* (12th ed. 1985, J. Martin), pp. 781-9; Spry *Equitable Remedies* (3rd ed. 1984), pp. 491-502, 528-32. The *Mareva* order is now dealt with by s. 37(3) Supreme Court Act 1981.
15. Respectively, *Gulf Oil (GB)* v. *Page* [1987] Ch. 327 (GA): *Church of Scientology of California* v. *Miller, Times*, 23 October 1987 (CA); *Att.-Gen.* v.

190   *Employment Rights in Britain and Europe*

Guardian Newspapers Ltd. [1987] 3 All E.R. 316 (HL); *X* v. *Y* [1987] 1 All E.R. 648.

16. *Supreme Court Practice* (1985) Vol. 1, 0.29/1/2. See generally, *Hanbury and Maudsley Modern Equity* (12th ed., J. Martin, 1985) Chap. 24.

17. Lord Upjohn sets out the principles in *Redland Bricks Ltd* v. *Morris* [1970] AC 652.

18. Hoffman J. in *Films Rover International* v. *Cannon Film Sales* [1986] 3 All E.R. 772, 785.

19. *Patel* v. *Smith (Eziot) Ltd.* [1987] 1 WLR 853 (HL). For Turner LJ see *Att.-Gen.* v. *Sheffield Gas Consumers Co* (1853) 3 De G.M. & G. 304, 320. On cases where the injunction is not in aid of a proprietary right, see Spry *Equitable Remedies* pp. 326-9. The modern injunction retains its powers for the landowner even when it is a delinquent local authority: *Waverley BC* v. *Hilden* [1988] 1 WLR 246 (eviction of gypsies who were 'trespassers' while the council 'sought to enforce its property rights', p. 257).

20. See, e.g., R. Dworkin, *Taking Rights Seriously* (1977), pp. 31-9, 69-70. To ignore the interlocutory process does not take rights seriously enough.

21. *Shelfer* v. *City of London Electric Lighting Co.* [1895] 1 Ch. 287, 315-6, Lindley LJ.

22. F. Frankfurter and N. Green, *The Labor Injunction* (1932), p. 201.

23. See W. Gould, *A Primer of American Labor Law* (1982), Chap 2 and 8.

24. S. Lynd, 'Government Without Rights' 4 Ind. Relns. Law Jo. 483, 486 (1981) on *Boys Markets Inc.* v. *Retail Clerks* 398 US 235 (1970).

25. *Ford Motor Co.* v *AUEF and TGWU* [1969] QB 303; on the cases after the Second World War, see P. Davies and S. Anderman, 'Injunction Procedure in Labour Disputes' (1973) 2 ILJ 213, 219-228; continued on the NIRC (1974) 3 ILJ 30.

26. See *Boston Deep Sea Fisheries* v *TGWU, Times,* 13-21 March and 9 April 1970 (CA); *Aston Transport Ltd.* v. *Cowdrill* (unreported), Foster J, 15 October 1971; *Coopers Road Services* v. *Jones* (unreported) Goulding J, 30 September 1971. In *Hull and Humber Cargo Co.* v. *TGWU Times,* 16 December 1971, Brightman J refused a mandatory injunction, by reason of the plaintiff's delay, but allowed short notice of one day for an *inter partes* motion. Foster J. on the *ex parte* motion in *Torquay Hotel Ltd.* v. *Cousins* [1969] 2 Ch. 606 (CA), stressed the court's discretion not to hear the defendant. See Wedderburn *The Worker and the Law* (1986, 3rd ed.), pp. 687-90.

27. *Clark* v. *Heathfield* [1985] ICR 203, 205 (CA); and (No. 2) [1985] ICR 606, 609.

28. *Bayer* v. *Winter* (No. 2) [1986] 2 All E.R. 43, 46.

29. *Gouriet* v. *UPW* [1978] AC 435, Lord Wilberforce p. 484.

30. *Barretts & Baird (Wholesalers) Ltd.* v. *Institution of Professional Civil Servants* [1987] IRLR 3; B. Simpson (1987) 50 MLR 506; Wedderburn (1987) 16 ILJ 1, 19-21. For a matrimonial *ex parte* injunction granted on a Sunday, see *Re N* (No. 2) [1967] Ch. 512 (husband restrained from taking children abroad; the urgency was apparent). The *ex parte* injunction should be preceded by notice on the previous day with a writ, summons and affidavit: Practice Note [1983] 1 WLR 433. But again there is an exception in cases of 'urgency', which is regularly used in labour injunctions: see Wedderburn, *The Worker and the Law,* p. 687-8; Bowers and Duggan, *The Modern Law of Strikes,* p. 148, who say 'most judges' clerks are very understanding of the need for urgency in strike cases, and the judges are obliging in accommodating parties at short notice', referring to experience of such applications over the weekend and on Christmas Eve.

31. *Ryder* v. *Mills* [1850] Parl. Pap. 67 Sess. 3, ×/11 p. 479.

32. Lord Diplock *NWL* v. *Woods* [1979] ICR 867, 879 (HL).

33. Goff LJ, *Beaverbrook Newspapers* v. *Keys* [1978] ICR 582, 589 (CA).

34. Respectively, Lord Denning MR *PBDS (National Carriers)* v. *Filkins* [1979] IRLR 356 (CA); and for a rare case on the relevance of the unfairness of a dismissal: *Shipside Ruthin* v. *TGWU* [1973] IRLR 244 (Donaldson P., NIRC).

35. *CPR* v. *Gaud* [1949] 2 KB 239 (CA).
36. Lord Denning MR, *Star Sea Transport of Monrovia* v. *Slater* [1978] IRLR 507 (CA).
37. See *Emerald Construction* v. *Lowthian* [1966] 1 WLR 691 (CA); *Daily Mirror Newspapers* v. *Gardner* [1968] 2 QB 762 (CA); *Square Grip Reinforcement* v. *MacDonald* 1966 SLT 232; ibid. (No. 2) 1968 SLT 65 (Ct. Sess.); *Cunard SS* v. *Stacey* [1955] 2 Lloyd's Rep. 247 (CA).
38. F. Davidson, *The Judiciary and the Development of Employment Law* (1984), p. 192.
39. *Thomas* v. *NUM (South Wales)* [1986] Ch. 20; *Mercury Communications Ltd* v. *Scott Garner* [1984] Ch. 37, 93.
40. *Monsanto plc* v. *TGWU* [1985] IRLR 406 (CA).
41. *Financial Times*, 5 February 1988; and see *Sealink Ltd v. NUS*, *Independent*, 5 February 1988; and see S.A. Auerbach (1988) 17 ILJ 227.
42. See Wedderburn, *The Worker and the Law* Chap. 8; and on 'economic duress': *Universe Tankships* v. *ITWF* [1983] 1 AC 366; Wedderburn (1982) 45 MLR 556.
43. See *Torquay Hotel Ltd.* v. *Cousins* [1969] 2 Ch. 106 (CA); *Stratford* v. *Lindley* [1965] AC 269 (HL); *Hadmor Productions* v. *Hamilton* [1983] 1 AC 191 (HL); *Dimbleby and Sons* v. *NUJ* [1984] 1 WLR 427 (HL); *Merkur Island Shipping* v. *Laughton* [1983] 2 AC 570 (HL).
44. Lord Diplock, *Porter* v. *NUJ* [1980] IRLR 404, 406.
45. See e.g. *Meade* v. *Haringey LBC* [1979] ICR (CA); and *Harold Stephen Ltd* v. *PO* [1978] 1 AER 939 (CA). For the earlier period, see *O'Connor (Alan Page) Ltd* v. *Clarke*, *Times*, 21 January and 12 February 1953.
46. Warner J, *Solihull MB* v. *NUT* [1985] IRLR 211, 214. See too *Associated Newspapers Group* v. *Wade* [1979] ICR 664; *Prudential Assurance* v. *Lorenz* (1971) 11 KIR 78; *Porter* v. *NUJ* [1980] IRLR 404 (HL); *Shotton* v. *Hammond*, *Times*, 26 October 1976, Oliver J.
47. *Cavendish House* v. *Cavendish-Woodhouse Ltd.* [1970] RPC 234, 235; see too *Ford Motor Co.* v. *AUEF and TGWU* [1969] 2 QB 303; *Thomson* v. *Deakin* [1952] Ch. 646, 660, 671 ('a prima facie case, or if you will, a strong prima facie case').
48. *Stratford* v. *Lindley* [1965] AC 269, 338. It is true this test was there agreed by counsel; but that concession was made because the legal profession understood this to be the test on earlier authority. The subsequent use by Lord Diplock of this 'concession' to invalidate the test bordered upon the specious.
49. *American Cyanamid Ltd* v. *Ethicon Ltd* [1975] AC 396, 407, hereafter '*Ethicon*'. Note that *Kerr on Injunctions cit.* (1927) treated patent cases (of which *Ethicon* was one) as special in several respects, pp. 307-26.
50. O. Kahn-Freund, *Labour and the Law* (3rd ed. 1983, P. Davies and M. Freedland, eds.), p. 362. Kahn-Freund also expressed the view that if there were no 'violation' of the law, no injunction would be granted; the plaintiff must 'satisfy the court that a breach of contract or trust or a definable tortious act or the violation of a concrete right is threatened': *Labour and the Law*, p. 360. This was an excessively optimistic view on his part even before the *Ethicon* decision.
51. *Fellowes* v. *Fisher* [1976] QB 122; also *Hubbard* v. *Pitt* [1976] QB 142 (Lord Denning M.R., dissenting). See P. Wallington, 'Injunctions and the Right to Demonstrate' [1976] Camb. L.J. 86.
52. *NWL* v. *Woods* [1979] ICR at p. 884. For Lord Scarman, see ibid., p. 889.
53. *Continental Grain Co.* v. *Islamic Republic of Iran Shipping Lines* [1983] 2 Lloyd's Rep 620, 623, *per* Ackner LJ (mandatory injunction).
54. See TUC *Report 1976*, p. 75; Employment Protection Act 1975, Schedule 16 III, para. 6.
55. *NWL* v. *Woods* [1979] ICR at pp. 879-81 (Lord Diplock); pp. 889-90 (Lord Scarman); *BBC* v. *Hearn* [1977] 1 WLR 1004, 1016; Wedderburn (1978) 41 MLR 80; Simpson (1980) 43 MLR 372. See too Clerk and Lindsell, *Torts* (15th ed. 1982, and Fifth Supp. 1987; 16th ed. 1989 forthcoming) para. 15-34.

56. Ibid., pp. 879-82; and see *Duport Steels Ltd.* v. *Sirs* [1980] 1 WLR 142 (HL); *Mercury Communications Ltd* v. *Scott-Garner* [1984] Ch. 37, 82, 92; *Marina Shipping* v. *Laughton* [1982] 2 QB 1127 (CA); *News Group Newspapers* v. *SOGAT* [1986] IRLR 337, 355; *Hadmor Productions* v. *Hamilton* [1983] 1 AC 319, 324-5.

57. *NWL* v. *Woods* [1979] ICR pp. 881-2 (as corrected in *Duport Steels* v. *Sirs* [1980] 1 WLR 142, 147): *Express Newspapers* v. *McShane* [1980] AC 627, 694 (Lord Scarman) 685 (Lord Wilberforce *dubitante*); also *Duport Steels* v. *Sirs* [1980] 1 WLR at p. 166 (Lord Fraser). See too Simpson (1980) 43 MLR 327; Wedderburn ibid. 319; Lord Denning MR in *Beaverbrook Newspapers* v. *Keys* [1978] ICR 582, 586-7; *Star Sea Transport of Monrovia* v. *Slater* [1978] IRLR 507.

58. *Films Rover International Ltd* v. *Cannon Film Sales* [1986] 3 All E.R. 772, 782, 785.

59. *NDLB* v. *Sabah Timber Co.*, *Times*, 30 September 1987 (CA); *Associated Newspapers Ltd.* v. *Insert Media Ltd.* [1988] 1 WLR 509 (Hoffman J; no injunction where merely proof of damage without cause of action); *South Carolina Insurance* v. *Assurantie Maatshappij* [1987] AC 24 (HL).

60. Geoffrey Lane LI, *Stephen (Harold) Ltd* v. *PO* [1978] 1 All E.R. 939, 944.

61. *Shotton* v. *Hammond*, *Times*, 26 October 1976; *Taylor and Foulstone* v. *NUM (Yorkshire Area) and NUM* [1984] IRLR 445 (the case which was the base of the later contempt of court by the national NUM).

62. *Rules of Supreme Court* (1985), p. 619; RSC O. 41 r.5; and (on cross-examination) O. 38 r.2(3).

63. See *House of Spring Gardens Ltd.* v. *Waite* [1985] FSR 173 (CA); and Scott J. in *Bayer* v. *Winter* (No.2) [1986] 2 All E.R. 43, 46. Compare, too, *Re A Company* (No. 001424/1983), *Times*, 21 June, 1984 (contempt).

64. Lord Diplock in *Garden Cottage Foods Ltd* v. *Milk Marketing Board* [1983] 2 All E.R. 770, 772-3; *Hadmor Productions* v. *Hamilton* [1983] 1 AC 319 (HL); *Mercury Communications* v. Scott-Garner [1984] Ch. 37 (CA). On the earlier position, see Ormerod, *cit.* note 4, *supra* pp. 131-4, citing especially Lord Atkin and Lord Wright in *Evans* v. *Bartlam* [1937] AC 473, 480, 484.

65. Lord Diplock in the *Garden Cottage Foods* case, ibid. p. 777 ('there could hardly be a clearer case of damages being an adequate remedy').

66. *Evening Standard Co. Ltd* v. *Henderson* [1987] ICR 588, where Lawton LJ felt the ability of skilled personnel to 'snap their fingers at their old employers' was today a 'most unsatisfactory situation in the world of master and servant': pp. 594-5.

67. *Morris* v. *NUM (Midlands Area)* (unreported) 22 August 1984; *Clarke* v. *Chadburn* (No. 1) (unreported) 25 May 1984; ibid. (No. 2) [1984] IRLR 350.

68. *Powell* v. *Brent LB* [1987] IRLR 466 (CA); *Hughes* v. *Southwark LB* [1988] IRLR 55; *Irani* v. *Southampton & SE Hampshire HA* [1985] IRLR 203; *City and Hackney HA* v. *NUPE* [1985] IRLR 252. *Dietman* v. *Brent LB* [1988] IRLR 299 (CA); *Ali* v. *Southwark LBC* [1988] IRLR 100. See too K. Ewing and A. Grubb, 'The Emergence of a New Labour Injunction?' (1987) 16 ILJ 145, who may be over optimistic about the range of both injunction and judicial review since in many cases the employer will express loss of confidence in the employee. In *Hughes* v. *Southwark LB*, above Taylor J rejected the argument that damages were adequate for social workers in whom the employing authority did retain 'great confidence' but whom it ordered to work in a new area in breach of contract (one with more child abuse cases) by reason of the 'loss of job satisfaction, distress and other factors which are not compensatable at common law'. The result that the area would remain understaffed was a 'public interest' he could not there take into account.

69. Employment Act 1982, s. 15 and s. 16 (limits between £10,000 and £250,000, according to size of union). See May L. in *Mercury Communications* v. Scott-Garner [1984] Ch. 37, on the damages point. Compare *Shipping Company Uniform Inc.* v. *ITWF* [1985] IRLR 71, 76 (Staughton J).

70. Griffiths J, in *Express Newspapers Ltd.* v. *Keys* [1980] IRLR 247, 250; and see Lord Diplock in *Duport Steels Ltd.* v. *Sirs* [1980] ICR 161, 184.

71. I. Spry, *Equitable Remedies*, pp. 464-9; *Att.-Gen.* v. *Wright* [1988] 1 WLR 164.
72. *NWL* v. *Woods* [1979] ICR at pp. 879-81.
73. In *Stratford* v. Lindley [1965] A.C. 269 (HL), the interlocutory injunction was still in force at least four years later: *Stratford* v. *Lindley* (No. 2) [1969] 1 WLR 1547 (CA).
74. Dillon LJ *Mercury Communications* v. *Scott-Garner* [1984] ICR 74, 125.
75. *Dimbleby & Sons* v. *NUJ* [1984] 1 WLR 427, 431-2.
76. *Cayne* v. *Global Natural Resources plc.* [1984] I All E.R. 225 (CA); *Thomas* v. *NUM (South Wales)* [1985] 2 WLR 1081, 1112; [1986] Ch. 20, 68-9; *News Group Newspapers* v. *SOGAT* (No. 2) [1986] ICR 181; cf. *J. Michael Design Ltd.* v. *Cooke* [1987] 2 All E.R. 332; and note 39 above. Lord Denning recognised the problem in the (non-industrial) picketing case of *Hubbard* v. *Pitt* [1976] ICR 308, 320 (diss.).
77. *Clarke* v. Heathfield [1985] ICR 203 (CA); (No. 2) ibid., 606. On the problems in receivership procedure and sequestrations in the trade union cases, see the authoritative review by G. Lightman, 'A Trade Union in Chains' [1987] Current Legal Problems 25. No receivership of a union had previously been ordered (before 1971) by reason of s. 4. Trade Union Act 1871, see Wedderburn, *The Worker and the Law*, pp. 738, 744.
78. *International General Electric Co. of New York* v. *Customs & Excise Commsrs*. [1962] Ch. 784, 789. See S. De Smith *Judicial Review of Administrative Action* (4th ed. 1980, J. Evans), p. 523.
79. *Clarke* v. *Chadburn* [1984] IRLR 350, 352. It must be noted that even the remedy of declaration may be the subject of contempt proceedings if it is defied; see the somewhat anomalous decision in *Webster* v. *Southwark LBC* [1983] QB 698.
80. *White* v. *Kysych* [1951] AC 585, 596 (PC).
81. *Leigh* v. *NUR* [1970] Ch. 326.
82. *Esterman* v. *NALGO* [1974] ICR 620: *Lawler* v. *UPW* [1965] Ch. 712. See Davies and Freedland, *Labour Law: Text and Materials* (1984 2nd ed.), p. 607.
83. Notable swallows are *Longley* v. NUJ IRLR 109 (CA), and *Hamlet* v. *GMBAT* [1986] IRLR 293; and see *Walsh* v. NUPE, *Times* 22 March 1988, CA.
84. See Spry, *Equitable Remedies*, pp. 241, 395-7; *Williams* v. *Roberts* (1850) 8 Ha. 315; *Moody* v. *Cox* [1917] 2 Ch. 71.
85. *News Group International Ltd* v. *SOGAT* (No. 2) [1987] ICR 181, 228-31; and *Loosely* v *NUT* [1988] IRLR 157 (need of dishonesty or sharp practice). Compare *Chappell* v. *Times Newspapers* [1975] 1 WLR 482 (CA) where the worker failed partly because he would not 'do equity'; *Cory Lighterage* v. *TGWU* [1973] ICR 339 (CA); and *Morgan* v. *Fry* [1968] 2 QB 710 (CA), where Lord Denning MR took account of the plaintiffs' being 'troublemakers'.
86. Contempt of Court Act 1981, s. 14(1). On the Queen's Remembrancer, see s. 16(1) (2). On the uncertainties surrounding principles for sentencing for civil contempt, see the caution of Mustill LJ, *Re SA Conversions* (1988) New Law. J.R. 169, CA.
87. Trade Union and Labour Relations Act 1974, s. 2(c). On 'martyrdom', see Wedderburn, *The Worker and the Law*, pp. 56-7, 672, 736, 745. On the *O'Shea affaire* in Australia, see W. Creighton, W. Ford, R. Mitchell, *Labour Law, Materials and Commentary* (1983), pp. 913-5; see too pp. 774-80.
88. See *Le Monde*, 1 August 1987 (Creteil); *Cour Cass.* 4 July 1986, *SNECMA c. Allain*, 1986 *Dr. Soc.*. 75; also Trib. Bobigny, 21 November 1987, *Air Inter c. SNOMAC*, 21 November 1987 (the second interlocutory injunction); rv'sd Cour d'appel, Paris, 27 January 1988, *Dr. Ouvrier* 166 (quashing the Bobigny decision and restricting the Creteil judgment to its special facts). See generally B. Teyssié, *La Semaine Social Lamy*, 374, 7 September 1987, pp. xxiii-xxxix; J.E. Ray, 'La Responsabilité des Syndicats' 1987, *Dr. Soc.* 426-31; J. Pélissier, 'La Grève, liberté très surveillé' 1988 *Dr. Ouvrier* 59; J. Deprez, 'L'Existence de revendications préalables' 1986 *Dr. Soc.* 610 [see below Chapter 10, pp. 286-9, 314-6].

89. C. Hebraud 1972, *Rev. Trim. Droit Civ.* 174. On *astreinte* see the Law of 5 July 1972, art. 7, as amended by the Law of 9 July 1975; G. Couchez *Procedure Civile* (4th ed. 1986) pp. 38-40 (juge des réferés); and J. Jacob (ed.), *Trends in the Enforcement of Non-money Judgments and Orders* (1985), pp. 161-3; also pp. 167-8 on Italy, pp. 254-5 on Holland (and for the English editor's incredulity about a system working without the sanction of contempt of court, pp. 37-9).

90. F. Chabas and P. Jourdain, 'Régime de la Réparation' 1986 *Jur. Chasseur Civile* F. 224-2, p. 3; it is quite separate from damages, p. 18; on appeal courts see p. 21; and see D. Dennis *Encyclopaedie Dalloz de Procedure; Tit. 'Astreinte'.*

91. Art. 5, law of 5 July 1972.

92. For a short account, see M. le Galcher-Baran, *Les Obligations* (5th ed. 1986, ed. P. Level), pp. 134-6.

93. *The Due Process of Law* (1980), p. 9.

94. F.A. Mann, 'Contempt of Court in the House of Lords and the European Court of Human Rights' (1979) 95 LQR 348-9.

95. See *Oswald on Contempt* (3rd ed. 1910); Halsbury *Laws of England* (4th ed.), Vol. 9, p. 2; G. Bowrie and N. Lowe, *Law of Contempt* (2nd ed. 1983), Chap. 1; A. Arlidge and D. Eady, *Law of Contempt* (1982), pp. 33 *et seq.*, C. Harnon, 'Civil and Criminal Contempts' (1962) 25 MLR 179.

96. Mainly in providing a right of appeal in criminal contempt in the Administration of Justice Act 1960, s. 13. The distinction between civil and criminal contempts seems to have originated in the 17th century, and appears not to be recognised in Scotland: *Report of Committee on Contempt of Court* (1974, Cmnd 5794) para. 22.

97. See, for example, *Linnett* v. *Coles* [1987] QB 555 (CA); *Re (A Minor)* [1986] 16 Fam. Law. 187 (CA); *Lamb* v. *Lamb* [1984] 14 Fam. Law. 60 (CA). The limit is set by: s. 14 Contempt of Court Act 1981.

98. *Trade Union Immunities* (1981 Cmmnd 8128) p. 36; see too, Wedderburn, 'Freedom of Association and Philosophies of Labour law' (the 'GCHQ Lecture' for 1988, below Chapter 8).

99. *Heatons Transport Ltd* v. *TGWU* [1973] AC 15 (HL: rules on authority to be read with other union documents and practice); *Express & Star Ltd.* v. *NGA* [1986] ICR 589 (CA: 'nod and wink', using a common law test on servants or agents); *Thomas* v. *NUM (S. Wales)* [1985] IRLR 136, 152; *Howitt Transport* v. *TGWU* [1972] IRLR 93 (union liable for acts even of members: Donaldson P.); *Kent Free Press* v. *NGA* [1987] IRLR 267, 277. Contrast *Therm-A-Stor* v. *Home Insulation* [1982] Com. L.R. 244.

100. *Kent Free Press* v. *NGA* [1987] IRLR 267 (0.45 r.7(2)(3)) requiring service displaced; and r.7(7) introduced in 1962 was held to give the courts a 'discretionary dispensating power', p. 273); *Express Newspapers plc* v. *Mitchell* [1982] IRLR 465 (defendant could not obey order but he could 'have done something'). Compare the approach in *Beeston Shipping* v. *Babanaft International* [1985] 1 All E.R. 923 (CA: strict compliance with rules on notice required); *Phonographic Performance* v. *Tsang, Times*, 17 May 1985 (CA). *Parra* v. *Rones* (1986) 16 Fam. Law. 262 (CA: strict requirement of proof of reasons for committal); *Linkleter* v. *Linkleter, Times*, 12 June 1987 (CA: defective order for committal should be cured only exceptionally); *Wright* v. *Jess* [1987] 1 WLR 1076 (CA: non-recording of dispensation of service excused).

101. See Lawton LJ, *Express and Star* v. *NGA* [1986] ICR at p. 595, approving Cross J, *Phonographic Performance* v. *Amusement Caterers* [1964] Ch. 195, 198-9; *Con-Mech (Engineers)* v. *AUEW* [1973] IRLR 331, and below note 115.

102. Bingham LJ *In Re H., Times*, 1 April 1988; *Savings and Investment Bank v. Gasco Investments* B.V. [1988] 2 WLR 1212, 1227, Purchas LJ, CA. See too, Mustill LJ *Re S.A. Conversions Ltd.* (1988) New Law J.R. 169, 170 (on sentencing in the 'very special field of civil contempt').

103. *Re Bramblevale* [1970] Ch. 128 (CA); *Savings & Investment Bank* v. *Gasso Investments BV* [1988] 2 WLR 1212 (where the CA is firm about the distinction);

Dean v. *Dean* [1987] 1 FLR 517 (CA). The action for contempt, however, is a process quite separate from any prosecution: *Szezepanski* v. *Szezepanski* (1985) 14 Fam. Law. 120 (CA), *Caprice* v. *Boswell* (1986) 16 Fam. Law. 52 (CA).

104. Cross J., *Phonographic Performance Ltd.* v. *Amusement Caterers (Peckham) Ltd.* [1964] Ch. 195, 198-9.

105. Lord Diplock, *Att.-Gen.* v. *Times Newspapers* [1974] AC 273, 308 (HL). See too, R. Kidner, 'Sanctions for Contempt by a Trade Union' (1986) 6 Leg. Studies 18, esp. pp. 27-30; and J. Griffith, *The Politics of the Judiciary* (3rd ed. 1985), pp. 112-8.

106. Arlidge and Eady, *Law of Contempt*, p. 48 ('only in very recent times' have fines been imposed); Wedderburn, *The Worker and the Law*, p. 715, n. 6. The release of the dockers' shop stewards in 1972 without purging their contempt, because the union had been found liable and open to coercion (*Heatons Transport* v. *TGWU* [1973] AC 15) and it was therefore in the public interest to release them, *Times*, 27 July 1972; J. Griffith, *The Politics of the Judiciary* (3rd ed. 1985), pp. 66-7, stretched to the limit the power of the court to release a contemnor when there was no longer any point in coercing him to obey the order. So too, the court may accept he has 'purged' his contempt even where there is no apology: *Read (Transport) Ltd* v. *NUM (S. Wales)*, *Times*, 19 March 1985; and see Lightman, op. cit., note 77, pp. 47-9.

107. *Z Ltd.* v. *A-Z* [1982] QB 558, 579-584 *per* Eveleigh LJ; *TDK Tape Distributors (UK)* v. *Videochoice* [1986] 1 WLR 141, 144.

108. See *James* v *Cliffe*, *Times*, 16 June 1987 (CA; Lawton LJ. *Express & Star* v. *NGA* [1986] ICR pp. 595-6.

109. For Australia, see *Australian Meat Industry Employees Union* v. *Mudginberri Station* (1986) 66 ALR 577; (1988) 6 Int. Lab. L.R. 332 (H.Ct). On the *Mudginberri* case, see M. Pittard (1988) 1 Aust. Jo. Lab. Law 23 ('unions were realising for the first time since the 1960s the full impact that use of existing law [on secondary boycotts] had upon unions', p. 34). Lightman, op. cit., note 77, treats contumacious civil contempt as fully criminal in England (p. 28), but *quaere* whether the courts have finally taken this step. Compare Arlidge and Eady, *Contempt of Court*, pp. 30-48, 72-80.

110. As in *Austin Rover* v. *TASS* [1985] IRLR 162, an incident where the TGWU was fined £200,000 some weeks after the end of the dispute: Wedderburn, *The Worker and the Law*, pp. 77-8.

111. In *Taylor* v. *Foulstone* v. *NUM (Yorkshire Area)* [1984] IRLR 445, the plaintiffs finally discontinued the action long before proceedings about the contempt, sequestration and receivership were completed.

112. RSC. 0.52, note 52/1/2; *Roberts* v. *Albert Bridge Co.* (1873) LR 8 Ch. App. 753; *Anon* (1808) 15 Ves. 173.

113. *Att.-Gen.* v. *Times Newspapers* [1974] AC 273, 307-8; Lord Scarman in *Home Office* v. *Harman* [1983] 1 AC 280, 319 (HL), and Lord Diplock p.307.

114. *Yianni* v. *Yianni* [1966] 1 WLR 120, 124, Cross J.

115. *Heatons Transport* v. *TGWU* [1972] ICR 285, 296, 320; *Con-Mech (Engineers)* v. *AUEW* [1973] IRLR 331; (No. 2) ibid 333; (No. 3) ibid 335; and [1974] IRLR 2, 4; see Wedderburn, 'Contempt of the NIRC' (1974) 37 MLR 187; N. Lewis 'Showdown for NIRC' (1974) 3 ILJ 201. On the NIRC see too *Davenports Brewery* v. *TGWU* [1973] ICR 632, 639; *Howitt Transport* v. *TGWU* [1973] ICR 1, 11; Wedderburn (1973) 36 MLR 226.

116. See Salmon L.J. *Jennison* v. *Baker* [1972] 2 QB 52, 64.

117. *Con-Mech (Engineers)* v. *AUEW* (No. 2) [1973] IRLR, pp. 334-5.

118. *Clarke* v. *Chadburn* [1984] IRLR 350, 353.

119. *Poje* v. *Att-Gen. British Columbia* [1953] 2 DLR 705 (Supt. Ct.); *Re Tilco Plastics Ltd* v. *Skurjat* [1966] 57 DLR (2d) 596, 625; *Skeena Craft* v. *Pulp and Paper Workers* [1971] 17 DLR (3d) 17, 20; *Re Att-Gen. Nova Scotia* v. *Miles* (1971) 15 DLR (3d) 189, 193; and the pioneer study by A. Carrothers, *The Labour Injunction in British Columbia* (1956), pp. 11-23.

120. *Re British Columbia Govt. Employees' Union* [1985] 5 WWR 421.
121. RSC 0.113; *Univ. Essex* v. *Djemal* [1980] 2 All E.R. 742 (CA). On identifying pickets see A. Auerbach, 'Legal Restraint of Picketing' (1987) 16 ILJ 227. On Order 113 and representations, see *Amey Roadstone Corpn.* v. *Purdey* [1986] Current Law Yearbook, para. 2654.
122. RSC 0.15 r. 12. See *EMI* v. *Kudhail* [1985] 11 FSR 36, criticised by Auerbach, op. cit., p. 232
123. *M. Michaels (Furriers)* v. *Askew, Times,* 25 June 1983 (CA); *UK Nirex* v. *Barton, Times,* 14 October 1986; see Auerbach, 'Legal Restraint of Picketing' (1987) 16 ILJ 227, and also (1988) 17 ILJ 46. In the Wapping dispute the judge refused representative proceedings partly because he considered that the branches to be represented were separate trade unions in law within s. 28(1) TULRA 1974: *News Group Newspapers* v. *SOGAT* (No. 2) [1986] ICR 181, 221-5.
124. *Z Ltd* v. *A-Z* [1982] 1 QB 558, *per* Eveleigh LJ p. 578. On the need for *mens rea* and the 'knowledge' of a corporation: ibid, pp. 581-3.
125. *Seaward* v. *Patterson* [1897] 1 Ch. 545, 554; *Scott* v. *Scott* [1913] AC 417, 458, *per* Lord Atkinson (preferring civil contempt); *Z Ltd* v. *A-Z Ltd* [1982] 1 QB pp. 580-1; see G. Lightman, op. cit., n. 77, pp. 27-8; and C. Harnon (1962) 25 MLR pp. 182-4.
126. *Hopkins* v. *NUS* [1985] ICR 268, 276-7.
127. TUC *Report* (1985), pp. 40-62. The plan was put to the receiver and sequestrators who – not surprisingly – threatened to initiate proceedings for contempt if it was undertaken. No court decided the issue, though those same officers would have had access for private consultation with the judge.
128. *Taylor* v. *NUM, Times,* 20 November 1985; Auerbach (1987) 16 ILJ 227, 239.
129. See, Lightman, op. cit., note 77, pp. 40-1, 45-6, arguing that advisers are not liable unless they are contumacious, which appears to be the only view consistent with the authorities before 1985.
130. *Eckman* v. *Midland Bank* [1973] 1 QB 519; *Messenger Newspapers Group* v. *NGA* [1984] ICR 345. Lightman, op. cit., note 77, p. 34, argues persuasively that the duty to co-operate with the receiver is more limited.
131. Lord Templeman *Att.-Gen.* v. *Guardian Newspapers Ltd* [1987] 3 All E.R. 316, 353; Lord Ackner, p. 359 (damages not an adequate remedy: p. 360). For the final judgment in the subsequent action: *Att.-Gen.* v. *Observer* [1988] 3 WLR 776, HL.
132. *Att.-Gen.* v. *Newspaper Publishing* [1987] 3 All E.R. 276; see Donaldson MR, pp. 297-300; Lloyd LJ, pp. 306-309; Balcombe LJ, pp. 311-2. Compare *UK Nirex Ltd* v. *Barton, Times,* 4 October 1986. See note A on p. 197.
133. Ibid. Donaldson MR p. 296; Lloyd LJ, p. 308 and p. 307 ('the destruction, in whole or in part, of the subject matter of the action itself'); Auerbach (1988) 17 ILJ 46.
134. Ibid., p. 294. Balcombe LJ retains the normal classification: pp. 311-4.
135. See *Tilco Plastics Ltd* v. *Skurjet* (1966) 57 DLR (2d) 596; *Catkey Construction* v. *Moran* (1969) 8 DLR (2d) 413. 'A general order of this sort binds people who have no advance knowledge of the proceeding and thus no chance to influence the scope of the order as it might affect them'; H. Arthurs, D. Carter, and H. Glasbeek, *Labour Law and Industrial Relations in Canada* (1981), p. 244. One such injunction in Quebec led to the imprisonment of 40 union leaders: p. 245. These practices 'weakened the respect in which the courts are held by a large segment of society ... where social injustice and class have been imparted to them, whether with or without sufficient reason': K. Swann, 'The Labour Injunction in Alberta' (1976) 9 Alb. L.R. 1, 21. Contrast the approach in *Township of Sandwich West* v. *Bubin Estates* (1987) 30 DLR (4th) 477.
136. *The Labor Injunction* (1930), p. 123. See too, B. Aaron, 'Labor Injunctions in State Courts, II', 50 Va. L. Rev. 1147 (1964); and for a more managerial view, H. Perritt, *Labor Injunctions* (1986).

137. *Att-Gen.* v. *Newspaper Publishing* [1987] 3 All E.R., pp. 301-2.

138. *Hadkinson* v. *Hadkinson* [1951] p. 285 (CA); *Bettinson* v. *Bettinson* [1965] Ch. 465.

139. *Clarke* v. *Heathfield* [1985] ICR 203 (CA); *Clarke* v. *Heathfield* (No. 2) [1985] ICR 606 (Mervyn Davies J). Warner J stated the normal principle in *NUM* v. *NUM (Nottingham Area)* (unreported) 19 December 1984; see Lightman, op. cit., note 77. p. 37.

140. See Lightman, op. cit., note 77, p. 43 (on *Taylor* v. *NUM*, *Times*, 20 November 1985) and p. 48 (Mervyn Davies J, *Clarke* v. *Heathfield*, 11 June 1986).

141. On the further judicial steps in the Seamens' Strike, see Auerbach (1988) 17, ILJ, 227.

142. B. Aaron, op. cit., 50 Va. L. Rev. 1147, 1158 (1964); see too A. Schatzki, 'Some Observations About Standards Applied to Labor Injunction Litigation' 59 Ind. Law. Jo. 565 (1984).

143. Earl Brown 9 Ind. Rel. Law Jo. 497, 502 (1987).

144. Creighton, Ford, Mitchell, op. cit., note 87, p. 779.

145. See Wedderburn, 'The New Politics of Labour Law' in W. McCarthy (ed.), *Trade Unions* (1985, 2nd ed.) pp. 521-30.

146. *Rookes* v. *Barnard* [1964] AC 1129, 1117, on s. 3 (limb 2) Trade Disputes Act 1906, later s. 13(2) TULRA 1974, then repealed by s. 19 Employment Act 1982; see Wedderburn, *The Worker and the Law*, pp. 612-3.

147. *Sunday Times*, 6 August 1972.

148. Griffith, op. cit., note 1, p. 68; Vol. 865 Parl. Deb. HC, cols. 1089-91, 1291-7.

149. Spry, *Equitable Remedies* (3rd ed. 1984), p. ix.

150. Lord Goff, *South Carolina Insurance* v. *Assurantie Maatschappij* [1987] AC 24, 44; C. Forsyth [1988] Camb. L.J. 177; and see *Lee* v. *Walker* [1985] 1 All E.R. 781 (CA).

151. See Wedderburn 'Labour Law – From Here to Autonomy?' (1987) 16 ILJ 1, 22-9; K. Ewing 'The Right to Strike' (1986) 15 ILJ 143; cf. D. Howarth, 'The Autonomy of Labour Law – A Response to Professor Wedderburn' (1988) 17 ILJ 11.

152. M. Dooley, quoted by C. Summers and H. Wellington, *Labor Law Cases and Materials* (1968), p. 168.

[A. On nn. 132-7 above, see now *Att.-Gen.* v. *Times Newspapers* [1991] 2 WLR 994 (HL) upholding, if not widening, the offence as stated by the CA; to nullify the purpose of the main order was an 'interference with the administration of justice'; even the most liberal judgment accepts that contempt may now be committed by a named defendant, an aider or abettor, and also 'gratuitous third parties' (Lord Oliver, p. 1020). The Law Lords expressly discuss the labour law consequences of this last *Spycatcher* judgment.]

8

Freedom of Association and Philosophies of Labour Law: The Thatcher Ideology

The United Kingdom has never had to face that chasm between public and private law which for long denied state and other public servants in so many other countries a place in the realm of collective bargaining. No *Beamte* (still without a right to strike) no *fonctionnaires* or *agents publics* placed under special restriction, no need of special laws, like those in Sweden, 1965, or Italy, 1983, to bring the municipal and state official imperfectly into collective labour law, no claim by the State that its 'sovereignty' is infringed by collective bargaining, found even in the United States.[1] Administrative discipline is of course exercised over such employees, not least in the civil service; but subject to the legal rule that the Crown may 'dismiss at pleasure', that merely parallels the private employer's power to legislate for his workplace – subject to broadly the same laws and, above all, to the power of the employees' collective intervention through a trade union. This unique history, consequential upon the perceptive decision of a frightened ruling class in 1917 to follow the path advocated by the Whitley Committee towards collective consultation in the public sector, and therefore inevitably towards collective bargaining, has made developments in the labour law of the public sector of central importance. Indeed, the attitude of government in Britain towards public sector industrial relations is, in many ways, a touchstone of its labour law policies.

What, then, is the historical significance of 'GCHQ'? Civil servants employed there to work on secret spy communications had long been permitted, indeed encouraged, to join autonomous,

Based on the 'GCHQ Lecture' for 1988 given at the invitation of the First Division Association of Civil Servants, 29 February 1988. First published (1989) 18 Industrial Law Journal 1.

national trade unions. There was a 'well-established practice of consultation', as Lord Fraser put it.[2] On 25 January 1984 'all that was abruptly changed'. Without consultation, the government announced new conditions of service, imposed immediately, 'the effect of which was that they would no longer be permitted to belong to national trade unions.' How will the historian see this ban on union membership? The government claimed that this step, taken, as the ILO was to decide, in breach of the most fundamental Convention on freedom of association, had been taken because of the needs of 'national security' at the communications centre of its security services. It managed to persuade both the Law Lords and European Commission on Human Rights that this reason had motivated and justified its action – despite the breach of what Lord Roskill called the employees' 'legitimate expectation of consultation' with their unions, albeit they were 'in strict theory ... dismissible at will' by their employer the Crown.

Whatever the merits of the spy centre litigation and of the ultimate dismissal in 1988 of those who insisted on maintaining union membership, it is useful to ask how that abolition of freedom of association at GCHQ will be seen in the broad pattern of the policies developed since 1979. Will the historian see its emphasis as more relevant to spy-catching or to union-thrashing? Is it part of the picture identified by one commentator who saw the government 'working towards a time when the unions, at any rate as they are today, have ceased to exist and have become instead, genuine friendly societies, divorced from their present connection with industrial relations'? Their role in wage bargaining now 'meaningless', they should become associations designed 'to offer to their members real opportunities in insurance, health care, mortgages and travel'.[3] In that helpful context, the events of 1984 serve as a focus to contrast two different philosophies in labour law policy – the traditional analysis and a more recent, alternative analysis. After briefly identifying the traditional analysis, we turn to that new analysis and its origins, and to its relationship to the labour legislation of the 1980s.

I The Traditional Analysis

In the beginning, when the word was with Mr (now Lord) Prior, he said introducing the first Employment Bill in 1979: 'Our approach is essentially a pragmatic one.'[4] And the Prime Minister remarked: 'If necessary, we will legislate further.'[5] It was possible to believe that policy involved a pragmatic 'trade union reform', step-by-step, on the evidence of what was thought necessary for a better 'balance' in industrial relations law. The old targets of 'good industrial relations' and reform of collective bargaining seemed to have a place. Above all, Prior himself justified legislation by reference to the analysis of the employment relationship which expressed the central point of consensus within the 'traditional analysis'. He trod that common ground when he said:

> The law should always give full recognition to the inherent weakness of the individual worker *vis-à-vis* his employer, to the need for him to be organised in a union and to the need for his union to have such exceptional liberties as may be necessary to redress the balance.

That was 'fundamental', though he added that this 'privilege' must be 'restricted to what is necessary'.[6] There might be objection to such liberties being thought in this century 'exceptional', but there seemed to be common ground; and strong though the criticism was of what became the 1980 Employment Act, the predominant case made for it appeared at least to accept that workers have a right to effective combination in trade unions because of the very nature of the employment relationship. That view had over the previous century become a national and international norm supporting 'freedom of association' in its employment context. The weakness of the individual worker, wrote Fox, makes the individual agreement for sale of his labour power 'asymmetric', an exchange 'which cannot be gauged by reference to the so-called *contract* of employment'.[7] The individual employee's position of subordination, involving (save in exceptional cases) 'submission' to the command of the employer, is clothed, Kahn-Freund said, by 'that indispensable figment of the legal mind, the contract of employment'.[8] Combination in autonomous organisations is therefore, in a free society, a need and a right for those employed. Britain, the very home of collective bargaining both in the private and the public sector, has done much to export that 'traditional analysis' to the world, not least to the ILO and the other centres of international standards. Some will find unnecessary, even tedious, a rehearsal of such elementary norms. They are recalled because they are relevant to what has happened, far more relevant than theories and debates about 'abstentionism' or 'regulation'.

Some observers, it is true, perceptively detected an 'impetus towards non-unionisation'[9] in the early years after 1979; but the traditional analysis continued to appear in official rhetoric. By 1982 the Secretary of State, Mr Tebbit, spoke of two aims: 'safeguarding the liberty of the individual from the abuse of industrial power' and 'a more balanced framework of industrial relations law'. He added he had 'no quarrel' with the TUC's claim to three basic rights for workers – to combine collectively, to bargain collectively, and to withdraw labour. He went on to comment that he was *not* legislating on 'the internal organisation of trade unions ... this time at any rate'.[10] The plans for 1984 and 1988 were, it is clear, already under discussion.

The blessing given by Prior, however, to the analysis which validates trade unions out of the very nature of the employment relationship becomes more difficult to discover in later ministerial statements. Instead, a different analysis found that its time had come. Its challenge was, moreover, facilitated by the unique historical character of British labour law; and because this alternative analysis has derived great advantage from the idiosyncratic nature and the odd semantics of that legal structure, those must be outlined in order to set the stage.

II Varieties of Labour Laws

When the industrial revolution faced British law with the emergence of modern trade unions, it took one step later paralleled by all the comparable systems in Western Europe, but not a second. The first step was the repeal of penal laws rendering trade unionism illegal, just as in France, 1884, Germany, 1869, Italy, 1889. Britain began the process in 1825, though the Master and Servant Acts making breach of the employment contract a crime were not finally repealed until 1875. Some of the penal provisions were special enactments (like the Combination Acts 1799-1800); many others derived from the ordinary common law. But most of the other comparable European countries took the second step – one which unions in Britain rarely demanded, and have generally believed they could do without – namely, the establishment of 'positive rights' for workers to organise collectively, sometimes with a specific right to bargain (as in Sweden) or to strike (as in the modern French and Italian constitutions).

Whatever the reasons for that crucial divergence,[11] the countries that ended up with constitutional or similar 'positive rights' for trade unions had to take a third step. The rule that workers break their employment contracts by taking industrial action – or, equally important, threaten to break those contracts by explicit or implied threats to strike – had to be changed. Instead, it was necessary to adopt the principle, in some form, that absence from work in industrial action did not break employment contracts but 'suspended' them. So, in France, as long as the employee remains within the constitutional rights to organise and to strike, in particular avoids *faute lourde* (serious misconduct), he or she does not break the employment contract merely by the act of striking. We may note that it has taken many years in such countries for the law to approximate the legal position of the civil servant or other public official – some have even now not done so – but in private law the suspension principle has been a commonplace from Spain to Sweden, the German Federal Republic to Italy.

How different in Britain. Industrial action is invariably a breach of the employment contract, a common law rule as fundamental today as it was in 1800. A threat to strike is invariably a threat to break the contract; the only way out is to give notice to quit and resign from the employment.[12] The employer does not normally sue his striking employees for damages, but he may dismiss the worker for the breach, an unthinkable lawful power in systems with a 'right' to strike. And, of course, he may refuse to pay wages, as the House of Lords has resolutely reaffirmed, even in a go-slow or other action short of a strike: 'If the worker declines to work, the employer need not pay.'[13]

What parliament did provide in Britain, between 1871 and 1906, and modernised in 1974, was protection against a limited range of common law liabilities that made trade union organisation and action illegal. These statutory provisions for industrial liberties came to be called – unhappily – the 'immunities'. The first was contained in the Act which affirmed the lawful status of unions, not by enacting any right to 'freedom of association' but by exempting them from the common law doctrine of 'restraint of trade' (an exemption which even today, in section 2(5) of TULRA 1974, is the basis of our industrial 'freedom of association'). It is often overlooked that lawful trade unionism would be impossible without that protection from the doctrine of restraint of trade.

From 1871 onwards, freedom of association in Britain was created not by rights but by immunities. When it came to industrial action, parliament enacted an 'immunity' in 1906, not for the workers themselves, but for the organisers of strikes, granting protection from liability in a particular range of torts, notably conspiracy and inducing breach of employment contracts. So-called 'immunity' against these liabilities protected union officials in the courts so long as they acted 'in contemplation or furtherance of a trade dispute' (the once golden formula of our labour law). Also, after the *Taff Vale* case had shown – to the surprise of most lawyers at the time – that unions could be struck down by massive awards of damages and costs in civil actions, a more general protection was accorded to unions and their funds against liability in tort. But 'immunities' face a common law which does not stand still. As Lord Donaldson MR has said: 'The common law is a living thing. Its principles may not change but its application conforms to changing circumstances.'[14]

Stripped of mystification this means that from time to time living judges create new liabilities out of older principles. When they do that, the 'immunities' which parliament has enacted for trade disputes many years earlier can be outflanked, as happened to the immunity for inducing breach of employment contract. For some 50 years no one thought of suing union officials for inducing the breach, not of the employment contracts (where the 1906 Act protected), but of the commercial contracts disrupted in the dispute. As the Donovan Report pointed out, no one knows why the earlier immunity was so limited.[15] In the 1960s judges accepted extensions of the tort liability that outflanked it for strikes interfering with commercial contracts.[16] They also created another new liability – dubbed the tort of 'intimidation' – out of the very threat to strike itself.[17] Nothing in the 1906 Act protected either. The legislation of 1974–76, passed to repeal the Industrial Relations Act and, broadly, to restore the traditional structure, therefore revived the earlier trade dispute immunities in a modern form to match the renewed creativity of the common law judges. Parliament provided an immunity in trade disputes for threats to strike and for inducements to break or interfere with commercial, as well as employment, contracts. There was little point in renewing protection for the latter if that protection could be once more outflanked by liability for the former.

As Lord Scarman described it: 'Briefly put, the law now is back to what Parliament had intended when it enacted the Act of 1906 – but stronger and clearer than it was then.'[18] The function of such laws, whatever their form, was to assure some liberty to organise, to bargain and to strike; there was, and is, no other protection against common law liability. Such a view, though, was not representative of the judges. More characteristic was the judgment of Lord Diplock, who saw these trade dispute immunities as 'intrinsically repugnant to anyone who has spent his life in the practice of the law', openly affirming that their effects 'have tended to stick in judicial gorges'.[19] This relationship of the common law judge to industrial liberties which present themselves in his court as exceptions to the 'ordinary law of the land' has long been the curse of British labour and it offered an exceptional opportunity for the new analysis.

III The Alternative Analysis

In the very same year as these judgments, the first government led by Mrs Thatcher was elected. In that year too a leading author of the alternative philosophy completed a major three-volume work, described shortly afterwards by the Prime Minister herself as 'absolutely supreme'.[20] He had already in his earlier work had great influence upon many Cabinet ministers, and he took a very different view of employment and 'freedom of association'. Trade unions enjoy, he claimed, 'unique privileges' in all Western European societies – we should note at the outset that the thesis is not confined to Britain. These privileges can, and do, put governments into a position which 'must before long destroy the whole market order, probably through price controls which accelerating inflation will force governments to impose'.[21]

It had begun to happen in most European countries 'by the 1920s'. But the 'acquisition of privilege has nowhere been as spectacular as in Britain', largely by reason of the Act of 1906. 'The whole basis of our free society is gravely threatened by the powers arrogated by the unions.'[22] In 1980 he added:

> There can be no salvation for Britain until the special privileges granted to the trade unions three-quarters of a century ago are revoked. Average real wages of British workers would undoubtedly be higher and their chances of finding employment better, if the wages paid in different occupations were again determined by the market, and if *all limitations* on the work an individual is allowed to do were removed ... [The] legalised powers of the unions have become the biggest obstacle to raising the living standards of the working class as a whole ... They are the prime source of unemployment. They are the main reason for the decline of the British economy in general.[23]

In 1984, he called for 'a libertarian anti-labour union movement of workers', to combat the trade union 'monopolists'.[24]

These are big claims. The conclusions do not depend upon surveys or evidence to Royal Commissions but upon an avowed discovery of the true nature of industrial society and of 'freedom' itself. Trade unions create a unique form of 'monopoly'; they are always a coercive restraint upon the market. In this they differ from other monopolies, for 'much enterprise monopoly is the result of better performance, while *all* labour monopoly is due to the coercive suppression of competition.' Companies are acceptable as personified aggregations of capital, so long as company management is required to act only 'as trustees for the shareholders', and *not* 'for the public or social interests' – the very concept is rejected. Under these conditions, their role is not harmful because they promote competition.[25] Corporate enterprise fits into the necessary system of 'private ownership and individual decision as to the use of resources'; and even oligopoly, with big companies, is not therefore inconsistent with competitive markets.[26]

The Political Economy of Hayek

This is the voice of Professor Friedrich Hayek. It is not claimed in what follows that his doctrines concerning political economy were the sole determinants of Government policy in the 1980s. Economists will point to Friedman or to Walters, even to Minford; others to Nozick, even to Scruton. What is suggested here is that the pedigree and meaning of the new labour laws of the 1980s can be found in a unique and astonishing manner in the writings of Hayek. His position, elaborated over some forty years, is emphatically not based on arguments of empirical inquiry to set against the traditional analysis or to determine the way to 'good industrial relations'. His is a stance of total and at times bitter opposition to that analysis as a whole, couched in terms of truth and error. Three aspects are particularly relevant.

First, the individual employment contract has no special character; it is but one contract among many, to be governed by common principles of 'freedom of contract' and the general law. The employed person has chosen by his contract to have 'the regular income for which he sells his labour'; he must therefore do 'the bidding of others', in contrast to the 'independent' entrepreneur. The employee's freedom depends on choice between 'a great number and variety of employers', and that can be achieved only in a competitive market. The pressures of organised groups such as trade unions on that market create distortions and must therefore be ended. Cyclical unemployment can be reduced by 'appropriate monetary policy'. The state may provide a bare 'uniform minimum' for those in distress on proof of 'need', but no more.[27]

'[The] real exploiters in our present society are not egotistic capitalists or entrepreneurs, and in fact not separate individuals, but organisations which derive their power from the moral support of collective action and the feeling of group loyalty.' It is the *group*, by its collective pressure, which is noxious and individual interests which count and must be protected. The call for 'freedom of organisation' ('hallowed by its use as a battle cry' over the years, especially by 'labour unions') carries overtones that are 'in conflict with the reign of law on which a free society rests'. This is why the powers of such groups 'will probably require limitations by general rules of law far more narrow than those it has been found necessary to impose by law on the actions of private individuals'.[28] It is not a question of balance, of organisations being too strong or too weak, or of the vulnerability of individual employees. Such group organisation is in itself a threat to law and to society. The very term 'freedom of association' must be reinterpreted because 'this term has in fact lost its meaning and the real issue has become the freedom of the individual to join or not to join a union' – a proposition supported by a rare (and inaccurate) empirical assertion that the 'sole cause' of industrial disputes is 'as often as not' an attempt by unions to 'force unwilling workers to join'.[29]

Secondly, it follows that unions must be stripped of their legal 'privileges'. A privilege is a 'right conferred by special decree (*privi-legium*) [*sic*] which others do not have and not for an objective possibility which circumstances offer to some but not to others'. The privileges that create 'special rules for particular classes' (like workers or the poor) are the worst examples.[30] The common law rule of 'restraint of trade' must be generally enforced so as no longer to legitimise the 'organisational activities' of unions,[31] For they 'coerce' individual workers, upset the market, depress real wages and increase unemployment, as has happened in 'most countries of Europe'.[32]

This is not an attack upon particular, modern 'privileges'; there is no detailed critique of the Acts of 1974-76 set against that of 1906. The call is for repeal of all immunities, including those of the early, first-stage legitimation of unions, such as the immunity from restraint of trade given in Britain in 1871. All must go. Indeed, the traditional Rights of Man – freedom of speech, of the press, of religion, of assembly and of association – must be reconsidered so as to sterilise them against collectivism. 'They have only one valid objective; they are intended to protect ... simply individual liberty in the sense of the absence of arbitrary coercion.'[33] But at this point a more threatening note enters. The abolition of collective 'privilege' may not be enough. Stronger laws may be needed in 'certain employments' (they are not specified, but some area of essential services seems to be indicated). In those occupations workers should be required to take on 'long-term obligations' banning strikes, and any 'concerted attempts' to break those obligations should be made 'illegal'.[34] Freedom of contract is not enough. The state steps in here with stiffer penalties.

Given all that, trade unions may be permitted to continue. The concession, however, is guarded. Unions should be confined either to organising the consent of workers choosing between the alternative offers of their employer (though, naturally, each 'at the same cost') or to the 'oldest and most beneficial activity of the unions', that of 'friendly societies'. Even so, Hayek leaves open the question whether unions are justified on 'a larger scale than that of the plant or corporation'. After all, the practicability of 'industry-wide or nation-wide bargaining ... would almost certainly disappear if the basic coercive power of the unions were removed'.[35]

Lesser acolytes of Hayek's school have applied his precepts strictly, declaring: 'modern unionism in its typical form is a challenge to the authority of the state, and in particular an affront to the rule of law.'[36] Or, again: 'Ideally, what is needed for the emancipation of labour is the enactment of the principle underlying the British Combination Acts of 1799 and 1800 ... adapted to the 1970s.'[37] In 1985 the Director General of the Institute of Directors deplored the way 'collective bargaining tends to debase labour' and demanded the repeal of the 'Trade Disputes Act 1906' [*sic*] in order to re-establish the 'law of contract' (that is to say, the law which, without the immunities, makes trade union action unlawful). By 1988 such writers became confident enough to demand not only the outright abolition of all such 'immunities' but also the end of protective legislation on unfair dismissal, maternity rights, redundancy pay and trade union activities at work, with a view to employers 'offering' to each worker a 'flexible' individual contract more suited to the market.[38]

Such writing manifestly misdescribes the liberties of British labour relations law, misusing the negative form of the immunity to prove that it has the substance of a 'privilege' – rather as if an Act that gave slaves an immunity against recapture were interpreted as necessarily granting them a 'privilege'. It also portrays an astonishingly naïve belief in the neutrality of the principles of common law and the equivalent laws that preceded trade union emancipation on the Continent.[39] Such laws were, not unnaturally, based upon the ideology of the time, above all the ideology of contract and property dominant in the last two centuries. As Vice-Chancellor Malins said in 1868: 'The jurisdiction of this court is to protect property.'[40] How could it have been otherwise? It was a crime in 1872 for a workers' combination to create 'such annoyance and interference as would be likely to have a deterring effect upon masters of ordinary nerve' – the liability first provided with a trade dispute immunity in 1875 – simply because that group activity disturbed the order of the market and of the property relations then seen as sacrosanct by the common law. That, too, was why the United Order of Boilermakers was in 1867 adjudged an illegal association 'in restraint of trade', the judgment which led to the immunity of 1871.[41] The rights of private property are the natural base of the common law, just as they are the core of Hayekism. Both treat its legitimacy as an indisputable foundation of the social order.

Nor does this school of thought waste much time on the greatest legal 'privilege' of all, that bestowed on companies by way of limited liability. Lord Diplock observed recently that in all 'trading countries', the law permits 'the creation of corporations as artificial persons ... to enable business to be undertaken with limited liability in the event of the business proving to be a failure'. Hayek agrees that limited liability is on his own definition a privilege; but the law should do little more here than insist upon disclosure of corporate affairs to the public and upon the absolute right of shareholders to control.[42] Companies will then play their proper role in the competitive market. This picture, together with a simplistic reliance upon 'freedom of contract', may look rather antique in today's world of pyramid corporate groups, oligopoly and transnational capital; but it is the basis on which he takes a third step, one which brings us to the notion of 'error'.

Society, State and Constitution

In Hayek's view, the common law as a body of distilled wisdom, with its judge established as one organ 'by which the spontaneous order grows', normally requires legislative change only where there has arisen some distortion, 'some past development based on error', or because of 'some more general requirements of justice'.[43] Otherwise, it forms part of a natural social order. 'Liberalism' itself is 'inseparable from the institution of private property'. That 'presupposes the enforcement of rules of just conduct' (that is *general* rules) 'and expects a desirable spontaneous order to form itself'. But 'justice' and the 'rule of law' have nothing to do with balancing group interests. Criticism of the way judges uphold the 'system of several property' are misplaced, for that system protects those who own and those who do not; and the very development 'on which modern civilisation depends was made possible only by the institution of property'. The state therefore has a duty to defend the spontaneous order.[44]

But that defence must be executed in the proper way. Coercive public law and social planning are undesirable. They will be 'oppressive' to individuals. This perception springs, in turn, from a basic tenet, where his analysis of society combines with Hayek's more general philosophical position on the nature of humankind itself. The character and fragmentation of human knowledge, he asserts, deny to any ruler the opportunity of a comprehensive view of society, in particular industrial society. No one can ever *know*, therefore, what is of 'value to society'. The term 'social justice' is devoid of meaning, an illusion usually cloaking the interests of groups. Previous social policies which have taken into account, or (worse) encouraged, interest groups are not open to debate; they are 'demonstrably false'. To seek any 'balance' between interest groups is 'demonstrably irrational and inefficient and unjust in the extreme'. The optimum condition men and women can seek, given the division of labour in industrial society and the nature of human knowledge, is in the nature of things the competitive market. 'Altruism' and 'solidarity' are objectionable: 'It is these two instincts, deeply imbedded in our purely instinctive or intuitive reactions, which remained the great obstacle to the development of the modern economy.'[45]

Here is an intellectual system that lays claim, honestly but not without some arrogance, to the only true understanding of justice, rationality, the rule of law, social order, political economy and the nature of knowledge – all in one closed system. Opponents are listed as a line of 'false prophets', from Auguste Comte, St Simon, Kelsen or Freud to Marx and Gunnar Myrdal. All are guilty of 'errors' or hold 'erroneous' views. The suggestion by Galbraith (who is both wrong and 'naïve') that there is 'no alternative' to public management in modern economic affairs 'just is not true'. And of course: 'The whole idea that we can replace the market by central planning is based on intellectual error.'[46]

All this is reflected in his ideal political constitution, which may seem a long way from labour law but is important and revealing. There would be two assemblies: a governing assembly for ordinary legislation and a superior legislative assembly to maintain the general principles of 'just conduct'. The latter would have members aged 45 to 60, one-fifteenth elected every fifteen years, preferably from age-group 'clubs' (people who had kept contact after their school days – 'and, perhaps, national service'). Members would share not party affiliations but the 'outlook of a generation'. Both assemblies would be subject to a supreme constitutional court, which would decide questions of legislative competence and – more important for the market order – more often pronounce 'that nobody at all was entitled to take ... coercive measures not provided for by general rules of just conduct'.

But what about threats to the order so established? For them the middle-aged Assembly would have an emergency committee in 'permanent existence'. What kind of emergency becomes clear in the next step. For under this system of governance – geriatric, autocratic, and dependent (as is Hayek's wont) upon the judges' intuitive understanding of 'justice' – the 'anti-social activities' of those 'now euphemistically called "social partners" ' (in what the traditional analysis called collective bargaining) would disappear. Since individualist market-capitalism is the real and only 'democracy', it is necessary to enshrine it in the political constitution.

> Once it is clearly recognised that socialism as much as fascism or communism inevitably leads into the totalitarian state and the destruction of the democratic order, it is clearly legitimate to provide against our inadvertently sliding into a socialist system by constitutional provisions which deprive government of the discriminating powers of coercion even for what at the moment may generally be regarded as good purposes.[47]

Hayek's state must be a strong and a vigilant state. It must have a constitutional power to defend the natural order against not only positive 'coercive' planning or groups that endanger the market, but also against the threat even of socialism-by-inadvertent-consent. Conceived as libertarian, the doctrine ends by denying liberty to those who would change its economic doctrines. The 'constitution of liberty' must deny liberty to those who do not share his beliefs.

Hayek did not of course write the 'step-by-step' programme of labour law for 1980-88; but one would need to be juridically tone deaf not to pick up the echoes of his philosophy in recent policies and pronouncements. They extend beyond industrial relations of course, to include the Prime Minister's ambition to 'get rid of socialism as a second force' in British politics and to institute a choice between two parties which both believe in 'economic freedom'. And to the claim: 'There is no such thing as society. There are individual men and women and there are families.'[48]

Nor is it difficult to identify the same philosophy second-hand in the publications of the Centre for Policy Studies, Institute for Economic Affairs, and Adam Smith Institute. It is not the purpose here to join the debate about the precise character of this now dominant ideology or its relationship to other versions of the 'rule of law',[49] nor to assess how far the economic doctrines of others have been combined in social policy with it. But the record on its face suggests that the character of labour legislation since 1979 can be better understood – and its future course probably better predicted – by reference to this framework set up by Hayek than to any other. It helps, for example, to explain what some regard as the paradox of a government associated with the rhetoric of deregulation and individualism turning increasingly to state regulatory measures. This mixture of market forces and strong government, displaying a determination to put down those who might disrupt the 'spontaneous order', is quintessentially Hayek.

Freedom of Association and the Lawyers

We should note parenthetically that there is a parallel issue tucked away in the technicalities of the legal debate here and abroad which tends to fortify the Hayekite camp. It hardly needs explanation that the term 'freedom of association', as used in this paper, includes a right to organise in autonomous trade unions that are able to be effective in representing their members. But that is not the only legal interpretation that has currency. Amongst lawyers one can find two quite distinct interpretations, one purposive, one emasculating. To be meaningful in a purposive sense, the term connotes protection for the collective aims of the association, though to what extent remains open for argument in a given situation. The right to form trade unions in the law of many Western European countries takes account of this factor and invariably includes within it an area of protection for *some* aspects of collective action, for example a right or liberty to bargain or to strike. The legal systems differ in precise content. But in varying degrees some such content is intrinsic to *la liberté syndicale*, to *libertà sindacale*, and to *Koalitionsfreiheit*. So too in Sweden, the basic right to associate includes the right to 'take advantage' of union membership and to 'work for' the organisation. So too, the ILO regards the opportunity to bargain and some kind of right to strike as essential elements in 'freedom of association' itself.[50]

But others, including the Law Lords in 1970 and the Canadian Supreme Court in 1987, have held that a constitutional 'freedom to associate' bears no such meaning. It is no more than a right to associate together, not a right to do anything at all in association. It is not infringed, therefore, by legislation banning collective bargaining or strikes.[51] The members of the union can still 'associate' for other purposes. Here it is important not to overestimate the European Convention on Human Rights, which in Article 11 guarantees everyone's right of freedom of association, 'including the right to form and to join trade unions for the protection of his interests'. The Strasbourg Court of Human Rights has held that this right, by itself, does not necessarily give rights to bargain, still less to strike. Each state is left a 'free choice' on that matter.[52] Such an interpretation risks reducing freedom of association to a mere freedom of assembly, an empty right to meet together. It is significant that judges who take that second, emasculating view – that workers can exist in 'association' without any industrial rights to bargain or to strike, without infringement of the right to 'freedom of association' – always point out that they can still pursue 'friendly society' objectives. Nor is it surprising to find that those propounding individualist philosophies interpret this freedom with emphasis, like Hayek, upon the right to *dissociate*. All these attitudes to freedom of association involve not legal interpretations but ideological assertions.

IV The New Labour Law Programme

If we turn to the government's labour legislation, we find that the main statutes of 1980, 1982, 1984, 1986 and 1988, together with the many Orders and Regulations after 1979, can now be seen in a framework very different from that described at the outset by Mr Prior. They are consistent only with the alternative analysis. The threads of the programme may be unravelled here under five headings: 1. *Disestablishing Collectivism*; 2. *The Deregulation of Employment Law*; 3. *Union Control and Ballots for Individuals*; 4. *Enterprise Confinement*; and 5. *Sanctions Without Martyrs*.

1. Disestablishing Collectivism

First, the government has removed most of the measures designed since the turn of the century to support collective bargaining and to prop up collective organisation, frequently (as has been the British style) by imposing articulated minimum conditions. For example, the Fair Wages Resolution, supportive of low-paid workers was rescinded in 1982. Unilateral arbitration for minimum conditions related to collective bargaining, available in some form since 1940, was repealed in 1980. Various statutes ensuring minimum 'fair wages' were repealed between 1980 and 1984. Wages Councils' powers (originating in 1909, protecting nearly 3 million workers' minimum conditions) were reduced in 1986 to setting one basic rate; young workers were excluded; and wages inspectors were reduced by administrative means by 35 per cent since 1979. No ILO obligations could be given priority over the repeal of such laws; so here the government denounced two ILO Conventions. Legal impediments to the market rates and special laws for particular classes of workers had to go. In 1988, local authorities were prohibited from any consideration of fair wages, training or employed status of contractors' workers in offering public contracts – a step readily explicable on a Hayekite understanding of 'freedom of contract'. Local authorities must not inhibit the spontaneous market order.

When Earl Gowrie said of this part of the policy as early as 1980: 'We want to get back to the voluntary system,' he was using 'voluntary' in the Hayekite sense.[53] We now know, in the public sector at least, that if voluntary collective bargaining itself produces inconvenient results it will be abolished outright by law. The abolition by statute in 1987 of teachers' rights of collective bargaining, condemned by the ILO Committee of Experts as a breach of Conventions 98 and 151, was followed by proposals for a negotiating structure in which the official management side would have the ultimate power to impose conditions when 'it has already offered the maximum that can be afforded,'[54] a direct parallel to Hayek's function for unions to organise workers' choice between the employer's alternative offers 'at the same cost'.

Let us stay in the public sector. It has seen the gradual growth of imposed obligations that try to ban 'concerted attempts' to strike in particular areas of employment (the attempt, for example, to impose a no-strike condition on nurses' unions for negotiations with the government and the refusal in 1988 to allow individual nurses taking industrial action access to regrading appeal machinery). New liabilities control industrial action in telecommunications; the 1983 manifesto commitment to legislate on 'essential services' has been neither implemented nor renounced.[55] The 1988 Employment Act treads the same path when in section 30 it 'deems' Crown servants to have a contract of employment for the purpose of allowing the government to sue persons who induce a breach of them. No 'balance' here to secure the civil servant's right to sue his or her employer on this 'contract'. The demand made of workers in the public sector who resist is one of unconditional surrender, as in the case of the miners; and to the new restrictions on picketing is added a national police strategy and a Public Order Act 1986, applying the diagnosis that serious industrial disorder is henceforth to be treated as public disorder. Deregulation leads to reregulation by a state determined to protect the market order.

The weak duty to bargain placed generally on employers in 1975 when recommended by ACAS – a short-lived attempt to extend collective negotiation – was repealed in 1980 (without, it must be said, great opposition).[56] But it is the peculiarity of the British situation that no further legal steps were needed therefore to facilitate a process of non-recognition or even de-recognition of trade unions, at any rate in the private (including the growing, privatised) sector. Those who want to encourage deunionisation need only the right economic conditions. Neither process is, as yet, the rule; withdrawal of recognition is the exception, as ACAS has made clear; but, as its Chairman has also said, one would be 'blind if one does not recognise' that deunionisation was on the increase; the 1987 *Report* showed the trend continuing with 'many managements ... re-examining their relationships with trade unions', and the chairman of the CAC and spokesman for the CBI have seen in management's style of increasingly individualised labour relations in 1988 a threat to collective bargaining itself.[57] A TUC Report of 1986 showed that the process of privatisation encouraged the trend.[58] Non-unionism in the private sector is not confined to Wapping, D.C. Thomson or IBM. Though the extent is a matter of dispute, reports in 1987[59] suggested a significant increase in important companies, with low union density in various sectors: and derecognition which 'was once extremely rare is now becoming more commonplace'.[60]

Privatisation and other pressures for decentralisation or 'flexibility' demand that unions today should move further towards enterprise unionism, while in some types of 'single union' agreements the identity of the bargaining union owes more to the preference of the employer granting organising rights to a union even before any workers have been hired than to any democratic choice by the workers themselves. It is this climate that now reinforces the importance of an absence of a legal duty to bargain with a union democratically 'representative' of the workforce, either in the American 'majoritarian' or the French 'proportional' sense. Indeed, our law has little knowledge of that concept of 'representativity' so fundamental to debates in other modern systems, as in France or Italy. Moreover, in jurisdictions where the tide of industrial relations and the very concept of freedom to organise still favour collective organisation and bargaining, the absence of any overall duty to bargain is less significant (there is none in Italy or in Germany, while the duty imposed in 1982 in France is weak). That is even more significant where the social system has maintained, as in Italy, a thrust towards genuine 'tripartism' in economic and social affairs. The very meaning of the law, or of the absence of a law, is dependent on that type of social context. In Britain, law and society have each encouraged the other to deregulate the labour market.

2. Deregulation in Employment Law
This factor is important, too, in the 'deregulation' of the individual employment relationship. In other European systems increased 'flexibility' has sometimes introduced wider managerial prerogatives, but it does not always end legal regulation. In Britain 'flexibility' is taken to be a synonym for deregulation by repeal. By contrast, when more 'flexibility' was introduced in Germany,

France and Italy on part-time and 'atypical' employment, significant legal protection for such workers remained. The German Act of 1985, for example, includes controls over the use of fixed-term contracts and over employment contracts with 'beck-and-call' working hours (*Kapovaz*), while the Italian law of 1984 gives part-time workers priority rights to full-time jobs and the right to have certain conditions of work determined by collective bargaining. What is important is that regulation is natural to such systems; the residual law is built upon it, unlike the unlimited freedom of contract natural to the residual British common law. So too, the Italian law of 1977 on restrictions over women's heavy and night work allowed for variation by collective agreement.[61] Not so the British Sex Discrimination Act 1986; its deregulation was characteristically abrupt and total in levelling down, whatever the real position of women – the most vulnerable and least unionised workers – in the labour market. In 1987 a consultative document gave notice of legislation (now in the 1989 Bill) to repeal, too, dozens of legislative provisions that have for decades protected the working hours of young workers.[62] Such regulation is now said to be 'obsolete'. Everyone must be free to choose – old or young, strong or weak, employee or employer.

The government also consulted about repealing the old laws banning women from underground work in mines – an 'urgent matter' because repeal required denunciation of yet another ILO Convention and provisions in the European Social Charter (so urgent was it that the Convention was denounced in the middle of consultations 'to clear the way for possible changes' in the Bill of 1989). The government even felt that it was no longer 'appropriate' for the law to demand seats for female shop assistants (its unbridled zeal to deregulate causing it to overlook the fact that this provision of the Shops Act 1950 had been overtaken in 1963 by a levelling-up in the seats-for-all section 13 of the Offices, Shops and Railway Premises Act). In ancient Rome, fearful of the safety of the state against a return of Hannibal's elephants from Carthage, Cato the orator declaimed at the close of every speech: '*delenda est Carthago*' ('Carthage must be wiped out'). Today, it portrays an elephantine devotion to doctrine to proclaim that the well-being of British society rests upon the maxim: *delenda est ancillarum sedile* ('seats for shopgirls must be wiped out').

The sex equality laws themselves, though, now constitute the main impediment to the policy of market deregulation, especially in the form of EEC law, in Article 119 of the Treaty and Directives 75/117 and 76/207. (There is no such bulwark supporting the race discrimination laws.) The government's response, here as in social security law, has been to comply slowly, even minimally, with these obligations and their interpretation by the Luxembourg Court. Witness the 1983 equal value regulations and the Sex

Discrimination Act 1986. Other EEC obligations have received similar treatment, as in the 1981 Transfer of Undertakings Regulations, which an unscrupulous employer can easily evade (though it may be doubted whether this Directive, 77/187, has produced dramatic change in any other jurisdiction).[63] Draft Directives that touch upon employers' prerogatives have been blocked; the 'Vredeling' draft Directive has been pushed off the agenda (though the 'European Company' project has crept back on to it); the Delors initiative for a social dimension to the internal market after 1992 has been resisted. On the other hand, one initiative which the government has launched in Brussels has been a fierce 'campaign' to challenge draft regulations as unduly restrictive and to insist upon a special 'Task Force' there to protect the interests of employers from interference. British influence was also applied in 1986 to get rid of 'unnecessary administrative restraints' and to ensure that the qualified majority procedures under the Single European Act should not apply to 'the rights and interests of employed persons'. It is small wonder that the TUC has become a convert to Community social action.

British deregulation has a further, specifically Hayekite, characteristic. From 1979 onwards there has been creeping erosion of the floor of rights on employment protection, hand-in-hand with a gradual reduction of social security rights towards a bare floor on proof of need. Apart from basic legislation on health and safety (which he did regard as necessary) and a bare minimum for the needy, Hayek is against all such laws. We have accordingly seen a diminution of maternity rights, the removal of protection against unfair deductions from wages, the alleviation of the employer's burden of proof, extension of the employee's qualifying period to two years and similar changes in unfair dismissal law. These last hit hardest at the millions of 'atypical' workers (temporary, casual, short-term, fixed-term, homeworkers and the like, even when they are lucky enough to be 'employees') not to speak of 'trainees' whom the Secretary of State now has untrammeled discretion under the 1988 Act to designate as 'employees' or not (without advice from the unions after the waspish abolition of the Training Commission – the latest of the tripartite bodies to go).[64]

But just as important as the fact has been the *manner* of British deregulation. Time and again, the government's assertion that such legislation is a 'burden on business' deterring recruitment by employers has been met by research evidence that such deterrence is non-existent or minimal; it has replied that its own evidence, although 'anecdotal', is otherwise and sufficient to proceed.[65] The distaste for systematic evidence, for what might be called traditional 'Donovan' testimony, was evinced especially in the legislation extending the categories of non-unionists protected from discipline or dismissal in a union membership agreement;

that did not await the publication of the authoritative survey
commissioned by the government. Since 1982 the trend has been
towards legislation by assertion of truths. Evidence has
increasingly taken a back seat.

3. Union Control and Ballots for Individuals

With the closed shop we come to a third area, control of the union
itself and the place of ballots. Here we find an emerging policy
after 1982 increasingly concerned not with any balance of interests
but with an *a priori* assumption about what the market in its
industrial relations dimension should be like. To the extension of
the protected categories of non-unionists who should be free from
discipline or dismissal in a closed shop, legislation itself effected in
1982 with little reference to the surveys that showed the width of
categories already exempted by many such agreements, was added
the requirement of a ballot. Although an absurdly high majority
was required (80 per cent of the electorate of 85 per cent of the
voters) many took this ballot as the condition for 'fair' dismissals to
be a means of validating closed shops. At the same time, but less
noticed, the 1982 Act amended the law generally, *outside* closed
shops, to place non-unionism on a par with, or in some ways
superior to, trade unionism. The Act moved into that territory, in
Mr Tebbit's words, to provide the 'most comprehensive ...
statutory protection for non-union employees we have ever had in
this country'.[66]

This was a crucial shift in 1982 away from the traditional analysis
of which the main objective became explicit only later. That
objective was to secure the paramount rights of the non-unionist.
In the 1988 Employment Act the closed shop ballot is not further
refined in order to be a better mechanism to validate the UMA; it
is abolished entirely. The ballot was an interim measure on the
road to abolishing this hated practice. The Act deprives union and
employer alike of all lawful, industrial pressures to enforce a UMA
agreement. Formal freedom of contract is preserved by permitting
such agreements to be lawful, even if in practice unenforceable; all
the collective pressures to make them effective are outlawed.
Indeed, it seems doubtful how far under section 10(2) of the Act
the union can exercise pressure on the employer for any special
benefits for its own members.

Strike ballots have undergone a similar fate. By the Trade Union
Act 1984 a majority in a ballot (with obligatory questions written
by government on the union's ballot paper, on which the union is
since 1988 forbidden to add its comments) was made a condition
for retention of the central immunity in trade disputes. That
applies where the organisation of union industrial action is an
inducement to break employment contracts (as it normally is). The
1988 Act, however, empowers a dissident union member, in the

absence of such a supportive ballot, to sue in the courts whether or *not* the action is in breach of any employment contract. Its circular definition of industrial action ('any strike or other industrial action' by employees: section 1(7)) confirms that any and all forms of organised, collective pressure on the employer are caught, without exception – bans on voluntary overtime, collective protests about unsafe workplaces, concerted withdrawals of goodwill. All need a ballot if the union supports the action, on pain of a court order. Under section 1 of the Act wherever a group of workers make a demand supported by their union with an implied threat to take action (and that is not difficult to prove) a dissident member can obtain a court order whether or not there is evidence that the action threatened itself would be by any rule of the general law unlawful. Breach of the employment contract is no longer the bound of illegality. Now it is not the unlawful act but the group pressure, the collective organisation *itself*, that is the target. The link with Hayek is immediate.

The link becomes stronger. Even if a strike ballot has obtained a majority, the 1988 Act, in section 3, prohibits a union on pain of paying compensation from lawfully expelling or penalising in any way a dissident member by reason of his opposing, or going to work in defiance of, the majority decision to strike albeit in breach of his obligations under the contract in the union rules. Illegal 'unjustifiable discipline' also arises if a member is disciplined for refusing, in relation to a strike, to break any requirement of his employment contract (even if that is a new obligation introduced for strike breaking) or for accusing union officials of illegality unless the *union* can prove the assertion was false and made in bad faith. To deny an association the liberty without penalty to expel a member who contravenes rules that are (under the general law) lawful rules is to deny to it the very essence of a 'voluntary' and 'free' association. Indeed, to relieve the member of his obligations under a lawful contract (the union rules) might at first sight be thought even to go beyond principles of 'freedom of contract'. But Hayek supplies one further maxim to save the day, one which is manifestly the basis for section 3: 'No principles of collective conduct which bind the individual can exist in a society of free men.'

We recall that the 'real exploiters' are the unions and that instincts of 'solidarity' must be displaced, along with 'altruism'. The individual must be freed by the state from the rules of the group no matter how democratic their adoption, and from loyalty to the group in any conflict. The individual must be made superior to the group, ballot or no ballot, and relieved of the obligation of solidarity with his fellows. To create the 'free society' the state must deny the very existence of his obligations to the group. His contract with the group is to be voidable at his option. The last battle ahead, says Hayek, is 'for the abolition of *all* coercive power to direct individual efforts'; and if you ask – as the traditional analysis would – why this does not lead to legal curbs on the coercive power of his employer too, to whom the employee is subordinate, the reply is ready to hand: '[Employed persons] are protected by the need of the employer to create working conditions which will secure him the necessary flow of new recruits.'[67] Freedom for the individual worker *is* the labour market.

Mr Fowler expressed the point in the House of Commons when explaining section 3: 'We believe that an individual has a right to choose whether to go on strike and that right is *paramount*.' Ironically, he argued, too, that the very fact that in our system the individual worker has no 'immunity' against his breach of employment contract (i.e. no right against the employer to choose to strike) is itself the *reason* why the union must not have the right to 'coerce' him by insisting upon his contractual union obligation to join the majority who do strike in breach of their employment obligations. The employer's powers must be retained, and the individual employee must retain *his* power to 'choose' what to do – unfettered by the obligations owed to his group but fettered by his employment obligations.[68] The law imposed by the state steps back a century to abolish the binding, legal force of working class organisation. That is precisely the path marked out for it by Hayek.

This insistence that so-called individual rights must always prevail, and be made by the state to prevail, against the association or group – and in particular against the union – is the latest marker clearly to characterise the new British labour law. The trade union is seen as the obstacle to the competitive market and a threat alike to individuals and to private property. No argument can succeed thereafter which complains about the union's treatment being 'special'. Time and again, in the debates on the various Bills, ministers faced the complaint: 'You don't do that to companies,' or 'You don't ban that for golf clubs.' Such arguments missed the point. The unionised group of workers receives special treatment because of what it *is*. In debates on the Act of 1988, whether it was to justify the tightening up of ballot requirements for the unique regulation of political funds; or to impose the unprecedented legal control over elections to the principal executive committee (now to include anyone who 'may' under rule or in practice attend committee meetings); or to impose special legal rules about indemnifying officials (permissible for all other associations on a discretionary basis and not subject of proven complaint even in the miners' strike); or to impose the extraordinary provision where each individual member is given the right to inspect accounting records relating to union assets for the previous six years not only in the books of the union, but also those held by every branch from Lands End to John O'Groats (when shareholders have no right at all to inspect such records) – the reply was the same. It did not rest on surveys or evidence. As one minister most succinctly put it: 'Trade unions are unique institutions.'[69]

The normal rules of argument and analogy by now have no application. The traditional analysis treated unions as one among many voluntary, contractual associations, where special legal provisions had to be justified. That was why, in 1974, union rules were made into fully enforceable contracts, parallel with other associations, without re-enacting the limitations which had for a century after the Act of 1871 made most of those rules unenforceable directly in the courts. Other systems of law, including those with specialised labour courts (Germany, for example) deal with internal union disputes in the ordinary civil courts for just that reason. Unions are placed alongside other contractual associations. In the new British regime, however, unions are 'unique' institutions which require more narrow 'limitations' (to use Hayek's word) than the laws customary for such associations, not because of what they have done, but because of what they are – working class groups.

The strict regulation of unions' internal organisation which started in the 1984 Act is extended to such a degree in 1988 that it must be questionable under the terms of ILO Conventions 87 and 98, and clearly will provide unimagined opportunities for harassment by any dissident, individual member, whether a Rookes genuinely aggrieved or an Osborne set up for the job. For this he will have – in pursuit of the same logic – the right to call on the state to help him, in the form of the new Commissioner for the Rights of Trade Union Members. The new policy, here as elsewhere it must be noted, is quite different from that of 1971. There is to be no State 'Registrar' this time round. That would be to commit the venal sin of corporatism. The state retains its formal distance by assisting the 'individual' (except perhaps when state approval is needed for scrutineers of union ballots under section 15, which does seem to cross the line into corporatism). It is the function of this special state officer to assist the individual in suits launched against a union (on causes of action suitably enlarged by state enactment) because it is the task of the state to protect the market for individuals. The formal doctrinal purity behind the Act's structure does credit to the converts. As Goldthorpe has pointed out, such legal harassment, while it may not destroy a union, can undermine its 'capacity for strategy'.[70] The rules of the game are changed so that, with the state as dealer, the card of 'individual rights' trumps the group trick every time.

4. Enterprise Confinement

When we come to the fourth area of the legislation on the

destruction of the trade dispute 'immunities', we find that it, too, now rests not on any argument of 'balance' of industrial power, but squarely on an attack upon immunities as 'privileges'. Even so, the form of the developing legislation is worth attention. The central 'immunities' protecting inducing breach of contract and like torts (that is, liberties to take or threaten industrial action in Britain) have been restricted by a succession of steps based largely on a common principle – in 1980 the ban on 'secondary', or solidarity, action and picketing away from the worker's own workplace; in 1982 the redefinition of trade dispute to confine it to disputes between workers and their *own* employer; the banning in 1982 of action to help workers in another employment gain union recognition, or even consultation, from *their* employer.[71] At this point, it is critical to remember that wherever there is even a serious argument that workers have acted without 'immunity', judges will grant an interlocutory injunction, in procedures (it must be said) that are quite unfair, to stop the industrial action. So, it was enough for Mercury Communications in the British Telecom dispute to show that, under the new definition, the union was arguably pursuing a political rather than an industrial dispute, in order to get an injunction. This labour injunction is the courts' contribution to the policy in action. It is the point where the common law approach to union organisation and to protection of property makes contact with the new analysis. No judges have been heard to say that these new laws stick in their 'judicial gorges', as the old immunities did.[72]

The common principle running through this part of the legislation is more than consistent with Hayek's concern that, if trade unions are to continue, they may need to be confined to the plant or to the enterprise. The principle is that the needs of the market demand the confinement of workers' influence within each enterprise – the doctrine of enterprise confinement. At every step, the news laws do just that. They prohibit the export of workers' collective influence beyond the boundaries of their own employment unit, itself defined by the employer. If the latter sets up a subsidiary company to run part of the enterprise, the range of industrial liberty for employees is immediately redefined. Trade disputes, industrial action, pressure for recognition – these new rules of the game confine lawful activities of combinations of workers within gates erected by their own employer. The aim is to produce enterprise associations and to break with the 'coercive' pressure of wider, workers' organisation. The effect of separate corporate employers was made clear by the Law Lords in the *Dimbleby* case. In this way the limits of lawful industrial action, as the Wapping dispute vividly illustrated, can be set by the employer.

It is, in this context, of particular importance to the public sector whether the Crown will remain one undivided employer, or whether new laws or administrative measures will be introduced to make each Ministry or designated area into a separate employer. The GCHQ story reminds us that attempts to do that might be made unilaterally by Order in Council as well as by legislation. Introduction of different legal 'employers' into segments of the central public sector could have devastating legal consequences for civil service unions. More widely, in an era of internationalised capital, the new approach rules out, under British law at any rate, any countervailing power of unions across national frontiers (as the ITWF quickly discovered in the series of decisions banning its traditional action through boycotts imposed by British workers against flags-of-convenience ships whose third-world crews so often enjoy iniquitous conditions of employment – thereby asserting a common fellowship in perhaps the purest kind of solidarity action).

It is worth noting that in the hey-day of the traditional analysis Conservative lawyers did not always regard such sympathetic action as evil. One report in 1958, of which a reputed author was the young Lord Donaldson, conceded that secondary action was 'politically, socially and economically justified if, without it, employees will have insufficient bargaining power' (though the writers thought this was not the case at the time by reason of 'full employment').[73] There was even a hint of that approach in the way Mr Prior argued the case on 'secondary action' in 1979-80. This particular piece of enterprise confinement was, he seemed at times to suggest, something of an exception to workers' general liberty to organise wider action. Today, however, action taken in solidarity with other workers outside the enterprise is banned as a sin against competition. The Hayek doctrine is embraced in all its rigour.

The principle of enterprise confinement is still further refined by section 17 of the 1988 Act which introduces a doctrine of 'workplace confinement'. Under it, each separate place of work must produce its own majority in a separate ballot before industrial action is lawful there. The 'separate place of work' test is narrower even than the unit of employment. The government, under pressure from employers who were concerned about fragmen- tation of convenient working arrangements, had to permit exceptions. These they ultimately drafted (after parliamentary debates of gargantuan confusion) in terms of allowing an aggregate ballot where all the workers to be balloted are of the same occupational category or have a 'common factor' in their terms and conditions (even if not the same factor linking each pair of them, provided no such worker in an employment unit is excluded from voting). The extent to which this section ('the gibberish clause', as Lord McCarthy called it) permits aggregate ballots across what are industrially 'bargaining units' is not entirely clear. Unless the exceptions apply, separate majorities at separate workplaces are required for lawful industrial action. The object of the ballot, once again, is not to discover the collective view and enforce it. For an individual, however he votes, is given, as we have seen, legal support to brush aside the majority decision. The aim, on the contrary, is to make lawful, group action by workers as difficult as possible.

This step-by-step salami-slicing of the workforce to designate permissible limits of collective organisation is a quite logical development of the new philosophy, one with which traditional analysis can hardly find common ground and one which reason would suggest has further steps in mind in pursuit of its logic. Other developments in the labour market go with the same grain. Indeed the grain itself may be thought to have an economic, rather than a legal, imperative. The fragmentation and segmentation of workers into 'core' employees surrounded by peripheral, less secure workers (often on part-time or other 'atypical' contracts) promotes the same tendency in the workforce. It is no part of the new programme to concern itself with protection for more peripheral workers. But it is not unthinkable that its next step might be to confine permitted collective bargaining for all workers, or selected groups of workers, to each separate plant or workplace, with exceptions that suit influential groups of employers in (say) engineering or electrical contracting. The draft *Code of Practice on Industrial Action Balloting 1988*, with its demands that unions explain the employer's case to their members and new obligations limiting ballots which would traditionally have been thought inappropriate for a 'Code' and which, the TUC pointed out, would mean in practice the end of ballots and lawful industrial action, shows that the policy's spring of invention is not dry.

5. Sanctions Without Martyrs

Fifthly, we come to the rest of the law on trade unions themselves, those 'unique' institutions which must receive unique attention. Debates on the Acts have increasingly revealed that the case for control – be it special control of political expenditure (not applied, after all, to any other association), control of internal elections or control of industrial action – has been less and less supported by appeals to 'abuses' or evidence of neglect. Today Ministers decreasingly ask for briefs that list union practices their audience might find objectionable. A few, isolated incidents are thrown in; but the argument is now based more upon the bare principle of 'individual' versus 'union'. It was to be expected that the protection given to the union against tort liability in 1906 after the shock of *Taff Vale*, would be an early target, a 'privilege' to be abolished. Indeed, the omission of this item from the 1980 Act and its inclusion in 1982 suggests that it was in that year that traditional analysis gave way finally to the thrust of the Hayek philosophy in the legislation. There had, it is true, been considerable debate about the scope of this particular protection in traditional debate. The Webbs had disapproved of this solution to the problem in 1906. The Donovan Report in 1968 proposed that the need to save unions from catastrophic loss of funds through awards of damages and costs might be met by retaining an immunity limited to trade disputes. It was a matter of balance. But some protection was needed.

When in 1982 this protection was repealed and unions were again made liable in tort, they were also made subject to a special, strict code of law about those for whom they were vicariously liable. In a sense the 1982 Act did recognise that a problem exists – the problem that unions may be wiped out by the law of tort – because it limited the damages obtainable against a union (e.g. to £250,000 for larger unions).[74] But the effect of that is limited; it applies only to each set of proceedings, and not to costs or sequestration. Much more important is the central place of this legal change in the overall scheme. For this is the key that makes the new system work. The substitution of union liability for the liability of officials is aimed at avoiding the 'martyrdom' problem. Under the Industrial Relations Act, the imprisonment of the five dockers' shop stewards in 1972 demonstrated the risks of 'self-inflicted martyrdom'.[75] Sanctions against officials, and above all imprisonment for contempt, become the focus in industrial conflict for even greater agitation by members. This is a lesson of general experience, from the *O'Shea* case in Australia to the Kent miners' leaders in 1941. Lord Denning warned in 1980 that in industrial cases the 'weapon of imprisonment' for contempt of court must never be used again: 'Some better means must be found.'[76]

That means was found in the priority accorded to unions as defendants in tort actions. Already, in the Supreme Court Act 1981, procedures had been changed so as to avoid imprisonment of officials who did not pay fines (wheeling out the Queen's Remembrancer to enforce in the county court). But that was not enough to make the new liabilities bite (especially as such fines are often paid by anonymous business men). So, although officials might still be fined, after 1982 the civil sanctions were to apply primarily to the property of the union, through damages and injunctions for liability and fines or sequestration on contempt. Such sanctions can be made to work best in a system where trade unions derive their strength from membership and the contributions of members. Where unions have few funds and their strength is based more upon support than on membership, as in France, such weapons are comparatively less powerful, especially if the courts possess (as there) less draconian powers in what we call cases of civil contempt and if the union's *patrimoine* (main property) is protected (as there) from attachment. In Britain, however, the membership and property base of the trade union movement offers to the legal process a sharp point of leverage, one readily grasped by the 1982 Act.

The reintroduction of the union as defendant, above all in the common case where an interlocutory injunction is the remedy sought, has proved how justified were the fears of parliament in 1906 when it provided protection against the *Taff Vale* doctrine of tort liability. It is in these injunction cases that the texts of labour law come to life. Only two years after the 1982 Act Lord Diplock ruled that the new Act made it easier for a judge to exercise his discretion and grant an injunction to an employer who had an arguable cause, because the case was now more likely to 'proceed to trial and final judgment where the defendant is the trade union itself and not a mere individual office-holder in it'.[77] So, in the 1980s the sweeping reductions of the immunities readmitted the tides of the common law and put the union, its property and its organisation increasingly at risk, a law based and judicially developed upon those very principles which saw unions as an improper restraint of trade in the market and industrial action as an unlawful interference with contracts and property rights, parallel to the Hayek formula. The exposure of union property to civil liability under that common law is the key which makes the machinery work. The interlocutory labour injunction is the oil that makes the engines hum smoothly.

V. Labour Law, Association and Freedom

The old common law doctrines fit the bill for the new philosophy precisely because they lean, once de-immunised, in favour of property and the 'individual' and against any combination of group action by individual workers. Whereas in 1980 it might have been possible to think of debating the new inroads upon immunity as questions of degree, a relative matter about 'where the limits of industrial action should be drawn',[78] now immunities are seen as 'privileges' *tout court* for the first time in consistent government policy since the First World War (for even Mr Baldwin rejected the employers' demands in 1927 to emasculate them). Now government asks not whether immunities are to be discarded, but whether any should be retained. 'Democracy' in unions is not concerned with balancing majority and minority rights; it is a field in which the 'individual' must (subject to his employment obligations) be made 'paramount', where the law must relieve him of consequences for breaking a contract precisely because the contract is one based on 'group loyalty'. Elsewhere, the special character of the employment contract and the special need and right of the worker to organise collectively, once acknowledged, is now increasingly rejected.

The same creed finds *all* regulation of conditions of work inherently bad (except, Hayek teaches, health and safety legislation – is it just coincidence that that was the only major area of employment law which the United Kingdom government would agree to being included explicity in the new majority-voting procedures of the Single European Act?). Regulation of terms and conditions, whether by statute or by collective bargaining, is an obstacle to market competition, a 'burden on business' (the phrases of Hayek and Lord Young differ only in their lucidity). It inhibits the 'spontaneous order' and, therefore, the good society – and, therefore, 'freedom' in the only meaning that is known or permitted. The pragmatic and positivist traditions are squeezed out because they were an 'error'. The restoration of employer prerogative and property rights is a necessary part of jettisoning legal and collective controls over labour – over young workers' hours, unfair wage stoppages, the union going-rate or minimum conditions for the sweated trades. Social security laws must be made into a bare subsistence minimum, and collective organisation by workers must be squeezed until it is lawful only in a narrower and narrower compass, confined within the enterprise, preferably in a friendly society role.

These are not propositions for pluralist debate. They are a closed system, a gospel or creed for those who cannot be expected to parley with the enemy within. If the necessary laws cannot all be passed at once, but only step-by-step, that has the advantages of allowing repetition of its phrases – 'trade union power' or 'privilege' – to sound self-evident with time and of inducing the proponents of different versions of the traditional analysis to think (as they have in self-delusion thought) that they are still able to engage in some version of the traditional debate. History shows how hard it is to reintroduce shared assumptions once they are driven off the agenda. While some kind of trade unions will no doubt continue to be permitted, their continuance provides a convenient enemy to be blamed for disasters in time of recurring inflation or renewed unemployment, their leaders (like George Orwell's Goldstein) 'commanders of a vast shadowy army', hate figures in official demonology. Each step, though, is intended to be as far as possible irreversible, eliminating any alternative, preventing the threat of even an inadvertent-slide-into-error that would, by definition, destroy the market order.

The face of the alternative philosophy is stamped on the new labour laws. Like Hayek, it propounds not *a* version of *a* free society, but *The* Version of *The* Free Society. The function of the state is to secure a model of 'spontaneous order', creating conditions for individuals to provide for their own needs in manners not known to authority,[79] but as individuals, never in effective groups (unless they are corporate capitalist groups). For any reader of Hayek, there is little here that is intellectually original. What is original today is the single-minded political application of the original revelation.

Hayek's Prolegomena and its Sequel

Indeed, it happens that some thirty years ago Hayek himself spelt out the immediate, first steps to be taken in order to abolish trade union 'coercion' of the market. They were: a. The end of all legal 'privileges' of unions and the strict application of all 'general rules of law'; b. a ban on 'picketing in numbers' and on all closed shop, preferential hiring or similar restraints of trade; c. an end to the legality of secondary strikes and boycotts; d. special laws to protect non-unionists ('to reinstate the principles of free association in the field of labour'); e. the rescission of 'all legal provisions which make contracts' negotiated with union representatives 'binding on all employees' in an enterprise. None of these prohibitions, he taught, would offend the doctrine of 'freedom of contract', because that freedom has limits, one of which is the 'general rule' of the common law banning contracts 'in restraint of trade'. Moreover, watch must be kept on the demand for further 'privileges' by employees 'such as security of tenure', which he believed they came to demand as of right by reference to the conditions of 'public servants'.

That was his programme propounded in Chicago in 1959 for the 'changes needed to restrain the harmful powers of the unions', so that the market could work, the primary steps necessary 'if a free society is to be preserved'.[80] Today the programme has a familiar look. It is an approximation of the agenda for the British legislation of 1980-88. But this was a first instalment. It may be expected that the programme in Britain also has further ambitions. Once we understand the nature of the philosophy, it is less fanciful to expect more and more legislative instalments. Moreover, under the Acts of 1980 to 1988 the Secretary of State can issue Codes to guide the courts. In 1988 the Engineering Employers Federation demanded a new Code to impose new, and unfair, procedures on unions in the ballots required for lawful industrial action, demands reflected in the draft *Code of Practice* published a few months later. Further experiments with such Codes, perhaps regulating union elections, nominations or candidatures for office, could accompany future Bills.

So too, the same logic would point in the direction of new controls over union activities, perhaps tightening the screw on union income derived from agreements with employers for a 'check off', or adding sanctions as teeth to 'restrictive practice' inquiries (after the experiment of the 1988 reference of media unions' practices under the Fair Trading Act 1973, s. 79). Or we may see new limitations upon unions' political funds, possibly the reimposition of 'contracting-in'; measures rendering the closed shop and union preference illegal *per se*; the abolition of immunities either for all workers or for specified groups. We might see measures to limit the right to hold ballots for industrial action in specified situations – thereby giving the government a partial solution to the elusive problem of strikes in 'essential services' – or measures following the precedent set for teachers by placing a ban upon collective bargaining in other recalcitrant parts of the public sector.

Such measures would once more be advanced in the name of 'protecting the individual' and, by 1992 when the 'single market' threatens more sharply the margins of British capital, of the need for 'flexibility' to meet competition. At the same time we can expect a social security net set tighter and a narrowing of the floor of workers' individual employment protection rights, with perhaps a few prizes for unions that concentrate on friendly society functions (possibly an increase in the traditional tax advantages for 'provident' benefit funds for unions that do not strike). The common law will continue to be comfortable with such a programme. Its vision fits hand in glove with that mixture of individualism and artificially enforced, spontaneous social order which has often characterised the dominant strain of philosophy propounded by English common lawyers, with the 'half-conscious belief', as Laski put it, that the 'Common law provides, so to say, a law behind the law which is enacted by parliament' – a secret umpire in place behind the bench to protect its version of the social equilibrium.[81]

It is not surprising that the judges' law of 'contract, tort and property' is perceived by the Hayek school as its umbilical link with the 'fundamental law' that is part of the spontaneous order.[82] Many – though not all – English lawyers have similarly long regarded trade unionism as itself a privilege, enjoyed on social and legal sufferance whatever parliament may have said. They were, it could be said in their defence, misled in their training by the peculiar form in which statute law enshrined in the 'immunities' of apparent privilege such freedom of association as British workers have ever had. But this long common law tradition, based on property, contract, individualism and the 'natural' social order, may perhaps be part of a socio-economic culture which has made England, in particular, the most fertile soil for the political expression of Hayek's philosophy – rather than Scotland and Wales where group loyalties are perhaps more strongly felt in all social classes. As for Western Europe across the Tunnel, there the deeper roots of statist corporatism have put the democracies of the Continent in the past at more immediate risk of a different authoritarian threat to pluralist democracy, the threat posed in the form of fascism. Today, the absence – as yet – of any Hayekite victory in the ideology governing those countries is the most important factor touching the future of the Community and of labour law within it.

There is now, therefore, a challenge to those who do not accept the new faith on law and the labour market, who continue to assert the value of free and effective association, affirming both the need for collective combination as a condition of freedom for employed individuals and the right to organise together in protection of their occupational interests and against exploitation in a pluralist democracy. If they hold that the concept of 'social justice' is not wholly meaningless, they will also refuse to accept that the limitations on human knowledge, real though they undoubtedly are, preclude all possibility of managing a free society in the general interest. Yet, thrown into confusion by the newly dominant philosophy, they have found that their old arguments will not do: the chosen citations from Donovan, carefully assembled statistics or analyses of countervailing power, national and multinational – all have lost their magic. At times this was because they overlooked their need for positive state intervention to protect freedom of association and minimum standards in the labour market. But more generally, they have failed to identify the new analysis for what it *is* and have acted as if the terms of the debate had not changed.

It is here that a perspective on Hayek may assist. But there is still the uncomfortable question: what are they to do? Some refuse to argue with zealots about faith. (Will they then take to the hills and surrender the field of democratic debate?) Others claim that, given the success of the new creed, one must be realistic and adopt its language and grammar as one's own. (Have they calculated that the adoption of Hayekite syllogisms produces Hayekite conclusions?) The traditional analysis had within it – as does Hayek's system – statements of value. Many who were drawn to it affirmed that men and women are not bounded merely by perpetual priority for individual greed and acquisition, that group loyalties do have their own validity and that an adult democracy does allow for choice beyond the market. For labour law this must inevitably mean – like it or not – in conventional terms an era of more intense politicisation. Assumptions are no longer freely shared. The game has been moved off the old board and no player can have his bid heard, let alone recapture the lead, who is shy about casting his principles to 'stand the hazard of the die'.

The philosophy of Hayek and its importance for the new labour law has gone too long unemphasised, especially by those of us whose first task is to analyse and explain the legislation. It does not explain everything, but it illuminates much. What is more, its relevance to legal policy makes doubly relevant the new critique of marginal economic theory which reintroduces social and industrial relations as crucial factors in theories of productivity and wage determination.[83] If that critique is right, when wages and the economy refuse to behave according to the truths of the market philosophy we can expect the legal machineries of the state to be called upon increasingly by government to intervene in face of what it must perceive as erroneous distortions. In such developments the perils for autonomous trade unionism can only increase. But there is, too, a parallel danger that under the sway of that philosophy a generation could arise in schools, colleges and universities (where the state intervenes with curricula and guidance to guard against inadvertent slippage into 'error') which knows of few employment laws except those that protect property and the market, whose members are each intent upon individual acquisition, obedient to the spontaneous order, part of no group other than an age 'club' entered in school or in 'national service', with little or no knowledge of the dignity that informs collective mutual endeavour in the free association of men and women in society and at work. Were such a day to dawn, the events at GCHQ would come rightly to be perceived as a milestone, a turning point in 1984 along a path that rendered 'freedom of association' meaningless. It is fitting then that GCHQ should be annually remembered.

Notes

1. On public servants in labour law see, G. Camerlynck, G. Lyon-Caen, J. Pelissier, *Droit du Travail* (13th ed., 1986) pp. 976 *et seq.*; G. Ghezzi and U. Romagnoli, *Il diritto sindacale* (2nd ed., 1987) pp. 190, 291 *et seq.*; W. Däubler *Arbeitskampfrecht* (2nd ed., 1987) pp. 466 *et seq.*; Folke Schmidt, *Law and Industrial Relations in Sweden* (1977) pp. 97, 178 *et seq.*; B. Hepple, Chap. VII in Wedderburn and W.T. Murphy (eds.), *Labour Law and the Community* (1982); H. Edwards, R. Clarke, C. Craver, *Labor Relations in the Public Sector* (1979, on 'sovereignty' pp. 23-43); T. Schooley (1987) Ind.Rels. Law Jo. 283 (public sector right to strike in the United States); B. Hepple and P. O'Higgins, *Public Employee Trade Unionism in the UK, The Legal Background* (1971); Wedderburn, Chap. 6 in B. Aaron and Wedderburn (eds.), *Industrial Conflict; A Comparative Legal Survey* (1972); G. Morris, *Strikes in Essential Services* (1986); H. Hughes 'The Settlement of Disputes in the Public Service' (1968) Pub. Admin. 45.
2. *Council of Civil Service Unions* v. *Minister for the Civil Service* [1985] ICR 14, 21 (HL); and Lord Roskill, pp. 46-7. On the dispute see Gillian Morris [1985] *Public Law* 177; on the ILO and GCHQ (Case 1261), see Susan Corby (1986) 15 ILJ 161; on the European Human Rights Commission's rejection of a TUC complaint: S. Fredman and G. Morris (1988) 17 ILJ 105. The ILO Committee of Experts has maintained pressure on the U.K. government to 'take action to enable the workers at GCHQ to enjoy the freedom of association in trade unions under [Convention 87]': *Report (III, 4A)*, 1988, 75th Sess., p. 180 [below p. 353].
3. B. Levin, 'Tucking in to the TUC', *Times*, 14 December 1987. See too, Philip Basset, 'Deunionisation Marches On', *Financial Times*, 25 January 1988: 'GCHQ

230   *Employment Rights in Britain and Europe*

is only one example of deunionisation.' Those giving up union membership at GCHQ were paid £1,000; one-day demonstrations did nothing to deter the government from transferring some dissenting civil servants and dismissing others: *Financial Times*, 12 October, and 7 and 8 November 1988.

4. Parl. Deb. HC 17 December 1979, col. 59.
5. *Times*, 22 April 1980.
6. Parl. Deb. HL 21 May 1979, col. 824
7. *Beyond Contract: Work, Power and Trust Relations* (1974), p. 191.
8. *Labour and the Law* (now 3rd ed. 1983, P. Davies and M. Freedland), p. 18. This individual contract is a 'command contract under the guise of an agreement': O. Kahn-Freund, 'Introduction' to K. Renner, *The Institutions of Private Law and their Functions* (1949), p. 28; cf. R. Lewis (1979) 8 ILJ 202.
9. P. Kahn, N. Lewis, R. Livock, P. Wiles, *Picketing; Industrial Disputes, Tactics and the Law* (1983), p. 214.
10. Parl. Deb. HC 8 February 1982, cols. 743-4.
11. On the reasons for this, see Wedderburn, *The Worker and the Law* (3rd ed. 1986), pp. 20-7.
12. Henry J., *Barretts and Baird Ltd* v. *Institution of Professional Civil Servants* [1987] IRLR 3, 8; cf. *Boxfoldia Ltd* v. *NGA* [1988] IRLR 383. An Italian employer may not dismiss or penalise workers for exercising their constitutional right to strike, whether or not union rules are broken, a ballot is held or notice is given: *Cort. Cass.* No. 6831, 8 August 1987.
13. Lord Templeman in *Miles* v. *Wakefield MDC* [1987] ICR 368, 391 (HL), who also said: 'Industrial action is largely a twentieth century development introduced with success by the Bermondsey matchworkers at about the turn of the century' (a somewhat idiosyncratic account of British labour history). The worker also receives no pay in systems where the contract is suspended.
14. *Hennessy* v. *Craigmyle Ltd* [1986] ICR 461, 468.
15. *Donovan Royal Commission Report* (Cmnd 3623, 1968) p. 233.
16. See *Stratford* v. *Lindley* [1965] AC 269 (HL); *Torquay Hotel Ltd* v. *Cousins* [1969] 2 Ch. 106 (CA); Wedderburn, *The Worker and the Law*, Chap. 8.
17. *Rookes* v. *Barnard* [1964] AC 1129 (HL).
18. *NWL* v. *Woods* [1979] ICR 867, 886.
19. *Duport Steels Ltd* v. *Sirs* [1980] ICR 161, 177.
20. Parl. Deb. HC, 10 March 1981, col. 756.
21. F.A. Hayek, *Law, Legislation and Liberty* (1979) – cited below as '*LLL*' – Vol. III, p. 144, and Vol. I, p. 142 (the 1906 Act 'conferred on the labour unions unique privileges').
22. F.A. Hayek, *The Constitution of Liberty* (1960) – cited below as '*COL*' – pp. 268–9.
23. F.A. Hayek, *1980s Unemployment and the Unions* (1980, IEA) p. 58 and p. 52 (emphasis supplied); see too his *A Tiger By the Tail* (2nd ed., 1972, IEA).
24. F.A. Hayek, 'Jobs: The Basic Truths We Have Cast Aside', *Times*, 7 August 1984. See too Hayek's earlier political tract (as he later called it) *The Road to Serfdom* (1944), answered by B. Wootton in *Freedom Under Planning* (1945). On Hayek's influence: J. Burton (ed.), *Hayek's Serfdom Revisited* (1984); N. Barry, *Hayek's Social and Economic Philosophy* (1979); E. Butler, *Hayek* (1983); and (after this paper was written) A. Gamble, *The Free Economy and the Strong State* (1988); below n. 49.
25. Hayek, *LLL*, Vol. III, pp. 82-3.
26. Hayek, *COL*, p. 124. He had earlier gone to the logical conclusion that a company should not be allowed to hold *voting* shares in another company because of the risks to entrepreneurial competition and to the interests of individual shareholders: see *Studies in Philosophy, Politics and Economics* (1967), Chap. 22, 'The Corporation in a Democratic Society', pp. 309-10, written in 1960. But this idea, which would make corporate groups much more difficult to handle and be

unacceptable equally to industrial and to finance capital, significantly finds no place in his later writing.

27. Hayek, *COL*, pp. 120-1, 300-3 ('socialism' would produce one big employer); and see the remarkable essay on 'Social Security', ibid., pp. 285-305, where the case for a free national health service is rejected ('The manner in which state medicine has been used in Russia as an instrument of industrial discipline gives us a foretaste of the uses to which such a system can be put': pp. 298-300).

28. Hayek, *LLL*, Vol. III, pp. 89-90, and p. 96.

29. Hayek, *LLL*, Vol. III, p. 96; *COL*, p. 268.

30. Hayek, *LLL*, Vol. III, p. 73, and Vol. I, p. 142.

31. Hayek, *COL*, p. 275, and *LLL*, Vol. III, pp. 86-7. He nowhere ventures into the changing economic and legal character of the restraint of trade doctrine between 1600 and the modern century; cf. G. Treitel, *Law of Contract* (7th ed., 1987), pp. 345-69.

32. Hayek, *COL*, p. 271.

33. Hayek, *LLL*, Vol. III, pp. 110-1.

34. Hayek, *COL*, p. 269.

35. Ibid., pp. 275-7. Francis Place believed unions would disappear if made lawful in 1824. S. and B. Webb believed the friendly society role was the one that would dwindle: *Industrial Democracy* (1902) Vol. II, p. 826. Lord Prior has joined those who think it will become primary: *Financial Times*, 9 November 1988.

36. Arthur Shenfield, *What Right to Strike?* (1986, IEA) p. 44. See too L. Neal and L. Bloch, *The Right to Strike in a Free Society* (1983, Centre for Policy Studies), on the need to militarise key posts in essential services.

37. W.H. Hutt, *The Theory of Collective Bargaining, 1930-1975* (1975, IEA), p. 119.

38. Sir John Hoskyns, Institute of Directors, *Times*, 13 February 1985; for total abolition of the immunities, see C. Hanson and G. Mather, *Striking Out Strikes* (1988, IEA) (all employment relations should be individualised; and strike ballots should be abandoned because they confer a 'spurious legitimacy' on strikes); and R. Tur Chap. XVI in Wedderburn and W.T. Murphy, *Labour Law and the Community* (1983) advocating 'life without immunities' for unions.

39. See B. Hepple (ed.), *The Making of Labour Law in Europe* (1986); B. Aaron and K. Wedderburn (eds.), *Industrial Conflict, A Comparative Legal Survey* (1972).

40. *Springhead Spinning Co* v. *Riley* [1868] LR 5 Eq. 551, 558.

41. Respectively *R.* v. *Bunn* (1872) 12 Cox 316, and *Hornby* v. *Close* [1867] 2 QB 153.

42. See Lord Diplock, *Dimbleby & Sons Ltd* v. *NUJ* [1984] 1 WLR 427, 435; and Hayek, 'The Corporation in a Democratic Society', n. 26 above, pp. 306-9.

43. Hayek, *LLL*, Vol. I, p. 89, pp. 119-20 (on judges and 'nomos'), and generally Chaps. 3-5.

44. Hayek, *Studies in Philosophy, Politics and Economics* (1967) p. 165, *LLL*, Vol. I, p. 121. Hayek coined his own word, 'catallaxy' to designate that 'special kind of spontaneous order produced by the market through people acting within the rules of the law of property, tort and contract', *LLL*. Vol. II, p. 109, which was fundamental to his thinking. See too his *The Confusion of Language in Political Thought* (1968), pp. 28–31. Compare C. Veljanovski in W. Twining (ed.), *Legal Theory and Common Law* (1986), p. 223. On judges, *LLL*, Vol. I, pp. 112-21.

45. Hayek, *LLL*, Vol. I, pp. 11-19, Vol. II, p. 96, and Vol. III, pp. 92, 95-6, 170. On 'altruism' see his 'Science and Revolution' in *Knowledge, Evolution and Society* (1983, Adam Smith Institute), p. 31; and 'our inevitable ignorance' making planning forever impossible, ibid. pp. 19-20. On 'justice' see *LLL*. Vol. II. Chaps. 8, 9; and his impassioned onslaughts upon 'social justice': *LLL*, Vols. II, pp. 65-98, and III, pp. 75-7, 90-7, 170-4, and *COL*, Chap. 2. The 'just law' is inexorably linked to the market, and without an 'insight into what the scoffers still deride as the

"invisible hand" the function of rules of just conduct is indeed unintelligible, and lawyers rarely possess it': *LLL*, Vol. I, p. 114.

46. Respectively Hayek, *LLL*, Vol. III, pp. 174-6, p. 50 and pp. 93-6; *Knowledge, Evolution and Society* (1983) p. 54; so too, p. 55; and *The Fatal Conceit* (1988). On the crucial concept of 'spontaneous order' and its questionable legal application, see *LLL*, Vol. III, Chaps 1-5. Hayek himself presents his epistemology, sociology, morality, 'just' law and political economy as one inevitable, unified system. For a good example, see *The Counter-Revolution of Science* (1959 ed.), p. 9 integrating Part 1, 'Scientism and the Study of Society' (because no centralised authority can ever *know* about all needs and resources, some 'mechanism' is required to utilise them, 'precisely the function which the various "markets" perform', pp. 176-7) and Part II, 'The Counter-Revolution of Science'.

47. See Hayek, *LLL*, Vol. III, pp. 112-26, 137-44, and 151.

48. *Financial Times*, 19 November 1986, and *Observer*, 27 December 1987. For early publications of the school, see for example: K. Joseph, *Solving the Union Problem is the Key to Britain's Recovery* (Centre for Policy Studies, 1974); K. Joseph and J. Sumption *Equality* (1976); the policy plan of N. Ridley, *Economist*, 27 May 1978; *The Omega File* (Adam Smith Institute, 1985, collection of earlier Omega reports).

49. That debate is of course relevant to the present enquiry, but cannot be adequately pursued here. See n. 24 above, and R. Levitas (ed.), *The Ideology of the New Right* (1986), especially A. Gamble, Chap. 1 'The Political Economy of Freedom'; N. Bosanquet, *After the New Right* (1985); and S. Hall and M. Jacques (eds.), *The Politics of Thatcherism* (1983); and now A. Gamble, *The Free Economy and the Strong State* (1988); R. Skidelsky (ed.), *Thatcherism* (1988). On the 'Rule of Law', see J. Griffith, *The Politics of the Judiciary* (3rd ed., 1985), Chap. 12; I. Harden and N. Lewis, *The Noble Lie: The British Constitution and the Rule of Law* (1986); R. Miliband, 'Activism and Capitalist Democracy', Chap. 2 in C. Harlow (ed.), *Public Law and Politics* (1986); J. Jowell and D. Oliver (eds.), *The Changing Constitution* (1986); and now K. Ewing, Chap. 8 in C. Graham and T. Prosser (eds.), *Waiving the Rules; The Constitution Under Thatcherism* (1988).

50. See ILO Convention No. 87, 1948, and for detailed references to these paragraphs, Wedderburn, 'Freedom of Association or Right to Organise?' (1987) 18 Ind. Rels. Jo. 244. On the European Convention on Human Rights, see M. Forde (1983) 31 America Jo. Comp. Law 301. For Sweden, see Joint Regulation of Working Life Act 1976, Art. 7.

51. *Collymore* v. *Att.-Gen. Trinidad* [1970] AC 538 (PC); *Re Public Service Employee Relations Act* [1987] 1 SCR 313; *Public Service Alliance of Canada* v. *R.*, ibid. 424; *Retail Wholesale & Dept. Store Union* v. *Govt. of Saskatchewan*, ibid. 460 (Sup.Ct.); T. Christian and K. Ewing (1988) 17 ILJ 73.

52. See Wedderburn, op.cit. (1987) 18 Ind. Rels. Jo. 247. The European Social Charter, 1961, does guarantee rights to bargain and to strike (Arts. 5 and 6) but is not within the jurisdiction of the Strasbourg court. On the Convention and the right to dissociate: *Young James and Webster* v. *UK* [1981] IRLR 408: Wedderburn, *The Worker and the Law*, pp. 362-81.

53. See Employment Act 1980, s. 19; Wages Act 1986, Part II; *Employment Gazette* 1987, p. 213; ILO Conventions No. 26 and No. 94; Earl Gowrie, Parl. Deb. HL, 20 May 1980, col. 902; Local Government Act 1988, ss. 17-20; and generally, Wedderburn, *The Worker and the Law*, Chap. 1.

54. Pay and Conditions of Teachers Act 1987, and *Teachers Pay and Conditions* (Cm. 238, 1987, p. 34); S. Fredman and G. Morris (1987) 16 ILJ 10 and 215; ILO Committee of Experts, *Report III (4A) 1988*, 75th Sess., p. 212.

55. On the Telecommunications Act 1984, as a possible model for essential services: Hazel Carty (1984) 13 ILJ 165; on nurses, *Times*, 28 July 1983, and *Financial Times*, 17 November 1988. See generally, Gillian Morris *Strikes in Essential Services* (1986); and see, Education Reform Act 1988, s. 222; Coal Industry Act 1987.

56. Employment Act 1980, s. 19.

57. D. Smith, Chairman ACAS, *Financial Times*, 23 October 1987; ACAS *Report 1986*, pp. 26-7, and *Report 1987*, p. 17; Professor Sir John Wood, CAC, and R. Price, CBI, *Financial Times*, 28 and 29 October 1988.

58. TUC, *Bargaining in Privatised Companies, 1986*; *Financial Times*, 22 December 1987 (National Freight Corpn).

59. See *Financial Times*, 19 February, 19 March, 4 and 24 April, 26 and 28 May, 16, 20 and 29 June, 13 and 22 August, 3 September, 22 October, 17 December 1987 (Heinemann, Octopus Publishing, Scottish Agriculture Industries, Docklands Light Railway, Nelson-Burgess, Tioxide, Norfolk Capital and Stakis Hotels, Coca-Cola, Schweppes, Midland Montague and Barclays BZW).

60. B. Towers, 'Derecognising Trade Unions' (1988) 19 Ind. Rels. Jo. 181; see P. Beaumont (1987) 25 BJIR 323; A. Sproull and J. McInnes, ibid., 335; L. Cairns 'New Towns Unionisation' *Financial Times*, 23 April 1987; P. Beaumont, *The Decline of Trade Union Organisation* (1987); ACAS *Annual Report 1986*, p. 12. But compare J. McInnes, *Employee Relations in Large Manufacturing Plants in Scottish New Towns* (1987).

61. Especially Acts 903/1977 and 273/1984; see T. Treu, 'Recent Developments of Italian Labour Law' (1985) 10 *Labour and Society* 27; S. Sciarra and Wedderburn, Chap. 6 in A. Pizzorusso *Law in the Making* (1988); and the useful annotation to *Nitti c. Veterie Meridionali, Foro it.* (1986), I p. 2676 in (1988) 6 Int. Lab. L.R. 15. On part-time and the Italian Law 863/1984; F. Carinci, R. de Luca Tamajo, P. Tosi, T. Treu, *Il diritto sindacale* (1987, 2nd ed.) pp. 162-4. On the German Act of 1985, M. Weiss, *Labour Law and Industrial Relations in the Federal Republic of Germany* (1987) pp. 46-50. On France, J. Savatier, 'Le travail à temps partiel', Dr. Soc. 1988, 438; J. Pélissier, 'Le travail intermittent', Dr. Soc. 1987, 93.

62. Sex Discrimination Act 1986, s. 7; *Restrictions on Employment of Young People and Removal of Sex Discrimination* (Consultative Document, 1987, DE) and *Releasing Enterprise* (Cm. 512, 1988) paras 7.5.1 *et seq.*; Employment Bill 1989, Chaps. 7 (women) and 8 (young workers). For denunciation of ILO Convention 45 (women's underground work), see Parl. Deb. HC, 26 May 1988, Written Answers, col. 314. For a different style when Sweden denounced this Convention, see N. Valticos, *International Labour Law* (1979), p. 175 (need to maintain satisfactory conditions for women workers).

63. See *BIFU* v. *Barclays Bank* [1987] ICR 495, 503. On the Single European Act, see Art. 100A of the amended Treaty. For the 'Task Force', see *Encouraging Enterprise* (1987) Chap. 3; *Releasing Enterprise* (Cm. 512, 1988) paras 1.8 *et seq*.

64. Employment Act 1988, s. 26. The Training Commission created by Part II of this Act out of the Manpower Services Commission, but with a minority of union representatives instead of tripartite parity, was wound up in September 1988 after the TUC Congress resolved to oppose the new Employment Training scheme. Its final dissolution is provided for in the Employment Bill 1989.

65. See for example, W. Daniel and E. Stilgoe, *The Impact of Employment Laws* (1978); R. Clifton and C. Tatton-Brown, *Impact on Small Firms, etc.* (1979, DE); S. Evans, J. Goodman and L. Hargreaves, *Unfair Dismissal Law* (1985, DE); and the remarkable series of government papers on deregulation: *Employment* (Cmnd 9474, 1985); *Lifting the Burden* (Cmnd 9571, 1985); *Burdens on Business* (1985); *Building Businesses, Not Barriers* (Cmnd 9794, 1986); *Encouraging Enterprise* (1987), Chap. 3; *Releasing Enterprise* (Cm. 512, 1988). On the closed shop, see S. Dunn, J. Gennard, *The Closed Shop in British industry* (1984).

66. N. Tebbit, Secretary of State for Employment: Parl. Deb. HC, 8 February 1982, col. 742.

67. For these arguments: Hayek in, respectively, *LLL*, Vol. III, pp. 151-2, and *COL*, p. 447.

68. N. Fowler, Secretary of State for Employment, Employment Bill Standing Committee F, Parl. Deb. HC, 1 December 1987, cols. 203 and 208. On the Employment Act 1988, Part I, see E. McKendrick (1988) 17 ILJ 141; J. Bowers

and S. Auerbach, *A Guide to the Employment Act 1988* (1988).

69. Mr Nicholls, Parliamentary Under-Secretary for Employment, Employment Bill, Standing Committee F, Parl. Deb. HC, 8 December 1987, col. 274.

70. In J. Goldthorpe (ed.), *Order and Conflict in Contemporary Capitalism* (1984), p. 338, citing A. Pizzorno in C. Crouch and A. Pizzorno (eds.), *The Resurgence of Class Conflict in Western Europe since 1968* (1978).

71. Employment Acts 1980, ss. 16, 17 and 1982, ss., 14 and 18. The 'gateways' to legality for secondary action in s. 17(3) and (4) of the 1980 Act, much relied upon by Mr Prior at the time, were soon proved to be of little or no value: see *Dimbleby and Sons Ltd* v. *NUJ* [1984] 1 WLR 427; *Merkur Island Shipping Corpn* v. *Laughton* [1983] 2 AC 570 (HL). See too, s. 9 of the 1982 Act, amending Employment Protection (Consolidation) Act 1978, s. 62, which increased the risk of a striker being dismissed by confining the group to be considered to those currently on strike at his establishment: see P. Wallington (1983) 46 MLR 310.

72. See Wedderburn, *The Worker and the Law*, pp. 684-705; *Mercury Communications Ltd* v. *Scott Garner* [1984] Ch. 37 (CA); *Dimbleby and Sons Ltd* v. *NUJ* [1984] 1 WLR 427, HL; and above n. 19. On the evasion of s. 17(1) of the Trade Union and Labour Relations Act 1974, which tried to curbe *ex parte* injunctions in trade disputes, see *Barretts & Baird Ltd* v. *IPCS* [1987] IRLR 3, and B. Simpson (1987) 50 MLR 506.

73. Inns of Court Conservative Society, *A Giant's Strength* (1958), p. 26.

74. Employment Act 1982, ss. 15, 16; provident funds and political funds unavailable to finance industrial action are protected: s. 17. The Act also introduces a special code of vicarious liability for unions: s. 15(3)-(7).

75. *Trade Union Immunities* (Cmnd 8128, 1981), p. 36; and see *Democracy in Trade Unions* (Cmnd 8778, 1983) pp. 14-15; Wedderburn, *The Worker and the Law*, pp. 56 *et seq.*, 77 *et seq.* and 530-40. For fines on officials, see *Kent Free Press* v. *NGA* [1987] IRLR 267.

76. *The Due Process of Law* (1980), p. 39.

77. *Dimbleby & Sons* v. *NUJ* [1984] 1 WLR 427, 432, reconsidering his earlier statements about the 'realities' of labour injunctions in *NWL* v. *Woods* [1979] 1 WLR 1794, 1305. On the attempt by Parliament to intervene in contested injunction cases, in s. 17(2) of TULRA, see Wedderburn, *The Worker and the Law*, pp. 687-93.

78. Trade Union Immunities (Cmnd 8128, 1981), p. 92.

79. See Hayek, *LLL*, Vol. II, pp. 36, 38 and Vol. III, Chap. 5.

80. Hayek in *COL*, pp. 277-9, and p. 123. 'Yet the situation is not hopeless,' he added. 'The present position of the unions cannot last; for they can function only in a market economy which they are doing their best to destroy.' All that was needed was 'a return to the principles of the rule of law' and a 'change of economic policy' away from the 'thicket of arbitrary controls'. To preserve 'a free society', there must be 'strict prevention of all coercion': pp. 279, 283-4.

81. H.J. Laski, *Trade Unions in the New Society* (1950), p. 126. Lawyers have a 'nostalgia' for the law before the 1906 Act. '[The] attitude of our courts in trade union cases is ... unintelligible except as the expression of a mental climate which has never freed itself from the belief that trade unions are organisations threatening the equilibrium of a society built upon the principle that the means of production must remain in private hands': H.J. Laski, *The State in Theory and Practice* (1954), p. 174. On the courts, see too especially J.A.G. Griffith, *The Politics of the Judiciary* (3rd ed., 1985). On the relationship of the common law to the law of labour relations, see Wedderburn (1987) 16 ILJ 1; and see M. Vranken, 'Specialisation and Labour Courts' (1988) 9 Comp. Lab. LJ 497.

82. P. Johnson, *The Recovery of Freedom* (1980), p. 183; and see the uncompromising demand to return to the 'ordinary law of contract and tort in industrial relations' in C. Hanson and G. Mather, *Striking Out Strikes* (1988, IEA). Hayek's own regard for common law judges reaches back to 1623 when, he noted with

approval, they declared 'monopoly' to be 'against the common law and the liberty of the subject', *COL*, pp. 167-8.

83. For a stimulating review, see W. Brown and P. Nolan, 'Wages and Labour Productivity: The Contribution of Industrial Relations Research to Understanding Pay Determination' (1988) 26 BJIR 339 and P. Nolan and P. Marginson, *Skating on Thin Ice? David Metcalfe on Trade Unions and Productivity* (1988, Warwick Paper in Industrial Relations No. 22).

9

The Italian Workers' Statute: British Reflections on a High Point of Legal Protection

'In the post-war era,' it was claimed by an Italian authority in 1979, 'a transnational labour law scholarship has arisen on the same level as that in comparative civil or comparative constitutional law.'[1] It was a bold claim. Comparative civil law or commercial law often finds familiar institutions in neighbouring industrial societies – limited liability, for example – whereas labour law, rather like family law, penetrates into, and depends upon, deeper and more delicate social roots. The comparative method has been, until recently, more limited in Britain than in some other countries, though it is now accepted as a way, not of importing solutions – few are foolish enough to try that – but of extending our agenda and our horizons. At a time of possible change in labour law in Britain and in the Community, it may be useful to cast an eye comparatively on the Italian *Statuto dei lavoratori* (the 'Workers' Statute') of 1970, first for the rich material it contains and, secondly, as a way of reassessing British experience in the second half of the 1970s and, through that, prospects for the 1990s.[2]

In the very first proposals of 1969 introducing the original Italian Bill to protect 'workers' freedom and dignity, trade union freedom, and freedom of action in the workplace', a reference is found to

the tendency in all countries for labour law to reach a higher level of development. We need think only ... of the report presented to the British government by the Donovan Commission, and the new

A revised version of a paper to the conference celebrating 20 years of the 'Workers' Statute', *Lo Statuto dei lavoratori e l'Europa*, 17-20 May 1990, at the Faculty of Law and Department of Private Law in the University of Palermo. Revisions have increased the Italian, and decreased British material. First published in (1990) 19 Industrial Law Journal 154.

recognition of trade union status in last December's proposals by the French government.[3]

Comparative labour law had by then not travelled so far in England. Except for a reference to the French *Conseils de Prud'hommes*, the Donovan Royal Commission Report itself had little transnational or comparative content, notwithstanding the inclusion of Kahn-Freund himself among its members. Nor did ministers' speeches proposing British employment laws of the 1970s include allusions to European experience; and none have done so in the 1980s, except for momentary uses of comparative references marred by infelicity.[4]

In fact, we now see that, although broad parallels in the labour law developments of the last two decades can be found in Western Europe and that in some senses the 1970s were in all those countries the 'decade of the unions',[5] there was no equivalent ambition in all of their labour law systems to advance to levels uniformly 'higher'. The developments in Britain after the Donovan Report of 1968 and in Italy with the *Statuto* of 1970 may be useful points of departure for a tentative contribution to comparison. In general terms, they expressed comparable ambitions in respect of employment protection for workers and rights for trade unions. But how far were these ambitions made concrete in laws sufficiently adapted to stick and to last in the national conditions? How far were their differences attributable to different union structures (ideological pluralism in Italy and 'unitary' multi-unionism in Britain)? And what was their legacy in the 1980s? How far does a comparison between these two very different systems offer a line of inquiry – answers are too much to hope for – on the place of labour law in the 1990s, especially after the European Community's 'Social Charter' of December 1989 which, despite the 'abstention' of Britain from its signatories, is bound to be, along with the more limited 'Action Programme' of the Commission, a declaration of profound importance for the Community.[6]

The Italian Statuto *and British Laws of the 1970s*

An initial difficulty besets the attempt at such a comparison. In Italy, the policies of labour law over the last two decades appear, at least to the visitor, to have a homogeneous history, a consistent series of periods. They were, one of their architects has said, constructed by way of 'alluvial deposits'.[7] In contrast, British policy after 1970 took the path of three zig-zags: the direction of 1971-74, when the Conservative government's Industrial Relations Act attempted to institute a more regulated legal structure, though on a recognisably traditional base; then 1974-79, when a Labour administration returned to traditional 'abstentionism', but with added promotional elements and a floor of individual guarantees; and lastly, the Thatcher administration after 1979, which has pursued twin methods to 'set the market free' (a logical expression of the neo-liberal philosophy which owes so much to Hayek),[8] with, in the Italian sense, 'pure' deregulation of workers' employment protection guarantees along with progressive de-collectivisation of the labour market, in particular by sharp reductions in trade union liberties and the removal of minimum labour standards.

It is in the second period, 1974-79, that we might expect initially to compare the philosophy of the *Statuto* with British law, especially the Employment Protection Act 1975, not least because both periods of legislation avowedly sought to be 'promotional', to encourage unions and collective bargaining. In doing so, it is useful to adopt the device of distinguishing 'individual' from 'collective' law, though only for schematic purposes, for Italian authors are ever quick to point out that 'reality is different in the sense that rights that are individual (starting with the [Italian] right to strike) are destined to operate, that is to be made effective, in a collective dimension.'[9] But in both of the national legislations there can be found an intention to introduce, on the one hand, new employment rights for individual workers, with a union presence in their enforcement and, on the other, interventions to promote and to support trade union organisation in the workplace, and thereby collective bargaining.

Individual Employment Rights

If the British legislation of 1974 to 1978 is comparable at the individual level, it is at once seen to be weaker. For the first time in Britain it was affirmed that the small steps taken earlier, in the 1960s, should lead to the worker's receiving protections touching the very foundations of the employment relationship to which the 'contract of employment' must give way, though we can now see that 'contract' continued to control the plot from below as effectively as old Hamlet's ghost.[10] The legislature confirmed and reinforced provisions introduced in the previous decade concerning dismissal, especially the right to payments in a 'redundancy' (that untranslatable term of art now central to English law) and rights against 'unfair dismissal'. But, for reasons which are still not wholly clear, 'qualifying periods' requiring continuous employment with one employer were, with a few exceptions, retained as a condition of the worker enjoying these rights. For 'unfair dismissal' the six months period, increased to two years in 1985 by the new legislation as part of its 'deregulation' of the market, became a crucial factor, not least for 'atypical' workers. In Italy attention has concentrated on a different kind of threshold, the numerical test on the size of the workforce (Art. 35).

Rights of maternity leave with pay for women workers accompanied legislation to enforce equal pay for men and women (on 'like' work) – Community law later compelled a change to work of 'equal value' in amendments which appear to be more effective than the Italian constitutional provisions supplemented by the laws of 1977 and of 1984[11] – and to a ban on employment discrimination on grounds of sex and of race. In Italy the *Statuto*, oddly, did not go this far. It banned discrimination against workers on grounds of union membership or activity or participation in strikes and on religious or political grounds (Art. 15). But it did not add to the general constitutional ban on sex discrimination; grounds of race, language and sex were added to Article 15 only in 1977. British law also protected, for the first time, rights to 'reasonable' time off work for public duties (so too, the wider Arts. 31 and 32 of the *Statuto*) and for trade union activity (paid in the case of a shop steward) again mirrored in the strong provisions of Articles 23 and 24.

In 1975, with the same philosophy, the Employment Protection Act aimed to protect against dismissal or discipline by reason of activity for an independent trade union at work, provided it was carried on outside working hours. In contrast to the Italian approach, this did *not* include strike or other industrial action (see Arts. 14, 15, 16). For Italian law, the strike is an individual right, exercised collectively, and therefore at the very core of 'trade union activity'. But British law tried to use the individual right to bolster collective organisation; dismissal for trade union activity therefore afforded a remedy even if the worker had no qualifying period of employment. These elementary provisions illustrate the divergent bases on which the British law and the *Statuto* built. In Britain the classical foundation of 'freedom of contract' was barely disturbed; the 1975 legislative additions were a small annexe to the common law edifice of employment relationships, whereas the *Statuto* constituted, in individual terms, it has been said 'a primitive version of a Charter of *habeas corpus* for the worker' (citing Arts. 2, 3, 4, 5, 6, 8, 9, 14 and 15) while in other provisions 'it introduced more specifically a nucleus of modification inside the normative structure of the individual employment relationship itself' (Arts. 13, 18).[12] The amendment of the Civil Code concerning a worker's right to the 'job' for which he was hired, and to higher tasks (and pay) under certain conditions, went to the core of employment law. So too did the legislative control of disciplinary procedures (Art. 7).

It is perhaps useful for those who believe that Britain has suffered from extreme over-protection of workers' rights to note how the horizons of the Italian legislation are altogether wider. No law in England introduced anything like Article 8 banning the employer from inquiries into a worker's opinions (on union affairs as much as on religion or politics) whether on recruitment or during the employment; 'a quite new principle in the area of legal rules protecting the private life of the worker'.[13] Nor was there anything as bold as protection from security guards, from audio-visual monitoring, and in medical examinations (Arts. 2, 4, 5). Whereas the *Statuto* spoke of protection of the humanity and dignity of the subordinate worker, the British legislature protected a floor of rights for someone who was perceived as essentially a subordinate, not perhaps a commodity, but not a person whose dignity it was the job of legislation to safeguard, and there was no British constitution to make it think differently (proposals for the *Statuto* were anchored in the constitution of 1948: see Art. 1). On the other hand, the British wisdom of the time was wont to suggest that legislative control of, for example, disciplinary procedures might evince a lack of confidence in the ability of unions and collective bargaining to control abuses. Even so, from the outset it was clear that the provisions on dismissal in Britain lacked adequate remedies, without which no 'right' is worth the time of the legislature. As is now well known, the reinstatement of the worker 'unfairly dismissed', although intended to be a primary remedy, is ineffective; the number of workers who obtain reinstatement (even through conciliation) has been small and the rest have to be content with modest compensation (in 1988-89 the median award was £1,732). Contrast Article 18, where the minimum is five months' pay, a failure to carry out an order of reinstatement leads to pay for every day of default and, if he is a union official, the employer may have to pay additional sums to the national retirement fund.[14]

In the *Statuto* Article 18 built on the base of the law of 1966 which first introduced a modern law on 'unfair dismissal' (itself enacted on the basis of an agreed national, collective accord – a contrast with Britain where the dominant pressure leading to legislation in the period preceding 1970-71 was not that of employers and unions, but of the civil service).[15] The effectiveness of reinstatement orders in Italy seems to be much higher than in Britain, more so in the North and in medium and larger enterprises; but, perhaps more significant, it appears that some three-quarters of the effective reinstatement orders result in a continuation of the employment relationship for more than one year.[16]

Workers' Union Rights at Work

Similarly, the British law on 'interim' orders, to maintain employment of workers illegally dismissed by reason of trade union activity, has been relatively ineffective, partly because of the difficulty of proving that the dismissal of the worker is likely to have been caused by any 'trade union activities'. Such a provision is light years away from the regime whereby the employer is subject to severe penalties for any act which constitutes *condotta antisindicale* in Article 28 (anti-union acts), where even penal penalties may result. The *Statuto* understood that only effective remedies give life to the bones of substantive principle.

Article 28 is one of the most remarkable provisions in modern European labour law. The extent of protection for workers and unions and (as modified by the law No. 847, 8 November, 1977, and in the context of the reformed procedures of law No. 533, 11 August 1973, giving a special 'labour jurisdiction' to the local judge (*Pretore*))[17] the availability of the legal process to the local trade union, are striking features of the 1970 law. It was enacted to 'guarantee the effective enjoyment of trade union rights and, more generally, to protect from all attacks the union presence in the enterprise and to ensure respect for union freedom and activities'.[18] Italian labour jurisprudence is replete with case law evidencing the full ambit given by the courts for that purpose to Article 28.

As we move into this realm of union rights there is, therefore, less ground for comparison. Britain has no constitutional rights to organise in trade unions or to strike; in Italy, the Constitution guarantees the first in Article 39 and the second in Article 40. For British workers in trade unions liberties have for a century been expressed as 'immunities', granted by parliament to shield the union organisers against the major incidents of criminal and civil liability which would be otherwise imposed by judges under the 'common law'. To have asked the British legislature in 1974-75 to enact something like Article 28 would have been seen as the equivalent of asking it to build the Colosseum. Yet, if we can disengage ourselves from the authoritarian legislation of the 1980s, we must not forget that after 1976 the width of the immunities and the organisational strength of British unions made it arguable (and often led them to argue) that they needed no such protection as they enjoyed in practice 'liberties' permitting them to be at least as effective as trade union movements abroad with wider, positive 'rights'.

In Italy the law is couched in rights and judges so understand them. Indeed, the relative freedom from strict precedent has allowed these judges to scrap some of the limitations previously attached by interpretation to the constitutional rights. The best example of recent decades has been the repudiation in 1980 of a doctrine of 'unjust damage' or 'proportionality' (doctrines influenced by German juridical doctrines on strikes) previously employed as a limit on the right to strike. This notable decision of the appellate judges even rejected the need for any *a priori* definition of a 'strike' whatever, holding that the constitution meant it to be understood as used, and as developed dynamically, in 'everyday language'.[19] British union liberties were, in contrast, built largely as exceptions to the 'ordinary law of the land' (whose creative judges dynamically outflanked them from time to time) and most judges, perhaps most lawyers, still perceive them really to be so. That is the core of the case now often presented for 'positive' rights.

There is a further difficulty in making comparison. Such laws depend – above all in labour law – upon courts applying them in the spirit of the legislation (the British advocates of 'labour courts' have not yet addressed this issue); there is no guarantee that, faced with Italian rights, British courts would reach Italian solutions. The reforms in Italy did not stop, therefore, at substantive law. The process of the labour jurisdiction was radically transformed in 1973, especially by the construction of a more informal one-man 'labour court' in the guise of the local *Pretore* in a special 'labour jurisdiction' (no one seems to have argued there was need of a tripartite tribunal) with a quick, more informal, oral procedure; this reform is often referred to as an integral part of the success of the *Statuto* in action. Certainly it appears to be true that most courts have accepted it, above all the local *Pretori*, whose interim orders to enforce violations of Article 28 must be given within two days and normally rest undisturbed during appeals (the first appeal since 1977 goes back to the *Pretore*). This procedure gives all the advantages of 'interlocutory' surprise to the union or the worker plaintiff, not, as in Britain, to the employer.

The question of the relationship between bench and legislator touches not only the substantive law and the procedures of the court. It involves the nature of the 'judge'. The British judge is not, like the Italian, a career judge, though we do have career magistrates. He (more rarely she than in Italy) is appointed normally in middle-age after a successful career as a barrister (now sometimes a solicitor). In the higher civil courts, he and the barrister before him belong to the same club. Not so in most Continental countries. The Italian judge chooses a career on the bench when young, receiving his or her first appointment normally well before thirty years of age.[20] Few would dare to suggest that this produces a less independent judiciary, though British eyebrows tend to be raised at the tendency of the Italian judiciary to regard itself as part of society to the extent of forming associations, even trade unions (which in the national culture necessarily take on the colours of competing ideologies, as with the left-oriented '*Magistratura Democratica*').[21] The characteristics of national judges and their training are crucial to any comparison.

On the substantive law, examples of decisions on 'trade union activity' and some applications of Article 28, make plain the stark differences in the law, where the nature of the judicial traditions and structure are not irrelevant. A British worker who in 1978 was penalised for promoting a petition against unsafe conditions at the place of work after discussion in the local union branch was held to have undertaken activity insufficiently connected with the union to be a 'union activity'; so too, in 1983 workers dismissed by an employer because of his 'fury' at the demand of a union to be recognised at his factory were also not protected without a qualifying period because the reasons for the dismissals had no relevance to the workers' individual 'trade union activities'.[22] Such jurisprudence would be impossible under Article 28 (as well as other provisions of the *Statuto*, for example, Article 15). A threat by an Italian employer to his tobacconist managers that he might not renew their employment after a strike in 1981 resulted in severe penalties; an employer was held guilty by the final appeal court in 1982 for sending written rebukes to his employees on strike who, on the orders of the union, had taken the stamp out of the time-card clock; and, while there is no general duty to bargain so that mere refusal to bargain or 'recognise' does not fall within Article 28, an employer who chooses to bargain with non-union representatives is in breach (he could not, said the appeal judges in 1976, 'leap over the union representation', the *rappresentanza* present under Article 19 and deal with the workers directly).[23] This last case is of especial interest in industrial practice today when employers in Britain and elsewhere are excluding unions by developing 'direct' involvement of their employees in some sectors.[24]

Not everything, though, is plain sailing. In some decisions the courts have tended to require a subjective intention to injure union interests, a requirement vigorously rejected by the commentators who include with Article 28 all behaviour displaying 'opposition to a conflictual relationship' (as against 'opposition *in* conflict'),[25] and they have retained certain limitations on 'abnormal' strikes, such as rapid 'hiccup' strikes, where the test of legitimacy tends today to be whether this unusual exercise of the right to strike damages only production or damages the 'integrity' or 'productive capacity' of the enterprise, in which case an employer's conduct may be excused under Article 28, even to the extent of closing down the plant.[26] The majority view also appears to maintain the ban on the legitimacy of most forms of action short of a strike, where there is no 'cessation of work' (as in a work-to-rule).

What is of special interest comparatively is the tension which the legal history reveals between elements even in the Italian judiciary and unions and many commentators. The *Statuto* contains in Article 28 procedural rights for local union bodies to appear in court largely because the case law of the 1950s had rejected the right of unions to represent a grade of workers; and whereas the move away from restrictive definitions of a 'strike' in the decision of 1980 are widely welcomed, the new limits are equally criticised (in particular, the distinction between damage to 'production' and to 'productive capacity' which is said to be virtually meaningless).[27] One can find parallel tensions in France between, on the one hand, restrictive judicial interpretations of the right to strike and, on the other, critical unions and commentators.[28] Judges in capitalist societies appear, understandably perhaps, to have moments (which are hard to predict even in Britain – they do not necessarily coincide with party political developments) when their instinct is creatively to restrict strikes. But in France and Italy the issue is made more diffuse by the absence of a doctrine of strict precedent. Minority judges more easily maintain their fiercely independent critique even of new trends in appellate courts. And the spirit of the exchanges is manifestly different in quality from that which has infused the interventions by British judges in the pendulous oscillation between creativity and immunity since 1871 and, more lately, in narrow interpretations of workers' rights even in a period of deregulation. One does not in those countries find basic union rights 'sticking in the judicial gorges'.[29] It is this difference, not 'judicial creativity' *per se*, that suggests the need for further inquiry into the diverse character, careers and training of the judiciary and into the courts' traditions in different countries (for this is not a simple matter of personal 'judicial bias').

The Law and Collective Labour Relations

At first the two countries appear to be altogether beyond comparison when we come to industrial conflict and the 'right' to strike. In industrial action invariably the British worker *breaks* his contract of employment; in Italy the contract of the striker is suspended. In Britain a union or any other person may have protection against tortious liability for inducing the worker's breach of contract so long as he acts in furtherance of a 'trade dispute' within the statutory definition; the legislature in 1974-78 merely modernised these 'immunities' to match new civil liabilities which had been imposed by the courts in the 1960s.[30] In Italy the constitutional right to strike vests in each worker individually, though exercised collectively.[31] It is of course precisely this area of the British law which has received greatest attention from the new legislation of 1980-90; most 'immunities' have been sharply restricted, others repealed, and the definition of a licit 'trade dispute' has been sharply narrowed. In Italy, the limiting fact is the concept of 'strike' itself, encompassing all cessations of work, even if primary demands in an employment-related dispute are aimed at the public authorities, not the employer (very different from even the traditional British 'trade dispute').[32] Moreover, the employer in Britain can lawfully dismiss all his workers who are on strike, and the legislation proposed in 1990 gives him power to dismiss them individually and selectively, unless the union adopts the strike and holds the obligatory ballot – *if* it can do so in time (for it cannot escape liability itself where it endorses the action without a ballot; whereas by repudiating it, the union will *ipso facto* confirm the employer's power to dismiss). As we have seen, the employer who attempted to do this in Italy would be brought to book within a few days.

Although the rapid development of Italian collective bargaining in the decades after 1950 increasingly made possible meaningful comparisons with the older British industrial practice (on shop stewards, for example)[33] the combination of constitutional rights and the *Statuto* made direct comparison on the law of industrial conflict impossible. Articles 14, 15, 16 and 28, for example, build upon the sure foundation of Articles 39(1) (union freedom of organisation) and 40 (right to strike) of the Constitution; Article 28 intervenes to protect trade union activity *'dall' esterno'*, while the procedural reforms in the *'rito del lavoro'* (labour procedure) in 1973 created special, quick procedures available to unions and workers. It is not unimportant, when we return to the position in the Community, first to record the distance which divides these two systems of law in respect of workers' collective rights. We may also note that the Committee of Experts of the International Labour Organisation in April 1989 expressed the view that in six different ways British law fell, even before 1990, below the minima of the two basic Conventions, Nos. 87 and 98, on the right to freedom of association (which imports some right to strike) and the right to bargain.[34] Where Italian jurisprudence is now concerned with what seem to English eyes finer points of a right to strike, even marginal issues such as the legitimacy of articulated strikes affecting *'produttività'*, cases in the English courts – and especially actions by the employer or a third party to obtain interlocutory injunctions, which are more readily available in our courts than any other in Europe, and sanctioned by penalties more draconian[35] – still reflect uncertainty on an effective liberty to strike itself.

There may be, though, advantage in pursuing comparison, however difficult it is. For the British legislation (especially the Employment Protection Act 1975) had parallel aims to those of the *Statuto* in a purpose of *'legislazione di sostegno'* (legislation supportive of collective bargaining) which was widely shared in Europe at the time. Nor was all of it, on its face, weaker in formulation. Unions 'recognised' for bargaining by the employer, for example, had the right to demand disclosure from him of certain types of information necessary for collective bargaining (rights to information still rest generally in Italy on collective agreements), in addition to the rights of consultation on proposed 'redundancies' which the Community Directive 129/1975 demanded. There is perhaps a special irony in the fact that the British legislation demanding mere consultation satisfied the Directive, whereas the Italian laws, which envisaged an opportunity to bargain about the dismissals themselves, did not and were, to the annoyance of many Italian writers, rejected by the European Court of Justice as insufficient to implement the Directive.[36]

But the face of legislation can deceive. For example, the right to information for the recognised British union never went further than the subjects on which the employer was already bargaining (and he can today always adjust the ambit) and the employer's obligation to consult about proposed redundancies imposes no substantial limit on his freedom to reduce the workforce by dismissal. What is more, Britain has never enjoyed any general legal obligation on the employer to 'recognise' a union for bargaining. It is true, of course, that by the 1970s both in Italy and in Britain the process of bargaining was well rooted in a 'voluntary' system and that in the past this would have been regarded, in Britain as in many other countries, as sufficient.[37] But as though to anticipate the difficulties of a future decade (when the problem of 'non-recognition' – often partial derecognition – is gradually becoming more insistent)[38] the British legislation of 1975 here accelerated in the fast lane past the *Statuto*, which after long debate had chosen to introduce neither a general right to information nor a duty to bargain.[39]

When we search for norms which are 'promotional' or 'supportive', the *Statuto* is usually the stronger. In the British laws there is nothing approaching the 'r.s.a.' (*rappresentanza sindacale aziendale*) of Article 19, giving a unionised group the right to operate in the enterprise within the 'ambit' of a 'representative' union after the workers have taken the 'initiative' to constitute it (a concept badly served by the official translation 'works union'; the English equivalent should perhaps be 'a unionised presence in the workplace'). Nor are there any equivalent workers' rights of "assembly" (Art. 20), referendum (Art. 21) or *proselitismo* (Art. 26, an individual right to canvass for the union and to collect subscriptions), let alone the limitation on the employer's prerogative to transfer officials to other workplaces (Art. 22), which British employers would have resisted implacably, or the rights of joint regulation on a range of matters (*e.g.* Arts. 4, 7 and especially 9 on health and safety). The *Statuto* was rightly seen as marking a strong move away from 'constitutional abstentionism'. Indeed, in these last articles it was thought to be a form of incipient 'industrial democracy'.

But on the duty to bargain the *Statuto* 'abstained', choosing deliberately not to impose it. The debates of the time make it clear that appreciation of problems arising from the American 'duty to bargain in good faith' was an element in that decision. The British law (after debates less strong in comparativism) appeared to leap forward across the chasm that separated the 'abstentionism' of its past from its visions of the future. The Act of 1975 provided that where a union was 'recommended' after inquiries by ACAS, an employer was under a legal duty to bargain with that union. Was the British legislature here, contrary to the expected contrast in cultures, less pragmatic than the Italian on what has become a central aim that workers, as the Social Charter requires, should have a right to collective bargaining? Without an obligation to 'recognise' a union, the employer can in legal terms in Britain reduce union rights to consultation or information – even where they are enacted to implement Community law – to things writ in water. The obligation to bargain was a juridical keystone to the 'promotional' or 'supportive' character of British legislation.

By 1980, however, that law had proved so defective that its repeal by the Thatcher administration in 1980 encountered little opposition even from the unions. The judges had interpreted its ill-drafted provisions restrictively, not to say perversely, employers had obstructed its application[40] and the problem of adequate remedies (on which the *Statuto* was ingenious) was never solved.[41] Most important of all, ACAS itself had hit upon no agreed criteria for 'recommending' a union for bargaining (the CBI and TUC representatives on the council never agreed on the rules of the game). In the context of employer resistence and competitive multi-unionism this was a mortal wound. Perhaps, but only perhaps, all might have been different had the law been based upon overall agreement between employers and unions, rather like the accord preceding the Italian law 604 of 1966 on unfair dismissal and many later 'pre-negotiated' laws. But this well-known European method of transforming agreement into law has been notably lacking in Britain in all periods.[42] The era of the 'social contract', and the legislation of 1975 which rested partly upon it, had been based upon pacts between the unions and the Labour government.

Supportive Legislation and Policies of Intervention

By not intervening in regard to the duty to bargain, and the many correlative difficulties about bargaining parties and their conduct, the *Statuto* paradoxically achieved an intervention which has been stronger and more lasting. Alongside the protections of union activity and the right to strike (Constitution Arts. 39, 40; *Statuto* Arts. 14, 15, 16 and 28) the 1970 law created the *rappresentanza sindacale aziendale* constituted by the workers' initiative (a crucial factor) but linked to the confederal representative unions or, sometimes but less important, to other local bargaining unions

(Article 19). 'This constituted a change of direction from the abstentionism of the 1950s and 1960s ... an interventionist policy to support the confederal unions.'[43]

But it was also a victory for imprecision. A British statute of such a character would have been unthinkable without the inclusion of complex criteria for the selection of the union or unions, the nature of the body at enterprise level and the rights and duties of all the parties, something more like the detailed German Works Constitution Act 1972. Perhaps the nearest any proposal has come to it was that for a 'Joint Representation Committee' in the Bullock Report.[44] But even that is a poor analogy because Article 19 allows for various *'rappresentanze'* at a plant if that emerges from the workers' initiatives. Such a result is to be expected from ideologically pluralist unionism. There is, of course, no point of reference in Britain equivalent to that of the *'confederazioni maggiormente rappresentative'* (most representative unions). This concept is not majoritarian, like the American elected bargaining agent; rather, as in France, unions may achieve 'representative' status merely by affiliation to one of the ideologically divided national confederations. In Britain, an equivalent renvoi to affiliates-of-the-TUC would have solved little (at any rate without transformed 'Bridlington' procedures).

As so often in labour law, the nature of the answers, and of the very legal problem itself, is shaped primarily by the structure of the labour movement. But not wholly. On occasion the legal system itself sets prior problems, as with the power of the High Court on injunctions and 'contempt of court', or in Italy with the prior definitions of aspects of the employment relationship in the Civil Code. More important, the interventions of the state, if it is insistent, cannot always be resisted whatever the shape of the movement and whatever the nature, one suspects, of the pre-existing law. An Italian Mrs Thatcher – were such a being imaginable – would be determined to repeal most of the promotional and supportive sections of the *Statuto*. The *Statuto* cannot be proffered as an immutable tablet of stone, though some Italian writers risk seeing it in that way. In the Trade Union Act 1984 and Employment Act 1988 the British government introduced stringent controls over the *internal* affairs of trade unions (over elections, scrutineers, liabilities of officers, powers of discipline, etc.), unthinkable and unconstitutional in Italy and in most other European countries.[45] These, and the Bill of 1990 which increases those controls and imposes vicarious liability beyond normal limits, have not accompanied pre-negotiated benefits for unions: quite the reverse.

It has been of primary importance for the success of the *Statuto* that the structures of Italian trade unionism were sufficiently flexible and democratic to give real life to so Delphic a formula as the r.s.a. of Article 19, which requires no more than an 'organised nucleus' of workers for its constitution.[46] That basic structure introduced by law in 1970 enabled the system to develop new forms of relationship between law and collective bargaining in the decades which followed. Henceforth, the legislature could proceed on the basis that there was a substructure of legitimate and protected trade unionism in the enterprise upon which it could rely and build. That result was in no way achieved – quite apart from the restrictive laws to come in the 1980s – by the British legislation of 1974-78, and remains one of the most difficult aspects in Britain for any alternative policy of promotional legislation.

Reflexive Regulation, the Market, Inflation and the Statuto

The strength added by a guaranteed trade union presence within the system had many indirect effects upon existing law, not least by reason of its inclusion of the doctrine of '*inderogabilità in peius*' (prohibition of conditions below those in the statute) and repeal of all earlier contrary provisions (Art. 40). But it was also the base without which the 'crisis legislation' of the 1970s, when the terms of the labour market changed, could not have taken the form which it did. The use of reflexive law in the 'crisis laws' was matched in the later period of 'flexible legislation' leading into the 1980s. These processes of legislative 'intervention' were made possible by the availability of the *rappresentanza*.[47] The process of referring legislative standards for implementation and even variation to local bargaining, begins with the *Statuto* itself; for example, Article 4 envisages plant agreement on audio-visual mechanisms, Article 6 for searches, Article 12 for the operation of social assistance institutes, and so on. Thereafter the threads of the interlocking relationships between law and collective bargaining become more frequent and more complex. They shine through such laws as those on night work for women (Law 903/1977, allowing collective arrangements to vary the legislative ban); on integration of salaries and the gradual decrease in the indexation of wages (the famous *scala mobile*; Laws 797/1976, 91/1977, and 297/1982); on derogations from workers' rights in times of crisis in the enterprise (Law 215/1978).

So too, in the later period laws aiming at greater 'flexibility' used a reference to plant agreements both to implement and, where desired, to vary the norms laid down. The method is prominent in the new laws on fixed term contracts and *contratti formazione lavoro* ('work training contracts': Laws 79/1983, and 56/1987 Art. 23) and on 'solidarity contracts' which tried to increase employment opportunities by combining state aid with local agreements. The same is true of legislation on part-time employment (Law 863/1984, which affords full employment protection rights to such workers with a priority right to full-time employment when available and promotes negotiation with a union on the major aspects of the structure of part-time employment in the enterprise) and on the *quadri* (lower management and technical workers, Law 190/1985).[48]

> The central feature of this experience is, without doubt, found in the intense and interconnected relationship between legislative requirements and the varied manifestations of free collective bargaining ... contractual norms are conceived as a natural prolongation of legislative rules, as an element of integration of a complex character, and to them was assigned a composite function, one of concretisation of matters assigned by the legislator, but also a means of integration, of adaptation and of specification of the legal content.[49]

None of this would have been possible without the '*rappresentanza*'. Perhaps we may evaluate the importance of this base laid by the *Statuto* and of the method thereby made possible in the later legislation over such a wide area of social policy, by considering the equivalent period in Britain immediately after the oil crisis. What were the measures taken here equivalent to the Italian laws on, for instance, the tapering off of wage indexation, the fragmentation of the labour market, integrated salaries, solidarity contracts and the *Cassa integrazione guadagna* (that idiosyncratic fund for workers suspended – not dismissed – by reason of redundancy), all of them related both to 'flexibility' and to wider policies on inflation and incomes? As far as labour law is concerned, the answer is: none. Instead, there had grown up a tradition of managing the incomes side by imposing restraint on wages separately from, and outside, the British corpus of law on labour relations.

Without doubt, it was true in the 1970s that 'successive governments throughout the post-war years have been centrally concerned with the control of inflation ... (whilst) maintaining a high level of employment,' more than with 'Donovan' style problems.[50] But the means employed were not integrated into labour law. Thus two attempts were made to impose wage-restraint by law, in 1966-69 by a Labour government, in 1972-74 by a Conservative government; but in each Act, to the understandable applause of those defending the autonomy of bargaining, care was taken to shield the legislation from any effect whatever upon the law on collective bargaining and strikes. The same was true of the extra-legal attempts to impose 'pay norms' earlier back to 1948 and later in 1974-79.[51] When the unions co-operated with the pay norms, whether imposed by laws or in quasi-legal form, they exacted no great price which underpinned their strength or legitimacy. For these they continued to depend largely upon bargaining strength at the workplace.

By 1977 the 'social contract' between unions and government disintegrated.[52] Labour was to lose power after what is now known as the 'winter of discontent' of 1978-79 (that debased reference to *Richard III*). The successor government of the 1980s denied the very existence of an official 'pay policy'; so to act would distort the market rates for labour (though no government can avoid a policy in the public sector, as a series of strikes in that sector have testified). The conventional wisdom of the era was – and may soon be again – that 'wage-push' is the decisive element in increasing inflation, but no effort was ever made to link the interventions of the law, or the 'quasi-law' on pay norms, with those of collective bargaining rights. The reason usually given for this was that the law 'abstained' from regulation of collective bargaining (Conservative governments, too, have usually supported 'voluntarism') and that answer stood despite other features of 'integration'. Even the Conservative government of 1971-74 came to draw a sharp distinction between its legislation on pay restraint to counter inflation and its Industrial Relations Act 1971, although critics saw the two as arms of one policy.

But it would be interesting to know how far the institutions of internal government administration also played a part in the maintenance of this distinction. Labour law was the domain of the Ministry of Labour, now the Department of Employment; but inflation was territory in the hands of the Treasury. In the former there were still civil servants ready to defend the old traditions of 'abstention'. With hindsight, it may be wondered, too, whether a closer link between inflation policy and labour law would necessarily have been to the disadvantage of the unions or whether, had the structure of collective bargaining come to be utilised integrally as a point of reference in fiscal and other measures, the place of the unions might in the end have been stronger. Whether the problems of competitive multi-unionism would ever have allowed them to demand anything as flexible and imaginative as the *rappresentanza* we cannot know.

On the other hand, it would be visionary to believe that an administration led by Mrs Thatcher, with the breadth of social support which it has undoubtedly enjoyed, would have had difficulty in rescinding any such protections, just as it has dismantled 'immunities' and protections of minimum standards from the Fair Wages Resolution to Wages Councils rates for those under 21 in order to remove 'burdens on business' and 'distortions' of the market identified in laws and agreements alike supporting the 'going rate', employment guarantees or apparently corporatist collective arrangements. In other words, plain though it appears to a foreign observer that the *Statuto*, and especially the *rappresentanza* was the indispensable base on which the policy of '*deregolazione contrattata*' (deregulation by agreement) could be built, it is not so obvious that such an institution would remain intact whatever the political circumstances (if, for example – unthinkable though it now is to most Italians – a government emerged which decided to break with traditions of industrial consensus). Further, if it is correct to think that the r.s.a. was the crucial invention, one might ask whether proposals for further changes in labour law which are currently the subject of intense debate in Italy – on the nature of unions, the redefinition of the 'representative unions', the possible interlocking of various union 'self-regulation' codes concerning industrial conflict with new legal supports or sanctions, and on similar new 'rules of the game' – may come to be measured by the effect they might have upon that base of the law introduced in 1970.

Labour Law, Recognition and Deregulation

We may note two further features, one an effect traceable to the *Statuto*, the other a more general consideration relevant to any comparative assessment. First, we have noted that the *Statuto* did not impose any general duty to bargain, but ensured that the *rappresentanza* clung like a limpet to the walls of every enterprise. After that, the substantive and procedural elements in the law and the facts would normally produce bargaining. In a British context, any legislation of similar kind which left matters to be settled or adjusted by collective bargaining, would encounter the objection that, there being after 1980 no legal obligation on the employers to bargain, they could set the later laws aside by simply refusing to bargain. The answer to that, Italian experience suggests, may not necessarily be a new, global duty to negotiate. It is one of the more interesting features of the Italian 'crisis' laws and subsequent reflexive measures that they appear not to impose in every case clear *duties* to bargain as one might expect in order that the collective bargaining fulfil the task assigned to it by statute. Rather, they have been analysed as in the main bringing about an 'onus' to bargain on the employer: 'The bargaining power of the collective union presence, which operates under the guidance of the promotional legal norms, can bring about the inevitability of negotiation also on the part of the employer.'[53] The statutory law allows or calls for local agreement on certain issues knowing that the *rappresentanza* is there.

It is precisely here, however, that other Italian writers have come to raise a further problem, one which 'arises from the lack of adequate rules of legitimation for the union parties who are called upon to realise legal results in collective agreements, in an area of activity undertaken in the public interest'.[54] In so far as collective bargaining has now been given a public function, that of authorising arrangements or variations, does not the need arise, they ask, to enact 'norms at a second level about the *rappresentanza*'? Does not devolution of state powers to collective bargaining demand – 'like it or not' – some new rules to replace the flexibilities and the formlessness of the *rappresentanza*? An observer from England – who by this stage of the inquiry might as well be a man from Mars – may be tempted to note that one of the intrinsic reasons for the failure of the 1975 law in Britain, giving ACAS power to recommend a union for bargaining status, was that it included no such secondary rules. That parallel does not imply, however, that a different jurisdiction must define its answers in the same way. Naturally, there will be other factors specific to each, in Italy, for example, the constitution; it is said (not without dissenters) that

> a law which claimed to determine analytically the forms of the trade union presence in the enterprise would certainly be invalidated on grounds of unconstitutionality for violating the principle of union freedom [under Article 39 of the constitution].[55]

Deregulation and Legal Cultures

Secondly, however, in so far as we have touched upon the fashionable topics of 'flexibility' and 'deregulation', a word is required about a specific difference in legal structure and technique which is part of the inheritance of the *Statuto* and its lack of a counterpart in Britain, and which makes a difference to the nature of the labour law debate in the two jurisdictions. The political choices of the last decade are obvious enough. In Italy the legislation of 'flexibility' accompanied a policy of '*garantismo flessibile*' (flexible, as against rigid, employment protection for workers). The policy was described, in an influential paper of Professor Giugni, as aiming to combine '*gli obiettivi di socialità con gli obiettivi di efficienza*' (objectives of social purpose with objectives of efficiency).[56] In Britain, on the other hand, we find what Italian writers describe as 'pure' deregulation, step after step of protection repealed, to the point in 1989 of permitting industrial tribunals to impose a deposit of £150 as a condition of pursuing a complaint against dismissal before it, to relieve 'burdens on business'. Such changes will 'be disproportionately felt by employees in smaller and under-organised establishments who make up the largest category of unfair dismissal complainants'.[57] Elsewhere we see the increased employer's power to dismiss strikers *en masse* or, from 1990, even selectively; the illegality encountered by a union enforcing its (lawful) rules against blacklegs and by industrial action not strictly confined to the workers' own unit of employment (the only code in Europe to ban all sympathy action), all part of a consistent attempt to de-collectivise the labour market and increase managerial power.[58]

But there are other, and in a longer perspective more interesting, features inherent in the legal and social systems and not dependant primarily upon the political choices of the day. Put simply, it is easier to deregulate in Britain, and rather more difficult to regulate, because of the nature of the legal culture itself. In a common law jurisdiction, the dominance of 'freedom of contract' is marked, in Britain more than marked; there is a 'near-obsession with contract, contract law and contract-thinking which at present pervades employment law'.[59] Here one finds no articles of the Civil Code defining a 'subordinate employee' or marking out the normal incidents to be expected of the contract of employment. The very concept of an 'employee' is full of uncertainties. The *legal* concept of *'l'inquadramento'* (the categorisation of workers, of greater importance in Italy) is inaccessible to English lawyers (the nearest we get is 'blue collar' and staff, a distinction of little legal content), while concepts, based on the Civil Code, of *'qualifica'* (broadly, the occupation for which a worker is qualified) and *'mansione'* (the job, but with a legal base: see Article 13 of the *Statuto*) have British equivalents in industrial relations rather than in the limited concepts known to the law.[60] Italian collective bargaining and Italian deregulation are unintelligible without some reference to this legal base. 'Deregulation' in our system presents itself primarily as a process merely of *repeal* of laws which have impinged upon the 'free' contractual system. If the European dialogue is not to be one for the deaf alone, we need to specify more carefully just when and where this difference between the systems matters: the labour law of one built from the outset upon juridical foundations, but in the other evolving in the shifting sands of 'freedom of contract'.

When, for example, the Italian system is faced with a policy of articulated deregulation, the need for a 'reregulation or reformulation' of norms[61] is not merely a matter of policy. It is a juridical necessity. In order to deregulate, this system *must* reregulate. And that process must be something more than the result that comes about automatically in Britain when repeal of the statute opens the gates to uncertain 'reregulation' by the common law tide. Amendment of the basic building blocks in the Civil Code is a momentous event (as in Art. 13 of the *Statuto*). So too, the only way in which the part-time employment contract could be accepted into the Italian system in a process of flexibilisation was by legislation which not merely removed old norms but substituted a plethora of new ones (employment protection rights for the part-time worker, priority if full-time jobs emerge, collective bargaining about the structure of hours, etc.: Law 863 of 1984). No doubt the policies of government, employers and unions were crucial to the precise form of that law; but the needs of that legal system itself promoted open debate about the new balance of interests of the parties involved. In the common law system, bare repeal allows for deregulation by slogans about 'freedom'.

The debate which necessarily ensues in the Italian system prompts a search for 'uniform treatment and protections in the entire "family" of relationships entered into by subordinate workers'.[62] In the British system there is no such family. Unless legislation intervenes, the common law will permit whatever relationship the parties define – part-time, fixed term, temporary, or even an unclassifiable employment relationship *sui generis* (as courts have recently dubbed arrangements that seemed to fit no known category of work relationship and whose terms were devised by employers' advisers to attain the best results of flexibility for them).[63] Legislative control of the employment relationship or its incidents is here the exception; there is no connecting concept of subordination within the structure of the common law. Only contract. The position of 'trainees' has illustrated the problem. The young worker under training may be an employee or he may not, according to the contract. Some do not even have a contract at all.[64] The importance of this uncertainty must be measured against the fact that so many employment protection rights are enjoyed only by those under a 'contract of employment' *stricto sensu*. The insecurity felt by parliament was indicated by the Employment Act 1988 which, instead of taking the opportunity to resolve their general legal status, in section 26 gave the minister a wide power to designate any group of trainees as employees or not, as he saw fit, case by case, for the purposes of the Act. Thus, in regard to the 'atypical' workers who are now becoming all too typical of parts of the labour market, in the tertiary sector above all, British law cannot match the economic realities of casual, seasonal, unclassifiable, temporary, part-time, fixed term, or homeworkers. There never seems to be an occasion to debate the issue in terms of a 'family' of relationships (to try to do so would be thought donnish, and not just by the government.) In each category, some are employees in law; some are not. Even if they are employees, many cannot attain the continuous employment required to enjoy the main employment protection rights (in 1988 official figures showed that at least 60 per cent of part-time workers were excluded).[65]

In a similar manner, the picture offered by a common law system psychologically predisposes towards deregulation. Legislation has not ceased to bear the mark of an intruder in the home of the common law. It is the common law that still lays claim to straight normality, statute is the deviant. Similarly, the 'immunities' which since 1906 have alone made lawful industrial organisation and action for workers are often spoken of as 'privileges' by many, including many judges. So too, when laws are repealed which have long protected the hours of work and conditions of young workers, from rest periods to night work, as in 1989 (contrary to international standards), this can the more easily be represented as a 'return to freedom of contract' between young workers and employers.[66]

Labour Law and The Community after 1992

The vivid contrast between British policies of stark deregulation, which are given this assistance by our legal culture, and the development of policies of 'bargained legislation' and maintenance of consensus in Italy in pursuit of social guarantees along with economic efficiency in the labour market, is also of importance in regard to the introduction of the 'internal market' in the European Community in 1992. The adoption of the Social Charter by eleven member states (Britain's failure to sign is unlikely to deprive the document of its importance) and the Commission's Action Programme to bring (a few) parts of it into effect, have heightened the significance of such different national approaches to policy. There can be no question in the foreseeable future, of course, of total 'harmonisation' of the labour laws of all member states; and even if there were, the provision in the Treaty, as amended in 1987, preventing majority voting in the Council on the rights and interests of employed persons (Art. 100a(2)) would make any such aim impracticable. On the other hand, Community legislation has long been thought necessary in certain areas of the labour market. Take, for example, the employer's duty to consult with unions about proposed redundancies (Directive 75/129), or on rights of workers and unions in the transfers of undertakings (77/187) and the provisions on workers' rights in insolvencies (80/987), and on issues relating to equal treatment of men and women (76/207, 86/378).

Two justifications are commonly offered for such measures. The first relates to the 'social dimension' of the market or the 'welfare' of the workers concerned, the second to the need to prevent unequal conditions of competition. Thus, it has been said of the redundancy Directive that, quite apart from 'welfare' considerations, if a country can authorise redundancies on less stringent conditions than other countries 'its industry will be given an incalculable advantage'.[67] This is not the place to analyse the rich material in the Commission's Action Programme,[68] but many of the proposals made in it bear the marks of both justifications. For example, in proposing a Directive on the approximation of laws of member states concerning the conditions and hours, especially a ban on night work, for young workers (Chap. 11), it pursues the logic of a 'social dimension' of the internal market in tandem with that of preventing competitive advantage by exploitation of the young; so too, with the proposals for an additional ten Directives on health and safety of workers where Community law is extensive (Chap. 10: 'recognising the dangers not only to health and safety [of workers] but also to the business environment and the labour markets of divergent health and safety conditions').

More important for present purposes are the precise proposals made – and not made – concerning collective labour relations. The principle of 'subsidiarity', whereby the Community leaves to the domestic laws of member states those matters more appropriately dealt with by them than by Community law, is applied by the Commission very differently in various areas. In regard to workers' rights to information and consultation, proposals for an 'instrument' which might become Community law figure strongly; the ghost of the draft 'Vredeling' Directive is invoked as the basis of this initiative.[69] Moreover, the attitude to workers' participation in decision-making matches the parallel proposals on the 'European Company' in the draft Regulation and Directive now before the parliament, with their optional 'models' of forms of workers' participation.

When we turn, however, to the other matters under this heading – freedom of association, collective bargaining and the right to strike – the Commission proposes no action for binding Community legislation. It does, it is true, intend to promote and extend the 'social dialogue'; but that it must do in any event under the Treaty (Art. 118b). This void in the proposals is a matter of enormous significance to Britain, arguably less to Italy where these rights are established. As there is no obligation on the employer to recognise a union, it is arguable even now that Britain is not in compliance with the Directives concerning redundancies and transfer of undertakings, because by derecognition he can under the implementing legislation escape from the duty to consult.[70] Much more serious is the Commission's intention to take no action to enforce by Community obligation a floor of collective rights in regard to bargaining and the right to strike. We have seen that the ILO Committee of Experts has judged that the British law on strikes (even before the measure of 1990) and in one respect the law on collective bargaining (the prohibition on school teachers' negotiations) falls below the minimum required by the standards of the ILO Conventions on freedom of association and the right to bargain (Nos. 87 and 98). Significantly, the preamble to the Charter declares that it draws 'inspiration' from the ILO Conventions, a feature which might have prompted the attention of the Commission to such failures. As for collective bargaining, not only is there no general duty on employers to bargain; the employer can evade many protective rights offered to workers or unions by the simple expedient of refusing to recognise a union, or by reshaping the area on which he is prepared to bargain.[71]

By refraining from proposals for Community action to place a floor below which employers in member states are not allowed to fall in collective labour relations, the Commission may be thought to have negated the very principles which offer justification for the earlier Directives. Apart from the question of workers' 'welfare', the enormous divergences in the national laws on trade union freedoms, bargaining and strikes would appear to be capable of offering 'incalculable advantages' to employers in some countries as against others in the single competitive market. The British employer who exercises his Community freedom to set up an establishment in Italy finds the legal environment a traumatic experience. Moreover, it is not apparent whether even the 'social dialogue' can operate efficiently and in analogous ways in countries where employers do, and those where they (or some of them) do not, recognise even an 'onus' to bargain with recognised trade unions.[72] The arguments, therefore, for a reasonably common floor of equivalent standards to labour law in the internal market are based not only on 'welfare' but also on the bottom line of competition. Pressure for a 'European floor of rights' is bound to grow, especially from those who fear that their less protective employment laws will expose their workers to a dimension of 'social dumping'.[73] They will argue that what is sauce for consultation on redundancy is sauce, in due course, for atypical workers, collective bargaining and the right to strike.

For the debate, therefore, on the Social Charter in Britain the differences between the national systems are of primary relevance and the legacies of the *Statuto* are now of particular interest; a system of law which supports, promotes and underpins a union presence at the workplace could hardly be of great significance, not merely in terms of narrow policies at home but in the construction of a genuine internal market in the Community. Many now hold the view that nothing can solve this particular problem in Britain except an overall, *general* duty to bargain on employers, while to that it is often replied that experience between 1975 and 1980 shows that this type of obligation cannot work, especially cannot be enforced, in the British system.[74] Yet here in the Community we find a member state, also lacking a general duty to bargain, but with the practice of bargaining supported by legal structures which derive from its constitution and from the *Statuto*, the latter having invented an ingenious institution as a novelty in 1970 which has become a foundation of its modern law and practice. An alternative policy in British labour law, if there ever is one, would be wise to search for the lessons of that development.

Let it be repeated, to avoid misunderstanding: the *rappresentanza* cannot be copied in Britain. But it is worth further study with a view to seeking equally ingenious institutions that might stick appropriately in Britain. So too is Article 28. It would, one must admit, be unusual for policy at Westminster to be guided to new havens by the hesitant tracks of comparative labour law. But such travels can lead adventurous legislators into unfamiliar territory where they may be visited with the vision of new ways ahead. So it was with the *Statuto*. It may be doubted whether even its authors, who understood the need for a comparative, 'transnational' study of labour law, could have predicted the importance which the *rappresentanza* would come to acquire later in the subtle developments of their own labour legislation and practice. But they did their homework, eschewed timidity and were rewarded for their audacity. That, at any rate, has comparative relevance for the British legislative imagination in 1992.

Notes

1. G. Giugni, 'Diritto del lavoro'. *Enciclopedia del novecento* III (1979), p. 946.
2. See the Appendix for extracts from the Workers' Statute.
3. In the presentation by the Minister of Labour (Brodolini) and of Justice (Gava), *Disegno di legge (Senato della Repubblica*, 24 June 1969. Doc. 738) p. 2; 'Donovan' Royal Commission *Report* (Cmnd 3623, 1968).
4. For example, the government proposed the new powers of dismissal in clause 7 of the Employment Bill 1990 in order to give British employers 'the same freedom to respond to unofficial action as employers in West Germany' (1990) *Employment Gazette* 3. But dismissed unofficial strikers are not denied access to the German courts, and their dismissal needs consultation with, sometimes even the consent of, the Works Council: M. Weiss, *Labour Law and Industrial Relations in the Federal Republic of Germany* (1987), Chap. VII. So too, confusing use is made of snippets from various systems in *Unofficial Action and the Law* (Cm. 821, 1989), pp. 2-3.
5. See G. Baglione and C. Crouch, *European Industrial Relations. The Challenge of Flexibility* (1990).
6. See the Social Charter as finalised on 8 December 1989, in House of Lords EEC Select Committee *Report: A Community Social Charter*, 5 December 1989. (Paper HL 6-1, 3rd Report 1989-90); and in Wedderburn, *The Social Charter, European Company and Employment Rights* (Inst. of Employment Rights, 1990); and the Commission's *Action Programme* (COM (89) 58, 27 November 1989); extracts in (1990) *European Industrial Review and Report* 193, 26; 194, 26; and 195, 23.
7. G. Giugni, *Lavoro, legge, contratti* (1989), p. 305 (originally 'Il diritto del lavoro negli anni '80' (1982) Giorn dir. lav. rel. ind. 373).
8. Wedderburn, 'Freedom of Association and Philosophies of Labour Law' (1989) 18 ILJ 1 [above Chapter 8].
9. T. Treu in G. Arrigo (ed.), *Lo Statuto dei lavoratori: un bilancio politico* (1977), p. 43.
10. See the recent review by S. Honeyball, 'Employment Law and the Primacy of Contract' (1989) 18 ILJ 97.
11. The treatment of '*parità*' in the Italian books seems to be brief to English eyes: see F. Carinci, R. De Luca Tomajo, P. Tosi, T. Treu, *Il rapporto di lavaro* (2nd ed., 1985), pp. 119-22; G. Ghezzi and U. Romagnoli, *Il rapporto di lavoro* (2nd ed., 1987), pp. 97-8, 209-11, 274. On indirect discrimination and British developments: F. Albisinni, 'Due leggi inglesi sulla questione femminile' (1976) Riv. giur. lav., 1, 341; and M.V. Ballastrero, *Dalla tutela alla parità* (1979) and 'Il

lavoro e i lavori delle donne' (1986), Pol. Dir., 233 [and now Law no. 125, 10 April 1991].

12. L. Mariucci, *Le fonti del diritto del lavoro* (1988), to which I am much indebted.

13. S. Sciarra, 'Art. 8' in G. Giugni (ed.), *Lo Statuto dei lavoratori: commentario* (1979), p. 79. On employment and private life, beliefs and conduct, see G. Giugni. Chap. 4, Folke Schmidt (ed.), *Discrimination in Employment* (1978).

14. See L. Dickens, M. Hones, B. Weekes, M. Hart, *Dismissed* (1985): see (1990), *Employment Gaz*. 213-8; in 1988-89 out of 17,870 unfair dismissal cases, 11,814 were settled or withdrawn: 5,786 went to a hearing of which 2,166 succeeded; the remedy of reinstatement or re-employment was awarded in 58, ACAS records a 'success' rate by conciliated settlement of 70 per cent in 1989, but it is not clear how many of the settlements involved re-employment: ACAS *Report 1989*, Table 10.

15. J. Clark and Wedderburn, Chap. 6 in Wedderburn, R. Lewis and J. Clark (eds.), *Labour Law and Industrial Relations* (1983), p. 175.

16. See M. Rocella, 'Reinstatement of Dismissed Employees in Italy' (1989) 10 Comp. Lab. Law Jo. 166, who demonstrates the relative success in three regions of reinstatement orders; T. Treu, '*Una ricerca empirica sullo Statuto dei lavoratori negli anni 80*' (1984) 23 Giorn. D.L.R.I. 497.

17. G. Tarzia, *Manuale del processo del lavaro* (3rd ed., 1987), p. 267, and see Chap. III, on law no. 533 of 11 August 1973, (which gives the *Pretore* special training and 'powers comparable to the powers of the criminal courts' in the labour jurisdiction): G. Certoma, *The Italian Legal System* (1985), p. 456. The granting of *locus standi* under Art. 28 to the local union organ having an interest, which was in part a reaction to earlier judicial restrictions, derived in part also from study of the even wider standing which French unions have in cases concerned with a collective or, in some instances, an individual interest: *Code du Travail* Arts L. 411-11 (collective interests). L. 123-6 (sex equality), L. 124-20 (foreign workers). L. 127-6 (group employers), L. 135-4 (application of collective agreements), L. 721-19 (homeworkers): G. Lyon-Caen and J. Pelissier, *Droit du Travail* (14th ed., 1988), pp. 703-10.

18. M. Grandi and G. Pera, *Commentario breve allo Statuto dei lavoratori* (1987), p. 149.

19. Cass. 30 January 1980, no. 711, FI 1980, I, 25; G. Giugni, *Diritto sindacale* (8th ed., 1988), pp. 244-50; Wedderburn, *Report on Legislative and Judicial Restrictions on Trade Union Action and the Right to Strike* (Paris 1989), now in (1990), 1 Rev. Int. du Droit Comp. 37, 48, 63, 95-6.

20. G. Certoma, op. cit., n. 17 above, 72-3; Wedderburn, 'Le législateur et le juge' in *Les Transformations du Droit du Travail: Études Offertes à Gérard Lyon-Caen* (Dalloz, 1989).

21. See G.F. Mancini, 'Politics and Judges: the European Perspective' (1980) 43 MLR 1.

22. *Chant* v. *Aquaboats* [1978] ICR 643 EAT: *Carrington* v. *Therm-A-Stor Ltd* [1983] ICR 208 C.A. (pet. disallowed [1983] 1 WLR 190, HL).

23. See respectively, Pret. Montefiascone 29 June 1981, G. It. 1982, I, 2; Cass. no. 1037, 18 February 1982; Cass. no. 1366, 5 April 1976, FI 1976. I, 1132. On conflicting approaches to the legitimacy of 'articulated' strikes, see F. Santoni in Fl. 1985, I, 502 (on Cass. no. 419, 26 January 1985, and Trib. di Term. Imerese, 7 June 1985).

24. See ACAS *Report* 1989, pp. 11-12; *Labour Research*, April 1988, p. 13.

25. F. Carinci, R. De Luca Tomajo, P. Tosi and T. Treu, *Diritto Sindacale* (2nd ed., 1987), p. 192.

26. See Wedderburn, *Report on Legislative and Judicial Restrictions*. (etc.) (Paris, 1989) n. 19 above; now in 1990, no. 1, Rev. Int. du Droit Comparé 37.

27. G. Giugni, *Diritto Sindacale*, op. cit., pp. 106-7, 246-9.

28. See Wedderburn, 'Le législateur et le juge' in *Les Transformations du Droit du Travail*, op. cit. n. 20, above.

29. See Lord Diplock, *Express Newspapers Ltd* v. *McShane* [1980] AC. 672 at p. 687.
30. R. Rideout, *Principles of Labour Law* (5th ed., 1990), Chap. IX; Wedderburn, *The Worker and the Law* (3rd ed., 1986), Chaps. 7 and 8.
31. See G. Giugni, *Diritto sindacale*, op. cit., Chap. 12.
32. See [Chapter 10 below]. The Italian Law 146 of 12 June 1990, now requires up to ten days notice of strikes in certain essential public services, in order to 'balance the exercise of the right to strike against other interests protected by the Constitution'. Self-regulating codes of procedure are required from unions (many already have them) on pain of exclusion from bargaining, and workers failing to observe minimum requirements may be suspended for certain periods (the remuneration going to the national unemployment fund). Requirements of minimum services are imposed and notice of alternative arrangements must be given to consumers by the enterprises. The law establishes a new conciliation function for the Minister, with power to issue 'ordinances' in case of prolonged conflict which can lead to pecuniary penalties for workers, and a Commission ('nine experts in constitutional and labour law and in industrial relations') to promote agreement between the parties and the workers concerned on minimum services and to report on the conduct of strikes and self-regulation codes. Art. 28 of the *Statuto* is applied (curing earlier doubts) to the whole sector and to acts by employers infringing collective agreements. [See also p. 353 below.]
33. See the invaluable article by S. Sciarra, 'The Rise of the Italian Shop Steward' (1977) 6 ILJ 35. The *rappresentanza* of Art. 19 (discussed below) was not, of course, built out of the air. Part of its genius was to give legal expression to industrial realities. In the late 1960s the official 'internal works committees' were overtaken by unofficial '*consigli di fabbrica*' (factory councils) a name which harked back to the councils proposed by Antonio Gramsci in 1920 as 'the territory of workers' self-government'; G.F. Mancini, Chap. 1, S. Serfarty and L. Gray (eds.), *The Italian Communist Party* (1980), p. 10. The pre-existence of the *consigli*, which had a wide variety of constitutions, facilitated the introduction of the *rappresentanze* (into which many councils were converted) under Art. 19. Such developments gathered pace after the 'hot autumn' of 1969, when in two years union membership rose by 20 per cent.: P. Lange, G. Ross, M. Vannicelli, *Unions, Change and Crisis: French and Italian Union Strategy and the Political Economy, 1945-1980* (1982), Chap. 2; and generally, G. Giugni, 'Recent Trends in Collective Bargaining in Italy', (1971) Int. Lab. Rev., no. 4, 307. The Italian law deliberately avoided the French structure where the external union has complete control of its *section syndicale d'entreprise*. Instead, it built in the need for a workers' initiative. The operation of the rsa within the 'ambit' of a larger union allowed for "realisations over a vast range of models and solutions' (F. Carinci, R. De Luca Tomajo, P. Tosi, T. Treu, *Dirrito sindacale* (2nd ed., 1987), p. 141; see too n. 53, below). Today's problems reflect both the failure of the three main union confederations (CGIL, CISL, and UIL) to merge, as had been planned in the 1970s, and the emergence of 'autonomous' (breakaway), unions and dissident rank and file movements within those unions, both of which groups tend to be referred to as 'COBAS' (*comitati di base*). In 1990 a COBAS of railway workers was, in a breakthrough for such groups, admitted to official collective bargaining for the first time: *Repubblica*, 20 May 1990.
34. The text of the Experts' observations of 28 April 1989, is contained in K. Ewing, *Britain and the ILO* (Instit. of Employment Rights, 1989).
35. See for a survey of judicial novelties in the use of injunctions and of contempt of court, Wedderburn, 'The Injunction and the Sovereignty of Parliament' (1989) 23 *The Law Teacher* 4.
36. G. Ghezzi and U. Romagnoli, *Il Rapporto di lavoro*, op. cit., n. 11, pp. 318-9; G. Pera, *Diritto del lavoro* (3rd ed., 1988), p. 530. On the remarkable condemnation of Italy by the court, see *EC Commisssion* v. *Italy* (8 June 1982) [1982] ECR

2133; a second judgment of 6 November 1985, (FI, 1986, IV, 109) confirmed it. But collective dismissals in breach of the Directive have been held to be actionable directly; Cort. cost. no. 140, 1984; Pret. Tornio 19 March 1984, Fl, I, 2640. On British duties to disclose and consult, see Employment Protection Act 1975, ss. 17, 99; and Transfer of Undertakings (Protection of Employment) Regulations 1794 of 1981, regs. 10, 11.

37. B. Veneziani, *Stato e autonomia collettiva* (1986) 86, 141 *et seq*.

38. See T. Claydon, 'Union Derecognition in Britain' (1989) 27 BJIR 214, and n. 24 above.

39. See T. Treu, *Condotta antisindacale e atti discriminatori* (1974), pp. 66-78.

40. On judicial attitudes, see B. Simpson, 'Judicial Control of ACAS' (1979) 8 ILJ 69; on the *Grunwick affaire*, P. Elias, B. Napier, P. Wallington, *Labour Law, Cases and Materials* (1980), pp. 29-59. On fears that the duty to recognise might be 'too heavy a burden' for the British system: K. Wedderburn (1978) 13 Israel Law Rev. 435, 456.

41. Art. 36 of the *Statuto* makes use of severe administrative remedies against those in receipt of contracts or subsidies from public authorities, an interesting parallel to suggestions made by some unions (which did not, however, get off the ground) during the debates on 'industrial democracy' in Britain in the 1970s: see P. Davies and Wedderburn, 'The Land of Industrial Democracy' (1977) 6 ILJ 191, 205-209.

42. See Wedderburn and S. Sciarra, 'Il contratto collettivo come accordo e come legge' (1989) Riv. di dir. civ. 45, also as 'Collective Bargaining as Agreement and as Law' in A. Pizzorusso, *Law in the Making* (1988), pp. 186-237.

43. L. Mariucci, *Le Fonti del diritto del lavoro* (1988), p. 39.

44. See the 'Bullock' Committee Report on *Industrial Democracy* (Cmnd 6706), Chap. 10.

45. See E. McKendrick, 'Employment Act 1988, Part I' (1988) 17 ILJ 141. On the comparison see: 'Trade Union Democracy and Industrial Relations' (1988) 17 Bull. Comp. Lab. Relns. (X. Blanc-Jouvan p. 7, M. Weiss p. 27, G. Giugni p. 39, F. Valdes Dal-Re p. 75 and Wedderburn p. 145).

46. See G. Giugni and P. Curzio in G. Giugni (ed.), *Lo Statuto dei lavoratori: commentario* (1979), p. 322.

47. S. Sciarra, 'Plant Bargaining and Recent Deregulatory Trends in Italy' (1987) 8 J. Comp. Lab. Law 123.

48. T. Treu, 'Recent Development in Italian Labour Law' (1985) 10 *Labour and Society* (ILO) 27.

49. G. Ferraro, 'Fonti autonome e fonti eteronome nella legislazione della flessibilita' 1986 32 Giorn. DLRI 667, 677.

50. P. Davies and M. Freedland, Introduction to O. Kahn-Freund, *Labour and the Law* (3rd ed., 1983), p. 4.

51. See Wedderburn, 'Labour Law Now: A Hold and a Nudge' (1984) 13 ILJ 73.

52. J. Clark, H. Hartmann, C. Lau, D. Winchester, *Trade Union National Politics and Economic Development* (1980).

53. See the analysis in S. Sciarra, *Contratto collettivo e contrattazione in azienda* (1984), pp. 84-108. The laws contain a great variety of formulae in referring matters to local agreement. Many other legal problems of course remain, especially as Art. 19 does not lay down any specific form for the *rappresentanza*. For example, there may be a number of *rappresentanze* in the one plant. The 'federal pact' of 1972 aiming at unity between CISL, CGIL and UIL saw a unified plant *consiglio* as the basic union structure, but including non-members who 'wish to participate of their own free choice'. A union, however, has no right to designate a group as the 'r.s.a.' from outside the plant (Cass. no. 1256, 21 February 1984); it must 'recognise' a group already emerging from the workers' initiative: G. Giugni, *Diritto sindacale*, op. cit., pp. 90-1, Appendix I, 271. But can a collective agreement structure the r.s.a., for example by requiring a minimum number of members to be enrolled in a union before a local group is so recognised, thereby increasing certainty for the

employer? This has been attempted in agreements in the financial sector, which require eight enrolled members before there is a legitimate *rappresentanza*. Recent decisions have accepted such practices as lawful (e.g. Cass. no. 6807, 16 November, 1983; Cass. no. 1418, 18 February, 1985, Riv. it. dir. lav. 1985, II, 395) though earlier decisions did not (Cass. no. 4718, 5 November, 1977; see too below, text to n. 55). The 'r.s.a.', apart from its specific functions (e.g. under Arts. 4, 6, 20, 21, 23-24, 25, 27), has almost unlimited general functions in representing the interests of workers: '*plurilegittimazione*' (multi-legitimacy), as G. Ghezzi and U. Romagnoli put it: *Diritto sindacale* (2nd ed., 1987), pp. 97-100. It must never be forgotten that the r.s.a. is required to spring from an 'initiative' of the workers, though it must then operate within the 'ambit' of a 'representative' union, as specified by Art. 19(a) or (b).

54. M. D'Antona, R. De Luca Tomajo, G. Ferraro, L. Ventura, *Il diritto del lavoro negli anni 80* (1988), p. 30.

55. G. Giugni, *Diritto Sindacale*, op. cit., p. 91. Recent proposals by the unions (CGIL, CISL and UIL) for a new form of *Consiglio aziendale delle rappresentanza sindacale* ('Cars'), half to be elected by union members and half by all workers, were strongly criticised as not solving the problem of 'organisational legitimacy and electoral legitimacy'; that is said to need further legislation to 'complete' and structure Art. 19: L. Mariucci, 'La rappresentanza sindacale' (1990) LD 129; D'Antona, 'Diritti sindacali e diritti del sindacato' (1990) LD 247, who cites the British legislation of 1984-88 (P. Davies (1988) LD 329) as hostile to the unions but giving rise paradoxically to 'a kind of "corrected" single channel,' for example in strike ballots, and to a 'modernisation' of union structures, pp. 258-9. The current Italian debate notably overlaps the traditional British debate about 'single channel' representation, but one must have in mind the participation of non-union members in the *rappresentanza*.

56. G. Giugni, 'Il diritto del lavoro negli anni 80' (1982) 15 Giorn. dir. lav. rel. ind. 373, in *Lavoro, leggi, contratti* (1989) 293, 334.

57. Employment Act 1989, s. 10; S. Deakin, 'Equality under a Market Order' (1990) 19 ILJ 1, 16. For the argument that a more regulatory labour law can be more efficient and just, see S. Deakin and F. Wilkinson, *Labour Law, Social Security and Economic Inequality* (Inst. of Employment Rights, 1989).

58. See especially the Employment Act 1982, ss. 9 and 18; Trade Union Act 1984, ss. 1-11; Employment Act 1988, ss. 1-3; Employment Bill 1990, cl. 4 and 9.

59. S. Honeyball, op cit. (1989) 18 ILJ 97, 108.

60. See the Civil Code arts. 2082-2126. On 'job', 'work' and 'employment' in British law: see *Wood* v. *Cunard Ltd, Times*, 7 May 1990, CA; Employment Protection (Consolidation) Act 1978, s. 153. The fact that the statutory law rests on an extraneous base of 'contract' also accounts for other difficulties, e.g. in s. 140 ibid.; *Logan Salton* v. *Durham CC* [1989] IRLR 99, EAT (separate contract not within s. 140). Judicial approaches to the employer's contractual prerogative to alter conditions 'undermine collective negotiation': B. Bercusson, 'Les Relations Professionnelles et le Droit du Travail' *Travail et Emploi*, 1987 No. 3, 15, 19 (on *Gilham* v. *Kent CC* [1985] ICR 227 CA).

61. G. Giugni, 'Giuridificazione e deregolazione nel diritto del lavoro italiano' (1986) 30 Giorn. D.L.R.I. 317, now in *Lavoro, leggi, contratti* (1989), pp. 337, 352; also an English version: 'Juridification and Deregulation in Italian Labour Law' (1987) 8 Comp. Lab. Law. Jo. 317.

62. M. D'Antona, R. De Luca Tomajo, G. Ferraro, L. Ventura, *Il diritto del lavoro negli anni 80*, n. 54, 2.

63. See *Ironmonger* v. *Movefield Ltd.* [1988] IRLR 466.

64. See Wedderburn, *The Worker and the Law* (3rd ed., 1986), pp. 118-20 and 509-11.

65. Department of Employment Evidence to the HC Employment Committee, 7 June 1989. 'Part-time Employment' (viii 155-156), p.270; and see C. Hakim (1989) 18 ILJ 69, and R. Disney and E. Szyszczak (1989) 18 ILJ 223.

66. Employment Act 1989, s. 10, and S. Deakin, op. cit. (1990) 198 ILJ 11-13.
67. G.F. Mancini, 'Labour Law and Community Law' (1985) 20 Irish Jurist 1, 12.
68. See Wedderburn *The Social Charter, European Company and Employment Rights* n. 6 above.
69. See C. Docksey, 'The United Kingdom and the Vredeling Directive' (1986) 49 MLR 281.
70. See D. Wyatt, 'Enforcing EEC Social Rights in the United Kingdom' (1989) 18 ILJ 197; B. Hepple, 'The Crisis in EEC Labour Law' (1987) 16 ILJ 77; B. Hepple and A. Byre, 'EEC Labour Law in the UK' (1989) 18 ILJ 129.
71. G. Bain and L. Dickens, 'A Duty to Bargain?' Chap. 3 in R. Lewis (ed.), *Labour Law in Britain* (1986).
72. See Wedderburn, op. cit., n. 68. above, pp. 29-42 and 64-70, on the failure of the Commission to propose minimum collective labour standards.
73. U. Mückenberger and S. Deakin, 'From Deregulation to a European Floor of Rights: Labour Law, Flexibility and the European Single Market' (1989) ZIAS (*Zeitschrift für ausländisches und Internationales Arbeits und Sozialrecht*) 153; and see Wedderburn, 'The Social Charter in Britain – Labour Law and Labour Courts?' (1991) 54 MLR (forthcoming).
74. On the issues of union recognition and 'representation' see W.E.J. McCarthy, *The Future of Industrial Democracy* (1988, Fabian Soc. No. 526) and *Freedom at Work* (1985, Fabian Soc. No. 508), pp. 27-33.

Appendix: Extracts From 'The Workers' Statute'

Law No. 300, to make provisions respecting the protection of workers' freedom and dignity, trade union freedom and freedom of action within the workplace, and provisions respecting placement. Dated 20 May 1970.

Part I Workers' Freedom and Dignity

1. *Freedom of opinion.* Irrespective of their political or trade union opinions or religion, workers shall be entitled to express freely on the premises where they carry on their activity their personal opinions, respecting the principles of the Constitution and the provisions of this Act.

2. *Sworn watchmen or guards.* It is lawful for an employer to employ a private force of sworn watchmen or guards ... only for the purposes of protecting the property of the undertaking.

It shall be unlawful for sworn guards to report workers for acts or facts which are unconnected with the protection of the property of the undertaking.

It is unlawful for an employer to order the guards referred to in the first paragraph of this section to supervise the work, and such guards shall not be entitled during working hours to enter the workplace where the work is performed, except for exceptional reasons on specific grounds, the reasons for which are clearly stated and connected with the duties specified in the first paragraph of this Article ...

3. *Supervisory staff*. The names and specific functions of staff members whose duties involve supervision over the work shall be communicated to the workers concerned.

4. *Audio-visual equipment*. It is unlawful to use audio-visual and similar equipment for supervising and controlling the workers' activity at a distance.

Such tele-control and supervision equipment and installations (closed-circuit television, etc.) which are necessary for organisation, production or industrial safety, but which could also be used for supervising the worker's activity at a distance, shall be installed only after the consent of the works unions has been obtained or, in their absence, of the works committee. Where such agreement has not been obtained, the Inspectorate of Labour shall decide the case at the employer's request, specifying, where applicable, the mode of utilising such equipment ...

5. *Medical examinations*. It is unlawful for an employer to check by medical examination the aptitude for physical work of an employee or his incapacity arising out of sickness or accident. Medical check-ups in the case of absence on grounds of illness shall be carried out only by the inspectorate services of the competent welfare institutions, which shall be obliged to carry out such check-ups at the employer's request. The employer shall be entitled to have a worker's physical aptitude examined and ascertained by the public authorities and specialised institutions governed by public law.

6. *Personal searches*. Searches of the worker's person ('frisking') shall be prohibited, except where they are indispensable to protect the property of the undertaking and are connected with the nature of the tools, raw materials or products involved.

In such cases, personal searches may be conducted only if carried out at the exit to the workplace, that the worker's dignity is respected, that such searches are carried out discreetly and are made in conjunction with the systems of automatic pre-selection applying to the entire staff or groups of workers.

The circumstances in which personal searches may be conducted and the manner in which they are to be carried out (subject to the conditions laid down in the second paragraph in this article) shall be the subject of an agreement between the employer or the works unions or, failing this, the works committee. In the absence of such agreement the Inspectorate of Labour shall decide the matter at the employer's request.

7. *Disciplinary sanctions*. The disciplinary rules respecting sanctions, the offences for which each such sanction may be imposed and the procedures with respect to notification of such sanctions shall be

brought to the notice of the workers by posting up in a place accessible to the entire staff. They shall be in conformity with the provisions of labour agreements or contracts of employment on the subject, where such exist.

The employer shall not impose any disciplinary measure on any worker without giving him prior notice of the charge brought against him and without having heard him state his defence. The worker may be assisted by a representative of the trade union association of which he is a member or to which he is affiliated, or a person engaged by him to assist in his defence.

Without prejudice to the provisions of Act No. 604 of 15 July 1966, no disciplinary sanction involving a definitive modification of the employment relationship may be imposed; any fine imposed shall not exceed four hours' basic wage; any suspension without pay shall not exceed ten days' duration. In no case shall disciplinary sanctions more serious than verbal reprimand be imposed until after five days have elapsed as from the date of the written report of the offence concerned.

Without prejudice to the similar procedures laid down in collective industrial agreements and the possibility of instituting proceedings before the courts, a worker upon whom a disciplinary sanction has been imposed may demand within the following twenty days (or request the union of which he is a member or to which he has given a power of attorney for this purpose to put forward such demand) the establishment, through the intermediary of the provincial labour and full employment office, of a conciliation and arbitration board composed of a representative of each of the parties and a third member appointed by mutual agreement (or failing agreement, by the director of the labour office). The disciplinary sanction shall be suspended until the board takes a decision. If the employer fails to appoint his representative on the board referred to in the preceding paragraph within the ten days following notice served on him to do so by the labour office, the disciplinary sanctions shall be null and void.

8. *Inquiries into workers' opinions unlawful.* It is unlawful for an employer, with a view to admitting a worker to his employment and for so long as the employment relationship continues, to carry out or cause to be carried out any inquiry concerning the worker's political, religious or trade union opinions, or concerning any facts not relevant to an assessment of the worker's aptitude for his occupation.

9. *Protection of health and safety.* The workers shall be entitled to exercise inspection and supervision through their representatives over the observance of the statutory provisions respecting the prevention of industrial accidents and occupational diseases, and

the right to promote research into, the organisation and application of all measures for the protection of their health and personal safety.

10. *Workers pursuing studies*.[1] Workers pursuing studies, registered with and regularly attending classes in primary, secondary or vocational schools (whether such schools be public, state-approved or authorised to award the certificates or diplomas prescribed by law) shall be entitled to special hours of work to enable them to attend such classes and prepare for examinations; they shall not be compelled to work overtime or during weekly rest periods. Workers pursuing studies, including those attending universities, shall be entitled to days off work on full pay in order to sit for examinations.

11. *Cultural, recreational and social activities*. All cultural, recreational and social activities carried on within the undertaking shall be managed by bodies on which the workers shall be represented in the majority.

12. *Welfare clubs, etc*. The welfare clubs and social assistance bodies approved by the Ministry of Labour ... shall have the right to carry on their activities inside the undertaking on a footing of equality, in accordance with arrangements to be made in plant agreements.

13. *Tasks assigned to worker*. The following shall be substituted for Article 2103 of the Civil Code [on workers' jobs]:

The worker shall be assigned tasks for which he was recruited, or tasks falling within a higher category to which he was later promoted, or tasks equivalent to those which he last performed, without any reduction of remuneration. If the worker is required to perform higher duties, he shall be entitled to receive the remuneration corresponding to such activity, and such transfer to a higher post shall become definitive (unless he was assigned to the post to replace an absent worker entitled to reinstatement) after a period prescribed in collective agreements, in any case not exceeding three months. He may be transferred from one production unit to another only for cogent reasons connected with technical requirements, organisation and production.
Any agreement to the contrary shall be null and void.

Part II Freedom of Association

14. *Right of association and right to carry on trade union activities*. The right to establish trade union associations, to join such associations and to carry on trade union activities is guaranteed to all workers within the workplace.

15. *Discriminatory acts*. Any agreement or act for any of the following purposes shall be null and void:

a. to make the employment of a worker subject to the condition that he joins or refrains from joining or leaves a trade union association;

b. to dismiss a worker, or to discriminate against him as regards the attribution of qualifications or functions or with respect to transfers or disciplinary measures, or to cause him any other prejudice on account of his membership of a trade union, his trade unionist activities or his participation in a strike.

The provisions of the preceding paragraph (b) also apply to agreements or acts involving political or religious discrimination.[2]

16. *Collective discriminatory measures of a financial nature*. It is unlawful to grant any financially favourable treatment of a discriminatory nature within the meaning of Article 15.

At the request of any workers who consider themselves to be victims of the type of discrimination referred to in the preceding section (or that of the trade union associations representing them) the *Pretore*, if he is satisfied that such facts are authentic, shall order the employer to pay to the Pension Adjustment Fund an amount equivalent to the amount of the discriminatory financial awards illegally granted, for a period not exceeding one year.

17. *Employer-financed trade unions*. It is unlawful for employers or their associations to establish or support, financially or otherwise, any workers' trade union association.

18. *Reinstatement in employment*.[3] Without prejudice to the procedure referred to in Article 7 of Act No. 604 of 15 July, 1966, the judge, in his order declaring a dismissal to be without effect under Article 2 of the said Act, shall cancel any dismissal he finds to be without sufficient cause or justification or declare such dismissal to be null and void under the above-mentioned Act, and shall order the employer to reinstate the worker in his post.

The worker concerned shall be entitled to damages for any prejudice suffered as a result of his dismissal declared to be without effect or null and void under the preceding paragraph. In any case, the compensation awarded by way of damages shall not be less than five months' wages (the wages being determined according to the provisions of Article 2121 of the Civil Code). An employer who does not obey the order referred to in the preceding section shall be bound in addition to pay to the worker concerned his full remuneration arising out of the employment relationship as from the date of the order until the date of the worker's reinstatement.

If on being offered reinstatement by the employer the worker does not return to his post within 30 days, the employment relationship shall be deemed to be terminated ...

In the case of dismissal of any worker referred to in Article 22, the judge may, at any stage of the proceedings, on the joint demand of the worker and the trade union of which he is a member or which he has appointed to represent him, make an order for the said worker's reinstatement in his post if he is of the opinion that the evidence submitted by the employer is not pertinent or insufficient.

The order referred to in the preceding paragraphs may be appealed against immediately in a counter-plea submitted to the same judge who made the order ... The order may be quashed by the judge hearing the case.

In the case of the dismissal of any worker referred to in Article 22, an employer who fails to execute a judgment referred to in the first paragraph of this article or fails to carry out the order referred to in the fourth paragraph (if such order has not been appealed against or has been upheld by the judge who originally issued such order) shall be bound in addition to pay to the Pensions Adjustment Fund, for each additional day of failure to execute the judgment order, an amount equal to the worker's pay for that day.

Part III Trade Union Activity

19. *Establishment of works unions ['rappresentanze'].* Trade union representation at the plant level (works unions, shop stewards, etc.) may be established on the initiative of the workers, in each production unit, within the ambit of:

a. the associations affiliated to the most representative confederations at the national level;

b. the trade union associations, not affiliated to the above-mentioned confederations, which are signatories to the national or provincial collective agreements applying in the production unit concerned.

In undertakings where there are two or more production units, co-ordinating bodies may be established by the works union.

20. *Assemblies.* The workers shall be entitled to meet within the production unit where they are employed, outside working hours (also during working hours, up to a limit of ten hours a year, for which they shall receive their normal pay). More favourable rules may be laid down by collective agreement.

The meetings (which may include all the workers or certain groups of workers) shall be convened by individual or collective invitation, by the works unions or shop stewards within each production unit, having on their agenda trade union questions and employment problems, in accordance with an order of priority of convocation of which the employee shall be notified. Members of the leadership of the trade union which established the works union, not employed in the undertaking may attend the meetings on condition that prior notice to this effect is given to the employer.

Subsequently other modes of exercising the right of assembly may be stipulated in collective agreements or at the level of the undertaking.

21. *Referendum.* The employer shall be obliged to permit the holding of referendums (within the undertaking but outside hours of work) either of a general nature covering the entire staff or for certain categories, on questions connected with trade union activities, through the intermediary of the entire framework for the trade union representation of the workers in the undertaking, all the workers belonging to the production unit and the category concerned being entitled to participate.

Subsequent other modalities for holding referendums may be stipulated in collective agreements, including those at the level of the undertaking.

22. *Transfer of officials of works unions.* Transfer from one production unit to another of officials of the works unions referred to in Article 19 or of candidates for election to works unions or members thereof may be made only with the prior authorisation of the trade union associations of which they are members.

23. *Paid leave of absence.* The officials of the works unions referred to in Article 19 shall be entitled, for the purposes of the duties of their office, to paid leave of absence.

Unless there are more favourable provisions in the collective agreements, the following persons at least shall be entitled to the leave of absence referred to in the first paragraph: [a, b and c are omitted, which set out different numbers of officials for undertakings of different sizes.]

The paid leave of absence referred to in this section shall not be less than eight hours a month in the [larger] undertakings referred to in clauses (b) and (c); in the undertakings referred to in clause (a) such unpaid leave shall amount to not less than one hour per year and per staff member. A worker who wishes to avail himself of the right laid down in the first paragraph shall notify the employer to this effect in writing 24 hours beforehand as a general rule, the notice being transmitted through the works union.

24. *Unpaid leave.* The trade union officials referred to in Article 23 shall be entitled to unpaid leave in order to participate in trade

union negotiations or to attend congresses or meetings of a trade union nature, for periods not exceeding a total of eight days a year ... [also after notice to the employer].

25. *Right to post up notices.* Works unions shall be entitled to post up in appropriate places which the employer shall be obliged to provide in areas easily accessible to all the workers, on the premises used by the production unit, published material, documents, notices and communications connected with trade union matters and labour interests.

26. *Trade union dues.* Workers shall be entitled to collect contributions and engage in publicity and recruitment for their trade union organisations within the workplace, as long as they do not interfere with the normal activity of the undertaking. The workers' trade union association shall be entitled to collect, by means of check-off from wages, the trade union dues which the workers have agreed to pay in the manner prescribed in collective industrial agreements, guaranteeing secrecy of payment of his dues by the worker to the trade union association of his choice.

In undertakings where the employer-employee relationship is not governed by collective agreements the worker shall be entitled to ask for the trade union dues to be paid to an association indicated by him.

27. *Premises for works unions.* In production units where 200 workers or more are employed the employer shall provide on a permanent basis for the works unions, to enable them to carry out their functions, a suitable room or the like within or close by the production unit concerned. In production units where a lesser number of workers is employed the works unions shall be entitled to be allowed the use of suitable premises for their meetings, if they so request.

Part IV Miscellaneous Provisions

28. *Restraint of anti-trade union conduct.* If the employer shows by his conduct that he intends or attempts to hinder or limit the exercise of freedom of association and trade union activities or the right to strike the *Pretore* [local judge] within whose jurisdiction the conduct complained against took place may, at the suit of the local organs of the national trade unions concerned, summon the parties within the following two days and take a summary deposition of the facts at issue. If he is of the opinion that there is an infringement of the provisions of this paragraph he shall order the employer by an immediately executory judgment stating the grounds on which it is based, to cease and desist from his illegal

conduct and to redress any grievances or obviate the effects thereof.

The said order shall not be annulled until the *Pretore* hands down a judgment in his office as labour judge, under the procedure initiated according to the following paragraph.

Appeal may be made against the order to the *Pretore* in his office as labour judge within the fifteen days following notification of the same to the parties; the judgment awarded by the *Pretore* shall be immediately enforceable.[4]

An employer who fails to obey the terms of the order referred to in the first paragraph or the judgment handed down on the appeal shall be liable to the penalties provided for in Article 650 of the Penal Code.

29. *Amalgamation of works unions* [omitted]

30. *Local and national trade union officers' paid leave.* Members of the leadership (provincial and national) of the associations referred to in Article 19 shall be entitled to paid leave in accordance with the stipulations of the contract of employment, in order to attend meetings of the associations concerned.

31. *Unpaid leave of absence for workers holding public office by election or exercising trade union functions on the provincial or national level.* A worker who is elected as a member of the national parliament or a regional parliament or elected to other public office shall obtain unpaid leave of absence at their request at any time during, or for the entire duration of, their term of office. This provision shall also apply to workers required to exercise trade union functions at the provincial or national level.

Periods of unpaid leave of absence as provided for in the two preceding paragraphs shall be taken into account at the request of the worker concerned for calculating [pension and sickness benefits] ...

32. *Leave entitlement of workers elected to public office.* Workers elected to office as municipal or provincial councillors and who do not wish to be granted unpaid leave shall be authorised, at their request, to be absent from work for the time strictly necessary to carry out their official functions, without any reduction in remuneration ...

Part V Provisions Respecting Placement [omitted]

Part VI Final Provisions: Penalties

35. *Scope.* In the case of industrial and commercial undertakings, Article 18 and Part III of this Act (except Article 27, first

paragraph) shall apply to every registered office, headquarters, establishment, branch, subsidiary firm, office or independent workshop where more than fifteen workers are employed. The said provisions shall likewise apply to agricultural undertakings employing more than five wage earners.[5]

The above provisions shall also apply to industrial and commercial undertakings which, within the territorial limits of a commune, employ more than fifteen workers and to agricultural undertakings which, within the same territorial limits, employ more than five workers; they shall apply even if each production union considered separately does not fulfil these numerical requirements.

Without prejudice to the stipulations of sections, 1, 8, 9 and 14 to 17 inclusive above the provisions of this Act shall be applied to shipping companies with respect to crew, by collective agreement.

36. *Obligations of companies receiving state subsidies, etc., and companies awarded public works tenders*. In the provisions for state subsidies, etc., within the meaning of the legislation in force to be granted to contractors carrying out an organised economic activity and in the specifications, articles and conditions respecting the carrying out of public works by tender, a specific clause shall be inserted stipulating the contractor's obligation to provide or have provided for his workers conditions at least as favourable as those stipulated in the collective agreements for the corresponding category and zone.

This obligation shall be respected both while the work is being performed and at later stages, throughout the entire period during which the contractor receives subsidies and credit facilities from the state, within the meaning of the legislation in force.

Any failure to meet this obligation discovered by the Inspectorate of Labour shall be reported immediately to the Minister whose department granted the subsidy, etc., or awarded the tender. The department concerned shall take the necessary steps, which may include cancellation of the subsidy or tender; they may also, in the case of serious cases or a repeated offence, debar the undertaking concerned for a period not exceeding five years, from any possibility of receiving further subsidies, credit facilities or tenders.

The provisions of the preceding paragraphs shall also apply in the case of financial aid or subsidies, credit facilities or tenders given by public bodies; in this case the Inspectorate of Labour shall report any offences directly so that sanctions may be imposed.

37. *Application to employees of public bodies*. The provisions of this Act shall also apply to the work and employment relationship of employees in the service of public bodies which exclusively or

principally carry on a business or financial activity ... [and] of employees of other public bodies, unless such questions are administered differently by special provisions.

38. *Penal provisions.* Any person infringing Articles 2, 4, 5, 6, 8, and 15, first paragraph, clause (a), shall be liable (unless the offence is a more serious one) to a fine of not less than 300,000 and not more than 3,000,000 lire or a term of imprisonment of not less than fifteen days and not more than one year.[6]

In serious cases the fine and the term of imprisonment may be imposed simultaneously.

If the fine laid down in the first paragraph of this section appears insufficient in view of the financial situation of the guilty employer (even if the maximum amount is imposed) the court shall have power to increase the fine up to five times the amount ...

39. *Payment of fines to the Pensions Adjustment Fund.* All amounts paid by way of fines shall be paid over to the Workers' Pension Adjustment Fund.

40. *Repeal of contrary provisions.* All provisions contrary to this Act are repealed. Such repeal shall be without prejudice to more favourable provisions for the workers contained in collective agreements and agreements with trade unions.

41. *Tax exemption, etc.* All documents required for the application of this Act and the exercise of rights thereunder, and all formalities, deeds and documents respecting judgments arising out of the application of this Act shall be exempt from registration and stamp duty and all other taxes and duties.

Notes

1. Extended to all workers in vocational training by Law No. 845 of 21 December 1978.
2. And to discrimination on grounds of race, language or sex: Law 903 of 9 December 1977.
3. This text is the original Art. 18, which has recently been replaced by the version enacted in Law 108 of 11 May 1990; see Art. 35, n. 5 below.
4. As amended by Law 847 of 8 November 1977.
5. Law 108 of 11 May 1990, has rewritten Art. 18 of the *Statuto* so as to vary the threshold previously applicable under Art. 35. It applies the remedy of reinstatement to employees if the employer employs more than fifteen workers (or five in agriculture) in enterprises within the 'commune', even if there are fewer workers in the particular workplace, and to all employers who employ more than 60 workers. Part-time workers are now included (Art. 1). Where the dismissal is invalid the judge orders reinstatement and not less than five months wages in compensation, but the worker may opt for fifteen months wages instead of reinstatement. Art. 2 applies to workers below these thresholds (except in

certain non-profit making enterprises) rights to compensation against unfair dismissal under Law 604 of 15 July 1966. All discriminatory dismissals in breach of Art. 15 of the *Statuto* are made void, irrespective of motive, with a remedy of reinstatement (Art. 3). The law bears the marks of legislation passed hurriedly to avoid the constitutional procedure of referendum, threatened by certain groups in an attempt to abolish thresholds.

6. As revised by Law 689 of 24 November 1981.

10

The Right to Strike:
Is There a European Standard?

> Where [industrial] action is lawful ... individual employees should
> have the right, as in other European countries, not to be dismissed
> for that action. (Labour Party, *Looking to the Future*, 1990).

There is a real prospect that in the 1990s British labour law will be
fundamentally reformed. With this in mind, would-be reformers
often say that a new code of law for employment and industrial
relations must adopt 'European' standards, in particular guaranteeing a 'right to strike'. This is an admirable sentiment, not least
because our laws on strikes were adjudged in 1989 to fall below the
minimum standards set by Conventions of the International
Labour Organisation on freedom of association.[1] The cry naturally
goes up: Out with immunities, bring in the positive rights they have
in Europe. But there are snags, the most obvious being that there
is no one European labour law, certainly no one 'right to strike'. In
the twelve Member States of the European Community (often
referred to as 'Europe') there are twelve systems of labour law
with notable, sometimes radical differences. How far can common
standards be found beneath this diversity? This question may help
to clarify issues that will arise in the reform. That is the main
purpose of what follows. It is not an attempt to devise answers for
a programme, rather an effort to see how far a comparative look at
some European systems helps to refine the questions, many of
which have not yet begun to be asked.[2]

The Right to Strike as an International Value

But everyone – or nearly everyone – in Western Europe supports a

---

An unpublished paper delivered in London, 20 January 1990, expanded and
updated to January 1991. I am very grateful to Hélène Cohen for drawing my
attention to some of the French material used in this revised paper.

'right to strike' (soon perhaps in Eastern Europe too).[3] It is rightly regarded as a democratic value. As Kahn-Freund pointed out in 1931: 'The fact that both fascist and communist dictatorships have prohibited industrial conflict is surely no coincidence.'[4] Such a right is recognised by the United Nations International Covenant on Economic, Social and Cultural Rights. Most of the Community states are parties to the Council of Europe's Social Charter of 1961, which also recognises a 'right to collective action' for workers and employers; and all of them have ratified the International Labour Organisation's Convention on Freedom of Association No. 87, 1948, under which a right to strike has been consistently held by the ILO, its Freedom of Association Committee and its Committee of Experts to be: 'one of the essential means available to workers and their organisations for the promotion and protection of their economic and social interests as guaranteed by Articles 3, 8 and 10 of the Convention'.[5] All except the United Kingdom adopted the European Community Social Charter in 1989 which affirms that 'the right to resort to collective action in the event of a conflict of interests shall include the right to strike'.[6]

But even a cursory look discloses wide variations in the acceptable ambit accorded to the right, even in the international instruments. The Council of Europe Social Charter and the European Community Social Charter both restrict its application to disputes which arise out of conflicts of 'interests', as opposed to disputes about 'rights' (e.g. interpretation of agreements) and therefore make it subject to 'peace' obligations arising from collective agreements.[7] This, as we shall see, is not the uniform general rule in the domestic laws of Western Europe which it is sometimes thought to be.[8] Under the ILO Convention on Freedom of Association the national law may also impose limitations requiring disputes about legally binding texts to be solved only by the courts, but this principle does not permit a government to submit all strikes to arbitration or to exclude from legality all strikes protesting at social and economic conditions. So too, although restriction by way of obligatory strike-notices or strike-ballots is permissible under the Convention, these are accepted only so long as the procedures are not unduly onerous.[9] More important, the ILO has extended the legitimacy of strikes in defence of workers' occupational and professional interests beyond the boundaries of working conditions or other matters which may be settled by collective agreement; the right to strike, in its jurisprudence, extends to peaceful protest on social matters which are of direct concern to them.[10] This is part of the ILO analysis which regards a right to strike as part of the right to freedom of association.

The Community Social Charter, however, permits the exclusion by national law of 'the armed forces, the police *and* the civil service' (art. 14), but the ILO has been resolute in permitting the exception from rights to freedom of association of the police and armed forces (Convention 87 art. 9) but not of the entire government service (see too, the Council Social Charter, article 5). The right of the latter to strike, however, may be much more severely restricted,[11] and those in essential services may be specially regulated without contravention of the Convention; but their right to take industrial action should not be totally excluded. We shall see that this reflects a common pattern outside Britain – though it must be added that when we come to discuss the public sector, we shall find that British law has long been one of the more liberal systems; indeed, not so long ago it was sometimes difficult for British comparative lawyers to persuade Continental colleagues that public or State employees were part of 'labour law' at all. To that we return below.

So too, where a minimum service is required as a condition of legality, the category of 'essential service' is narrowly interpreted by the ILO and the minimum service should be negotiated with the workers concerned.[12] But both under the ILO Convention and the Council of Europe Charter, the dismissal of strikers for the very act of engaging upon legitimate industrial action is regarded as an infringement of the right to strike which is inherent in freedom of association itself. The law should hold that in a legitimate strike the contract of employment is suspended, not broken.[13] But everything there rests upon the meaning of a legitimate strike.

Before we can come to legitimacy, there is the meaning of 'strike' itself. As we shall see, many national systems of law accept, in theory at any rate, nothing less than a *total* cessation of work. They reject the go-slow, work-to-rule, ban on voluntary overtime, work-without-enthusiasm, 'thinking-strike'[14] and the innumerable other forms of industrial action 'limited only by the ingenuity of mankind'.[15] The Council of Europe Social Charter has been interpreted as not including the more limited forms of action within its right to strike.[16] We shall see that many national systems insist upon a complete cessation of work. On the other hand, the ILO has taken the view that such forms of action short of a full strike may be subjected to special limitations only where they cease to be peaceful.[17] This expansive tendency in ILO jurisprudence is of particular importance. Under the Community Social Charter many of these questions remain to be decided, if they ever are; but the Preamble to that Charter directs attention both to the ILO Conventions and the Council of Europe's Social Charter as sources from which 'inspiration should be drawn' and, therefore, presumably guidelines obtained for interpretation. The dominant place of interpretations by the ILO (an agency of the United Agency), as against the often narrower understandings of the European instruments, is of some importance for the future.

Clearly, one would expect the Community Charter at least to accept the principle that the exercise of a legitimate right to strike leads not to breach, but to suspension of the employment contract.

The British Liberty to Strike

British law has never measured up to any of these standards. It has never known a 'right' to strike, only a liberty of industrial action in which the organisers are protected from some common law liabilities. It escaped censure for that in its 'classical' period of 1906 to 1970 largely because its curious structure of 'immunities' in trade disputes from liabilities in criminal law and in tort provided trade unions in practice with a reasonably wide freedom of action. The legislation of the 1980s though, as we have seen, by squeezing the area of legality protected by those immunities, finally incurred the censure of the ILO Experts in 1989.[18] We may come to see this as the final phase of its transformation.

The development of the law on strikes in Europe has been classified as involving three phases: first, the strike is treated as a crime: second, the strike becomes a 'liberty' or freedom; and thirdly, there emerges a right to strike, the phase when the law necessarily delimits and defines the strike.[19] On this basis, the classical British system has been left retarded in the second phase. Excluding the grip of restraint of trade in 1871 and some relevant criminal liabilities from trade disputes in 1875, it provided the unions with their very legality by means of immunities; the style was confirmed for the organisers of strikes in 1906 and again in 1974 with immunities in trade disputes from such torts as inducing breach of, first contracts of employment, then later all contracts (in order to meet the expansion of tort liability by the courts), together with in the classical period complete protection of the union itself in tort, though not its officials.[20] The legislation of the 1980s played a different tune but – in contrast to the band of 1971 – on the same classical instruments. Immunities were narrowed, for example by demands for strike ballots in industrial action called by the union, by the ban on secondary action, on action to secure negotiation through the aid of another employer, and on action for the reinstatement of unofficial strikers. The definition of the golden formula ('acts done in contemplation or furtherance of a trade dispute') was itself amended restricting legality to disputes with the workers' own employer which relate wholly or mainly to their own employment; and the general protection of the union from tort liability was withdrawn, returning to *Taff Vale* in the sense of making it the primary defendant in litigation, vulnerable to injunctions, damages and sequestration, hoping thereby to solve that problem of individual 'martyrs' which had dogged the legislation of 1971-74.[21]

In this legislation – both in the classical period and in the 1980s – it was necessary to define a 'strike' or 'industrial action' only rarely. The only meaningful definition employed is that concerned with the freezing of the employee's service for the purposes of continuous employment qualifying him for such rights as redundancy payments or unfair dismissal.[22] Elsewhere, the legislation of the 1980s felt compelled to describe a strike for the purpose of the new rule requiring a union strike ballot and giving a union member a right to call for one; but this produced nothing more meaningful than the definition of a strike as a 'concerted stoppage of work' (apparently, here, for any purpose at all, when the normal meaning limits it to some pressure on the employer) plus the useless circular definition: 'industrial action means any strike or other industrial action by persons employed under contracts of employment'.[23] In general, the legislation both of 1974-78 and of the 1980s was able to leave strikes and industrial action undefined, even though the rights of employees not to be unfairly dismissed might depend on their interpretation;[24] and one remarkable result was that the courts came to regard as 'industrial action' in that area of unfair dismissal any concerted activity putting pressure on the employer whether or not it was a breach of the workers' contracts of employment.[25] That result was remarkable because, with rare exceptions such as a ban on voluntary overtime, both full strike action and limited action such as a go-slow or work-to-rule, invariably constitute a breach of the contract of employment in the British system.[26]

Suspension or Breach of Contract

It is in this common law feature that the absence of any 'right' to strike is most clearly exposed. 'The essence of a *right* as opposed to a *liberty* to strike', it has been claimed, 'is that those exercising the right are protected against any prejudice or detriment in consequence of having struck, particularly at the hands of the employer.'[27] While the organisers of strikes – indeed, 'any person' acting in furtherance of a trade dispute – might have protective immunities when acting 'in contemplation or furtherance of a trade dispute', in Britain the workers have always remained liable for their breach of contract – and, it turns out, possibly even for torts based upon a breach, either as a threat or in the form of 'unlawful interference' (or possibly even as the civil equivalent of the criminal act which once rendered strikes criminal conspiracies).[28] It is to be remembered that until 1875 this breach was – and had been for five centuries – a crime. The criminal texture of 'master and servant' jurisprudence is still clearly echoed beneath the surface of employment law today. In British legislation, therefore, the code words normally used for industrial action have referred to 'inducing breach of an employment contract', lapping over into associated tort liabilities such as procuring breach of other contracts, intimidation by threats to break a contract, conspiracy or unlawful interference. These have been the natural reference points. Perhaps because they were such an odd basis for a modern law on strikes, in the last two decades they caused commentators, trade unions, government and even employers to consider an alternative base to British law, a structure of 'positive rights', including possibly even a right to strike.[29] In 1981 the Green Paper issued by Mr (now Lord) Prior in his last gasp in office appreciated that such a step, were it taken, would create a 'need to insulate any legal right to strike from the common law ... [which] could mean developing a completely separate system of law with its own sanctions'.[30]

By the 1980s, academic writers increasingly supported a change to a right to strike (that is, a right to withdraw labour in combination, not the curious common law idea of a 'right' of *individual* workers to 'strike' by terminating the employment with or without combination).[31] Some enthusiasts were so keen on the idea that they fell victim to formalism, assuming that the change-over to a form of positive rights to strike would automatically solve the difficulties and make the judges' common law 'secondary to those rights'.[32] This is not the case. By itself, there is 'no guarantee that a system of positive rights would confer greater legal freedom' to strike.[33] To think otherwise is to ignore a century of legal history in which common law courts have regularly cut down the ambit of protections in immunities; there can be no guarantee they would not approach 'rights' similarly. Indeed, our experience of common law courts everywhere suggests that they habitually narrow the ambit of such positive rights as the right to freedom of association.[34]

The practical question, therefore, was and is: what are the conditions under which 'positive rights' can best resist common law liabilities, old and new, and introduce a liberal and stable system?[35] A look at Continental systems shows us that the adoption of a 'right' to strike, although it provides a modern platform, does not solve (as is often assumed) all the associated problems, for example those relating to remedies for strikers improperly dismissed. In France, for example, no principle is today more fundamental than the rule that the employment contract of a worker legitimately exercising his constitutional right to strike is suspended, not broken, unless he is guilty of serious misconduct (*la grève ne rompt pas le contrat de travail sauf faute lourde imputable au salarié* [a strike does not break the contract of employment unless the employee is guilty of serious misconduct]: art. L. 521-1 Code du Travail). In 1985, the legislature supplemented this rule by enacting that the dismissal of such a striker is '*nul de plein droit*' (null and void).[36] From this it is often thought to follow that such a dismissed worker must be entitled to the remedy of reinstatement, in the same way as the trade union or workers' representative who is in France protected by a special, strong and specific legislative status.[37] But even today the availability of this remedy to the ordinary striker is only recently established.[38] The extent of the right and the remedies associated with it must, like the definition of a legitimate strike, rest with the policy of the legislature and, in this area in France, the interpretations of the courts. If we demand that the primary remedy for strikers illegally dismissed be reinstatement, we must say so explicitly.

There has though been a debate about 'positive rights' in Britain, which, even if it has been muffled beneath the noise of battle on the Thatcher legislation, has clarified two points of departure. First, legal systems are not all 'immunities' or all 'rights'; they change their balance gradually. For example, even in the constitutional systems there has been an evolution, step-by-step. What is regarded as a cornerstone of the system may be relatively new. Take the doctrine of 'suspension of employment contract' in France. As recently as 1938, more than seventy years after the origins of a positive freedom of association, French courts still applied doctrines similar to those used by British courts today, namely that the strike is a breach of contract giving the employer a right to damages and even dismissal. One year later, however, the relatively unimportant 'Court of Arbitration' adumbrated a doctrine of suspension; then, after the war, when a *right* to strike was recognised by the Preamble of the 1946 constitution, the suspension doctrine came to be accepted and in 1950, just when all courts were at last ready to adopt it, a law was enacted with what is now a central text of the *Code du Travail* (art. L.521-1). In the early years, though, commentators had to argue the case that a legitimate strike could not be a breach of contract since it was the exercise of a constitutional 'right'.[39] So too, the doctrine of suspension developed gradually in West Germany where in 1955 the courts found that employment contracts must be suspended in strikes made lawful (inferentially) by the 1949 Constitution (art. 9.3); but, like the Swedish Labour Court, the German courts later inferred equally that contracts are suspended in lock-outs too, having recognised a parallel right for the employer to lock-out (though now under restrictions imposed by later cases to ensure proper application of their doctrine of 'parity of weapons').[40] On the lock-out, too, courts have had to make choices which may come as a new shock if positive rights are introduced in Britain.[41] But whether the employer should be allowed to lock-out is a different question altogether from the ambit of the right to strike. In France and Italy, far from regarding the lock-out as parallel to the strike the law begins by questioning its legality altogether. The right to strike is recognised by both French and Italian constitutions ('within the ambit of laws that regulate it'); not so the lock-out. Even the 'defensive' lock-out is normally illegitimate; and the Cour de Cassation, the highest civil court of appeal, has limited the occasions when even *force majeure* will permit its use.[42] The absence of the lock-out and presence of the strike among the rights constitutionally protected in Italy is held to stem juridically from

> the unequal condition of employers and workers, giving to the latter but not to the former the right to suspend the employment relationship ... a choice found in other constitutions (such as in Portugal and Spain) and contrary to the doctrine found in German jurisprudence of 'parity of arms' in industrial conflict. In consequence, a law confirming a right to lock-out would be unconstitutional ...[43]

This view reflects more accurately the power relationship at work. Italian writers are prone to argue therefore that ratification of such instruments as the Social Charter of the Council of Europe or European Community, which appear to equate the rights of workers and employers in industrial conflict, does not mean that the right to lock-out must be equally recognised.[44]

The second clarification is the lesson that form does not determine the content of rights – or remedies. Proposals for reform, on 'rights to strike' or on 'labour courts' can be evaluated only through examination of a precise content. They may then be profitably considered in a comparative setting where unfamiliar systems will help us draw up what is bound to be an unfamiliar agenda. If the moment is ripe, therefore, for a new development in British law an examination of the diverse European systems will help to expand the agenda.

Limiting Factors in Labour Laws

For the most part, then, adoption of a right to strike would require British labour law to define a number of concepts, and thereby policies, which have so far gone largely undefined or defined only implicitly. We have got by with relatively antiquated legal mechanisms: the traditional trio – common law liabilities; 'immunities' in trade disputes from some of those liabilities; and, in the 1980s, abolition or restriction of the 'immunities'. The debate on 'positive rights' has not always addressed the content of the rights to be created, but it has clarified central peculiarities of our law about strikes. As we have seen, in a comparative context the central peculiarity is the dominant precept that workers who take strike or other industrial action normally act in *breach* of their employment contracts (as opposed to the suspension of contract which applies to legitimate strikes in most of the twelve Community countries).[45] There are exceptions where there is no such breach (as with bans on voluntary overtime) but we need not stop over these, especially because the precise frontiers of the duties in the employment contract are often fuzzy and the employer seeking an injunction to stop the strike needs to persuade the court only that there is an *arguable* case, not a clear case, that a breach of contract was induced or committed.[46] Thus, although it was uncertain whether teachers were bound to perform the out-of-class duties they refused to undertake, it was arguable that they were; therefore an injunction was granted against the union which had organised their abstention.[47]

Whether or not there is a strike notice, 'a breach of the contract of employment', as Donovan recognised in one passage, 'will normally result'.[48] Strike notices are normally no more than announcements of impending breach of employment contract, not notices to terminate the employment; workers going on strike do not ask for their cards; union officials do not normally possess the authority to terminate the jobs of their members and will be put to proof of it if they claim to have it.[49] It is true that the Industrial Relations Act 1971, provided that a strike notice equivalent in length to proper notice to terminate cured the breach; but this applied to only one of the many 'unfair industrial practices', did not apply to action short of a strike and was cancelled out by a 'peace' clause in a relevant collective or other agreement. The idea that it protected a wide 'right to strike' was correctly judged to be 'misleading'.[50] The point of departure in at least nine (or ten, if Ireland is included) of the twelve member states of the European Community is completely different from the British because in those jurisdictions a legitimate strike involves not breach, but suspension of the employment contract.[51] Where there is a constitutional right to strike, it would indeed be illogical to permit it to be curbed by contractual obligation, not least where its purpose is to protect the weaker party; contract must give way to fundamental rights; their normal exercise cannot as such amount to breach of contract.[52]

This contrast best illustrates the difference in what may be termed 'limiting factors' in the laws about strikes. In Britain the main formula of our law since 1906 has given protections not to the strikers themselves but to the organisers of strikes – union officials or others. This has turned around whether they acted '*in contemplation or furtherance of a trade dispute*'. The definition of a 'trade dispute' has been the main factor limiting acceptable from unacceptable industrial action.

Let us first clear away a problem about the whole concept of 'trade dispute'. Unhappily it was created by Kahn-Freund and perhaps accepted by many of us too easily. He made the suggestion nearly fifty years ago – and never withdrew it – that the entire 'trade dispute' formula is flawed, based upon a 'theory of society and of politics' which is 'untenable'. The reason was said to be that the division required by the formula is not one which is in accordance with any true sociological category; there is no clear line in modern society between 'economic action' and 'political action'. So, he argued, British strike law rests upon a mistaken division between the political and the economic, 'the sphere of the "State" and the sphere of "Society" '; and the attempt to make the distinction work was, he asserted, 'doomed to failure'.[53]

I have lately come to find this argument erroneous. It rests upon the premise that the validity of *legal* boundaries on the legitimacy of strikes must coincide with frontiers which are sociologically *true*. One may accept that the line between the 'economic' and the 'political' in modern industrial societies is indeed impossible to draw with any certainty. But all systems of labour law must and do have such a cut-off point or limiting factor, equivalent to a division between the 'political' and the 'economic'. Whether or not it accords with any true sociological analysis (if indeed any such analysis is possible) some such legal line is unavoidably drawn by and for the law. The acceptable strike is accepted not because it is sociologically true, but because the policy of the particular legal system puts it on one side of an inevitable line. None of the Western European systems, for example, grants legitimacy to strikes which have purely 'political' purposes within the meaning each conventionally gives to that term; but their understanding of what constitutes a 'political' stoppage varies greatly.

The fact is that the division between 'economic' and 'political' is conventional, not ontological. Once the different limiting factors are compared, it is apparent that it is not sociological veracity which is at stake but adequacy in a particular legal policy. In the British case we have the definition, and in 1982 the redefinition, of 'trade dispute' and the nature of the 'political' strike changed with the redefinition.[54] In France, the right to strike is permitted for the defence of the workers' occupational interests and the admixture of political objectives is accepted – but to a different degree in civil and in criminal courts.[55] The Italian constitutional right to strike does not extend to 'pure' political strikes, but such strikes enjoy a 'liberty' in the system, making them immune from the penal code unless they 'subvert the constitution or impede the free exercise of legitimate authority which is the expression of the sovereign will of the people'.[56] And the full right to strike applies, as we shall see, to strikes in pursuit of 'politico-economic' demands, cases which in Britain would be excluded from 'trade disputes' even under the 1906 definition. In all these systems it is possible to argue for a wider or a narrower definition – but not on the basis of what is the 'true' political sphere. The argument is about what should, within the social and legal system of the given society and applicable values, be the action permitted by this limiting factor.

But in systems where a right to strike is recognised, limiting factors are not expressed merely in regard to the objectives of the industrial action. The primary limitations tend to appear in the definition of a legitimate 'strike' itself, just that area in which British law has little experience. What is a 'strike'? Does it include all types of peaceful industrial action? And after that: must it be preceded by notice, or by a ballot? We can see the point if we take France and Italy, systems very similar in structure but rich in differences.

The widest right to strike in Western Europe is guaranteed by article 40 of the Italian Constitution. Here a 'strike' includes action not only for economic aims against the employer (in furtherance of a 'trade dispute') but also for 'politico-economic demands'. For example, strikes are lawful when the demands are for better public housing or regulations on safety at work, or a better social security system, even though the pressure is directed primarily at public authorities: that is 'all demands regarding the interests of the workers which are protected by Title III of the Constitution' (on economic interests).[57] This formulation is wider both as to parties and as to content than the traditional British 'trade dispute' formula. Even in its 1906 traditional form the British limiting factor required a dispute with some employer or other; in its 1982 form it must be a dispute with the workers' *own* employer. Not so Italian law where the key factor is pursuit of the interests of workers as such. Moreover, in any action that prejudices the position of strikers the Italian employer risks infringing the worker's right under the Workers' Statute 1970 not to be penalised for taking part in a strike and the right of worker and union to obtain an immediate injunction for any form of 'anti-union' conduct, a crucial procedural feature of the Italian system administered, not by a special labour court, but by a section of the normal judiciary.[58]

The French development lies somewhere in the middle. The starting point is similar. As in Italy, the French constitution states that the right to strike may be limited by legislation; but no general laws have been enacted.[59] It is the judiciary here too which defines 'strike', delimiting the exercise of a constitutional 'right' which vests in the individual but is exercised collectively, suspending the employment contract. But the courts in France are not, as they are in Italy, subject to review by a constitutional court (the *Conseil Constitutionnel* controls only the propriety of legislation). The more restrictive definition of a strike adopted by the Cour de Cassation has been: 'a concerted stoppage of work aimed at pressing ascertained occupational demands [*revendications professionnelles*] on the employer, which he refuses to satisfy'.[60] There must be occupational demands on the employer; the link with the employer is more strict than the Italian interpretation of the same constitutional formula. But modern French jurisprudence has slackened the requirement that strikers must wait for the employer's response; now they may strike before it is known.[61] Nor is a strike notice required, save for the five-day notice obligatory in the public services.[62]

But the question which tests the limiting factors of all such systems is: what is a strike? Does that limiting factor allow partial as well as full stoppages of work. In principle, the legal system in both France and Italy replies that a strike entails a 'concerted abstention *from* work', not a faulty execution of the job while *at* work. The cessations may be regular and frequent (*débrayages répétés*); but they must be something more than 'work executed in a go-slow or in ways that are deliberately defective'.[63] In both these systems, the innumerable forms of partial industrial action, 'action short of a strike' in the new British structure,[64] are not given the constitutional protection accorded to a 'strike' proper. They remain unlawful breaches of the employment obligations. This is perhaps the most important lesson which British pursuers of 'positive rights' encounter. Having been accustomed to the law treating full and partial action equally to the detriment of the worker, they are sometimes surprised and disappointed not to find the precise opposite in the Continental systems. On the contrary, they can expect their opponents to argue that, if there is to be a positive right in Britain, it should apply only to 'full stoppages' not to action short of a strike. The distinction is in practice hard to apply, as the Italian and the French experience shows; but it is drawn nearer home by the Irish statute on unfair dismissal, where it is deemed to be unfair to dismiss selectively one or more of the employees taking part in a strike or other industrial action, but industrial action is confined to 'lawful action' while strike is not.[65]

Of course, this is not the end of the story. In Italy until 1980 the courts had also excluded from the constitutional right many forms of 'articulated' stoppage, such as 'hiccup strikes' (repeated stoppages over time) or 'chessboard strikes' (rapid stoppages in one place after another) – forms of action which sometimes defy the distinction between 'full' and 'partial' stoppage – especially if they caused disproportionate damage to the enterprise (using a concept of proportionality parallel to that controlling the legality of strikes in the German system) and dependant in part upon the concept of 'abuse of right'.[66] But in 1980 Italian judges adopted a new jurisprudence, holding that the constitutional right to strike is not to be restricted by the proportionality of damage or even by an *a priori* definition. 'Strike' now includes, therefore, all forms of action within the meaning of 'the concept derived from everyday language in its social context', so long as the stoppage does not infringe parallel constitutional rights.[67] This is a flexible and dynamic test. Today, therefore, short but repeated stoppages are constitutionally legitimate whatever the damage to production, though the majority view still excludes a go-slow or work-to-rule involving no clear absence from work, along with other ingenious action, such as the 'inside-out' strike (*sciopero alla rovescia*) where workers insist on work the employer does not want.[68] But at a certain point – and no-one is quite sure what it is – if damage is caused by these articulated strikes to the very '*produttività*' or '*integrità*' (the essential productive capacity or essence) of the plant, the workers may trespass on the constitutional rights of the employer and cease to enjoy protection. Commentators puzzle over this distinction, saying the law is 'difficult to state'.[69] The problem is not made easier for a British observer by a judicial system which does not have a strict principle of *stare decisis* or precedent; but more important is the realisation that positive rights can produce legal puzzles as difficult as the British immunities and consequent complexities castigated by the Experts of the ILO.[70] As we shall see later, the notion of 'balancing' the right to strike against other constitutional rights has come to be central in the Italian law on essential services. Short of adopting a written constitution, it is difficult to see how that aspect of the debate could have any analogue in Britain.

But here as elsewhere the logic of a system is not to be stated so simply. There are particular doctrines to be taken into account, and more important the surrounding principles of law as they attach to labour law. On the first, we may take the problem of '*auto-satisfaction*'. In the deceptive case of *Bardot* in 1978, workers had stopped work on three successive Saturdays. Their demand was: an end to Saturday working. Surely this was a lawful strike. The Cour de Cassation held it was not.[71] It had already held: 'The workers' right to strike does not allow them to execute their employment under the very conditions which they are demanding, in breach of those required by their contracts of employment.'[72] The demand on the employer must be for something different from that which the stoppage accomplishes. One cannot believe an Italian court would accept that reasoning. French commentators have castigated the ban on '*auto-satisfaction*' as an example of judicial enforcement of the social discipline denounced by Foucault,[73] but the French judges have insisted upon it, holding in 1989 that short stoppages by railway workers on Friday afternoons were unlawful because their demand was for the maintenance of rest periods at just that time (while, in a judgment on the very same day, deciding that stoppages on successive Saturdays at an IBM plant were lawful because the strikers were complaining not about Saturday work, but about increased overtime).[74]

On the other hand, the French system tends to work through the contractual consequences with rigorous logic. When employment contracts are suspended in a strike, no wages are payable and no work need be offered. But in a case of 1985, workers who had stopped work for a week successfully recovered their wages for that period. Their demand was for a machine to be made safe that had crushed a colleague's hand. The employer claimed he need not pay them because they were on strike; therefore the work-wage bargain was suspended on both sides: their contracts were suspended, they need not work, he need not pay. But the court disagreed. The demand motivating the stoppage was that the employer should repair his own breach of duty and provide safe machinery, which it had taken him a week to do. Their stoppage in response to that breach was justified under their contractual employment conditions. They were under no duty to work but their contracts were not suspended; it was not a strike; they were entitled to their pay.[75]

Legal Sources and Labour Movements

These elements of two neighbouring systems are but the tips of twin icebergs increasingly difficult for visitors to understand the more they look beneath the surface. If it is hard to explain to a British observer the logic of French trade unionism, where ideological pluralism and the consequent right to choose a union or not to join any union,[76] means that membership strength may be less important than support in elections for workers' representatives, it is equally hard to outline to a French counterpart the Disputes Principles and Procedures ('Bridlington') under which the worker's right to choose his union can, as the House of Lords upheld,[77] lawfully be constrained by an expulsion necessary to effect a TUC Disputes Committee Award. In France that right to choose a union is elevated to the level of a constitutional principle. How could it be otherwise in a system where it would be unthinkable to put pressure on a Catholic to leave the Catholic CFTC in order to induce him to join the Communist CGT even if the latter organises workers in that workplace? The language and the very logic of 'union security' is governed by the character of trade union organisation in the different systems. The same is true in part of the right to strike. It has been said: 'there exists a correspondence between the juridical structure of the right to strike and forms of union organisation: in a regime with union pluralism ... the strike must be put outside the competition of particular unions.' It cannot be a union monopoly and must therefore, as it is in France and Italy, be an individual right. This, it is said, is the way we may explain the difference between the doctrines on strikes in France and Italy and those, of a 'collective' type, dominant in Germany or Scandinavian countries.[78] We have already met the precept of which this reminds us, crucial to comparative inquiry and daily more relevant as 1992 approaches: if you wish to understand a country's labour law, first examine its labour movement and industrial history. The sources of today's structure are to be found not in the legal but in the social history.[79] But important though this link is between labour law and the pattern of the labour movement, it is wrong to exclude other factors; they are not irrelevant to the law's developing shape. For instance, the existence or absence of written constitutions in comparable countries cannot be ignored, as Kahn-Freund's survey of the 'impact of constitutions on labour law' made plain, though his most important conclusion was the ease with which judges everywhere can 'read their own notions of policy into the bill of rights'.[80]

But the point goes beyond the macro level of constitutions to the micro level of specific legal rules. Take vicarious liability. When will the trade union be liable for unlawful industrial action or for illegal acts committed in lawful strikes? In Britain this question has often arisen from picketing; in France and Italy it more often arises from an ensuing occupation of the workplace (the sacrosanct proprietary rights protected by the tort of trespass are tinged in those countries by a concept of the workplace as a common field of battle).[81] But in France and Britain, the initial premises about liability appear to be similar. It is useful to follow their logic, starting from similar premises but by subtle twists in neighbouring paths ending in practice in very different results.

As we have seen, the British union official is not, in law, the agent of his members unless the rules give him authority to be such.[82] But before the union's liability in tort was nullified by the full protection accorded in 1906 (and again in 1974) the reverse principle was employed: the official was an agent of the union. The union was liable on the ordinary principles of agency where a local official or body of the union acted within its authority as agent for the whole union under its rules and practices.[83] When the protection against tort liability was lifted, first the courts extended the range of vicarious liability through a more flexible concept of implied authority,[84] then the legislature devised a special code of vicarious liability for unions, not in the law of tort generally but specifically for tort liabilities in industrial action only.[85] That code it tightened in 1990 to make union funds liable for the acts of *any* 'official' (including branch officials) authorised or not, or even acts of any 'person' with whom such an official consorted in the co-ordination of industrial action, unless the union goes through a complex and cumbersome procedure of repudiation, including prompt written communication in the required words to each union member and employer involved.[86]

In France the principles of the ordinary law on associations and vicarious liability make for a different outcome when applied in labour law. Two crucial judgments of 1982 insisted on applying rigorously the classical doctrine that the union does not stand in a relationship of principal and agent to striking members, nor agent and principal, nor (which is crucial) to local 'union delegates', even though they are appointed by the union with the task of representing it and the interests of the workers *vis-à-vis* the employer,[87] nor even to the *sections syndicales* in the enterprise.[88] This means that the union cannot be automatically liable for their acts vicariously under article 1384 of the Code Civile. If the union is to be liable the plaintiff must prove the three requirements under article 1382 of the Code: fault, damage and a causal link between these two. One might think this was, even so, not so far from the British position; the law of tort normally gives a remedy for breach of duty which causes damage.[89] But once relieved of any liability as principal ('*commettant*') the union in France can be liable only for 'its' acts – that is to say acts of its 'organs', its general assembly, central committee, president or general secretary acting within their normal competence.[90] The union is liable if such an organ expressly instigated, incited or authorised acts which cause the damage suffered by the employer or the non-strikers (the two plaintiffs most often found), as in the *Trailor* decision.[91] But organising a strike is not by itself enough to engage responsibility for wrongful acts in it that fall outside 'the normal exercise of the right to strike', especially because in taking strike action the workers (including the union delegate) are exercising their own individual rights to strike. Thus, in a leading decision in 1990 the court said it was not sufficient to prove that a local union body supported members who occupied the plant in the union's name, since that did not amount to participation by the union itself in further illegal acts that caused the damage alleged (locking the doors of the plant) nor for union officers to adopt a passive attitude in face of illegal acts done by strikers, even though the union had called the strike.[92] 'The union is not at fault for not preventing illegal acts; only positive instructions make it liable.'[93]

The maintenance of this attitude to union liability by the Cour de Cassation is the more remarkable in face of frequent attempts by lower courts to erode it (sometimes by treating delegates *à l'anglaise* as agents of the union) and of recent extensions of personal liability. Since the celebrated *Corfu* judgment of 1972, where a union delegate was held personally liable for wrongfully obstructing the entrance to a works,[94] an increasing number of civil actions for damages have succeeded against individual strikers for unlawful 'strikes' or illegal acts done in the course of lawful strikes, such as occupations or infringements of the 'right to work' of non-strikers, sometimes resulting in damages of millions of francs. (These damages are in principle enforceable *in solidum*, i.e. in full against each worker made defendant in the action.) Workers' representatives and union delegates are not immune from this personal liability; but, again, the liability must be for personal acts which cause the damage.[95] In 1982 the French parliament was sufficiently concerned about the extensions of liability to propose an 'immunity' providing – in terms very familiar to the English lawyer – that civil liability should arise only from penal wrongs or acts manifestly not connected with '*the normal exercise of the right to strike*' (it might almost have read 'manifestly not in furtherance of a trade dispute'). But the Constitutional Council declared this part of the Bill to be unconstitutional, infringing constitutional principles of 'equality' – whereupon the courts, in a manner indicative of the power and independence of the French judges, themselves restated the rule that damages could not be recovered for a 'normal exercise of the right to strike'.[96]

Thus, French law restricts the liability of the union to a greater extent than the British rules on vicarious liability. To some extent this is natural to a labour law system dealing with unions which are very poor in resources. Indeed, French law protects the core of the union's property against seizure in legal proceedings – a precedent ignored equally by those who castigated the protection of British unions' funds from tort liability in 1906 and 1974 and by those who after its withdrawal in 1982 proposed labour law reforms without reintroduction of that protection (for fear of putting unions above the ordinary law of the land – forgetting that union rights are always introduced to rise above the levels of the ordinary law).[97] In France, though, some individual workers suffer from this legal structure; it may be that the problem of 'martyrs' in industrial conflict – which was made famous in England by the dockers' shop stewards in 1972 and which the new British laws largely solve by the simple tactic of making the union and its funds the primary target in litigation – is still to be solved in France.

But it is not possible to say that the narrower ambit of union liability in regard to vicarious liability depends largely, or even primarily, upon different structures or organisation in the labour movements of the two countries. Even before the Thatcher legislation sharply turned the screw of vicarious liability on British unions, first in 1982 then more savagely in 1990, the content and style of the law here was different from that in France by reason of the approach of the common law, on the one side, and the *Code Civil* and *droit commun*, on the other, to principles of vicarious liability. These principles can of course be developed liberally or restrictively. French judges proved between 1972 and 1990 that they are quite as capable of extending the liabilities of pickets or of strikers as the English courts. But the Cour de Cassation in the critical judgments on appeal has so far refused – despite considerable pressure in the decisions of some of the Courts of Appeal below it – to stray outside the classical French doctrines on this subject.[98] In seeking lessons from European experience, it is necessary to note that differences such as these spring largely from legal, not from industrial, sources; and within the legal causes we must include the judges who refused to be very 'creative' to extend union liability. Within the framework of the system set down by the hands of the labour movement, the law builds its own corridors. This mixture of social and legal sources also contributes to the shape of the law on strikes as such, for example the questions which all the systems face when one group of workers supports another in taking industrial action. We look first at that matter before turning to the typology of the systems as 'organic' and 'individualist' and to the distinction between so-called 'disputes of interests' and 'disputes of rights'.

Sympathy, Secondary or Solidarity Action

How far is industrial action lawful when the employer involved is not that of the workers taking the action but of other workers whom they are supporting. Here systems tend to edge along a spectrum of rules, mixing colours as they go. Broadly, they tend to emphasise either the shared 'interests' of the two or more groups of workers involved or the degree to which the second employer is an 'ally' of the first. The Italian courts accept solidarity action as legitimate provided workers act in defence of what they perceive to be their interest in the primary dispute. This is to be expected since, as we saw, the demands of the strikers, though related to their employment, need not in Italian law be aimed primarily at their own employer. The test is whether 'the victory or defeat of the primary group would have, more or less, some degree of importance for the second group'.[99] This represents a logical rule for a system which regards the right to strike of central constitutional importance; but, as we shall see, it may also have contributed to the developments of 1990 when new limitations were imposed upon strikes affecting a wide range of essential public services. In Spain the test, the 'interests' of the workers involved, is similar. So too in France – but with a more objective understanding of 'interest' for *grèves de solidarité externe* (external solidarity strikes). Demands by the initial strikers must relate to the interests of those who take the action elsewhere in solidarity, though it is sufficient if they do so indirectly. But in the curious area of '*grèves de solidarité interne*' (internal solidarity strikes) rather stricter rules apply; for example that strikes by workers about an injustice done to a colleague even in the same enterprise have been held to be unlawful when the strikers had no interest of their own to assert or to protect.[100]

At the other end of the spectrum, German law allows for sympathy action – in theory. Judgments accepting it are hard to find; but it has been judicially said to be justified if the second employer has become in an economic sense a 'part of the undertaking' or an ally of the first employer, a doctrine which makes its appearance also in the United States.[101] Swedish law is somewhat broader,allowing sympathy action where the union fulfils its own rules, where it does not infringe any 'peace obligation' in collective agreements and where the first strike is itself lawful. Moreover, if the first strike occurs abroad, the Swedish Labour Court has been known (though not consistently) to relax these principles, as in the case of a strike to support a boycott of goods from Chile, on the ground that workers have no opportunity to influence the social policies of a foreign country where the dispute originates – a rare example of a national system taking account of transnational realities.[102] In marked contrast is the British statutory definition of a trade dispute as amended by the Thatcher government in 1982 to tie the legality of disputes to facts which affect the interests of workers in Britain, matched by the increasingly narrow approach of the courts to the legality of industrial action abroad.[103]

The most remarkable provision on solidarity action is found in Denmark where the Labour Court permits solidarity strikes contrary to the peace obligation if a ballot has been held and notice has been given, so long as it is altruistic. Secondary strikers must *not* have a material interest of their own in the primary dispute, an exception which originated in the historic Compromise Agreement of 1899 and Rules of 1908, still as amended the basis of dispute settlement. The Danish test of altruism is at the infra-red end of the spectrum; most countries accept sympathetic strikes only if the workers have an interest of some kind in the primary dispute. In Ireland it must now by law be approved not only in a ballot but also (remarkably) by the Irish Congress of Trades Unions.[104] Yet the Danish approach can readily be defended. For example, action by port workers is often taken (in Scandinavia, for instance) to help the third world crews of flag-of-convenience ships, often little more than prisoners in such vessels employed on atrocious conditions.[105] Under the 1980s legislation this became unlawful in Britain. It is arguably a right which should be restored. Indeed, the restrictive British law on secondary strikes has since 1980 wandered off to the ultra-violet end of the spectrum. As the ILO Committee of Experts said in 1989, British law 'makes it virtually impossible for workers and unions to engage in any form of boycott activity or "sympathetic" action against parties not directly involved in a given dispute', thereby contravening the ILO Convention of 1948 on freedom of association.[106] When the 1990 Employment Act added to the offence by banning all forms of secondary action, British law in comparative terms seemed to lurch off the spectrum into a juridical black hole. Permission for secondary action against an 'ally' of the primary employer turns up in the system of industry-wide bargaining in Germany (as part of what may be called a 'pitched tents' vision of industrial conflict). In part it appeared in the special 'gateways' to legality in the 1980 British Act, often called the 'first-customer-or-supplier' exception and now repealed by the 1990 legislation. But it is less evident in the 'individualist' systems of Italy, Spain and France. There the dominant concept is one of workers' interest – logical enough, when what is at stake is the individual worker's constitutional right – and whether the support of one worker by another is a struggle in which both have a sufficient interest. The differences between these systems arises in great measure from the degree to which the presence of an interest is tested objectively or subjectively.

On the other hand, the concept of support between connected workers is not absent from traditional concepts employed in Britain, Sweden and Denmark. Proposals for a positive right to strike in Britain would inevitably raise the question: What tests are to be adopted for lawful sympathetic or solidarity or secondary action? And why? Should they rest upon workers' interests or upon employers' alliances? Or a mixture of the two? The very semantic presentation hints at predetermined choices. The terms 'solidarity' and 'sympathy' point towards workers' interests, while the American 'secondary' approach highlights instead the distinction between two employers and two employment areas. Comparative inquiry suggests that the latter, whatever its other qualities, more readily lends itself to dense thickets of legalistic regulation, especially in the definition of employers who are 'allies'.[107] In truth, changes in the employment pattern should never be the reason for limiting the right to strike. Where workers employed in five plants by one employer wake up to find that each plant is now run by a separate subsidiary company as the 'employer', nothing has changed for them and nothing should change for their rights. Community law requires a transfer of rights on a transfer of an undertaking. The right to strike in support of one another should equally not be affected.

But too narrow an interpretation of 'interest' can stultify this part of the right to strike in a form that would fail ILO requirements (it appears to have gone a long way in Greece).[108] While the emphasis of a system is bound to be on one or the other, there is no *a priori* reason why both elements should not be incorporated. Should not workers have the right to take action in support of colleagues employed across the street whose employment affects their working lives? Should not port workers have the right to offer altruistic aid in their desire to assist the oppressed crews of flag-of-convenience ships? Should not the transnational alliances of employers' groups be inspected for their real alliances rather than their corporate appearances? The spectrum becomes more blurred if we inquire into the employer's right to replace strikers during disputes. In broad terms, the organic systems, based on the link with collective contract and in Germany with 'parity of arms', tend to give stronger rights to the employer and to the employers' association (the prominence of such associations compared with their relative demise in Britain is not unimportant to the way the Labour Courts in Germany and Sweden see the issues). In Italy and Spain, the employer who uses strike-breakers risks committing 'anti-union' acts, while in France the law specifically prohibits the hiring of *temporary* replacement workers, but does not ban engagement of permanent employees with normal rights against dismissal or the use of temporary workers already hired before the strike. In Denmark workers required to break strikes by taking over work have an extended right to strike even in breach of peace obligations; but in Germany the right to use strike breakers extends to the use of state officials (the *Beamter*, who constitute about half of those in the public sector but enjoy no right to strike whatever, and whose place in the system stems more from the history of the state of Prussia than of ordinary German labour relations). Further inquiry into specific rules in the different systems risks unprofitable fragmentation.

What is perhaps immediately noteworthy is that, whatever their other differences, all these European systems reserve some area of legality for solidarity or sympathetic action of some kind. Only the British Act of 1990 has sought to make it wholly unlawful. When reform of that law comes, attention will need to be given to the way 'interest' and 'ally' tests are combined, and their balance in the frame of workers' and unions' overall rights (for example their rights to participate in the taking of decisions). Again, since British employers operate much less than the German in associations, in bargaining industry-wide or in strike insurance, the courts must have the competence and duty to identify 'allies' among companies hidden by separate corporate veils, whether in a formal group or not. So too, as we have seen, the nature of the 'interest' required between groups of workers should not rule out, in defined cases, action on an altruistic basis. Even if an acceptable combination of the 'ally' and 'interest' tests can be found, the question will nevertheless arise whether sympathetic action should be required to be supported by a separate ballot even where the primary action was taken by workers who had held a ballot. If a right to strike is created which inheres in the individual workers, it is difficult to see why they should not be free to exercise it without a further state-imposed ballot where they have an interest in common with others in the primary dispute. On the other hand, there may be a stronger case for demanding an obligatory period of notice for certain types of solidarity action. But these problems raise the question – in whom is the right to strike to vest? In the worker? Or in the union? Those questions raise an issue more familiar to other European systems than to ours.

Organic and Individualist Rights to Strike

The differences in legal culture complicate comparisons, let alone harmonisation, of the labour laws in the member states of the Community, each deeply rooted in a specific social fabric. As we have seen, the link between the national legal structure and the development of a particular labour movement explains some, but not all, of the diverse features of modern rights to strike. The most obvious is the emergence of the peculiar 'immunities', stemming primarily from the nature of the British trade union movement between 1850 and 1906, the very year in which the Labour Party was born but British trade unions were already able to influence the political establishment despite the absence of universal male franchise. No single factor makes comparison more difficult than the fact that ours was the only European labour movement to grow to maturity exclusively as an industrial movement, with no parallel political party seeking to mobilise the new working class.[109] That is the reason our law on industrial action cannot fit into one of the customary frameworks; the fact that the legal culture has entwined itself around this 'voluntary' heritage greatly complicates the problems of legal policy.

Outside Britain, a division is customarily made between two types of union movement which broadly correlates with two types of right to strike: the 'organic' and the 'individualist'.[110] In the 'organic' systems unions are based upon membership in centralised, unitary or bipolar centres, such as the DGB and DAG in Germany, the LO and TCO in Sweden or LO in Denmark. In these systems the law vests the right to strike *not* in the individual but in the union. A variant found in Portugal is to vest the right in a union but permit groups of workers to exercise the right to strike where there is no effective union.[111] By contrast, in the 'individualist' systems, as we have seen in France, Italy or Spain, unions have grown up divided by ideological or religious pluralism. In Italy, for example, the main confederations (reading from left to centre) are the CGIL, UIL and CISL, divided ideologically but at times attaining a high degree of unified action. Here the right to strike is necessarily the legal property of each individual worker, albeit that it can be exercised only collectively with others.[112]

The modern German right to strike was constructed by the courts largely out of the few words in the constitution guaranteeing to everyone 'the right to form associations for the maintenance and improvement of working and economic conditions' (article 9.3), in the light of its other sections (especially art. 2). The courts require that a strike must be called by a union strong enough to exercise 'pressure'; that is indeed the mark of union legitimacy in the bargaining system. But the right to strike is further limited; it must be exercised only as the *ultima ratio* or last resort, directed against an employer on an issue on which a collective agreement can be made and restrained within action which is 'proportional' to the aims and to the need to maintain 'equality of arms' between unions and employers (who have a parallel right to lock out). If it fails to meet these conditions, it is a tort under the Civil Code.[113] Although action short of a full strike occurs – in a famous case an opera company took industrial action by singing at 'half voice' – it is virtually impossible to justify as lawful under these criteria. Of course, such a legal base does not prevent the courts from deciding that where the right to strike (or to lock-out) is lawfully exercised, the collective right is dominant and employment contracts are suspended.[114] The doctrine of suspension is not the preserve of the 'individualist' systems.

Sweden also falls into the 'organic' camp. The constitution guarantees a right of industrial action both for unions and associations of employers, so long as its exercise does not contravene obligations incurred by law or by contract, including collective agreements (art. 17). Such agreements impose a 'peace obligation', as they do in Germany, and this must not be infringed. A union must observe its own rules in calling a strike, and give notice of a strike to the State Conciliator (except in claims for unpaid wages). But the Joint Regulation at Work Act of 1976 which extended the right of unions to bargain collectively (even to the point of giving them a certain 'priority of interpretation' of collective agreements, i.e. to impose their interpretation until the Labour Court holds otherwise) created a special right to take strike action if the employer refuses to negotiate a 'joint regulation' agreement over the wider area (art. 44). Generally no strike, lock-out or 'other comparable action' is allowed to challenge the validity or interpretation of a collective agreement, or induce an alteration of it, or support a strike by another union which it is not allowed to take.[115] Union members are bound by the same rules and the union is obliged to press them to end any action in breach of a 'peace obligation', just as the employers' association must press its members to do so. On the other hand, non-unionists are permitted to join in a strike called properly by a union. Legal action against individual workers for 'wildcat' strikes is rare, but one finds it, for example in the action brought against 920 workers in 1990 when, the court being too small, the case was adjourned to the 'house of culture'.[116]

All this sounds rather regimented and corporatist, and so it is. But it has another side. One must set in the balance the very real workers' rights, in Sweden both in collective bargaining and in minority representation on company boards possessed by workers through their union, and in the vast structures of 'co-determination' on company supervisory boards and, more important, in the Works Councils, a structure which is an article of faith for unions and workers – and even for many employers – in Germany. Moreover, even in an unlawful, unofficial or 'wild-cat' strike, where the employment contract *is* broken, the employee cannot be dismissed unless (in Sweden) the employer proves it is objectively necessary to terminate the employment or (in Germany) unless the Works Council is consulted and the employer proves serious fault.[117] This made groundless a claim that powers to dismiss unofficial strikers selectively, enacted for the British employer in the Employment Act 1990 (s. 9), were needed to give to him the 'same freedom to respond to unofficial action as employers in West Germany'.[118]

What is more, while the organic systems do not leave the unofficial striker defenceless, he may well fare worse under an 'individualist' system. Thus the individual French worker who has gone on strike at the call of his union but by exceeding the 'normal exercise' of the right to strike has been guilty of *'faute lourde'*, may be liable to dismissal and, worse, in damages to the tune of millions of francs at the suit of the employer or non-strikers. The Swedish employee, on the other hand, who has responded to his union's call to engage in a strike which turns out to be illegal finds that the Labour Court leniently awards lower damages, if any, against him; the fault is perceived to lie with the union, so that even unofficial strikers in Sweden find that the normal limit of damages against individuals is SK200 (£20), a traditional, and now mystically symbolic, figure in that Court.[119] A notable feature of Scandinavian labour law is the difference between the Swedish and the Danish Labour Courts. The latter has a much higher 'tariff' for breaches of peace obligations. In 1989 it charged skilled workers at the rate of DKr 32 per hour (just under £3) and DKr52 if there was any failure to obey an order. This court puts up its 'tariff' from time to time and fines the unions much larger sums – the brewery workers' union was fined DKr10 million (some £900,000) for encouraging members to strike after a collective agreement had been made.[120] But even this 'toughest' of the Scandinavian Labour Courts does not dispose of the powers to punish for contempt of court which the English High Court enjoys.[121]

Indeed, the law on dismissal under which the individual employee on strike has fared worst is the British. At common law his repudiatory breach of contract justifies summary dismissal, and since the 1970s the legislation has allowed him to seek a remedy for unfair dismissal only where the employer dismisses (or re-employs) employees taking part in the strike or industrial action with him on a selective basis.[122] After rendering it easier in 1982 for the employer to manipulate this machinery, the Thatcher legislation gave him power in 1990 to select 'unofficial' strikers for dismissal at his whim without any right to complain to an industrial tribunal of unfair dismissal.[123] The policy reason for maintaining this position in 1974 was the desire to keep the merits of strikes out of the tribunals, or more important out of the appellate courts, which would otherwise inevitably build up a body of principles on 'reasonable strikes'.[124] It may be questioned now whether this decision was wise, though at the time it seemed to be so given the attitude of the judges to industrial action and in the light of the immediate past experience of the NIRC. A different choice was made in Ireland in the statute of 1977, which allowed dismissed strikers to challenge the fairness of dismissal;[125] but it is unlikely that British experience would have matched the relatively small amount of litigation on that provision.

More important, consideration of the Swedish and German systems must not create the belief, as it commonly does, that a system which is 'organic' in the sense that lawful strikes are vested exclusively in the hands of trade unions, must contain other features of the same kind, such as 'peace obligations' or the *ultima ratio* rule. In the law as reformed in 1982 in Greece, for example, the right to strike is constitutionally vested in 'lawfully established trade unions'.[126] But there is no 'parity of arms' doctrine. Indeed, lock-outs are prohibited. The objects of legitimate strikes are *not* confined to matters which can be the subject of collective bargaining; nor is sympathy action outlawed (indeed, representative official unions have an extended right of solidarity action against multi-national enterprises where the action abroad can affect domestic working conditions); and in principle interlocutory injunctions are banned (the courts appear to have little difficulty in intervening in other ways).[127] On the other side of the coin, the Minister of Labour has power under a law of 1955 to refer disputes to compulsory arbitration; for 45 days no industrial action is allowed and the awards are legally binding; further limits of this kind were imposed in 1985 but repealed in 1988 after ILO objections.

The ILO does not consider – perhaps surprisingly – that the monopoly right of official unions to call lawful strikes is necessarily an impairment of the right to strike.[128] Indeed, some organic features of that kind are found in most of the individualist and unclassifiable systems. They arise from pressures for order in the labour market, not dissimilar to the pressures for union security (including the closed shop). In Ireland, where the law rests upon a structure of immunities bequeathed by British labour law, legislation of 1941 established that the right to negotiate collective agreements is confined to unions authorised by licence; the main immunities from tort liability were also restricted to such authorised unions;[129] and Irish legislation of 1990 retains preferential treatment for authorised unions in regard to enjoyment of the immunities.[130] In that respect, the system is 'organic'. Individualist systems could hardly adopt such an openly discriminatory system. Nevertheless, legal distinctions between unions do appear. In France, for example, only representative unions' can give the five-day notice required to legitimise a strike in 'public services' under the law of 31 July 1963.[131] The notion of a 'representative' union is not bounded by 'majoritarian' concepts; here a union may qualify by being affiliated to one of the national 'representative' confederations or recognised at the level of the enterprise of service by a series of tests which look to its effectiveness as a union.[132] Realistic commentary accepts that this type of legal distinction 'renounces strict respect for trade union pluralism and its corollary, equality between unions'.[133]

On the other hand, the 'representative unions' in Spain which enjoy a certain priority and numerous advantages (for example, in enterprise bargaining) under the LOLS of 1985,[134] normally depends more directly upon proof of a percentage of support by voters in the elections for workplace representatives. This affords them advantages, but not a legal monopoly, in the calling of strikes. The status derives from the acquisition of 10 per cent of the votes at enterprise or national level (or 15 per cent in an autonomous Commune); but other subsidiary tests are used; and affiliation to a national 'representative union' may, in French fashion, also be enough.[135] In Italy 'the more representative unions' (*i sindacati maggiormente representativi*) are also privileged; indeed, 'they have become one of the corner stones on which the legislation about Italian industrial relations is based.'[136] The union rights in the Workers' Statute of 1970, for example, largely apply only to local union bodies working 'within the ambit' of representative unions.[137] But they do not depend on electoral support for their status. They are there defined by reference to affiliation to one of the national 'representative' unions (mainly CGIL, CISL and UIL)[138] or as a union which signs national or provincial agreements applicable to that enterprise. Like the French concept, the Italian is a relative concept, tending to shift meaning in different applications; but it has not identified a privileged group in respect of strikes. Instead, out of the furious debate of the 1980s on the 'representativeness', in every sense, of unions came Law 146 of 12 June 1990, discussed below, on 'essential public services'. Under it agreements signed by some unions can affect the right of other unions or workers to take strike action (in respect of the notice required, for example); in most cases it appears these unions would be 'representative', but some writers question whether it is constitutional for the state to delegate this power to them (under arts. 39 and 40 of the Constitution).[139] It may well be that the 1990s will see a redefinition of '*rappresentatività*'.

In France and Italy the right to strike, as we saw, necessarily vests in the individual worker. The 'peace obligation' is therefore of lesser importance. The union cannot bargain away a worker's constitutional right to strike, especially by agreements it has made; and the worker may be guilty of wrongdoing in the light of what he knows to have been agreed. In Italy the union itself may be liable for breach of an express peace clause; but, though quite common in the 1960s, such clauses fell into disuse through union opposition in the 1970s and are now found very rarely. According to majority opinion, such a clause binds only the union body which signs it – not intermediate union bodies or individual workers – and then only to the extent of the explicit, 'relative' obligation to keep the peace on matters covered by the agreement.[140] So too in France clauses in an agreement to give notice or to engage in conciliation before a strike is called are binding on the union but only if they involve delays of such duration that the right to strike is not effectively extinguished. But where union strike action is undertaken in breach of such a clause, the union is contractually liable for the breach. The same jurisprudence holds that individual workers (including union delegates) may also be liable, but only if they knowingly cause the agreement to be broken so as to be guilty of *faute lourde* (as when they are promoters of a strike which they know will break an agreement to give notice).[141]

We can see therefore that although the peace obligation is found, it is less prominent; and it makes little sense even to discuss 'unofficial' strikes in these individualist jurisdictions where the right vests in the worker not the union. Far from being central to the system, as in Germany or Sweden, the peace clause is marginal. The *faute lourde* of individual workers who knowingly strike in breach of an agreement is crucial, for in face of it the employer has extensive powers: he may dismiss each worker summarily, lawfully lock them out, make deductions from pay, and if he re-engages them he can require them to sign an undertaking to work normally, while in addition each may be liable in damages *in solidum* (for the whole amount) for loss caused to him or to other employees or even (though this happens rarely) to third parties. Here the French system in practice protects the worker less than the Italian in which such sanctions as dismissal are said, in face of such protections as articles 15 (ban on discrimination) and 28 (ban on employer's 'anti-union' conduct) of the Workers' Statute 1970, to be possible but 'theoretical'.[142]

On the other hand, in Italy the new provisions on strikes in 'essential public services' in Law no. 146, 12 June 1990, mean that workers in that widely defined sector can be made subject to 'disciplinary', monetary sanctions for contravening requirements on strike notices or on the maintenance of a minimum service during a dispute, where the requirement may have been set by a collective agreement (arts. 2, 4: penalties 'proportionate to the gravity of their offence' but not dismissal or a variation of their employment contracts). Their trade unions may also be penalised, for instance temporarily deprived of union rights (including the check-off otherwise guaranteed by the Workers' Statute) and suspended from bargaining (for at least one month), for the same offence. The statute lays down minimum standards but it is envisaged by it, and equally by the government and the major unions, that collective agreements will set standards above the compulsory floor (e.g. collective agreements may require a strike notice longer than the ten-day minimum required by the Law, art. 2(5)). Although such penalties do not in the strict sense arise from breaches of 'peace clauses' in the agreements themselves, where they stem from such provisions in collective agreements they have a parallel effect in practical terms on workers and unions in this sphere of 'constitutionally protected' rights and interests (health, safety, transport, information, communications, education and the like) which the new law attempts to 'balance' against the constitutional right to strike. Collective agreements seem likely increasingly to shape workers' and unions' duties under the guidance of a 'Commission' (arts. 12, 13: the *Commissione di Garanzia* discussed below in the section on public services). We cannot yet know how all this will work, for instance, whether a union temporarily barred from official bargaining will turn effectively to unofficial pressures; but there is a parallel in functional terms between these limitations upon the legitimacy of strike action and those set by 'peace clauses', not least because of the involvement of unions in what is intended to be a species of joint administration, building on the earlier practices of union 'self-regulation' (*autoregolamentazione*). We may, however, also note that workers in this sector can be subjected to higher penalties – up to £200 a day – for failing to provide a minimum service required by an ordinance (*precettazione*) issued by a Minister or a regional Prefect under the guidance of the Commission, in revised procedures by which the law aims to protect the same constitutional interests from 'a proven danger of grave and imminent injury' (arts. 8, 9).

Although caution is required in its use, the distinction between the individual and the organic right to strike is useful as a point of departure and a safeguard against false comparative judgment. It helps to explain, for example, why 'unofficial' action is a wholly inappropriate category in, say, France or Italy and why the Green Paper of 1989,[143] was less than helpful in citing isolated provisions from the laws of West Germany, Denmark or Sweden out of their organic context. Curiously, traditional British labour law did once confront the issue of 'peace clauses'; in 1974 parliament prohibited their incorporation from collective agreements into individual employment contracts unless five special conditions were met.[144] This was odd in two ways. First, our courts have leaned strongly against incorporating procedural requirements relating to industrial action into individual contracts.[145] Secondly, even if the prohibition or restriction is not translated from the collective agreement to the individual employment contract, industrial action by the worker invariably remains a breach of his employment contract, just as it would have been if he had broken the peace obligation. The incorporation of the peace obligation seems to make no difference. There is little judicial support for the – perhaps logical – argument that incorporation of a peace procedure should imply a right to strike once it is exhausted. The origin of the 1974 provision was probably an erroneous belief that insertion of such obligations by *express* provision was unusual and 'artificial'.[146] This piece of British legal history reminds us too of the elementary distinction between the right to strike of the worker and the right to organise strikes (which may or may not inhere in the union alone).

Disputes of Rights and Disputes of Interests

In similar vein the distinction between 'disputes of interests' and 'disputes of rights'[147] – often illustrated by the difference between a wage claim and a dispute about interpretation of an agreement – means much less in 'individualist' systems, even though the collective agreement is a binding contract. French writers state firmly that, although civil responsibility may fall on a union or a delegate or even a worker for breach of an agreement, the right to strike itself is not limited by the fact that the dispute is about

> rights or interpretation which could be taken to the courts ... and the same is true of a strike breaking out even though a collective agreement has been signed or renewed ... The right to strike is not subordinated to the possibility of a legal action, nor to collective bargaining.[148]

French judgments which disqualify 'internal solidarity' strikes within the one enterprise in protest against dismissal of a colleague which was not 'manifestly' unlawful, do so not primarily because the dismissed worker might take the dismissal to the *conseil de prud'hommes* but because the strikers were held to have pursued no occupational interest of their own.[149] The same general rule applies in Belgium but largely, it seems, for the quaint reason that Belgium has never had its *Taff Vale* judgment – unions sign agreements that include 'peace clauses' but they have no legal personality and cannot be sued in the courts.

This overlap between issues which are justiciable but which may still be the subject of legitimate strikes, demonstrates the falsity of the common assumption based on shallow formalism that wherever disputes over rights are taken 'into the courtroom' they are necessarily removed from the area of legitimate industrial action[150] – though that has not prevented even recent reforms from explicitly adopting the distinction between 'rights' and 'interests' disputes as the basis of strike law (in New Zealand and in some respects in Portugal, for instance).[151] British law has not incorporated this principle. A valid trade dispute can exist about the rights and wrongs of an alleged 'unfair dismissal', though the recent removal of immunity from strikes for which 'one reason is the fact or belief' that an employer has exercised his new power of selective dismissal over unofficial strikers shows how easily something like it can be adopted.[152] The latest Irish legislation appears to move a step in that direction by making exhaustion of procedures (whether legally binding or not) relating to individual employees' employment a condition of retention of the basic immunities.[153]

It is in the organic systems that the distinction between conflicts of interests and conflicts of rights becomes critical, and then normally in its 'relative' form (that is, extending only to matters covered by the agreement; in one of its rare phases of 'creativity' in the 1930s the Swedish Labour Court made great use of 'implied' or 'invisible' peace obligations which showed how devastating a wider interpretation can be). Here, say the German courts

> industrial conflict is complementary to collective bargaining ... industrial action is only allowed in so far as its purpose is the achievement of a collective agreement and the achievement of aims that can be regulated by a collective agreement.

But the courts have shown a tendency to interpret the scope of agreements narrowly (an agreement stating starting times for work did not 'regulate' hours; therefore the peace obligation did not prevent strike action about working hours; nor was that action invalidated because it aimed to render forthcoming legislation on hours ineffective).[154] The Swedish courts agree; a strike over the interpretation of a collective agreement or (with few exceptions) to demand a new agreement before the old one has expired or in breach of procedures applicable under it – a conflict of rights – is unlawful (except, oddly enough, in this jurisdiction in the special case of the non-payment of workers' wages). Here, the limiting factor – the very concept of the legitimate strike – differs profoundly from that in the individualist systems, even though in the latter the force of the collective agreement is not ignored. There are not, of course, in reality merely two ideal types. The Netherlands falls into the organic camp (despite its union pluralism) but with the important proviso that conflicts of rights usually go not to the ordinary courts, but to agreed joint arbitrations commissions. In Spain a system at first sight individualist has struggled to limit the force of 'peace obligations' bequeathed by a law of 1977 which fits uncertainly with later legislation.[155]

In general terms, though, the distinction between 'rights' and 'interests' disputes is important to a minority of West European systems (in Germany and Scandinavia and in some measure Portugal), is unknown to others (Britain and Ireland) and in the rest (France, Greece, Italy, Luxembourg, the Netherlands and Spain) is, in the words of the European Commission's survey, 'a theoretical distinction' which does 'not have much importance at the practical level'.[156]

It has been little noticed that the European Community's Social Charter explicitly adopts the organic, not the individualist, model. Article 13, as we have seen, declares that the right to collective action, including strikes, arises in the event of a 'conflict of interests' and 'subject to the obligations arising under national regulations and collective agreements'. That would represent a novel limitation on the right to strike as known in Italy, France, Belgium, Spain or even Britain. One may say the point is not of immediate consequence because the 'Action Programme' of the Commission includes no proposals to harmonise this area of labour law in the Community. Nevertheless, it is important for a new agenda in Britain, especially for those who have supported the Charter without reservation.

Allan Flanders once wrote that Britain had shown, industrially and legally, a 'lack of concern for the distinction between conflicts of interest and conflicts of rights, which is fundamental in European labour law'.[157] It is fundamental to German and Swedish law, but not to Italian or French law. Moreover, the British system has been a mish-mash, incorporating 'organic' features – protection of the union from all tort liability (until 1982) – but on the other hand fiercely individualist precisely because it has not limited liberties to withdraw labour to 'conflicts of interest' or the liberty to organise stoppages to official groups. Or, to adopt a different tack, the British system is heavily organic in that it protects the organisers, not the workers; but individualist-organic in that any person can be an organiser. The golden formula of acts done in furtherance of a trade dispute traditionally referred to acts 'connected with', and now in its tarnished form since 1982 refers to acts 'wholly or mainly relating to', employment conditions; both are wider than the organic logic that bans strikes when a collective agreement exists covering the issues in dispute. Before we adopted every word in the Social Charter, we should perhaps have considered whether we mean to make the big change in our law which would be effected by enacting a right to strike limited to the area of 'disputes of interests'. At the time points of that kind tended to be brushed aside in an understandable, but not altogether commendable frenzy to support the Charter and nothing but the Charter. Yet strangely, the same point appears to arise for a number of other systems of labour law apart from the British, not least the French and Italian.

The models of organic and individual systems are not of course immutable. In real life systems become mixed. In 1963, for instance, an atypical organic element was grafted on to French strike provisions by the law that requires strikes in the widely-defined public services to be called only on five days' notice by a 'representative trade union' (a phrase which broadly means a union affiliated to one of the five national confederations or with sufficient support at local level: Code du Travail art. L.521-3).[158] Again, Spain is an individualist system; its pluralist unions are divided ideologically and regionally and its Constitution of 1978 guarantees a right to strike – thought not a right to take other forms of industrial action – exercisable by workers 'in the defence of their interests' (art. 28.2). This the constitutional court has interpreted to mean an individual right to strike which cannot be wholly extinguished by 'peace clauses' in agreements.[159] But the *Ley Organica de Libertad Sindical* (The General Law on Trade Union Freedom) 1985, expressly promotes the status of unions in their role as strike initiators at various levels, whether or not they are 'representative' (a status for which the basic test in Spain is receipt of 10 per cent of votes in elections for workers' representatives); the same law provides, too, protections parallel to the Italian against an employer's 'anti-union conduct' with severe criminal sanctions.[160]

The aim of inspecting this typology is not to find some 'natural' place in the spectrum in which British law can be safely tucked. On the contrary, it encourages us to expect the British reform to have elements of both. Most systems contain contradictory elements inserted by moments of their own history. Some are remarkable, such as the exception in Denmark permitting strikes in breach of the peace obligation if the strikers act in order to remedy a 'threat to life or welfare or a gross offence to workers' honour' (an ancient formula the Labour Court has not unexpectedly interpreted narrowly). The systems are, in other words, the result of historical process; some, like Ireland or the Netherlands, are now difficult even to place on the spectrum at all. The Netherlands, having virtually no legislation on industrial conflict, left its High Court to make up the laws about strikes.[161] Its trade union movement has been divided on political and religious lines, once three, but now two main confederations divided on these lines.[162] Despite that pluralism the pattern of its law is not individualist. The High Court invented a right to strike (which it later justified retrospectively by reference to the Council of Europe's Social Charter, art. 6(4), when it was ratified by the Netherlands in 1980) but vested it in the trade union in the German style.[163] Despite its union pluralism, the organic legal base makes 'unofficial' strikes for the most part unlawful. That is an unusually mixed character; but there is no reason why a new British law about strikes should not incorporate elements from both 'organic' and 'individualist' models. What matters is that in constructing new limiting factors we have a sense of what is made impossible by our own history and of our purposes for the future.

But the inspection of other systems brings home further issues, particularly for any British government which sought to introduce strongly organic features. The success of the organic systems, for example, has depended to a far greater degree than individualist systems upon the central organisation of their trade union movements. Sweden, Denmark, Austria and Germany are obvious illustrations. It would be utterly impossible to run a German system of industry-bargaining and organic strike law with French-style trade unions. And vice-versa. In terms of being a competitive movement there are aspects of the British trade union movement which resemble the latter rather than the former. More, if the limits of the Social Charter of 1989 were followed, what meaning would we ascribe to 'obligations arising under collective agreements' (peace obligations taken from the organic systems as a limit on the right to strike)? Does this mean legally enforceable obligations? If so, the limitation will have little impact in Britain since the law presumes there is no intent to create legal relations at collective level unless otherwise stated in writing.[164] But Community bodies, including the Court of Justice, have a habit of regarding this principle of a 'gentleman's agreement' as a route of possible evasion by Britain from Community principles, as was demonstrated in the law of sex discrimination when Britain was forced to enact a provision for bringing collective agreements before a court even though they were at collective level unenforceable.[165] On the other hand, if peace clauses in collective agreements which were not contractually enforceable between the parties were made into legal limitations on the right to strike, the law would have a destabilising effect upon collective bargaining likely to be of greater impact even than the ill fated statute of 1971.

British Law in a European Framework?

The classical British law about strikes seems to fit nowhere in this schema, neither 'organic' nor 'individualist', even though (as we saw) the model of 1906 has traces of both elements, 'individual' in that the act given immunity in furtherance of a trade dispute can be the act of '*any person*', not merely of a trade union, but 'organic' when the union and its funds were for most of the period until 1982 protected against all tort liability – and, perhaps too, because after 1982 they became the primary target of liability. The strike laws of the 1980s were claimed to protect the 'individual'; for example, the Acts of 1980, 1982, 1984, 1988 and 1990 were said to protect individual members against their union, even setting up a Commissioner to support cases in the courts to that end alone; and the 1989 measure was claimed to liberate workers from outmoded regulation at work, 'free' once again to negotiate individually with their employer on, for example, night work.[166] But the bulk of the legislation affecting workers' rights to take combined action in and through their unions cannot be categorised under that heading. For instance, the 1980s programme introduced, alone in Western Europe, laws in which state controls intervened deep inside internal trade union affairs (from the prohibition of 'unjustifiable' union discipline allowed by lawful rule-books to regulation of elections and vetting of election scrutineers) – intervention from which even the organic systems refrain.[167]

A more careful reading of the new policy suggests that it has a further function for the state, the 'protection' of individuals primarily where that also debilitates the union in the labour market, in order more generally to sustain a market free from 'distortions' caused, as Hayek insists, primarily by the strength and 'privileges' of collective labour.[168] While general policy favours decentralisation and the individualisation of employment relations, an inevitable trend of this legislation on strikes and internal union affairs must, paradoxically, be towards state-regulation with a special kind of 'organic' legal system. So, in 1982 union liability in tort was revived, making injunctions and damages against them, not their officials, the primary remedy for employers. But in 1984 and 1988 unions were given a special position in relation to strike ballots, and by 1990 the union's official endorsement or repudiation of industrial action determines the legal power of the employer himself to dismiss individual employees and to do so selectively (though in practice, because ballots cannot be organised by the union overnight to make lawful its endorsement of unofficial action, the employer can say 'heads-dismissal-for-you; tails-an-injunction-for-your-union'). To retain the legality of their actions, unions must send to members statutory mumbo-jumbo formulae on strike ballot forms or on notices repudiating industrial action.[169] More of the same is forecast for 1991. To this extent, officially abhorring corporatism the state's labour law system acquired new organic, corporatist features.

The creation of a 'right' to strike would require new choices which it is pointless to consider in terms merely of 'retaining' or 'repealing' parts of the 1980s legislation. The balance of individual and organic elements in a new system would need its own justification and its own negotiation. Would lawful strikes require notice, and would notice protect against certain remedies (like the Irish provisions in the Act of 1990 allowing strike notice to prevent interlocutory injunctions)? Could the individual's *right* to take concerted strike action be extinguished by a 'peace' clause and, if so, under what conditions? Should there be a ballot before such limits are imposed on individual employment contracts? If strike ballots are required, what is their impact on action previously taken without union support? What answers are given to the famous questions in Donovan about the consequences of suspending the contract of employment?[170] For example, when does suspension end? What is the employer permitted to do during suspension? What elements in our actual or desired collective bargaining practices point in one direction or the other? What are the implications of our choices for union structure and management prerogative? How would the right to strike relate to obligations on an employer to 'recognise' a trade union (for example, where there are workers who object to a particular union being the bargaining agent)? If there is a procedure for obliging the employer to bargain with a union, does it import limits on the right to strike for recognition? What relationship should the new law about strikes have to dispute settlement?

Such questions cannot be answered merely by adopting a preference for positive rights to strike or looking for a European standard. But there may be fewer mistakes if experience elsewhere is consulted. The difficulties are exacerbated by the fact that reform of British labour law in the 1990s will need to grapple also with traditional problems of the system, none of which can be easily defined in terms of the structures we have been discussing. These older problems, inherent in the interplay of legislative immunities and the common law developed by the courts (which have been inflamed by legislation of the 1980s when, instead of providing immunities, it progressively stripped them away), have been addressed elsewhere in greater detail.[171] The three central problems, none of them created by the legislation of the 1980s, must however be mentioned: interpretation of the immunities, creation of new liabilities and the judges' remedies, especially interlocutory injunctions. The common law courts interpret 'trade dispute' immunities narrowly, inevitably so because the immunities appear as special defences, exceptions to the 'ordinary law of the land'. So they have been since 1906 in the law of tort, since 1875 in criminal law. Even industrial liberties expressed in positive form are treated by the common law judge as an immunity, not because he is 'biased' (it is fruitless to discuss the matter in those terms) but because he can see it in no other way. The 'right' to picket peacefully is introduced in the legislation with: 'it shall be lawful'. But judges treat that as an 'immunity'.[172] The only major occasion in recent legal history when the Law Lords adopted a liberal interpretation of the golden formula on which the immunities rest, was in a trilogy of judgments retaining a wide meaning of 'furthering' trade disputes given between October 1979 and February 1980, just when the first Bill was already passing through parliament to truncate those very immunites. Lord Diplock explained, without beating about the bush, that the modern immunities were 'intrinsically repugnant' to the common lawyer, and Lord Salmon said: '... if this be the law, surely the time has come for it to be altered'.[173] No judge has expressed a similar view of any part of the 1980s legislation which achieves its ends by reintroducing the dominance of the common law in trade disputes. The creation of a positive right to strike would answer that problem only if it were interpreted by courts which did not adopt these attitudes, above all the appellate courts.

Secondly, when it suits the logic of the common law and (as barristers tend to say) fits the 'climate of opinion', judges create new liabilities in tort. Not surprisingly, these are not to be found among the liabilities for which parliament had enacted an immunity. Moreover, in face of a new tort, the judges tend to interpret uncertain provisions in the statute restrictively, even if this means reducing it to a pointless or unnecessary section. Such was the case in 1964 in *Rookes* v. *Barnard* where a union official, admittedly protected in a trade dispute under the 1906 Act from liability for *inducing* his members to break their employment contracts by striking, was found liable by the Law Lords for the separate, scarcely known and therefore unprotected, new tort of 'intimidation' because he had joined with them in a *threat* to break their contracts.[174] His inducement of the breach was protected by parliament; but not, the Law Lords found, discovered in a burst of creative law making, his jointly threatening to do that very same act. A subsection of the 1906 Act protecting 'interference' with contracts in trade disputes was held to have been inserted in the Act by parliament to give immunity against a different tort which might exist, though that liability was found not to exist at all. It was no accident that a rash of such judgments appeared in the 1960s, by which time conventional wisdom warned of the perils of 'union power'.

The tradition of expanding categories of tort liability in a manner hostile to unions has been a regular feature of our labour law since the nineteenth century, hibernating in periods of judicial 'abstention' (sometimes for decades) but never dying out. Even Kahn-Freund was lulled by the non-interventionist period before the early 1960s into the belief that 'the 1906 Act contained an exhaustive list of the "economic" torts' (i.e. that the judges would create no more new ones) – but he admitted that this theory was 'blown sky high' by the *Rookes* case.[175] The same common law tradition bloomed once again in the Court of Appeal's 'dock strike' judgment of 1989, where the judges created yet another new tort, adding together a non-actionable inducement of a breach of statutory duty by the dockers and an 'intent to injure' to produce liability in the union.[176]

It is by extensions of liability of this kind that the common law courts have long asserted their hegemony. That was the reason why in 1906 parliament felt it necessary to grant to the union itself a blanket protection in tort, which was repealed in 1982. There was no point in granting trade dispute immunities against a list of liabilities if new ones were regularly invented; much better to deal with tort *tout court* (at a stroke). True, that had the unhappy result of protecting a union against even such torts as defamation, but officials would remain liable for that and similar torts. Unhappily, in the 1980s the debate on this difficult issue was degraded into the loaded question: 'Should the unions be above the law?' Usually, it was added that the Crown could since 1947 be sued in tort. A moment's thought exposes the impoverished quality of such questions. If 'the law' – here it is the common law – is such that it makes it impossible for a body to fulfil its socially acceptable functions, then that 'law' should be changed. People who asked questions about unions being 'above the law' did not seriously want a strong trade union movement, free from the judge-made protean liabilities of tort law. The central problem of British labour law has been to ensure that employment rights, including a right to strike, are securely placed outside this tradition. That is why, despairing of an answer to the oozing omnipresence of such liabilities, the debate began to turn to proposals for 'labour courts'. But just as a system of 'positive' rights solves nothing in itself, the label 'labour court', as has been suggested elsewhere, still leaves all to play for.[177]

The third problem is intimately related to court procedure: the power of the High Court to grant in its discretion interlocutory injunctions banning strike action on, at best, a few hours' notice, depriving the union of the chance to strike while the iron is hot, backed by the nuclear deterrent of punishment for 'contempt of court', and on proof by the plaintiff of no more than an arguable case – not a clear prima facie case, just a 'serious question to be tried'.[178] Such injunctions are theoretically interim until trial; in reality they determine the issues in many industrial disputes. The frail attempt in 1974 (s. 17(1) TULRA) to moderate even the *ex parte* injunction, granted before the union knows anything about it, failed; the competence of the judge to act in 'urgent' cases had to be retained; so we find an injunction granted in 1987, without notice to the union, over the telephone, from the judge's home on a Sunday afternoon.[179] A further provision (s. 17(2)) which attempted to modify the range of labour injunctions in contested hearings has had scarcely any effect. And in its 'dock strike' judgment of 1989 the Court of Appeal went further by requiring judges always to consider the 'public interest' which, it made clear, weighs in the balance in favour of granting an injunction against strikes of any magnitude. Such a test makes out of a dispute between private parties an issue of public law.

It is the *discretionary* character of this remedy which is crucial, and the fact that the same discretion is applied in all types of case, from copyright and patents to nuisances and trade disputes. The judges patrol this territory jealously, guarding their right to grant the remedies of 'equity' based upon concepts of property and contract, applying them as they see it justly to the circumstances of each case and never blushing when they create new procedural rules. In 1975, the hurdles were lowered so as to require the plaintiff to prove, not a prima facie case, but only a 'serious question' of liability. That was done in a case about patents, not about labour law. But lacking any autonomy, labour law is at the mercy of new rules, above all new procedural rules, created in the other corners of the seamless judge-made web that is the common law, substantive and procedural. The courts have expanded, too, the area of punishable contempt, inventing a new doctrine of 'anticipatory contempt' requiring third parties to abstain from acts which might assist a union *if* it were to disobey an order – *if* one were made. So we find the bank of one union in 1988 finding it to be necessary to apply to the court for an order preventing the movement of its client union's funds, in case it should one day move the funds in contempt of court.[180] Interlocutory procedure is notoriously unsatisfactory. One judge remarked, as he granted an injunction to ban industrial action by train crews in 1989: '... this is a decision I am driven to take at this late hour and after insufficient argument and certainly insufficient consideration'.[181] If the legal arguments are complex and uncertain after a quick hearing, the judge will grant the injunction to maintain the '*status quo*'; he will often say to the union: 'You might win at the trial,' when the likelihood is either that there will be no trial or that it will come on months or years after the injunction has helped to defeat the strike. Even a 'speedy trial' delayed for a few weeks or (which is much more rare) days cannot normally undo the damage of an immediate order stopping industrial action. Moreover, appeals can extend the interlocutory proceedings and during them an interim injunction will run to maintain the '*status quo*' in the plaintiff's favour.[182]

What is less widely recognised is the difficulty of controlling judicial discretion by legislation. The judges see themselves – in a sense within the logic of the common law, correctly – as even-handed, exercising the same discretion equally in *all* forms of social conflict. It is precisely that which they see as just within the logic of the common law and precisely that which a new labour law should not accept. That is the core of the problem: an 'equitable' discretion applied to strikes which is based upon principles of

preservation of property. A new labour law must displace that
process. But any attempt, however modest, to remove strikes from
the ambit of that discretion may once more encounter in England
the accusation that unions are being put above the 'ordinary law of
the land'; and the same accusation will be levelled at reforms which
upset the balance natural to common law ideology, whether it
forms part of the introduction of positive rights to strike or the
more difficult venture into 'labour courts'. Any reform will need a
Secretary of State of courage and character equal to that of
Michael Foot and his ministers who put TULRA and its
amendments on to the statute book in 1974 and 1976, in bloody
battles which tested their resolve and are now too little
remembered.

Interestingly enough, a parallel jurisdiction has recently shown
that an effort to cure these imbalances can be made. Between 1985
and 1990 a similar debate took place in Ireland. Government
proposals for a modified system of positive rights were overtaken,
on a change of administration, by a Bill to replace the 1906 Act but
to retain a system of immunities. Protection of unions (which are
licensed for bargaining) from tort liability continues to operate for
acts done in furtherance of a trade dispute; and for the immunities
from economic torts the definition of trade disputes remains wide;
but union rules are required to contain provision for secret ballots
to support industrial action.[183] But on injunctions a more
venturesome approach is taken. Where a strike has the support of
a union ballot and at least one week's notice has been given to the
employer, the latter is prohibited from obtaining an *ex parte*
injunction and (even more important) the court 'shall not grant an
injunction restraining the strike or other industrial action where
the respondent *establishes a fair case* that he was acting in
contemplation or furtherance of a trade dispute'.[184] Despite its
problems of interpretation, this statute requiring no more from the
defendant than a 'fair case' that he *acted* in furtherance of such a
dispute and not that he has a trade dispute *defence*, is an
experiment of which British reformers should take close account.

Comparative Creativity of the Courts

It must be added that British and Irish Judges are not alone in
expanding the civil liability of unions or strikers. Except perhaps
for the Swedish, all European courts exercising a jurisdiction over
strikes have had recent periods of 'creativity'. The Federal
German Labour Court is noted for its changes of doctrine – first
applying a doctrine of 'social adequacy', then a decade later
jettisoning it for a test of 'proportionality' to legitimise strikes;
disallowing, then allowing, then limiting 'warning strikes'; first
treating lock-outs as equivalent to strikes, then inventing a
separate mathematical formula (based on the number of workers

involved) for their legitimacy.[185] Even Italian courts, to the outrage of the commentators, have granted such injunctions. In a notorious decision of 1981, the judges even limited strikes for the workers involved to 'one occasion per year'.[186]

The pressures for wider liabilities are well illustrated in France. In 1986, the French Cour de Cassation approved decisions in interlocutory cases by first instance *juges des référés* with an interlocutory jurisdiction to grant injunctions in face of 'manifest wrongdoing' (in the form of procedure on *requête* it may even be *ex parte*)[187] even though those decisions, in the exercise of the judges' discretion, were overtly based upon an assessment of the reasonableness of a union's demands when it gave the strike notice required in the public services. This open intrusion into the merits of the industrial dispute itself was so unusual that later cases have drawn back to the more traditional rule that the judge has no competence to decide the reasonableness of the parties' claims in the industrial dispute.[188] Thus a strike otherwise legitimate will not be subject to an injunction because it is called on a date inconvenient to a section of the public.[189] Nor can the employer always obtain an immediate order when the strikers have occupied the plant – though such an order is proper as the occupation is 'manifestly illegal'[190] and the solution of procedural problems here disclose parallels with the English developments.[191] But some *juges* exercise their interlocutory discretion in a different way, for example to refuse an order for immediate evacuation, and instead to appoint an expert third party to examine the dispute, to conciliate and attempt to bring the parties to an agreement.[192] And even with an order of expulsion against workers in occupation, the employer may find that the police will not execute it immediately if there is a risk of disorder.[193]

French and Italian commentators have complained of the occasional regressive creativity of their judges; but confronted with the British experience they may count themselves lucky. The comparison, even so, is useful, for it suggests another question: since the return to stricter principle in the French courts was made possible because the courts are not strictly bound by even higher courts' decisions (at least in the strict manner of our theories of precedent) should a British labour court dealing with strikes be set free from the strict doctrine of precedent save as to matters of jurisdiction?

Even more important, the French judge in a civil case does not enjoy the equivalent powers of punishment for contempt of court. In some cases, such as occupations and sit-in strikes, penal sanctions may eventually be imposed; but normally in the ordinary civil case, a failure by a union or other defendant to obey an order of the court is sanctioned by an *astreinte*. This is a sum payable not as a fine to the state, but to the plaintiff – *if* he chooses to return to the court to demand its 'liquidation'.[194] We have seen that the Swedish Labour Court operates in most cases within the ultimate sanction of modest damages. German Labour Courts may impose fines for failure to obey an order which can, if not paid, in the last resort result in imprisonment. But none of the Continental courts with civil jurisdiction over strikes possesses anything like the British High Court's draconian power – once again a discretionary power – to punish and coerce a defendant for contempt, by fines, imprisonment, sequestration and receivership, and even to extend the area of criminalised behaviour.[195] Once again, this power exists equally in all types of civil case, but it falls with especial force upon unions. In the literature of comparative procedure, the British participants are to be found expressing disbelief that a High Court can retain its dignity, almost its virility, without powers to punish for contempt, and punish on an increasingly criminal footing, the very powers which consolidate the unfairness of the labour injunction.[196] One certainly cannot know the nature of any court, epecially a 'labour court', without knowing what are its ultimate powers of sanction.

Public Sector and Essential Services

But there is one area in which the British liberty to take industrial action had a head start and in practice remains more liberal than most. Surprisingly, perhaps, that is in the public sector.[197] In all Continental countries the public employee is historically, and remains in the current law, a separate legal species from the employee in the private sector. There could be no debate, as in Britain, about whether he had a contract 'of employment'. He was, and in great measure is, broadly speaking governed by public not private law, adjudicated in separate administrative courts; whereas the employee in the private sector is governed by private law, labour law administered in the ordinary or labour courts. To some extent, the subsequent history may be seen comparatively as a trend to 'privatise' the public employee's rights countered by pressures to confine the 'ordinary' employees' right to strike, as soon as it becomes established, within a web of 'public' duties. So, it has been said, there has been an 'osmosis' of public to private (elements of job security, though the private employee never attains the guarantees known to these public officials) as well as from private to public (rights of organisation, of bargaining and sometimes to strike).[198]

The Continental state official traditionally occupies a position imbued with duties of loyalty in return for the secure job (often for life). He could not be allowed a right to strike. That is still true of the German *Beamter*.[199] The phenomenon is not confined to European countries. In the United States the Federal employee who goes on strike commits a crime – so the issue does not neatly divide the common law from civil law countries – and most state and municipal employees have no right to strike.[200] Applying Blackstone's doctrine that the sovereign 'can do no wrong' in a fashion never adopted in modern British labour law, an American court could say of school teachers employed by a Board of Education (which as a municipal body exercised 'some part of the sovereignty entrusted to [government]'): 'To say that they can strike is the equivalent of saying that they can deny the authority of government and contravene the public welfare.'[201] President Reagan justified the doctrine in a speech during the period when he had hundreds of striking Federal air traffic controllers dismissed and prosecuted: 'None of us in government can strike against you, the sovereign people.'[202]

These doctrines, and the more modern versions mentioned below, have not been applied to the rights of the British civil servant; our law is unusual in that regard. It is true, of course, that no question of their 'right to strike' could arise in Britain, because no such general right exists, and that the precise legal status of the British civil servant in the employment of the Crown is still uncertain, especially on the question whether he or she has a 'contract' of employment. More, contract or no contract, it is clear that the Crown has the legal right, reaffirmed in the GCHQ case, to 'dismiss at pleasure', and to displace normal rights (such as trade union consultation rights) in pursuit of 'national security'.[203] But labour legislation normally applies, with suitable adjustments, even to these state employees at the core of the public sector, as in recent provisions 'deeming' that they have employment contracts for the purpose of subjecting their unions to tort liability for inducing breach of contract in a strike and thereby to injunctions.[204] And even where the laws do not apply,[205] this is often at the wish of the civil service unions through whom strong trade unionism has long afforded protection. Recent developments have sometimes had a Continental hue. For example, school teachers took a step towards the status of *Beamter* when their unions' long-standing collective bargaining rights were abolished in 1987, but government alleged this would last only for a few years.[206]

For the most part, British law about strikes in the 'public sector' – both at its core in the civil service and for other public employees in public agencies, nationalised industries or local authorities – has the same roots as for the private sector. That result was produced partly by reason of the legal tradition, especially the place of the 'Crown' and its relationship to the single system of courts and, even more, by the pattern of collective organisation of which the origins date back to 1917 when the liberal reports of the Whitley Committee changed gear from the 'Commissioners for Industrial

Unrest' just one year before, and swung public policy behind the
view that trade union organisation was desirable in the public
sector. British law has had little to say about 'essential services' or
'public services' (they are not of course the same – not every public
service is essential, nor are all essential services public), save for
the powers which government can take under the Act of 1920 to
maintain supplies for the community[207] – though it is to be noted
that wide use has been made of the Crown's prerogative powers to
use troops in aid of the civil authority (central executive
organisation stands ready to use them) and that the police were
organised as a national force in the miners' strike for the first, but
probably not the last, time.[208] But what has been unacceptable,
and is expressly banned by the 1920 Act, is civil conscription in
industrial disputes, a position not shared in other advanced
jurisdictions, as we shall see.

The starting point for the Continental public employee, certainly
in the core area of state officials, has been a status quite different
from an employment contract. In return for the benefits of their
status, they were originally subject to a public law prohibition on
bargaining and strike action alike. Even today, the German
Beamte is denied both those rights as they apply to other workers
(including public employees who are not *Beamte*). But in most
such countries, collective labour law for the public sector has crept
gradually closer to ordinary labour law and there have gradually
evolved wide, if qualified, rights to organise, to bargain and to
strike in the public sector, even in state employment. Even so, we
find the weight of the past in the most advanced system. In Italy,
for example, the *legge quadro* (framework law) modernising
industrial relations throughout the public sector still requires the
results of bargaining to find their final legal expression through
decrees which 'receive' the collective agreements and make them
binding.[209]

The unprepared British visitor experiences surprise at seeing
systems which have advanced with such bold steps towards a
collective bargaining or 'voluntary' model in which collective
organisational rights and even constitutional rights to strike have
been acquired by public employees, still retaining limitations
which are the heritage of a strict statist tradition. This is one reason
why it is dangerous, in the British context at least, to make the case
that the 'state' is a 'unique' employer as if that is necessarily
relevant to the rights of those employed by it.[210] Each state is
unique; but – as an employer – the British is less unique than
average. And many other types of employer are unique.
Multinational oil companies hardly share many features with a
one-man Salomon Ltd, except for the personality ascribed by law.
Yet we do not argue on that ground for diverse employment laws
for their employees. Why should we then suggest different

employment terms – especially as to strikes – when we are confronted by three different groups of workers doing the same work – let us say, refuse collectors, one group employed by a privatised Wandsworth plc, a second by Surrey County Council Filth Department, and a third by a Ministry of Environment (direct labour) Garbage Task Force? One employer is private, the second municipal, the third state. The workers' jobs are the same. Differentiation in workers' rights should be made according to workers' functions, not the fortuitous nature of their employers' legal status. The latter produces a ridiculous whirligig of workers' rights if their employers are nationalised and privatised.[211] Such considerations, together with a failure to appreciate the manner in which public employee unions operate at national and local level, made unconvincing the later American literature which tried to turn the 'sovereignty' argument for banning public employees' strikes into a more modern format: arguing that public employers were thereby subjected to improper pressure by one pressure group or that such strikes 'distort the political process' by an 'alien force in the legislative process'.[212]

The French system still bears many traces of that approach. But in the famous *Dehaene* judgment, 1950,[213] the administrative courts reversed their earlier doctrines to allow the right to strike to extend to civil servants. It cannot be too strongly emphasised what a radical step the decision was in that socio-legal climate. But the *fonctionnaire* did not thereby attain the level of industrial rights enjoyed by the British civil servant. The courts confirmed that special limits can still be imposed on the exercise of the right to strike: 'as on all other rights, to avoid an abusive exercise of it or one that contravenes the requirements of *l'ordre public*'. Thus, quite apart from the law of 1963 requiring notice of strikes (and banning 'rolling strikes') in the *'service publics'* – a term which here has a very wide definition [214] – the French *fonctionnaire* (civil servant) can be disciplined and suffer disciplinary deductions from salary for striking. Some of the most complex law, involving even constitutional challenges, in both Italy and France have concerned the precise calculations of such deductions, (especially for strikes of less than one day).[215] Of course it is true that the British civil servant can be made subject to administrative penalties under the code applying to him; but the French sanctions are wider. Indeed, there are further administrative sanctions to require the maintenance of a minimum service, a 'continuity of service' (France)[216] or, as in Italy, to avoid risks which threaten functions or services considered 'essential by reason of their pre-eminent general interest'.[217] Naturally, specific laws ban strikes in most countries by the armed forces and various branches of the police;[218] in France, air controllers and radio and television workers are also subject to strict control and minimum service obligations;[219] and in Italy similar limitations fall on seafarers, nuclear industry workers and air traffic controllers.[220]

More surprising perhaps is the survival of powers of conscription (*réquisition*) of strikers to maintain the service or work abandoned in a strike, stemming in France from wartime measures.[221] British labour law knows well of wartime restrictions which linger, but these have tended to be tolerated only while they are not used.[222] In France this power has been used, though rarely. It requires a ministerial order, but it can then be delegated to the local administration; it cannot be used except for 'needs of the nation', and the administrative courts will annul it if those needs are not fully proved (e.g. if the need for continuity of service is absent) or if it is defective in form. Nevertheless, it is a draconian power and a failure to answer to a lawful *réquisition* entails criminal sanctions and even loss of the job.[223] Similar powers exist in Italy and Portugal. The scope in Italy is, if anything, greater in the *precettazione* (call-up), a power to conscript strikers put into the hands of local Prefects to issue ordinances about 'buildings, local police matters or hygiene to protect public health and safety'. The power was created by a fascist decree of 1934 but held to be constitutional in 1977 on the grounds that, as the Constitution provided for a right to personal safety (article 32), a constitutional interest was created to which the right to strike (article 40) must give way.[224] The *precettazione* has been used more often in recent decades: against workers on boats to the islands, in hospitals, and in other transport 'so long as public opinion was in support' (though a recent attempt to use it against striking train crews proved once again that penal provisions rarely solve disputes).[225] As we shall see, in 1990 it was swept up into an attempt to legislate generally on essential public services.

These powers of coercion, widely accepted from left to right as limitations on the individual right to strike, have been little noticed in British comparative labour law. Yet they reflect the sort of debate we could expect to face if we adopted a system of positive rights in Britain. Even symapthetic writers wonder today whether the right to strike is the best weapon for public sector workers, 'the most effective way' of promoting their interests compared with 'other forms of dispute resolution (free from government control)' such as arbitration.[226] Pressure to solve disputes by arbitration might more easily find expression in the conditions attached to positive rights than is possible in a system of immunities. It is to be hoped that the debate on positive rights will bring this issue out into the open. On the one side a system with rights to bargain and to strike in the 1990s surely ought to take account of the problems normally addressed under this heading. On the other, it will be said, and correctly said, that in the wrong hands these 'conditions' could seriously damage the very right to strike itself.

It may well be that the Conservative manifesto commitment of 1983 to legislate on strikes in 'essential services' has not been implemented precisely because the Thatcher administration saw the questions begged thereby: is the corollary of such a law compulsory arbitration for the workers concerned (as we saw, the ILO would regard it as essential)? Must the government commit itself in advance to accept independent arbitration or, at least, mediation as the price of any such intervention? To a Thatcher government tied to Hayek it probably seemed preferable to go on squeezing the immunities within the traditional legal structure and fight it out whenever necessary against the enemy within. But if an alternative government wishes (as it should) to reform the legal structure by including a right to strike, it must have a full, not doctored, agenda. Indeed, later developments in Italy sharpen some of the questions. *Precettazione* has not been abandoned. It has been modernised as part of the new Law on the Right to Strike in Essential Public Services (no. 146, 12 June 1990). Just as the Workers' Statute represented the boldest attempt in Europe in 1970 at labour legislation promotional of both union rights and workers' individual rights (many of them gradually moved now into the public sector too), so Law 146 of 1990 must be seen as a bold attempt to retain the right to strike but socialise it expressly by clearer public boundaries. Indeed, it is crucial to understand its ingenuity comparatively, within its own tradition. Merely translated into English it looks foolhardy.

That is not to say that other jurisdictions have not taken steps of a similar kind, all of which depend upon a sufficient social consensus. For instance, a mixture of legislation and voluntary agreements was adopted for the same purpose in Sweden when state and municipal employees finally won rights to bargain and to strike in 1965 (later extended in 1976 to take account of the legislation in the private sector). Two central agreements were concluded in 1971, under which unions and public employers have set up boards at central and municipal level, jointly composed, to determine when industrial action is unacceptable. For example, codes were agreed on rules about stoppages and threats to food supply and medical care. Parallel parity boards were also established for the private sector.[227] In 1971, faced with the threat of a breakdown of these institutions, the Swedish government passed legislation to continue existing collective agreements in some public sectors by law until a settlement could be reached. More recently, confronted in 1990 with a failure to agree in national pay negotiations, it proposed a pay freeze and curbs on the right to strike itself – a remarkable innovation, even proposing a breach of the individual '200 kroner' rule – but parliament rejected the measure.[228]

Other countries have relied on legislation, sometimes even

constitutional provision. In Spain, for example, the constitution itself recognises that the right to strike can be limited by measures 'guaranteeing the maintenance of essential services for the community'.[229] In conjunction with a law of 1977, it gives the government powers to ensure their maintenance; but the range of 'essential services' is determined specifically by what can be seen to be interests 'of which protection is guaranteed by the constitution itself'.[230] The courts have insisted that there must always be some 'proportionality' between the sacrifices imposed on strikers and on the consumers, and have often accepted that the proper level of minimum service is that which is supplied by the union, either in negotiation with employers or even unilaterally.[231] The technique of limiting the area by reference to 'constitutionally guaranteed interests' is a key to the Italian experiment.

There is, of course, an obvious link between laws on essential services and bargaining and disputes settlement in those sectors where it may be most difficult for workers taking action to retain the support of 'the public'. Little original thinking has emerged in Britain in that area in the 1980s; and it is not clear what we may expect from the 'communication' of the Commission of the European Communities on the development of collective bargaining and agreements 'with special reference to the settlement of disputes'.[232] By the 1980s, the main Italian trade union confederations had begun to adopt voluntary 'codes of practice' to maintain certain services in industrial conflict, especially in transport.[233] Such voluntary 'codes' are not of course unknown in Britain (in local authorities and the health service, for example) but in Italy they began not only to be of wider application but to have legal support. The *legge quadro* of 1983 restructured and supported collective bargaining in the public sector and at the same time built in procedural requirements demanding that to bargain in the public sector, a union must have adopted a code of 'self-regulation' (*codice di autoregolamentazione*) with provision for at least two weeks notice of strike action and for the maintenance of 'indispensable services necessary to protect the constitutionally defined rights of others'. The courts did recognise that these self-regulatory codes, although unilateral union statements, had some legal force; for example, where a code had been broken, they permitted an employer (Alitalia) lawfully to take action against strikers which might have been 'anti-union conduct'.[234] On top of this, the law of 1983 encourages the conclusion of 'cooling off agreements' given force by decree in the public sector.

This was the setting for the enactment, after a two year debate, of Law 146 of 1990. It applies to all those within its scope, whether juridically in 'private' or 'public' employment (the 1983 law being amended accordingly).

That scope is defined by reference to 'essential' services that fall within certain 'personal rights protected by the constitution', e.g. rights to life, health, liberty and safety, freedom of movement, social welfare, education and freedom of communication (art. 1). These headings are expanded by a list of examples.[235] The right to strike is to be 'balanced' against the need for *prestazioni indispensabili*' (bare minimum services) in these areas. Consequently, at least ten days' notice of a strike is required, giving the date and an indication of its duration, and employers and workers are required to see that a minimum service is assured (art. 2); the employing body must notify the public about details of the minimum service five days before the strike. The law envisages that self-regulation codes will continue to be effective and that collective agreements will be made with union representatives above these minimum requirements. In this way, the legal intervention is presented as a legal framework for voluntary action.

But the sanctions are not weak. Workers who wrongfully strike contravening these provisions may suffer disciplinary sanctions, including monetary penalties; and unions or unofficial groups which call or support strikes in violation of the procedures will lose certain rights to carry on union activity and be excluded from bargaining for two months from the cessation of their conduct (article 4). In addition, where there is a 'danger of grave and imminent damage to the constitutionally protected personal rights', the minister or his delegate, after attempts at conciliation, may by ordinance require the minimum services to be performed, with financial penalties up to £200 per day (arts. 8, 9, the new *precettazione*).

Further, a 'Commission of Guarantee' (*Commissione di Garanzia*) of nine experts in industrial relations or labour law is being established, with a variety of functions. In the conflict itself, the CG is to assess the use of the strike weapon as against the protected interests, to attempt conciliation, to express its views on the merits and to make its own proposals for settlement of the dispute; it may refer to the President of the Assembly its views on the observance of self-regulation or of the collective agreements about minimum services and of interests of consumers (art. 13). The views of the *Commissione* are obviously to be important in decisions about imposing monetary penalties (article 4) or the *precettazione* (article 8). Further, where the conflict reveals a dispute between unions (or unofficial groups) about compliance with the law, the *Commissione* may within fifteen days consult the workers concerned out of working hours by secret ballot; but it is also to propose its own solutions to the inter-union dispute (article 14). The commentary of Italian writers suggests that this new law is not seen as an infringement of the individual right to strike; this is perhaps one of the more interesting aspects for the English observer, who notices that those who approve the new Law invariably consign their trust in the judiciary to see to it that it is not used as an engine of oppression. But there may be some doubt whether by preferring the agreements of some unions in respect of procedures about strikes (on strike notices etc.) it circumscribes the constitutional rights of other unions (under article 39 of the constitution).[236]

It should not be thought that steps to make the right to bargain conditional on acceptance of new conditions are unknown elsewhere. In Britain the most severe prohibition in the public sector was in the Pay and Conditions of Teachers Act of 1987 which abolished entirely the machinery of collective bargaining for school teachers, though in face of ILO condemnation the government said it would be only for a few years. A more direct parallel arose in Ireland. There the 1990 statute requiring unions generally to hold strike ballots in support of industrial action sanctioned the absence of a ballot not only by the loss of trade dispute immunities but also by loss of the union's status as authorised and 'licensed' to bargain.[237]

The Italian developments have occurred within a social policy of consensus and tripartism. Paradoxically, this most conflictual of European industrial cultures has taken the lead in introducing 'flexibility' into its labour market by policies of consensus and 'pre-negotiated legislation',[238] and has now attempted to readjust the practical effect of basic rights of workers and their unions concerning essential services in respect of the constitutional right to strike, until now regarded as the widest in Europe. The commentary on this latest move is full of reference to Kahn-Freund's last work in his depressed final years, where he regarded society as so far having changed its character that (despite the continuing need of the freedom to strike) the strike itself had taken on the guise of 'an internecine civil war ... between the worker as a producer and the worker as a consumer', requiring affirmation of 'the need for the freedom to strike and at the same time the need for a considerable restraint in its exercise'.[239] If that were the dominant note of a reform of the British law, no doubt the result would be a very restricted right to strike indeed. Parallel problems have been encountered in Ireland where, when workers and unions have attempted to rely upon the Constitution (article 40.3)[240] for a right to take industrial action, the courts have on occasion said 'innocent persons could not be damnified' by exercise of it, including third parties whose contracts were affected.[241] To balance the right to strike against third parties' rights in that way would reduce it to 'a pointless phenomenon of industrial relations'.[242]

Initiatives such as the Italian cannot, of course, be imported, especially when one sets off from a constitution which affirms not only the right to strike and a right to freedom of association in trade unions, but also a right to 'remuneration which must be in proportion to the quality and quantity of the work and sufficient to provide the worker and his family with a free and dignified existence' (art. 36: a provision no doubt imperfectly attained in practice, but of central importance to workers' rights). They do, however, stimulate useful questions. How far would the introduction of a positive right to strike in Britain deal *ab inito* with limits to which it was to be subjected in a balance with other fundamental personal rights and interests? Or would it remain subject to the very different, common law limitation which English judges have recently deployed, the requirements of the common law 'public interest'?[243] Perhaps it will be argued that, in order to escape from the suffocating effects of concepts of that kind, there should be from the outset a balancing of interests in the way in which the right to strike is formulated? Provision, in other words, for 'essential services' and the like (even if only in special forms of conciliation) in the same legislation. To that end it might be of value for British trade unions themselves, in their own experiments with codes of *autoregolamentazione*, to put forward their own proposals for a balanced right to strike after 1992.

Rights to Strike, Disputes Settlement and European Standards

Not only is there no one European pattern for the law about strikes; there is greater variety than on any other major labour law principle. Nor is it surprising that the differing developments offer us no simple plan of guidance for reform. On the other hand the very variety of the models in just these few countries of Europe offers illustrative and diverse ways of implementing international standards. If reform aims to create a right to strike, there are clearly many different formal options consistent with the ILO Conventions and a new system must attempt to maintain and improve on those standards within the logic of its own history. Moreover, the system with closest affinities to our own, in Ireland, has after a five-year debate rejected proposals for a 'right to strike' and retained instead a system based on the immunities, while at the same time attempting to place severe new limits on the labour injunction. That is an experiment of which the results must be closely monitored. We know too that British labour law need not be shy about offering a precedent on the basic labour law which governs public employment; but on the other hand, we should watch carefully the experiments in various jurisdictions to find answers to disputes in 'essential services', a problem area likely to become more acute.

Whether specialist labour courts are adopted or not, the

interpretation and application of a new labour law code deserves tribunals suited to the ambitions of policy.[244] If there is greater confidence in the court that has jurisdiction, there is every reason for the rights of a reformed system to be constructed with more than an eye on the settlement of disputes. In this area, Britain has a boon in its experience with voluntary third-party involvement, especially ACAS; although it is one that can be improved, few systems offer a superior agency. But it is notable how the pace of advance of machinery for dispute settlement has advanced now in European reforms. Part of the Italian law of 1990 is an attempt to build an adequate machinery for conciliation and prevention of disputes in essential public services, not least through the *Commissione di garanzia*; and in the same year, Ireland has established a 'Labour Relations Commission' with overall responsibility for a conciliation and advisory service, issuing codes of practice, appointing 'equality officers' and nominating 'rights commissioners' (who decide unfair dismissal claims), able to 'offer its services' at its own initiative in a dispute ahead of the 'Labour Court' which previously had primary conciliation and arbitral functions.[245] We may note too that the Community's European Commission expressed a special interest in machinery for dispute settlement in its Action Programme under the Community Social Charter and this, together with the pursuit of the 'social dialogue', may well lead the Commission to propose one day Community level machinery to assist in the solution of transnational or multinational disputes (for example the labour relations and 'social dumping' dimensions of foreign capital making investments in various States). The structure of ACAS has remained essentially the same since 1975; it may be time to ask whether its potential, and that of the CAC, can be further developed.

Most other national systems, though, set out from the base of a written constitution, and we must have it in mind that we cannot make up for that loss in British labour law by adopting a 'Bill of Rights' which is full of individual, but lacking collective rights (as is normally the case) or of collective rights that are pulped down by common law interpretation.[246] Even if common law principles were excluded from British labour law (a technical task of some difficulty) and even if the common law courts did not try to regain jurisdiction, whether by way of new wrongs, torts or 'economic duress', or new procedures of review (and we have seen that judges in Western Europe all have a tendency to innovate where labour law meets the *droit commun* but that English judges far outstrip the rest in invention to regulate unions) and even if that bane of the common law, the labour injunction, were banished (a problem of some complexity, little less than an attempt to teach common law judges the perspectives of a liberal French *juge des référés*), still history suggests – indeed, insists – that the High Court would continue to adopt the attitudes of the common law towards property, contract and combination. A century of experience makes it reasonable to believe it would continue to intervene in industrial conflict with that recognisable 'half-conscious belief that the common law provides, so to say, a law behind the law which is enacted by parliament'.[247] Trade unions, therefore, would be wise to consider the advantages of 'labour courts' but unwise to accept them on the spot before ascertaining they are not (as they need not be) the High Court without Jacobean costume. That is an issue which goes to the roots of a whole tradition and structure, not to the personal 'bias' of this judge or that.

Comparison also demonstrates that no new British law on strikes could refer to one simple overall model. The models help us know what we are doing rather than what to do. Further, they are useful as descriptions, rarely as prescriptions. Remember Kahn-Freund's doctrine of 'abstention' of the law. In the 1950s that was an original and convincing portrait of the classical British system in peace time during the first half of the century. But it gradually became less helpful as the social consensus which (almost) accepted trade unions was smashed by a change in middle-class opinion and by judicial interventions in the 1960s, then by legislative pressure in 1971 and finally by the ferocious onslaught of the 1980s. As a prescriptive model, moreover, it was never more than a questionable guide to what a system ought to be, in what he called a 'mature' system of industrial relations;[248] and British labour law can never return to (if, indeed, it ever really adopted) the 'non-intervention' which excludes statutory regulation to the degree of the abstentionist prescription.

On the other hand, comparison with other systems helps to moderate the now fashionable view that 'non-intervention' in Britain is dead. If the eye focuses on an insular perspective a belief in its death may be understandable but in a comparative context such reports appear, like those about Mark Twain, to be an exaggeration. Regulation has not ousted the primacy of the common law – that is part of the problem. In the 1980s parliament joined forces with the extreme doctrine of 'freedom of contract' which distinguishes our labour law from those systems which set out from a 'positively-regulated and comprehensive paradigm of employment', both in legislature and courts.[249] British (especially English) legal vision has no such pattern nor any in-built knowledge of the reality of that subordination which is at the heart of employment. The 1980s legislation went with that common law grain. An attempt by legislation in the 1990s to create positive rights to organise, to bargain and to strike will cut across it, and will be fiercely resisted – not least by offers of careful compromise.

But in looking for useful models, it would be wrong to think Britain should look only to the 'organic' systems, just because one can find affinities in (say) Germany or Sweden based upon collective 'contracting'. Not only are British collective agreements not normally intended to be 'contracts', British bargaining is much more decentralised, in certain respects more similar to the Italian. Moreover, both the organic and individualist models include expressions of a variety of relationships between collective conflict and collective bargaining. At enterprise level there is more collective bargaining in (individualist) Italy than in (organic) Germany, where at this level we enter the special realm of Works Council agreements. Nor should we forget the extent to which the social orders in Germany and Sweden provide legal rights for workers, including participation in the enterprise. To put it concretely, any proposal to adopt the limitations of German strike law – with its 'peace' obligations, proportionality and *ultima ratio* tests – which does not contain too some proposals for German style worker-participation, must explain why the latter are omitted.

Again, collective agreements are legally binding in France and Italy, as in Sweden and Germany; but the effect upon strike law is limited in the former but central to the latter. No doubt: 'Strikes are inevitable in a system of collective bargaining';[250] but the link chosen between collective bargaining and strikes is one which affects the whole system of industrial relations law and practice. In devising a positive right to strike one must take account of workers' rights in the system as a whole. Even within the 'organic' camp itself, sympathy strikes are lawful under very different conditions in Germany, Denmark, Sweden and the Netherlands (the last with pluralist unions). Nor does the fact that bargaining is subjected to government policies – whether open or disguised 'incomes policies' – justify limitations imposed for that purpose. Curiously, British incomes policy legislation has always, on a bi-partisan basis, avoided any serious impact upon the formal legal structures of freedom to strike.[251] Lastly, an 'organic' system depends upon its unions. It may be questionable whether it would, in any event, be possible to propose an 'organic' system for Britain, vesting the right to strike in unions alone, without changes in union structure with a different system of registration.

There is, therefore, a strong case for an incoming 'right to strike' to set off primarily from an *individualist* logic, especially if a central objective is to protect workers against dismissal for going on strike. Indeed, in British industrial culture that is a thread of continuity. The balance of the 'immunity' legislation in its trade dispute defences was individualist as far as the freedom to organise strikes went. On the other hand it is true that the definition of 'strike' in a system of positive rights would inevitably be the main limiting factor. That was one reason which led to the workers' representatives agreeing that there should be no express right to strike in the ILO Convention on Freedom of Association in

1948.[252] It is the consequence which the Italian courts were persuaded to minimise in 1980 when they adopted, as we saw, the principle that the constitutional meaning of 'strike' should be defined by reference to nothing more than the changing meaning of 'everyday language'. We have seen that this inevitably raises not only the definition of 'strike' but also the legality of action short of a full stoppage. Since judicial invention was undertandably unable to introduce a positive right to strike in England[253] – if the effort has been more successful in Ireland it rests on the constitution – positive rights require legislation.

It does not follow that there is no longer need of any legislative protections in the form of 'immunities'. Economic torts must either be abolished or excluded from the terrain of 'industrial conflict', both substantively and procedurally; and we must stop new common law inventions being strewn like mantraps across the path of industrial negotiation. Canadian judges, for example, had the sense to exclude 'economic duress' from industrial relations;[254] the English courts knew so little about industrial bargaining that they did not recognise the affinities between it and their conception of 'duress'. Such developments suggest that any positive right to strike will need immunities to protect its flanks.

One point is clear: there can be no 'right' to strike in a reformed system, organic or individualist, unless the effect of its exercise is to suspend, not to break, the contract of employment. This is the legal formulation which workers would recognise more clearly in the legitimate demand: 'No more Wappings'. That is why the definition of 'strike' becomes so important. Outside the area of the full strike the worker will be back to breach of the employment contract, unless the law makes special provision. But there is no reason why a set of 'immunities' should not supplement the right to strike, for there will be cases where action short of a strike should be protected. For example, in a dispute about the introduction of new technology workers should have – one hopes will have – the right to consultation through their union representatives (at Community level a proposed Directive is already in draft for a European Works Council in undertakings of 'European scale' for that purpose). If an employer fails to consult but insists on installing the machinery and the workers take industrial action short of a strike (say, a ban on overtime or a work to rule) their breach of contract and the organisers of their action should be protected from civil liability in the dispute. Similarly, where workers are taking lawful sympathetic action in support of others, their employer might prefer them to have the right to express that solidarity in the form of action less than a full stoppage: a one-day work to rule might be preferable to a one-day stoppage, and if so the question arises why it should not be lawful.

It may be said that a better way to achieve this objective would be to define the 'strike' as including all full *and partial* stoppages of work in a dispute. This is an arguable approach, though it is interesting that most of the systems with a positive right appear not to adopt it. This issue requires further debate, but it is clear that such a definition at this stage of development in Britain might be regarded as unnecessarily wide. It would be more important to ensure that in such cases of action short of a strike the discretion of a court would not be too easily available to the employer for an interlocutory injunction.

Of course a labour court might well makes its refusal of relief conditional on industrially helpful steps, possibly a ballot being held of the workers taking sympathetic action as soon as it was possible to do so fairly in stable conditions. So too, where essential services are involved in a dispute, it would be for consideration whether a labour court should have the right to insist, as a condition of its judgment, that steps towards conciliation be taken or even that a minimum service be maintained (defined not by it but by ACAS) as a method of attenuating a full stoppage. In most cases where an employer sought an injunction, one could imagine such a labour court inquiring first into the steps he had taken to prevent or settle the dispute. Certainly, if he had refused to recognise a union the court would seek to know why. In such procedures, a labour court might use discretion in a new manner which touched the central policies of the system.

Once a set of legal rights is established for workers, administered by tribunals that have broken from common law blinkers, it might well be possible to negotiate a progressive and more stable machinery for the legal end of industrial relations. That is why in defining the right everything depends on the precise terms. We might even expect employers to consider acceptance of a 'right' to strike provided that it was defined narrowly – and, no doubt, that a right to lock-out is also provided. They might be expected to argue that a right to strike is acceptable only if it consists in a concerted cessation of work for defined economic objectives (but not action short of that) preceded by a period of notice (stating the starting date and likely duration) after the support of a union ballot of workers taking part. To such strikes substantive protection and procedural assistance against the excesses of the labour injunction might be offered. Such guidelines could in practice produce a law more restrictive of industrial liberties than that of the classical period 1906 to 1970; and it could be narrowed still further by the High Court (or even by 'labour courts' or 'industrial courts' if inadequate skill is exercised in their constitution and establishment so that they are no more than the old courts in disguise).[255] But that outline of conditions is no more than a *pot pourri* of elements – out of context – imported from Ireland, Italy and France.[256] False comparativism of that kind is likely to appear increasingly in the debate, as we saw it did in the Green Papers of 1989. The nature and purpose of each element must be questioned. Has it been established, for example, even now just what are the purposes of 'strike ballots' and whether it is practicable to demand a ballot before every strike in any acceptable labour law system?

In the wide variety found in Europe, most systems took an original model from their own early labour movement and remain tied in certain respects to that original pattern; but they acquired a mixed character, sometimes from intentional adaptation, sometimes by the impact of a constitution or the legal culture. There is room for innovation, not least to implement values derived from international standards; but experience suggests the desirability of securing industrial rights by a degree of social consensus (in Italy for example through 'pre-negotiated legislation'). Curiously, because the origins of British labour law have been conflict rather than negotiation, we are short of experience compared with other systems – compared with France, Italy or Germany, little of our labour law legislation this century has been 'pre-negotiated'. We score high marks comparatively in the use of machinery for settlement of disputes (at any rate, we did before 1980); the customary comparison is justified between the conciliation tradition in Britain which began in 1896 and the chapters of French law on conciliation, mediation and arbitration, elegantly expressed but mouldering on the page. But negotiation by consensus of employment legislation is another matter. Perhaps the only major modern example in Britain is the law on unfair dismissal (and that was less a consensual project than a package sold and piloted by the civil service).[257] Here we see all the advantages and disadvantages of a divorce between 'state' and 'society'. The 'Social Contract' is a poor thing set against the comparable models in Scandinavia, Austria, the Netherlands, Germany, or even Italy and France; and the tradition of voluntarism in collective bargaining, for all its merits, can prevent sensible co-ordination of contractual and legislative norms, with the latter referring issues to the former, a technique now found widely throughout the Continent.[258]

Recent Italian experience also demonstrates that there are periods when deliberately strong measures can be introduced against employers (one thinks, for example, of article 28 on 'anti-union conduct' in the Workers' Statute 1970) but it must be doubtful whether the 1990s will be such an era in Britain (whether, for example, sequestration is likely to be a successful sanction on employers as a solution to the difficult problem of 'non-recognition').[259] Cracking this nut of non-recognition will be the most severe test of ingenuity in Britain. Labour law must be adjusted so that recognition of a union by an employer becomes the norm. Yet we are bound to be driven by conflicting pressures: the desire to establish recognition as a general practice clashes with the difficulty (experienced from 1975 to 1980) of making a *general* duty to recognise stick in a system such as ours. If we can devise an appropriate 'duty to recognise' (with an appropriate sanction) well and good.

But it may help us keep our balance if we remember that it is in the labour laws of only a minority of Community states that we find a general obligation to bargain. Indeed, it is one of the worst comparative errors current in Britain to believe that 'in Europe' there is always a legal obligation to bargain. Far from it. Neither Germany nor Italy has such a general duty to 'recognise' a union in their labour laws (France is only beginning to explore the problems of their law of 1982) but law and practice combine in other ways to make bargaining the norm in both of those countries.[260] Such experience plainly suggests that in every measure taken, even in legislation outside the area of labour law, the effect upon recognition of trade unions must be kept in mind.

There is, too, a need to convince a sufficient segment of enlightened management of the need for a higher plane of workers' rights in Britain as the basis of a new settlement in labour law. This will not be easy; for a decade they have been put in the legal saddle. Perhaps the laws governing employers who are their competitors in Europe – who compete with them only too successfully – most of which enshrine rights to strike, should be put on the agenda in search of a stable system in Britain. Paradoxically, too, a closer union in the European Community is unlikely to help with collective labour law issues in the medium term. Nor will it shift the agenda for reform on to a European plane in the foreseeable future. The reason is that the Commission's *Action Programme* on the 'Social Charter' treated collective labour law as subject to the principle of 'subsidiarity', including the right to strike, though it expressed a special interest in dispute settlement machinery. But generally there will be relatively little harmonisation in this area. Indeed, the technical task of harmonising the twelve rights to strike would be alarmingly difficult. But it is strange that the *Action Programme* has left to our national systems the most difficult problem of all: the relationship between the law and collective bargaining itself. It is just at that point that help from Community level might be most helpful in setting standards.

This means that the central contradiction of the internal market will remain with us for a long time: capital, largely international-ised and increasingly mobile (the employers), on the one side, but, on the other, each of the trade union movements stubbornly held by national anchors and with them, their collective labour laws.[261] In the longer term this must inevitably be a contradiction at the heart of the Community. When some employers must, and others need not, bargain with unions, or when some public officials enjoy a right to bargain and to strike while for others such rights are modest or missing, or when some workers can exercise a wide right to strike while others enjoy a liberty to strike below the level of minimum standards, the market arguably provides neither a 'level playing field' for competition nor a secure base for the Commission's 'social dimension'. For the moment, however, the Commission and the member states appear content with that.[262] It is true that the Commission intends to promote the 'social dialogue' – it is obliged to do so under the Treaty (art. 118b) – and that this appears likely to include a non-binding 'communication' giving a higher place to collective bargaining than has hitherto been seen in policies addressed to the 'social parties'. Such initiatives will necessarily touch upon industrial conflict and settlement of disputes. Indeed, the offer of transnational machinery to assist in the solution of disputes – a European ACAS, perhaps – may one day prove to be the first effective intervention at Community level on the subject.

Whatever else, a right to bargain and a right to strike, within ILO standards, must one day become as much a Community value as the right to equal pay. It is essential that any such Community standards escape the unnecessary minor restrictions in the Social Charter which have been rather overlooked in Britain. The most important of these is the restriction of the right to strike to 'conflicts of interests' and within 'the obligations arising under ... collective agreements'. We have seen that the exclusion of 'conflicts of rights' from the ambit of a legitimate right to strike is in practice emphatically not a common European standard. The historian may therefore find it surprising that British unions did not, however faintly, enter some reservations on that point (more important in the long run than the 'right not to join a union') when embracing the Charter. In fact, the labour movement in Britain adopted the Charter on rather short-term considerations, understandably delighted and dazzled in a dark hour by the prospect of political help 'from Europe' to defeat Thatcherism. (Who could guess she herself would resign later in 1990?) Historically, though, it has commonly been the trade union wing of the labour movement which has played the role of guardian of long-term perspectives: one may think, in their very different ways, of the Mond-Turner talks or the revolt over *In Place of Strife* or the refusal to register in 1972. In 1989, however, there was thought to be no room for characteristically careful caveats. Before the scope of the principle of 'subsidiarity' could be fully gauged or such points as 'conflicts of interests' adequately assessed, it was decided that the Social Charter must be accepted without any qualification.

Of course, recognition at Community level of a floor of conditions applicable to a 'right to strike' is not likely to become relevant until other steps towards political and economic union are taken (if they ever are taken) under a revised Treaty. For a long time after 1992 'subsidiarity' will continue to apply and the Community will leave this field to domestic initiatives alone. So it is British law which must create for its own jurisdiction positive rights to organise and to strike and (if we can solve the problems attaching to it) a general obligation to bargain or (whether we can or not) a series of legislative pressure points – as in Germany and Italy – prodding reluctant employers into both bargaining with unions and acceptance of union representatives for workers as of right in grievance procedures. A policy of reform in Britain must initiate rights on strikes at ILO standards immediately the opportunity appears; and management must be involved in a debate about the various standards found in Europe and asked why ours have been so low in the area of collective rights. For that task we can prepare ourselves by improving the level of debate now, using more precise comparison with particular systems and models, avoiding generalisations about 'Europe' which are unhelpful and ready to reject false analogies and inappropriate parallels.

An exposure to different ways of thinking about employment rights, especially about rights to strike, will not automatically provide our answers. But it will help to identify problems, especially transnational problems, and illuminate purposes that are common, but very differently expressed, in the various labour movements and in the legal dimensions of industrial relations systems in Europe.[263] Behind the kaleidoscope of the institutions we do see – from time to time – common standards or ambitions. Such an inquiry in Britain may help to ensure that our reforms are less insular, better informed and more capable of providing a right to strike needed in a system inspired by international standards and in contact – as our system now is not – with the diverse languages of liberty which are part of a shared European heritage.

Notes

1. Committee of Experts, *Report of the Application of Conventions* (Report III, Part 4A, 1989 ILO), pp. 235-41, on the UK legislation of 1980-88 falling below arts. 3 (workers' right to organise their activities; public authorities to abstain from interference), 8 (law of the land not to impair freedom of association) and 10 (defining workers' organisations); see K. Ewing, *Britain and the ILO* (1989). The Employment Act 1990 compounds the offence by extending the employer's right to dismiss unofficial strikers and making unlawful strikes by other workers in their defence: s. 9.
2. For general surveys, which do not however always agree, see European Commission, *Etude Comparative des Dispositions Regissant les Conditions de Travail dans les Etats Membres de la Communauté* (SEC (89) 11 37, 30 June 1989)

and *Resumé* (SEC (89) 926 final 20 June 1989); R. Blanpain (ed.), *International Encyclopaedia of Labour Law* (1979-83); *Striking Rights in Europe* (Bargaining Report, December 1989, Labour Research Department, 5); *The Regulation of Industrial Conflict in Europe; Strikes and Lock-outs in 15 Countries* (EIRR Report 1989).

3. There are some who regard any industrial action at all as no more than a gross breach of workers' contractual obligations: see C. Hanson and G. Mather, *Striking Out Strikes* (1988); A. Shenfield, *What Right to Strike?* (1986). This is a logical extension of the philosophy of Hayek predominant in the UK since 1980: see Wedderburn, 'Freedom of Association and Philosophies of Labour Law' (1989) 18 ILJ, 1 [above Chapter 8]. On the public sector, see below n. 197.

4. O. Kahn-Freund, *The Social Ideal of the Reich Labour Court* (1931) translated in R. Lewis and J. Clark (eds.), *Labour Law and Politics in the Weimar Republic* (1981) p. 154.

5. Committee of Experts, *Report on the Application of Conventions* (1989 ILO) above n. 1, p. 237; and many CFA decisions since 2nd Report, 1952, Case No. 28 (UK/Jamaica), see *Freedom of Association; Digest of Decisions of the CFA* (3rd ed. 1985, ILO) paras 361-485 ('ILO *Digest 1985*'); and R. Ben-Israel, *International Labour Standards; The Case of Freedom to Strike* (1988) especially pp. 37-128; N. Valticos, *Droit International du Travail* (2nd ed. 1983, Dalloz).

6. Art. 13; see *Social Europe* 1/90 (EC 1990); Wedderburn, *The Social Charter, European Company and Employment Rights* (1990). See too, 'European Community Law and Workers' Rights – Fact or Fake in 1992?' (forthcoming in 1991 Univ. Dublin L.R.).

7. Council of Europe *Social Charter* art. 6(4); European Community *Social Charter* art. 13. The latter makes it subject to 'national regulations'; and art. 31 and the Schedule of the former allow national restrictions prescribed by law necessary in a democratic society for protection of the rights and freedoms of others or for the protection of public interest, national security, public health or morals.

8. Below p. 304. But New Zealand has now adopted this test of legality for strikes and lock-outs in ss. 230, 233, 234, Labour Relations Act 1987. Compare the Irish Industrial Relations Act 1990, s. 9(2).

9. See *ILO Digest 1985*, above n. 4, paras 381-5, 419-20.

10. Ben-Israel, op. cit., pp. 94-6; *ILO Digest 1985*, op. cit., para. 368, especially 214th Report, 1982, Case 1081 (Peru).

11. Under the ILO Convention the right to strike of public servants can be denied but only if it is 'confined to public servants acting in their capacity as agents of the public authority or to services which would endanger the life, personal safety or health of the whole or part of the population': Committee of Experts *Report etc.* (1989 ILO) above n. 1, p. 167, condemning the German law denying the right to all *Beamter* and their use as strike breakers. The Council's Charter, art. 6(4), does not permit the right to strike to be denied to civil servants: O. Kahn-Freund in *Laws Against Strikes* (1972, eds. O. Kahn-Freund and B. Hepple), p. 15.

12. See above n. 5, *ILO Digest 1985*, paras. 365, 393-415; R. Ben-Israel, op. cit., above n. 4, pp. 106-16. See the continuing contravention by Greece, Committee of Experts *Report*, above n. 1, p. 172; and on many of the ILO requirements the series of CFA cases involving Greece: 160th Rep. 1977, Case No. 834; 199th Rep. 1980, Case No. 910; 204th Rep. 1980, Case No. 961; 214th Rep. 1982, Case No. 1021; 217th. Rep. 1982, Case No. 1091; 233rd Rep. 1984, Case No. 1224. The ILO rejected the UK submission that a later Convention, No. 151 1978, cut down the rights of civil servants to freedom of association under Convention No. 87, in the *GCHQ Case*: Case No. 1261, 1985; and see Committee of Experts *Report on Application of Conventions* (1985, ILO, Report III Part 4) p. 193. And on the *GCHQ* case before the Council of Europe and generally, S. Fredman and G. Morris (1988) 17 ILJ 105; but *GCHQ* was of course concerned with the right to trade union membership, not to strike. On the 'trade union activities' protected in British law, see *Fitzpatrick* v. *British Railways Board* [1990] ICR 674, CA.

13. Committee of Independent Experts on the European Social Charter *Conclusions I* (Strasbourg 1969-70), p. 39; N. Valticos, *International Labour Law* (1979), p. 95; *ILO Digest 1985*, above n. 4, paras 443-4; Committee of Experts *Report* (1989 ILO) above n. 1, pp. 138-41 (UK). [See note A, p. 353 below.]

14. A form of action found in the 1980s in the North of England where workers who had for many years regularly considered improvements in working methods and made valuable suggestions to management, refused to continue to do so until certain demands were met.

15. Donaldson P. *Seaboard Airlines Inc.* v *TGWU* [1973] ICR 458, 460 (NIRC).

16. O. Kahn-Freund, 'Reflections on the European Social Charter', *Miscellanea W.J. Ganshof Van der Meersch* (1972), p. 151.

17. *ILO Digest 1985*, above n. 5, para. 367; R. Ben-Israel, op. cit., n. 5, pp. 116-8.

18. See above n. 1, and generally Wedderburn, *The Worker and the Law* (1986 3rd ed.) Ch. 1.

19. P. Calamandrei, 'Significato costituzionale del diritto di sciopero' (1952) 1 Riv. Giur. Lav. 221.

20. See Conspiracy and Protection of Property Act 1875, s. 3; Trade Disputes Act 1906, ss. 3, 4; Trade Union and Labour Relations Acts 1974-76, ss. 13, 14, 15 (TULRA); Wedderburn *The Worker and the Law* (1986 3rd ed.) Chs. 1, 7 and 8. The very legality of the union rests still on an 'immunity' from restraint of trade: s. 2(5) TULRA 1974, modernising ss. 2, 3 Trade Union Act 1871.

21. See primarily, Employment Act 1980, ss. 16, 17; Employment Act 1982, ss. 12-18; Trade Union Act 1984, ss. 10, 11; Employment Act 1988, ss. 10, 17, Sched. 3; Employment Act 1990, ss. 4, 6, 7, 8, 9, Sched. 2.

22. See Employment Protection (Consolidation) Act (EPCA) 1978, Sched. 13, para. 24.

23. Employment Act 1988 s. 1 (7); Trade Union Act 1984 s. 11(11).

24. See s. 62, EPCA 1978, and s. 62A, ibid., added by s. 9 Employment Act 1990.

25. *Power Packing Casemakers* v. *Faust* [1983] ICR 292 CA; a breach of contract is not required here for industrial action or 'lock-out': *Express and Star* v. *Bunday* [1988] ICR 379 CA.

26. *Rookes* v. *Barnard* [1964] AC 1129, HL; *Simmons* v. *Hoover* [1977] QB 284. (On the place of the *Rookes* case, see Chapter 1 of this volume, pp. 12-18.)

27. P. O'Higgins on 'The Right to Strike' in J. Carby-Hall (ed.), *Studies in Labour Law* (1976), p. 117.

28. *Rookes* v. *Barnard* [1964] AC 1129, HL; *Barretts and Baird (Wholesale) Ltd.* v. *IPCS* [1987] IRLR 3 (Henry J explaining how this may have been the result of the repeal of s. 13(3) of TULRA in the 1980 Act s. 17(8)); and see Clerk and Lindsell *Torts* (1989 16th ed.) para. 15-15, 15-20; Wedderburn, *The Worker and the Law* (1986 3rd ed.), Chap. 8. The concept of 'illegal act' derives directly from common law thinking when a breach was a crime and a combination so to commit an 'illegal act' therefore a criminal conspiracy: see Brett J in *R.* v. *Bunn* (1872) 12 Cox C.C. 316, 339-41.

29. See e.g. Wedderburn, *The Worker and the Law* (1965), p. 286 (proposing an end to the doctrine that strikes break the contract of employment); and *Trade Unions in a Changing World – The Challenge to Management* (1980, CBI discussion document), p. 22.

30. *Trade Union Immunities* (Cmnd 8128, 1981) p. 90 (government discussion of positive rights). Compare the belief in the 'immunities', only four years after *Rookes* v. *Barnard* [1964] AC 1129, HL, in the *Donovan Royal Commission Report on Trade Unions and Employers Associations* (Cmnd 3623, 1968) para 935.

31. See for example, K. Ewing, 'The Right to Strike' (1986) 15 ILJ 143. On the curious British tradition ascribing a 'right to strike' to the individual worker so long as he gives notice to *terminate* the employment, see: Stuart-Smith LJ *Associated British Ports* v. *TGWU* [1989] IRLR 305, 318, CA; so too, the Inns of Court Conservative Society, *A Giant's Strength* (1958), p. 17. The Hohfeldian error is patent.

32. P. Elias and K. Ewing, 'Economic Torts and Labour Law' [1982] Camb. LJ 321, 358. [See too, Chap. 5.]

33. P. Davies and M. Freedland, *Labour Law: Text and Materials* (2nd ed. 1984), p. 786.

34. See *Collymore* v. *A-G.* [1970] AC 538 PC, and the Canadian Supreme Court in *Re Public Service Employee Relations Act* (1987) 38 DLR (4th) 161; T. Christian and K. Ewing, 'Labouring under the Canadian Constitution' (1988) 17 ILJ 73, on the dangers of a Bill of Rights; Wedderburn, 'Freedom of Association or Right to Organise?' (1987) 18 Ind. Rel. Jo. 244 (Chapter 6 of this volume).

35. See Wedderburn, 'The New Politics of Labour Law' (1983, Durham University Lecture), now in W.E.J. McCarthy (ed.), *Trade Unions* (2nd ed. 1985) 497-532; and Wedderburn, *The Worker and the Law* (3rd. ed. 1986), 847-56. [On 'labour courts', see below Chapter 11.]

36. Code du Travail art. L. 521-1; the addition in paragraph 3 was made by law no. 85-772, 25 July 1985.

37. See G. Lyon-Caen and J. Pelissier, *Droit du Travail* (14th ed. 1988), pp. 762-81 (*statut protecteur*).

38. See on this complex problem: J.-E. Ray, 'La réintegration du grèviste illégalement licencié' 1989 Dr. Soc. 349; the decision in *l'affaire Talbot*. Soc. 31 March 1982, appeared to leave the employee to his remedy in damages unless the employer agreed to re-engagement, but it was argued that the new art. L. 122-45, as amended in 1985 (declaring null and void any discipline or dismissal by reason of origins, sex, family situation, ethnic, national or racial attachment, political opinions, union activities or normal exercise of the right to strike or of religious convictions) must give rise to compulsory reinstatement (though this may not always be in the employee's interest). On unlawful dismissals in other systems, see below n. 117. Since this paper was revised, the Cour de Cassation has finally decided that the remedy of reinstatement is indeed available for workers dismissed for taking part in a lawful strike, even in interlocutory proceedings in which they also obtain compensation: see J-E. Ray 'La réintegration du salarié grèviste illégalement licencié' Dr. Soc. 1991, 64; Soc. 10 October 1990, *Sté. Thermo Formage Mediterranéen c. La Rocca*, Dr. Ouvr. 1990, 495 ('the employment contract not having been in law interrupted', the court can properly order its continuance); see also Soc. 26 September 1990, *Cie. Lyonnaise des Goudrons et des Bitumes c. André*, Dr. Ouvr. 1990, 457 (reinstatement after dismissal for workers who exercised their right to withdraw from work in face of danger but also stopped work completely with further demands on the employer; stoppage held to be a 'strike'; on various laws about stoppages in face of dangerous working conditions, see below Chap. 11, note 23).

39. See P. Durand, Dr. Soc. 1948, Chron. 262, 264; see H. Sinay and J-C. Javillier, *La Grève* (1984 2nd ed. Dalloz), pp. 293-9.

40. M. Weiss *Labour Law and Industrial Relations in the Federal Republic of Germany* (1987), pp. 135-6; F. Schmidt, *Law and Industrial Relations in Sweden* (1977), p. 74.

41. The lock-out is treated in Britain as parallel to the strike for the purposes of 'freezing' continuity of employment (EPCA 1978 Sched. 13, para. 24) but since 1982 a precise general parallelism has been broken because it has a different definition of 'relevant' employees in regard to the right of the employer to dismiss 'fairly' employees affected (s. 62 EPCA 1978). Now the employer has a new right to dismiss selectively and without challenge in the tribunals employees on unofficial strike: new s. 62A EPCA 1978, see s. 9 Employment Act 1990.

42. See, e.g., *Ballard c. Sté, A.E. France*, Soc. 4 November 1989 (national electricity strike not sufficient); G. Lyon-Caen and J. Pelissier, op. cit., n. 37, pp. 1028-33; H. Sinay and J.-C. Javillier, *La Grève* (2nd ed. 1984), pp. 452-75.

43. G. Giugni *Diritto sindacale* (7th ed. 1988), p. 260. But in face of illegal industrial action the employer may acquire a right to engage in a 'retaliatory'

lock-out (*serrata di ritorsione*) of uncertain ambit: ibid. pp. 262-6; G. Ghezzi and U. Romagnoli *Diritto sindacale* (1987 2nd ed.), pp. 234-43. In Spain the Constitutional Court has adopted a position similar to the Italian, permitting a lock-out only where needed to protect the safety of persons, goods or the plant and limited to a period necessary to remedy the danger and assure the resumption of work: Judgment 11/81, 8 April 1981; J. Cruz Villalón, 'El ejercicio del derecho al cierrepatronal', *La Ley Relaciones Laborales* 1986 II, 627.

44. See G. Ghezzi and U. Romagnoli, op. cit., pp. 235-6; and G. Giugni 'Art. 39' in G. Branca (ed.), *Commentario della costituzione: Rapporti economici* (1979) pp. 268-84 (on the relationships of the constitutional right to strike, art. 39, and freedom of economic enterprise, art. 41, in connection with international instruments).

45. Ten member states, if Ireland is included, have doctrines of suspension; Britain and Denmark do not; see EC *Comparative Study* ... (1989 above n. 2). On Ireland, see A. Kerr and G. Whyte, *Irish Trade Union Law* (1985) 246; *Becton Dickinson & Co.* v. *Lee* [1973] IR 1 (Sup. Ct.); the Constitution may imply suspension. But the Industrial Relations Act 1990, s. 12, retains the trade dispute immunity for inducing breach of an employment contract. On strikes and industrial action by (lawful) acts short of a strike under the Unfair Dismissal Act 1977, ss. 1 and 5, see ibid., pp. 210-13; M. Redmond, *Dismissal Law in the Republic of Ireland* (1982), pp. 35-9, 210-8.

46. *American Cyanamid Co.* v. *Ethicon Ltd.* [1975] AC 396, HL; Wedderburn, 'The Injunction and the Supremacy of Parliament' (1989) 23 Law Teacher 4; above, Chapter 7.

47. For such an injunction granted where the breach was uncertain but arguable, and the uncertainty both of facts and law weighed as usual against the defendant, see *Solihull MB* v. *NUJ* [1985] IRLR 211.

48. *Donovan Report* (Cmnd 3623, 1968) para. 937. For the civil consequences, see *Barretts and Baird (Wholesale) Ltd.* v. *IPCS* [1987] IRLR 3; B. Simpson (1987) 50 MLR 506; for the detailed case law, see Clerk and Lindsell *Torts* (16th ed. 1989) Chap. 15 (Wedderburn). But the employer's damages for the breach of contract are limited: *NCB* v. *Galley* [1958] 1 All E.R. 91 CA; see too, nn. 115-140 below.

49. *Boxfoldia Ltd* v. *NGA* [1988] ICR 752: 'a member "authorises" the union to decide on official industrial action .... (and) to communicate its decisions to employers and others .... It does not follow, however, that .... the union is thereby authorised to act as his agent .... to exercise rights of termination upon notice', *per* Saville J, p. 758. A similar problem would arise if a positive right to strike did not suspend the contract. There is of course no rule of law that prevents a 'strike notice' from being a notice to terminate, if that is its correct interpretation: see P. O'Higgins [1968] Camb. L.J. 223; K. Foster (1971) 34 MLR 275.

50. B. Simpson and J. Wood, *Industrial Relations and the 1971 Act* (1973), pp. 333-4.

51. On Ireland, see n. 45 *supra*. See generally Wedderburn 'Legislative and Judicial Restraints on Trade Union Activity and Rights to Strike' (Report to International Soc. of Labour Law and Social Security, Symposium, 13 September 1989, Paris), published as 'Limitation Législative et Judiciaire en Matière d'Action Syndicale et de Droit de Grève' (1990) *Revue Internationale de Droit Comparé* No. 1, 37, and in *Le Droit du Travail: Hier et Demain* (Soc. Lég. Comparée, 1990) 35-112.

52. G. Giugni, *Diritto Sindacale* (1988), p. 216. For the classic analysis of strikes and suspension of the individual employment contract, see X. Blanc-Jouvan, 'The Effect of Industrial Action on the Status of the Individual Employee', Chap. 4 in B. Aaron and K. Wedderburn, *Industrial Conflict – A Comparative Legal Survey* (1972).

53. O. Kahn-Freund, 'The Legal Framework', Chap. II, A. Flanders and H. Clegg, *The System of Industrial Relations in Great Britain* (1954), p. 127. The argument

does not appear in his later writings; by 1979 he came to see trade disputes in essential services differently: 'Socially (but by no means legally) speaking, the employer is .... no more than the agent of the consumer, the instrument of the public', *Labour Relations, Heritage and Adjustment* (1979), p. 76.

54. Employment Act 1982, s. 18, redefining s. 29 TULRA 1974; on the severe effect of changing a few words, causing industrial action to become 'political' in the eye of the law, see: *Mercury Communications* v. *Scott-Garner* [1984] Ch. 37 CA.

55. Soc. 10 March 1961; a different chamber of the Cour de Cassation accepted the legitimacy of a strike where the political objectives were predominant: Crim. 29 October 1969; H. Sinay and J.-C. Javillier, op. cit. *La Grève* (1984), pp. 223-7. A distinction permitting political strikes 'in defence of Republican principles' is criticised by commentators: G. Lyon-Caen and J. Pélissier, *Droit du Travail* (1990 15th ed.), p. 1037.

56. Cort. cost. (Constitutional Court) 13 June 1983, no. 165/83; 27 December 1974 no. 290/74; 28 December 1962, no. 123/62; see Wedderburn (1983) 12 ILJ 253. In a 'mixed economy' the economic zone cannot easily be divorced from the political: G. Pera, *Diritto del Lavoro* (3rd ed. 1988) pp. 224-5.

57. Cort. cost. 14 January 1974, no. 1/74; and 28 December 1962, no. 123/62; G. Giugni, *Diritto sindacale* (1988), pp. 239-42 (strikes for better housing, transport, health services etc. are within the right to strike properly so called).

58. Respectively art. 15 and 28, *Statuto dei lavoratori*, Law 300, 20 May 1970; see Wedderburn, 'The Italian Workers' Statute, Some British Reflections' (1990) 19 ILJ 154; and on the labour jurisdiction of the *Pretore*, 'The Social Charter in Britain – Labour Law and Labour Courts' (1991) 54 MLR 1, n. 203 ff. (below Chapter 12).

59. It must be noted that important laws in both countries limit strikes in the public sector: see in Italy, Law no. 146/90, 12 June 1990 on essential public services, touching on constitutionally protected rights; in France the law of 31 July 1963 (C.T. art. L. 521-2 *et seq.*) requiring notice and banning 'rolling strikes' in a widely defined area of public services (G. Lyon-Caen and J. Pélissier, *Droit du Travail* (1990 15th ed.) pp. 1074-7) below n. 62.

60. Soc. 21 March 1973; Soc. 16 October 1985; see generally G. Lyon-Caen and J. Pelissier *Droit du Travail* (1990 15th ed.), pp. 1021-8.

61. See *SARL Sogarde c. Cousin* Soc. 11 July 1989, Rev. Jur. Soc. Oct. 1989, 477; and Soc 24 March 1988; see J.-C. Javillier *Manuel du Droit du Travail* (1990 3rd ed.) pp. 407-8; G. Lyon-Caen and J. Pelissier, op. cit., n. 60, p. 1026; and see especially J. Deprez Dr. Soc. 1988, 649, on the fluctuations in the jurisprudence on this point.

62. The French law of 31 July 1963 bans 'rolling strikes' and demands five days notice from a 'representative' union (during which time, by an amendment of 1982, the parties are under a duty to negotiate) in widely defined areas of public services. The Italian Law no. 146/90, 12 June 1990, requires a notice of at least 10 days for strikes in a wide area of essential public services (or longer if agreed in collective agreements) stating the starting date and indicating the proposed length of the strike; makes a minimum service obligatory; and requires the enterprises providing services to give notice to the public of details of the service to be provided. Various civil penalties can be suffered by unions and workers infringing these obligations.

63. The formula used by the Cour de Cassation: Soc. 5 March 1953, Dr. Soc. 1953, 226. In Italy, the right to strike does not extend to 'concerted slow-downs', non-collaboration, 'pedantic' work-to-rule or obstructionism: Giugni op. cit. (1988), pp. 256-8. The employer has the right to slow down the pay of go-slow workers: Cass. 9 July 1980, no. 4263. Faced with incomplete performance in industrial action, the British employer is entitled to pay nothing, unless he orders or accepts the work done: *Miles* v. *Wakefield MBC.* [1987] AC 539 HL; *Wiluszynski* v. *Tower Hamlets LBC* [1989] IRLR 259, CA.

64. See for example the need to pose separate questions in a ballot on a strike and

on action short of a strike: Trade Union Act 1984, s. 11, amended by Employment Act 1988, s. 1(5), Sched. 3, para. 5(8), and Employment Act 1990 Sched. 2, paras 2, 3.

65. See ss. 1, 5(2) Unfair Dismissal Act 1977: M. Redmond, *Dismissal Law* (1982), pp. 212-7.

66. French, and in the past Italian, courts have reserved to themselves the right to disqualify stoppages which intentionally damage the enterprise to an inordinate degree, but in both systems this partly reflects the well known civilian concept of 'abuse of right': see G. Lyon-Caen and J. Pélissier, op. cit. (1990 15th ed.) pp. 1036-8; 29. *Rychter* Soc. 16 July 1964, D. 1964, 705 G. Lyon-Caen; Soc. 4 February 1988; Soc. 7 March 1989, Dr. Ouvr. 1989 415 (*grève thrombose, paralysing strike*). One question for British courts in a positive rights system would be whether they could adopt a doctrine of abuse of rights.

67. Cass. (Corte di Cassazione; High Court of Appeal) 30 January 1980 no. 711/80. On the need for a cessation of work: Cass. 28 March 1986, no. 2214/86, F.I. 1986 I 900, 904; but there are indications that less than a full abstention may be accepted: Cass. 9 March 1984; G. Ghezzi and U. Romagnoli, *Il diritto sindacale* (2nd. ed. 1987), pp. 251-2.

68. Cass. 30 October 1984 no. 5558/85; G. Giugni, *Diritto sindacale*, op. cit., n. 43, 256-8.

69. G. Pera, op. cit., n. 56, pp. 229-31; G. Ghezzi and U. Romagnoli, *Il diritto sindacale* (2nd. ed. 1987) pp. 202-4, 251-2; F. Carinci, R. de Luca Tamajo, P. Tosi and T. Treu, *Il diritto sindacale* (2nd ed. 1987) pp. 382-3, for rather different evaluations of the decision 711/80.

70. See the ILO Experts *Report on the Application of Conventions* (1989) III (Part 4A), p. 241; K. Ewing, *Britain and the ILO* (1989); and below p. 353 Note A.

71. Soc. 23 November 1978, D. 1979, 304, J-C. Javillier.

72. *Usinor* Soc. 15 June 1978, D. 1979, 25, P. Langlois; G. Lyon-Caen and J. Pélissier, op. cit. (1990 15th ed.) 'Auto-satisfaction des revendications', pp. 1039-4.

73. H. Sinay and J-C. Javillier, *La Grève* (2nd ed. 1984), p. 178.

74. See the two decisions Soc. 21 June 1989, D. 1990 Somm. 167, *SNCF c. Coudurier*, and *IBM c. Cortes*; contrast Soc. 27 June 1989 *SA Fonderie Pasquet c. Sotto* (strikes lawful when coinciding only fortuitously with the period strikers demanded should not be worked).

75. Soc. 11 December 1985, (1985) 6 Int. Lab. Law R. 317; contrast Soc. 10 December 1986 (employer not at fault in regard to state of workplace).

76. 'Every employee, whatever their sex, age or nationality has the right freely to join the union of their choice': Code du Travail art. L. 411-5, based on the Preamble to the Constitution.

77. *Cheall* v. *APEX* [1983] 2 AC 180, HL; B. Simpson (1983) 46 MLR 353; (free choice of union limited by right of union members not to associate with applicant). But British law after 1990 enshrines a right not to be refused employment by reason of union membership or non-membership, though the right is enforceable only by an action for compensation in an industrial tribunal and does not extend to blacklists on union activities: ss. 1-3 and Sched. 1, Employment Act 1990.

78. L. Mariucci, 'Il conflitto collettivo nell'ordinamento giuridico italiano' (1989) 41 Giorn dir di lav. e di rel. ind. 1, 17, and see on earlier developments, pp. 4-14.

79. As with the origins of the 'immunities' in Britain: Wedderburn, *The Worker and the Law*, (1986 3rd ed.) Chap. 1 [below Chapter 11].

80. O. Kahn-Freund, 'The Impact of Constitutions on Labour Law' [1976] Camb. L.J. 241, 270.

81. See further Wedderburn, op. cit., (1990) *Revue Internationale de Droit Comparé*, pp. 62-4; and J. Savatier, 'L'Occupation des lieux du travail' Dr. Soc. 1988, 655, for a full review of the current French position.

82. See *Boxfoldia Ltd* v. *NGA* [1988] ICR 752, above n. 49.

83. *Airey* v. *Weighill*, *Times*, 11 February 1905, CA: the union was liable for local branches or officials only if the 'wrongful acts have been ordered, authorised or ratified by the central body': T. Sophian, *Trade Union Law and Practice* (1927), p. 75. The approach was distinctly 'top down'; see generally, Wedderburn, '*The Worker and the Law*, Chap. 7.

84. *Heatons Transport (St Helens) Ltd* v. *TGWU* [1973] AC 15, HL where the Law Lords affirmed a 'bottom up' approach; but see the uncertainties left by the different decision in *General Aviation Services* v. *TGWU* [1976] IRLR 224, [1985] ICR 615, HL. The approach of the CA in the *Heaton* case, that authority for the wrongful act must be found in authorisation from 'the top' of the union, is closer to the French approach, below n. 88.

85. Employment Act 1982, s. 15; with a limitation on damages up to £250,000 in one proceeding according to the size of the union, s. 16.

86. Employment Act 1990, s. 6, substantially amending s. 15 of the 1982 Act.

87. See Code du Travail art. L. 412-4 to -17; G. Lyon-Caen and J. Pélissier, *Droit du Travail* (1990 15th ed.), pp. 830-40.

88. Soc 9 November 1982 *Sté Dubigeon Normandie c. Synd CGT*, and *Trailor c. Mme Abadie* ibid., D. 1982, 621 and D. 1983, 531 H. Sinay; Dr. Soc. 1983, 173, 275 J. Savatier; Dr. Ouvr. 1983, 275, F. Samito. G. Lyon-Caen and J. Pelissier *Droit du Travail* (1990 15th ed.), pp. 1065-8: 'union delegates are neither organs nor officers nor agents of the union', p. 1067. It seems the courts will take the same view of the members of the 'Comité de Groupe' who are (exceptionally) designated by the unions: op. cit., p. 788. [See below p. 353 Note B.]

89. On the comparison of art. 1382 Code Civil and the common law, see A. Tunc, *La Responsabilité Civile* (1981), pp. 11-18.

90. See J-M Verdier *Syndicats et Droit Syndical* (1987 2nd ed.), pp. 288-92: the union is not liable where a union officer contravenes the rules of the union: 289, n. 6.

91. Above n. 83: the union organised and instigated obstructions by pickets; see, G. Viney Dr. Soc. 1988, 416; and Soc. 21 January 1987; but see Soc. 23 June 1989 (the mere presence of a union official is not enough).

92. Soc. 17 July 1990 *U.L. CGT c. Générale Sucrière* Dr. Ouvr. 1990, 375; three judgments held the union of the enterprise (*Syndicat CGT de la Générale Sucrière Nassandre*) and regional union (*Syndicat CGT des Raffineurs de Sucre Marseille*) not liable, even though *délégués* and local union officers organised the strike in the course of which an occupation and illegal acts occurred; the union had not 'by any instruction or any other means been the origin of the illicit acts'; passivity in face of illegal obstructions by strikers is not enough: Soc. 23 June 1988 *Sté Sapro c. Charbolet*, Dr. Ouvr. 1988 446, F. Saramito. The legal result would have been totally different under the British Employment Act 1982, s. 15 as amended by s. 6, Employment Act 1990.

93. P. Waquet (Conseiller) *Report* in the *Sté Générale Sucrière* cases, 17 July 1990, in Dr. Ouvr. 1990, 375.

94. Soc. 8 February 1972, D. 1972, 656 J. Savatier; and G. Durry, 'La responsabilité civile des délégués syndicaux' Dr. Soc. 1984, 69; it matters not whether or not they acted as union delegates, they are personally liable for their own fault (e.g. the wrong of infringing the right to work): Soc 26 July 1984, *Casino Guichard c. Perrachon*.

95. For judgment *in solidum* of large sums, see *Di. Fruschia c. Arnaud* Soc. 6 June 1989, Dr. Ouvr. 1990, 31, F. Samarito (padlocking of plant by strikers contravening non-strikers' rights to work; seven strikers liable to 37 non-strikers for loss of their salaries). See also Soc. 8 December 1983 (perishing of goods; union delegates personally liable for fault in knowingly instructing specialist workers to break collectively agreed safety measures and join the strike, ruining the goods). But where a delegate was not party to all the wrongful acts, the Cour de Cassation held that he was not liable for all the damage done: Soc 23 June 1988 *Sté Sapro c. Charbelet*. [See too, p. 353 below, Note B.]

96. Cons. const. 22 October 1982, on art. 8 Law of 28 October 1982; Dr. Soc. 1983, 162, J. Hamon; and Soc. 9 November 1982 *Sté Dubigeon Normandie c. Synd CGT*, and *Trailor c. Mme. Abadie ibid*, n. 88 above.

97. See J-M, Verdier on 'l'insaisissabilité partielle du patrimoine syndical' (freedom from sequestration of trade union property) in *Syndicats et Droit Syndical*, Vol. I (1987 2nd ed.), pp. 295-8 (protected items are the property needed for meeting rooms, libraries and training courses: C.T. art. L.412-12). Similarly, see the pragmatic approach in A. Jeammaud Dr. Soc. 1978, 119 (note on *Ferrodo* Soc. 17 May 1977).

98. See Wedderburn, 'Le législateur et le juge' in *Les Transformations du Droit du Travail; Études Offertes à G. Lyon Caen* (1989 Dalloz), pp. 123-157.

99. F. Carinci *et al.*, op. cit., *Il diritto sindacale*, above n. 69, p. 393.

100. G. Lyon-Caen and J. Pelissier, op. cit., (1990 15th ed.) above n. 37, pp. 1026-8; H. Sinay and J-C, Javillier *La Grève* (1984), 204-7. On *Solidarité externe*: Crim. 23 october 1969; Crim. 12 January 1971 Dr. Soc. 1971, 547, J. Savatier. On *solidarité interne*: n. 148 below.

101. M. Weiss, op. cit. above n. 40, p. 138; 1 AZR 468/83, 5 March 1985, (1985) 5 Int. L.L.R. 56; and see 1 AZR 219/86, 12 January 1988, (1988) 8 Int. L.L.R. 58; 'The scope of the exceptional cases is much too narrow to allow solidarity strikes to become a relevant feature of industrial conflict': *Annotation*, p. 62. On the 'ally doctrine' in the United States, see D. Leslie, *Labor Law* (1986), pp. 125-36. On Britain: *Dimbleby* v. *NUJ* [1984] 1 WLR 427 (HL, no ally test for company group).

102. AD. 1980 Nr. 15; AD. 1984 Nr. 91, (1984) 4 Int. L.L.R. 65; Folke Schmidt, op. cit. above n. 40, p. 177. But in 1989 the Labour Court reverted to a narrower approach, disallowing industrial action where a ship's crew was covered by a foreign collective agreement: (1990) 202 EIRR 8.

103. Employment Act 1982 s. 18, amending s. 29 TULRA 1974. On the courts see *Dimskal Shipping SA* v. *ITWF* [1990] IRLR 102 CA (application of English principles on 'economic duress' to industrial action lawful in Sweden, Neill LJ dissenting); and in France the Cour de Cassation has enforced an arbitration clause against an employee working in Gabon (Soc. 17 June 1982) and a clause renouncing the right to strike by a worker going to work in South Africa: Soc. 16 and 17 June 1983, criticised by G. Lyon-Caen and A. Lyon-Caen, *Droit Social Internationale et Européen* (1991 7th ed.), pp. 54-5.

104. See s. 14 (2) (e) Industrial Relations Act 1990.

(105. Wedderburn, op. cit. (1990) Rev. Internat. de Droit Comparé, pp. 79-82.

106. ILO Experts Report III ((Part 4A) *Report on the Application of Conventions* (1989) p. 238; see K. Ewing, *Britain and the ILO* (1989, Institute of Employment Rights) Appendix, text of the Experts' Report.

107. See, for example, the remarkable jurisprudence in the United States on secondary boycotts, the ally doctrine, common situs problems, hot-cargo clauses, etc. outlined in L. Merrifield, T. St. Antoine, C. Craver, *Labor Relations Law: Cases and Materials* (8th ed. 1989), pp. 338-421.

108. Apart from the special case of multi-national companies provided for in Act 1264 of 1982, solidarity action, although legalised by that Act (for officially recognised unions), appears to be limited by the courts to stoppages which directly promote the strikers' work-related interests (Thessaloniki High Court 4392/1987) and which do not cause the enterprise irreparable damage (Athens C.A. 10599/1987); *The Regulation of Industrial Conflict in Europe* (EIRR, 1989), p. 26.

109. See Wedderburn, *The Worker and the Law*, n. 35, Chap. 1, and 'Industrial Relations and the Courts' (1980) 9 ILJ 65 (above Chapter 3).

110. See especially on 'organic' systems, O. Kahn-Freund, 'The Right to Strike' in G. Wilner (ed.), *Jus et Societas* (1979), pp. 201-19.

111. On Portugal, EC *Comparative Study ...* (1989), above n. 2, 74; *The Regulation of Industrial Conflict in Europe* (1989, EIRR) 41.

112. See L. Mariucci, 'Il conflitto collettivo....' (1989) 41 Giorn. dir. di lav. e di rel. ind. 1, op. cit., above n. 78.

113. M. Weiss, *Labour Law and Industrial Relations in the Federal Republic of Germany* (1987), pp. 130-8: art. 823, Civil Code (based on negligence).

114. Decisions of the Great Senate of the Federal Labour Court: 28 January 1955, BAG 1 291 GS 1/54 AP nr. 1; and (on lock-out) BAG 21 April 1971 GS 1/68 AP nr. 43, art. 9 GG Arbeitskampf. Suspension is also the rule in Sweden: Swedish Labour Court, AD. Nr. 11 1972.

115. Folke Schmidt, *Law and Industrial Relations in Sweden* (1977), pp. 160-90; S. Edlund and B. Nyström, *Developments in Swedish Labour Law* (1988), pp. 31-4.

116. The *Saab Scandia* case: (1990) 198 EIRR 10.

117. Sweden, AD Nr. 31 1975, (1975) 1 Int. L.L.R. 277; and Germany, 1 AZR 20/75, 28.1. 75, AP Nr. 51, (1975) 3 Int. L.L.R. 270 ('such dismissals must normally be preceded by a warning': Annotation, p. 273).

118. *Employment Gazette*, January 1990, 3.

119. AD 1975 Nr. 31; AD 1981 Nr. 5 and Nr. 10. On the special Scandinavian approach to damages as 'bot', see T. Sigeman (1987) 8 Comp. Lab. Law Jo 155 (somewhere between compensation and a fine).

120. See *The Regulation of Industrial Conflict in Europe* (EIRR, 1989) 15.

121. See Chapter 7 of this volume.

122. See s. 62 EPCA 1978; *Mackenzie* v. *Crossville Motors* [1990] ICR 172; *P. & O. European Ferries* v. *Byrne* [1989] IRLR 254, CA; above n. 25.

123. See respectively s. 9 Employment Act 1982, amending s. 62 EPCA 1978; s. 9 Employment Act 1990 (inserting new s. 62A).

124. Some saw the formula as protecting the employer (Phillips J, *Thompson* v. *Eaton* [1976] 3 All E.R. 383, 388), others as protecting the employees (O. Kahn-Freund in G. Wilner (ed.), *Jus et Societas* (1979), pp. 209-12; compare O. Kahn-Freund and B. Hepple, *Laws Against Strikes* (1972)). The changes in 1982 made it much more difficult to uphold the latter view, as the Wapping *affaire* made clear (5,000 staff dismissed when on strike, partly engineered by employer, against transfer of the *Times* to new site); the employer can also wait for the strike to crumble and then dismiss the hard core: s. 9 Employment Act 1982; P. Wallington (1983) 46 MLR 310). On remedies in France, above n. 38.

125. M. Redmond, *Dismissal Law*, op. cit., pp. 212-19; A. Kerr and G. Whyte, *Irish Trade Union Law* (1985), pp. 210-3; Unfair Dismissals Act 1977 ss. 1, 5(2).

126. Constitution art. 23(2) ('to be exercised by lawfully established trade unions for the purpose of defending and promoting the economic and, in general, work-related interests of working people'); strikes are regulated by Act No. 1264/82 under which unions must be accredited by a court; arbitration is governed by Act No. 3239/55. Compare the licensing of unions in Ireland: A. Kerr and G. Whyte, op. cit., Chap. 2; and now ss. 9, 16 and 20-22 Industrial Relations Act 1990.

127. A. Pappaionnou, 'Greek Labor in the 1980s' (1990) 11 Comp. Lab. Law Jo. 295, 304-7.

128. See ILO Committee on Freedom of Association, 160th Report, 1977, Case 834 (Greece) para. 198; Ben Israel, op. cit., n. 5, p. 121. On compulsory arbitration, ibid., 217th Report, 1982, Case 1089 (Greece) para. 241; and Committee of Experts *Report on the Application of Conventions* (1989) Report III (Part 4A), p. 277 (repeal of 1955 law and Convention No. 98, 1949).

129. Kerr and Whyte, op. cit., n. 125, pp. 53-62. The Act of 1941 appears to have been motivated by an attempt to reduce the number of unions; but the date is also in the war time period when, as a neutral, Ireland had many British based unions operating in it.

130. See s. 9 (1) Industrial Relations Act 1990; immunities in respect of peaceful picketing or inducing breach of employment contract (ss. 11, 12) and protection of the union from tort liability in trade disputes (s. 13) apply only to authorised unions. The Act also amends the monetary deposits which a union must put up

(according to size) to obtain a licence: s. 21, Sched. 3. The Registrar must inform the Minister about the persistent disregard by a union of the new rule that strikes must be supported by a ballot, and the Minister may revoke the union's negotiation licence: s. 16(5).

131. Code du Travail art. L.521-3; if the union organises a strike without the notice, it incurs civil liability: Soc. 6 February 1985.

132. On the difficult concept of 'representativity' (which is relative and variable in different areas of application) see G. Lyon-Caen and J. Pélissier *Droit du Travail* (1990 15th ed.), pp. 714-27 (at enterprise level the union must prove its proportional effectiveness; the court will look to its membership, support in elections of workers' representatives, independence, experience and even patriotic attitude during the wartime occupation: Code du Travail art. L. 133-2).

133. J-M. Verdier, *Syndicats et Droit Social*, Vol. 1 (1987 ed.), p. 473, and see on the concept pp. 479-560.

134. La Ley Organica de Libertad Sindical 11/1985, 2 August 1985: on the background, F. Valdes dal-Ré, 'Representación y representatividad sindicales en España', 1988 *La Ley: Relaciones Laborales* II, 145-158 (electoral support is not the only test; a union may acquire the status because it is in a confederation of unions which has 'representative' status at national level, similar to the Italian and French concept; this is sometimes known as representatives 'by radiation', 155).

135. M. Rodriguez Piñero and J. Cruz Villalon, 'La legge spagnola sulla libertà sindacale' (1987) 33 Giorn. di dir. del lav, e di rel. ind. 77, 89-103. Spanish labour law knows of a wide variety of workers' representatives at any one workplace, and diverse treatment of different unions is not necessarily illegal discrimination: T.C. 108/1989 8 June 1989, and 84/1989 10 May 1989: (1991) 9 Int. L.L.R. 21 and 28.

136. G. Giugni, *Diritto sindacale* (1988 7th ed.), p. 82; also pp. 87-8 for the relative meanings in various contexts. The Italian system is fluid, where the Spanish is more legalistic: M. Casas Baamonde, 'Sulla rappresentatività sindacale' (1990) Lavoro e Diritto 449.

137. See Wedderburn (1990) 19 ILJ 154 (Chapter 9 above).

138. On other national unions the position is not entirely clear: F. Carinci, R. de Luca Tamajo, P. Tosi, T. Treu, *Diritto sindacale* (1987, 2nd ed.), pp. 114-6; and Cass. no. 1320/86, 1 March 1986.

139. See L. Mariucci, 'La legge sullo sciopero nei servizi pubblici essenziali; problemi chiusi e aperti' (1990) Lavoro e Diritto 533, 546-7, who also questions the position under art. 39 of the Constitution (on *libertà sindacale*: freedom to organise in unions).

140. G. Giugni, *Diritto sindacale* (1988, 7th ed.), pp. 156-9. But a minority view would bind all lower (i.e. plant) union bodies covered by an industry level collective agreement, even by an implicit peace obligation (F. Santo-Passarelli, 'Pax, pactum, pacta servanda sunt', 1974 Mass. Giur. Lav. 374) and in one decision the court held individual workers bound because of the terms of the clause agreed by a plant committee (Cass. No. 357/71, 10 February 1971): F. Carinci, R. de Luca Tamajo, P. Tosi, T. Treu, *Il diritto sindacale* (1987, 2nd ed.), pp. 287-94; G. Ghezzi and U. Romagnoli, *Il diritto sindacale* (2nd ed., 1987), pp. 154-6 (who reject all but the narrowest efficacy of 'truce clauses'). See too the valuable survey: L. Mariucci, 'Il conflitto collettivo' (1989) 41 Giorn. di dir. del lav. e di rel. ind. 1, 12. When the 'triangular accord' of 22 June 1983 required unions not to reopen demands on pay for 18 months, plant demands in contravention of this agreement were not seen as illegal.

141. See: Soc. 5 and 6 May 1960; and *Sté Tanneries de Sireuil* Soc. 8 December 1983 (the case of perishable goods); H. Sinay and J-C. Javillier, op. cit., n. 32. pp. 252-7; G. Lyon-Caen and J. Pélissier, op. cit., n. 37, pp. 1048-9, 1064-5; J-C. Javillier, *Manuel: Droit du Travail* (3rd ed. 1990), p. 410; but compare J-M Béraud, 'Le rôle des délégués en cours de grève' Dr. Soc. 1988, 666. Recently French judges have firmly upheld the rule that a worker is not liable for causing a

breach of procedures in a collective agreement unless he acts deliberately or knowingly incites others to commit such a breach: Soc. 10 October 1990 *Sté. Thermo Formage Mediterranéen c. La Rocca*; Dr. Ouvr. 1990, 495 (strikers dismissed but reinstated). Liability is stricter in English law (see on 'turning a blind eye', *Emerald Construction Co.* v. *Lowthian* [1966] 1 WLR 691, CA; and *Falconer* v. *ASLEF* [1986] IRLR 331), though possibly not so strict in Scotland: *Roseleigh Ltd* v. *Leader Cars* 1987 SLT 355 (commercial dealings); but contrast *Square Grip Reinforcement Ltd.* v. *Macdonald* 1968 SLT 65 (principles not unlike the English applied to union officials).

142. G. Pera, *Il diritto del lavoro* (1988, 3rd ed.), p. 237; on the *Statuto dei lavoratori* see Wedderburn (1990) 19 ILJ 154 Chapter 9 of this volume, pp. 234-75. The French employer's powers are listed by G. Lyon-Caen and J. Pélissier, op. cit., n. 37 (1990, 15th ed.), p. 1041, and their increasingly strict application by the courts strongly criticised by J. Pélissier, 'La Grève: Liberté Très Surveillée' Dr. Ouvr, 1988, 59. On liability *in solidum*, see below p. 353, Note B.

143. *Unofficial Action and the Law* (1989 Cm. 821) 2-3, 'Overseas Experience'.

144. See s. 18(4) TULRA 1974.

145. See *National Coal Board* v. *NUM* [1986] ICR 736; see Wedderburn, *The Worker and the Law* (3rd ed. 1986), Chap. 4 on 'incorporation'.

146. O. Kahn-Freund, *Labour and the Law* (3rd ed. 1983, eds. P. Davies and M. Freedland), pp. 176-7. For a case where collectively agreed provisions appeared to be appropriate to bind workers in regard to an overtime ban, see *Camden Exhibitions Ltd* v. *Lynott* [1966] 1 QB 555, CA.

147. The jurisprudential validity of the distinction between rights and interests disputes in this crude form may be questionable (see K. Wedderburn, 'Conflicts of Rights and Conflicts of Interests in Labor Disputes' in B. Aaron (ed.), *Disputes Settlement Procedures in Five Western European Countries* (1969), pp. 65-90; but that issue cannot be pursued in this paper.

148. G. Lyon-Caen and J. Pélissier, op. cit., (1990, 15th ed.) n. 37, 1028; on clauses requiring notice, see nn. 140 and 141 above. On *grève de solidarité interne*, see ibid., p. 1027; Soc. 18 March 1982; Soc. 27 November 1985; J. Deprez Dr. Soc. 1988, 143, and above n. 100.

149. So too, a stoppage in protest against discipline of a worker who had fired a paint gun, without challenging the fact that this was *faute lourde* and not in pursuance of any demands of those taking action, was held not to fall within the right to strike: Soc. 30 May 1989, *Boultam c. Norinco*; but a stoppage protesting against a dismissal will be legitimate where it contests the employer's threat to 'the stability of employment and the interests of the workers generally': Soc. 27 February 1974.

150. J. Schregle, 'Labour Relations in Western Europe: Some Topical Issues' (1974) 109 Int. Lab. Rev. 1, 11-12.

151. Under the New Zealand Labour Relations Act 1987 (No. 77) s. 234, a strike or lock-out is unlawful: 'if it concerns – (a) a dispute of rights ...'; and the right to strike is based explicitly upon 'disputes of interest' (ss. 230, 233). On Portugal see EC *Comparative Study* ... (1989) above n. 2, p. 72.

152. Employment Act 1990 s. 9(2).

153. See Industrial Relations Act 1990 s.9(2)-(4).

154. M. Weiss, op. cit. above, n. 40, 132; on lawful preparation for strike action over working hours, see the Federal Labour Court: 1 AZR 404/88, 27.6.1989, ZIP 1989 1356; (1991) 9 Int. L.L.R. 480 (action sufficiently 'proportional' and not unlawful as a 'political' strike; anti-trust legislation does not apply to labour relations). On Sweden and the 'invisible peace clauses' of the 1930s, see D. Fischer in A.H. Goransson *Kolektivitavtalet som Fredspliktsinstrument* (1988, English résumé).

155. See S. del Ray Guanter, *Negociación Colectiva y Paz Laboral* (1984), pp. 305-315; but compare T. Sala Franco (ed.) *Derecho del Trabajo* (5th ed. 1990)

pp. 202-4 on *el deber de paz* (the peace obligation). The position of peace clauses in Spain allows for doubt: EC *Comparative Study* ..., above n. 2, pp. 69-70.

156. EC, *Comparative Study*, above n. 2, p. 72.

157. A. Flanders, *Management and Unions* (1970), p. 99.

158. See art. 3, law of 31 July 1963; H. Sinay and J-C. Javillier, op. cit., *La Grève* (1984) Title 4 Chap. 1; G. Lyon Caen and J. Pélissier, op. cit. (1990 15th ed.), pp. 1071-7.

159. Constitutional Court: T.C. 11/81, 11 April 1981; see M. Rodriguez-Piñero 'Le Tribunal Constitutional Espagnol et le Droit Syndical' in *Transformations du Droit du Travail: Etudes Offertes à Gérard Lyon-Caen* (1989 Dalloz), pp. 114-22; S. del Rey Guanter, *Negociación Colectiva y Paz Laboral* (1984) Section II, on the apparent limitations by peace obligations and conflicts of interests in earlier laws: above nn. 135, 155.

160. Ley Organica de Libertad Sindical, 1985 (LOLS) arts 12-15; J. Cruz Villalon 'La legge spagnola sulla libertà sindacale' (1987) Giorn di dir. del lav. e di rel. ind. 79. In Italy the special judicial procedure (a hearing within two days) and the severe sanctions on anti-union conduct, in art. 28, were the 'most important practical novelties introduced by the whole law [of 1970]': G. Giugni, op. cit., n. 43, p. 104.

161. See further, Wedderburn, 'Legislative and Judicial Restraints (etc) ....' (1990) Rev. Int. du Droit Comp. 37, 79; on Denmark see (1988) 175 EIRR 13.

162. A third 'non-denominational' federation has now been created alongside the two largest union federations (Catholic and socialist); there is also one managerial federation: (1990) 202 EIRR 8.

163. High Court: Hoge Raad 22 April 1988, NJ 1988, 952, (1988) 8 Int. L.L.R. 394; and 30 May 1986, NJ 1986, 688, (1986) 6 Int. L.L.R. 4; Hof Amsterdam 13 April 1972 (memorandum from L. Van Der Heuvel).

164. TULRA 1974 s. 18; *Dimskal Shipping* v. *ITWF* (No. 2) [1990] ICR 694, CA.

165. See Sex Discrimination Act 1986, s. 6.

166. See S. Deakin, 'Equality and the New Market Order' (1990) 19 ILJ 1; E. McKendrick, 'The Rights of Trade Union Members' (1988) 17 ILJ 141.

167. See the revealing Symposium, 'Trade Union Democracy and Industrial Relations' (1988) 17 Bull. Comp. Lab. Relns., especially France (X. Blanc-Jouvan, 7), Germany (M. Weiss, 27), Italy (G. Giugni, T. Treu, 39) Spain (F. Valdes Dal Re, 83), Sweden (C. Hemström, 95), Britain (Wedderburn, B. Bercusson, 107), United States (C. Summers and J. Bellace, 145) and a comparison by M. Biagi, 199-206.

168. See the detailed analysis in Wedderburn, 'Freedom of Association and Philosophies of Labour Law' (1989) 17 ILJ 1 (Chapter 8 above).

169. See Trade Union Act 1984, s. 11 (3) as amended by Sched. 3, para. 5(8) (strike ballot), and s. 15(5A) Employment Act 1982 added by Employment Act 1990, s. 6 (words required for repudiation).

170. See *Donovan Report* (Cmnd 3623, 1968) para. 643. See too, on procedures and industrial action, S. Anderman, 'The Status Quo Issue and Industrial Disputes Procedures' (1975) 4 ILJ 131.

171. See Wedderburn, *The Worker and the Law* (1986 3rd ed.) especially Chaps 1 and 8; 'Industrial Relations and the Courts' (1980) 9 ILJ 65 (Chapter 3 of this volume); and 'The New Policies in Industrial Relations Law', Chap. 2 in P. Fosh and C. Littler *Industrial Relations and the Law in the 1980s* (1985); also 'The Social Charter in Britain – Labour Law and Labour Courts?' (1991) 54 MLR 1 (Chapter 11 below).

172. Wedderburn, 'The New Politics of Labour Law', 1983, in W.E.J. McCarthy, *Trade Unions*, (2nd ed. 1985) 514-27 (Chapter 4 above).

173. *Express Newspapers* v. *McShane* [1980] AC 672, 690 HL; *Duport Steels* v. *Sirs* [1980] ICR 161, 177 HL; *NWL* v. *Woods* [1979] ICR 367 HL; see especially B. Simpson (1980) 43 MLR 327 (and Chapter 3 above).

174. *Rookes* v. *Barnard* [1964] AC 1129, HL; see for the details of this case, K.

Wedderburn, 'Intimidation and the Right to Strike' (1964) 27 MLR 257; compare
L. Hoffman *Rookes* v. *Barnard*' (1965) 81 LQR 116 (Chapter 1 above).

175. See *Quinn* v. *Leathem* [1901] AC 495, HL; *Taff Vale Railway Co* v. *ASRS*
[1901] AC 426 HL. For O. Kahn-Freund's shock, see *Labour Law: Old Traditions
and New Developments* (1968), pp. 69-70; and for one of the many expressions of
distaste for *Allen* v. *Flood* [1898] AC 1, HL, see Lord Devlin *Samples of
Lawmaking* (1962), pp. 11-14. See too, Wedderburn, 'The Social Charter in
Britain; Labour Law and Labour Courts' (1991) 54 MLR 1, 39-40 (see Chapter 11
below).

176. *Associated British Ports* v. *TGWU* [1989] 1 WLR 939 CA; reversed on other
grounds ibid., HL (the reliance upon motive in this judgment reopens old battles
about *Allen* v. *Flood* [1898] AC 1; see *Clerk and Lindsell on Torts* (1989 16th ed.),
Chap. 15, paras 15-20, n. 45 (and Chapter 1 above).

177. See Wedderburn, 'The Social Charter in Britain – Labour Law and Labour
Courts?' (1991) 54 MLR 1, (Chapter 11 below).

178. *American Cyanamid Co.* v. *Ethicon Ltd* [1975] AC 396, HL; on the
interlocutory injunction generally and the difficulty of limiting discretionary
remedies by legislation, and on contempt of court in relation to this, see
Wedderburn, 'The Injunction and the Sovereignty of Parliament' (1989) 23 *Law
Teacher* No. 1, 4 (Chapter 7 below).

179. In *Barretts and Baird (Wholesale) Ltd* v. *IPCS* [1987] IRLR 3 (in these
proceedings a different judge later discharged the injunction because there was not
even an arguable case for the plaintiff).

180. *Midland Bank* v. *NUS*, 28 April 1988; see for two invaluable discussions, S.
Auerbach 'Injunction Procedure for the Seafarers' Dispute' (1988) 17 ILJ 227, 231,
and G. Lightman 'A Trade Union in Chains' (1987) *Current Legal Problems* 25
(who exposes the new dimensions created in 'contempt of court' during the miners'
strike litigation). [See now p. 197 above, Note A.]

181. *London Underground* v. *NUR* [1989] IRLR 341, 342, Simon Browne J. On
injunction procedure and creeping extensions of criminalisation, see Wedderburn,
'The Injunction and the Sovereignty of Parliament', op. cit. (1989) 23 Law Teacher
4, 34-6 (Chapter 7 above). The United States Supreme Court has shown a
determination to retain the lines of distinction between criminal and civil contempt:
Hicks ex. rel. Feiock v. *Feiock* 108 S. Ct. 1423 (1988).

182. In the dock strike of 1989 the legal proceedings exhausted the period of four
weeks allowed for a strike after the ballot, forcing the union to ballot its members
again. The Employment Act 1990, s. 8, recognised this problem by permitting the
court to extend the period for a short period when litigation has led to an injunction
being granted but later discharged.

183. See the Irish Industrial Relations Act 1990, respectively ss. 9, 13, 8 and 14-17.

184. Industrial Relations Act 1990, s. 19(1) and (2). These provisions do not apply
to entering or damaging 'the property of another' or action likely to cause death or
personal injury: s. 19(4). *Quaere* whether 'property' is limited to real property. If
not, the employer might always be able to use this exception. Further, the employer
will presumably try to obtain his injunction before the process of the ballot is
completed; or perhaps persuade a third party (possibly a compliant union member)
to make an *ex parte* application.

185. See M. Weiss, *Labour Law and Industrial Relations in the Federal Republic of
Germany* (1987), pp. 132-9, 141-3.

186. Cass. 24 January 1981, 568/81. Such decisions 'exceed the boundaries of the
judicial function', not least by dealing with hypothetical future situations: G.
Giugni, *Diritto sindacale*, op. cit., n. 43, pp. 250-1, who also doubts the propriety
of interlocutory injunctions under art. 700 Codice Civile because they intervene 'in
the course of the industrial conflict' and implicitly authorise the employer to use
disciplinary sanctions against the workers.

187. Arts. 808, 809, 812 of the new Code de Procedure Civile; G. Couchez,

Procédure Civile (1986 4th ed.), pp. 35-51. See Wedderburn (1991) 54 MLR at pp. 29-30 (Chapter 12 below). On judicial creativity in labour law, see the Annotation to Soc. 13 December 1988, *Sté Bidermann c. Comité Central d'Enterprise*, in (1991) 9 Int. L.L.R. 580: 'Are there any longer lawyers who consider that judges do not create law?'.

188. Cass. (Ass. plén.) 4 July 1986; see J-E. Ray 1988 D. 477; G. Lyon-Caen, Dr. Soc. 1986, 745; and the reassertion of the traditional rule by the Paris Court of Appeal, 27 January 1988, D. 1988 Jur. 351, (1989) 8 Int. Lab Law. R. 400; and A. Jeammaud and M-C. Rondeau-Rivier, 'Vers une nouvelle géométrie de l'intervention judiciaire' D. 1988, 299.

189. *Air Inter* TGI d'Evry, 20 December 1989 (strike called at time of heaviest holiday traffic), Dr. Ouvr, 1989, 280.

190. Soc. 21 June 1984, Dr. Soc. 1985, 19, J. Savatier; *Syndicat CFDT c. S.A. Auto. Peugeot*, TGI Mulhouse, 9 October 1989 (unconditional order to evacuate factory obtained *ex parte* and upheld; illegal occupation a sufficient 'trouble manifestement illicite'; but a state conciliator had been appointed).

191. The *Peugeot* decision, TGI Mulhouse 9 October 1989, cit. n. 190, is one of many in which, when the names of occupying workers are not known, courts have permitted orders to be made *ex parte*, sometimes against unnamed defendants; see too *Ferodo* Soc. 17 May 1977; and Soc. 21 June 1984; J-C. Javillier, *Manuel: Droit du Travail* (1990 3rd ed.), pp. 408-9. Compare the developments in the English courts: S. Auerbach, 'Legal Restraint of Picketing; New Trends, New Tensions' (1987) 16 ILJ 227.

192. For a strong use of these powers under the new *Code de Procedure*, see *Sections syndicales CFDT (etc) de RVI Annonay c. Rénault* TGI Privas, 13 October 1989; but the court must not compel the employer to negotiate about agreements beyond his legal duty: TGI Paris 2 October 1989, ibid. Dr. Soc. 1990, 173. See A. Jeammaud and M. Le Friant, 'La Grève, le Juge et la Négociation' Dr. Soc. 1990, 167, 176; but compare for a different approach favouring a wider liability, B. Teyssié, Dr. Soc. 1988, 562, 569-71.

193. G. Lyon-Caen and J. Pélissier, *Droit du Travail* (15th ed. 1990), pp. 1045-6.

194. G. Couchez, *Procédure Civile* (4th ed. 1986), pp. 175, 157, 215-6. For a useful outline on *astreinte*, see D. Harris and D. Tallon, *Contract Law Today, Anglo-French Comparisons* (1989), pp. 268-70.

195. See the accounts in Wedderburn, *The Worker and the Law* (3rd ed. 1986), pp. 705-48; and 'The Injunction and the Sovereignty of Parliament' (1989) Law Teacher 4, 22-31 (Chapter 7 above, pp. 174-86).

196. See U. Jacobsson and J. Jacob (eds.), *Trends in the Enforcement of Non-Money Order Judgments and Orders* (1988). On increasing criminalisation, see too Wedderburn (1991) 54 MLR 1, 24-5, notes 122-129, (Chapter 11 below).

197. On the British law in the public sector, see now S. Fredman and G. Morris, *The State as Employer* (1989), especially Chaps 3 and 10. See the seminal study by B. Hepple and P. O'Higgins, *Public Employee Trade Unionism in the UK; the Legal Framework* (1971). See too the useful Symposium on strikes and essential services: (1988) 39 Giorn. dir. di lav. e di rel. ind. T. Blanke 493 (Germany), A. Lyon-Caen 515 (France), R. Simpson 527 (Britain), F. Valdes dal Re 551 (Spain).

198. M. Rusciano 'L'Unificazione normativa del lavoro pubblico e del lavoro privato' (1989) 42 Giorn. di dir. del lav. e di rel. ind. 143, 147-9. Administrative lawyers in Italy see labour law as having made public law recognise social facts, not least the implications of public sector union organisation: A. Battigliani (1990) 45 Giorn. di dir. del lav. e di rel. ind. 39.

199. M. Weiss, *Labour Law and Industrial Relations in the Federal Republic of Germany*, op. cit., pp. 23, 139-40, and see 143 (such civil servants may lawfully be used as blacklegs to break the strike of other workers, e.g. postal workers). Attempts have been made to justify this on the ground that the state as employer cannot lock out.

200. See H. Edwards, R.T. Clark, C. Craver, *Labor Relations in the Public Sector*

(3rd ed. 1986) and Supp. 1989, pp. 532-632; W. Gould, *A Primer on American Labor Law* (1982), Chap. 10. There is no common law right to strike and none has been created for the public employee by the Constitution: *Utd Fedn of Postal Clerks* v. *Blount* 325 F. Supp. 879, aff'd, 404 U.S. 802 (1972). The crime is enacted by 5 USC sec. 7311(3) and 18 USC sec. 1918. Every Federal employee must take an oath swearing not to strike (5 USC sec. 3333) and Executive Order 11491 disallows any unions that 'assert the right to strike against the government of the United States' (ss. 2, 19).

201. *Norwalk Teachers Assocn.* v. *Board of Education* 83 A. 2d. 482, 487 (1951). For an earlier review of United States law in the context of five European countries, see B. Aaron and K. Wedderburn (eds.), *Industrial Conflict: A Comparative Legal Survey* (1972), Chap. 6 (Wedderburn) 'Industrial Action, the State and the Public Interest'.

202. *Government Employee Relations Reporter* (3 August 1981); C. Olson 'Right to Strike in the Public Sector' (1982) *Labor* 494; their union, PATCO, was broken by decertification and its members banned indefinitely from Federal employment: *Wagner* v. *Office of Personnel Management* 783 F. 2d. 1042 (Fed. Cir.) *cert. den.* 106 U.S. 3276 (1986).

203. *Council of Civil Service Unions* v. *Minister for the Civil Service* [1984] 1 WLR 1174, HL; *R.* v. *CSAB ex parte Bruce* [1988] ICR 649 (CA on other grounds [1989] ICR 171); and see *McLaren* v. *Home Office.* [1990] IRLR 338, CA.

204. Employment Act 1988, s. 30.

205. See ss. 99, 138 Employment Protection (Consolidation) Act 1978, including rights to complain of unfair dismissal but excluding rights to a redundancy payment, because the legislation 'is really no more than a minor counterpart in the private sector for provisions long since current in the public sector': P. Davies and M. Freedland, *Labour Law: Text and Materials* (1984 2nd ed.), p. 567.

206. Teachers' Pay and Conditions Act 1987. The German *Beamter* are excluded from the normal law of collective bargaining and their terms of work are governed by 'the Federal legislator' and the administrative courts (M. Weiss, op. cit., n. 40, p. 23, though negotiation does in fact take place).

207. See on the Emergency Powers Act 1920, G. Morris, Chap. 3, *Strikes in Essential Services* (1986).

208. See on the former K. Jeffery and P. Hennessy, *States of Emergency* (1983); S. McCabe and, on the latter, P. Wallington, *The Police, Public Order and Civil Liberties* (1988).

209. Law no. 93 of 29 March 1983; G. Pera, op. cit. n. 56, pp. 274ff.; a presidential decree puts the agreements into formal legal effect. There is 'considerable perplexity' about how the government falls under a duty to enact in the decree just the same terms as in the agreement: G. Giugni, *Diritto sindacale* (1988 7th ed.) pp. 206-7; but it is said that some amendment to the form of the agreed terms is possible: F. Carinci, R. de Luca Tamajo, P. Tosi, T. Treu, *Diritto sindacale* (2nd ed. 1987), p. 329.

210. See for example, S. Fredman and G. Morris, 'The State as Employer: Is it Unique?' (1990) 19 ILJ 142, and (1991) 107 LQR 298.

211. See the parallel difficulties on employee participation in nationalised industries privatised in France: G. Lyon-Caen and J. Pélissier, op. cit. (1990 15th ed.), pp. 913-8.

212. See, for instance, the convincing answers given to H. Wellington and R. Winter 'Structuring Collective Bargaining in Public Employment' 79 Yale L.J. 822 (1970), by J. Burton and C. Krider, 'The Role and Consequences of Strikes by Public Employees' 79 Yale L.J. 418, 422-32 (1970). Many American municipalities have adopted laws which permit bargaining but not strikes, for example the 'Taylor Law' in New York in 1967; so too, the Federal Executive Order 11491, 1969.

213. Cons. d'Et. 7 juillet 1950; G. Lyon-Caen and J. Pélissier, op. cit., n. 37, 1071-82. Previously, the right to strike had been denied to public servants: Cons. d'Et. 22 octobre 1937.

214. On the details, see B. Aaron and K. Wedderburn, *Industrial Conflict: A Comparative Legal Survey*, op. cit., n. 201, pp. 373-5.
215. See the summary in J-C. Javillier, *Manuel: Droit du Travail* (1990 3rd ed.), pp. 404, 418-9 (a legislative intervention would not be out of place since different types of calculation now govern three types of public employee). A complex compromise was also struck in Italy in Law 312 of 11 July 1980: G. Giugni, op. cit., n. 43, 221-5 (allowing for larger deductions where a short strike has longer effects). The extensive litigation and argument about deductions from pay testifies to the importance of short-term industrial action in these public sectors.
216. See *Syndicat National des Fonctionnaires* Cons. d'Et. 16 December 1966 (administrative judges ensure that measures are limited to what is required as minimum service). Public authorities may hire temporary workers for the minimum service (Cons d'Et. 18 January 1980; postal service) – which the employer may not do under 'private' labour law: Code du Travail art. L.124-2-2.
217. Corte cost. 123/62, 28 December 1962, one of a line of cases rendering unconstitutional relevant parts of the fascist Penal Code; so too, 222/76, 3 August 1976 (statutory level of service essential to running psychiatric hospital precluded strike). Some remaining articles of the Code (especially art. 330, making collective abandonment of public service a crime) have been repealed by Law no. 146, 12 June 1990, art. 11, see below n. 235.
218. In Britain: Police Act 1964, especially s. 53(1) (incitement to disaffection); but see the threat made in 1988: S. Fredman and G. Morris, *The State as Employer* (1989), p. 400; and on workers in the nuclear industry, see R. Lewis (1978) 7 ILJ 1.
219. Laws of 27 December 1947 and 28 September 1948 (police); 13 July 1972 (armed services); 2 July 1964 and 31 December 1984 (air traffic controllers); and 7 August 1974, 29 July 1979, and 31 December 1984 (radio-television).
220. 382/78 of 11 July 1978, art. 8 (military forces); art. 1105 Navigation Code; Law 121/81 of 1 April 1981 (police); and Law 242/80 23 May 1980 (air controllers); and implicitly for nuclear workers in Decree 185 of 13 February 1964.
221. Law 11 July 1938 and Ordonnance 6 January 1959 (in recent years the *réquisition* appears to have been used much less frequently than the *precettazione* in Italy, below n. 224.
222. Order 1305 of 1940 making strikes in trade disputes into crimes was repealed in 1951 after prosecutions (both of which failed) against unofficial strikers in the docks and the gas industry: see O. Kahn-Freund in M. Ginsberg (ed.), *Law and Opinion in England in the Twentieth Century* (1959) p. 256.
223. See G. Lyon-Caen and J. Pélissier, op. cit., n. 37 (1990, 15th ed.), pp. 1078-9.
224. Corte cost. no. 4, 12 January 1977; see G. Giugni op. cit. n. 43, 234-5; see too, for a demand from radical authors for, not the abolition, but the democratisation of the *precettazione*: G. Ghezzi and U. Romagnoli, *Diritto sindacale* (1987 2nd ed.), p. 262.
225. G. Giugni, *Diritto Sindacale* op. cit., p. 235; for a criticism see, G. Pera, *Diritto del lavoro* (1988 3rd ed.), pp. 247-9.
226. K. Ewing (in a review of Fredman and Morris, op. cit.) (1990) 19 ILJ 270: 'How long will it take the ambulance staff to recover money lost during a dispute which might well have been settled by arbitration?' For such arbitration to avail it must, of course, have the co-operation of the government of the day, which was not the case in the ambulance dispute.
227. Folke Schmidt, *Law and Industrial Relations in Sweden*, n. 40, pp. 192-6; S. Edlund and B. Nyström, *Developments in Swedish Labour Law*, op. cit., n. 115, 35. On the current debate on the 'Swedish model', see G. Rehn and R. Meidner in (1990) 195 EIRR 11.
228. See on the government's proposals (1990) 194 EIRR 10, and on damages above n. 119; and on the eventual austerity package: (1990) 197 EIRR 9.
229. See M. Rodriguez-Piñero in *Les Transformations du Droit du Travail; Etudes Offertes à Gérard Lyon-Caen* (1989 Dalloz), pp. 114-120.

230. F. Valdes dal Re 'Diritto di sciopero e servizi essenziali della communità in Spagna' (1988) 39 Giorn. di dir. del lav. e di rel. ind. 551, 558-64 (criticising the Constitutional Court for permitting excessive delegation of the powers on essential services, 571).

231. T.C. 17 July 1981, n. 26/81 (Constitutional Court); T.C. 5 May 1986 n. 53/86; and T.C. 3 February 1989, n. 27/89, *La Ley (Relaciones Laborales)* 1989 I, 680 (measure going too far on essential services unconstitutional as suppressing the right to strike). But compare the remarkable recent Bill in Greece, coming into effect in 1991, which extends the range of 'essential services' and transfers to management the right to designate the minimum service and the workers who must provide it, together with the right to vary these designations during the strike: see (1991) 204 EIRR 20. These rights were previously held by the union, subject to arbitration in case of dispute. The same Act will extend the employer's power to dismiss employees participating in any unlawful strike and even in a lawful strike if there is 'intimidation' of non-strikers interfering with their right to work.

232. EC Commission *Action Programme Relating to the Implementation of the Community Charter of Basic Social Rights for Workers* (Com (89) 568, 27 November 1989) Part II, p. 30.

233. Art. 11, Law 93/1983, 29 March 1983; G. Giugni op. cit. n. 43, 236. For a list of the codes based on 'autoregolamentazione' in 1986, see ibid., pp. 387-97: they included schools, central and local government, health service, vets, and transport, with self-imposed limitations about strike notices, length and form of stoppages and maintenance of minimum service. This tendency towards negotiation of new 'rules of the game' is found, too, in collective agreements and 'Protocols' in the private and public-commercial sectors in the 1980s: ibid., pp. 28-9 and Appendix II. It was an important precursor of the Law of 1990, above, pp. 302-4, 320-5.

234. F. Carinci *et al.*, op. cit., n. 69, 404-11; P. Roma 13 June 1987, F.I., I 2227. See on these developments, the analysis by S. Sciarra, 'Il conflitto fra gruppi nei servizi pubblici essenziali' 1988 Lav. Dir. 667.

235. In art. 1(2) including services in public health, urban refuse, energy, administration of justice, transport by rail, air and sea (to the islands), social security, certain bank services, public schools and universities, telecommunications and radio-television services as well as the environment, cultural heritage, and customs' control of animals. Services such as food production are not included; one might think that Constitutional protection of personal health and safety would lead to their inclusion; but they are not of course 'public' services.

236. L. Mariucci 'La legge sullo sciopero nei servizi pubblici essenziali' (1990) Lavoro e Diritto 533. See for a more critical approach to the earlier Bills of 1988, G. Garofalo 'Sulla titolarità del diritto di sciopero' (1988) 39 Giorn. di dir. del lav. e di rel. ind. 573 (there may be infringements of equality among unions under art. 39 or art. 40; but the right to strike as such is not infringed by such measures; it is not unlimited: 'no one has ever contended .... that it would be legitimate for a doctor on strike not to minister to an injured casualty', 575).

237. Industrial Relations Act 1990, ss. 16(2)(5), 17(1).

238. G. Mariucci, *Le Fonti del Diritto del Lavoro* (1989), pp. 47-57; G. Giugni, op. cit., n. 43, pp. 22-7.

239. O. Kahn-Freund, *Labour Relations; Heritage and Adjustment* (1979), p. 78.

240. Kerr and Whyte, op. cit., n. 45, pp. 246-8. It is not yet definitely ascertained that the Constitution may be invoked in support of industrial action; but it is established that the Constitution 'imposes limitations' upon it: 247.

241. *Talbot (Ireland) Ltd* v. *Merrigan, Irish Times*, 11 April 1981; see Kerr and Whyte, op. cit., 247.

242. M. Redmond, *Dismissal Law* (1982), p. 2, n. 43.

243. See *Associated British Ports* v. *TGWU* [1989] IRLR 305 CA (reversed on other grounds, [1989] 1 WLR 939, HL).

244. See on labour courts, 'The Social Charter in Britain – Labour Law and Labour Courts?' (1991) 54 MLR 1 (Chapter 11 below).

245. Industrial Relations Act 1990, ss. 24-43 (Ireland).

246. See Wedderburn 'Freedom of Association or Right to Organise?' (1987) 18 Ind. Rel. Jo. 244 (Chapter 8 above).

247. H.J. Laski, *Trade Unions in the New Society* (1950), p. 126, a 'half-conscious belief' of the courts and most English lawyers.

248. See O. Kahn-Freund in *The System of Industrial Relations in Great Britain* (1954, eds. A Flanders and H. Clegg), pp. 43-5, the classic statement of *prescriptive* 'abstentionism', which finds more muted expression in his later works; see too, his 'Labour Law', *Law and Opinion in England in the Twentieth Century* (ed. M. Ginsberg, 1959); R. Lewis, 'Kahn-Freund and Labour Law; An Outline Critique' (1979) 8 ILJ 197.

249. U. Mückenberger and S. Deakin, 'From Deregulation to a European Floor of Rights' (1989) ZIAS 153, 163.

250. *In Place of Strife*, (1969, Cmnd 3888), p. 25, adding (adumbrating Donovan): 'Reform of collective bargaining will remove many of these causes of strikes.'

251. See Wedderburn, 'Labour Law Now – A Hold and a Nudge' (1984) 13 ILJ 73-77.

252. R. Ben Israel, *International Labour Standards; The Case of Freedom to Strike* (1988), Part II.

253. See Lord Denning MR, *Morgan* v. *Fry* [1968] 2 QB 710, 727-8, CA. On the literature on a right to strike in Britain, see (1991) 54 MLR notes 85-132 (below in Chapter 11). On Ireland: see A. Kerr and G. Whyte, *Irish Trade Union Law* (1985), pp. 230-48.

254. See *Manalaysay* v. *The 'Oriental Victory'* [1978] 1 FC 440, 446. Compare *Universe Tankships Inc. of Monrovia* v. *ITWF* [1983] 1 AC 366, HL; Wedderburn (1982) 45 MLR 556; *Dimskal Shipping* v. *ITWF* (no. 2) [1990] ICR 694 CA.

255. See the discussion in Wedderburn (1991) 54 MLR 1 (Chapter 11 below).

256. Though there are undoubtedly infelicities in it, the writer stands by the general argument of 'The New Politics of Labour Law' (Durham University Lecture, 1983), Chapter 4 of this volume.

257. See J. Clark and Wedderburn in Wedderburn, R. Lewis and J. Clark (eds), *Labour Law and Industrial Relations* (1983), pp. 175-8.

258. See Wedderburn and S. Sciarra, 'Collective Bargaining as Agreement and as Law: Neo-Contractualist Tendencies and Neo-Corporative Tendencies' in A. Pizzorusso (ed.), *Law in the Making* (1988), pp. 186-237.

259. See for example, K. Ewing, 'Trade Union Recognition – A Framework for Discussion' (1990) 19 ILJ 209.

260. In Italy the decision not to adopt such a general duty was a conscious one in 1970 (see Wedderburn, 'The Italian Workers' Statute' (1990) 19 ILJ 1 (Chapter 9 above, especially n. 53) and S. Sciarra, *Contratto collettivo e contrattazione in azienda* (1984) pp. 84 ff. on the legal pressures on the employer to negotiate). The German Federal Labour Court has recently had occasion to reassert that there is no duty to bargain in its jurisdiction: 1 AZR 142/88 14 February 1989, NZA 1989, 601; (1991) 9 Int. L.L.R. 475: the union can 'take conflict measures' in face of a refusal to bargain; but the constitutional guarantees (art. 9.3) would be infringed if the employer rejected the union and 'actively impeded its activities as an organisation'. In France, the *lois Auroux* introduced a duty to negotiate in 1982 (now Code du Travail art. L. 132-27) but the courts appear to be giving employers a discretion as to the level at which it is carried out: Crim. 30 January 1989, *Dunkirk CFDT c. Wright* (1991) Int. L.L.R. 471.

261. See Wedderburn, 'The European Community and Workers' Rights – Fact or Fake in 1992?' (Moran Memorial Lecture, Trinity College Dublin, 6 December 1990, forthcoming in (1991) Univ. Dublin LJ1. For a similar view in a different system: S. Sciarra, *Notizario giuridico* 1990 no. 8, 28 ('freedom to bargain, beyond being part of trade union freedom [*libertà sindacale*], also becomes, in the modern era of labour law, a further specification of that absolute value', 32).

262. See Wedderburn, *The Social Charter, European Company and Employment Rights* (1990 Institute of Employment Rights); and 'The Social Charter in Britain – Labour Law and Labour Courts?' (1991) 54 MLR 1 (Chapter 11 below).

263. On the relationship between different understandings of 'freedom of association' and 'social rights' in the Community, see the useful, if sometimes disturbing, discussion by S. Sciarra 'Regulating European Unions: An Issue for 1992' (1990) 11 Comp. Lab. Law Jo. 141.

NOTE A. On nn. 13-18 and 106 above: The ILO Governing Body adopted on 27 February 1991, the 277th Report of the Freedom of Association Committee, including Case No. 1540, *National Union of Seamen* v. *United Kingdom* (where some 2,000 seamen on strike were dismissed). The Committee found that British law in the Employment Protection (Consolidation) Act 1978 (as amended in 1982) and, still more, in the Employment Act 1990, giving the employer power to dismiss workers in the course or at the conclusion of a strike or other industrial action, contravened the elementary principles of freedom of association in Convention No. 87, 1948. It rejected the UK government's argument that the Convention meant that an employer was permitted to dismiss workers during the strike, but not after it.

NOTE B. On nn. 88-96 and 142 above: The Cour de Cassation reaffirmed its relaxation of the *in solidum* principle on damages for unlawful acts in industrial conflict, holding that the requirement of causality makes an individual worker liable only for damage that can be ascribed to his or her unlawful acts: *Robin c. Sté. Les Papeteries de Maudit* Soc. 30 January 1991. The application of joint and several liability is therefore now uncertain. On the other hand, the principle which requires a wrongful act to be done by an 'organ' before the union is liable, and that the union delegate in the enterprise is not the agent of the union, has been strictly maintained: *Sté. Kaolins du Finistère* Soc. 19 December 1990. See for a more detailed comparison with British law, Wedderburn 'Vicarious Liability and *Responsabilité Civile* in Strikes: Comparative Notes' (1991) 20 ILJ (September).

11

The Social Charter in Britain: Labour Law – and Labour Courts?

> Then Mrs Melrose Ape stood up to speak. A hush fell in the ballroom beginning at the back and spreading among the gilt chairs ... 'Brothers and sisters,' she said in a hoarse, stirring voice ... (It was one of her favourite openings.) 'Just you look at yourselves,' she said. Magically, self-doubt began to spread in the audience ... But suddenly on that silence vibrant with self-accusation broke the organ voice of England, the hunting-cry of the *ancien régime*. Lady Circumference gave a resounding snort of disapproval: 'What a damned impudent woman,' she said.[1]

When Lord Chorley, in whose honour this paper is given, held the Cassel Chair it was, of course, still called the Chair of Commercial and Industrial law. No apology is needed then for its theme – that it is time for British labour law to take a good look at itself, to examine its own structure.

A premature invitation to self-analysis, Freud tells us, risks a response of 'resistance, rejection and indignation'.[2] One must 'wait for the right moment at which you can communicate your interpretation to the patient with some prospect of success' to avoid, as it were, receiving a Circumference response. But, whatever the risks, it is no longer premature to invite analysis, not of the transient policies of particular governments past, present or future, but of the structure of British labour law: for a century almost unchanged, but now subject to pressures for change from the impending single market in Western – perhaps Eastern – Europe, from comparisons with other systems that are inevitable and insistent in an internationalised economy and from its own domestic contradictions.

A revised version of the nineteenth Chorley Lecture delivered on 6 June 1990 at the London School of Economics and Political Science. First published in (1991) 54 Modern Law Review 1.

It is the comparative dimension which has often been lacking from our discussion, by which I mean not the foolish search for institutions to import from elsewhere but the stretching of the imagination and of the agenda by inquiry into unfamiliar legal treatments of familiar social problems and in so doing to follow the argument wherever it leads. Even the Donovan Commission's Report in 1968 was sparing in such inquiry, despite the presence of Otto Kahn-Freund,[3] in contrast to the comparative inquiries which have preceded major labour law reforms elsewhere.[4] Even when our debates have had parallel discussions in France, as when the redefinition of 'trade dispute', that central pillar of our labour law, coincided with the novel proposal there of an 'immunity' to exclude civil responsibility for acts which were no more than a 'normal exercise of the right to strike', scarcely a word of comparative inquiry crossed the Channel, in either direction.[5]

Now the European Community's Social Charter of Fundamental Rights has appeared at a moment when the transnational economy puts national laws in a new frame.[6] Signed by only eleven of the twelve member states and then merely as a solemn declaration of principles, it has nevertheless already become an important reference point for labour law and even for collective bargaining.[7] Parts of it have been selected by the Commission in its Action Programme for proposed enactment as binding Community law by 1993.[8] This will inevitably affect the style, substance and structure of our labour law. The purpose of what follows is to draw together some threads about that structure; about the direction of Community law; about our industrial relations and trade union law, and finally about 'labour courts', which is where we may find resistance to be deepest.

Origins and Sources of Labour Laws

British labour law still bears the three leading characteristics which it had acquired by 1875, when like other European systems, in parallel but not contemporaneously, it passed through the repeal of repressive penal laws on unions and in employment to elementary freedoms to combine collectively. Those three features may be said to be, broadly, first a formal 'freedom of contract' in defining the employment relationship and most of its consequences (that 'figment of the law'[9] which became the lawyer's modern cloak for subordination); second, a slender cushion of legislative protections (starting with the Factories Acts and Factory Inspectorate, the great contributions to the 'method of legal enactment' promoted by Tory reformers and unions alike); third, basic liberties for those whose need was to organise in industrial combination (those of whom Kahn-Freund said: 'On the labour side, all power is collective power'[10]) common in function with the trade union rights secured in other democracies but radically different in form in the attempt to protect freedom of association, not as in most other countries by positive rights, but in a negative way by the 'immunities' from some – certainly not all – common law liabilities.[11]

The emphasis of this legal structure – the breadth of the freedom of contract accorded to the parties to the employment relationship, the limited nature of regulatory protection once the nineteenth century legislation on safety and on the hours of women and young workers was in place, and the negative or 'privileged' character of the immunities governing collective freedoms – makes it look peculiar to those from other systems. By itself, that is no reason to change it. For decades it did work, within the social consensus or the imposed balance of social power of the time. But the question of change assumes a new insistence today, not least through questions posed by new comparisons. Not only does collective labour law elsewhere in Western Europe tend to be couched in positive rights and duties, the building blocks of employment law are there differently regulated. There the law has tended from the outset to circumscribe the types of employment relationship available, even if today they can more readily be reshaped by collective bargaining.

Take the Italian Civil Code. It recognised three types of employee: workers, white-collar staff, and managers. Other types of contract are possible, though the Code defines freedom of contract outside the recognised forms of contract as accords designed to protect 'meritorious interests' and, in modern interpretation, is held to subject the individual employment contract to the terms of collective agreements more favourable to the worker.[12] But social and economic change demanded greater flexibility. This flexibility was achieved, not by abolishing the definitions and leaving employment relations to the unguided results of so-called 'contract', but by legislation which in 1985 introduced into the Code a fourth recognised category – the intermediate grades (*i quadri intermedi*: roughly, lower management and technical staff). But, having invented the new category, it then referred its precise application and meaning back to collective bargaining.[13] Autonomous collective bargaining is as strong in Italy as in Britain; but its comprehension requires a firmer grasp of the legal building blocks.

Similarly, the law in such jurisdictions sets a wider floor of conditions at work. In ten of the twelve Community states, for instance, legislation limits maximum hours of work; nine have general legislation limiting overtime and night work.[14] The Commission's Action Programme proposes binding regulation on maximum working hours throughout the Community, to implement the Charter's aim of a right to a 'weekly rest period' and, with few exceptions, an end to night work by the young.[15] The place for regulation in the Community labour market is at once raised on any comparative agenda. For such laws do not necessarily restrict effective and autonomous bargaining. German unions are slightly ahead of their counterpart engineering unions in Britain in their industrial campaigns for a 35 hour week; and recently in France, the new laws regulating temporary work were used as the floor of a comprehensive national agreement between unions and employers on the subject.[16] Even a nodding acquaintance with Italian practice, especially in the last two decades, confirms the 'intense inter-relationship between legislative regulation and diverse manifestations of collective autonomous action' to the point where 'contractual norms come to be conceived as a natural extension of legislation, as one element integrated into a single phenomenon.'[17] In truth, a glance abroad suggests that the relationship between legal intervention and collective bargaining is not always that of crudely opposed magnetic poles, as is often assumed in Britain.[18]

The modern British assumption has been that the way to regulate working hours is not legal regulation but collective bargaining. True, from the nineteenth century on we limited the working hours of women and of young workers by law in an increasing range of workplaces;[19] and the regulation of men's hours too was a trade union objective until relatively recently. As late as 1893, legislation gave to the Board of Trade powers to regulate the hours of railwaymen, but it was the same legislation which helped the Amalgamated Society of Railway Servants, virtually destroyed in its fight for recognition in 1890, to increase its membership by 90 per cent in the next six years.[20] This precedent, suggesting that such statutory intervention is consistent with increased union strength and collective bargaining was to be overlooked in coming decades. But by 1920 Britain felt unable to ratify the first ILO Convention for a legal 48-hour week which it had helped to promote;[21] the line was, with very few exceptions, drawn short of legislation on the working hours of adult men. Legal control was thought proper only for the working hours of women or young workers. Today the massive deregulation in the Employment Act 1989 has withdrawn protection even from these 'exceptional' cases.

On the other hand, we take it for granted today – employers, unions and state alike – that legislation should be the primary method to protect other conditions at work. Above all, safety and accident prevention at work are dealt with in that way, by all legal means available: criminal and civil sanctions, powers for inspectorates, administrative machinery under the Health and Safety Commission, and rights for workers' safety representatives[22] – though as yet with no clear right for workers to stop work when they reasonably apprehend danger at work.[23] The Commission's proposal for ten new Community Directives on safety at work created less anxiety in Whitehall than the rest of the Action Programme, for this is regarded there as a field where, unlike other working conditions, laws must regulate them. Following Hayek, even labour lawyers of the Chicago school today differ from Nassau Senior by embracing the propriety of this particular legal intervention in the market.[24] In this area the programme of the Thatcher government may justly claim to be a continuation of traditional policy. At any rate, acceptance of regulation on safety, but not on maximum working hours (save for specially vulnerable groups of workers) became part of 'voluntarism'. But it may owe as much to history as to logic. To most labour law systems in Western Europe – and now to the Charter and the Action Programme – history has bequeathed wider boundaries for a legally regulated floor in the employment relationship,[25] boundaries arguably more suited to today's labour market.[26]

Labour Law Systems in the Community

This is not the only way the British structure stands out from the others, albeit they are also highly diverse *inter se*. There are the well-known peculiarities in the law on industrial relations. The basis of Kahn-Freund's analysis in 1954 and 1959 of an 'abstention of the law' from British industrial relations was (it is often forgotten) the view that British social structure was 'exceptionally stable'.[27] But the period in which the organic structure of our labour law was built, the 50 years before 1920, was not a period of uniform stability; far from it – the military in Trafalgar Square in 1886, the great lock-out of 1897, in 1907 a threat of chaos on the railways, in 1913 justified fears of a revolution, 'a time of remorselessly rising tension, of impending doom'.[28] What we find in that formative period is not a special stability, but a unique coincidence of social factors which sired a peculiar legal structure. Like other European systems, our employment relationships had to be torn free from criminal sanction and become the subject of civil obligation in the guise of 'contract' – a contract, as Fox puts it, into which there were 'carried over the personal status relations characteristic of the master-servant model'.[29] The common law tradition continued to import the master's prerogatives, parallel to the subordination in other jurisdictions which characterised 'the new status of the worker whose freedom of contract is in effect only a formality'[30] – an approach still central to the British courts' attitude to employment legislation.[31]

So too, in the two decades before 1890 all comparable European systems experienced the successful struggle for the bare legalisation of trade unions. But the British system had already struck out on a path of its own.[32] Britain was set apart in many ways: it had no written constitution; there was, among the ruled as among the rulers, a sharp addiction to the ideology of *laissez faire*. But the crucial difference for labour law was the fact that 'on the Continent unionism developed simultaneously with the mass *political* labour movement and its parties.'[33] The decisive factor was that here 'trade union organisations came first and the political movement much later, on the Continent the sequence was the reverse.'[34] An industrial movement emerged here, unaccompanied by working-class political parties, with demands (to which parliament in part acceded, significantly before the completion of adult male franchise) not so much for rights as for a protected space. If we watch that space carefully, we see it filled not by rights of association, but by Disraeli's immunities against criminal liabilities and then the immunities against specified civil liabilities in 1906, the very year late in the process when such a political party was finally born, after the foundations of our labour law were laid.[35]

That is why we have 'immunities' in trade union law, not rights. They were the outcome of specific social relations. It was useful to rationalise them, as Kahn-Freund did brilliantly, as 'collective *laissez faire*' – while they worked, while they were sustained by the accepted balance of power and of social values. One may now – perhaps one now should – ask whether this is a sufficient reason to keep them.

This somewhat idealised, but revealing, historical vignette reminds us that the language of a labour law system can be learned only from its social history, above all the history of its labour movement. Without a smattering of that vocabulary comparative conversation is impossible. The fact that the right to strike in the Federal Republic of Germany and in Sweden is 'organic', that is, vests in the organisation or trade union alone, is inexplicable without a grasp of the centralised development of their unitary unions;[36] while in France and Italy, understanding the history of labour movements divided by ideological and religious pluralism is crucial to a grasp of the 'individualist' principle, that the right to strike is the property, not of the union, but of the individual worker.[37] To the Italian lawyer it is a fundamental verity, to the German a gross error, to hold that: 'the right to strike vests not in the union or any other association, but in the individual worker as such, even though this legal right is bound to be exercised in a dimension that is necessarily collective.'[38]

Of course, such diverse systems may also share principles not shared by the common law. To take an important example, all four of those systems agree that a legitimate exercise of the 'right to strike' (as it is differently understood in each, both in scope and character) entails not the breach, still less the termination, of the workers' employment contracts, but only a suspension of them until the conflict is ended, temporarily excusing the employer and the striking employees from performance. The point about breach of contract tends to be dealt with curtly, for example in Italy by the maxim '*qui jure suo utitur, neminem laedit*' (he who exercises a right is not liable to a person thereby damaged).[39] Today it appears to all of those systems to be a central principle – indeed, few principles are more fundamental to the French law than *la grève ne rompt pas le contrat de travail sauf faute lourde imputable au salarié* (a strike does not break the contract of employment unless the employee is guilty of serious misconduct).[40] But it was not always so; even in France the doctrine of suspension was first adumbrated in 1939 and firmly established only in 1950.[41]

Today, however, the French jurist is mystified to hear the English lawyer hold that, while the organisers of industrial action may have an 'immunity' from liability for many economic torts in a trade dispute, the striking employees themselves have no such immunity and are invariably in breach of their contracts unless they give notice to make themselves unemployed; that is, to surrender their jobs as the condition of a lawful strike. As a Lord Justice of Appeal said only recently: 'if [the workers] give notice *terminating* their contracts … a strike would be lawful.'[42] In 1906 Sir Charles Dilke had perceived the central importance of immunity in trade disputes from the tort of inducing breach of contract; but no-one proposed that the breach of contract by workers should itself be cured by the invention of a right to strike.[43] Nor was such a right to strike demanded.

But it would be absurd to think that the history of each labour movement writes its labour law system on tablets of stone. It writes the vocabulary, but other factors change the story, even the grammar: periods of war, new constitutions, social movements, changes in employers' organisation, in technology and in patterns of capital, and in relations of production national and now, above all, international. New doctrines are grafted on, like the suspension of employment contracts in strikes. Legal systems come to cut across the original typologies. So we find that in (organic) Germany and (individualist) France and Spain the Ministry of Labour may 'extend' collective agreements to bind new employers. But no such administrative extension of contractual agreements is permitted in (organic) Sweden or in (individualist) Italy.[44] In Britain weak forms of 'extension' by way of unilateral arbitration existed from 1940 to 1980 but, except in time of war, they were never accepted by employers as natural to the system.[45]

In this general setting, the Action Programme signals a moment of change in proposing new areas for legal regulation. For example, it is proposed there should be greater legal control of working hours – a maximum of eleven hours in 24, at least one rest day in seven, a maximum eight hours' night work in 24 on average in a fortnight, a ban on two consecutive night shifts, limits on overtime by night workers in heavy work, specified breaks in rotating shifts, with further regulation on health assessment and safety especially for night workers and possible exemptions by law or collective agreement provided the workers enjoy compensatory rest periods over a six months period.[46] So too, regulation is proposed, including more formal employment contracts, to protect the so-called 'atypical' or 'precarious' workers who do not enjoy a 'standard employment relationship' – the part-time, seasonal, casual, homeworking, lump-labour, temporary, agency, fixed-term, or 'task' workers, now increasingly all too typical of some segments of the labour market. In 1951 the ratio of part-time to full-time workers in Britain was 1 to 25; by 1989 it was nearly 1 to 4.[47] These workers are overwhelmingly women, many not organised in unions, four-fifths in service industries, the majority not enjoying the 'main employment protection rights', especially protection against unfair dismissal, either through lack of qualifying work periods or by not having 'contracts of employment' at all.[48]

The Commission followed the plan set out in its Action Programme for a Community floor of rights for part-timers, on written contracts, training, equality in occupational pensions and social security and for many terms and conditions of employment to be parallel or proportional to the conditions of full-time workers, with three proposals for Directives in 1990, the fate of which is still uncertain.[49] The important point is that the Action Programme was adamant that there must be a common floor of regulation on 'atypical' work relationships so as to avoid 'problems of social dumping and ... distortions of competition at Community level'; and some of the proposals for implementation of that programme invoke the procedures of the amended Treaty which permit the adoption of Community laws by a majority in the Council of Ministers.[50]

Deregulation and the Common Law

To most other member states such proposals will come as less of a shock. Italian law already gives part-time workers a longer list of employment rights, proportional to those of full-time employees, including rates of pay; the employer must give them priority to full time vacancies, is prodded to negotiate on their hours and jobs with a union, and can require overtime only within the terms of a collective agreement.[51] France, too, requires consultation with the *comité d'enterprise* (works council) on part-time workers, according to them 'the same rights as for full-time workers', proportional salary and the same priority to switch to full time work.[52] A law of 1986, introduced as a measure of 'flexibilisation', permitted the hiring of workers with indeterminate hours, but only within a standard employment contract and under a collective agreement.[53]

The fixed-term contract presents a similar picture. Indeed, in Germany where the law provides a 'positively-regulated and comprehensive paradigm of employment',[54] it was the courts which first refused to recognise the validity of a fixed-term hiring unless the employer gave an 'adequate reason' why it should not be a full-time, open-ended contract, a very different approach to 'freedom of contract' from ours. When the German legislature sought more flexibility in 1985, it relaxed these rules but retained a restriction on the term of the fixed-term contract of eighteen months, sometimes renewable but only once. And French courts have applied strictly the controls adjusted in 1986 over part-time or fixed term contracts, holding for example that a failure to provide the required written contract for a fixed term contract turned it into a contract of indeterminate length.[55]

Of course, political policies seeking to respond to labour market pressures for greater 'flexibility' have varied. At one end of the spectrum, Italian policy has adjusted its level of employment protection rights, which after the Workers' Statute of 1970 had reached perhaps the highest point of any comparable European system, in pursuit of what one of its architects described as 'objectives of social purpose combined with objectives of efficiency'.[56] A measure of deregulation has been achieved by way of social consensus in 'bargained legislation' or 'deregulation by agreement' founded upon 'institutional support for the management of the labour market by consent'.[57] At the other end of the spectrum, there has been no bargaining about the recent deregulation of British employment protection, starting though it did from a lower level, in the quest to remove 'burdens on business' which government policy has claimed to find in our employment laws.[58]

But there is a more important point here than the social and political policies pursued by the different governments. Whatever its political colour, any British administration would find itself starting out from special premises in its legal and social culture. At Westminster the Germany and French laws of 1985 and 1986 have the air, not of deregulation, but of regulation. The nature of those systems is such that, when legislation for 'flexibility' is introduced, the need arises automatically for a *re-regulation* of the developing employment relationships. Where the building blocks are ordained by law – as in Italy, where the very concept of the 'job' or of 'occupational qualification' and the categories of standard employment relationships are described in the Civil Code itself – the legislature cannot allow a bare deregulation to leave the Code void.[59] There must be a new model, a readjustment of interests. But in a common law system, whose colours history has nailed to a wider concept of 'freedom of contract,' deregulation is presented largely as repeal of statutory regulation, as a return to the 'ordinary law of the land.' There may be a re-regulation, but often it is no more than a reoccupation of terrain by the common law. And an overall, readjustment of interests, a re-regulation, is not an item natural to the agenda. That is a separate agenda.

The greater stability of these other labour law systems – it is the British system which has pursued a zig-zag path of contrasting policies since 1970, far more violent than the swings of policy in France, much more volatile than the Italian or German system – is no doubt to be explained largely by more general social causes; but one may venture to think that a contribution has been made by the legal culture itself. But, it is said, the British legal building blocks are, by comparison, infinitely malleable. That is at once the virtue and the bane of the system, a Protean quality which affects both legislature and courts. Examples are ready to hand. In 1988 parliament faced the chaotic legal status of 'trainees' – they may or may not have a contract; they may or may not have a contract 'of employment'; in the absence of special provision, they may fall outside even the laws protecting workers on safety at work.[60] But it did not deregulate their status in a new model (like the 'work-training' contracts in Italy or in France) or even readjust the half-forgotten contract of apprenticeship. It threw up its hands, not for the first time, and gave the minister power to categorise groups of trainees as 'employees' or not-employees, almost as the mood takes him.[61] The episode reinforced the case long made by scholars in the field for replacing the anarchic common law building-block, the 'contract of employment', a concept long in terminal crisis, by a new legal category of work-relationship, more suited to the needs of modern employment.[62]

The potency of this style of freedom of contract constricts parliament in other ways, for example in the difficulty which it meets in banning contracting-out of statutory protection because of the primacy given to the (often mythical) 'intention of the parties'.[63] In 1988 the Employment Appeal Tribunal showed once again how profound the difficulties are, and how ambiguous is the 'intention of the parties'. An ageing clerk of works had been interviewed for a job by a company for the duration of building work; he was hired through an agency which took over his tax deductions and insurance contributions and told him of other arrangements for 'the client'; he was subject to one week's notice from either the company or the agency, but then was taken on for a second project by a subsidiary, which eventually dismissed him. None of the parties had 'really directed their minds to this issue of a contract of employment'. If he had a contract of employment he would enjoy the right to complain of an unfair dismissal. But the court was quite unable to find a 'contract of employment': 'We can think of no contract of service, properly so called, remotely resembling the contract which existed between [the agency] and the applicant.' His was a 'contract *sui generis*'. So he had no such rights.[64] That is the kind of labour law which cannot last much longer.

This common law tradition also governs the judges' interpretation of parliament's employment protection laws. It is now an old tale told by many scholars of different viewpoints, how the interpretation of employment protection laws has been dominated by a tradition out of kilter with their purpose: by assumptions that the common law will continue to operate on the statutory material, by skewing the meaning of 'dismissal,' by inserting concepts of managerial authority which have 'sterilised' the law on unfair dismissal, by adhering to notions of 'contract' or of 'service' which do not reflect the nature of the social relationship, all to such a degree that reform of the legislation will predictably collapse if it is built on these foundations of the common law.[65] The decisions under review are, we may note, primarily those of the Court of Appeal, the High Court and the Employment Appeal Tribunal; occasionally, too, those of the House of Lords.

But how can we exclude the impact of this common law tradition on employment law? No doubt legislation could be better drafted and better interpreted.[66] But the problem goes deeper than this, to the assumptions and the administration of the system of justice itself. That is why even this area of 'individual' employment law has prompted a debate about the introduction of 'labour courts' (as they have usually been called). The industrial tribunals have not had the remit of displacing this tradition; indeed, they have been put in its tutelage. But it is widely recognised that once issues of industrial relations pass from 'informal' procedures into the hands of courts, 'those courts should be plainly recognised as having a task different in function from the traditional court'.[67] The reform of employment law raises the question of reform of the procedures and the machinery of justice. Before coming to that issue, however, we must touch on the two other questions: first, the future development of Community law after the Social Charter and, secondly, our domestic law that governs the delicate fabric of industrial relations and, in particular, of industrial conflict.

The Logic of Community Labour Law

The Commission's Action Programme has selected a substantial part of the Charter for immediate Community Directives – safety at work, 'atypical' employment, working hours, protection of young workers, freedom of movement, disabled workers, possibly social clauses in public contracts, and workers' rights to consultation and information parallel to the participation rights proposed in the draft European Company Directive.[68] In addition there are the programmes on vocational training, sex equality and job creation. On the other hand, no Community intervention is proposed now on other parts of the Charter, such as a minimum wage ('it is not the task of the Community to fix a decent reference wage,' but the Commission may deliver a non-binding 'opinion' on practices which do not afford a decent standard of living), and the right to freedom of association, the right to bargain collectively or the right to strike – though those rights are declared to be 'vital in the field of industrial relations.' These matters are left to national laws under the principle of 'subsidiarity,' that principle of feline inscrutability and political subtlety whereby the Community is supposed to act only when 'objectives can be reached more effectively at Community than at national level'.[69]

But Community law has already penetrated deeply, even if not yet effectively, into the structure of collective labour relations. Two Directives of 1975 and 1977, for example, require member states to oblige employers to consult with workers' representatives over redundancies and on the transfer of the employing undertaking.[70] Nor are the incursions of the large new body of law about equal pay and sex equality without their relevance. The justifications offered for such measures have always included two elements: the 'welfare' of the workers concerned and the creation of conditions for 'undistorted competition' – broadly the reasons advanced for international labour standards by Robert Owen more than 170 years ago.[71] The two are interwoven in the concept of a 'social dimension' of 1992, and the Action Programme says that 'the economic, industrial and social aspects of the internal market form a whole.'[72] But since the Treaty of Rome was signed in 1957 there has been tension between welfare and competition. Can the market's invisible hand alone do the job of harmonising social systems? Or must the process be steered, and if so how far – especially if, as the Commission has long held, there must be 'equalisation in an upward direction'? The Spaak Report which preceded the Treaty saw 'a progressive coalescence of social policies' as the *result* of competitive forces in a common market; intervention would be needed only for 'correcting ... the effect of *specific* distortions'.[73] The compromise in the Treaty broadly adopted that view of social costs; there would be an improvement in working and living conditions resulting from the 'functioning of the Common Market' and the procedures in the Treaty, subject of course to the principles of equal pay for men and women and holidays with pay.[74]

But the need to stop 'distortions in competition' has grown more intense as competition from outside the Community has grown. By

1985 Professor Mancini, then an Advocate General, now a judge of the European Court of Justice, said of the Directive on redundancy consultation:

> Admittedly, reductions in staff are a terrible thing, and to stand idly by in the face of unemployment ... would be unworthy of our Europe, which is the heir to enlightenment and suffused with the notion of welfare. Yet, like it or not, upstream from enlightenment and welfare there is no getting away from the conditions of competition. If a country can authorise redundancies on less stringent conditions than other countries, its industry will be given an incalculable advantage. And it is against the advantage that war is being declared.[75]

This argument, that employers in one state gain advantages if its labour or social laws permit them to engage in employment practices below the essential standards required in others, cuts across schools of political economy. Whether regulation is seen – to take the three main views – as a natural part of a 'social market', or as an undesirable 'burden on business', or as the pre-condition for a labour market to operate effectively, all schools agree that regulation is not neutral.[76] The need for a 'level playing field' of competition therefore requires a broad equivalence in labour standards. For some the minimum level would move upwards, for others the obligatory requirements would be low; but none could agree to standards which allow incalculable advantage only to some.

The Action Programme justifies the need to enforce such standards, not necessarily in detail but through minimum provisions, by appealing *both* to the welfare of workers *and* to preventing 'distortions of competition'. Measures are needed on atypical workers to prevent the dangers to employment terms which may cause 'social dumping' and to prevent 'distortions of competition at Community level'; on working time to improve firms' 'competitiveness' and to avoid undue diversity harming 'the wellbeing and health of workers'; on working conditions of those sent to another country to avoid 'disadvantages for workers' and 'distortions of competition'; on social clauses in public contracts to assure fair competition, efficiency and equal treatment for workers; on consultation rights for workers to strengthen competitiveness 'in a context which is socially accepted'; on safety to protect workers and avoid dangers 'to the business environment of divergent health and safety conditions'.[77]

From a different standpoint, the CBI has insisted that imposition of a common legal duty to bargain 'would potentially disrupt industrial relations, requiring companies to decide a wide range of issues through collective bargaining rather than individually with employees ... [when] competitors outside the EC would not be constrained or burdened in the same way'.[78] But from that standpoint, the logic of the argument must apply, too, inside the single market. Thus, the employer in France who is now subject to an obligation to bargain may be suffering conditions of 'distorted competition' against his rival in Britain, who is not so subject.[79] Indeed, it is hardly likely that all distortions of competition of the next decade can be excluded by Directives on sex equality, employee's rights in insolvency, redundancy and transfers of undertakings alone. While those who call for 'universal legal standards' on social security, employment protection, non-discrimination, collective representation and minimum pay through the Community are not likely to see their calls answered in the early years of the single internal market,[80] like it or not, the pressure towards more extensive regulation of labour standards is likely in the medium term increasingly to affect both employee protection and also collective labour relations. 'The Commission will intervene whenever it sees the need for harmonisation in areas where national or occupational initiative alone will not be enough.'[81] Plans for the future shape of British labour law would be wise to take this into account.

Positive Rights, Immunities and Injunctions

It is in collective labour relations that the British heritage has been singular because freedom of association, for the reasons outlined, took the form of 'immunities'. There is undoubtedly something unattractive in a modern democracy about expressing as 'immunities' fundamental liberties to organise, to bargain and to strike – the three central freedoms – not least when those who wish to decollectivise the labour market seize on the legal form of the 'immunities', without examining their social function, as a shallow semantic proof that they import 'special privileges'.[82] Such policies lead to calls for the abolition of all trade dispute 'immunities' and the designation of the strike as a 'crude breach of contract', in substance for an end to lawful strikes.[83] In the Social Charter the democratic freedoms to organise, to bargain and to strike are expressed quite deliberately as 'rights'.[84] Moreover, their content is linked through its preamble with international minimum standards in the Conventions of the ILO, from which the Charter draws 'inspiration', standards of rights which are, the ILO Committee of Experts has held, contravened by British law on strikes in the 1980s, especially in its ban on most secondary action, the legality of dismissal of striking workers and its narrow concept of the limiting factor of the system, a legitimate trade dispute.[85]

In any reform of labour law there is now manifestly a case, if only on grounds of certainty, for adopting a clear code of positive rights and duties on industrial relations generally and industrial conflict in particular alongside immunities. After the legislation of the 1980s, the day has gone when a Royal Commission could be sustained in its conclusion that the immunities can in practice enshrine a satisfactory 'right' to strike (even then perhaps optimistic four years after *Rookes* v. *Barnard*).[86] The legal form of 'immunities' no longer seems able alone to protect the substance of industrial autonomy from the state; the historical reason for not drafting the legal structure in terms of positive rights has therefore disappeared, and the need to legislate primarily in the language of rights, with immunities playing a necessary but supportive role, demands fresh inquiry into the administration of labour law in state agencies. For in real life rights exist only in the decisions of courts which enforce them.

But a change in legal form alone means little. Proponents of positive rights have at times given the impression that the change in form automatically solves substantive problems.[87] When the new wrapping comes off, the legal contents revealed may be in practice narrowly or widely drawn, and narrowly or widely interpreted. Not everyone, for example, would accept the logic of the French courts who have imported into their constitutional right to strike the doctrine of *autosatisfaction*, under which a strike must not itself achieve the bargaining demand. So, workers demanding an end to the working of overtime on a Saturday act lawfully if they strike for the day on Friday, but unlawfully if they strike on a Saturday.[88] Nor can the distinction between 'disputes of interest' and 'disputes of rights,' which is fundamental to only a minority of Continental systems (i.e. to those whose law enshrines an 'organic' right to strike), be accepted in the absolute form in which it appears in the Social Charter. But these details apart, as the Charter also shows, the language of 'positive rights' implies a minimum content, both the right to organise the strike and the right of the individual worker to stop work. It is, therefore, unthinkable that the exercise of a '*right* to strike' could now import a breach of the contract of employment. Having taken that step, one is into 'positive rights' territory. Such a general change of direction necessitates a 'release from the disciplines of the common law'.[89]

Positive rights are not entirely novel. They were proposed in the 1960s;[90] and a government Green Paper of 1981 acepted that, if a positive right to strike were introduced, 'there would be a need to insulate ... [such a] right to strike from the common law ... This could mean developing a completely separate system of law with its own sanctions and with separate courts to administer and enforce those sanctions.'[91] Government was prepared to put labour courts on the agenda in 1981 for this reason, just as in 1965 industrial tribunals were proposed as 'a nucleus of a system of labour courts' for individual disputes, not by employers or unions, but by the Ministry of Labour.[92] The conversion of many trade unions to the need for a new code of employment rights is relatively recent. But it is now widely argued, here too, on collective labour law that the law must be rescued from 'the common law tradition.'

Because that same 'common law' is embodied (and highly personalised) in the judiciary, however, one point must at once be made crystal clear. This analysis does *not* impute 'bias' to judges. That explanation at once mis-states and understates the problem. That great, and highly conservative judge, Scrutton LJ, said in his famous lecture of 1923 that it was difficult to ensure impartiality between litigants 'one of your own class and one not of your class', much more difficult than in the Commercial Court. This problem, he affirmed, arose from the 'habits you are trained in, the people with whom you mix'. But he prefaced his remarks by saying: 'I am not speaking of conscious impartiality.'[93] Nor – emphatically – am I.

We must concentrate, as he did, not on marginal questions of personal prejudice, but on common law habits, training and traditions – habits learned in pupillage, training reinforced in practice, traditions transmitted in the bones and briefs of each generation. A comparative framework is once again useful because it makes us ask the unfamiliar question: What is 'a judge'? In any comparison with Continental systems, we are made to remember the importance of the judge's pedigree. In England he is a member of the same club as the barrister before him, part of the same tradition, institutionalised in a common pattern of Inns, practice and judging. This is much less true of the Continental career judge; not necessarily more radical, but equally independent, his (and significantly much more often, her) roots lie in the choice to become a judge made at a young age. The career judge in some jurisdictions undoubtedly bring to bear on the work in court a different relationship with the wider society.[94] It is impossible not to detect this difference when examining the role of the courts even in such parallel institutions as the British industrial tribunals and the German Labour Courts, or even more, in the patterns of French *jurisprudence*, Italian *giurisprudenza* and English case law, where what Griffith has called the 'remarkable consistency of approach' of English judges contrasts with their counterparts in a manner not to be explained merely by reference to the doctrine of precedent, and even in the structures which recently legislative reforms have prescribed for the processing of labour litigation.[95]

More, because the British system grew up with immunities not rights, the common law tradition has never been compelled, as other judicial systems have been, to assimilate the realities of subordination in employment or the consequent need and justification for collective organisation and action. In that tradition such organisation and action is an 'exception' from the ordinary law, to be justified in each case. Ineradicable traditions of thought and habit are therefore at the centre of the problem, exemplified in two well known areas: first, the outflanking of parliament's 'immunities' in trade disputes by creative decisions – if you like, by new liabilities in tort – and, secondly, the unjust procedures governing remedies in industrial conflict.[96]

It is here we encounter the real difficulty of 'insulating' any new structure of substantive law in the existing courts. One can indeed understand that the common law judge, with this background, finds it hard to accept that his common law torts, old and new, are to be shut out. Faced with 'immunities' protecting industrial action, Lord Diplock acknowledged frankly that they 'have tended to stick in judicial gorges' and were 'intrinsically repugnant to anyone who has spent his life in the practice of the law,' that is the common law.[97] The problem is not limited to strikes. In the short period when employers were obliged to negotiate with unions specified by ACAS – in effect, a rudimentary duty to bargain – one judge subjected the whole scheme to a strict interpretation because it was analogous to a 'compulsory acquisition of property'.[98] The latter type of case shows how the ordinary courts are unsuited to the comprehension not merely of immunities but also of collective rights.

The tale of the immunities has been often told. The fact is that from the moment the immunities were invented in 1871, decision after decision has produced new liabilities out of the hat to outflank them, most commonly (but not only) in tort, each adding a twist to the skein of the liabilities restricting trade union activity in the 'ordinary law of the land'.[99] There were, it is true, periods of relative judicial 'abstention' – during the two world wars[100]; after the General Strike to 1939, when trade unions were weak; and during the 1950s, when middle-class opinion appeared momentarily to accept strong trade unions.[101] It was natural perhaps in the early 1950s to think this 'non-intervention' normal, but experience since has demonstrated that each of those periods was exceptional. For a much longer period, in the nineteenth and early twentieth centuries and again from the 1960s until today, with one major exception, the tradition has created more liabilities to the disadvantage of trade unions than were ever dreamed of by parliament.

If anyone believed this creative tradition to be dead, recent events have shown them wrong. Born in 1869 of Sir William Erle, nurtured by *Quinn* v. *Leathem* and *Taff Vale* in 1901, encouraged by *Osborne* in 1910, reborn in *Rookes* v. *Barnard*, 1964, nourished the next year in *Stratford* v. *Lindley*, succoured by *Torquay Hotel* v. *Cousins* in 1969, replenished by 'economic duress' in *Universe Tankships* in 1982, it flourished again in the Court of Appeal judgments in the 'dock strike' case of 1989.[102]

Indeed, the 1989 extension of liability by the Court of Appeal –

what the trial judge dubbed a tort which would be created 'from the deliberate infliction of injury upon the plaintiff's property or business by a non-tortious inducement of a non-tortious breach of duty'[103] – relied upon an 'intention to injure' to turn what was lawful into unlawful means. That is the very ingredient central to evasions of the exceptional decision in 1898, *Allen* v. *Flood*,[104] a decision for which Lord Herschell was never forgiven in refusing to extend liability to a union official who had done nothing unlawful, and for which Lord Halsbury had his revenge in *Quinn* v. *Leathem* in 1901. By 1904 it was judicially recognised that the Law Lords had been 'getting round' *Allen* v. *Flood* ever since it was decided.[105] The customary judicial attitude was still pursued sixty four years later when Lord Devlin complained that the decision had 'dammed a stream of thought that I believe would have had a beneficial effect on the law of tort'; there was 'no going back now on *Allen* v. *Flood*. But all the same only a tenuous barrier holds back the flow *Allen* v. *Flood* stopped up.'[106] His speech in *Rookes* v. *Barnard*, opening new paths to fresh pastures of economic tort liability, followed two years after.[107] No one could say that Lord Devlin was the most retrogressive of judges; his devotion to the common law was in some areas more than tinged with liberalism. But experience both here and in other common law jurisdictions demonstrates that for the architects of a new labour law in Britain to place its administration in the hands of that kind of common law judicial machinery would be an act of folly.[108]

Side by side with substantive law stand unjust interlocutory remedies, notably the 'labour injunction'; this is also part of 'common law' tradition in the wider sense to include discretionary equitable remedies. The labour injunction upholds the '*status quo*' until full trial but, as Frankfurter and Greene demonstrated in 1932, the interlocutory ban against striking while 'the iron is hot' and (what is sometimes forgotten) the interim injunctions awarded during the hearings and appeals, help the employer to win the industrial dispute – whether or not the subsequent trial is in lawyer's terms 'speedy' (and usually there is no trial at all) and whether or not the union would win it after the full legal procedures have been deployed:

> The suspension of activities affects only the strikers; the employer resumes his efforts to defeat the strike and resumes them free from the interdicted interferences. Moreover, the suspension of strike activities, even temporarily, may defeat the strike for practical purposes.[109]

We find the same mixture of inappropriate principle and robust creativity here too.[110] For example, the classical rule was that a plaintiff won his injunction only if he proved a '*prima facie* case'. But in 1974 the Law Lords moved the goal posts. Today the plaintiff need prove no more than an arguable case – 'a serious question to be tried,' something not frivolous or vexatious, a test which in the complexities of uncertain tort liability and outflanked immunities hands the first fruits of victory to most applicants for an injunction in industrial disputes.[111] That new rule was laid down not in a labour law case, but in a case about patents (where it may, or may not, be a sensible rule)[112] but it had to be applied across the board. Nothing illustrates better the way labour law is vulnerable to novelties introduced in other parts of the seamless common law, a lack of autonomy far greater than in most comparable systems.[113]

If the evidence (on affidavit, not matching the standards of a trial) offers just an argument, no more, that the union might have done wrong, the injunction is granted if the balance of convenience is in the applicant's favour. Judges are not troubled by uncertainties; difficult points of law or uncertainties in the evidence must be reserved 'until trial'.[114] Meanwhile the industrial action is stopped or the time allowed to implement a strike ballot is exhausted, especially if there are appeals.[115] Judges freely admit that the procedures lead to injunctions awarded 'after insufficient argument and certainly insufficient consideration'.[116] As for that 'balance of convenience' which must favour the successful applicant, the claim by the employer or third party that there is a threat of 'irreparable harm' to his business cannot be matched by the union. The reason is not, as some trade unionists think, because the judge will not listen, but because the traditional exercise of discretion in favour of the *status quo* is static and based on property[117]; the 'equitable principles' cannot allow industrial conduct to be measured against standards of continuing industrial relations where the interests of property dictate otherwise.[118]

The *central defect* – and it is one that is difficult for parliament to correct within traditional procedures – lies in the fact that the *same sort of discretion is applied to all types of social conflict*. Even statutes limiting injunctions are assumed to leave with the judge the traditional residual discretion, for example in case of urgency. The attempt to modify the new test invented by the Law Lords in 1975 has been a notorious failure.[119] But in 1974 parliament also legislated to stop the practice of granting injunctions *ex parte* in trade disputes. That, one might think, was a venture reasonably likely to find favour. Yet in a trade dispute case of 1987 we find an injunction granted *ex parte* against a civil service union, without its knowledge, over the telephone, from the duty judge's home, on a Sunday afternoon – an injunction discharged a fortnight later because argument finally proved that the plaintiffs had not even an arguable case.[120] In addition to all this, the Court of Appeal has now laid it down that the judge's discretion must always take account of the 'public interest',[121] thereby, it would seem, turning every such action between private parties in industrial disputes into a question of *ordre public*. The lesson of the labour injunction is clear. Legislation can touch the application of this High Court discretion only marginally. One must doubt whether new procedures to match the new code of industrial rights and duties could be administered satisfactorily by these tribunals.

It is important to note that the power of the interlocutory labour injunction owes much to the doctrine of 'contempt of court', again a phenomenon peculiar to the common law – 'a great power, a power to imprison without trial, but it is a necessary power', as Lord Denning has it.[122]

The orders of the courts must – let there be no doubt – be upheld. But there are many ways of doing that. No Continental labour courts, not even the German, have powers as great as those which the common law tradition gives to the High Court, from fines to sequestration, and certainly not in interim hearings; this is a feature which tends to baffle the common lawyer reared on the belief that without these ultimate deterrents in the discretion of the judge the populace will rebel.[123] Yet respect for the decisions of those courts is not destroyed. The Swedish Labour Court has always used the sanction of damages; and where, as in France, enforcement of civil orders is achieved primarily by *astreinte* (a money penalty paid to the plaintiff) the opportunities to settle the dispute and waive payment are increased.[124] Although the classical principles on 'civil contempt' allow for a somewhat parallel waiver by the plaintiff,[125] there has recently been a significant, but patchy trend towards the criminalisation of all types of contempt.

The distinction between 'civil' contempt (which permits parties to compromise) and 'criminal' contempt (which does not) has been firmly upheld in recent commercial cases,[126] but it has been vigorously rejected in trade union cases since the National Industrial Relations Court began the fashion.[127] It is in fact astonishing that, both in Britain and in other common law jurisdictions, the range of avowedly criminal liabilities for contempt has been extended by judicial fiat, most notably in industrial contexts.[128] Even the liability of third parties for contempt has been extended. A little noticed decision during the miners' strike of 1984-85 held that an adviser to a union could be in contempt of court for what he had done even before the union was subject to any liability, creating the hitherto unknown wrong of 'anticipatory contempt'.[129] One bank therefore felt compelled to ask the court for directions about moneys held for a union client, without its client being liable at all.[130] Other extensions, such as the new scope of receivership established in the miners' strike, are better known.[131] These extensions have been creatively designed by the courts to police industrial disputes by rigorous enforcement of interlocutory orders which are, it must be recalled, made on evidence of an 'arguable' liability from which the union might even be able to prove itself free at a full trial. They are developments in the common law *genre*, unhelpful to the settlement of disputes; they have redoubled distrust in the present legal process; they are part of a machinery of justice which needs overhaul.

The Need for Labour Courts

These factors suggest a need for specialised industrial courts, or 'labour courts' as they have usually been called, in order to give labour law some autonomy from the common law tradition. Scholars have put the point in different ways. For this purpose it may prove 'indispensable' to secure 'the introduction of fully fledged Labour Courts'.[132] 'The solution [to the problem of control of private bureaucratic power] seems to lie in a mixture of agencies independent of the ordinary courts.'[133] 'Tripartism ... the natural and preferable way of administering and enforcing individual rights at work' should be extended to 'disputes arising out of the application of collective labour law'.[134] More bold: a 'step towards a European labour law would be the generalisation of a labour court system, covering all levels, under the administration not of a justice department but of an employment department'.[135] Boldest so far: 'The trend towards specialisation in labour dispute settlement is persuasive in inclining towards a specialist labour tribunal or court at Community level – comprising, for example, expert judges from national labour court systems.'[136]

In the light of such pronouncements by scholars of varied viewpoints, no one can say 'labour courts' are not now on the agenda. Indeed, as was the case with the adoption of programmes for 'positive rights', it may even be that some proponents of an idea whose time appears to have come do not always attend to the enormous difficulties in its path. There is no doubt that an 'experiment with labour courts would be a high risk strategy', one nevertheless starts with the question: 'without some such step, how can labour law ever be administered on any basis other than the common law?'[137] Acknowledging the risks, the dangers and the difficulties, the years appear to have made more cogent tentative proposals for labour courts advanced two decades earlier.[138] Indeed, when the question is posed in terms of the common law courts, everything which has gone above demands that the proposal be examined not merely as a label or gimmick, but thoroughly and positively.

But what is a 'labour court'? And what sort do we need? Although there is some descriptive literature about them, these quesions have been less discussed.[139] A labour court is largely what you make it. The *genus* is usually taken to include any tribunal with specialised functions and expertise in employment and labour relations, but that is a very broad description. The National

Industrial Relations Court (NIRC) of 1971 in Britain falls within it, but it was very different from what is now being proposed. Labour courts in Sweden, Germany, France and Italy are very different from one another. Each grew up, or was introduced, for particular purposes. Some deal only with individual employment disputes, others with all types of dispute. Some (as in Germany) have specialist appellate courts, others the ordinary courts of appeal (as in France and Italy, in the former normally in a special 'social' division), some (as in Sweden) have no appeal machinery at all, though they may act (as in Sweden again) as both first instance courts for most labour cases and as appeal courts for the few that originate elsewhere.[140]

An argument for labour courts must, therefore, define an appropriate species. After all, if you want to adopt a dog and would like to have a corgi, you do not want to end up with a rottweiler. At the risk of offending those who have come to adopt this meritorious proposal with zeal, it must be said at the outset that the adoption of an inappropriate species of labour court, reflecting uncertainty about the object of the exercise, could do more harm than good. Indeed, there may be some who still feel at the end of the argument: 'Better the High Court we know than the Industrial Relations Court we do not.' Some have concluded that reform of traditional industrial justice must wait for the 'reform of civil procedure in general'.[141] If challenged, the common law 'legal system is likely to win, indeed it will win', though that may be a 'misfortune'.[142] Answers must therefore be found to those who ask: what will be the jurisdiction, scope or composition? If the case for labour courts has merit as an answer to the problem of the common law courts, it plainly suggests that their jurisdiction should include both individual and collective employment disputes. In that event, we need not one court but a series of tribunals (including tribunals tailored to the needs of Scotland and Northern Ireland). They must, of course, be informal, flexible, speedy, cheap and accessible – those are the traditional requirements of labour courts everywhere. To that end we could retain the industrial tribunals, reformed at minimum along the lines of the 'Justice' and the Warwick Reports,[143] with appeals from them brought before the central labour court, or more accurately one of its divisions. (To that extent, in this sector of its jurisdiction there is no objection to building on a reform of the Employment Appeal Tribunal; but the proposal as a whole is, as will be seen, different from converting the EAT itself into the labour court, for under the guidance of its presiding High Court judges it has been integrated into the common law tradition.)[144]

The court could also, like the Swedish Labour Court, itself sit in divisions as a first instance court on 'collective' disputes. Since individual employment protection can be expected to rest upon a much expanded statutory base, stemming both from Westminster and from the Community, the labour court would have as one of its major tasks ensuring a balance in the system not only through the development of a co-ordinated structure of individual employment rights but by the protection and promotion of autonomous negotiation between the collective parties including, but not confined to, collective bargaining. Similarly, among its primary concerns would be the maintenance of close relations with the conciliation service in ACAS and a determination to dispose of remedies to promote settlement of disputes – in the evocative phrase of Gérard Lyon-Caen: *fondé sur la conciliation, la discussion plus que sur la juridiction* (based on conciliation, talks rather than judgements).[145]

Some proposals have very different objectives. For example, Lord Donaldson's 'radically new approach', proposing that the courts should be used in their 'traditional role' but with the power to decide 'who is right' in industrial disputes, to 'investigate the grievances,report to the public and recommend and, if necessary, enforce solutions'. To the objection that 'disputes of interest are not justiciable', he responded: 'I disagree.'[146] That kind of compulsory arbitration of the industrial merits, found in the laws of Australia since 1904 and in the writings of Sidney Webb (when Beatrice was not around),[147] was a subterranean current in the operations of the NIRC. But it is no more relevant to the objectives of the present agenda than a retreat to Order 1305. It is no accident that Scrutton LJ defined his problem of 'impartiality' in terms of labour disputes: 'This difficulty does not arise in the Commercial Court.'[148]

Current proposals envisage a system that aims at the maintenance of continuing collective industrial relations, resolving disputes in a manner different from that of 'the traditional court',[149] through a network of courts and tribunals free from the common law tradition, established not to enforce their view of the judges' appreciation of the merits in industrial conflicts but to apply a fair set of ground rules both substantive and procedural – in the full knowledge that in the sense of rules and procedures applied fairly within a broad consistency, some aspects of 'legalism' are unavoidable; but in any other sense it is to be eschewed[150] – recognising as a primary source the authority of autonomous bargaining and the virtues of conciliation, and therefore wherever possible using reflexive processes to promote agreement between the parties.

Most labour courts share the aim of conciliation; for example they all build in a conciliation stage, though in very different ways: sometimes conciliation by the legal president (as in Germany, very actively), or by a separate group of the lay judges (like the French *conseillers prud'hommes*), or by use of, or in conjunction with, bipartite or tripartite machinery set up by employers and unions (as with Italy) or through a separate autonomous conciliation and mediation service (in Sweden and Britain).[151] The successful experience here with ACAS could be expected to lead to the continuation in Britain of this last method, rather than any closer participation in conciliation by the court itself, along with further development of machineries for dispute resolution (to which a high priority must be given, as the Social Charter suggests).[152]

On remedies, we may have much to learn from practice elsewhere. In difficult industrial disputes a labour court would wish to avoid the kind of traditional judgment which cuts technical legal knots and leaves the parties to get on with the job of living together afterwards as best they can, and even more wish to abstain from the crude favouring of one side which the present practice of interlocutory injunctions entails. It is worth examining, for example, the practice of some *juges des référés* (judges with interlocutory jurisdiction) in France who in their interlocutory jurisdiction to prevent as a matter of urgency a 'manifestly illegal disorder',[153] grant conditional orders in the dispute, requiring employers to agree to such steps as negotiation or conciliation. In other cases they have made their injunctions conditional upon the inspection of the workplace by an expert where it is the cause of a dispute.[154] In such ways, a court may make a positive contribution to resolution of the underlying dispute, instead of firing an injunction at one party on formal, substantive grounds, compounded in Britain by a discretion guided by proprietary interests, leaving the parties to pick up the pieces. By contrast, the absence of such articulated and specialised remedies or procedures can cause difficulties from the outset for a labour court.[155] The 1987 reform of the New Zealand Labour Court, for example, is already being adjudged unsatisfactory, largely because it left that court tied to traditional common law remedies of injunction and contempt of court, including sequestration.[156]

The New Zealand experience may be of special relevance if only because a British labour court is bound to have some interlocutory jurisdiction. The *ex parte* injunction must go in industrial disputes. But any court must have some interim competence. This should, however, be carefully limited in such disputes and guided by new concepts of discretion. The labour court must not be born swathed in *Kerr on Injunctions*. The precise limitations demand careful study. One proposal, for example, already made is that a party should have the right to claim a speedy, full trial. This might be a useful part of a wider reform,[157] but it cannot in itself be a complete solution. Indeed, if both sides were to have such a right it might be welcomed more by an employer who in the nature of things is better prepared to go to court from the start, having chosen his moment to launch the interlocutory proceedings; and it is doubtful whether even reformed procedures for discovery of documents or for 'further and better particulars' could ever make a speedy trial in layman's terms 'immediate', so that the union would be left (in the absence of further reform) still subject for many weeks to the initial injunction – in the period that the 'iron is hot' and the dispute often won or lost.

Without a doubt, a labour court could have no truck with a standard of proof for such interlocutory remedies as is based upon the 1975 standard of a 'serious question to be tried'. But that and similar changes in the rules of procedure and evidence would by themselves change little; they are hardly worth creating a labour court to administer. They need to be put into a broader frame of imaginative reform. There are numerous measures worth investigating, such as the use of conditional orders (for example, allowing the court to require as preconditions of an order certain procedural steps, such as discussion with ACAS or other expert intervention in a dispute, or the revocation of dimissals connected with a dispute), or requiring refusal of an order where maintenance of minimum services is assured by the union or through ACAS,[158] or permitting refusal where the employer has acted in a manner inconsistent with a code of industrial behaviour, including dismissals or unfair discipline of employees or refusal to negotiate with a representative union. Modest steps such as these have in effect already been put on the agenda by the common law courts; it was, after all, the Court of Appeal which said in 1989 that the 'public interest' must always be considered in the granting of injunctions, though its understanding of the phrase would not be that adopted by a labour court since its view of strikes and the public interest 'could turn the balance of convenience into a mere formality'.[159] There are other areas to be considered; for example, where the courts grant an interlocutory injunction now they do so on terms of a 'cross undertaking in damages', to compensate the defendant if it turns out he was in the right all along; but in industrial cases everyone knows this is of no value to the union.[160] There is no reason why a scale of realistic monetary compensation (quite apart from costs) should not be fixed for an employer who abuses the labour court by obtaining an interim order to which further inquiry shows he was not entitled.

But what would be the relationship of the labour court to the rest of the machinery of justice, given that the object is to assure to it a reasonable autonomy?[161] This question has to be answered in two parts, one easy and one more difficult. First, in order to be free from judicial review by the High Court, the central labour court with its different divisions must enjoy a status at minimum equivalent to a part of the Supreme Court of Judicature. Short of that it could have no autonomy at all. The proposal is quite different, therefore, from any plan to substitute a new name of 'Labour Court' on the door of a division of the High Court or of the Employment Appeal Tribunal which, though tripartite, has for all its virtues played a full role in constructing the difficulties from which escape is now sought. More vexed though, secondly, is the question of appeals from the labour court even if it has that status, a point central to the whole venture. Appeal courts can control the whole system; and comparative inquiry suggests that non-specialised appeal courts (even where the common law tradition is not dominant) need unexpected qualities of sensitivity not to undo the work of specialised courts. That is why even British labour law has had occasional experience of expert bodies to which a conclusive industrial jurisdiction was entrusted on specialised questions, without further appeal.[162] These, it will be rightly said, are slender precedents; yet they do allow us to consider the issue on principle and to jettison sentiment for a functional approach. The Swedish Labour Court works – and in its system works well – without any appellate machinery; while in Germany there are two tiers of specialised appellate labour courts matching the federal constitution, with the legal judges in the majority at Federal level.[163] In Britain it is undeniable that the Court of Appeal and the House of Lords Judicial Committee have – in the nature of our system – been the outstanding protagonists of the common law tradition in labour law.[164] Nor would that be changed by adding a few wingpersons to the bench (a minority is the usual proposal) or giving the appeal courts power 'to enlist the assistance of an industrial member',[165] except possibly for the worse by clothing old habits with a fresh legitimacy.

If the new labour court is to be part of a solution, it is scarcely logical to hand over its decisions at the outset to the control of courts which are prominent parts of the problem. There is, in other words, a compelling case that decisions of the specialist labour courts should not end up in the hands of the common law Court of Appeal or Judicial Committee of the House of Lords. That is inherent in the reason for choosing labour courts. The layman's answer, to allow appeals to those appellate courts but limit them to 'questions of law,' would hardly change the *status quo* and put little or no brake on their power. As the Master of the Rolls said recently, 'the absence of evidence to support a finding of fact has always been regarded as a question of law.'[166] Indeed, one may think that it is often the job of lawyers to ensure that the really big cases do involve questions of law. But there is ground for believing that the Swedish system works as it does partly because of the scale of the market involved.[167] The extensive litigation in the British industrial tribunals would not be likely to decrease with the increasing range of employment protection and the labour court, it may be said, could hardly be expected to carry out its first instance and appellate work on the scale required without some error creeping in. If an appellate body were in consequence thought necessary, there would be no need to rupture the logic of the system. The legislature could still make it abundantly clear (and give delegated powers to rectify perverse interpretations muddying the waters) that the jurisdiction of ordinary appellate courts is excluded. In other words, the specialised labour court should have the resources to deal with appeals by a further adaptation of its structure.

Many courts constitute special or 'full' chambers or divisions, often with an increased number of judges, for special occasions. The French *Cour de Cassation*, for example, in which labour law appeals are normally heard in the 'Social Chamber,' can (and in some cases must) sit on important matters of principle in *Assemblée plénière* (a Full Court), and the Swedish Labour Court has a similar capability.[168] There is a case for constituting a Full Bench of the labour court as the day-to-day appellate court, if need be with a majority of legal judges, composed of members who had not participated in the case below. But there the process of appeal would normally stop. It may be asked: What about the Law Lords? To which, with no disrespect to them, the question must be put in response: What is their function in a system of law based upon specialist judicial administration – in particular when the assumptions and general principles which they will quite understandably bring to bear are those of a common law which the system was devised largely to exclude?

There is one final area in which such a function can, however, be found, though it should be shared. That goes to the special case of allegations that the labour court has exceeded its remit. So absolute was the victory of the common law courts in England that we are not, as are those who have separate types of court (administrative, labour, commercial courts, etc.), accustomed to the problems of a conflict of jurisdictions (thought it must be added that English courts have long lived happily with the separate courts in Scotland and Northern Ireland, with the Law Lords usually able to iron out any difficulties). With a new domestic separation of jurisdictions, the question is therefore properly put: 'Should the Labour Court have the final word on its own jurisdiction or should there be some kind of Conflicts Tribunal?'[169] Since the first conclusion is teasingly indicated to be unreasonable, we are clearly invited to adopt the second. This we probably should do, but in a special form.

Few have felt their blood run cold at the mention of a *Tribunal des Conflits* since Jennings exploded Dicey's account of administrative law in France and England.[170] A pragmatic approach suggests that a new problem needs a new, articulated tribunal. On disputes about jurisdiction a final competence might well be accorded, for example, to a chamber of the Judicial Committee of the Privy Council composed jointly of Law Lords and legal judges of the labour court, none of whom had been earlier concerned with the cause in hand, presided over by the

Lord Chancellor. There is a case for references on such matters, certificated as of public importance, to be allowed to 'leap frog' direct to this Jurisdiction Chamber of the Judicial Committee. Use of the Judicial Committee for similar purposes has long been part of projects on Scottish devolution, i.e. to act as the court deciding constitutional issues; and such arrangements would be strikingly less difficult to introduce than the new relationship between our courts and the European Court of Justice in the Community, yet that relationship has now settled down. It may be said that the 'powerfulness of the opponents of change' will obstruct any such reform, but that view is based on the belief that 'the common law tradition will remain dominant'.[171] The prediction may be correct; but it is a crystal ball into which it may be premature to gaze before we have even drawn up an adequate agenda for reform. Nor should opponents of such change include the judges, for courts that have encountered little difficulty in absorbing the profound effects of s.2(4) of the European Communities Act 1972,[172] should encounter no obstacle to the loyal application of legislation properly enacted by parliament for an adjustment of domestic jurisdictions.

Comparative Questions on Labour Courts

A comparative perspective – one, let it be repeated, useful not for importation of solutions but for discovery of questions which may help find solutions – demonstrates that this has so far been an agenda for a rather conservative programme. For example, we have said nothing about procedural reforms, everywhere crucial in labour law – 'class actions' (e.g. in sex discrimination cases) or the right of a trade union to appear whenever a 'collective interest' is in issue even if the complaint is in form individual, a procedure notably successful in France in the long established *action syndicale* and in rather different forms in Italy.[173] In the latter, the right of the union locally to obtain swift remedies for 'anti-union' conduct has been adjudged 'the decisive instrument of guarantee' both for specific union rights and for the conditions needed to sustain effective union activities in the enterprise.[174] Such points can only be briefly registered here, but if the regulated base of the system of employment law is to increase, as seems likely, and collective labour law restructured within a framework largely of positive rights, such procedural considerations become more pressing. As Italian experience has shown, the best of labour laws is effective only when matched by adequate procedures and sanctions, and these may have to be adapted by introducing very special provision for labour cases, not least in adjusting the concept of the *status quo* during proceedings to safeguard the interests of employees, individual and collective.[175] The many proposals for reform of the

British industrial tribunal procedures testify to the growing interest in this area, though 'reform' has hardly been the mark of practice in the 1980s.[176]

But what about the structure of the court? It is often assumed rather than argued that a labour court must be 'tripartite', like the industrial tribunals, with a legally qualified chair and wingpersons from employee and employer panels. This may well be a desirable format, but there are some questions still worth asking.[177] For example, who should nominate or select the panels of wingpersons? Is there a case for the panels to have an elected element? Should there be, as has been suggested, wings representing other interests, consumers or the unemployed? Should not the legal chairs (both of industrial tribunals and labour court) themselves be appointed by a machinery which contains a tripartite content, as in Germany?[178] But there are bigger questions than these. Tripartism has many virtues but some reasonably successful labour courts are not tripartite at all. The French *Conseils de prud'hommes* sit with equal numbers of employers and employees without any legal judge, except when a local judge is called in to resolve a deadlock, though then only on the points of disagreement between the lay judges.[179] What is more, these judges in the *Conseils* are all elected; workers over sixteen (whether or not unemployed) vote in each geographical and sectional constituency every five years during working hours in elections which are significant for the unions that propose candidates,[180] – '*juridiction élue, paritaire, conciliatrice*' (a magistracy elected, bipartite and conciliatory). Indeed, the bipartite character of the *Conseils* is sometimes said to foster a certain 'social consensus'.[181] Perhaps the sociologists will discover the same quality in the tripartite industrial tribunals now that there has been no repetition of the precedent of 1972, when the TUC successfully called for union nominees to leave the tribunals in protest against unfair legislation – an acceptance of the view from the Lord Chancellor downwards that, being judges, they are in no sense 'representatives'.[182]

There is little evidence that majority opinion in Britain would prefer a bipartite to a tripartite structure (though it may never have been asked; it has certainly never been asked whether it would prefer to elect some of the lay panel members).[183] But the question still arises: what *kind* of tripartism? There is more than one. Are we satisfied with the simple tripartism we have or should we provide stronger resources within the court itself?

There is, for example, what may be called '*fortified tripartism*', illustrated by the Swedish Labour Court. That tribunal normally sits with seven members: two legal judges ('with a legal training and long experience as judges') with two employers and two employees as wings, but with a seventh member, an expert with 'specialised knowledge of conditions of the labour market'.[184] 'Fortified tripartism' of this type opens up possibilities of specialisation and of better specialised knowledge of the case in hand. The French *Conseils* lean in the direction of further specialisation by sitting in five separate occupational sections to which the lay judges are separately elected, including now a special section for the technical or managerial *cadres*.[185] Such an idea is not wholly foreign to British practice. For some time demands have been made for specialist wings in discrimination cases in the tribunals, and one English judge with experience of the EAT has called for 'a selected core of *chairmen* and members' with specialised training and experience, to 'sit on race and sex discrimination cases'.[186] Official practice indeed already seeks to select a wing-woman in sex discrimination cases, and for race discrimination cases it favours a person 'experienced' in race relations (though parallel logic might have suggested someone black).[187] But the parties have no legal right to demand such composition of the tribunal (though, if it is more fair, logic might suggest they should have the right to do so).[188] It has, on the other hand, been rightly observed that, in the British setting, a provision for specialised training even of those who sit on race or sex discrimination cases needs care, for 'if badly handled a recommendation such as this might appear to be a sophisticated form of jury knobbling.'[189]

But important though they are, such cases do not stand alone as categories inadequately understood by the present system of industrial justice, and it has been therefore suggested that 'there may be a case for specialisation in one or two other complex areas.'[190] Labour courts commonly feel the need for experts and a procedure should, as it does in Italy and France, meet that need.[191] Indeed, in Britain the problem of the expert is already insistent in another dimension. In equal pay cases, we have had to turn to the independent expert, given a special status, paid for by public funds, taken from a list drawn up by ACAS (no nominations – overtly – allowed here) to whom the tribunal is obliged to refer issues as a witness to advise it, though he may be cross-examined and the parties may produce one expert of their own.[192] It is perhaps no accident that it is in these cases, along with the dismissal of trade unionists, that commentators find the 'individualist, common law bias of judicial decision-making' least well-suited.[193] In fact, with compulsory expert witnesses here and growing demands for expert wingpersons or even expert chairmen there, a problem has arisen which should not be transferred to a new labour court. While it may not be possible to adopt the same solution for the tribunals, there is a strong case for adding to the first instance and appellate sittings of the labour court itself a suitably expert member, Swedish-style as a lay judge, to fortify tripartism – not so much on the wing as in the midfield.

In general, the orthodox explanation of the role of the lay wings is that they are members of the court, not representatives, who bring their special experience to bear. Without doubt they try to do that; it would be wrong to overlook the efforts of some wing members to keep the tribunals informal and realistic. But it would also be myopic not to recognise that, although in some cases they may outvote the chair, the legal chair usually controls that outcome. Dissents, it is reported, occur in only 4 per cent of tribunal cases and even then they occur without the traditional dissenting judgments[194]; it is rare for the lay members to outvote the legal chair who is in theory *primus inter pares* (first among equals) but who is normally dominant, as is the itinerant High Court judge who presides over the EAT for just a few years before he is whisked back to the High Court.[195] This is the common experience of bare tripartism everywhere, with a lawyer in the chair and significant legal representation of the parties; in German labour courts control by majority votes of the wings is regarded as 'theory', because 'it is the professional judge who normally dominates the panel', while in the Swedish Labour Court, with its 'fortified' structure, dissents have been much more common.[196] Tripartism has nowhere by itself been an answer to excessive legalism. An industrial tribunal has often been described by the buzz words: 'an industrial jury'.[197] But that is a dangerous analogy. Far from being remote from the lay jurors, the legal chair retires *with* the jury. In the jury room he is judge and jury. The introduction of fortified tripartism might make a contribution to combat these difficulties in a labour court and, if there were ever the resources to introduce it below, even to assuage the undue legalism of some of our tribunal chairs. More generally, the experience of tripartism demonstrates the critical role which the legal chairs of the labour court would play and why special attention must be paid to them, their career and their training.

Until recently, the idea of 'training' judges tended to make hackles rise in the Strand. Today, however, it is increasingly accepted as necessary, not merely in criminal matters but also, for example, to administer the new policies of family law. The Judicial Studies Board with a budget increased by £500,000 has instituted a series of seminars for 1,000 judges irrespective of rank – from justices clerks to High Court judges – conducted by psychiatrists, academics and welfare officers, on how to handle disputes concerning children. The aim is said to be to produce a 'corps of children's judges' with a common approach,[198] a task, the judge chairing the programme has said, that means 'a fundamental change in what people like myself have been doing for the past thirty years'.[199] Continuous training would be no less essential for the judges of a labour court, at a much more intensive level than the initial training and refresher courses for tribunal chairmen and three-day course with a few half-day, annual refreshers now given to lay members.[200] Those who sit on the appellate division should always have had, or be given, experience of sitting as chair of a tribunal;[201] and all members of the court would need to continue with courses and social experience, even (if fortified tripartism were adopted) the experts.

But there is a limit to what one can unlearn by training. It is in the recruitment of the new legal judges that the experiment is likely to succeed or fail. There is no reason why in the long run at least part of the judiciary of the labour court should not be recruited at a rather younger age, spending a period of years in tribunals, forming a core of career judges with more women and an improved social and ethnic composition.[202] Such a core of industrial judges would, of course, take some years to put in place. The question inevitably arises about the initial establishment of the labour court, and it is to that issue that the immediate attention must be paid.

We may note, first, that informed specialisation with training of the judiciary, is now the mark of perhaps the most successful 'labour court' in Western Europe, one which is not tripartite. The Italian *Pretore* is a local judge, in large urban areas one of a group, who takes on the 'labour jurisdiction' moulded by the procedural reforms of 1973 and 1977 which supplemented the Workers' Statute of 1970.[203] Any comparison of success rates of workers in litigation[204] must, of course, take account of the more extensively protective quality of the substantive law there, as well as the traditional stance of that legal system to reject compromises or 'renunciations' by workers of their vested rights under laws or collective agreements ('*l'inderogabilità*').[205] But there can be little doubt that the procedural reforms of 1973, which considerably modified that principle, were vital to the effective enforcement of the new substantive rights and remedies in the 1970 Act, including reinstatement in dismissal cases.[206] They provided procedures in a one-judge labour court which are informal and speedy (hearings sometimes take place inside the workplace itself) and – a major change in this jurisdiction – are mainly oral, in addition to a variety of conciliation methods including tripartite or 'joint' commissions of employers and unions.[207]

This experience may suggest that, useful though it undoubtedly is, in a given case, tripartism is not always a matter of principle. Curiously, Italy once had tripartite tribunals, the *probiviri*, set up in 1893 under French influence for categories of workers (*operai*, but not white collar *impiegati*) who 'at the beginning of the early, uncertain steps in collective bargaining, had to resolve disputes according to equity', referring to early collective agreements and to 'good sense'.[208] But these courts were abolished by the fascist regime in 1928 which imposed the *Magistratura del lavoro* with powers of compulsory arbitration.[209] There appears to have been no pressure to revive them. But after the democratic constitution of 1948, which prohibited 'special judges' but allowed 'specialised sections of judges for particular matters, as well as the participation of suitable citizens from outside the judiciary' (art. 102) – a formula which might have allowed for certain types of tripartite experiment – the labour jurisdiction was left in the hands of the ordinary civil judges, the *Pretori*, with appeals going to normal appeal courts, ultimately to the *Corte di cassazione*, and on constitutional questions to the Constitutional Court. The law of 1973 recognised the need for specialisation and training. It introduced the subject of labour law into the examinations for the judiciary and obliged the Ministry of Justice 'to organise courses of training each year for judges who specialise in the subject'.[210]

Difficulties have naturally been encountered; commentators criticise the judges, especially appeal judges, since in a system of career judges lacking *stare decisis* (or more accurately, operating with a relaxed concept of precedent) at first instance the young *Pretori* often display a varied and liberal approach, in terms that are not unfamiliar to English ears: their training has not led to a proper application of the new procedures, or they have interpreted legal concepts in an unrealistic manner, limited the right to strike by doctrines of 'unjust damage' or, more generally, retained 'an archetype in the procedural model' which is 'the child of an individualist concept of industrial conflict'.[211] On the other hand, accounts given by the judges themselves (by no means unsympathetic to the collective aspirations of the Workers' Statute and the laws which have followed it), other commentaries and now empirical work suggest that the administration of the law had indeed changed since 1973, not least in the speed of the process and in introducing new limits to managerial prerogative, and has formed the basis of the success of the new labour law.[212]

The interest, therefore, in the Italian experience here is not that we have found some flawless Eldorado of labour jurisdiction, but that we have evidence of a system which made co-ordinated changes to substantive law and procedure in this specialised sector of the administration of justice which were, for all the differences of legal, social and industrial culture, not wholly different in quality and extent from those which would need to be undertaken in Britain if the agenda outlined in this paper were pursued – and it did not fail. It took patience and courage, and there was opposition to the venture, including constitutional challenge;[213] and if it be said that middle opinion of the mid-1970s was more favourable to such ideas than in the decade that followed, as the British debate about 'industrial democracy' may also testify,[214] we should reflect that the 1980s have now gone, leaving us with the need for imagination directed to a new decade in which society itself is likely to change in unimaginable ways. In Britain the creation of a stable labour law system will need similar qualities.

British Labour Courts: Where Could We Start?

For a British labour court, then, one might aim at a status which gives it the necessary autonomy, both in primary and appellate functions, with an informed, trained and comprehending industrial magistracy, which includes a core of career judges recruited at a younger age attracting a better sexual, ethnic and social composition for at least this part of the judiciary. But it may be objected that this is a pipe dream. Is it practicable? Where could we even begin to staff these new specialist courts with suitable members of experience?

It would not be easy. But we are fortunate. There is one rich resource, already an established part of our labour law process, respected by employers, workers, unions and government. It is the Central Arbitration Committee (the 'CAC'). Anchored in the informal arbitral traditions of the old 'Industrial Court' of 1919,[215] the CAC received the hardest tasks of the 1970s legislation in its statutory jurisdictions – awards on union recognition, disclosure of information in bargaining, unilateral arbitration, the Fair Wages Resolution and the impact of equal pay on collective agreements and pay structures, in addition to its voluntary arbitration jurisdiction.[216] In those areas it had to operate as something like a court. It is a tripartite body in which two of the lay members ('persons whose experience is as representatives' of employers or of employees appointed by the Secretary of State from nominations by ACAS – a significantly different procedure from the tribunals) sit with the chairman or a deputy chair, also appointed by him after consultation with ACAS.

The wing members clearly play a significant role in the committee, contributing to the aim of deciding cases in a fair 'pattern' without legalistic 'rigidity'.[217] Moreover, while the chairman may not himself put the adoption of labour courts as his top priority, few can doubt that it is the lead given by him and the deputy chairmen that has secured interpretations of legislation which adopt a 'problem solving approach', acknowledge the role of 'semantics and logic' but insist on a priority for 'industrial relations practice', leaning against solutions which do not facilitate and improve collective bargaining.[218] In broad terms, this does of course imply an attitude to substantive industrial and employment issues,[219] but it is one which could, and experience shows has, successfully run an arbitral tribunal which has in its statutory jurisdictions a labour court competence of the kind under discussion in this paper.

Indeed, as Davies and Freedland have written recently, in the 1970s the CAC acquired

> some title to be regarded as the new collective labour court,
> complementing the work of the industrial tribunals in the individual
> sphere. More important ... the CAC developed its powers in a
> genuinely radical way and made a significant break from the 'court
> substitute' model of adjudication which, as we have seen, has
> dominated the approach of the industrial tribunals ...[220]

It is generally agreed that the CAC in adopting an 'active
problem-solving approach',[221] goes 'to great pains to locate the
problem that is before it and its solution to the problem firmly on
the industrial relations context out of which the problem has arisen
and in which the proposed solution must succeed or fail'.[222]
Careful studies in the 1970s of its sophisticated decisions in the
statutory jurisdictions, many of them now unhappily repealed,
found that its 'flexible and realistic attitude and its policy of
attempting to make industrial relations sense of the law, bodes well
for the future'.[223] Its awards frequently address the immediate
problem in a way that leaves the parties able to come back to it,
and its independence of government, asserted by statute and
reaffirmed in its first Report, was proved abundantly in the face of
income policies.[224] It broke with the tradition of its predecessor,
the Industrial Court, which after its first year never gave reasons
for its awards, but (save where required by statute) only to the
extent of inserting a paragraph explaining the 'general considerations' which it had taken into account.[225]

This is not to say that one agrees with every decision of the
CAC,[226] and it is true that the CAC was overturned on a few
occasions by the High Court as having reached impermissible
interpretations of the statute to be applied and therefore
misdirected itself in law.[227] On those occasions, however, the
difference between the two tribunals served to illustrate starkly the
diverse approaches, the CAC's problem-solving and functional
emphasis on the one hand, the High Court's strict letter of the law
on the other. The comparison illustrated yet again the unsuitability
for this jurisdiction of the High Court. The sharpest illustration
arose in a case on equal pay. Faced with the job of making sense of
equal pay in relation to collective agreements, with a jurisdiction to
declare what amendments must be made in a discriminatory
agreement, the CAC's approach took it into a broad consideration
of the wider pay structures into which, the High Court held, it was
not entitled to go in the absence of overt discrimination in the
agreement. An authoritative commentatory showed that this
'rather brusque treatment' by the court, albeit the legislation was
not happily worded, was the best one could expect: 'Perhaps it is
unfair to expect the Divisional Court overnight to develop a more
sophisticated form of judicial review. Perhaps also it was
unrealistic to expect parliament to have foreseen in 1970 how

sensitively the Committee would come to grips with equal pay issues in 1975 ...'[228]

The study constituted a concrete illustration of the reasons why judicial review of a labour court by the philosophy of the High Court is unthinkable, and *a fortiori* the need not to import that philosophy with its judges into the labour court itself. In any event, between 1976 and 1983 (when the bulk of its work was done before the statutory jurisdictions came to be eroded) the CAC issued some 2,000 awards of which nineteen were challenged in the High Court; and of these six only were quashed.[229] Almost all of its statutory jurisdictions have now been repealed by the legislation of the 1980s. But the CAC itself survives. This gives us enough experienced chairs (not excluding some of the deputies without formal legal qualification) and able wings to staff several divisions of a labour court immediately, including at least one in Scotland and still leave members for the committee's arbitration work.

So there is before us no pipe dream but a practical case to be answered. The rationale for labour courts is the need to administer a reformed labour law code free from the common law tradition and to provide, not a new governess in that school of correction like the National Industrial Relations Court, but an informal specialist court which respects autonomous bargaining, embraces individual and collective rights in the labour market, promotes settlements and reinforces the stability of a new type of employment, with the juridical independence to do its job. Given that, there can be no doubt about the base on which to build. With a choice between common law courts and a flexible tripartite tribunal of the proven calibre of the CAC, the architects of a British labour court system would be foolish not to select the resources of the CAC as their point of departure. Indeed, the argument puts the burden of proof on those who reject that choice. Its chairman already has the status of a senior specialist judge in the field; and if it is said that such a court must be presided over by someone with the 'status of a High Court Judge', there would be no problem about making the necessary, formal appointment of the chairman. In these days of professional reform, there are some in the Temple who would applaud. No doubt policy makers would come under strong pressure to choose a judiciary more generally grounded in common law habits. It must be said that to succumb to such pressures would be a failure in perception, imagination and nerve. Indeed, it might be better not to begin on the project, for a fudged reform with all the ultimate disappointments of raised expectations would risk leaving labour law worse not better administered, less not more stable, in the hands of common law courts. The failure would be the more indefensible when we have before our eyes a well of alternative experience on which to draw for success.

The next reform of British labour law is likely to be no ordinary reform. Community, comparative and domestic pressures are, we have seen, likely to make inevitable a new structure that secures autonomous bargaining and industrial rights and duties within patterns of regulated employment guarantees suited to a modern labour market – a labour law for 2000. The argument suggests that the administration of that system through fair and flexible procedures requires a specialised labour court free from the common law tradition. By chance, the kernel of such a court lies ready at hand in the Central Arbitration Committee, already practised in a rule of law administered informally and with sensitivity to pluralist values and to the industrial facts of life, under whose wing reformed industrial tribunals could be sheltered and enhanced for their tasks. It is a remarkable opportunity, a fortunate circumstance, one which should not be squandered by faltering steps which hand the baton back to those who have always held it in their grip but no longer have the right to carry it.

Notes

1. Evelyn Waugh, *Vile Bodies* (1930), p. 100.
2. S. Freud, *Two Short Accounts of Psycho-Analysis* (1926, Penguin ed. 1970) p. 134.
3. *Report on Trade Unions and Employers Associations* (Cmnd 3623, 1968); the main comparative concern was with the French *Conseils de Prud'hommes*.
4. As with the inquiries in Italy which preceded the 'clean break with foreign experience' concerning union representation in the enterprise in art. 19 of the 'Workers' Statute' 1970: see L. Mariucci, *Le Fonti del diritto del lavoro* (1988), p. 93; Wedderburn, 'The Italian Workers' Statute: British Reflections', [Chapter 9 above]. See too now the valuable comparative survey, M. Biagi, *Rappresentanza e democrazia in azienda* (1990), especially pp. 73-81, 313-320.
5. Employment Act 1982, s. 18, amending s. 29, Trade Union and Labour Relations Act 1974 (TULRA). On France, see Wedderburn, 'Le Législateur et le Juge' in *Transformations du Droit du Travail; Etudes Offertes à Gérard Lyon-Caen* (Dalloz 1989), pp. 136-55; M. Forde, 'Bills of Rights and Trade Union Immunities' (1984) 13 ILJ 40. The proposed immunity was declared unconstitutional by the *Conseil Constitutionnel* (Constitutional Council) (22 October 1982) but was in effect reintroduced by the courts for acts constituting a 'normal exercise of the right to strike' in *Synd. CGT c. Sté Dubidgeon Normandie* Soc. 9 November 1982; J. Savaiter Dr. Soc. 173; G. Lyon-Caen and J. Pélissier, *Droit du Travail* (1988 14th edn) pp. 1036-9; H. Sinay and J-C. Javillier, *La Grève* (1984) 2nd edn), pp. 374-8 [and above p. 292].
6. *Community Charter of Basic Social Rights for Workers* (1990; below 'the Social Charter'; see Appendix 3 of HL Select Committee on the EC 'A Community Social Charter', 3rd Report, 5 December 1990, welcoming the Charter in its final form of 8 December 1990). The Community *Social Charter* must not, of course, be confused with the Council of Europe 'Social Charter' of 1961, arts 7(8) and 8(4)(b) of which the UK denounced in the light of the Employment Act 1989.
7. See the GMB negotiators' 'check list' in *Getting Ready for the European Social Charter* (GMB 1990). By May 1990 the GMB had negotiated an agreement with a German company opening a plant in Birmingham which incorporated the

principles of the Social Charter: *Financial Times*, 22 May 1990.

8. *Communication from the Commission Concerning its Action Programme Relating to the Implementation of the Community Charter of Basic Social Rights for Workers* (9978/89. COM (89) 568 final; 29 November 1989). For an expansive view on the 'extensive' impact this 'massive' programme would have on the UK, see E. Vogel-Polsky, 'What Future is there for a Social Europe Following the Strasbourg Summit?' (1990) 19 ILJ 65; B. Bercusson, 'The European Community Charter of Fundamental Social Rights' (1990) 53 MLR 624; but compare the assessments in B. Hepple, 'The Implementation of the Community Charter of Fundamental Social Rights' (1990) 53 MLR 643; Wedderburn, *The Social Charter, European Company and Employment Rights* (1989, Institute of Employment Rights); and below n. 70.

9. O. Kahn-Freund (ed.) K. Renner, *The Institutions of Private Law and their Functions* (1949), p. 166.

10. O. Kahn-Freund, *Labour and the Law* (3rd ed. 1983; eds P. Davies and M. Freedland), p. 17.

11. See Wedderburn, *The Worker and the Law* (3rd ed. 1986), Chaps 1, 7 and 8.

12. See especially *Codice Civile* arts 1322, 2077, and the incisive explanation of law and agreements as 'sources' and the place of the principle of 'inderogability' of collective agreements by L. Mariucci, *Le fonti del diritto del lavoro* (1988) pp. 99-103; cf. G. Vardaro, 'Funzioni e livelli dei contratti collettivi' Lav. Dir. 1987, 229 (collective agreements have 'assumed in a real sense the form of normative sources with their own base independently of a delegation or reference from statute.' 240); and below n. 205.

13. *Codice Civile*, art. 2095, modified by the Law no 190 of 13 May 1985 ('the conditions for belonging to the category of *quadri* shall be established by national or plant collective bargaining in respect of each branch of industry and for each particular establishment of enterprises,' art. 2(2); such agreements were to be concluded in the first instance within one year, art. 3). See F. Carinci, 'L'Evoluzione storica' in *L'Inquadramento dei lavoratori* (Quaderni di dir. del lavoro e delle rel. ind. 1987) pp. 11-40. See too, other regulatory articles of the Code in arts 2096-2113 (which invalidates 'renunciations' or 'compromises' by workers to their disadvantage of rights derived from laws or collective agreements).

14. See EC, *Etude Comparative des Dispositions Régissant les Conditions de Travail dans les Etats Membres de la Communauté*. (1989, SEC (89) 1137 final) Part II, Chap. V; extracts in 1990 189 EIRR 31; ibid. 190, 29; ibid. 197, 29; R. Blainpain, E. Köhler (eds.), *Legal and Contractual Limitations on Working Time in the EC States* (1988) Chap. IV. There is no general legislation on working hours in Denmark and the UK, none on night work hours in Denmark, Ireland and the UK, none on overtime in Italy, Denmark or the UK. The long standing British controls over hours of vulnerable workers, ie women and workers under 18, have been repealed by ss 9 and 10 Employment Act 1989; see S. Deakin, 'Equality under the Market Order' (1990) 19 ILJ 1, pp. 7-13 (noting too, the denunciation of ILO Convention 45 of 1935 on underground work by women). ILO Conventions of 1990 require social protections for workers on night work, including consultation with union representatives about schedules, especially for women workers.

15. See *Social Charter*, arts 8, 20, 22; *Action Programme* (Part II), Chaps 2 and 11.

16. On the recent French collective agreement, with a 'self-destruct' clause if the law is changed, see: 1990 EIRR 197, 18 (and on the effects on subsequent law reform: ibid., 198, 5). On the German 35-hour week campaign in engineering: 1990 EIRR 198, 11. In Britain, the CSEU achieved 132 agreements cutting hours in its campaign, targeting companies one by one in engineering, but many had productivity and other offsetting provisions: IRRR, 1990 Pay and Benefits Bull. 258, 8; some 566 workplaces were covered: *Bargaining Report* 97 (LRD, July 1990) 10, where 34 of the agreements are analysed.

17. G. Ferraro, 'Fonti autonome e fonti eteronome nella legislazione della flessibilità' (1986) 32 Giorn. dir. lav. rel. ind. 667, 677. It must of course be

remembered that this result is more likely in systems which, subject to more favourable conditions, give the collective agreement an automatic effect on terms of employment affected (e.g. in France, *Code du Travail* art. L 135-2; Italy, *Codice Civil* art. 2077).

18. See Wedderburn and S. Sciarra, 'Collective Bargaining as Agreement and as Law: Neo-Contractualist and Neo-Corporatist Tendencies of Our Age' in A. Pizzorusso (ed.), *Law in the Making* (1988) pp. 185-237 (also (1989) 35 Riv. di dir. civ. 45-102). The Webbs' belief that the 'method of enactment' would supplant the 'method of collective bargaining' (*Industrial Democracy* (1902), pp. 796-806) is not therefore supported by an approach to regulation which recognises a stronger role for law but sees 'a separation of functions and roles between law and collective agreement in the hierarchy of legal sources', ibid., pp. 236-7.

19. B. Hutchins, A. Harrison, *A History of Factory Legislation* (1903); Wedderburn, *The Worker and the Law*, pp. 401-12. Exemptions were available and were regularly granted, but usually on conditions which gave the Inspectors a useful competence to afford to such workers some social protection, for example in the availability of transport after late night shifts. On state intervention and partial employment, see now E. Szyszczak, *Partial Unemployment: The Regulation of Short-Time Working in Britain* (1990), especially Chaps 4 and 5.

20. Railway Servants (Hours of Labour) Act 1893. The Act helped to cut the long hours worked by railwaymen and, by reason of the machinery introduced, helped to establish the new union: H. Clegg, A. Fox, A. Thompson, *A History of British Trade Unions Since 1889; Vol. 1, 1889-1910* (1964), pp. 229-39, an essential period for the understanding of the Taff Vale Railway battle of 1900-1: ibid., Chap. 8; J. Saville (ed.), *Essays in Labour History* (1960).

21. A. Alcock, *A History of the ILO* (1971), pp. 14-21, 50-5. On the factors which led the British government not to legislate generally on working hours in 1920, see H. Phelps Brown, *The Origins of Trade Union Power* (1983), pp. 117-9.

22. Now in particular, the Health and Safety at Work Act 1974, and the burgeoning Community law, especially following the 'Framework Directive' on safety at work, 89/391 of 12 June 1989.

23. Art. 8(4) of the 'Framework' Directive of 12 June 1989, 89/391, provides that workers have the right to stop work 'in the event of serious, imminent and unavoidable danger' without suffering 'any disadvantage' or 'harmful ... consequences'. In debates on the Employment Bill 1990, the government argued that this right already exists because 'it is unlawful to work in unsafe conditions' and 'simple refusal to work in unsafe conditions does not constitute industrial action' (T. Eggar, Minister of State, Standing Cttee D Parl Deb, 20 March 1990, cols 391, 393; see too, Parl. Deb. HL, 12 July 1990, cols 504-18). The meaning of 'industrial action' in s. 9 of the Act on unfair dismissal, as in s. 62 Employment Protection (Consolidation) Act 1978 ('EPCA'), does not turn on breach of the employment contract but arises from concerted pressure upon the employer (*Power Packing Casemakers* v. *Faust* [1983] ICR 292, CA; *Express & Star Ltd* v. *Bunday* [1988] ICR 397, CA). A stoppage by workers refusing to operate vehicles that were dangerous in breach of the criminal law has been held to be a 'strike' within s. 62 (*Wilkins* v. *Cantrell & Cochrane Ltd* [1984] IRLR 483, EAT). The assertion that a 'simple' stoppage over safety is not 'industrial action' therefore seems to be defensible in this context only if it puts no pressure on the employer to rectify the danger. Even under the common law, a contractual right to stop work requires 'a high degree of unanticipated danger': M. Freedland, *The Contract of Employment* (1976), p. 239; *Ottoman Bank* v. *Chakarian* [1930] AC 277; and it is unclear even then whether employees have a right to suspend the contract, rather than rely on the employer's repudiatory order to work at an unsafe place as a ground for a lawful termination. Workers faced with a breach that is criminal can rightly claim a 'constructive dismissal' but not, it seems a suspension of the contract: *Reid* v. *Camphill Engravers* [1990] ICR 435. Current English law appears therefore not to comply fully with the Directive,

which does not limit the right to stop work to cases where there is no 'pressure' on the employer. French law affords a right to stop work where workers have *'a reasonable belief* that there is a grave and imminent danger to health or safety': *Code du Travail* art. L 231-8-1 (added in 1982).

24. See F. Hayek, *Law Legislation and Liberty* (1979) Vol III, p. 115, and pp. 41-54, 81, 142; Wedderburn, 'Freedom of Association and Philosophies of Labour Law' (1989) 18 ILJ 1, 8-14, 34-35. The Chicago school is, however, insistent that other employment protection legislation must be excluded: R. Epstein, 'In Defense of Contract at Will' (1984) 51 Univ. Chic. LR 947.

25. See B. Hepple (ed.), *The Making of Labour Law in Europe* (1986) Chap. 3, and T. Ramm, Chaps 2 and 6.

26. See U. Mückenberger and S. Deakin, 'From Deregulation to a European Floor of Rights; Labour Law, Flexibilisation and the European Single Market' (1989) 3 ZIAS (Zeitschrift für ausländisches und internationales Arbeits- und Sozialrecht) 153 ('The long term aim is the achievement of a new form of individual security for workers, which takes priority over market forces and over the individual contract of employment': p. 201).

27. O. Kahn-Freund, 'Labour Law' in M. Ginsberg (ed.), *Law and Opinion in England in the Twentieth Century* (1959), p. 216: see too his Chap. II, 'Legal Framework', in A. Flanders and H. Clegg, *The System of Industrial Relations in Great Britain* (1954).

28. H. Phelps Brown, *The Growth of British Industrial Relations* (1959), p. 332, and generally Chap. VI; G. Dangerfield, *The Strange Death of Liberal England* (1935) Part 2. Chap. 4; A. Fox, *History and Heritage* (1985), Chaps 4, 5, 6.

29. A. Fox, *Beyond Contract; Work, Power and Trust Relations* (1974), p. 188.

30. B. Veneziani in B. Hepple (ed.), *The Making of Labour Law in Europe*, above n. 25, p. 72.

31. See for example, H. Collins, 'Capitalist Discipline and Corporatist Law' (1982) II ILJ 78 and 170: below, n. 65.

32. Wedderburn, 'Industrial Relations and the Courts' (1980) 9 ILJ 65, 66-9; A. Jacobs 'Collective Self-Regulation' Chap. 5. *The Making of Labour Law in Europe*, above n. 25.

33. E.J. Hobsbawm, *Worlds of Labour* (1984), p. 153; and on the grip of *laissez faire*, see his *Labouring Men* (1964) Chap. 14. In Sweden, unions affiliating to the central federation originally were required to be affiliated also to the Social Democratic Party: Folke Schmidt in B. Aaron and K. Wedderburn, *Industrial Conflict; A Comparative Legal Survey* (1972), p. 28.

34. O. Kahn-Freund (ed.), *K. Renner: The Institutions of Private Law and their Functions* (1949), p. 172, though later he somewhat resiled from this explanation for reasons that remain obscure: *Labour and the Law* (1977, 2nd ed.), p. 40. See too, Wedderburn, *The Worker and the Law*, op. cit., n. 11 above, pp. 21-7, and (1980) 9 ILJ 65; A. Fox, *History and Heritage*, op. cit., n. 28 above, Chap. 4.

35. Conspiracy and Protection of Property Act 1875, s. 3; Trade Disputes Act 1906, ss. 1-3; and see H. Pelling, *The Origins of the Labour Party* (1954) especially Chap. 10.

36. See O. Kahn-Freund, 'Strikes and the Law – Some Recent Developments in Western Europe' in *Jus et Societas; Essays in Tribute to Wolfgang Friedmann* (1979), pp. 201-19. 'Non-union strikes as such are ... illegal' in Germany: T. Ramm. ... '*Federal Republic of Germany*', *International Encylopaedia for Labour Law and Industrial Relations* (1979, ed. R. Blainpain), p. 196.

37. H. Sinay and J-C. Javillier, *La Grève* (2nd ed., 1984), Tit. 1 Chap. 2, and 'Le Droit Comparé de la Grève', ibid., Chap. 3; G. Giugni, 'L'Autotutela e il diritto di sciopero' Chap. 10. *Diritto sindacale* (8th ed. 1988).

38. G. Ghezzi and U. Romagnoli, *Il diritto sindacale* (2nd ed. 1987), p. 193.

39. G. Giugni, *Diritto sindacale*, n. 37, p. 216. A strike in Sweden is taken 'merely to suspend the duty of performance': Folke Schmidt, *Law and Industrial Relations in Sweden* (1977), p. 74.

40. *Code du Travail*, art. L 521-1. For the *locus classicus* on this question, see: X. Blanc-Jouvan, 'The Effect of Industrial Action on the Status of the Individual Employee', Chap. 4 in B. Aaron and K. Wedderburn (eds), *Industrial Conflict: A Comparative Legal Survey*, above n. 33.

41. See G. Lyon-Caen and J. Pélissier, *Droit du Travail* (14th ed. 1988), pp. 1001-4; and see Wedderburn, 'Laws About Strikes' (forthcoming in W. McCarthy (ed.), *Legal Interventions in Labour Law*, 1991).

42. Stuart-Smith LJ, *Associated British Ports* v. *TGWU* [1989] 1 WLR 939, 970, CA (reversed on other grounds, HL; B. Simpson (1989) 18 ILJ 234). Of Community member states, only Britain, Denmark and (perhaps) Ireland regard a legitimate strike as effecting breach, rather than suspension of the employment contracts: EC, *Etude Comparative (etc.), above*, n. 14; on Ireland, A. Kerr and G. Whyte, *Irish Trade Union Law* (1985), Chap. 8.

43. See on the 1906 Bill R. Kidner (1982) 2 Legal Studies 34; Wedderburn, *The Worker and the Law*, pp. 21-5; R. Harrison, *Before the Socialists* (1965), pp. 287-9; W. Cornish and G. de N. Clark, *Law and Society in England 1750-1950* (1989), pp. 328-36.

44. For detailed sources and the diverse natures of various national 'extension' machineries, and their absence from other systems, see Wedderburn and Sciarra in A. Pizzorusso, *Law in the Making*, op. cit., above n. 18, pp. 220-7; to explain these differences by 'traditional methods of collective bargaining (see O. Kahn-Freund, 'Labour Relations and International Standards: Some Reflections on the European Social Charter' in *Miscellanea W. Ganshoff van der Meersch* (1972) 131 p. 147) is an inadequate explanation of the variations: ibid., 223.

45. On the wartime Order 1305 of 1940 and its successor Order 1376 of 1951, see O. Kahn-Freund in A. Flanders and H. Clegg, *The System of Industrial Relations in Great Britain* (1954), pp. 83-100; on its successor, s. 8 Terms and Conditions of Employment Act 1959: K. Wedderburn and P. Davies, *Employment Grievances and Disputes Grievances in Britain* (1969), pp. 204-13. The most recent measure, Employment Protection Act, 1975, Sched. 11, was repealed by s. 19 Employment Act 1980. In so far as it came to rely after 1946 upon standards set by representative collective bargaining, the Fair Wages Resolution could be seen as a parallel institution (O. Kahn-Freund, 'Legislation through Adjudication' (1948) 11 MLR 269, 429; B. Bercusson, *Fair Wages Resolutions* (1978)); and on the various statutes incorporating 'fair wages' clauses, now repealed or nullified, Wedderburn and Davies, op. cit., pp. 199-203. The Resolution was rescinded in 1983. Local authorities are now prevented from using such standards in awarding contracts: Local Government Act 1988, ss. 17-20.

46. *Action Programme*, Pt. II Chap. 3 and, on young workers, Chap. 11 (building on the proposals of 1983, 'the adaptation, flexibility and organisation of working time' are crucial for 'the dynamism of firms ... the creation of employment ... and the improvement of their competitiveness ...': diversity of practice must not have an 'adverse effect on the well-being and health of workers' and needs 'minimum requirements,' or 'minimum reference rules,' about rest periods, overtime, etc. laid down at Community level,' pp. 18-9); and the Commission's proposals of 20 September 1990 (COM (90) 317 final, SYN 295); for a Directive on working time, which the British government called an 'arbitrary obstacle to new working patterns': *Financial Times*, 26 July 1990; (1990) EIRR 201, 14; see B. Hepple, *Working Time: A New Legal Framework?* (1990 IPPR). The proposal for a Directive demanding more formal written contracts, with 'greater transparency' on rights and obligations and references to the relevant 'law and/or collective agreement' (p. 19), could be of great importance especially for the growing tendency for individual bargaining in Britain, though unhappily public sector workers are to be excluded. In proposals of 25 July 1990 the Commission suggested obligations for both the employer and the 'user' in another State to whom he sends workers to ensure observance of the employment contract; the contract should

contain any relevant conditions laid down by law or in collective agreements in the 'host country' which are 'more favourable than those in force' in the country of origin (an interesting use of the formula in the Fair Wages Resolution 1946 and an adumbration of the kind of Community labour law British courts may have to apply: see below, nn. 214-6).

47. See *Evidence* to the HC Employment Cttee on 'Part-Time Employment' by the Dept of Employment, HC 270-viii, 7 June 1990, 150, especially 155; and *Evidence* of the TUC, HC 270-ix, 14 June 1990, 177; also the Government *Reply* to the Second Special Report, HC 485, 13 June 1990. The Commission's figures of 13 June 1990 showed that the Netherlands and Denmark had a higher percentage of part-time employees than Britain.

48. See the Dept of Employment *Evidence*, op. cit., n. 47 above, Table 14 ('45 per cent of part-time employees were eligible [in 1988] for the main employment protection rights,' p. 155). On the dispute about the right figure, see C. Hakim (1989) 18 ILJ 69 (who estimates that more part-timers are covered); R. Disney and E. Szyszczak (1989) 18 ILJ 223. On the reasons for predominance of part-time work among women: M. Metcalfe and P. Leighton, *The Under-utilisation of Women in the Labour Market*, IMS Report 172 (1989); and on the recent repeal of protective legislation, S. Deakin (1990) 19 ILJ 1, 5-11.

49. On 13 August 1990 the Commission proposed three Directives (COM (90) 228 final, SYN 280, 281), the first two for workers working over eight hours a week: (a) under art. 100 of the Treaty, proportional rights to full time workers in respect of training and social services, with employers obliged to give reasons in the employment contract for temporary work and to inform workers' representatives before using part-time workers; (b) under art. 100a, pro-rata 'social protection' in relation to full timers, eg on paid holidays, dismissal allowances, seniority payments, occupational pensions, etc (but not basic pay) with limits on the length of temporary employment relationships; and (c) under art. 118a, guaranteeing equal rights for all temporary workers on health and safety: see *Non-Standard Forms of Employment in Europe* (EIRR Report 3, 1990), pp. 59-67.

50. *Action Programme*, pp. 15-6; as for the proposed Directives, above n. 49, British government opposition (they are 'unrealistic and damaging to business and to jobs'; M. Howard, Secretary of State for Employment, DE Press Notice, 29 June 1990) objected to the use of Treaty articles in (b) and (c) which provide a 'Treaty base' for qualified majority voting in the Council of Ministers: see Wedderburn *The Social Charter, European Company and Employment Rights* (1989) op. cit., n. 8, pp. 52-5.

51. Law no. 863, 19 December 1984, especially art. 5, which applies to both 'vertical' and 'horizontal' part-time work; it is an offence for the employer to fail to deposit with the public authorities a copy of the written part-time contract. See generally, A. Maresca, 'Il part time,' Chap. 1 in M. D'Antona (ed.), *Occupazione flessible e nuove tipologie del rapporto del lavoro* (1988), pp. 31-76. In the 1987 collective agreement for engineering the parties 'recognise the principle of part time work, meaning working hours by day or by week less than those envisaged in the collective agreement for that type of worker, which can constitute a useful instrument for flexibility ... so far as it is used for the needs of the enterprise ... according to criteria of proportionality [of pay] within normal principles ...' (art. 5.6): F. Carinci, *Commentario del contratto collettivo dei metalmeccanici dell'industria privata* (1990), pp. 185, 191.

52. *Code du Travail*, art. L 212-4-2 to -5; G. Lyon-Caen and J. Pélissier, *Droit du Travail* (1988, 14th ed.) pp. 475-80.

53. Ordonnance of 11 August 1986, modified by law of 19 June 1987 (now in *Code of Travail* art. 212-4-8 *et seq.*); G. Lyon-Caen and J. Pélissier, *Droit du Travail*, n. 52, pp. 245-53; J. Pélissier, 'Le travail intermittent' Dr. Soc. 1987, 93-100.

54. U. Mückenberger and S. Deakin, 'From Deregulation to a European Floor of Rights' (1989) *ZIAS*, above, n. 26, p. 163.

55. On Germany, see M. Weiss, *Labour Law and Industrial Relations in the FRG* (1987), pp. 46-9. The law of 1985 was to last four years only, but has been extended for a further five years: 1990 EIRR, 185, 4. On France, see Crim. 25 February 1986; Soc. 13 November 1986, J. Savatier Dr. Soc. 1987, 407, and his 'Le travail à temps partiel; chronique de jurisprudence' Dr. Soc. 1988, 438-48; and now Law of 12 July 1990 (1990 EIRR 200, 27). For a comparative review of controls over fixed term contracts, see *Travail et Emploi*, 1989, no. 1, *Numéro Special: Formes d'Emploi*: M. Pedrazzoli (Italy) 1; M.E. Casas Baaomonde and F. Valdes dal Ré (Spain) 17; V. Merle (France) 25; U. Zachert (West Germany) 42. The picture in Britain (see P. Davies and M. Freedland, 32) was thought by the editor to be marked by 'the weakness of its employment legislation,' P. Koeep, p. 7.
56. G. Giugni, 'Il diritto del lavoro negli anni '80' (1982) 15 Giorn. dir. lav. rel. ind. 373, 408 (now in *Lavoro legge contratti* (1989), p. 334).
57. L. Mariucci, *Le fonti del diritto del lavoro*, op. cit. n. 4 above, p. 49, and generally Chap. II; S. Sciarra, *Contratto collettivo e contrattazione in azienda* (1985) Chap. II. The Italian movement has been towards a more 'flexibile' employment protection, but in some respects protection has recently increased. e.g. in thresholds for protection against unfair dismissal (Law 108 of 11 May 1990; Wedderburn (1990) 19 ILJ 154, 189 [see above Chapter 9].
58. See for further references, Wedderburn (1989) 18 ILJ pp. 20-3. British research, such as that by W. Daniel and E. Stilgoe, *The Impact of Employment Protection Laws* (1978) or S. Evans, J. Goodman, L. Hargreaves, *Unfair Dismissal Law and Employment Practice* (DE 1985), is matched elsewhere in concluding that deregulation does not necessarily lead to higher recruitment: see on Germany, C. Buchtemann, 'More Jobs through less Employment Protection?' (1990) 3 *Labour* 23.
59. Thus, Giugni can say that a 'full scale deregulation, understood as a reinstatement of a market equilibrium ... can have no convincing rational base ... not corresponding to the realities of the labour market ...': 'Giuridificazione e deregolazione nel diritto del lavoro italiano' (1986) Giorn dir. lav. rel. ind. 317, 331 (now *Lavoro legge contratti* (1989) 337, 353; English version (1987) 8 Comp. Lab. Law Jo. 389, 323-4).
60. On trainees in Britain, see the invaluable note by N. Wikeley, 'Training for Employment in the 1990s' (1990) 53 MLR 354, especially pp. 362-8. On apprentice or 'work training' contracts invented elsewhere: M. Weiss, *Labour Law and Industrial Relations in the FRG*, above n. 55, pp. 51-2; R. Pessi, Chap. III, 'Il contratto di formazione e lavoro' in M. D'Antona (ed.), *Occupazione flessibile ... etc*', above n. 51, pp. 77-109; G. Lyon-Caen and J. Pélissier, *Droit du Travail*, above n. 52, pp. 66-88 (and the new art. L 900-2 *Code du Travail*). See too, the symposium on 'Youth Employment' (1986) 24 BJIR 25-81.
61. Employment Act 1988, s. 26.
62. See, for a useful fresh look at the issue, H. Collins, 'Independent Contractors and the Challenge of Vertical Disintegration to Employment Protection Laws' (1990) 10 Ox. Jo. Leg. Studs. 353 (the only way out 'requires the mandatory imposition of these rights by reference to social and economic criteria,' p. 380); cf J. Clark and Wedderburn in Wedderburn, R. Lewis and J. Clark (eds), *Labour Law and Industrial Relations* (1983), pp. 144-55 ('A Crisis in Fundamental Concepts'): B. Hepple, 'Restructuring Employment Rights' (1986) 15 ILJ 67; and (1990) 11 Comp. Lab. Law Jo. 425, 439.
63. See s. 140 EPCA 1978; *Logan Salton* v. *Durham CC* [1989] IRLR 99, (prevalence of contract concluded 'without duress' and not a variation of existing employment contract, but with effect of excluding protection, distinguishing *Igbo* v. *Johnson Matthey Chemicals Ltd* [1986] IRLR 215, CA). On the 'intention of the parties,' see J. Clark and Wedderburn, op. cit., n. 62, pp. 152-4; H. Collins, op. cit., n. 62, pp. 372-6.
64. *Ironmonger* v. *Movefield Ltd* [1988] IRLR 461, EAT, pp. 463, 465, *per* Wood J

(the IT had held there was no dismissal in any event as it was a task contract). The arrangements had been used by the company for many years: p. 463.

65. See for some other sources of this long debate, P. Davies and M. Freedland, *Labour Law: Text and Materials* (2nd ed. 1984) pp. 361-71; B. Hepple, Chap. 16 in G. Bain (ed.), *Industrial Relations in Britain* (1983) and 'Restructuring Employment Rights' (1986) 15 ILJ 69; H. Collins, 'Market Power, Bureaucratic Power and the Contract of Employment' (1986) 15 ILJ 1, and 'Corporatist Discipline and Capitalist Control' (1982) 11 ILJ 170; H. Forrest, 'Political Values in Individual Employment Law' (1979) 42 MLR 361; Wedderburn, 'Labour Law: From Here to Autonomy?' (1987) 16 ILJ 1, 4-22; B. Napier, Chap. 12 and P. Leighton, Chap. 18 in R. Lewis (ed.), *Labour Law in Britain* (1986); U. Mückenberger and S. Deakin, 'From Deregulation to a European Floor of Rights' (1989) ZIAS 153, above n. 26; S. Deakin, 'Labour Law and the Developing Employment Relationship' (1986) 10 Camb. Jo. Econ. 225.

66. It is true that the HL has felt compelled to adopt new methods of interpretation under pressure from Community law and that other courts may be willing to follow, even into domestic law as such: *Litster* v. *Forth Dry Dock & Engineering* [1989] ICR 341, HL; *Hancill* v. *Marcon Engineering Ltd* [1990] IRLR 51, EAT; but the problems identified in the analyses cited, n. 65, go far beyond questions of statutory interpretation.

67. Sir John Wood 'Labour Relations Law – The Missing Pieces' (1990) 24 The Law Teacher 111, 121. This seems to be a prescription for more than reform of statutory interpretation, see below n. 132 *et seq*.

68. On the draft Regulation and Directive for the European Company, COM(89) final – SYN 218, 219, see the House of Lords EEC Committee, *Report*, 10 July 1990, Paper 71-1 (criticising the Treaty base for the proposals on worker participation, art. 54, which would allow for majority voting in the Council); Wedderburn, *The Social Charter, European Company and Employment Rights*, op. cit., n. 8. Chap. 5; B. Hepple, 'The Implementation of the Community Charter of Fundamental Social Rights' (1990) 53 MLR 643.

69. See the *Action Programme*, cit. Part 1, paras 3 and 6; Part II, pp. 15, 29-30 where the Commission declares it will prepare a non-binding 'communication' on collective bargaining; on the Commission's role in the 'social dialogue,' see art. 118b of the Treaty; and see B. Hepple, op. cit. (1990), n. 68, pp. 651-4. On workers' rights to information and consultation the Commission plans to propose a Directive for model European Works Councils in undertakings with establishments in more than one member state.

70. EEC Directives 75/129 and 77/187 leading in the UK to ss. 99-105 EPA 1975, and the Transfer of Undertakings (Protection of Employment) Regulations 1981, SI 1981 no. 1794. Whether the UK has adequately implemented the Directives since 1980, when all obligation to recognise trade unions was removed from the law, may be doubted since the obligations to consult are couched in terms only of recognised unions: see Wedderburn, op. cit., *The Social Charter, European Company and Employment Rights*, above n. 8, Chaps 3, 5, 6; B. Hepple, op. cit., above n. 68, (1990) 54 MLR pp. 648-51. On this and related issues, see C. Docksey (1986) 49 MLR 281; B. Hepple and A. Byre (1989) 18 ILJ 127; D. Wyatt (1989) 18 ILJ 197. This issue will arise in the revision of the 1975 Directive on collective redundancies promised in the *Action Programme* Part II, p. 19. The Commission has alleged a violation in the UK failure to impose an obligation to consult except where the employer chooses to recognise a union: s. 99 Employment Protection Act 1975 ('EPA'). The ECJ upheld a charge of a similar violation by Italy: Case 91/81. [1982] ECR 2133, and Case 131/84; see M. Garofalo (1990) 46 Giorn. dir. lav. rel. ind. 235, 258-71. On the earlier developments of harmonisation of Community labour law, see B. Hepple, Chap. II in J. Adams (ed.), *Essays for Clive Schmitthoff* (1983); J. Pipkorn, 'Comparative Labor Laws in Harmonising Social Standards in the EC' (1977) 2 Comp. Lab. Law 260. Compare, on the 'indepen-

dence of social policy': B. Bercusson, 'The European Community's Charter of Fundamental Social Rights of Workers' (1990) 53 MLR 624, 625, 638-41.

71. On the history of international labour standards, see T. Ramm, Chap. 7 in B. Hepple (ed.), *The Making of Labour Law in Europe* (1986).

72. *Action Programme* Part I, para. 9.

73. *Rapport des Chefs de Délégations, Comité Intergouvernemental*, 21 April 1956, Chairman P. Spaak, pp. 19-20, 60-1; O. Kahn-Freund, 'Labour Law and Social Security', Chap. VI in E. Stein and T. Nicholson (eds), *American Enterprise and the European Common Market: A Legal Profile* (1960) Vol. 1, pp. 301-19; and see his remarkable 'Sketch Map of Labor Laws in the Six' at pp. 361-442, to appreciate just how far labour law has come in Western Europe since 1960.

74. See especially arts 117-121 of the Treaty of Rome, as amended in 1987.

75. G.F. Mancini, 'Labour Law and Community Law' (1985) 20 (NS) Irish Jurist 1, 12.

76. See U. Mückenberger and S. Deakin, op. cit., above n. 26 (a review arguing for the third view); T. Eggar, Minister of State, *Evidence to HL EEC Committee, A Community Social Charter (with Evidence)* (HL Paper 6, 5 December 1989, 3rd Report), p. 16: control of wage rates and employment conditions would 'stop one of their competitive advantages' for poorer countries; J. Hendy, 'Treat the Charter as a Starter', *Times*, 2 January 1990.

77. *Action Programme*, Part II, pp. 16, 18, 23, 31, 48.

78. CBI *Evidence* to HL EEC Committee, in *Report*, above n. 47, p. 20. Some define 'social dumping' to mean 'that companies will invest where the wages and conditions are cheapest and thereby force the workers in other countries ... to accept lower standards', R. Blanpain (1990) 11 Comp. Lab. Law. Jo. 403. Others will see this as a natural feature of competition in a free Community market.

79. See in France, after the *Auroux* reforms, the law of 13 November 1982; *Code du Travail*, art. L 132-27.

80. U. Mückenberger and S. Deakin, op. cit., above n. 26, p. 202.

81. V. Papandreou, Commissioner for Social Policy, speech on 16 October 1989, *For a Social Europe* (ETUC 1989) p. 25. See too T. Treu, *Pubblico e privato nell' Europa Sociale* (1990) Lav. Dir. 320 (logic may point to total harmonisation of labour laws but there is little prospect of this happening); M. Weiss, 'European legislation on labour matters will be implemented only if the social parties and the different member states do not resist it' (1990) 11 Comp. Lab. Law Jo. 423.

82. See especially, F. Hayek, *1980s Unemployment and the Unions* (1980), p. 58, *The Constitution of Liberty* (1960), pp. 267-84, and *Law Legislation and Liberty* (1979), Vol. III p. 144; R. Tur, 'The Legitimacy of Industrial Action' in Wedderburn and W.T. Murphy, *Labour Law and the Community* (1982), pp. 155-64. For the place of Hayek, Wedderburn (1989) 18 ILJ 1 [above Chapter 8].

83. G. Mather, *Times*, 23 June 1989; C. Hanson and G. Mather, *Striking Out Strikes* (1988).

84. *Social Charter*, arts 11-14; but the right to strike is confined to 'conflicts of interest,' a limitation which is effective only in some member states, and art. 14 permits special limitations on all three rights for the armed forces, police and 'civil service' (the last representing an unsatisfactory principle applied in many Continental systems which began with a gulf between private and public employment law); see Wedderburn, *The Social Charter, European Company and Employment Rights* (1990, Institute of Employment Rights), pp. 398-43 [above Chapter 10].

85. *Report of the Committee of Experts*. ILO 76th Session 1989 Report III (Part 4A) pp. 234-41; K. Ewing, *Britain and the ILO* (1989, Institute of Employment Rights). The Committee also criticised the complexity of British law of which both 'the form and content' should be reconsidered, p. 241. Subsequently, the Employment Act 1990 has effected further contraventions by banning all secondary action and extending power for employers to dismiss 'unofficial' strikers selectively.

86. *Donovan Report* (1968, Cmnd 3623) para. 935; *Rookes* v. *Barnard* [1964] AC 1129, HL. [See Chapter 1 above.]

87. See on the need for caution about changing the legal form, Wedderburn, 'The New Politics of Labour Law' in W. McCarthy (ed.), *Trade Unions* (2nd ed., 1985) pp. 397-432; for a sceptical view: A. Wilson 'The Future of Labour Law: Positive Rights and Immunities' (1986) Industrial Tutor 27; and a more optimistic approach: K. Ewing, 'The Right to Strike' (1986) 15 ILJ 143.

88. See the cases of *Bardot* Soc. 23 November 1978, D 1979 304, J.C. Javillier; *Usinor* Soc. 15 June 1978, D 1979 25, O. Langlois; and *SNCF* Soc. 29 June 1989; H. Sinay and J.C. Javiller, *La Grève* (2nd ed., 1984) p. 178; Wedderburn, 'Laws about Strikes' in W. McCarthy (ed.), *Legal Interventions in Labour Law* (forthcoming 1991) [and see above, Chapter 10, p. 288].

89. K. Ewing, 'Positive Rights and Immunities' (1988) 10 Comp. Lab. Law Jo. 1, 35. On conflicts of rights and conflicts of interests in various systems, see Wedderburn, 'Laws About Strikes', W. McCarthy (ed.), *Legal Interventions in Labour Law* (1991 forthcoming); *The Social Charter in Britain, European Company and Employment Rights* (1990) pp. 39-42 and 'The Right to Strike – A European Standard?' (forthcoming papers 1991).

90. See C. Jenkins and J. Mortimer, *The Kind of Laws the Unions Ought to Want* (1968), proposing *inter alia* rights to organise and to bargain.

91. *Trade Union Immunities* (1981, Cmnd 8128), para. 376. The CBI discussion document, *Trade Unions in a Changing World; The Challenge for Management* (1980, chair A. Jarret), suggested that a positive right to strike might be enacted, subject to 'reasonable limitations.' A new policy 'should use whatever drafting format is appropriate to particular problems': Wedderburn, 'The New Politics of Labour Law' in W. McCarthy (ed.), *Trade Unions* (2nd ed., 1985), p. 524.

92. Ministry of Labour, *Evidence to the Royal Commission* (1965), p. 92; see J. Clark and Wedderburn in Wedderburn, R. Lewis and J. Clark (eds), *Labour Law and Industrial Relations* (1983), pp. 173-84. For unrelated, but interesting proposals to use munitions tribunals as arbitral 'labour courts', see G. Rubin, 'Labour Courts and the Proposals of 1917-1919' (1985) 14 ILJ 33, and (1977) 6 ILJ 149.

93. Scrutton LJ, 'The Work of the Commercial Court' (1923) I Camb. LJ 6, p. 8.

94. The Italian judge normally reaches the bench before 30 years of age and the highest position of a career by 53: G. Certoma, *The Italian Legal System* (1985), pp. 71-3; these judges also display considerable social activity, forming associations divided on normal ideological lines: G.F. Mancini, 'Politics and the Judges – The European Perspective' (1980) 43 MLR 1; so too in France: W. de Haan, J. Silvio, P. Thomas (1988) 16 Jo. Law Soc. 477. Swedish judges choose not to be practitioners within three years of their university degree: S. Strömholm, *An Introduction to Swedish Law* (2nd ed., 1988), pp. 39-40. In France the same division appears, but practitioners can switch to be judges in the ordinary courts. French judges enter the profession by competition, but there is also some recruitment from advocates and other professional persons at a later stage: G. Couchez, 'Le Personnel Judiciaire' Section II *Procédure Civil* (1988, 4th ed.). The lay judges of the *Conseils de Prud'hommes* are elected by employers, on the one side, and employees, on the other (on the history of the *conseils*, M. David 1974 Dr. Soc. (no.2) 3, 17). See too, B. Aaron (ed.), *Labour Courts and Grievance Settlement in Western Europe* (1971) on France, X. Blanc-Jouvan; West Germany, T. Ramm.

95. J.A.G. Griffith, *The Politics of the Judiciary* (2nd ed., 1985; 3rd ed. forthcoming), p. 31. On Germany, see E. Blankenburg and R. Rogowski, 'German Labour Courts and the British Industrial Tribunal System' (1986) Jo. Law and Soc. 67, 84; on France and Italy, Wedderburn, 'Le législateur et le juge' in *Les Transformations du Droit du Travail: Etudes Offertes à Gérard Lyon-Caen* (1989) 123, especially pp. 142-7. For recent procedural reforms which have substantially affected labour jurisdictions see: in Sweden, the Act on Litigation in Labour Disputes 1964, as amended by Acts of 1977-84; in Italy, the Law on Employment Disputes and Social Security Matters, Law no 533, 11 August 1973; G. Tarzia, *Manuale del processo del lavoro* (2nd ed., 1987); and in Spain, the Law on

Procedure in Labour Disputes, 521/1990, 27 April 1990 (for the employers' complaint of unconstitutionality, (1990) 199 EIRR 8).

96. For a full account of the positive law here, see Chapter 15 (Wedderburn) in R. Dias (ed.), *Clerk and Lindsell on Torts* (16th ed. 1989).

97. *Express Newspapers Ltd* v. *McShane* [1980] AC 672, 687; *Duport Steels Ltd* v. *Sirs* [1980] ICR 161, 177. It is true that in these cases the HL barred a particularly narrow interpretation of the immunities adopted by the Court of Appeal under Lord Denning MR but the terms of the Law Lords' opinions invited legislation to narrow them, which was indeed already before parliament: see B. Simpson (1980) 43 MLR 327; P. Davies and M. Freedland in J. Jowell and J.P. McAuslan (eds), *Lord Denning: the Judge and the Law* (1984). Parliament did not give unions 'rights', only 'immunity to lawbreakers': Lord Denning MR, *Express Newspapers* v. *McShane* [1979] ICR 210, 218 [see above Chapters 8 and 10].

98. Browne-Wilkinson J, *Powley* v. *ACAS* [1978] ICR 123, 135 (an analysis which in any event was questionable, since the individual worker still retained the 'right' in law to make whatever contract he chose with his employer); see generally, B. Simpson, 'Judicial Control of ACAS' (1980) 9 ILJ 125.

99. For an area of judicial creativity often forgotten (because intervention in the internal affairs of British unions has in the 1980s come to be dominated by legislation), see O. Kahn-Freund, 'The Illegality of a Trade Union' (1943) 7 MLR 172; *Edwards* v. *SOGAT* (1971) Ch. 354; and generally, Wedderburn, *The Worker and the Law* (3rd ed. 1986), Chaps 1 and 9.

100. See e.g. *Crofter Hand Woven Harris Tweed Co* v. *Veitch* [1942] AC 435, HL. It is also to be remembered that by reason of an agreement between the TUC and the Labour government, the 'wartime' period extended for labour law until 1951 when the ban on strikes in Order 1305 was at last rescinded after unsuccessful attempts to prosecute leaders of unofficial strikes conducted by the Attorney General, later Lord Shawcross. The facts of *Thomson* v. *Deakin* [1952] Ch. 646, CA, the high point of post-war abstentionism, occurred in the spring of 1952.

101. When that opinion changed, 'the social bottom was knocked out of the judges' attitude of "non-intervention" ': Wedderburn, 'Labour Law and Labour Relations in Britain' (1972) 10 BIJR 271, 277. The judicial decisions in the period immediately following the First World War contain divergent strains of policy and were in part probably affected by the social cohesion briefly desired in some circles after its slaughter: Wedderburn, *The Worker and the Law*, n. 11, pp. 31-3.

102. See Sir William Erle *Memorandum, Royal Commission on Trade Unions 11th Report 1867-9* (C 4123) 'The Law Relating to Trade Unions' pp. lxxi-ii; R. Hedges and A. Winterbottom, *The Legal History of Trade Unionism* (1930), pp. 46-62; *Quinn* v. *Leathem* [1901] AC 495, HL; *Taff Vale Rlwy Co* v. *Amal Soc. Rlwy Servants* [1901] AC 426 HL; *Amal Soc. Rlwy Servants* v. *Osborne* [1910] AC 87 HL; *Rookes* v. *Barnard* [1964] AC 1129, HL; *Stratford* v. *Lindley* [1965] AC 269 HL; *Torquay Hotel Co Ltd* v. *Cousins* [1969] 2 Ch. 106, CA: *Universe Tankships Inc of Monrovia* v. *Laughton* [1983] 1 AC 366 HL; *Associated British Ports* v. *TGWU* [1989] IRLR 291 (Millett J), [1989] 1 WLR 939 CA, reversed on other grounds HL.

103. *Per* Millett J [1989] IRLR p. 303; for the CA decision, [1989] 1 WLR 939, especially Stuart Smith LJ at p. 966 on intention; see B. Simpson (1989) 18 ILJ 234; *Clerk and Lindsell on Torts*, op. cit., n. 96, paras 15-20, n. 45.

104. *Allen* v. *Flood* [1898] AC 1 HL; *Quinn* v *Leathem* [1901] AC 495, HL.

105. Grantham J, *McGuire* v. *Andrews*, *Times*, 8 March 1904.

106. Lord Devlin, *Samples of Lawmaking* (1962), pp. 11, 12. He expressly recognises that the 'stream of thought' is that leading back to Sir William Erle by citing with approval Pollock's adoption of Bowen LJ, *Skinner* v. *Shew* [1893] 1 Ch. 413, 422: 'at common law there was a cause of action whenever one person did damage to another wilfully and intentionally without just cause and excuse,' a formula which gives the judge full scope to apply such policies, not least to trade

unions: compare the Court of Appeal in *Associated British Ports* v. *TGWU* [1989] 1 WLR 939 (reversed on other grounds, ibid. HL), above n. 103.

107. *Rookes* v. *Barnard* [1964] AC 1129, HL, pp. 1203-20. Lord Devlin even held open, pp. 1215-6, the prospect of liability arising from '*Quinn* v. *Leathem* without the conspiracy', a frontal attack on *Allen* v. *Flood* itself.

108. See for example interpretations of rights to freedom of association by the Law Lords in the Privy Council in *Collymore* v. *Att. Gen.* [1970] AC 538, PC (Lord Donovan) and the majority judgments in *Re Public Service Employee Relations Act, etc.* (1987) 38 DLR (4th) 161 (SCC); T. Christian and K. Ewing, 'Labouring under the Canadian Constitution' (1988) 17 ILJ 73; Wedderburn 'Freedom of Association or Right to Organise? (1987) 18 Ind. Rels Jo. 244; A. Kahn, 'The Canadian Charter, Freedom of Association and Labour Relations' (1989) 20 Ind. Rels Jo, 47 [but see now *Lavigne*'s case, 27 June 1991, SCC].

109. F. Frankfurter and N. Greene, *The Labor Injunction* (1932), p. 201.

110. For detailed authorities underpinning the argument in this section, see Wedderburn, 'The Injunction and the Sovereignty of Parliament' (1989) 23 The Law Teacher 4-44 [above Chapter 7], and *Clerk and Lindsell on Torts*, op. cit., above n. 96, pp. 822-4, 932-7.

111. *American Cyanamid Co* v. *Ethicon Ltd* [1975] AC 396, HL. The earlier rule is clearly stated by Lord Upjohn, *Stratford* v. *Lindley* [1965] AC 269, 338, but there were discrepancies in the way it was applied: S. Anderman and P. Davies 'Injunction Procedure in Labour Disputes' (1973) 2 ILJ 213, 219-28, (1974) 3 ILJ 30 (on the procedure in the NIRC).

112. See W. Cornish, *Intellectual Property* (2nd ed. 1990), pp. 38-40, 172-3.

113. Some judges recognised the massive change which the new formula would bring about in labour relations cases: e.g. Lord Denning MR, *Hubbard* v. *Pitt* [1976] QB 142, 178; see too, *Fellowes* v. *Fisher* [1976] QB 122, 130-40. On the contrast with the 'autonomy' of labour law in other systems, see Wedderburn (1987) 16 ILJ 1, especially pp. 11-13 on the *Perrier* decisions in France (Cass. Ass. Pl., 21 June 1974; approved in Cass. Ass. Pl., 28 January 1983) [above Chapter 5]; see too D. Howarth's response (1988) 17 ILJ 11.

114. See for example, *Solihull MB* v. *NUT* [1985] IRLR 211; Wedderburn, *The Worker and the Law*, pp. 698-701 and op. cit., n. 110. (1989) 23 The Law Teacher, pp. 17-22. The defendant union is frequently assailed with new evidence throughout the proceedings, even on appeal, requiring new affidavits in reply from union officers which may ultimately be turned against the union: see *Mercury Communications* v. *Scott Garner* [1984] Ch. 37, CA.

115. The Employment Act 1990, s. 8, recognises the injustice of the union's loss of its four-week period for the validity of a strike ballot by reason of litigation (as in *Associated British Ports* v. *TGWU* [1989] 1 WLR 939 HL); but the extra discretionary periods it allows are unlikely to be adequate in all cases.

116. Simon Brown J, *London Underground* v. *NUR* [1989] IRLR 341-342.

117. See the principles set out in Kerr on *Injunctions* (6th ed. 1927); I. Spry, *Equitable Remedies* (3rd ed. 1984); P. Pettit, *Equity and the Law of Trusts* (6th ed. 1989), pp. 462-524.

118. See *News Group Newspapers* v. *SOGAT* (No. 2) [1987] ICR 181.

119. On s. 17(2) TULRA 1974 (added in 1975), see Wedderburn, op. cit, n. 110 (1989) 23 The Law Teacher pp. 13-6; *The Worker and the Law*, pp. 687-96.

120. See s. 17(1) TULRA 1974, and *Barretts and Baird (Wholesale) Ltd* v. *IPCS* [1987] IRLR 3; see Wedderburn, op. cit., n. 110. (1989) 23 The Law Teacher pp. 9-11 [Chapter 7 above]; B. Simpson (1987) 50 MLR 506-10.

121. In *Associated British Ports* v. *TGWU* [1989] 1 WLR 939, CA; the HL reversed on other grounds and did not comment on either the expanded liabilities in tort or the new 'public interest' principle in interlocutory injunctions. Both would therefore be regarded as binding, especially in interlocutory motions, until the HL sees fit to pass upon them. Until this judgment there were grounds for thinking that

402   *Employment Rights in Britain and Europe*

some judges, including members of the Court of Appeal, felt that the unfair interventions against trade unions by interlocutory injunctions had gone too far: see *Hamlet* v. *GMBU* [1987] ICR 150; *Longley* v. *NUJ* [1987] IRLR 109, CA. Those were, however, cases concerned with internal union affairs.

122. Lord Denning, *The Due Process of Law* (1980), p. 9; see too the laudatory remarks of F. Mann (1979) 95 LQR 348-9. For more detailed discussion and authorities on contempt of court, see Wedderburn *The Worker and the Law*, pp. 705-17, and op. cit., n. 110, (1989) 23 The Law Teacher pp. 22-31.

123. See U. Jacobsson and J. Jacob (ed.), *Trends in Enforcement of Non-Money Judgments and Orders* (1985), pp. 37-9, 163, 238-9.

124. On Sweden: F. Schmidt in B. Aaron (ed.), *Labour Courts and Grievance Settlement in Western Europe* (1971), pp. 183-4; T. Sigeman, 'Damages and Bot' (1987) 8 Comp. Lab. Law Jo. 155 (on the special Scandinavian money payments as *bot*). On the *astreinte* see: M. le Galcher-Barran, *Les Oligations* (5th ed. 1986, ed. P. Level) pp. 134-6; D. Harris and D. Tallon, *Contract Law Today: Anglo-French Comparisons* (1989), pp. 268-70 and Wedderburn op. cit., n. 110 (1989) 23 The Law Teacher pp. 23-4. The French legislature expressly rejected a proposal to treat part of the *astreinte* as a fine payable to the State in the reforms leading to the new law of 5 July 1972. In certain cases, such as violence or continued occupation of a workplace, the enforcement mechanisms do involve the intervention of the public authorities: see J. Savatier, 'L'Occupation des lieux de travail' Dr. Soc. 1988, 655, especially pp. 659-62.

125. See Lord Diplock, *Att. Gen.* v. *Times Newspapers* [1974] AC 273, 308, HL; cp. R. Kidner 'Sanctions for Contempt by a Trade Union' (1986) 6 Legal Studs 18, 27.

126. See for example, *Savings and Investment Bank* v. *Gasco Investments BV* [1988] Ch. 422 CA; Mustill LJ in *Re SA Conversations Ltd* (1988) 4 BCC 384, 386-9.

127. See: Donaldson, P. *Heatons Transport* v. *TGWU* [1972] ICR 285, 296, 320; *Con-Mech (Engineers)* v. *AUEW* (No 2) [1973] IRLR pp. 334-5; Megarry J, *Clarke* v. *Chadburn* [1984] IRLR 350, 353. The move from civil to criminal contempt is sometimes made via the addition of such words as 'wilful' or 'contumacious' see e.g. Lawton LJ, *Express and Star* v. *NGA* [1986] ICR 589, 599.

128. On criminalisation in Canada, see *Poje* v. *Att. Gen. British Columbia* [1953] 2 DLR 705; *Skeena Craft* v. *Pulp and Paper Workers* (1971) 17 DLR (3d) 17; in Australia, *Australian Meat Industries Employees Union* v. *Mudginberri Station* (1986) 66 ALR 577; M. Pittard (1988) 1 Aus. Jo. Lab. Law 237; *Australian Consolidated Press* v. *Morgan* (1965) 112 CLR 483 (breach of interlocutory order); in Trinidad and Tobago, see R. Chaudhary (1981) ICLQ 260 (Industrial Court). In New Zealand the new labour Court applies a similar law and regards civil contempt as 'quasi criminal': *New Zealand Rlwys* v. *New Zealand Seamen's Union*, Goddard CJ, 6 October 1989 (transcript), the court imposed a fine for the union's 'defiance' of the court even though there had been a 'settlement agreement'; compare the fine on the TGWU after settlement of the Austin Rover strike of 1984, Wedderburn, *The Worker and the Law*, p. 77.

129. G. Lightman, 'A Trade Union in Chains' [1987] Current Legal Problems 25 (where other unreported cases on the miners' strike are revealed); *Taylor* v. *NUM*, *Times*, 20 November 1985. The liability of third parties had been extended in *UK Nirex* v. *Barton, Times*, 14 October 1986, beyond the classical liability for 'aiding and abetting a contempt': S. Auerbach, 'Legal Restraint of Picketing' (1987) 16 ILJ 227, 239.

130. See the invaluable account by S. Auerbach, 'Injunction Procedure in the Seafarers' Dispute' (1988) 17 ILJ 227, p. 231 on *Midland Bank plc* v. *NUS*, 28 April 1988, and pp. 234-6 on the extraordinary new judicial method of 'transferring' a sequestration order from one set of proceedings to another, *P & O European Ferries (Dover) Ltd* v. *NUS*, 1 February 1988.

131. Wedderburn, *The Worker and the Law*, pp. 728-38 [and see p. 353 above].

132. K. Ewing, 'Rights and Immunities in British Labour Law' (1988) 10 Comp. Lab. Law Jo. 1, 35; and 'The Right to Strike' (1986) 15 ILJ 143, 157-8 (proposing a Labour Court *as part of* the Queens Bench Division, on the model of the Commercial Court … a specialist jurisdiction … [with] specialist judges' and with no appeal to the Court of Appeal); see below n. 164.

133. H. Collins, 'Against Abstentionism in Labour Law' in J. Eekelaar and J. Bell (eds), *Oxford Essays in Jurisprudence* (1987 3rd Series), 79 p. 100. The use of the 'ordinary law of the land' and the ordinary courts in the policies of the 1980s, contriving to appear as deregulatory or 'abstentionist' makes a debate about labour courts inevitable: P. Davies and M. Freedland, 'Labour Courts and Reform of Labour Law', *In Memoriam Zvi Bar-Niv* (1987), pp. 71-2. It is interesting that earlier onslaughts by those courts did not create such a debate; the prominence and acceptance of a different regulatory base was perhaps the factor which made the difference.

134. W.E.J. McCarthy, 'The Case for Labour Courts' (1990) 21 Ind. Rels. Jo. 98, p. 110; there must be 'a more balanced legal element', p. 106.

135. U. Mückenberger and S. Deakin, op. cit. (1989) ZIAS 153, above n. 26, p. 207.

136. B. Bercusson, *Fundamental Social and Economic Rights: A Report to the EC Commission* (1989, European University Institute), p. 42.

137. Wedderburn, 'Labour Law: From Here to Autonomy?' (1987) 16 ILJ 1, p. 27; 'the topic must lose its taboo', p. 28 (it seems to have done so). As to the problems, see D. Howarth, 'The Autonomy of Labour Law – A Response to Professor Wedderburn' (1988) 17 ILJ 11, some of whose objections are discussed by W. McCarthy, op. cit. (1990) 21 Ind. Rels. Jo. pp. 104-10.

138. K. Wedderburn, *The Worker and the Law* (1965), p. 228: 'Such a [new] code of law would almost certainly need Labour Courts in which every section of the community could feel confidence.'

139. See, for example, descriptions in B. Aaron (ed.), *Labour Courts and Grievance Settlement in Western Europe* (1971); B. Aaron, 'Labour Courts and Organs of Arbitration', Chap. 16 in B. Hepple (ed.), *International Encyclopaedia of Labour Law* (1985); B. Essenberg (ed.), *Labour Courts in Europe* (1988 ILO); W. Blenk (ed.), *European Labour Courts: Current Issues* (1989 ILO); B. Hepple, 'Labour Courts: Some Comparative Perspectives' (1988) 41 Current Legal Problems 169; Folke Schmidt, *Law and Industrial Relations in Sweden* (1977); T. Ramm on 'Special Labour Courts' in B. Hepple (ed.), *The Making of Labour Law in Europe* (1986), pp. 270-5; for recent amendments in Italy and Sweden, see n. 95, above. See too, the valuable survey of British developments by P. Davies, *Arbitration and the Role of Courts: The Administration of Justice in Labour Law* (1978, British National Report, 9th International Congress, International Soc. for Labour Law and Social Security); and on the Industrial Tribunals, L. Dickens, M. Jones, B. Weekes, M. Hart, *Dismissed: A Study of Unfair Dismissal and the Industrial Tribunal System* (1985).

140. See the Act on Litigation in Labour Disputes, 1964 as amended in 1977 and 1984: the Labour Court has jurisdiction in cases arising from collective agreements, the 1976 Joint Regulation Act, and any other dispute where the parties are bound or an employee is covered by a collective agreement; other disputes are determined by the ordinary district court (Chap. 2, ss. 1, 2); no appeal lies from the Labour Court or from any decision to refer a case to it (ss. 4, 8); the Labour Court acts as an appeal court from the district court and has a discretion whether an order is to apply during appeal proceedings (ss. 12. 14). See too, nn. 163 and 184 below.

141. B. Hepple, op. cit., n. 139 (1988) 41 Current Legal Problems 169, 184-6.

142. Sir John Wood, 'The British Arbitrator: A Question of Style' in W. Gerschfeld (ed.), *Arbitration 1986: Current and Expanding Roles* (1987) 8, 17; but in his thoughtful advocacy of 'balanced reform', the need to change the character of the courts in the system is given a high place in his 'Labour Relations Law – The Missing

Pieces' (1990) 24 The Law Teacher 111, especially pp. 120-2. See, too, the interpretation of his advocacy of improved procedure, drafting and interpretation (Sir John Wood, 'The Collective Will and the Law' (1988) 17 ILJ 1) as opposition to labour courts by W. McCarthy, 'The Case for Labour Courts', op. cit. n. 134, pp. 107-9; see too, n. 218 below. D. Howarth, 'The Autonomy of Labour Law – A Response to Professor Wedderburn' (1988) 17 ILJ 11, poses pertinent sceptical questions some of which are addressed below.

143. The 'Warwick Report' in Dickens *et al.*, *Dismissed* (1985) op. cit. above n. 139; 'Justice', *Industrial Tribunals* (1987, Chairman B. Hepple). It is not overlooked that the two Reports are not in all respects at one, and that the 'Warwick Report' called for drastic changes in the tribunals, moving towards an institutionalised form of arbitration.

144. Even if at times it has addressed the policies of the legislation: Dickens *et al.*, *Dismissed*, op. cit. n. 139 above, pp. 187-9, 212-4, 286-9; cf Browne-Wilkinson J, 'The Role of the EAT in the 1980s' (1982) 11 ILJ 69. Some of the worst judgments, both legally and industrially, however, have come from the EAT: see e.g. *Marley* v. *Forward Trust Group Ltd* [1986] ICR 115, EAT; [1986] ICR 891 CA.

145. G. Lyon-Caen, 'Du Rôle des Principes Généraux du Droit Civil en Droit du Travail (Première Approche)' 1974 Rev. Trim. de Droit Civil 229, 231; see Wedderburn, op. cit., n. 137, (1987) 16 ILJ pp. 2-4, 25-8 [above pp. 107-9, 123-6].

146. See Sir John Donaldson (as he then was) 'Lessons from the Industrial Court' (1975) 91 LQR 181, 191-2, and 'The Role of Labour Courts' (1975) 4 ILJ 63, 68. On the advice along these lines given by him to government, see *Guardian*, 30 November 1983. But in general, the Donaldson proposals are 'highly individualistic in the common law tradition': B. Hepple, 'Labour Courts: Some Comparative Perspectives' op. cit., n. 139, p. 186. Compare O. Kahn-Freund: the settlement of trade disputes is 'not justiciable,' *Labour and the Law*, above n. 10, p. 138. On earlier proposals to make Munitions Tribunals into local arbitration courts: G. Rubin, n. 92 (1985) 14 ILJ 33.

147. See his *Memorandum* to the Royal Commission of 1906, Report, p. 18; H. Phelps Brown, *The Origins of Trade Union Power* (1983), pp. 49-50, ('compulsory arbitration, for all its being talked of, was not a practicable alternative course in 1906'). On compulsory arbitration in Australia, see R. McCallum, M. Pittard, G. Smith, *Australian Labour Law; Cases and Materials* (1990), Parts 2 and 3; and on the failure in that context of compulsory procedures under s. 37 Industrial Relations Act 1971, O. Kahn-Freund, *Labour and the Law* (1983 3rd ed., eds P. Davies and M. Freedland), pp. 147-53.

148. See op. cit. [1923] Camb. LJ p. 8, n. 93 above. Sir Thomas Scrutton was a renowned practitioner in the Commercial Court from its creation in 1895 until 1901; Lord Donaldson was a renowned judge of that Court before he became President of the NIRC in 1972. 'It is hard to envisage a more undesirable development than expressly making judges, even if assisted by expert wingmen, the arbiters of the rights and wrongs of industrial conflict': B. Simpson (1986) 49 MLR 796, 814.

149. Sir John Wood (Chairman of the Central Arbitration Committee), 'Labour Relations Law – The Missing Pieces', op. cit., above n. 67, p. 121; see too below n. 218.

150. See R. Munday, 'Tribunal Lore: Legalism and the Industrial Tribunals' (1981) 10 ILJ 146; but in this weak sense, 'legalism' may not effectively distinguish a 'court' from regulated arbitration: compare R. Rideout (a deputy chairman of the CAC) 'Arbitration and the Public Interest – Regulated Arbitration', Chap. V in Wedderburn and W.T. Murphy, *Labour Law and the Community* (1982); B. Aaron (ed.), *Dispute Settlement Procedures in Five Western European Countries* (1969); F. Schmidt, 'Conciliation, Adjudication and Administration' 45, and K. Wedderburn 'Conflicts of "Rights" and Conflicts of "Interests" in Labour Disputes' 65.

151. See: M. Weiss, S. Simitis and W. Rydzy, 'The Settlement of Labour Disputes

in the FRG' in T. Hanami, R. Blanpain (eds), *Industrial Conflict Resolution in Market Economies* (1984) 102 (a high rate of successful settlement is achieved, 105); A. Döse-Digenopoulos and H. Höland, 'Dismissals of Employees in the FRG' (1985) 48 MLR 539 (the system leads to dominance of the legal judges and profession, 556); E. Blankenburg and R. Rogowski, 'German Labour Courts and the British Tribunal System' (1986) 13 Jo. Law and Society 67, 82 ('Some Labour Court judges take conciliation attempts quite seriously; others despise them'). See too, *Code au Travail*, arts L 511-1, 515-1 (bureau de conciliation; bureau de jugement); G. Lyon-Caen and J. Pélissier, *Droit du Travail*, op. cit., n. 5, pp. 629, 639-40; F. Schmidt, *Law and Industrial Relations in Sweden* (1977), pp. 200-206; S. Edlund and B. Nyström, *Developments in Swedish Labour Law* (1988), pp. 28-44; G. Ghezzi and U. Romagnoli, *Il rapporto del lavoro* (2nd ed. 1987), pp. 335-64, and *Il diritto sindacale* (2nd ed. 1987), pp. 127-8; G. Pera, *Il diritto del lavoro* (3rd ed. 1988), pp. 597-604 (Law 533 of 11 August 1973 extended the available methods of arbitration and conciliation in labour disputes). On Ireland see: A. Kerr, G. Whyte, *Irish Trade Union Law* (1985), pp. 340-56 (the 'Labour Court') and the Industrial Relations Act 1990 ss. 24-33 (establishing the conciliation competence of the Labour Relations Commission).

152. See P. Davies, op. cit., n. 139, pp. 299-316; L. Dickens *et al.*, *Dismissed*, op. cit., n. 139, Chap. 6 and pp. 279-80; ACAS Report 1989 Tables 8-10.

153. The interlocutory jurisdiction under the new *Code de Procedure* especially arts 808, 809 and 812 (requête; *ex parte*), is more restricted than that of the High Court, see G. Couchez, *Procédure Civile* (4th ed. 1986) but is sufficiently parallel to raise interesting questions of remedial method. The judge has no jurisdiction to decide the reasonableness or legitimacy of the industrial claims put forward by either party to the conflict' (*l'affaire Air Inter*, C d'A Paris, 27 January 1988, D 188, 352, J.C. Javillier Dr. Soc. 243; A. Jeammaud, M. Rondeau-Vivier D 1988, Chron. 229; J. Ray Dr. Soc. 1988, 242), despite the decision of the Cour de Cassation, Ass. plén. 4 July 1986, to allow such a decision as one of fact (see, G. Lyon-Caen and J. Pélissier, op. cit. above n. 5, p. 1034; and comparatively with Britain: Wedderburn in *Les Transformations du Droit du Travail*, op. cit., above n. 5, pp. 147-51). On other jurisdictions, see Wedderburn 'Limitation Législative et Judiciaire en Matière d'Action Syndicale et du Droit de Grève' 1990, No 1 Rev. Internationale de Droit Comparé 37, pp. 104-7.

154. Approved by the Cour de Cassation, Soc. 26 July 1984; but the appeal court also approved the practice of other judges who, in cases of occupations, insisted on restoration of the employer's property rights (Soc. 21 June 1984, J. Savatier Dr. Soc. 1985, 19) or claimed they had no competence to impose conditions: J.C. Javillier, *Manuel de Droit du Travail* (1988), pp. 349-50; G. Lyon-Caen and J. Pélissier, *Droit du Travail*, n. 5, pp. 1015-6. The law of 31 July 1963 requires five days notices of strikes in *services publics* by a representative union, but this provision was declared in the law of 19 October 1982 to impose an 'obligation to negotiate' on the parties (*Code du Travail*, art. L 521-6). On the law and essential minimum services in Spain and Italy, see below n. 158.

155. See M. Vranken, 'Specialisation and Labour Courts: A Comparative Analysis' (1988) 9 Comp. Lab. Law Jo. 497, reviewing the New Zealand court, pp. 513-22.

156. See on the Labour Court under the New Zealand Labour Relations Act 1987, Part IX, J. Hughes (1988) 13 NZ Jo. of Ind. Relns 277-83, and R. Boast, ibid., pp. 33-9 (on interim injunctions 'no procedural changes of any kind,' thereby perpetuating the 'well-recognised tactical disadvantages faced by a trade union defendant,' p. 39); and, on substantive law, G. Anderson, ibid, pp. 21-31 (the Act tries to 'patch up an inadequate system' based on the common law; 'the state of the law on injunction remains virtually unchanged,' p. 30); see too, on New Zealand n. 128 above.

157. See for example, TUC *General Council Report 1990*, Section B Annex 1, para.

18 (need for 'immediate full trial to prevent employers seeking to win them merely as a stalling device').

158. This sensitive area will not be improved by ignoring it. British unions have experience of maintaining safety and emergency services during disputes: see G. Morris, *Strikes in Essential Services* (1986), especially Chaps 5 and 6; also Chap. 10, 'Collective Disputes', S. Fredman and G. Morris, *The State as Employer* (1989); on the different European backgrounds: K. Wedderburn, Chap. 6, 'Industrial Action, the State and the Public Interest' in B. Aaron (ed.), *Industrial Conflict, A Comparative Legal survey* (1972). In Spain the courts' agreement to union proposals for maintenance of 'essential services for the community' (a limitation on the right to strike under the Constitution, art. 28.2) was supported by the Constitutional Court decisions 11/81, 8 April 1981, and 26/81, 17 June 1981: M. Rodriguez-Piñero, 'Le Tribunal Constitutionel Espagnol et les Droits Collectifs des Travailleurs' in *Les Transformations du Droit du Travail; Etudes Offertes à Gérard Lyon-Caen* (1989 Dalloz) pp. 114-20; F. Valdes dal Rè, 'Diritto di sciopero e servizi essenziali in Spagna' (1988) Giorn. dir. lav. e rel. ind. 551; Wedderburn, op. cit., above n. 153, (1990) No. 1 Rev. Internationale du Droit Comp. pp. 82-6; E. Gonzàlez Biedma 'Los servicios de seguridad y mantenimiento en la impresa durante la huelga' (1990) *Relaciones Laborales La Ley* No. 9, pp. 8-38 (see the comparative treatment pp. 9-18), and 'El cumplimiento de los servicios de mantenimiento en caso de huelga', ibid. No. 10, pp. 9-46. In Italy, where art. 40 of the Constitution guarantees one of the widest rights to strike, Law 146 of 12 June 1990 requires the observance of procedures, including ten days' notice, where strikes affect essential constitutional rights on safety, health, transportation, education, and communications and establishes a Commission with powers to call a ballot of workers; bodies which contravene the new rules may be excluded from collective bargaining and workers made subject to penalties, but not to dismissal: Wedderburn (1990) 19 ILJ 154 op. cit. n. 4; and see (1990) EIRR 199, 21-2.

159. B. Simpson (1989) 18 ILJ 240, commenting on *Associated British Ports* v. *TGWU* [1989] 1 WLR 939; see too, the acceptance by some Law Lords that an injunction might be given despite the possibility of a defence where the effects of a strike might be 'disastrous' for an employer, the public or 'perhaps of the nation itself': *NWL* v. *Woods* [1979] 1 WLR 1294, 1307; *Express Newspapers* v. *McShane* [1980] AC 694-5; Wedderburn (1980) 43 MLR 319.

160. See Lord Denning MR *Hubbard* v. *Pitt* [1975] ICR 308, 320, in a case of non-industrial picketing; Wedderburn, *The Worker and the Law*, p. 691. The principle that an interlocutory injunction must not finally decide the case, however, is sidestepped by the technically correct, but fictional notion that the union's rights will not be 'finally decided' until full trial: *Thomas* v. *NUM (S. Wales)* [1986] Ch. 20.

161. Here pertinent questions are undoubtedly put by D. Howarth, op. cit., n. 137 (1988) 17 ILJ pp. 14-21.

162. The CO still has such a competence on union 'independence', EPA 1975 s. 8(12); the Registrar of Friendly Societies had power to decide complaints about union mergers (Trade Union (Amalgamations) Act 1964, s.4(8)) and on the political fund (Trade Union Act 1913, s.3(2)) without appeal, but in both cases an appeal on a point of law from the CO to the EAT was introduced by EPA 1975, s. 88, now EPCA 1978 s. 136. A parallel case was found on the Occupational Pensions Board in the Social Security Pensions Act 1975, s. 55(4), now repealed: Social Security Act 1989, Sched. 5. K. Ewing cites the formula in s. 7(8) Interception of Communications Act 1985, op. cit. (1986) 15 ILJ at p. 157; but he is right to doubt whether the ordinary courts would respect such a formula designed to exclude them from appeals in labour law.

163. In Sweden the Supreme Court has a residual supervision jursidiction (S. Strömholm (ed.), *An Introduction to Swedish Law* (2nd ed. 1988), pp. 40-1, 107-9; Act on Litigation in Labour Disputes, as amended 1985, Chap. 2, s. 7; F. Schmidt, *Law and Industrial Relations in Sweden* (1977), pp. 37-44); and in Germany the

Federal Labour Court is subject to the Federal Constitutional to which constitutional issues must be referred (on the courts, M. Weiss, *Labour Law and Industrial Relations in the FRG* (1987), pp. 96-103, 184-6; T. Ramm, 'The Federal Republic of Germany', *International Encyclopaedia for Labour Law* (1979, ed. R. Blanpain), pp. 210-1 and 'Corte costituzionale e diritto sindacale nella RFT' (1989) 42 Giorn.dir. lav.e rel. ind.269, illustrating the range of the court's interventions and the many cases waiting to be decided). Unlike the German Labour Courts and the Italian judges with a labour jurisdiction, decisions of the French courts cannot be impugned on constitutional grounds; the *Conseil Constitutionnel* deals with proposed legislation: above n. 5.

164. The importance of this point has been widely acknowledged in recent years: see K. Ewing, op. cit. above n. 132, (1986) 15 ILJ pp. 157-8, who advocates making the decisions of a new Labour Court placed *within* the Queen's Bench Division 'final,' thereby leaving the 'ordinary courts', including the Court of Appeal, 'snookered'. See also on appeals, B. Hepple op. cit. (1988) 41 Current Legal Problems pp. 183-4, for a proposal to take the EAT 'out of the ordinary court structure' and thereby prevent appeals to the Court of Appeal: see too 'Restructuring Employment Rights' (1986) 15 ILJ at p. 83. But the High Court would then acquire a competence of judicial review over such an arbitral body with statutory powers. Putting the labour court within the Queen's Bench Division might be difficult to draft in 'judge-proof' terms and might increase the difficulty of excluding the Court of Appeal. There is also, of course, the technical problem in drafting legislation that by reason of the accidents of 1873-75 the Judicial Committee of the House of Lords is not in the same position as the Court of Appeal which is part of the Supreme Court. These considerations may favour the inclusion of an appeals system within the labour court's own domain, e.g. to a Full Bench, with review by a special body, such as that suggested here, only in case of dispute as to jurisdictions, below nn. 168-170. For a 'labour court' in the grip of judicial review, see *Cadwell* v. *Labour Court* [1988] Ir. R. 283.

165. Lord Donaldson of Lymington MR, *British Coal Corpn* v. *Cheeseborough* [1988] ICR 769, 775 (appeal dismissed: [1990] IRLR 148, HL); and see his conclusions expressed in *Martin* v. *MRS Fastenings* [1983] IRLR 198, 199: 'The field of industrial relations has its own very specialised "know how" and this is something which, initially at least, is more familiar to Members of Parliament than to judges ... At the end of my term as President of [the NIRC] my regret was not that it was a mixed court of judges and industrial members, but that there was a right of appeal to the Court of Appeal which did not have similar advantages, albeit perhaps with the industrial members being in a minority.'

166. Lord Donaldson of Lymington MR, *British Telecommunications* v. *Sheridan* [1990] IRLR 27, 30; *per* Ralph Gibson LJ 'misunderstanding or misapplying facts may amount to an error of law', though he expresses the need for caution, p. 30.

167. In 1987 the total Swedish labour force was 4.4 million: S. Edlund and B. Nyström, *Developments in Swedish Labour Law* (1988), p. 18. Despite extensive legal aid (P. Henrik Lindblom in S. Strömholm (ed.), op. cit. above n. 163, pp. 139-41) it does not appear to be a very litigious society.

168. Law of 3 July 1967; G. Couchez, *Procédure Civil* (4th ed. 1986), p. 29. If the Swedish Labour Court finds that its decision will depart from a legal principle or interpretation previously adopted, it may refer the case or legal question 'to the Court in its entirety' (thirteen members): Act on Litigation in Labour Disputes, Chap. 3, s. 9.

169. D. Howarth, op. cit., above n. 137, (1988) 17 ILJ 11, 24.

170. See the celebrated passage in W. Ivor Jennings, *The Law and the Constitution* (3rd ed. 1947), pp. 210-4; Dicey's objection to the (formal) presidency of the Minister of Justice in the *Tribunal* is met by offering the Lord Chancellor, president in fact of the judicial House of Lords and the Judicial Committee of the Privy Council, also, of course, a member of the legislative House and a Cabinet Minister.

171. B. Hepple, op. cit. above n. 139, (1988) Current Legal Problems p. 186,

finding support in Sir John Wood, 'The British Arbitrator – A Question of Style', op. cit. at p. 17, see above n. 142; so too, the understandable doubts about the availability of enough persons of 'the appropriate calibre' to staff a labour court are no reason for 'abandoning the search in advance,' W. McCarthy, op. cit. (1990) 21 Ind. Rels Jo. p. 109, above n. 134. See too below n. 215 *et seq*.

172. See T. Hartley, *The Foundations of European Community Law* (1988), pp. 42-4, and sources there cited.

173. In France the *action syndicale* was recognised by the Cour de Cassation in 1913 and now allows the union to represent the 'collective interest', even if it is in issue only indirectly, which it may now do in any court: *Code du Travail* art. L 411-11; and see G. Lyon-Caen and J. Pélissier, op. cit. above n. 5, pp. 705-10, where the six further cases are set out when a 'representative' union can appear in court to defend the individual interests of a member, including sex discrimination cases (ibid. art. L 123-6), an inclusion specially relevant to Britain; for a detailed exposition, J.M. Verdier, *Syndicat et Droit Syndical*, Vol. I (1987 2nd ed.), pp. 583-663. In Italy a union may be asked to assist the court by the judge or by a party (*Codice di Procedura Civile* arts 421, 425, as substituted by Law 533 of 11 August 1973; G. Tarzia, *Manuale del processo del lavoro* (1987), pp. 120-8). But, more important, under art. 28 of the Workers' Statute 1970 (Law 300 of 20 May 1970, as amended by Law 847 of 8 November 1977), the local union body which has an interest has the right to sue in cases of 'anti-union conduct' (M. Grandi and G. Pera, *Commentario breve allo Statuto dei lavoratori* (1985), pp. 148, 161-171). On the Workers' Statute 1970 and the *rappresenatanza*, see Wedderburn (1990) 19 ILJ 154. These provisions are considered to be central to the 'defence of collective interests' (G. Ghezzi and U. Romagnoli *Il diritto sindacale* (2nd ed. 1987), Chap. 7, 174) and allow the collective dimension to be introduced into employment disputes properly: G. Giugni, *Diritto sindacale* (1988 7th ed.), pp. 106-7. In Sweden proceedings can be instituted by an organisation on behalf of a member where the dispute relates to a collective agreement or falls within the Joint Regulation at Work Act 1976: and, more important, a person suing a member or former member in any such case *must* join the union, which can defend the action even if the individual does not: Act on Litigation of Labour Disputes, Chap. 4, s. 5.

174. L. Mariucci, *Le fonti del diritto del lavoro* (1988), p. 40.

175. Many accounts of the 'labour jurisdiction' of the *Pretore*, below n. 203, take insufficient account of the importance of the bold reforms of procedure in labour cases in Italy, (see e.g. the 'Justice' Report (1987) op. cit., above n. 143, pp. 62-3). The most important were in Law 533 of 11 August 1973 (rewriting Title IV of the *Codice di Procedura Civile*) and the 1977 amendments to art. 28, Workers' Statute, Law 300, 20 May 1970, on 'anti-union conduct' by the employer, *inter alia* changing the rule that an appeal from an order had to be made within fifteen days to the ordinary tribunal into a provision that this appeal must be made, under the flexible and speedy procedures of 1973, to the same *Pretore* who first heard the case (Law 847 of 8 November 1977, arts 2, 3) and whose order normally stands during appeals: G. Tarzia, op. cit., n. 173, (1987) Chap. IV and pp. 267-75; G. Pera, *Il diritto del lavoro* (3rd ed. 1988), pp. 290-8. The orders of the *Pretore* are sanctioned by criminal penalties (up to three months' imprisonment) and given special publicity, in a process in which the union can claim damages: G. Ghezzi and U. Romagnoli, op. cit. n. 173, pp. 282-91 (the nearest Italian law comes to 'contempt' proceedings: F. Carinci, R. de Luca Tomajo, P. Tosi, T. Treu, *Il diritto sindacale* (2nd ed. 1987), pp. 197-200). The first order of the *Pretore*, in a 'summary process' of great orality, should be given within two days and the 'father' of the Statute states that although this period is often exceeded, it still leaves the labour procedure 'completely *sui generis*' and much quicker than ordinary procedure, while the sanctions are 'one of the fundamental innovations' which explain its effectiveness: G. Giugni, *Diritto sindacale*, op. cit., n. 37, pp. 105-7 (the sanctions apply also to sex discrimination cases, Law 903, 9 December 1977, 'but with less success', p. 107).

176. See the 'Justice' Report, op. cit. above n. 143, and L. Dickens *et al.*, *Dismissed* (1985) op. cit. n. 139. For a careful assessment of the problem of 'legalism' in the context of proposals for reform, see I. Smith and J. Wood, *Industrial Law* (4th ed. 1989), pp. 241-51. Legislative measures have been more in the style of charging employees a deposit of up to £150 for coming to the tribunal, para. 1A, Sched. 9 EPCA 1978, introduced by s. 20 Employment Act 1989: 'close to the average weekly wage of unfair dismissal applicants and several times the amounts dismissed workers are likely to receive in income support or unemployment benefit': S. Deakin (1990) 19 ILJ 1, 16.

177. The extension of tripartism is the essence of the case made by W. McCarthy, op. cit. above n. 134, (1990) 21 Ind. Rels. Jo. 98; on experience in the industrial tribunals, see L. Dickens *et al.*, *Dismissed*, above n. 139, especially Chap. 3.

178. The monopoly of the CBI and TUC in nominating to the panels of lay wings has been broken in the 1980s by inclusion of other bodies: the National Chamber of Trade, Institute of Directors, National Federation of Small Employers, Royal College of Nursing, EEPTU and UDM. Other, perhaps unlikely, constituencies have been suggested (consumer or unemployed 'non-combatants': see D. Howarth, op. cit. (1988) 17 ILJ 11, 25). Under the German Labour Courts Act, s. 18(1), the appointment of *Land* Labour Court judges (like others, young career judges, but nominated by the Labour Department, *not* the Department of Justice) must be approved by a tripartite committee composed of Labour Court Presidents and nominees of employers and employees: E. Blankenburg and R. Rogowski 'German Labour Courts and the British Industrial Tribunal System' (1986) 13 Brit. Jo. Law Soc. 67, pp. 83-6 (where the power of the German judge to control the highly informal procedure and to mediate throughout the case is contrasted with the 'formal adversary process' in the tribunals chaired by a solicitor or barrister of seven years' standing appointed by the Lord Chancellor). Federal Labour Court judges are appointed on proposals by the Labour Ministry and a committee of *Land* Labour Ministers plus persons elected by the Federal Parliament, in consultation with the Minister of Justice and the judges; all lay judges are appointed for four years from nominees of employers and unions: M. Weiss op. cit. above n. 55, p. 97.

179. Results of various elections by workers (to works' councils, safety committees, social security bodies and even the *conseils*) can be a residual or complementary test of a union's '*représentativité* ', that relative and difficult concept of crucial importance to French labour laws (e.g. on the capacity to conclude collective agreements): *Code du Travail*, art. L 133-2: G. Lyon-Caen and J. Pélissier, op. cit. n. 5, p. 692; but for a different emphasis on such elections and the test of *l'audience*, see J.M. Verdier, op. cit. n. 173, pp. 495-500. See the proportions of votes for candidates of various unions for the *Conseils de Prud'hommes* in 1987: J.C. Javillier, *Manuel Droit du Travail* (1988), pp. 251-4 (the abstention rate in the *Conseils* elections was 54 per cent).

180. G. Lyon-Caen and J. Pélissier, op. cit. (1988) above n. 5, pp. 625-43. On their development, see R. David, *Droit Social*, 1974, Special no. 2, 3; W. McPherson and W. Myers, *The French Labor Courts: Judgment by Peers* (1966); X. Blanc-Jouvan, Chap. I in B. Aaron (ed.), *Labor Courts and Grievance Settlement in Western Europe* (1971); B. Napier (1979) 42 MLR 270 and S. Van Noorden (1980) *Employment Gazette* 1098, on the 1979 reforms; A. Supiot, *Les Juridictions du Travail* (1987, Dalloz); and on current tendencies, J.C. Javillier, 'Les nouvelles tendances dans l'organisation juridictionelle' 1983, Journées de la Soc. de Législation Comparée 103. The number of cases of deadlock has increased, but it is smaller than the outside observer might expect. Since 1958, the giving of instructions to the lay judges (e.g. by a union) has been expressly illegal: see X. Blanc-Jouvan in B. Aaron (ed.), op. cit., n. 139 above, p. 22.

181. J.-P. Bonafe-Schmitt, 'Les Nouveaux Prud'hommes: Un Nouvel Enjeu Syndical?', *Travail et Emploi* 1983, No. 18, October, 84, 93.

182. Wedderburn, *The Worker and the Law*, pp. 264-8; L. Dickens, 'Tribunals in

the Firing Line' (1983) 5 Employee Relns No. 1, 27 (the TUC's policy of non-co-operation on the closed shop in 1984 was not implemented); J. McIlroy, *Trade Unions in Britain Today* (1988), pp. 87-91.
183. But if the view were adopted of L. Dickens *et al.*, *Dismissed*, op. cit. above n. 139, pp. 278-98, that there should be movement towards an arbitral system, the role of the chair, or at least of the legal chair, would come into question. See too the powerful arguments for a move in this direction by R. Rideout 'Unfair Dismissal – Tribunal or Arbitration' (1986) 15 ILJ 84, who would, however, maintain the tripartite model but with experts in the chair who need not be lawyers, pp. 90-4. If such arbitral bodies based on disciplinary agreements with exemption orders, as he proposes, came under the review jurisdiction of a labour court, it would be more than ever necessary for its composition to give it the necessary industrial expertise to avoid inappropriately legalistic interpretations. Such a move might also make easier an extension of protection to vulnerable, especially women, workers: see on that vulnerability, L. Dickens 'Falling through the Net' (1988) 19 Ind. Rels Jo. 142. It 'would be a mistake to move away from the tripartite structure with a legally qualified Chairman': 'Justice' *Report*, op. cit. above, n. 143, para. 4.5.
184. See respectively, P. Henrik Lindblom in S. Strömholm (ed.), op. cit. above n. 163, p. 110, and the Act on Litigation in Labour Disputes, Chap. 3, ss. 1, 2; F. Schmidt, op. cit. above n. 39, pp. 37-42, especially p. 41; normally the employee side consists in one LO member (blue collar) and one TCO (white collar); but where a particular bargaining area is concerned, a 'special composition' is adopted, e.g. two TCO members in a white collar case, or in private sector cases both employers may be SAF (the private sector employers' association) instead of one from the various public sector employers. Complex rules apply to further special compositions (e.g. only one local authority employer can sit), but there appears to have been no complaint about such arrangements. The court was opposed by the unions when created in 1928 but 'has long been an element of Swedish labour law enjoying the support of all parties concerned': L. Forsebäck, *Industrial Relations and Employment in Sweden* (1980), p. 47. On the history of the unions' change of attitude between 1928 and the first Basic Agreement in 1938, see F. Schmidt, *The Law of Labour Relations in Sweden* (1962), pp. 9-34.
185. The traditional sections are defined sectorally, whatever the job of the workers, i.e. industry, commerce and services, agriculture and '*activités diverses*': *Code du Travail*, art. L 512-2; the section for *cadres* was added by the reform law of 18 January 1979, and that category was extended in this context by the law of 6 May 1982. The normal jurisdiction of the *Conseils* includes all individual disputes arising from the employment contract (other than inventions); but this is of course wider than English ears might imagine since many rights (including the right to strike) are couched in individual terms.
186. See Waite J, 'Lawyers and Laymen as Judges in Industry' (1986) 15 ILJ 32, 41.
187. B. Hepple, 'Judging Equal Rights' (1983) Current Legal Problems, 71, 78-9. For a call for 'specialist tribunals', see J. Solomons in R. Jenkins and J. Solomons (eds), *Racism and Equal Opportunity Policies in the 1980s* (1987), p. 47; compare Lustgarten's doubts about 'negative legal sanctions', Chap. 2, R. Jenkins, Chap. 12; P. Gordon, 'Racial Discrimination; Towards a Legal Strategy?' (1982) 9 Brit. Jo. Law Soc. 127; V. Kumar, *Industrial Tribunal Applicants under the Race Relations Act 1976* (1986, CRE).
188. *Habib* v *Elkington* [1981] ICR 435, EAT (though 'it was clearly intended by the government of the day that someone who had the necessary special experience should be a member,' p. 440 *per* Slynn J; see Lord Jacques HL Deb vol. 375, cols 725-6, 15 October 1976).
189. I. Smith and J. Wood *Industrial Law* (4th ed. 1990), p. 250 n. 15, in their careful assessment of the 'Justice' *Report*, 1987, op. cit., n. 143, which suggested such specialist training, para. 3.16-3.24. The 'system of nominating by sponsoring organisations has failed to provide panels which are fully representative of

industry. It has failed abysmally to provide a sufficient number of women and black members,' ibid., para. 4.14 (of the panel members only 21 per cent were women and less than 1.5 per cent from the ethnic minorities: paras 3.16, 4.13).

190. 'Justice', *Report*, op. cit. para, 4.10, 'if jurisdiction is extended to non-employment cases, the members should have special knowledge and experience of the field in question, eg education, housing etc,' para 3.23(e). One might suggest that the problems of certain industries were also complex. At present the contribution of the lay wings is general rather than specific experience: L. Dickens, op. cit. *Dismissed*, above n. 139, p. 83.

191. The Italian labour judge (*Pretore*, below n. 203 *et seq.*) has power, of his own motion after hearing the parties or on application by a party, to appoint an expert to report within ten days on most issues in the cause and the same may be done on appeal: arts 424, 441 *Codice di Procedura Civile* (as amended in 1977, above n. 175; the report may be oral at first instance); see G. Tarzia, *Manuale del processo del lavoro* (1987), pp. 136-9, for the exceptions to the availability of *la consulenza tecnica* (technical advice). The position is similar in France: G. Couchez, op. cit. n. 153, paras 238-41, 369-73; N. Code Proc. Civ. arts 256-84.

192. Equal Pay Act 1970, ss. 1, 2; Equal Pay (Amendment) Regulations 1983, SI 1983 No 1794; Industrial Tribunals (Rules of Procedure) (Equal Value Amendments) Regulations 1983, SI 1983 No 1794; Industrial Tribunals (Rules of Procedure) (Equal Value Amendments) Regulations 1983, SI 1983 No 1807; Industrial Tribunals (Rule of Procedure) Regulations 1985, SI 1985 No 16, Sched. 2. L. McCrudden (ed.), *Women, Employment and European Equality Law* (1987). It has been doubted whether the special status of the expert's report complies 'with the EEC requirements which ensivages a purely judicial process': I. Smith and J. Wood, *Industrial Law* (1989 4th ed.), p. 396; but compare the Italian judge's competence to call for an expert, above n. 191. In the first three years, fewer than ten cases had completed these tortuous procedures: 'Justice' *Report*, op. cit., para. 3.25 (which recommends the 'removal of the independent experts', leaving the experts of the parties to fight it out: 3.27). Some EAT wings want the aid of an expert assessor: *Aldridge* v. *British Telecomms* [1989] ICR 791. 800-2.

193. L. Dickens and D. Cockburn, Chap. 19 in R. Lewis (ed.), *Labour Law of Britain* (1986), p. 560.

194. It seems to be constant at about this rate: B. Hepple, 'Labour Courts' (1988) op. cit. above n. 139, p. 173; and in G. Bain (ed.), *Industrial Relations in Britain* (1983) p. 411, citing 'COIT 1981'.

195. L. Dickens *et al.*, *Dismissed*, op. cit., above n. 139, pp. 71-3; B. Hepple, 'Judging Equal Rights', op. cit., n. 187, p. 78. It has been rightly observed that since appeals to the EAT are allowed on points of law only, it is odd that even in theory the lay members can outvote the legal judge: I. Smith and J. Wood, op. cit. above n. 192, p. 238. On control by the presiding judge, see J. Wood (1990) 19 ILJ 133.

196. M. Weiss, op. cit. above n. 55, p. 97; E. Blankenburg and R. Rogowski, op. cit. above n. 151, pp. 81-5. In the 1970s there were dissents in just under 20 per cent of Swedish Labour Court cases, many by employee lay members (F. Schmidt, op. cit., above n. 39, p. 40).

197. See Megaw LJ, *Bessenden Properties* v. *Corness* [1974] IRLR 338, 340; Lord Donaldson of Lymington MR, *Sheridan* v. *British Telecommunciations* [1990] IRLR 27, 30.

198. Frances Gibbs, *Times*, 8 May 1990, 'Act Takes Judges Back to School'.

199. Johnson J, *Times*, 5 May 1990.

200. 'Justice' *Report* op. cit. above n. 143, paras 4.10, and 4.16: 'Those who sit in specialised jurisdictions (e.g. discrimination) should receive special training.'

201. In 1987 most High Court or Court of Session judges presiding over the EATs had no previous knowledge of the tribunals or employment law: 'Justice', *Report* op. cit., n. 143, p. 51. The 'Warwick' survey found, in a small sample, that 31 per

cent of tribunal chairs were barristers or in judicial office and 47 per cent solicitors; only three of 38 were women; few had any industrial experience; many dismissed the need for training: L. Dickens *et al.*, op. cit., above n. 139, pp. 53-6. Reform of the judiciary is now demanded by both supporters and opponents of incorporating the individualist European Convention of Human Rights (Council of Europe 1951) into British law: see H. Kennedy, A. Lester QC and other 'Charter 88' lawyers, *Guardian*, 5 October 1990 ('otherwise the judiciary will continue to be staffed by white, male and middle-class lawyers'); J.A.G. Griffith, *Guardian*, 14 June 1990.
202. The 'Justice' *Report*, op. cit. there is 'a need for positive action to promote the appointment of more women and members of the ethnic minorities' (para. 4.8), and career entry for law graduates should be 'an alternative mode of selection of chairmen of tribunals' (para. 4.9).
203. See above nn. 93, 175, 191; G. Tarzia, *Manuale del processo del lavoro* (1987); Wedderburn, 'The Italian Workers' Statute', Chap. 9 above. It is notable that the informal labour procedures apply also to appeals, and the decision is given immediately with reasons later: arts 437, 438 *Codice di Procedura Civile*, as amended by Law 533, 11 August 1973. The public sector is rather different. Great strides have been made to approximate the position of the public employee who, as always on the Continent, begins in Italy by having a totally differnt status from the private sector employee and subject frequently to the administrative courts. The *legge quadro sul pubblico impiego* (framework law on public employment) Law 93 of 29 March 1983 (see. M. Rusciano and T. Treu in (1984) *Le nuove leggi civili commentate*, pp. 593-750) extended the industrial rights of public employees and contributed to a new balance between administrative and ordinary courts: G. Ghezzi and U. Romagnoli, *Il diritto sindacale*, op. cit. above n. 38, pp. 291-6; G. Pera, *Il diritto del lavoro*, op. cit. n. 175, pp. 269-78. In a creative jurisprudence, from a position where rights of action were frequently denied in this sector, unions came to acquire a *locus standi*, sometimes in the administrative, sometimes in the ordinary courts; and State and other public employees have rights to sue in one or other court, with union rights based on art. 28 of the Workers' Statute 1970 (above n. 173): G. Giugni, *Diritto sindacale* (1988 8th ed.), pp. 111-5 (a set of 'baroque and scarcely rational distinctions' in procedure which are now in need of reform); M. Rusciano, 'L'unificazione normativa del lavoro pubblico e del lavoro privato' (1989) 42 Giorn. dir. lav. e rel. ind. 143-67.
204. As with comparisons between the *Pretori* or the German labour courts and the British tribunals: E. Blankenburg and R. Rogowski, op. cit. (1985) 13 Jo. of Law and Soc. above n. 178, 67; on the relationship of the tribunals to different policies in substantive law, see P. Davies and M. Freedland 'Labour Courts and the Reform of the Law' in *In Memoriam Zvi Bar-Niv* (1987), pp. 43-58.
205. On the first, see Wedderburn, 'La legislazione di sostegno in Italia e Gran Bretagna' (1990) 45 Giorn. dir. lav. rel. ind. 59, and 'Lo Statuto dei lavoratori e L'Europa' (1989) Quaderni di dir, del. lav. e delle rel. ind. 71 ('we find a Member State of the Community which, though it has no general obligation to bargain, furnishes support for the practice of collective bargaining in a legal structure which derives from the Constitution and the *Statuto*,' p. 86); and for the highly technical rules on the second, which affected the availability of informal arbitration, now accepted more readily within the procedures provided by collective agreements, see G. Ghezzi and U. Romagnoli, *Il rapporto di lavoro* (1987 2nd ed.), pp. 330-45. The prohibition on compromises and 'renunciations' of rights which would in principle normally be 'inderogabili' (above n. 12) stems from art. 2113 *Codice Civile*.
206. See on reinstatement, M. Roccella, 'The Reinstatement of Dismissed Employees in Italy: An Empirical Analysis' (1989) 10 Comp. Lab. Law Jo. 166; G. Ghezzi and U. Romagnoli, op. cit. n. 205, pp. 303-14; and now art. 1, Law 108 of 11 May 1990, on 'Individual Dismissals', reaffirming in the case of those unfairly dismissed by all but the smallest enterprises the obligation of the employer to

'reinstate the worker in his job' (with an option for the worker to take compensation equal to 15 months wages instead). Employers with more than fifteen workers (including trainees or part-time workers under collective agreements: see above n. 51) in an establishment or in employment in the same 'commune' are covered. Smaller employers are obliged to reinstate or pay damages for unfair dismissal, but must give written reasons on request in default of which the dismissal is void: ibid., art. 2.

207. Arts 410, 411, *Codice di Procedura Civile*, as substituted by Law 533 of 11 August 1973, require use of one of the various methods of conciliation before the case is heard by the judge, and if it does not succeed a report is still drawn up stating any lines of a solution which might be acceptable ('specifying the amount to be paid to the worker', art. 412). The success of the reform is measured by the extent to which it has overcome difficulties created by traditional concepts barring a compromise by reason of the principle of 'inderogabilità': see G. Ghezzi and U. Romagnoli, *Il rapporto del lavoro* (2nd ed. 1987), pp. 355-68; G. Tarzia, op. cit. above n. 203, Chap. III. The amendment of the last paragraph of art. 2113 *Codice Civile*, by Law 533 of 11 August 1973, to allow for binding agreements in conciliation procedures within what are now arts 410 and 411, was a step of major importance (R. de Luca Tomajo, *La norma inderogabile nel diritto del lavoro* (1976); F. Carinci, R. de Luca Tomajo, P. Tosi, T. Treu, *Il diritto del lavoro* (1987 2nd ed.), pp. 340-7). These solutions have problems; for example, there are other articles of the Civil Code which may threaten the validity of such contracts: G. Ghezzi and U. Romagnoli, op. cit., above p. 336; but they may be less serious than those besetting the equivalent English law, which comes to the issue in the opposite way from a wider 'freedom of contract,' as in s. 140 EPCA 1978; see above n. 63.

208. G. Pera, op. cit., above n. 203, p. 592.

209. See for an account of attempts to outflank the *magistratura* and on Calamandrei's Civil Code of 1942, which avoided many of the demands of the dying fascist government: G. Giugni, Chap. IV, B. Aaron (ed.), *Labor Courts and Grievance Settlement in Western Europe* (1971, antedating the 1973 reforms).

210. Law 533 of 11 August 1973, arts 21 (training), and 23 (examinations).

211. See G. Ghezzi and U. Romagnoli, *Il diritto sindacale*, above n. 38, pp. 268-71; and G. Giugni, *Diritto sindacale*, above n. 37, pp. 244-7. In the 1970s the doctrine of 'unjust damage' was used to render all 'articulated' strikes unlawful; but since the decision in Cass. no. 711, 30 January 1980, the courts have avowedly given up this approach, affording to the term 'strike' its meaning in 'everyday language'. Even so, judges have since made use of a qualitative distinction between damage to production (*produzione*) and damage to the 'essential productive capacity' (*produttività*) to put strikes causing the latter outside the right to strike, and have imposed other limits greatly criticised by commentators: see Giugni, op. cit., pp. 246-51; Ghezzi and Romagnoli, op. cit., pp. 192-204, 224-35 (and on lock-outs, pp. 234-43); Wedderburn, op. cit. n. 153, (1990) Rev. Internationale de Droit Comparé 37, pp. 62-4, 94-7. In 1984, Giugni feared that Constitutional Court decisions might mean rejection of strikes which 'interrupted the public service,' or might even reintroduce criminal liablities: *L'intervento del giudice nel conflitto industriale* (1984, Assoc Ital di Diritto del Lavoro) 129, p. 134 (he was the main author of the new Law 146 of 12 June 1990, which attempts to build civil legal sanction into the unions' codes for 'self-regulation' of the right to strike in essential public services). This struggle in Italy against judicial novelties is not without parallel in France (see H. Sinay, 'La neutralisation du droit de grève?' Dr. Soc. 1980, 250; J. Pélissier, 'La grève: liberté très surveillée' Dr. Ouvr. 1988. 59; G. Lyon-Caen 'Réglementer le droit de grève?' D 1979, Chron. 255). Critics will rightly say that interventions by courts in this area in many countries are not to be overlooked in assessing the likely fate of a right to strike in a British labour court; but the interventions of the common law judges have been on the whole more extreme: compare, on the French and British case law, Wedderburn, 'Le législateur et le juge', op. cit. above n. 5.

212. L. Mariucci, *Le fonti del diritto del lavoro*, op. cit., above n. 4, p. 41; T. Treu (ed.), *L'uso politico dello Statuto dei lavoratori*, Vol. I (1975) with the results of a survey, pp. 201-310; and *Lo Statuto dei lavoratori: prassi sindacali e motivazioni dei giudici*, Vol. II (1976) especially Chaps II (M. Taruffo) on judicial reasoning and III (S. Scarponi) on lawyers and the conduct of cases. For the account of six *Pretori* of the Law of 1973 ten years on, see 'Intervista sulla giustizia del lavoro dalla riforma' (1984) 21 Giorn. di lav. rel. ind. 115-204, most of them concluding that the reforms had worked satisfactorily, though not in every way (e.g. on personal attendances, art. 417 *Codice Civile*). On the judicial approach to the remedy of reinstatement, and cautious comparisons with Germany and Britain, see: M. Roccella, op. cit. above n. 206 (1989) 10 Comp. Lab. Law Jo. 166.

213. G. Pera, *Il diritto del lavoro* (3rd ed. 1988), pp. 161-3; P. Lange, G. Ross, M. Vannicelli, *Unions, Change and Crisis* (1982) Chaps 3 and 4; and especially, G.F. Mancini, 'Lo statuto dei lavoratori dopo le lotte operaie del 1969' in E. Bartocci, *Sindacato classe società* (1975), pp. 303-45.

214. See the *Bullock Report* (1977, Cmnd 6076) (O. Kahn-Freund (1977) 16 ILJ 65; P. Davies and Wedderburn, ibid. 197) which was refrigerated by the White Paper *Industrial Democracy* (1978, Cmnd 7231). But the debate was kept alive by the EC proposals for the *Fifth Directive on Harmonisation of Company Law* (revised text see: DTI *Consultation Document* 1990), the *European Company* (proposed Regulation with a Directive on employee participation, COM (89) 268 final – SYN 218, 219; DTI, DE *Consultative Document*, 1989) and the amended 'Vredeling' proposals of 1983 (8256/1/83 COM (84) 159; see C. Docksey, 'Employee Information and Consultation Rights in the Member States of the EC' (1985) 7 Comp Lab Law 32, with useful national comparisons). The debate is refreshed by the *Action Programme*, Part II Chap. 7, pp. 31-4, above n. 8 *et seq.* with new proposals for an 'instrument' on workers' rights to information, consultation and participation. Provision for information, consultation and 'balanced participation' on safety has already been enacted in the 'Framework' Directive 89/392 of 12 June 1989, arts 10, 11; (1990) H and S Info. Bull. 14, 15.

215. See for the background, Lord Amulree, *Industrial Arbitration in Great Britain* (1929); Industrial Courts Act 1919, ss. 1-3; K. Wedderburn and P. Davies, *Employment Grievances and Disputes Procedures in Britain* (1969), Chaps 8-10.

216. Employment Protection Act 1975, ss. 3, 10; also ss. 16, 19-21, Sched. 1 Part II, and Sched. 11 (repealed, Employment Act 1980, s. 19); s. 3 Equal Pay Act 1970 (now repealed by s. 9 Sex Discrimination Act 1986); B. Bercusson, *Fair Wages Resolutions* (1978). On the body linking it to the old Industrial Court, the 'Industrial Arbitration Board,' see R. Simpson and J. Wood, *Industrial Relations and the 1971 Act* (1973), Chap. 8. On the rescission of the Fair Wages Resolution, see B. Bercusson (1982) 11 ILJ 271.

217. See for the operation and the methods of the CAC, the various writings of Professor Sir John Wood (below n. 218), who has been chairman since it began its work in 1976, here especially, 'The CAC – A Consideration of its Role and Approach' (1979) 87 *Employment Gazette* 9-17: 'No decision making body wants to produce a succession of awards which lack pattern or coherence. Yet the use of precedents, as seen in the courts and to a lesser extent tribunals, imposes a stifling rigidity,' p. 11. See too, R. Rideout (a deputy Chairman): 'Arbitration and the Public Interest: Regulated Arbitration' in Wedderburn and W.T. Murphy (eds), *Labour Law and the Community* (1982), pp. 54-9.

218. *Annual Report 1976*, para. 3.6. But when an industrial relations issue comes to the courts, they must be 'plainly recognised as having a task different in function from the traditional court. At the heart of that difference is the undoubted fact that the parties are very likely to remain in close relationship after the dispute has been decided': see Sir John Wood, 'Labour Relations Law – The Missing Pieces' (1990) 24 The Law Teacher 111, p. 121. See too, Sir John Wood, 'The Role of Neutrals in Interest Disputes' (1989) 10 Comp. Lab. Law Jo. 441, and (with B. Hepple, T.

Johnston) 'United Kingdom Report: The Role of Neutrals in Shopfloor Disputes' (1989) 10 Comp. Lab. Law Jo. 198; 'The British Arbitrator – A Question of Style' in W. Gerschfeld (ed.), *Arbitration 1986; Current and Expanding Roles* (1987), 270; 'Information for Bargaining' (1990) 40 *Federation News* 1; 'The Collective Will and the Law' (1989) 17 ILJ 1; 'The Case for Arbitration' 1980, Personnel Management, 52-5; 'Last Offer Arbitration' (1985) 23 BJIR 415; 'Pendulum Arbitration; A Modest Experiment' (1988) 19 Ind. Rels Jo. 244. Contrast the approach of his namesake Wood J, 'The EAT as it Enters the 1990s' (1990) 19 ILJ 133 (the lay members 'must be directed on the law' 138; but: 'All healthy law should develop' 141).

219. Sir John Wood, 'The concept of the rate for the job may have some weaknesses but it expresses a universal assumption as to fairness,' op. cit. n. 218, (1990) 40 *Federation News*, p. 6.

220. P. Davies and M. Freedland, 'Labour Courts and the Reform of Labour Law in Great Britain' in *In Memorian Zvi Bar-Niv: Collection of Essays on Labour Law* (1987) 41, p. 61.

221. B. Bercusson, op. cit., above n. 45, p. 47.

222. P.L. Davies *Report* (1978) op. cit. above n. 139, p. 325.

223. P. Wood, 'The CAC's Approach to Schedule 11, Employment Protection Act 1975, and the Fair Wages Resolution 1946' (1978) 7 ILJ 65, 83. See on the recognition jurisdiction, B. Doyle (1980) 9 ILJ 154; on awards and low pay, M. Jones (1980) 9 ILJ 28; compare O. Kahn-Freund, *Labour and the Law* (3rd ed. 1983, P. Davies and M. Freedland), pp. 113-8; and for contrasts with the High Court, R. Bendictus and B. Bercusson, *Labour Law Cases and Materials* (1987), pp. 476-87, 514-7. On the CAC's determination to respect the 'spirit' as well as the letter, see: *Central Council for Education in Social Work and ASTMS* Award 82/18; and for stress upon future industrial relations whilst respecting the technical legal issues: *Fife Health Board and ASTMS* Award 82/9, para. 23.

224. Employment Protection Act 1975, Sched 1, para 27; CAC *Report 1976*, para. 1. 4; J. Wood, op. cit., n. 217; O. Kahn-Freund, op. cit. above n. 10: 'The CAC is not of course a court ... Nevertheless, its spirit is judicial and so too, to some extent, is its procedure.' On incomes policy, see B. Bercusson, *Fair Wages Resolutions* (1978), pp. 486-97; Wedderburn 'Labour Law Now – A Hold and a Nudge' (1984) 13 ILJ 73, 74-8; and on ACAS, B. Weekes, 'ACAS – An Alternative to Law?' (1979) 8 ILJ 147, 153.

225. See on reasons for awards on disclosure of information, ss. 19(4), 20(2), Employment Protection Act 1975; but the CAC still explains its awards in 'General Considerations,' e.g. *General Accident Fire and Life plc and MSF*, Award 89/2; cp. H. Gospel and P. Willman (1981) 10 ILJ 10.

226. The writer is, for example, among the minority which has the misfortune to disagree with its refusal to include a right to a collective procedure in an award of terms and conditions: see e.g. *Commodore Business Machines (UK) Ltd and EETPU*, Award 78/339; *Phoenix Timber and TGWU*, Award 77/272, an attitude the roots of which seem to lie in *R* v. *IDT ex parte Portland UDC* [1955] 3 All E.R. 18, CA; and see now *National Coal Board* v. *NUM* [1986] ICR 936, Scott J (see Wedderburn, *The Worker and the Law*, op. cit., pp. 339-40; *contra* O. Kahn-Freund, *Labour and the Law*, above n. 10, p. 117: the CAC saw that to do so would be 'inconsistent' with the legislation).

227. See e.g. *R* v. *CAC ex parte BTP Tioxide* [1981] ICR 843; *R* v. *CAC, ex parte Deltaflow* [1979] ICR 657; *R* v. *CAC, ex parte RHM Foods* [1979] ICR 657. Other, unsuccessful, applications for judicial review failed since they were an attempt to use the High Court to appeal against the findings of the CAC: e.g. *R* v. *CAC, ex parte TI Tube Division Services Ltd* [1978] IRLR 183; but such litigation can in itself put horrendous obstacles in the path of effective action by such bodies, as happened to ACAS in the compulsory recognition procedures: e.g. *Grunwick Processing Laboratories Ltd* v. *ACAS* [1978] AC 655, HL; *UKAPE* v. *ACAS* [1981] AC 424

Employment Rights in Britain and Europe

HL; see B. Simpson 'Judicial Control of ACAS' (1979) 8 ILJ 69. The decision in
EMA v. *ACAS* [1980] 1 WLR 302 HL, came too late to save the day after repeal.
228. P. Davies, 'The Central Arbitration Committee and Equal Pay' (1980) 33
Current Legal Problems 165, p. 188, in an authoritative review of the High Court
decision in *R* v. *CAC, ex parte Hy-Mac* [1979] IRLR 461: 'The tone of the
judgments was one of disbelief, even outrage, at what the Committee had done.'
The provision in issue, s. 3 Equal Pay Act 1970, was repealed by s. 9 Sex
Discrimination Act 1986.
229. See I. Smith and J. Wood, op. cit. above, n. 189, p. 42. The transfer of some
CAC personnel to the labour court as judges would not, of course, deprive the
CAC, in the hands of those remaining, of its distinct arbitration role.

Glossary

AC	Appeal Cases
ACAS	Advisory Conciliation and Arbitration Service
All E.R.	All England Law Reports
ASTMS	Association of Scientific, Technical and Managerial Staffs
Ass. Plèn.	Chambers of Cour de Cassation in Full Session
AUEW	Amalgamated Union of Engineering Workers (also AEU)
ASLEF	Associated Society of Locomotive Engineers and Firemen
BJIR	British Journal of Industrial Relations
BOAC	British Overseas Airways Corporation
CA	Court of Appeal
CAC	Central Arbitration Committee
Cass.	Corte di Cassazione (Italian High Court of Appeal)
CBI	Confederation of British Industry
Ch.	Chancery Division
CIR	Commission on Industrial Relations
CLJ	Cambridge Law Journal
CO	Certification Officer
Comp. Lab. Law Jo.	Comparative Labor Law Journal (US)
CFDT	Confédération Française Démocratique du Travail
CFTC	Confédération Française des Travailleurs Chrétiens
CGIL	Confederazione Generale Italiana di Lavoro (Italian union)
CISL	Confederazione Italiana Sindacati Lavoratori
CGT	Confédération Générale du Travail
CGT-FO	Confédération Générale du Travail-Force Ouvrière
Cons. const.	Conseil Constitutionel (French Constitutional Council)
Corte cost.	Constitutional Court (Italian)
CRE	Commission for Racial Equality
Crim.	Criminal Chamber Cour de Cassation
CT	Code du Travail
D.	Dalloz
DKr	Danish Kroner
Dr. Soc.	Droit Social
Dr. Ouvr.	Droit Ouvrier
EAT	Employment Appeal Tribunal
EC	European Communities (also EEC)
ECHR	European Convention of Human Rights (and Court, Strasbourg: Council of Europe)
ECJ	European Court of Justice (EC: Luxembourg)
EEC	European Economic Community

EETPU	Electrical, Electronic, Telecommunication and Plumbing Union
EHRR	European Human Rights Reports
EOC	Equal Opportunities Commission
EPA	Employment Protection Act 1975
EPCA	Employment Protection (Consolidation) Act 1978
EIRR	European Industrial Review and Report
FWR	Fair Wages Resolution
GCHQ	Government Communications Headquarters
Giorn. di dir del lav.e di rel ind:	Giornale di diritto del lavoro e di relazioni industriali
GMB	General, Municipal and Boilermakers union
HL	House of Lords (judicial committee: final appeal court: Law Lords)
HS Info. Bull.	Health and Safety Information Bulletin (in IRRR)
ILJ	Industrial Law Journal
ILO	International Labour Organisation
Ind. Rels. Jo.	Industrial Relations Journal
ICR	Industrial Cases Reports
Intl. Lab. L.R.	International Labour Law Reports
IR	Irish Reports
IRLR	Industrial Relations Law Reports
IRRR	Industrial Relations Review and Report
IT	Industrial Tribunal
J	Judge of the High Court ('Mr Justice ...')
Lav. Dir.	Lavoro e diritto (Italy)
LC	Lord Chancellor
LIB	Legal Information Bulletin (in IRRR)
LJ	Lord Justice (Court of Appeal)
LOLS	La Ley Organica de Libertad Sindical (Spain)
LQR	Law Quarterly Review
LRD	Labour Research Department
MLR	Modern Law Review
MR	Master of the Rolls (judge in CA)
MSF	Manufacturing, Science and Finance union
NALGO	National and Local Government Officers Association
NCU	National Communications Union
NGA	National Graphical Association
NIRC	National Industrial Relations Court (Britain 1971–74)
NUJ	National Union of Journalists
NUM	National Union of Mineworkers
NUPE	National Union of Public Employees
NUR	National Union of Railwaymen
NUS	National Union of Seamen
NUT	National Union of Teachers
Ox. Jo. Leg. S.	Oxford Journal of Legal Studies
P.	President

PC (JC)	Privy Council Judicial Committee (mainly Law Lords)
QB	Queen's Bench Division
Riv. dir. lav.	Rivista di diritto del lavoro (Italy)
SK	Swedish Kroner
SOGAT	Society of Graphical and Allied Trades 1982
Soc.	Cour de Cassation, Social Chamber (France)
Sté.	Societé
TGWU	Transport and General Workers' Union
TUC	Trades Union Congress
TUPE	Transfer of Undertakings (Protection of Employment) Regulations 1981
UCATT	Union of Construction, Allied Trades and Technicians
UCW	Union of Communication Workers
UIL	Unione Italiana del Lavoro
VC	Vice Chancellor (High Court and Court of Appeal)
WLR	Weekly Law Reports
ZIAS	Zeitschrift für ausländisches und internationales Arbeits- und Sozialrecht

Index

37, 82-3, 85, 91, 174, 216-9, 308-9, 324; legitimation of, 41-50, 202, 358-9; liability, civil, of, 38-9, 79, 171-2, 202, 222-4, 279, 290-3, 328-31, 337-8, 370-1; damages and, 223, 291; protected property (*patrimoine*) and, 38-9, 206, 223-4, 291-2, 355 (*see also Taff Vale*, Employment Act (1982), Employment Act (1990)); litigate, right to (*action syndicale*), 124, 381-2, 408; martys and, 223, 337-8; 'New' and 'New Model', 46-8; pluralist and unitary, 41-7, 60-1, 69, 144, 289-92, 297, 301-2, 307-8, 359; multiunionism, 37, 324; in public sector, 316-25; registration, 14, 21, 36, 337; 'representative', in, 42, 47, 144, 213, 224, 248, 252, 269, 301, 344, 409; right not to join, 21, 23, 31, 91, 144-6, 153; *see also*, Closed shop, Dismissal, Immunities, Political activity, Right to strike, Strikes, Trade disputes

Trade Union Act (1871), 35, 36, 279

Trade Union Act (1913), 37, 49

Trade Union Act (1984), 12, 164, 216-7, 248-9, 263, 309

Trade Union and Labour Relations Act (1974-76), 12, 18-19, 49, 51-7, 79, 90, 95, 120, 160-8, 184, 202, 312, 372; employment contract, collective agreements and, s. 18(4), 90; injunctions, *ex parte*, s.17(1), 160, 312; injunctions, interlocutory, s. 17(2) 166-8, 185, 312; interference and s. 13(2), 120; inteference and s. 13(3), 18-19; minority government, 12, 52; pendulum and, 49, 56; protection outside trade disputes (ss. 13, 14), 95; restraint of trade s.2(5), 202; trade dispute, definition amended, s.29(1), 79

Trades Union Congress (TUC) 9-11, 20, 23, 166, 181, 213-5; 'Bridlington' principles, 248, 289

Trailor, l'arrêt (1982), 291-2

Trainees, status of, 110, 215, 249, 255, 363

Training, 33; of judges, 35, 369, 382, 385-6; of workers, 255, 363

Transfer of undertaking, employment protection and, 79, 122, 256, 367; *see also* European Community Directives

Treu, Tiziano, 238

Trinidad, 146

Tripartism, 80, 84, 213, 374, 379, 382-4, 385; 'fortified', 382-3

Turner LJ, 158

Twain, Mark, 327

Tynan v. *Balmer* (1967), 85, 92

Unemployment benefit, 37-8, 366

Unfair dismissal *see* Dismissal

Union membership agreement *see* Closed shop

United Nations, 141-2, 145

United States, 46-7, 94, 113, 160, 185, 198, 294; civil and criminal contempt of court, 347; Dooley, Mr and, 188; public employment, strikes and, 198, 316-17, 319; Reagan, President, 317; secondary action, ally doctrine, 294

Universe Tankships of Monrovia v. *ITWF* (1983) HL, 120-1, 329, 370

Unlawful interference *see* Interference, Intimidation, Tort

Upjohn, Lord, 155, 165, 173

Vicarious liability, 79, 177, 290-3, 353

Voluntarism: no return to old, 94; Thatcher policies as, 211-13; *see also* Abstention, Collective *laissez-faire*, France, *Heatons* case (1983), Non-intervention, Trade Unions

Wages, 202, 249, 325, 365; minimum wage, 325, 365

Wages Act (1986), 12

Wages Councils, 80, 211, 251; inspectorate, 211; objective suicide, 49; young workers excluded from, 211

Wales, 227

Wapping, 107, 174, 181, 213, 220, 329

Warwick Report (on industrial tribunals), 375

Webb, Sidney and Beatrice, 47, 53, 225, 376, 392

Whitley Committee, Reports of, 75, 198, 317-18

Wigham, Eric, 27

Wikeley, Nicholas, 396

Wilberforce, Lord, 161

Women, 33, 214, 239, 357, 361; industrial tribunals and, 411; maternity rights, 215, 239, 357; sex equality and privatisation, 214-5; underground work, 214; *see also* Employment Act (1989), Equal Pay, Non-standard employment, Sex discrimination

Wood, Sir John, and CAC, 364, 388-9, 409, 414-15

Woodcock, George, 36

Work to rule *see* Industrial action, Strikes

Workers, 24, 79, 151, 254-5, 324, 329, 365; consultation, participation and, 82, 329, 364-5; *see also* Contract of Employment, Non-standard employment, Social Charter, Freedom of association, Women, Young workers

Workers' Statute (1970) *see* Italy

Young, James and Webster v. *UK* (1981) *see* Railwaymen's case

Young, Lord, 227

Young workers, 211, 214, 249, 357